D1389894

Floating Charges in Scotland

EDINBURGH STUDIES IN LAW

Series Editor
Alexandra Braun, University of Edinburgh

Editorial Board
George Gretton, University of Edinburgh
John Lovett, Loyola University New Orleans
Hector MacQueen, University of Edinburgh
Elspeth Reid, University of Edinburgh
Kenneth Reid, University of Edinburgh
Lionel Smith, McGill University
Anna Veneziano, Universities of Teramo and UNIDROIT
Neil Walker, University of Edinburgh
Reinhard Zimmermann, Max Planck Institute for Comparative and International Private
   Law in Hamburg

Volumes in the series:

Jonathan Hardman and Alisdair D J MacPherson (eds), *Floating Charges in Scotland: New Perspectives and Current Issues* (2022)

Hector L MacQueen (ed), *Continuity, Influences and Integration in Scottish Legal History: Select Essays of David Sellar* (2022)

Guido Rossi (ed), *Authorities in Early Modern Law Courts* (2021)

John W Cairns, *Enlightenment, Legal Education, and Critique: Selected Essays on the History of Scots Law, Volume 2* (2015)

John W Cairns, *Law, Lawyers, and Humanism: Selected Essays on the History of Scots Law, Volume 1* (2015)

Paul J du Plessis and John W Cairns (eds), *Reassessing Legal Humanism and its Claims: Petere Fontes?* (2015)

Remus Valsan (ed), *Trusts and Patrimonies* (2015)

Eric Descheemaeker (ed), *The Consequences of Possession* (2014)

Neil Walker (ed), *MacCormick's Scotland* (2012)

Elaine E Sutherland, Kay E Goodall, Gavin F M Little and Fraser P Davidson (eds), *Law Making and the Scottish Parliament* (2011)

J W Cairns and Paul du Plessis (eds), *The Creation of the* Ius Commune: *From* Casus *to* Regula (2010)

James Chalmers, Lindsay Farmer and Fiona Leverick (eds), *Essays in Criminal Law in Honour of Sir Gerald Gordon* (2010)

Vernon Valentine Palmer and Elspeth Christie Reid (eds), *Mixed Jurisdictions Compared: Private Law in Louisiana and Scotland* (2009)

John W Cairns and Paul du Plessis (eds), *Beyond Dogmatics: Law and Society in the Roman World* (2007)

William M Gordon, *Roman Law, Scots Law and Legal History* (2007)

Kenneth G C Reid, Marius J de Waal and Reinhard Zimmermann (eds), *Exploring the Law of Succession: Studies National, Historical and Comparative* (2007)

Hector MacQueen and Reinhard Zimmermann (eds), *European Contract Law: Scots and South African Perspectives* (2006)

Elspeth Reid and David L Carey Miller (eds), *A Mixed Legal System in Transition: T B Smith and the Progress of Scots Law* (2005)

https://edinburghuniversitypress.com/series/esil

EDINBURGH STUDIES IN LAW
VOLUME 18

Floating Charges in Scotland

New Perspectives and Current Issues

Edited by
Jonathan Hardman and
Alisdair D J MacPherson

EDINBURGH
University Press

Edinburgh University Press is one of the leading university presses in the UK. We publish academic books and journals in our selected subject areas across the humanities and social sciences, combining cutting-edge scholarship with high editorial and production values to produce academic works of lasting importance. For more information visit our website: edinburghuniversitypress.com

Edinburgh University Press Ltd
The Tun – Holyrood Road
12(2f) Jackson's Entry
Edinburgh EH8 8PJ

Typeset in New Caledonia by
Cheshire Typesetting Ltd, Cuddington, Cheshire
and printed and bound in Great Britain

A CIP record for this book is available from the British Library

ISBN 978 1 4744 5872 6 (hardback)
ISBN 978 1 4744 5873 3 (webready PDF)
ISBN 978 1 4744 5874 0 (epub)

Contents

Foreword   vii

Editors' Preface and Acknowledgements   x

List of Contributors   xv

PART 1   THE HISTORY OF FLOATING CHARGES

1 The 'Pre-History' of Floating Charges in Scots Law   3
   Alisdair D J MacPherson

2 Borrowing on the Undertaking: Scottish Statutory Companies   62
   Ross G Anderson

3 The Genesis of the Scottish Floating Charge   102
   Alisdair D J MacPherson

4 The Story of the Scots Law Floating Charge: 1961 to Date   157
   George L Gretton

PART 2   THEORETICAL, COMPARATIVE AND POLICY PERSPECTIVES

5 Law and Economics of the Floating Charge   197
   Jonathan Hardman

6 Floating Charges and Moral Hazard: Finding Fairness for
   Involuntary and Vulnerable Stakeholders   228
   Jennifer L L Gant

7 Hohfeld and the Scots Law Floating Charge   271
   Jonathan Hardman

8 The Species and Structure(s) of the Floating Charge: The
   English Law Perspective on the Scottish Floating Charge   304
   Magda Raczynska

PART 3 PRACTICE, DOCTRINE AND THE FUTURE

9 The Ranking of Floating Charges   345
   Jonathan Hardman and Alisdair D J MacPherson

10 The Floating Charge and Insolvency Law   400
   Donna McKenzie Skene

11 The Empirical Importance of the Floating Charge in Scotland 442
   Jonathan Hardman and Alisdair D J MacPherson

12 Reform of the Scottish Floating Charge   473
   Andrew J M Steven

   Index   510

Foreword

The floating charge was introduced into Scots law in 1961 by the Companies (Floating Charges) (Scotland) Act of that year. That Act was passed largely in response to demand from the commercial world. It was thought that the introduction of the floating charge was necessary to take account of two elementary commercial facts. First, a modern company (and indeed any other commercial concern) will require to borrow money, if only to provide liquidity or working capital, and will require to grant security for its borrowings. Secondly, such a company will almost inevitably possess a large number of different types of property over which it can grant security. In this connection, it is significant that at the present day most property (in excess of 80 per cent of the total) is incorporeal or intangible: such property has no physical existence but only exists by virtue of the legal system, as in the case of debts or shares or intellectual property rights. Understandably, companies wish to grant security over intangible property and the floating charge has been seen as an easy and flexible means of achieving that result.

It is therefore hardly surprising that the floating charge has proved extremely useful in practice. This is shown by the frequency of its use. Nevertheless, the use of the floating charge has given rise to a significant number of legal problems, especially in relation to its interaction with other areas of law and legal institutions. These include contracts, property, insolvency and perhaps most notably diligence, where the notion of 'effectually executed diligence', first introduced by the 1961 Act, has been the subject of repeated litigation.

In large measure these legal problems originate at a conceptual rather than a strictly practical level. The floating charge is a concept derived from English equity and I think that the underlying problem is that English equity has a distinctive, flexible, conceptual structure that is not easy to translate into a system such as Scots law that is based on structures originating in Roman law. Nevertheless, while the difficulties may be said to originate at a conceptual level, they have important practical implications; that is well illustrated by the significant volume of Scottish case law on the floating charge. The 1961 Act has been repealed and re-enacted, with substantial modifications, but many of the problems remain, and litigation continues, often on fairly fundamental aspects of the floating charge.

For the law to go forward in a coherent and sensible way, it is essential that the past difficulties should be properly confronted and solutions devised that work well at both a theoretical and practical level. That is why the publication of this book is particularly to be welcomed. For the first time, the floating charge and its practical operation in Scots law are examined and analysed on a comprehensive basis. That, in my opinion, is essential if the underlying difficulties are to be properly addressed, whether by the courts or in new legislation. For this reason alone, this book must be warmly welcomed.

The analysis of the floating charge starts with its history (and indeed pre-history), which is essential background in any attempt to understand the charge. It is, furthermore, an interesting story considered purely as legal history. Thereafter conceptual and policy considerations are examined in detail. This is absolutely essential if the Scottish floating charge, and the conceptual and practical problems that have arisen from it, are to be properly addressed. For the first time, the book provides an economic analysis of the floating charge as it is used in Scots law and Scottish commercial practice. For a legal institution that is designed to meet important commercial requirements, in the form of the need for a comprehensive means of security that is capable of covering all assets, including intangible assets, it seems to me that an economic analysis is vital. This chapter of the book, therefore, fills an important gap in the existing legal analysis. At the same time consideration is given to the possible adverse effects of the floating charge: by conferring a security on certain creditors a charge may reduce or defeat the rights of other creditors or potential creditors. Frequently these will be persons in a weaker economic position, such as employees, and it is important, in my opinion, that any economic analysis should look at the economic disadvantages as well as the advantages of the floating charge.

I have already remarked that the problems with the floating charge in Scots law are largely conceptual in nature. For this reason I am pleased to see that the institution is subjected to a proper Hohfeldian analysis. I have long thought that this technique is of enormous benefit in any attempt to understand the law; by providing theoretical clarity it enables the practical application of the law (and law is ultimately a practical subject) to be properly focused.

The final part of the book is firmly focused on the floating charge as a practical institution of the law. The practical difficulties created by the floating charge have generally arisen in two areas, the ranking of floating charge rights *inter se* and the relationship between floating charges and the general law of insolvency. Both of these are considered comprehensively and in detail; this is the first time that such detailed consideration has ever been given to these important subjects.

Another important first for this volume is the empirical analysis of floating charges, based on data from Companies House. Especially if future reform of the law is to be considered, as I hope it will, that data is essential to establish the extent and detailed nature of the use of floating charges in practice. Such analysis should also be of great assistance to those charged with drafting floating charges, a topic that has perhaps not received the attention that it should. Finally, the final chapter of the book, written by a former Law Commissioner, considers possible reform of the law in future. As I have indicated, floating charges have given rise to a very substantial amount of litigation and both conceptually and in practice there remains considerable uncertainty about how they operate. For this reason, reform of the law will almost certainly be desirable and, indeed, necessary.

If effective reform is to take place, however, it is essential that the existing state of the law should be properly analysed and understood. This requires consideration of its origins, its history, its theoretical structure and its practical operation, especially in relation to its interaction with other legal institutions. That is precisely what this volume provides, for the first time.

For all these reasons this volume is greatly to be welcomed. It is the first edited collection to be devoted to floating charges as a separate subject, rather than as an aspect of company law or insolvency. It is written by a range of eminent contributors, who are all well known as experts in their respective areas. It is also the first work that has embarked on a properly critical and wide-ranging analysis of the law of Scotland in this area. As such it should provide a firm basis for future development or reform of the law. It will unquestionably be required reading for anyone dealing with floating charges and their consequences, and it is to be recommended to every practitioner dealing with commercial or insolvency law.

Lord Drummond Young
Edinburgh
September 2021

Editor's Preface and Acknowledgements

Floating charges were introduced into Scots law by the Companies (Floating Charges) (Scotland) Act 1961 as a response to the demands of commerce. Since their arrival, they have remained popular among banking and finance lawyers (and their clients) but have also proved controversial. Academics and judges, in particular, have frequently identified doctrinal and conceptual difficulties with floating charges and have criticised the dissonance between this form of security and wider Scots law. However, while much has been written about floating charges in Scots law, there has never been an edited collection on the subject providing various different perspectives and approaches. That is, until now.

One of us has previously written that 'there exists no holistic modern academic text that authoritatively covers a floating charge in Scotland' (J Hardman, *A Practical Guide to Granting Corporate Security in Scotland* (2018) para. 1–03), while the other, in a subsequently published monograph on floating charges, acknowledged that '[t]here is much scope for further work on the Scottish floating charge' (A D J MacPherson, *The Floating Charge* (2020) para. 1–09). This volume builds upon the work that has already been done on floating charges from a practical and doctrinal perspective and is a wide-ranging account of this contentious and fascinating security interest. By doing so, we believe that it provides a holistic account of the subject matter.

The work looks at floating charges from a number of different perspectives and is divided into three parts: (1) The History of Floating Charges (Chapters 1–4); (2) Theoretical, Comparative and Policy Perspectives (Chapters 5–8); and (3) Practice, Doctrine and the Future (Chapters 9–12). The first chapter is by Dr MacPherson and examines the position on floating security under Scots law prior to the introduction of the statutory floating charge; what may be referred to as the 'pre-history' of floating charges. It explores the rejection of general express hypothecs, including floating security, at common law as well as the emergence of the English floating charge and reactions to that development within Scotland. After briefly considering the Roman law position, the chapter spans a period from early Scots law up to the mid-twentieth century. In Chapter Two, Dr Ross Anderson focuses on statutory companies (i.e. companies created by private Acts of Parliament) and the creation of security over their undertakings. These companies were vitally important in the nineteenth and early twentieth centuries for financing large capital projects, particularly constructing and operating key infrastructure such as railways, harbours and tramways, but they are under-researched and often overlooked today. It is shown that these companies could create security that approximated modern floating charges in some respects. The third chapter is by Dr MacPherson and picks up from the first chapter by focusing on the arrival or 'genesis' of the floating charge in 1961. It does so through the examination of archival materials from the 1950s and early 1960s, which help to shed light on how the floating charge arrived in Scots law and why it took the form that it did. The consideration of some of the original provisions that were replicated in later legislation may also help with the interpretation of the current law. The fourth and final chapter in the historical part is by Professor George Gretton. He discusses the story of the floating charge since 1961, outlining the various developments, legislative and otherwise, and missteps along the way. Given his work on floating charges over a number of decades, we are delighted that his chapter includes his personal reflections on the subject.

The second part of the book is opened by Chapter Five, written by Dr Hardman. It contains a law and economics analysis of the floating charge in Scots law and seeks to demonstrate the economic advantage of the float-ing charge for market participants. This is an approach that has not previ-ously been utilised for floating charges in Scots law and produces interesting insights. The sixth chapter has been contributed by Dr Jennifer Gant and provides a welcome socio-legal perspective on the floating charge. In par-ticular, it examines moral hazard and considers how floating charges affect vulnerable and involuntary stakeholders, especially employees. Dr Gant assesses whether there are adequate protections for such parties to avoid the potential for abuse by floating charge holders, particularly in the context of insolvency. In the seventh chapter, Dr Hardman analyses the Scots law floating charge using the work of the celebrated American jurist Wesley Newcomb Hohfeld (1879–1918). On the basis of this, it is shown that much analysis and discussion of the floating charge is flawed. Consequences aris-ing from this conclusion are also identified. The eighth chapter has been written by Dr Magda Raczynska and provides an English law perspective on the Scottish floating charge. It identifies rough equivalencies between the two jurisdictions but argues that English law offers parties greater freedom regarding the terms of floating charges. This provides a useful comparative perspective of our floating charge from our southern neighbours' point of view.

The final part of the book begins with a chapter that the editors have co-written on the ranking of floating charges. Ranking is well-recognised as a complicated and troublesome area of law, especially when floating charges are involved. Chapter Nine therefore seeks to provide a relatively comprehensive consideration of the ranking of floating charges, including with reference to default rules, negative pledges, ranking agreements, distributions and issues involving circles of priority, offside goals and the doctrine of catholic and secondary creditors. The tenth chapter deals with the crucial relationship between floating charges and insolvency law and has been contributed by Professor Donna McKenzie Skene. The chapter offers a detailed examination of the enforcement of floating charges in the context of insolvency and discusses how various processes affect them. It shows that floating charges have had a considerable impact on the development of corporate insolvency law in the UK. Chapter Eleven has been co-written by the editors and presents novel empirical analysis of floating charges. Empirical work on floating charges has been sadly lacking over the years and this chapter seeks to address this gap. The chapter utilises data gathered from Companies House to draw conclusions as to the empirical importance of floating charges in Scotland. There is also discussion of some of the terms of a sample of floating charge instruments and consideration of the doctrinal implications of these. The final chapter of the volume, Chapter Twelve, is by Professor Andrew Steven and, fittingly, looks to the future by focusing on the reform of the Scottish floating charge. As well as considering previous reform attempts relating to floating charges and the Scottish Law Commission's moveable transactions project, Professor Steven discusses the potential routes for the reform of security rights and reflects on how these may affect the Scottish floating charge.

It appears that floating charges will remain a part of Scots law for the foreseeable future. As such, we are confident that this work will have not only scholarly value but also ongoing practical value. Floating charges continue to be used on a wide scale and have particular advantages as a form of security, including in relation to their enforcement capabilities, the flexibility that they provide the granter and grantee compared to other security interests, and their coverage of all types of property. One only needs to think of the difficulties that can exist in creating fixed security over certain classes of property, including the ever-more important digital assets, to understand the value of a security that can cover all of a debtor's property, of whatever type, whilst leaving the debtor free to deal with that property. We hope that this book will lead to further research in relation to rights in security, commercial law, commercial aspects of property law, company law and insolvency law, especially since floating charges are found at the intersection of all of these areas. We also hope that this work may provoke interest in utilising different methodologies for research in other parts of Scots law.

It is worth mentioning terminology. The chapters in this volume use a range of different terms, For the floating charge itself, you will see floating charge, floater, floating security and others. For the party receiving the floating charge, you will see recipient, creditor, holder, chargee and others. For the company granting the floating charge you will see company, granter, grantor, debtor and others. Each of these terms contains embedded connotations and denotations about the precise interaction between the parties to this arrangement – for example, 'creditor and debtor' clearly indicates that the relationship is wider than merely security granter and security holder, whereas 'granter and recipient' implies a narrower relationship. The essays in this book look at the same phenomenon from different perspectives. We therefore view the language deployed as part of the context for analysis. As such, we have deliberately not made terminology uniform throughout the volume but invite the reader to consider the terminology deployed by each author and how it influences, affects or otherwise reflects their core argument.

We are very grateful to the contributors of this volume for their faith in the project and for producing their high quality chapters. This is especially true given the difficulties and delays caused by the COVID-19 pandemic, which created unforeseen challenges in undertaking research and accessing resources. We also express our thanks to the Edinburgh Law Review Trust for their financial support and to the University of Aberdeen's Centre for Commercial Law for providing us with funds to employ research assistants. Those research assistants, Raiyan Chowdhury and Euan Reid, have our gratitude for their truly excellent work during the editing process. They made our own work much more straightforward than it could have been and we wish them well with their future careers. In addition, we thank our publisher Edinburgh University Press, and especially Laura Williamson, for their support and understanding, and the series editor, Professor Alexandra Braun for her encouragement. We also convey our gratitude to Lord Drummond Young for kindly agreeing to provide a foreword to this book. Finally here, we must thank Steven and Olivia, for their patience and support. Within individual chapters of this book, further acknowledgements have been included.

We have enjoyed editing and contributing chapters for this volume and we are keen that you also enjoy reading it.

Jonathan Hardman
Alisdair D J MacPherson
Edinburgh and Aberdeen
August 2021

List of Contributors

ROSS G ANDERSON is an Advocate and an Honorary Research Fellow at the University of Glasgow.

JENNIFER L L GANT is a Lecturer in Law at the University of Derby.

GEORGE L GRETTON is Emeritus Lord President Reid Professor of Law at the University of Edinburgh.

JONATHAN HARDMAN is a Lecturer of International Commercial Law at the University of Edinburgh.

ALISDAIR D J MACPHERSON is a Lecturer in Commercial Law at the University of Aberdeen.

DONNA MCKENZIE SKENE is Emerita Professor of Insolvency Law at the University of Aberdeen.

MAGDA RACZYNSKA is an Associate Professor at University College London.

ANDREW J M STEVEN is Professor of Property Law at the University of Edinburgh.

PART 1
THE HISTORY OF
FLOATING CHARGES

1 The 'Pre-History' of Floating Charges in Scots Law

*Alisdair D J MacPherson**

A. INTRODUCTION
B. SCOTS COMMON LAW
    (1) Roman law
    (2) Early Scots law
    (3) Institutional period
        (a) Corporeal moveable property
        (b) Heritable property
        (c) Incorporeal moveable property
        (d) Comparative law
        (e) General hypothec – doctrinal obstacles
C. ENGLISH LAW
    (1) English law and Roman law
    (2) Emergence of the floating charge
    (3) The floating charge controversies
D. THE 'ENGLISH' FLOATING CHARGE AND SCOTS LAW
    (1) The influence of terminology
    (2) Rejection of the floating charge
        (a) Late nineteenth century
        (b) *Ballachulish Slate Quarries Co Ltd v Bruce*
        (c) Commentary
    (3) Opposition to floating charges
    (4) Demand for floating charges?

* I am grateful to George Gretton, Andrew Steven, Andrew Sweeney, Scott Wortley and my co-editor for their comments on earlier drafts of this chapter and to Roddy Paisley for his assistance with some of the historical sources. I also wish to express thanks for observations provided by attendees of the Scottish Legal History Group Conference 2020 and the Scottish Property Law Discussion Group in October 2020, at which material from this chapter was presented. Any errors are, however, mine alone.

E. AGRICULTURAL CHARGES
    (1) Nature and operation
    (2) Contemporary commentary
    (3) Floating charges and agricultural charges
F. LATER DEVELOPMENTS
    (1) Increasing support for floating charges?
    (2) *Re Anchor Line*
    (3) *Carse v Coppen*
G. CONCLUSION

A. INTRODUCTION

An account of floating charges in Scots law should not begin merely with the arrival of the statutory floating charge in 1961. Rather, it is important to also understand the relationship between 'floating' security and Scots law prior to the Companies (Floating Charges) (Scotland) Act 1961. This can be described as the 'pre-history' of floating charges and is the focus of the present chapter.

The Scots common law rules on creating security rights are restrictive and long established. The position espoused principally by the institutional writers remains broadly applicable today. However, statutory creations, most notably the floating charge, have changed the landscape in this area. Exploring the reasons for Scots law's earlier rejection of security rights comparable to floating charges[1] can help us assess whether this remained a justifiable approach as time progressed. After examining the common law position in Scotland, including with reference to Roman law and early Scots law, the chapter will consider the development of the floating charge in English law. This form of security was explicitly rejected by Scottish courts but later served as a model when the reform of security over moveable property was being considered by the Law Reform Committee for Scotland (LRCS), which led to the introduction of the statutory floating charge.[2] The controversial status of the floating charge in English law, after it first appeared in the mid-to-late nineteenth century, may help explain why there was little pressure to introduce a similar security in Scots law until well into the twentieth century. Yet steps taken to address some of the controversy

---

1 Namely, express non-possessory security rights over a changing class of property (including future property).
2 See A D J MacPherson, 'The Genesis of the Scottish Floating Charge', Chapter 3 within this volume.

in English law, such as the requirements for registration of charges, laid foundations for floating charges to become more amenable in Scotland. Nevertheless, the prospect of floating security remained at least divisive, as shall be demonstrated in the context of the introduction of agricultural charges to Scotland in the late 1920s. At various points in the later parts of the chapter, consideration is also given to whether there was growing demand and favourability towards reforming Scots law to allow for floating security. Even if there was some increase in support, it was countered by hostility and the reassertion of judicial antipathy to floating charges in *Carse v Coppen*,[3] which is analysed in the final substantive section of the chapter. All of this assists in comprehending the background to the arrival of the statutory floating charge and provides insights into the course that reform ultimately took, by way of the legislative legal transplant of an adapted version of the English floating charge.

Given the potential scope of floating security, it is necessary to pay attention to all types of property in this chapter. However, although incorporeal moveable property and heritable property are considered at various points, the primary concern is corporeal moveable property. It is for this property type that debates about non-possessory security are usually most relevant. Such property has therefore largely been the centre point of discussion regarding the acceptability (or non-acceptability) of such security rights, including for the institutional writers and, later, the LRCS.[4]

B. SCOTS COMMON LAW

Histories of various types of security right in Scots law have been written by others.[5] Here, the focus is on security rights that could be deemed to

---

3 1951 SC 233.

4 See below for the views of the institutional writers and see MacPherson, 'The Genesis of the Scottish Floating Charge', Chapter 3, for the LRCS's focus on corporeal moveables.

5 See e.g. W M Gordon, 'Roman Influence on the Scots Law of Real Security' in R Evans-Jones (ed), *The Civil Law Tradition in Scotland* (Edinburgh: The Stair Society, 1995) 157; A J M Steven, 'Rights in Security over Moveables' in K Reid and R Zimmermann (eds), *A History of Private Law in Scotland*, Vol. I (Oxford: Oxford University Press, 2000) 333; A J M Steven, *Pledge and Lien* (Edinburgh: Edinburgh Legal Education Trust, 2008) Ch. 3; A Sweeney, *The Landlord's Hypothec* (Edinburgh: Edinburgh Legal Education Trust, 2021) Chs 2–4; J Burgoyne, 'Heritable Securities' in *The Laws of Scotland: Stair Memorial Encyclopaedia*, Vol. 20 (1992) paras 108 onwards. However, as Professor Gretton notes, 'The history of the Scots law of heritable security is one of considerable complexity, and has been subject to little research': K G C Reid, *The Law of Property in Scotland* (London: Butterworths Law, 1996) (G L Gretton) para. 112. See now also Scottish Law Commission, *Discussion Paper on Heritable Securities: Pre-default* (Scot. Law Com. DP No. 168, 2019) Ch. 2.

exhibit the characteristics of a floating charge: an express non-possessory security over changing property (including future property), that enables the debtor to deal with the property that is encompassed by the security.[6] Perhaps unsurprisingly given Scots property law's Civilian heritage, much of the discussion of security rights in Scots law, particularly with respect to moveable property, has taken place in the shadow of Roman law. And, in fact, the Scots law position can be viewed as something of a reaction against the Roman law of security rights. It is therefore to Roman law that we must first briefly turn.

(1) Roman law

Security rights in Roman law have been much discussed by scholars.[7] The Roman security rights regime became increasingly permissive[8] and allowed for the creation of security rights over property that the debtor continued to possess. This form of security has traditionally been referred to, in Scots law and elsewhere, as a hypothec, in contrast to pledge, where the creditor possesses the property in question.[9] In reality, the Roman usage of the terms 'pledge' (*pignus*) and 'hypothec' was inconsistent and the precise relationship of these forms of security is elusive.[10] Bankton notes that the terms

---

6 Without requiring the agreement of the security holder to release the property from the ambit of the security.

7 For a selection, see R W Lee, *The Elements of Roman Law*, 4th edn (London: Sweet & Maxwell, 1956) 175 onwards; R J Goebel, 'Reconstructing the Roman Law of Real Security' (1961) 36 Tul L Rev 29; W W Buckland, *A Text-book of Roman Law from Augustus to Justinian*, 3rd edn (rev by P Stein) (Cambridge: Cambridge University Press, 1963) 473 onwards; J A C Thomas, *Textbook of Roman Law* (New York: North-Holland Publishing Company, 1976) Ch. 25; M Kaser, *Studien zum römischen Pfandrecht* (Naples: Jovene, 1982); D Johnston, *Roman Law in Context* (Cambridge: Cambridge University Press, 1999) 90 onwards; H L E Verhagen, 'Ius Honorarium, Equity and Real Security: Parallel Lines of Legal Development' in E Koops and W J Zwalve (eds), *Law and Equity: Approaches in Roman Law and Common Law* (Leiden: Brill Nijhoff, 2014) 129. See also P Du Plessis, 'The *Interdictum de Migrando* Revisited' (2007) 54 *Revue Internationale des droits de l'Antiquité* 219. For consideration of the Roman law of security rights within a Scottish context, see e.g. Gordon (n 5); Steven, *Pledge and Lien* (n 5) paras 3–03 onwards.

8 Bankton, *Institute*, I, 17, 7, (1751; 1993), later referred to the 'infinite liberty' allowed by civil law in the granting of securities by debtors.

9 See e.g. Erskine, *Institute*, II, 6, 56 (1773; 2014); and Bell, *Commentaries*, II, 25. In this chapter, references to Bell's *Commentaries* are to the fifth edition (1826), rather than the commonly used seventh edition which was edited by John (later Lord) McLaren (1870). The fifth edition was the last published during Bell's lifetime and can therefore more appropriately be referred to in the context of the 'institutional period' below.

10 Steven, *Pledge and Lien* (n 5) para. 3–12 onwards discusses this. See the sources cited there.

were also 'often used promiscuously' within Scottish custom.[11] Nevertheless, for the sake of simplicity and consistency with most Scots law sources, the terms hypothec and pledge will be used in the traditional manner here (except where otherwise stated). Hypothecs may be subdivided into express hypothecs (by 'explicit convention of parties') and tacit (or legal) hypothecs (established by law from 'presumed consent').[12]

Roman law seems to have enabled parties to grant a general hypothec over a circulating body of assets, such as stock in a shop or stall. A passage from the Digest provides the most well-known authority for this[13]:

'When a debtor impignorated[14] a stall[15] to the creditor, the question was put whether this was invalid or whether by "stall" the merchandise in the stall was to be taken as impignorated. And if he sold goods from time to time, bought others, brought them into the stall and then died, could the creditor in the hypothec action[16] sue for all that was then on the premises, in view of the turnover of stock? Scaevola replied: What was in the stall at the debtor's death was subject to the security.'[17]

Some later writers have therefore stated that a floating charge was available in Roman law.[18] It has also been suggested that the Roman hypothec could

---

11 Bankton, *Institute*, I, 17, 2. Bankton himself uses the terms in an inconsistent way – see I, 17, 3. See also Erskine, *Institute*, II, 6, 56 and Hume, *Lectures 1786–1822*, Vol. IV (1955) 8. In Scots law, the term hypothec is, of course, most associated with the landlord's hypothec, a tacit form of security.

12 Erskine, *Institute*, II, 6, 56. Bell, *Commentaries*, II, 25, refers to a further sub-category of 'judicial' hypothecs. In Scots law, judicial security is diligence.

13 D.20.1.34.pr (Scaevola). See also D.20.1.15.1 (Gaius) and D.20.2.9 (Paul). These are all discussed by Verhagen (n 7) at 135 onwards. The following translation of D.20.1.34.pr is from A Watson (ed), *The Digest of Justinian*, Vol. 2 (Philadelphia: University of Pennsylvania Press, 1998), except that Watson uses the term 'mortgage' and variants thereof but 'mortgage' has a particular technical meaning in English law and should be avoided here. It has therefore been replaced with more appropriate terms. Further details are provided in the following footnotes.

14 The term 'pignori' is used in the Latin version. Watson translates this as 'mortgaged' but 'impignorated' is preferable. The term 'impignorated' has also been inserted at the end of the sentence in place of 'mortgaged' used by Watson. Given the context, impignorated is being used in a broad sense to mean non–possessory security.

15 'Tabernam.'

16 The Latin text is 'hypothecaria actione', therefore, 'hypothec action' is used in place of Watson's 'mortgage action'.

17 The more neutral 'security' has been used here in place of Watson's 'mortgage'. The Latin term used is 'pignori'.

18 For example, Buckland, *A Text-book of Roman Law* (n 7) 478; Verhagen (n 7) at 135 onwards. Goebel describes the relevant form of security as a 'pledge on floating stock in trade' – Goebel (n 7) at 47. See also V J M van Hoof, 'The "Generalis Hypotheca" and the Sale of Pledged Assets in Roman Law' (2017) 85 *Tijdschrift voor Rechtsgeschiedenis* 474 at 490–491. R R Pennington, 'The Genesis of the Floating Charge' (1960) 23 MLR 630 at 646 also compares and contrasts the English floating charge with the Roman hypothec.

be granted over all types of property: immoveable or moveable, corporeal or incorporeal.[19]

We should be cautious about attaching modern labels, such as 'floating charge', to Roman law security rights as it can lead us to unjustifiably imbue the Roman security with the characteristics of modern floating charges. Nevertheless, the general hypothec does appear to have had some of the defining features of the later floating charge. It was a non-possessory security available over a class of property, it could extend to future property and seems to have allowed the debtor to dispose of assets unencumbered by the security prior to the point where the security could be enforced. It could also be created by simple contract. There are, however, various aspects of the development of the two forms of security that differ and the right of a general hypothec creditor would have been conceptualised in a different manner to that of a floating charge creditor in English law.[20]

(2) Early Scots law

It is unclear to what extent the Roman law position on security rights was accepted into Scots law in the latter's early form. In the *Regiam Majestatem*, which dates from the early fourteenth century, it is stated that for a party to acquire a security right in property, the grantor can give possession of the item to be pledged to the creditor 'or he does not'.[21] This suggests the possibility of both possessory and non-possessory security; however, a separate reference is made to 'the King's court' not wishing to involve itself where there was a risk that the same property had been pledged multiple times,[22] which could only arise with non-possessory security rights (i.e. hypothecs). The court was apparently unwilling to give effect to hypothecs because of the possibility that the debtor had offered the property as security to various

---

19 See e.g. Verhagen (n 7) at 141–142; and the sources cited by Steven, *Pledge and Lien* (n 5) para. 3–15.

20 See below.

21 *Regiam Majestatem and Quoniam Attachiamenta* (ed and trans Lord Cooper) (1947) III, 2.

22 *Regiam Majestatem and Quoniam Attachiamenta* III, 4. This is very similar to the English law position outlined in *The Treatise on the Laws and Customs of the Realm of England Commonly Called Glanvill* (ed and trans G D G Hall) (Oxford: Oxford University Press, 1965) X, 8. Given the reference to the pledging of the property multiple times, pledge seems to be used in the *Regiam Majestatem* in its wide sense to include hypothecs (the Latin term 'vadium' is used in the text). Bell states that Scots law's 'repugnance' towards conventional hypothecs can be traced back to the time of Balfour and even to the *Regiam Majestatem* – Bell, *Commentaries*, II, 26. As discussed below, Lord President Cooper used similar language when referring to floating charges as 'utterly repugnant to the principles of Scots law' in *Carse* (n 3) at 239.

parties – resolving such disputes would be complicated and time-consuming and would cause uncertainty for litigating parties and prospective creditors. Limiting enforceability to possessory pledge would help to avoid these issues. It has, however, been suggested by some that express hypothecs might have been enforceable in ecclesiastical, local and private courts in early Scots law[23]; but, as Professor Steven notes, there is little evidence to support this.[24]

The *Regiam Majestatem* also states that pledge could be granted for moveable or immoveable property. This followed Glanvill, in English law, as well as the Roman law's unitary approach to property.[25] Likewise, Balfour grouped together 'movabill' and 'immovabill' property, stating that the debtor should put the creditor in possession (or sasine – the equivalent of possession for land).[26] Balfour's comment can be interpreted to mean either that hypothecs were, by his time, not legally available or that it was advisable to transfer possession for reasons of certainty and/or enforceability.[27]

Some later writers, such as Ross and Stewart, have suggested that in early Scots law it was even possible to create a general hypothec, and that the diligence of inhibition originated as a preventive measure to preclude the debtor from dealing with property that was subject to a general hypothec over their whole property.[28] While this is possible, it is largely a matter of speculation given the lack of evidence and, as noted above, the extent to which early Scots law admitted express hypothecs is disputed.[29]

Whatever the earlier legal situation was, the position changed so that the law itself did not generally give effect to express hypothecs (see below).

---

23 See Gordon (n 5) at 161 n 17; and the views of Lord Cooper in *Regiam Majestatem* (n 21) in the notes to III, 4.

24 Steven, 'Rights in Security over Moveables' (n 5) at 335 onwards. See also Sweeney, *The Landlord's Hypothec* (n 5) paras 2–07–2–08.

25 *Regiam Majestatem* (n 21) III, 2; *Glanvill* (n 22) X, 6. See Steven, 'Rights in Security over Moveables' (n 5) at 335 for discussion. As Steven notes, there were, however, some separate rules for heritable security.

26 J Balfour, *The Practicks of Sir James Balfour of Pittendreich*, P G B McNeill (ed) (Edinburgh: The Stair Society, 1962) Vol. I, 194. These Practicks were compiled in the later sixteenth century: they have been dated to 1579 but there were likely some additions until Balfour's death in 1583 (xxxii–xxxiii).

27 However, even before Balfour's *Practicks*, there seems to have been some form of preference for a landlord in items on the leased premises, i.e. a tacit security with characteristics of the landlord's hypothec – see Sweeney, *The Landlord's Hypothec* (n 5) paras 2–09 onwards. This can be considered an exception to the general position for hypothecs.

28 W Ross, *Lectures on the History and Practice of the Law of Scotland: Relative to Conveyancing and Legal Diligence*, 2nd edn (Edinburgh: Bell and Bradfute, 1822) 459–465; J G Stewart, *A Treatise on the Law of Diligence* (Edinburgh: W. Green, 1898) 525–526.

29 For further discussion, see J MacLeod, *Fraud and Voidable Transfer* (Edinburgh: Edinburgh Legal Education Trust, 2020) paras 5–68 onwards.

Furthermore, it seems as if, over time, the level of unitariness of security over different property types diminished as separate security regimes developed and diverged; comparing Roman law and early Scots law sources with the institutional writers and later Scots law sources seems to verify this.[30]

(3) Institutional period

(a) Corporeal moveable property

Amongst the institutional writers there was consensus that express hypothecs over corporeal moveables were generally not competent in Scots law. Stair provides the most well-known statement of this:

> 'But our custom hath taken away express hypothecations, of all or part of the debtor's goods, without delivery, and of the tacit legal hypothecations hath only allowed a few, allowing ordinarily parties to be preferred according to the priority of their legal diligence, that commerce may be the more sure, and every one may more easily know his condition with whom he contracts.'[31]

The impact upon 'commerce',[32] 'traffick'[33] and 'trade',[34] as well as the potential for encouragement of 'false credit',[35] are pointed to by writers of the period as justification for the rejection of hypothecs.[36] There seems to have

---

30 Gordon (n 5) at 159–160 states that if the *Regiam Majestatem* can be considered a historically accurate representation then it seems there was a time where 'no distinction was drawn between constitution of real security over land and over moveables'. He notes though that even at the time of that work a distinct law of heritable security was emerging.

31 Stair, *Institutions*, I, 13, 14. Stair cites *Cushney v Christie* (1676) Mor 6237 where it was held that under Scots law there is no tacit hypothec for the price paid for sold goods. And see *Ker of Greenhead v Scot and Elliot* (1695) Mor 9122 in which the court rejected the validity of a non-possessory security over sheep and other goods (symbolical delivery being held insufficient). See also Bankton, *Institute*, I, 17, 2–3; Erskine, *Institute*, III, 1, 34; Bell, *Commentaries*, II, 25–26. Stair's reference to 'hath taken away' may suggest that Scots law did once permit such security interests. Whether this is a reference to the position outlined in the *Regiam Majestatem* is unclear.

32 Stair, *Institutions*, I, 13, 14 and IV, 25, 1; Bankton, *Institute*, I, 17, 3. See also Hume, *Lectures*, Vol. IV (n 11) 32. It should be mentioned here that although Hume's *Lectures* is an important source it is not considered an institutional work – *Fortington v Lord Kinnaird* 1942 SC 239 at 253–254 per Lord President Normand; A Rahmatian, 'The Role of Institutional Writers in Scots Law' (2018) Jur Rev 42 at 51–52.

33 Bankton, *Institute*, I, 17, 3.

34 Hume, *Lectures*, Vol. IV (n 11) 3. Hume at 29 and Erskine, *Institute*, III, 1, 34 and *Principles*, III, 1, 13, also refer to trade but specifically in relation to tacit hypothecs.

35 Bell, *Principles*, § 1385.

36 A number of the terms used were largely synonymous (at least by the middle of the eighteenth century) – see e.g. S Johnson, *A Dictionary of the English Language*, Vol. I (1755) who writes in his definition of 'commerce': 'Intercourse; exchange of one thing for another; interchange of any thing; trade; traffick'. See also the entries for 'trade' and 'traffick' in Vol. II. The use of

been virtually no variation in position over the course of the institutional period, despite significant societal and economic changes,[37] and Bell notes that he was not aware of a single case in the Scottish case reports in which a party attempted to give effect to an express hypothec.[38] The writers of the period compare and contrast the Scots law position with Roman law, including with reference to commerce. Bankton, for example, expresses a belief that commercial issues were of greater concern to modern states than to the Romans, and Hume states that the 'commercial spirit' of his time was negatively disposed towards hypothecs.[39] Where conventional hypothecs were admitted – bonds of bottomry and *respondentia* (for ships and their cargo) – this could be justified as a desirable means of facilitating trade within a discrete context.[40] The Scots law rule on hypothecs was therefore not entirely inflexible and, given the trade-focused basis of the rule, further exceptions that actually supported commerce would logically be acceptable.

such terminology with this meaning can also be found in earlier Scottish sources, see e.g. the Diligence Act 1661 (c 344), which refers to 'trade' and 'traffique'.

37 For example, the Union of England and Scotland, the early stages of the Industrial Revolution and the growth of commerce across the country. The works of Adam Smith (1723–1790), the highly influential economist and philosopher, were also published during this period: most notably, *The Theory of Moral Sentiments* (1759) and *An Inquiry into the Nature and Causes of the Wealth of Nations* (1776). For details of Scotland's economic history, see e.g. S G E Lythe and J Butt, *An Economic History of Scotland 1100–1939* (Glasgow: Blackie & Son, 1975); T M Devine, C H Lee and G C Peden, *The Transformation of Scotland: The Economy Since 1700* (Edinburgh: Edinburgh University Press, 2005).

38 Bell, *Commentaries*, II, 26. But see e.g. *Ker of Greenhead* (n 31). The comment was also presumably subject to the exceptions of bonds of bottomry and respondentia – see below.

39 Bankton, *Institute*, I, 17, 3; see also Bell, *Commentaries*, I, 476. Hume, *Lectures*, Vol. IV (n 11) 29 and 32. And see the later description of 'hypothec' in G Watson, *Bell's Dictionary and Digest of the Law of Scotland*, 7th edn (1890, reprinted 2012), which also contrasted the Roman law with Scots law, the latter 'having regard to the inexpediency of such liens in a commercial and trading country, admits of but few hypothecs'. On a similar note, the philosopher David Hume (the uncle of Baron Hume) wrote in 'Of Liberty and Despotism' in *Essays, Moral and Political* (Edinburgh, 1741) at 175, that: 'Trade was never esteem'd an Affair of State, 'till within this last Century; nor is there any antient Writer on Politics, who has made mention of it'. In the period, there was much discussion about the country becoming a more commercial society, as well as the emergence of the stadial theory of societal development – see e.g. H Home (Lord Kames), *Historical Law Tracts* (1758); A Smith, *Lectures on Jurisprudence, Report of 1762–3*, R L Meek, D D Raphael and P G Stein (eds) (1978) 14 onwards; and see A Rahmatian, *Lord Kames: Legal and Social Theorist* (Edinburgh: Edinburgh University Press, 2015) Ch. 5 for discussion.

40 See e.g. Bell, *Commentaries*, I, 530 onwards and II, 26; Bell, *Principles*, § 452 and 1386. The 'encouragement of trade' was also a reason for the acceptance of tacit hypothecs relating to maritime matters according to Erskine, *Institute*, III, 1, 34. For brief historical details of the related topic of 'ship mortgages', including legislative developments, see G L Gretton, 'Ships as a Branch of Property Law', in A R C Simpson, S C Styles, E West and A L M Wilson (eds), *Continuity, Change and Pragmatism in the Law: Essays in Memory of Professor Angelo Forte* (Aberdeen, Aberdeen University Press, 2016) 367 at 394–397.

Nevertheless, as A J Sim has written, in relation to the general position: '[i]t was considered inimical to commercial stability and confidence that debtors should remain in possession of property over which their debts were secured'.[41] A party transacting with the owner of property would not know whether the property was subject to a security right (or multiple security rights). Bell recognised the importance of publicity in this context when he stated: 'it is against the principle and spirit of the law of Scotland to admit a real right or security which is not attended with some badge manifest and palpable'.[42] Similar points are applicable with respect to the general non-admission of tacit hypothecs. One solution would have been to use a register system. In *Ker of Greenhead v Scot and Elliot* (1695), the absence of registration was identified as a justification for the rejection of express non-possessory securities:

> 'The law has authorised sundry tacit hypothecks, as of the *invecta et illata in domum seu fundum* for the rent, but a hypothecation of a great flock of sheep, in security of a sum far below their value, *retenta possessione*, is unknown in law; and such pledges were very inconvenient, for there is no register to certiorate the lieges of such impignorations when they continue in the impleger's hand.'[43]

Yet as Erskine noted (albeit in the context of tacit security) it was 'impracticable to keep a record for moveables, by which purchasers may be ascertained of their danger'.[44] In the institutional period registration would not have seemed a realistic solution for express security rights, due to difficulties creating and maintaining a register for property that was so mobile and changeable and where there would have been considerable inconvenience recording in, accessing and checking such a register.

The lack of registration and consequent uncertainties for creditors regarding the possibility of existing security rights were serious problems with the Roman law of hypothecs (especially later Roman law).[45] The Scottish position was likely founded upon the idea that such problems would limit trade and the provision of credit due to the greater risks of non-payment that

---

41 A J Sim, 'Rights in Security over Moveables', *The Laws of Scotland: Stair Memorial Encyclopaedia* Vol. 20 (1992) para. 3.

42 Bell, *Principles*, § 1385 (this only appears from the 4th edn (1839) onwards); Bell, *Commentaries*, II, 26; see also Hume, *Lectures*, Vol. IV (n 11) 32 who praises earlier Scots for comprehending the 'great advantage' of not giving effect to encumbrances over corporeal moveables that were 'not published by the state of possession'.

43 *Ker of Greenhead* (n 31) at 9122.

44 Erskine, *Institute*, III, 1, 34.

45 See e.g. B Nicholas, *An Introduction to Roman Law* (Oxford: Oxford University Press, 1962) 153; F Schulz, *Classical Roman Law* (Oxford: Clarendon Press, 1951) 403 onwards; Zwalve (n 67) at 42.

creditors would encounter if security rights could already have been created without publicity. There was no doubt a belief that such a system would be open to abuse through fraudulent behaviour, leading to confusion and uncertainty. Instead, the certainty offered by generally only allowing possessory pledges was preferred.

There are, of course, economic advantages that can result from allowing parties greater freedom to use their assets as security (e.g. to grant multiple security rights over the asset) and to use their continued possession of such assets for productive economic purposes.[46] However, before the Industrial Revolution reached its stride, there was probably less need for the availability of non-possessory security over corporeal moveables. The growing value of moveables used for productive purposes in the context of the Industrial Revolution should logically have created more demand for non-possessory security so that the moveables could be used to raise finance but also continue to generate income. Yet, as noted below, the evidence for such demand in Scots law was sparse until much later. In any event, there was considered to be insufficient merit in non-possessory security to lead to its general introduction within the institutional period.

(b) Heritable property

For land there was already a functioning registration system in place, due to legislative intervention. An equivalent to actual delivery, known as sasine, had been devised at an early stage for the transfer of land and was also used for the creation of security rights in land. The giving of sasine originally involved a ceremony on the land, which was recorded in an instrument of sasine (a notarial deed)[47] and from 1617 recording of such instruments in the Register of Sasines was required to confer a real right.[48] As Bankton states, the form of security known as wadset was 'perfected, by infeftment duly registred [sic],

---

46 See J Hardman, 'Law and Economics of the Floating Charge', Chapter 5 within this volume, for an analysis of the economic value of the floating charge in Scots law.

47 These requirements lasted until 1845 and 1858 respectively, at which point conveyances became directly registrable – see K G C Reid and G L Gretton, *Land Registration* (Edinburgh: Avizandum, 2017) 7 for details.

48 Registration Act 1617 (c 16). See Reid, *Law of Property* (n 5) para. 640; Reid and Gretton, *Land Registration* (n 47) 1 onwards; and L Ockrent, *Land Rights: An Enquiry into the History of Registration for Publication in Scotland* (Edinburgh: Hodge & Co, 1942) for further information about the history of transfer and registration of land generally; and see Gordon (n 5) at 160 onwards for some historical details regarding the development of registration of heritable securities. See also H H Monteath, 'Heritable Rights: From Early Times to the Twentieth Century' in *An Introduction to Scottish Legal History* (Edinburgh: Stair Society, 1958) 156 at 183 onwards; and Ross, *Lectures* (n 28) 320 onwards.

[and] will stand good to the creditor, in prejudice of all posterior purchasers from the debtor, tho' he remained, in the civil, or even natural possession, because they may blame themselves that did not search the records'.[49] Over time, wadset was succeeded by other forms of security right for land, most notably bonds and dispositions in security and *ex facie* absolute dispositions qualified by back bond. However, for each of these, recording in the Register was required in order to confer a real right on the creditor.[50]

As Bell writes regarding heritable security rights: 'the whole law respecting the completion of real voluntary securities on land, is expressed in this one proposition, [t]hat the security requires to its completion a sasine duly recorded'.[51] The usage of equivalents to possession for security over land, most notably registration from 1617, was an example of Scots law overcoming the problems inherent in a lack of publicity where actual possession by a creditor was considered unsuitable or unproductive for them and/or for a debtor. Given the static and enduring nature of land in comparison to moveable property, as well as its generally greater value in this period,[52] it is not surprising that the registration of security rights over land was considered feasible while an equivalent register for moveables was not. If we consider a hypothec to be a non-possessory security, even if an equivalent to delivery to the creditor (such as registration) is used, then Scots law admitted, and admits, hypothecs over land. The current hypothec is, of course, the standard security, a statutory form of security.[53]

It is interesting to note that the term hypothec is nowadays more commonly used for security over land in continental jurisdictions[54] such as

---

49 Bankton, *Institute*, I, 17, 3. See also Stair, *Institutions*, II, 10, 1–2. And see Burgoyne (n 5) para. 109 on wadsets.

50 Recording or registration has also been required for standard securities since their introduction – Conveyancing and Feudal Reform (Scotland) Act 1970 Part II. For an overview of the history of heritable security in Scots law, see Scottish Law Commission, *Discussion Paper on Heritable Securities: Pre-default* (n 5) Ch. 2. And for discussion of the relationship between the pre-1970 Act forms of heritable security and the floating charge, see A D J MacPherson, *The Floating Charge* (Edinburgh: Edinburgh Legal Education Trust, 2020) paras 7–82 onwards.

51 Bell, *Commentaries*, I, 670. Bell gives a short history of the voluntary heritable securities at 670–673.

52 One piece of evidence for this is the large volume of case reports dealing with heritable property matters – see e.g. J J Waugh, 'Gleanings from the Eighteenth Century Law Reports' 1903 Jur Rev 164 at 175. In addition, the relative value of land seems to have been reflected in its use for the purposes of security – see e.g. S G Checkland, *Scottish Banking: A History, 1695–1973* (London: Collins, 1975) 5.

53 Conveyancing and Feudal Reform (Scotland) Act 1970 Part II.

54 See G L Gretton, 'Pledge, Bills of Lading, Trusts and Property Law' 1990 Jur Rev 23 at 23 n 2; and Scottish Law Commission, *Discussion Paper on Heritable Securities: Pre-default* (n 5) para. 3.18.

France[55] and Germany,[56] whereas in Scotland it is associated with security over moveables, especially the landlord's hypothec, a tacit security.[57]

(c) Incorporeal moveable property

For incorporeal moveable property,[58] the form of security available in the institutional period, and also in present-day Scots law, is a *fiducia cum creditore* type, whereby the right itself is transferred and the transferee is merely obliged to retransfer (retrocess) upon fulfilment of the secured obligation. For this reason, assignation in security is not considered separately from absolute assignation by a number of the institutional writers, with Bell's substantial treatment of assignation in security being the most notable exception to this.[59] In the paradigm case of claims (often referred to as debts), the institutional writers are clear that assignation followed by intimation to the claim debtor is necessary to transfer the property.[60]

Although intimation is, at best, a weak form of publicity (in that only one party is notified)[61] it can be considered an equivalent to delivery of corporeal moveables, as noted by Bell.[62] Since possession is not possible for incorporeal property, it may be said that, strictly speaking, the term hypothec is inapplicable. However, the extent to which publicity is necessary and desirable for this type of property, and what type of publicity is most appropriate, are valid points of discussion, and these parallel some of the issues regarding the admission of hypothecs in Scots law. There has

---

55 See the use of 'hypothèque' in France in Code Civil Arts 2393 onwards.

56 See the use of 'Hypothek' in Germany in BGB § 1113 onwards.

57 For detailed discussion of the landlord's hypothec, including from a historical perspective, see Sweeney, *The Landlord's Hypothec* (n 5).

58 The focus here is on personal rights.

59 See Bell, *Commentaries* II, 11, and 16 onwards.

60 Stair, *Institutions*, III, 1, 3; III, 1, 6 and III, 1, 43; Mackenzie, *Institutions* III, 5; Bankton, *Institute*, III, 1, 6–11; Erskine, *Institute*, III, 5, 1 and 8–9; Bell, *Commentaries*, II, 16–17. See R G Anderson, *Assignation* (Edinburgh: Edinburgh Legal Education Trust, 2008) Ch. 6 and para. 7–36; and MacPherson, *Floating Charge* (n 50) Ch. 9, for details on the necessity of intimation to transfer claims in security. See also Scottish Law Commission, *Report on Moveable Transactions* (Scot. Law Com. No. 249, 2017) paras 5.1 onwards.

61 R G Anderson and J W A Biemans, 'Reform of Assignation in Security: Lessons from the Netherlands' (2012) 16 Edin L Rev 24 at 34; Scottish Law Commission, *Report on Moveable Transactions* (n 60) paras 5.3 and 5.26. Perhaps more accurately it can be considered a private act involving a third party.

62 Bell, *Principles*, § 1459–1462. Bell describes the assignation and intimation transaction as most closely resembling the change of custody where corporeal moveables are being transferred and are held by a custodier first for the seller and then for the buyer (see § 1305).

been some debate regarding these matters in modern-day Scots law and, in fact, the Scottish Law Commission has recommended the introduction of registration as a means of creating security, by way of a subordinate right of 'statutory pledge', over certain types of incorporeal property (intellectual property and financial instruments) and there is also a desire that this could be eventually extended to claims.[63] Yet, in the institutional period there is a notable absence of consideration given to alternatives to intimation for creating security over incorporeal moveables.

With assignation, there is difficulty in creating security in relation to future property acquired by the cedent (assignor). The necessity of intimation creates practical problems. While present claims payable at a future point may be transferred these are not the same as other types of contingent or future claim, where the claim does not yet exist and it is not possible to identify who the claim debtor will be.[64] Even if the doctrine of accretion can facilitate a later transfer where the claim debtor has already received intimation of a purported transfer from cedent to assignee (prior to the 'cedent' actually holding the claim),[65] this depends upon a cedent knowing who the claim debtor will be, which is not always the case.[66]

(d) Comparative law

In his *Commentaries*, Bell expressly considers Scotland's non-admission of hypothecs in a comparative context. By doing so, he attempts to position Scots law within one of the mainstream legal currents in Europe and he imputes to the relevant laws of other systems in Europe the same commercial basis for the law as in Scotland. He states that in Europe's development from the Middle Ages 'the principal states ... were led to the encouragement of commerce' and thus departed from the Roman law on hypothecs, with conventional hypothecs having been proscribed 'in almost all the commercial states of Europe' or at least 'subjected to such restrictions as may

---

63 Scottish Law Commission, *Report on Moveable Transactions* (n 60). Even if the reforms are enacted, however, assignation in security would remain as an alternative means of creating security. See A J M Steven, 'Reform of the Scottish Floating Charge', Chapter 12 within this volume.

64 See e.g. Stair, *Institutions*, I, 3, 7; G L Gretton, 'The Assignation of Contingent Rights' 1993 Jur Rev 23; Scottish Law Commission, *Report on Moveable Transactions* (n 60) paras 5.81 onwards.

65 Stair, *Institutions*, III, 2, 1, appears to have considered accretion to be possible for assignations.

66 The intervening insolvency of the purported cedent may also defeat the operation of accretion. For the applicability of accretion to claims, see Anderson, *Assignation* (n 60) paras 11–46 onwards.

prevent material injury'.[67] In modern scholarship, Zwalve has written that although at the end of the fifteenth century the Roman security system had become part of the law of virtually all European countries except for England and Wales, over time there was a general trend (but with large differences across jurisdictions) towards the limitation or abolition of express hypothecs.[68] The criticism of the Roman law system by the likes of Voet may have been of some significance on this front.[69] These views would also no doubt have had some influence on the opinions of various Scottish lawyers, especially the many who studied law in the Netherlands during the institutional period.[70]

Bell states that under the applicable law in certain countries (such as in France, Spain, Germany and Holland) conventional hypothecs did not affect a bona fide purchaser.[71] He adds that, in other places (such as by the customs

67 Bell, *Commentaries*, II, 25. On hypothecs, generally, Bell refers to F dal Pozzo, *Observations sur le régime hypothécaire établi dans le royaume de Sardaigne* (Paris: Hachette, 1823). He also cites B Carpzov (Carpzovius), *Jurisprudentia Forensis Romano-Saxonica*, II, 23 (first published in 1638 in Frankfurt, but it is unclear to which version of this book Bell is referring). This source is referred to by W J Zwalve, 'A Labyrinth of Creditors: A Short Introduction to the History of Security Interests in Goods', in E-M Kieninger (ed), *Security Rights in Movable Property in European Private Law* (Cambridge: Cambridge University Press, 2004) 38 at 44 n 20, as evidence that in the Saxon territories of the German empire the maxim 'mobilia non habent sequelam' ('moveables cannot be traced into the hands of third parties') did not apply to general or special non-possessory security interests, except for what has been referred to as a 'floating charge' on the stock-in-trade of a shop.

68 Zwalve (n 67) at 43 onwards. Steven, 'Rights in Security over Moveables' (n 5) at 348, suggests that the continuity in the Scottish repudiation of hypothecs arose from the fact that the Roman law 'was acknowledged as unsatisfactory' and because a number of European countries rejected hypothecs to varying degrees.

69 See e.g. Zwalve (n 67) at 43 onwards, who cites the comments at Voet, *Commentarius ad Pandectas* (Geneva, 1757) XX, 4, 17. As Zwalve also notes (at 45), the Dutch Hoge Raad rejected Voet's view that the transfer of possession to the creditor was required to create security over moveables, yet Voet's position remained influential in practice. This was because practitioners were largely unaware of the court's opinions due to the absence of outlined reasoning and the fact that reports were not published until the twentieth century.

70 See e.g. J W Cairns, 'Importing Our Lawyers from Holland: Netherlands' Influences on Scots Law and Lawyers in the Eighteenth Century' in J W Cairns, *Law, Lawyers, and Humanism: Selected Essays on the History of Scots Law* Vol. 1 (Edinburgh: Edinburgh University Press, 2015) and Sweeney, *The Landlord's Hypothec* (n 5) paras 3–30 onwards and the sources cited there.

71 Bell, *Commentaries*, II, 25. But see above regarding the Saxon territories: of course, 'Germany' at this time consisted of a number of separate states. For Holland at least, it appears that good faith was not required in order for a purchaser to be protected, only that there was a transfer for value – see V J M van Hoof, *Generale Zekerheidsrechten in Rechtshistorisch Perspectief* (Deventer: Wolters Kluwer, 2015) 122 onwards.

of Paris and Orléans[72] and in England),[73] purported hypothecs did not even have an effect upon personal creditors (of the debtor). Scotland fell into this latter category and was therefore within one of the principal groups of the law of hypothecs in Europe. Bell was writing at a time when this area of law was in a state of flux. The French Code Civil (1804) required the transfer of possession in order to create an express security right over corporeal moveables.[74] As T B Smith later noted, the pre-Revolutionary French law 'lacked adequate machinery to secure publicity' and when the law was reformed it was thought that 'it would not be possible to carry out efficiently registration of express hypothecs over moveables'.[75] The French position was adopted by other states (including the Netherlands, Spain and Germany) over the course of the following century.[76] Despite the changing landscape (as well as the points made in his *Commentaries* regarding non-admittance and limitation of express hypothecs), Bell asserts in his *Principles* that, 'on the Continent', hypothecs (presumably tacit and express) were 'still largely admitted'.[77] As regards express hypothecs, the reality was that Scotland's position – giving hypothecs no effect, even against personal creditors – seems to have become more orthodox internationally as the nineteenth century progressed.[78]

72 For the customs of Paris and Orléans, Bell cites R J Valin, *Commentary on the Ordonnance de la Marine* (seemingly *Nouveau commentaire sur l'Ordonnance de la marine du mois d'août* 1681 (La Rochelle, 1776)) I, 341. At this point he also refers to J B C de Lucca, *Conflictus Legis et Rationis* (Rome, 1677).

73 For England, see further below. The assertion does not seem to pay sufficient regard to equity in English law.

74 See arts 2071 onwards CC (1804), and later arts 2119 onwards CC. From the early twentieth century exceptions to the rule developed and the French reforms of 2006 enable a party to grant express hypothecs so long as registration requirements are met – see arts 2333 onwards CC.

75 T B Smith, 'Historical Note' Appendix I to LRCS, *Eighth Report of the Law Reform Committee for Scotland* (Cmnd 1017: 1960) 13. See also T B Smith, *A Short Commentary on the Law of Scotland* (Edinburgh: W. Green, 1962) 472–474.

76 See Zwalve (n 67) at 47. As referred to by Zwalve, in Germany, the Bankruptcy Act of 1877 (*Reichskonkursordnung*) provided (at s. 14) that no preference was created where an attempt had been made to create a security over moveable property without the permanent transfer of possession.

77 Bell, *Principles*, § 1385. The word 'largely' was in the third edition (1833), having been absent in the second edition (1830), and references to F dal Pozzo, *Observations sur le régime hypothécaire établi dans le royaume de Sardaigne* (Paris, 1823) and Pothier, II, 945 were added (the reference to Pothier appears to be to R J Pothier, *Oeuvres complètes de Pothier: précédées dúne dissertation sur sa vie et ses écrits, et suivies dúne table de concordance*, J A Rogron and M Firbach (eds) (Paris, 1830)). For discussion of Bell's use of the works of Pothier (1699–1772), see K G C Reid, 'From Textbook to Book of Authority: The Principles of George Joseph Bell' (2011) 15 Edin L Rev 6 at 24–25.

78 As shall be seen below, towards the end of the century the position began to move in the opposite direction, at least in some jurisdictions.

Bell also refers to Scots law within a wider European context as regards heritable (immoveable) property. He states that, at the time, it was an 'almost universal' rule in continental Europe that hypothecs over such property had no efficacy 'unless entered into by solemn deed, and recorded'. In support of this, he cites a number of systems, including France, Germany, Holland and Spain.[79] Like Scotland then, registration of security rights over land in these jurisdictions was considered to be a viable regime that was more easily manageable than was the case for moveable property.

The Scots law position on express hypothecs was therefore certainly not exceptional and was in conformity with a number of other jurisdictions in Europe. The lack of exceptionality in the Scottish position would likely have further strengthened the view that it was appropriate and rational in the prevailing circumstances. Conversely, if the international current were to change due to economic developments or otherwise and Scots law was to be left adrift, then significant doubt could be cast upon the efficacy of the Scottish position.

(e) General hypothec – doctrinal obstacles

Throughout the institutional period then, the Scots law position on express hypothecs over corporeal moveables was clear and definite. They were rejected ostensibly to provide certainty within the field of commerce. The feared commercial problems noted above could largely be avoided where there was an act of publicity and the only apparently feasible means of publicity at the time for corporeal moveable property was to transfer possession. For heritable property recording in a register could serve this purpose, while the equivalent for incorporeal moveable property was, and is, intimation. Given the necessity of delivering the relevant corporeal moveable property, intimating an assignation to a particular debtor in relation to a specified debt and recording security over specific heritable property in the General Register of Sasines, a general hypothec over a particular class

---

79 Bell, *Commentaries*, II, 25. However, Bell states that these systems allowed for general security over this type of property, unlike in Scotland. For information regarding the relevant jurisdictions, Bell cites: Pothier, *Oeuvres posthumes de M Pothier* (Orléans and Paris, 1778) I, 426 (France); Carpzov (Carpzovius), *Jurisprudentia forensis Romano-Saxonica*, (in particular II, 23) (Germany); Van Leewin, IV, 7, 8–10 (which is presumably S van Leeuwen, *Het Roomsch Hollandsch Recht* (Amsterdam, 1780)), Voet, XX, 1, 9 (*Commentarius ad Pandectas*), and J van den Sande, *Decisiones Frisicae* (Leeuwarden, 1639) III, 12, 15 (Holland and Low Countries); d'Acosta and Rodriguez (Spain) (Bell seems to be referring to *Instituciones del derecho civil de Castilla* (originally published Madrid, 1771), although which version of this is not clear).

of potentially changing assets, even within one property type, was also not possible. Furthermore, these requirements (which necessitate the owning or holding of the property) meant that a security right over future property could not be created immediately from the point at which the property was acquired by the debtor.[80]

The separate regimes for creating security over different types of property inhibited the possibility of having a unitary security right over multiple pieces of property of varying types, or over all property of the debtor. Creating a security over even two pieces of property, where e.g. one is moveable and the other heritable, with only one act of publicity, is not available at common law in Scotland. And in Scots law generally, security rights create an immediate security right in the property in question and the debtor cannot transfer the property unencumbered by the security unless she has the security holder's permission. One notable (but partial) exception to the absence of security in Scots law covering multiple items of property is the landlord's hypothec, a security (albeit a tacit security) over a potentially changing body of moveable assets on the leased premises.[81] More broadly, the existing forms of security right were also increasingly seen as exhaustive and it was not considered desirable to allow for a voluntary general hypothec.

Due to all of this, the prospect of Scots law admitting a security akin to the general hypothec of Roman law was very distant. The law's objection to the existence of non-possessory security precluded the acceptance of a 'floating' security. Even as the nineteenth century progressed there was no indication of the law heading in a more liberal direction. This was in direct contrast to the position in England, from where the modern floating charge emerged. In addition, given the established common law position in Scotland, outlined in the institutional period, it is not surprising that Scottish courts were to later reject the validity of English-style floating charges.[82]

---

80 Subject to the limited contexts in which the doctrine of accretion could operate.
81 The landlord's hypothec was used as a model for enforcement when agricultural charges were introduced – see below. For discussion of when property is released from the landlord's hypothec, including historical consideration of this, see Sweeney, *The Landlord's Hypothec* (n 5) Ch. 9.
82 See below.

C. ENGLISH LAW

(1) English law and Roman law

It is of value to compare the Roman law of security rights to English law, since English law also ultimately developed general non-possessory security, in addition to possessory security. As specified by Millett LJ in *Re Cosslett (Contractors) Ltd*[83]:

> 'There are only four kinds of consensual security known to English law: (i) pledge; (ii) contractual lien; (iii) equitable charge and (iv) mortgage. A pledge and a contractual lien both depend on the delivery of possession to the creditor ... Neither a mortgage nor a charge depends on the delivery of possession. The difference between them is that a mortgage involves a transfer of legal or equitable ownership to the creditor, whereas an equitable charge does not.'[84]

It is tempting to draw parallels between security rights within English law and within Roman law, especially given the extraordinary influence of these two systems.[85] The possessory pledge of English law may be equated with the Roman *pignus* while the Roman hypothec at least has the non-possessory nature of an English mortgage or charge. As noted previously, several scholars have described the general hypothec of Roman law as a floating charge. And Professor Sir Roy Goode has referred to the Roman institution of hypothec as a 'robust ancestor of the equitable charge'.[86]

Examining security rights of a system through the prism of those we are most familiar with is, in some sense, inescapable. Yet care should be taken to avoid overstating the connection between security rights in the two systems. They developed independently, one arising from a legal system with a clearer distinction between real and personal rights and the other from a more opaque system featuring law and equity (and with markedly different chronologies). In addition, it is clear that there are security rights

---

83 [1998] Ch 495.
84 [1998] Ch 495 at 508. For discussion of the case from a Scots law perspective, see S P L Wolffe and W J Wolffe, 'Some Property Problems in Building Contracts', in A J M Steven, R G Anderson and J MacLeod (eds), *Nothing So Practical as a Good Theory: Festschrift for George L Gretton* (Edinburgh: Avizandum, 2017) 265.
85 Drawing parallels more broadly between English law and Roman law is not a new endeavour, see e.g. F Pringsheim, 'The Inner Relationship Between English and Roman Law' (1935) 5 CLJ 347.
86 R Goode, 'The Exodus of the Floating Charge', in D Feldman and F Meisel (eds), *Corporate and Commercial Law: Modern Developments* (London: LLP Professional Publishing, 1996) 193 at 195. Cf R Gregory and P Walton 'Fixed and Floating Charges – A Revelation' (2001) *Lloyds Maritime and Commercial Law Quarterly* 123.

in each system that are not directly comparable. For example, equating the hypothec of Roman law with the chattel mortgage of English law was rejected (rightly, given their distinctive natures) in the case of *Ryall v Rolle*.[87]

It has been suggested that the Roman law general hypothec and the English floating charge followed a similar evolutionary sequence.[88] As already noted, there are analogous characteristics. However, they were almost certainly conceptually different. Any statement regarding the nature of the Roman general hypothec is a matter of some speculation; however, the Romans may have considered the general hypothec to create an immediate right over any property subject to the security (including upon acquisition of property by the grantor), with the right being extinguished over property that was validly transferred to another party.[89] If this was the Roman conception, they would have, unlike in England, avoided the difficulties of identifying the pre-attachment nature of the security.[90] Under this construction, the Roman equivalent to the attachment event (when a floating charge becomes fixed) would simply have been the point at which the debtor lost the right to transfer property and the creditor could enforce.[91] Of course, we do not know enough about the Roman law hypothec to state precisely how it worked. The 'post-rationalisation' Civilian approach adopted here is, nevertheless, based upon reasonable supposition.[92]

It is possible that Roman law had an indirect effect on the changes in security rights in England in the middle of the nineteenth century, including the emergence of the floating charge. As well as the likelihood of certain English lawyers possessing knowledge of the Roman system, by virtue of the teaching of Roman law at Oxford and Cambridge, English judges (most

---

87 (1749) 1 Atk 165. A mortgage involves a transfer of property with the transferor holding the equity of redemption, whereas a hypothec involves the granting of a security right with the grantor retaining ownership. A *fiducia cum creditore* form of security in a Civilian system is more akin to a mortgage but the former technically only creates a personal right of redemption rather than an 'equity of redemption'. For some discussion, see Zwalve (n 67) at 49–50.

88 See Verhagen (n 7) at 141–142. By way of comparison, he refers to the relationships between transactional lawyers and the judiciary in creating the security, and the overcoming of the same difficulties: the objections towards non-possessory security, security over contractual claims and over future assets and the perceived need to identify specific objects of the security.

89 This would be consistent with the Roman law sources mentioned above. For another approach, see van Hoof (n 18) at 490–491.

90 See further below. 'Attachment' here equates to 'crystallisation' and is not being used in the 'attachment'/'perfection' sense.

91 There are also obviously practical distinctions between the modern floating charge and the Roman general hypothec, not least that the floating charge is largely limited to corporate entities and is embedded within a complex web of insolvency law.

92 Cf e.g. Pennington (n 18) at 646 who considers the Roman law hypothec to have only created a personal right, with a 'proprietary right' only being acquired 'by foreclosing'.

significantly within the Privy Council) had to decide cases in relation to parts of the British Empire with Civilian-influenced systems of law and they (and practitioners) were consequently exposed to rules under those systems.[93] In 1863 the Privy Council considered the case of *Tatham v Andree*[94] and had to determine the relevant law to apply in a Ceylonese matter.[95] It was held that a security by hypothecary bond before a notary over present and future goods was valid under the Roman-Dutch law applicable in Ceylon. The court examined authorities (including Voet, Grotius and Van Leeuwen) and noted that the general civil law rule was that the validity of a security did not depend upon the creditor's possession of the property; however, Roman-Dutch law had modified this so that if a debtor in possession sold or granted further security over the property then the creditor could not follow it into the hands of a transferee or grantee who had given value, thereby rendering the security ineffective.[96]

Despite the fact that this case was decided only a handful of years before the floating charge was formally accepted in English law, it would be bold to assert with any degree of certainty that there was a direct causal link. A decision of the Privy Council on Ceylonese law was of little weight in England (particularly in English equity matters) and the development of the floating charge may simply have been an internal response of English equity to address perceived commercial problems.

(2) Emergence of the floating charge

The English common law (in contrast to equity) is restrictive towards expressly created security interests without some form of possession (or equivalent). In general terms, that law only permits pledges, legal mortgages and contractual liens for tangible property and legal mortgages for

---

93 In addition, persons involved in trade between different parts of the British Empire (and beyond) would, at least in some cases, have had knowledge of the locally applicable law.

94 (1863) 1 Moore's PC (NS) 386.

95 Now Sri Lanka. The case is considered by J M Milo, 'Floating charge in civiele traditie. Het *Wetboek Napoleon ingerigt voor het Koningrijk Holland* als venster op verleden en heden van generale zakelijke zekerheidsrechten', in J H A Lokin, J M Milo and C H van Rhee (eds), *Tweehonderd Jaren Codificatie Van Het Privaatrecht in Nederland* (Groningen: Stichting het Groningsch Rechtshistorisch Fonds, 2010) 93 onwards.

96 At 408–410 per Lord Kingsdown. It should be noted that the English term 'mortgages' is used by the court in its judgment at various points. Cf the reception of the Roman-Dutch general hypothec in South Africa – V J M van Hoof, 'General Security by Means of Special Notarial Bonds' (2019) 82 THRHR 267.

intangible property.[97] Pledge and contractual lien require the pledgee or lienee to have possession of an asset while there is no possession requirement for mortgage.[98] The principal justification for the position regarding security over personal property seems to be that allowing the grantor to continue to possess goods where the grantee obtains an interest (without an overt or public act) could constitute a fraud upon creditors.[99] In relation to property subsequently acquired by the debtor, the common law requires a new act to create an interest in favour of the creditor and each item to be disposed of has to be released from the security by the creditor.[100]

Consequently, it was within equity that the floating charge developed. It was the flexibility and adaptability of the English system of equity that enabled the law to adjust to changing societal and economic circumstances and to offer a commercially focused response. Much has been written about the emergence of the floating charge in England in the middle of the nineteenth century.[101] It has been shown that there was a step-by-step process, which ultimately resulted in the acceptance of the floating charge by the courts.[102] Equity had for a long time accepted fixed security over present and future property with the grantor remaining in possession with power to deal with the assets in the course of business. This was, however, stopped by the case

97 See above. And see e.g. L Gullifer, *Goode and Gullifer on Legal Problems of Credit and Security*, 6th edn (London: Sweet & Maxwell, 2017) para. 1–05 onwards. The English charge is a product of equity. See also H Beale et al., *The Law of Security and Title-Based Financing*, 3rd edn (Oxford: Oxford University Press, 2018) para. 1.17 onwards. Yet there is some apparent inconsistency regarding which express security rights are available at common law – see Goode (n 86) at 195. It should be noted that the legal mortgage of choses in action is by legal assignment, which was not generally possible at common law but was made available by the Judicature Act 1873 s. 25(6), and see now the Law of Property Act 1925 s. 136.

98 Gullifer, *Goode and Gullifer* (n 97) paras 1–47 onwards. As stated at para. 1–48, 'It may still be theoretically possible to have a pledge of land, but such a security has not been encountered for centuries'.

99 See e.g. Goode (n 86) at 195. The acceptance of such security rights was resisted until the enactment of the Bills of Sale Act 1854, with its registration requirements.

100 See F Bacon, *The Elements of the Common Lawes of England* (1630) reg. 14; *Lunn v Thornton* (1845) 135 ER 587; Gullifer, *Goode and Gullifer* (n 97) para. 2–12, regarding security over future property; Pennington (n 18) at 631–632. See also G F Curtis, 'The Theory of the Floating Charge' (1941–42) 4 UToronto LJ 131 at 134.

101 See e.g. J Armour, 'The Chequered History of the Floating Charge' (2004) 13 Griffith L Rev 25; Curtis (n 100) at 131 onwards; Goode (n 86); R Nolan, 'Property in a Fund' (2004) LQR 120; Pennington (n 18). For an early twentieth-century Scottish perspective on the emergence of the English floating charge, see G W Wilton, *Company Law: Principal Distinctions between the Laws of England and Scotland* (Edinburgh: Hodge & Co, 1923) 9 onwards – 'The Floating Security of English Law'.

102 See e.g. E McKendrick, *Goode and McKendrick on Commercial Law*, 6th edn (London: LexisNexis, 2020) paras 25.01 onwards.

of *Graham v Chapman* in 1852.[103] For the floating charge to emerge, the decision in *Holroyd v Marshall*[104] in the early 1860s was therefore vital. In *Holroyd*, the House of Lords recognised the effectiveness of a charge over future property without a new act (the charge becoming immediately effective upon acquisition of the property).[105] Around this time, in the late 1850s and 1860s, parties contended that the wording of particular corporate debentures created security rights that included future property. However, the courts restrictively interpreted the debenture provisions, deciding that they either did not include future property or that the company could not deal with property (free from the security) without the agreement of the debenture holders.[106] For there to be a floating charge, the courts had to confirm that a charge could be created where the debtor retained the ability to deal with assets without the permission of the creditor. Combining security for the creditor with the unimpeded running of the debtor's business was of key importance.

The first case in which a floating charge was definitively held effective was *Re Panama, New Zealand and Australia Royal Mail Co* in 1870.[107] The decision was supported by subsequent cases, including *Re Yorkshire Woolcombers Association Ltd*.[108] In this latter case, Romer LJ (at 295) gave what has become the standard description of the English floating charge. He described it as: (1) a charge over a class of present and future assets; (2) with that class changing from time to time in the ordinary course of business; and (3) where the chargor can carry on its business in the ordinary way until some future event occurs (at which point the charge crystallises and attaches to particular assets). As specified in *Re Spectrum Plus Ltd*[109] and *Re Brumark Investments Ltd*,[110] it is this third characteristic that is considered crucial in distinguishing a floating charge from a fixed charge.

---

103 (1852) 138 E R 833. Gullifer, *Goode and Gullifer* (n 97) para. 4–02 n 16.
104 (1862) 10 HL Cas 191. And see the discussion of this case in *Tailby v Official Receiver* (1888) 13 App Cas 523.
105 Although the security in *Holroyd* has traditionally been assumed to be fixed, Gullifer, *Goode and Gullifer* (n 97) para. 4–02 ponders whether it could be categorised as floating as a result of *Re Spectrum Plus* [2005] UKHL 41, [2005] 2 AC 680. In *Holroyd*, the security is referred to as a 'mortgage'.
106 See Pennington (n 18) at 642–643.
107 (1870) 5 Ch App 318.
108 [1903] 2 Ch 284 affd *Illingworth v Houldsworth* [1904] AC 355. See also *Re Florence Land and Public Works Co* (1878) 10 Ch D 530 and *In Re Colonial Trusts Corporation* (1879) 15 Ch D 465.
109 (n 105) at paras 106–107 per Lord Scott of Foscote.
110 [2001] 2 AC 710 at paras 12–13 per Lord Millett.

There were a number of other floating charge cases in the late nineteenth century that provided further authority as to what the floating charge was and how it operated.[111] The first reported case in which the term 'floating charge' is actually used appears to be *Re Colonial Trusts Corporation*.[112] In this case and others of the period, 'floating security' was used interchangeably with floating charge and many reported judgments in fact refer only to the former.[113] Floating security can be considered as the general category of security interest, with the floating charge and the floating (equitable) mortgage being the two types of identifiable floating security.[114] Over time, the floating charge has become the dominant form of floating security.[115] Yet, the floating charge has not been fully defined and remains conceptually elusive. Much modern scholarship has focused upon the nature of the floating charge holder's interest in the charged assets prior to crystallisation.[116] Unfortunately, it is not possible to say that one interpretation has conclusively prevailed, although there is significant support for the view that the floating charge creates an immediate security interest (of some description) over assets encompassed by the charge.[117] The position after crystallisation is clearer: the floating charge becomes a fixed charge attaching to specific assets covered by the security.[118]

---

111 See e.g. *Re Florence Land and Public Works Co* (n 108); *Wheatley v Silkstone Coal Co* (1885) 29 Ch D 715; *Government Stock Co v Manila Railway Co* (1897) AC 81.

112 (n 108).

113 It has been suggested that 'floating' was 'rather a popular than a legal term' and that it originated in the USA – G W Wilton, *Company Law and Practice in Scotland* (Edinburgh: Hodge & Co, 1912) 189. Wilton later seems to have changed his view about the American origin of the 'floating' terminology – Wilton, *Company Law: Principal Distinctions* (n 101) 9.

114 See P Giddins, 'Floating Mortgages by Individuals: Are They Conceptually Possible?' (2011) 3 JIBFL 125; Beale et al., *Law of Security and Title-Based Financing* (n 97) para. 6.56. In F B Palmer, *Company Law*, 2nd edn (London: Stevens, 1898) the author uses the terms 'floating charge' and 'floating security' as synonyms, although principally uses the former expression (see e.g. at 212–213).

115 Although it seems as if a number of securities that are labelled as charges may actually be mortgages – Beale et al., *Law of Security and Title-Based Financing* (n 97) para. 6.56.

116 W J Gough, *Company Charges*, 2nd edn (London: LexisNexis, 1996) 97 onwards and 132 onwards; S Worthington, *Proprietary Interests in Commercial Transactions* (Oxford: Clarendon Press, 1996) 79 onwards; Nolan (n 101); Gullifer, *Goode and Gullifer* (n 97) para. 4–03; McKendrick, *Goode and McKendrick* (n 102) paras 25.04 onwards. For summaries of the various theories, see Beale et al., *Law of Security and Title-Based Financing* (n 97) paras 6.66 onwards; D Sheehan, *Principles of Personal Property Law*, 2nd edn (London: Bloomsbury, 2017) 355 onwards.

117 See Nolan (n 101); Giddins (n 114); Gullifer, *Goode and Gullifer* (n 97) para. 4–03; McKendrick, *Goode and McKendrick* (n 102) para. 25.07; Sheehan, *Principles* (n 116) 355 onwards.

118 See e.g. *N W Robbie* [1963] 1 WLR 1324; *Buchler v Talbot* [2004] UKHL 9, [2004] 2 AC 298, especially at para. 29 per Lord Hoffmann; Gullifer, *Goode and Gullifer* (n 97) para. 4–31.

As regards the origins of the floating charge, commercial considerations were a key factor in English courts' recognition of this type of security. Professor Pennington suggests that the speed of industrial and commercial expansion meant that by the third decade of the nineteenth century companies needed more capital but the corresponding expansion of credit created risks for investors leading to greater demands for better security, and the traditional forms of security were considered inappropriate and insufficient for circulating assets such as raw materials, manufactured goods, stock in trade and trade debts.[119] Certainly, the demands of particular commercial lenders were impactful in the move towards greater flexibility for security rights from the mid-nineteenth century onwards. However, Professor Getzler challenges the view that security over circulating assets was of vital economic significance. He notes that it was 'essential for the profitability of credit banking' but that it actually 'may have damaged the longer-term prospects of the economy'.[120] He also states that 'what market actors seek is not necessarily optimal for the market overall'.[121] While this is true, and must also be borne in mind as far as the introduction of the floating charge in Scots law is concerned, there was certainly an impression later that the Scottish economy at large was being disadvantaged in comparison to England by the absence of comparable security rights.[122] More widely, it is of interest that floating security was resisted in Scotland for a considerable period of time for commercial reasons but it was also commercial justifications that led to it being embraced in England, and later in Scotland too.

With respect to the form of the floating charge, Professor Pennington points to its origins in the statutory form of mortgage over an undertaking under the Companies Clauses Consolidation Act 1845, which applies to companies created by statute.[123] This style seems to have been later

---

119 Pennington (n 18) at 630–631. Pennington's statements on this seem to have been adopted by Lord Scott of Foscote in *Re Spectrum Plus Ltd* (n 105) in his brief history of the floating charge at para. 95 onwards.

120 J S Getzler, 'The Role of Security over Future and Circulating Capital: Evidence from the British Economy circa 1850–1920' in J S Getzler and J Payne (eds), *Company Charges: Spectrum and Beyond* (Oxford: Oxford University Press, 2006) 250.

121 *Company Charges: Spectrum and Beyond* at 227.

122 See MacPherson, 'The Genesis of the Scottish Floating Charge', Chapter 3, and Hardman, 'Law and Economics of the Floating Charge', Chapter 5.

123 Pennington (n 18) at 638 onwards. For further discussion of this, and the equivalent legislation for Scotland, see R G Anderson, 'Borrowing on the Undertaking: Scottish Statutory Companies', Chapter 2 within this volume, and MacPherson, *Floating Charge* (n 50) paras 4–21 onwards.

utilised by companies registered under the Companies Acts[124] when they
sought to give security that would not interfere with the carrying on of
their business. Within this context, scholars have pointed to the role of
legal practitioners in developing the floating charge and the receptiv-
ity of judges in accepting it and thereby adapting the law in this area to
the changing needs of society.[125] One writer, in the early 1940s, stated:
'The merits of judicial courage in the right places have never been better
illustrated'.[126] From the beginning of the twentieth century, the judiciary's
role in legal innovation with the floating charge was largely taken over by
the legislature. It has been suggested that the changes emanating from
parliament were driven by lobbying or populism and that few of them
created net social benefits and some, such as preferential debts, caused
losses.[127] However, it has been shown that costs were also caused by the
priority given to the floating charge by the judiciary and certain elements of
legislation such as registration 'probably created net benefits'.[128] It should
also be noted that judges played a role in the legislative process through
acting as members of committees reviewing the Companies Acts, which led
to further reforms, and by giving evidence to such committees (see further
below).

The history of floating charges in England is intimately bound up with
companies. It was the use of floating charges by companies that led to their
recognition by the courts and many subsequent developments with the floating charges regime only apply to incorporated entities. The Bills of Sale Act
(1878) Amendment Act 1882 essentially makes it impossible for an individual to create a floating charge (or floating mortgage) over 'personal chattels'
acquired after the execution of a bill of sale.[129] As a result of this, the law of
floating charges is often considered to be practically limited to corporate
entities.[130] However, personal chattels under the legislation are effectively
limited to goods and there are consequently other types of property not

---

124 The modern companies regime crucially arrived in this period, most notably with the Joint
   Stock Companies Act 1856 and the Companies Act 1862.
125 See e.g. Armour (n 101).
126 Curtis (n 100) at 150.
127 Armour (n 101) at 50–51.
128 Armour at 51.
129 See the 1882 Act ss. 4 and 5, in particular. However, the legislation does not seem to apply
   to oral agreements – see Beale et al., *Law of Security and Title-Based Financing* (n 97) para.
   11.04. The Bills of Sale Acts do not apply to companies – see Beale, para. 11.09.
130 See e.g. A L Diamond, 'A Review of Security Interests in Property' (The Diamond Report)
   (London: The Stationary Office, 1989) para. 16.15.

covered by the Acts – land, book debts,[131] other types of intangible property, as well as tangible personal property other than goods.[132] It therefore seems at least theoretically possible for an individual to grant a floating charge over, for example, all of their land and/or claims. Yet, the absence of registration for such security is highly undesirable and problematic, as it was for companies. The emergence of companies with registers applicable to them, as legal personalities, facilitated the registration of security that could apply to future property. This was also an important factor in the later introduction of the Scottish floating charge, the granting of which was (and is) limited to corporate entities.

(3) The floating charge controversies

Following its arrival, the floating charge was far from uncontroversial. There was pressure from various quarters to abolish or at least reform it. In 1881 the Associated Chambers of Commerce passed a resolution against companies being able to create security over future property (due to the preference this was giving to debenture holders over ordinary creditors).[133] While in 1896, in the landmark company law case of *Salomon v A Salomon & Co Ltd*,[134] Lord Macnaghten[135] stated:

> 'For such a catastrophe as has occurred in this case some would blame the law that allows the creation of a floating charge. But a floating charge is too

---

131 A general assignment of existing or future book debts (or a class of them) by a person engaged in business requires to be registered under the Bills of Sale Act 1878 in order to be valid against a trustee in bankruptcy under the Insolvency Act 1986 s. 344. This is a post-creation formality.

132 See Giddins (n 114) and the sources cited there. See also Beale et al., *Law of Security and Title-Based Financing* (n 97) para. 1.16. In addition, there is an interesting reference in a newspaper report from a bankruptcy court in 1869 (therefore pre-dating the *Re Panama* case) regarding an individual who apparently stated that when he offered to grant a mortgage over certain houses, 'only a floating charge existed on the property' – *The Times*, 5 October 1869, 9.

133 J B Jefferys, *Business Organisation in Great Britain 1856–1914* (Ayer Co Publishing, 1977) 256.

134 [1896] 11 WLUK 76; [1897] AC 22.

135 For biographical details see J A Hamilton (rev Hugh Mooney), 'Macnaghten, Edward, Baron Macnaghten (1830–1913)', *Oxford Dictionary of National Biography* (2004) available at *http://www.oxforddnb.com/view/article/34803* (last accessed 20 October 2021). Lord Macnaghten is an important figure in the development of the law of floating charges as he was involved in a number of leading cases in the late nineteenth and early twentieth centuries and provided some influential descriptions of floating charges – as well as his involvement in *Salomon*, see e.g. *Manila Railway* (n 111) at 86 and *Illingworth* (n 108) at 358. He was also a member of the Select Committee of the House of Lords that examined the Companies Bill – see *Report from the Select Committee of the House of Lords on the Companies Bill; together with the Proceedings of the Committee, Minutes of Evidence and Appendix* (1896–1899).

convenient a form of security to be lightly abolished. I have long thought, and I believe some of your Lordships also think, that the ordinary trade creditors of a trading company ought to have a preferential claim ... But that is not the law at present. Everybody knows that when there is a winding-up debenture-holders generally step in and sweep off everything; and a great scandal it is.'[136]

The subsequent Preferential Payments in Bankruptcy Amendment Act 1897 did not extend to ordinary trade creditors but gave rates, taxes and wage claims (all with certain limitations) priority over debenture holders with floating charges in the winding up or receivership of a company.[137] The justifications for the contents of the Bill that became the 1897 Act were discussed in Parliament: they included the fact that workers would have contributed to the production of the company's assets and should receive their arrears of wages in payment of this and that the relative loss to workers if the floating charge ranked ahead was significantly greater than the loss to a floating charge holder if the ranking positions were the other way around.[138]

In the context of the House of Lords Select Committee Report on the Companies Bill (1896–1899), there was some discussion about reserving a proportion of assets to pay ordinary creditors. To this end, there was a suggestion that one tenth of assets covered by debentures should be for the benefit of ordinary creditors and therefore non-chargeable.[139] This possibility was also mentioned by Lord Davey when examining a witness, who considered that it could be done but would lead to a diminution of security and higher interest payments in some cases.[140] The idea did not command sufficient support to be introduced at this time and a limited claim for ordinary (non-preferential) creditors ranking in priority to the floating charge

---

136 *Salomon* (n 134) at 53 per Lord Macnaghten. See also the later cases of *Re London Pressed Hinge Co Ltd* [1905] 1 Ch 576 and *Evans v Rival Granite Quarries Ltd* [1910] 2 KB 979 and the suggestion by Lord Davey in similar terms to Lord Macnaghten at HL Deb 2 Aug 1900, col 400–401. See too W Cornish et al., *Law and Society in England 1750–1950*, 2nd edn (London: Bloomsbury Publishing, 2019) 253–254.

137 Sections 2–3. This Act gave preferential creditors under the Preferential Payments in Bankruptcy Act 1888 priority over floating charge holders. Equivalent provisions were inserted into the Companies (Consolidation) Act 1908 and the Companies Act 1948. The current provisions are found within Sch. 6 and ss. 175 and 386 of the Insolvency Act 1986. And see also s. 464(6) of the Companies Act 1985 regarding Scots law.

138 See HC Deb 10 Feb 1897, cols 70–87. In particular, see the comments of G Kemp who moved the Second Reading of the Bill (at col 70 onwards). A suggestion that the preferential creditors should have priority over non-floating security interests was ultimately rejected.

139 *Select Committee Report* (n 135) (Session 1898), Appendix A (Memorandum submitted by J Smith, Inspector-General, Board of Trade) 166 (in observations).

140 *Select Committee Report* (Session 1897) para. 1217 (the witness was Stanley Boulter). And see Lord Macnaghten's general comments about reserving assets for certain creditors at para. 869.

holder did not appear until over 100 years later when the Enterprise Act 2002 introduced the 'prescribed part'.[141]

Another powerful criticism against floating charges was the absence of registration as a requirement for their validity. Without such publicity, other parties dealing with a company would not know whether such a charge (or charges) had been granted and therefore what risks there were in transacting with the company. The Davey Committee Report of 1895, in which the Companies Acts were reviewed, noted 'objections' to the power of a company to create floating charges, and stated that there was a 'nearly unanimous demand' for an efficient register of security interests granted by a company.[142] The committee decided not to recommend the prohibition of floating charges as long as an efficient register of charges was adopted.[143] They proposed that any relevant mortgage or charge not registered in the public register would be invalid against liquidators and creditors.[144]

In giving evidence to the House of Lords Select Committee on the Companies Bill in March 1897, Lord Justice Lindley[145] suggested that floating charges, due to their 'abuse' and the consequent unfairness rendered to unsecured creditors, should be limited to securing short-term loans.[146] In an

141 For the prescribed part, see Insolvency Act 1986 s. 176A (added by the Enterprise Act 2002 s. 252), and Insolvency Act 1986 (Prescribed Part) Order 2003 (SI 2003/2097). Reminiscent of the suggestion in the late nineteenth century, in 1982 the Cork Report recommended a 'ten per cent fund' for unsecured creditors derived from net realisations of assets subject to a floating charge but this was not introduced by legislation – *Report of the Review Committee on Insolvency Law and Practice* (Cmnd 8558: 1982) paras 1538 onwards.

142 Or at least for certain types of security interest: *Report of the Departmental Committee Appointed by the Board of Trade to Inquire what Amendments are Necessary in the Acts Relating to Joint Stock Companies Incorporated with Limited Liability under the Companies Acts, 1862 to 1890* (Cmnd 7779: 1895) (hereafter *'Davey Report'*) para. 43. The term 'mortgage' was used by the committee in this context but in a broad sense to include security rights such as floating charges.

143 *Davey Report* paras 45 onwards.

144 *Davey Report* para. 49. Companies themselves had to keep a register of charges under the 1862 Act but omission did not affect validity or priority, although directors could be fined for non-compliance – see the discussion at paras 46–47 of the *Davey Report*.

145 For biographical details see G H Jones and V Jones, 'Lindley, Nathaniel, Baron Lindley (1828–1921)', *Oxford Dictionary of National Biography* (2004) (online version – 28 September 2006) available at *http://www.oxforddnb.com/view/article/34535* (last accessed 20 October 2021). Lindley was one of the judges at the Court of Appeal stage in *Salomon* (n 134). He also appears to have been junior counsel for the appellant in *Re Panama* (n 107).

146 *Select Committee Report* (n 135) (Session 1897) para. 32 onwards. Another judge who gave evidence to the Committee was Romer J. For biographical details, see F D Mackinnon (rev by P Polden), 'Romer, Sir Robert (1840–1918)', *Oxford Dictionary of National Biography* (2004) (online *version – 28 May 2015*) available at *https://doi.org/10.1093/ref:odnb/35819* (last accessed 20 October 2021). Although Romer did not recommend abolition of floating charges altogether he believed that a floating charge should not affect unpaid or uncalled capital at the

appendix to the Select Committee Report, it was also observed that it was 'perhaps, a pity that [floating charges] were ever allowed, but the practice is too firmly established to alter … Publicity is now the only remedy'.[147] Other individuals, such as Francis Beaufort Palmer, were more positive. He noted how commonly used the floating charge was and referred to its 'immense advantage'.[148] He stated that 'the business of the country would be dislocated' if floating charges were abolished and also objected to tying the validity of every floating charge to its registration, due to fears of unintentional non-compliance as well as the burden and complication of compulsory registration.[149] Palmer's favourability towards the floating charge was also outlined within his *Company Law* where he referred to it having 'been recognized by the commercial community and by the investing public as of an eminently convenient type'.[150]

It was nevertheless decided that a public register should be introduced. Under the Companies Act 1900 s. 14(1)(d), 'a floating charge on the undertaking or property of the company' was to be void against the liquidator and any creditor of the company unless filed with the registrar for registration within twenty-one days after the date of creation.[151] If we look at this retrospectively from a Scottish perspective, the development of a registration regime was a crucial stage in the emergence of the floating charge as a potentially viable model to be introduced into Scots law. Although the gap between creation of security and registration would be at odds with the publicity principle of Scots law, the available registration

---

commencement of winding up, so as to give some protection for ordinary creditors (paras 200 onwards). In suggesting this, he indicated (at para. 204) that they should 'go back to the state of the law before the … decisions since 1862', but the meaning of this is unclear given the general lack of recognition of floating charges at that time.

147 *Select Committee Report* (n 135) (Session 1898) – Appendix A (Memorandum submitted by J Smith, Inspector-General, Board of Trade) 166.

148 *Select Committee Report* (n 135) (Session 1898) para. 649. Palmer had been a member of the Davey Committee – see e.g. *Davey Report*, iii.

149 *Select Committee Report* (n 135) (Session 1898) paras 651 onwards.

150 Palmer, *Company Law* (n 114) 213.

151 Various other security rights were also rendered void against a liquidator or creditor of the company if the registration requirements were not complied with. A 'mortgage or charge on any book debts of the company' was added as a further form of registrable charge by the Companies Act 1907 s. 10(1)(e). The current registration of charges regime, in Companies Act 2006 ss. 859A onwards, no longer provides an itemised list of the charges to be registered. Rather, charges granted by the company are registrable but there are exceptions. A registrable charge continues to be invalid against a liquidator and creditors of the company (and also now against an administrator) if the registration requirements are not met. For discussion, see A D J MacPherson, 'Registration of Company Charges Revisited: New and Familiar Problems' (2019) 23 Edin L Rev 153.

system could be a legitimising mechanism for express non-possessory security.[152]

Despite the introduction of the registration of charges regime in England and Wales, the floating charge remained divisive.[153] In 1906, the *Report of the Company Law Amendment Committee*, mentioned the 'extraordinary popularity' of floating charges and added that experience had shown that such charges had, to a significant degree, met 'the wants both of borrowers and lenders, and of the business world generally'.[154] Nevertheless, demands for abolition were acknowledged, and references were also made to cases in which 'fraudulent conduct' had benefitted floating charge holders at the expense of unsecured creditors.[155] The committee stated that if the practice of raising money by floating charges 'had recently commenced' or 'had been adopted only to a small extent' some of them would have been disposed towards prohibiting raising money by security upon future assets.[156] In reality, the majority were of the view that, in the main, floating charges,

> 'whilst facilitating largely the raising of money for industrial and co-operative and financial purposes, do not (especially having regard to the stringent provisions as to registration) interfere with the general creditors of the company to such an extent as to justify the recommendation of their abolition'.[157]

However, three members produced a minority report disagreeing with the majority view on the floating charge, pointed to instances showing that the

---

152 This would be especially true if the system was to be adapted for Scots law so that a security was only to be created, and thus have third party effect, upon registration. That was not true for floating charges under the law that was introduced in Scotland, nor is it the case under the current law.

153 See e.g. *Re London Pressed Hinge Company Ltd* (n 136) where Buckley J recognised the 'injustice' and 'mischief' caused by floating charges and considered the subject to be one which 'urgently requires attention' (at 583).

154 *Report of the Company Law Amendment Committee* (Cmnd 3052: 1906) para. 39. The report is often known as the 'Loreburn Report' after the committee's chairman, Robert Reid, Lord Loreburn. F B Palmer was also a member of this committee.

155 Loreburn Report paras 39–40.

156 Loreburn Report para. 41.

157 Loreburn Report para. 41. The majority suggested that the law should be amended to provide that a floating charge granted within three months of the commencement of winding up should be invalid, except to the extent of cash advanced at the charge's creation or later, together with interest at a rate not exceeding five per cent, but with an exception so that floating charges created in this period would be valid if it could be proved the company was solvent when the charge was created. This proposal was enacted by the Companies Act 1907 s. 13 (and was repeated in the Companies (Consolidation) Act 1908 s. 212). For some brief discussion of this change, see Wilton, *Company Law: Principal Distinctions* (n 101) 23. For subsequent changes in the law on this point, including extending the relevant period, see Companies Act 1948 s. 322; and the currently applicable Insolvency Act 1986 s. 245.

power to create floating charges could be 'greatly abused', suggested that the floating charge encouraged too much borrowing and 'reckless trading' and that it should not be possible to charge after-acquired chattels, or future book debts, or other property not in existence when the charge was created.[158]

Although the floating charge was divisive, it, nevertheless, continued to survive. And the prospect of its abolition seems to have diminished over time as it was subjected to greater controls and as it became ever more an established part of commercial practice in England. Yet its controversial status and the problems it had caused were known in Scotland and would have made the prospect of its introduction and acceptance there an unlikely one. Why, after all, would Scots law want to allow floating charges when many English counterparts suggested that they would consider disallowing them or abolishing them if they were not so well-established south of the border? Although the rationality of the Scots law position on express hypothecs would seem to have been reaffirmed, it should be noted that the criticism in England was largely limited to security over future assets rather than to all forms of non-possessory security.

D. THE 'ENGLISH' FLOATING CHARGE IN SCOTS LAW

(1) The influence of terminology

Given how integrated Scotland and England were, economically, culturally, politically and socially, in the later Victorian era and into the twentieth century,[159] it is no surprise that the emergence of the floating charge in

158 *Report of the Company Law Amendment Committee* (n 154) 27 onwards. One of the three authors of the minority report was Francis Gore-Browne, best known for *Gore-Browne on Companies*. For biographical details, see 'Sir Francis Gore-Browne, K.C.' *The Times*, 4 September 1922, 10.

159 Lord Watson, 'Recent Legal Reform' 1901 Jur Rev 1 at 11 stated that '[i]ntercourse between the two countries is now so constant, and they have so many interests and transactions in common, that it is highly undesirable that a citizen of either realm should come across a different system of law each time he crosses the Tweed'. He added, however, that '[t]he process of assimilation must be gradual, in all probability will be very slow, and complete identity of the two systems is a thing far outside the range of practical legislation'. Lord Rodger, 'Thinking About Scots Law' (1996) 1 Edin L Rev 3 at 16, referred to the mid-nineteenth century when 'the railway network was creating a British economy with British markets'. A high degree of economic integration between Scotland and England had, however, already been in place for quite some time: see e.g. I D Whyte, *Scotland before the Industrial Revolution: An Economic and Social History c1050–1750* (Oxford: Routledge, 1995) 332–333 – 'By the time Burns died in 1796 the Scottish and English economies were rapidly becoming so closely integrated that they cannot be considered in isolation'.

England created some interest north of the border. And, indeed, growing familiarity seems to have caused the judiciary in Scotland to begin to use the terminology of floating charges.

The first reported use of the term 'floating security' in Scotland seems to have been in the Outer House case of *Wilson v Guthrie*.[160] The judgment refers to an attempt to use a trust deed to create what the judge described as a 'floating security' over 'general assets' but which failed due to its intended applicability to *acquirenda*, for which it was suggested the trustees had a duty to seek 'chattel mortgages' from time to time as property was purchased. It is not entirely clear from the judgment but the judge (Lord Stormonth Darling) seems to have been considering certain aspects of American law.

Over time, the expressions 'floating security' and 'floating charge' appear to have seeped into the lexicon of Scots law itself. In *Traill's Trs*,[161] Lord Cullen described a creditor with a bond and disposition in security over land as having 'what may be called a floating security over the moveables of his debtor on the ground'.[162] In the same case, Lord Mackenzie stated that '[t]he conveyance in security by itself creates a floating charge which affects only the moveables on the ground at the time the diligence is done'.[163] These were of course applications of the English law terminology and concepts in order to better explain an existing Scots law phenomenon, namely poinding of the ground, which is discussed further below.[164] As we shall see, floating charges were also, of course, referred to when the courts had to determine their validity under Scots law.

Given that the term 'charge' was not a term of art in Scots law, it would have been more consistent with existing Scots law to have used the term 'security' when floating charges (and agricultural charges) were later introduced.

---

160 (1894) 2 SLT 338. The first reported Scottish case in which 'floating charge' was used appears to have been *Liquidators of the Scottish Drug Depot v Fraser* (1905) 12 SLT 757 but this was merely a passing reference to the Preferential Payments in Bankruptcy Amendment Act 1897, which used the term.
161 1915 SC 655.
162 1915 SC 655 at 666. Lord Cullen added that 'no actual *nexus* is put upon any particular moveables without a poinding of the ground executed while they are on the ground'.
163 1915 SC 655 at 671.
164 The application of the terminology of floating charges to other contexts was not limited to Scots law. Former Prime Minister H H Asquith suggested that 'a floating charge over the whole enterprise and industry of the inhabitants of German-Austria for years to come' was being imposed by way of treaty obligations following the First World War: HC Deb 14 Apr 1920, col 1714. See also HC Deb 25 Mar 1920, col 647; HC Deb 29 Apr 1920, col 1477.

(2) Rejection of the floating charge

(a) Late nineteenth century

In 1897, Gloag and Irvine, in their *Law of Rights in Security*, reaffirmed the position for creating security over corporeal moveables. They stated:

> 'It is a cardinal principle of the common law of Scotland that no real right to corporeal moveable subjects can be transmitted by voluntary conveyance, assignation or other transfer unless and until the transfer is completed by delivery of the subjects in question to the transferee.'[165]

Professor Steven cites Gloag and Irvine as evidence that the non-acceptance of hypothecs in Scots law was 'subsumed under a wider doctrine' of the creditor requiring possession in order to have a security over moveables.[166] It is important to recall that Scots law's rejection of hypothecs was underpinned by the policy standard that laws for rights in security should promote and not hinder commerce. It might have been advantageous overall for Scots law to continue to reject hypothecs but commercial, economic and legal developments, including in England, raise questions as to whether the Scots law position was hindering rather than facilitating commercial activity. While there was, and is, commercial value in adhering to the publicity principle, a viable alternative to possession that would enable a grantor to continue to use the property would diminish the commercial justification for rejecting hypothecs. Gloag and Irvine showed some recognition of this when stating:

> 'The law on the subject of security-rights over corporeal moveables is beset with difficulties; and is not, perhaps, in a very satisfactory state, as the result of its rules is often to deprive the owner of such property of the power to make use of it as a security for his debts. It is open to question whether the rigidity of the law of Scotland on this subject should not now be relaxed by the adoption of a system analogous to the English bill of sale.'[167]

Gloag and Irvine also refer to floating charges directly when they write that in Scots law, in contrast with English law, 'it is clear on principle, and settled by

---

165 W M Gloag and J M Irvine, *Law of Rights in Security Heritable and Moveable Including Cautionary Obligations* (Edinburgh: W. Green, 1897) 188. T B Smith uses this passage in 'Historical Note' Appendix I to LRCS, *Eighth Report* (n 75). Such sentiments are also found in the case law, see e.g. *Orr's Tr v Tullis* (1870) 8 M 936 at 950 per Lord Neaves, who contrasted the Scots law position with English law.
166 Steven, 'Rights in Security over Moveables' (n 5) at 349.
167 Gloag and Irvine, *Law of Rights in Security* (n 165) 187–188.

authority' that a floating charge debenture[168] without a specific conveyance or particular statutory authority for the company 'would be merely a personal obligation, and not a right in security at all'.[169] In support of their point, they cite the 1882 case of *Clark v West Calder Oil*[170] in which an attempt was made to assign in security mineral leases along with moveables on the ground.[171] The assignations were intimated to the landlords but the 'assignees' did not enter into possession of the property and the First Division held that a security had not been created due to the absence of possession. This case has been viewed by some as an attempt to create a floating charge.[172] In *Clark*, Lord Shand realised that if the purported non-possessory security was given effect to, and if debentures were used to create security over all of a company's assets (and the shares were all fully paid up), there would be no assets to meet the claims of general creditors. Consequently, he stated: 'I do not think that would be desirable. And the law in England has given rise, as I know, to much dissatisfaction, as well as to recent efforts for its amendment'.[173] The year after Gloag and Irvine's book was published, the House of Lords in *Inglis v Robertson and Baxter*[174] decided that the delivery requirement would extend to allowing a security right to be created by constructive delivery, where the goods were represented by a document of title, but intimation to a third party holding the property (e.g. a warehouse keeper) was required.[175]

The above-noted comments on hypothecs and floating charges by Gloag and Irvine were applicable to Scottish companies created under the Companies Acts. This is also true of the decision in *Clark v West Calder Oil*. However, Gloag and Irvine, and the judges in *Clark*, did recognise that companies in Scotland established by private Acts could create a security right with some characteristics of a floating charge, by virtue of provisions within

---

168 For the meaning of 'debenture' in Scots law at this time see Gloag and Irvine, *Law of Rights in Security* (n 165) 633 onwards. For a more modern account of the meaning of the term in Scots law see G L Gretton, 'Registration of Company Charges' (2002) 6 Edin L Rev 146.

169 Gloag and Irvine, *Law of Rights in Security* (n 165) 635–636.

170 (1882) 9 R 1017.

171 The terminology in the case is rather confused as regards forms of security and property types.

172 Wilton, *Company Law: Principal Distinctions* (n 101) 24–25, cites it as an example of the floating charge being 'so seductive in its attractiveness' that attempts were made to introduce it into Scots law. Indeed, in the case, *Re Panama* (n 107) was referred to in argument in support of the position that debenture holders should have priority over moveable assets of the company.

173 *Clark* (n 170) at 1035 per Lord Shand.

174 (1898) 25 R (HL) 70.

175 Cf *Hamilton v Western Bank* (1856) 19 D 152, and see the discussion at Scottish Law Commission, *Report on Moveable Transactions* (n 60) para. 25.4.

legislation such as the Companies Clauses Consolidation (Scotland) Act 1845 and the Companies Clauses Act 1863.[176] This is discussed further in Dr Ross Anderson's chapter.[177] It is worthwhile recognising here, however, that legislation regarding companies created by private Acts not only ultimately gave rise to the emergence of floating charges in English law more broadly, but enabled Scottish companies established by private Acts to create non-possessory security rights with similarities to floating charges.

(b) *Ballachulish Slate Quarries Co Ltd v Bruce*

In *Ballachulish Slate Quarries Co Ltd v Bruce*[178] a company that was incorporated under the Companies Acts had granted debentures and, in doing so, purported to charge its undertaking and property, including uncalled capital. The grantor entered liquidation and the case focused on whether a valid security had been created over the uncalled capital of the company. The First Division were of the view that an attempt had been made to create a floating charge. The court unanimously, and in the strongest possible terms, rejected this form of security. The Lord President (Dunedin) considered that the drafter of the relevant deeds had 'slavishly copied English forms' and that the terms used were 'not appropriate to the Scottish system at all'.[179] He did not wish to 'piece together nonsense' and stated that the whole method of creating a floating charge was 'absolutely foreign to our law'.[180] The other judges concurred. Lord McLaren stated: 'it is well known that such a floating security has no effect in the law of Scotland'.[181] Lord Kinnear considered it to be 'a case of bungled conveyancing' that failed to create

---

176 Gloag and Irvine, *Law of Rights in Security* (n 165) 629 onwards; *Clark* (n 170) at 1023 per Lord President Inglis and at 1033 per Lord Shand, who draw a contrast between the security rights that can be granted by companies to which these Acts apply and companies registered under the Companies Acts.

177 Anderson, 'Borrowing on the Undertaking: Scottish Statutory Companies', Chapter 2. See also MacPherson, *Floating Charge* (n 50) paras 4–28 onwards.

178 *Ballachulish Slate Quarries Co Ltd v Bruce* (1908) 16 SLT 48.

179 *Ballachulish Slate Quarries Co Ltd v Bruce* at 52 per Lord President (Dunedin). He did note that the English form taken was 'a very familiar one, namely, a document under which what is called a 'floating charge' is created'. He added that it was 'common knowledge' that a floating charge could be created over property in England. In *Bank of Scotland v Liquidators of Hutchison, Main, & Co* 1914 SC (HL) 1, a floating charge featured in the case but the court did not need to consider whether it would be a valid security under Scots law as it was granted by an English company (see at 4 per Lord Kinnear).

180 *Ballachulish* (n 178) at 52 per Lord President (Dunedin). For there to have been any valid security created, the intimation of the assignation of the uncalled capital would have been necessary. But it was not possible for there to be a floating charge with assignation and intimation.

181 *Ballachulish* at 52 per Lord McLaren.

a security right.[182] In order for there to be an valid security over uncalled capital, the court maintained that an assignation followed by effective intimation to the shareholders was required.[183] The judges rejected the attempt to create a floating charge because this form of security was at odds with the existing rules of Scots law. They appear to have considered the position to be so obvious and overwhelming that no attempt was made to examine the merits or qualities of a security of this type or the underlying reasoning behind its rejection in Scots law.[184]

The case evidences the doctrinal conservatism of the Scots law position in comparison to the flexibility and commercial responsiveness of English equity, which produced the floating charge. Referring to the Scottish approach as conservative is not, necessarily, a criticism. The floating charge could fit more readily within the English system of equity, whereas there would need to be considerable adaptation for such security to be coherent with existing Scots law. There would also need to be a particularly strong rationale to overturn the existing requirement for possession or intimation to constitute security over moveables. Although the floating charge may have brought certain commercial benefits in England (at least to some parties), it also had considerable negative aspects. As the floating charge was not available in Scots law, the legislative changes (for companies) used to remedy certain problems with the floating charge in English law were not applicable to Scotland. Somewhat paradoxically then, the absence of registration may have hindered the acceptance of floating charges in Scotland, yet the form of registration enacted by legislation to address concerns about the floating charge was not applicable to Scottish companies. It seems clear that for Scots law to feasibly accept a floating charge device there should be legislative intervention, most notably because judges could not create a system of registration and because there was a long-standing legal position, and if this was departed from it would create significant uncertainty.

The registration of charges requirements under the Companies Act 1900 were disapplied in relation to Scottish companies by s. 34(2) of that Act. It was later suggested that this provision had only been inserted during the Bill's progress due to the 'sudden discovery' that under Scots law floating

---

182 *Ballachulish* at 52–53 per Lord Kinnear.
183 *Ballachulish* at 52 per Lord President (Dunedin) and at 52 per Lord McLaren.
184 The lack of examination of the floating charge is referred to by A J P Menzies, 'Is the Creation of a Floating Charge Competent to a Limited Company Registered in Scotland?' 1909–1910 Jur Rev 87 at 87–88. See also J Hardman, *A Practical Guide to Granting Corporate Security in Scotland* (Edinburgh: W. Green, 2018) para. 6–03.

charges were not possible.[185] When the Bill that became the Companies Act 1907 was being discussed there were some concerns about the absence of a provision excluding Scottish companies from the registration requirements.[186] The Lord Chancellor stated that if it was the 'real wish of the people of Scotland' then such a provision would be inserted but he would not accept the legal profession's view, for what was being done 'was a part of high public policy'.[187] The 1907 Act did not contain such a provision[188]; however, the Companies (Consolidation) Act 1908 expressly stated that it was mortgages or charges created by English or Irish companies that had to be registered, thus excluding Scottish companies by implication.[189] The 1907 Act made changes to the registration of charges regime by, for example, adding the following to the list of registrable securities: mortgages or charges on any land, or any interest therein; and mortgages or charges on any book debts of the company.[190] These security rights were also required to be registered under the 1908 Act.[191]

If Scottish companies had not been excluded from the registration provisions then the possibility of floating charges being accepted into Scots law would have been more plausible. However, a number of issues would still have made the prospect doubtful: the fact that floating charges could be created without publicity, and only subsequently had to be registered for full effectiveness; the use of terminology and concepts that had no particular meaning in Scots law; and doubts about whether allowing floating charges was desirable overall (including from a commercial point of view). In any event, the prevailing view was that a Scottish company could not grant a floating charge.[192]

---

185 HL Deb 14 May 1907, col 759 (Lord Balfour of Burleigh). This was despite the reference in *Davey Report*, para. 50 that noted that the law of Scotland with respect to 'mortgages' would not be affected by the proposal to introduce registration.
186 HL Deb 14 May 1907, cols 758–759 (Lord Balfour of Burleigh). The registration clause in the Bill would repeal and replace the registration section of the 1900 Act (s. 14) but there was no equivalent to s. 34(2) of the 1900 Act within the 1907 Bill.
187 HL Deb 14 May 1907, col 760 (Lord Chancellor (Lorcburn)).
188 The Companies Act 1907 s. 10, repealed and replaced s. 14 of the 1900 Act. However, it is possible that the provision disapplying the registration of charges regime to Scottish companies could still have been interpreted to also apply to the new provisions.
189 Companies (Consolidation) Act 1908 s. 93(1).
190 Companies Act 1907 s. 10(1)(d) and (e).
191 Companies (Consolidation) Act 1908 s. 93(1)(d) and (e).
192 See also J Chisholm, *Green's Encyclopaedia of the Law of Scotland* Vol. 11 (Edinburgh: W. Green, 1899) 141–142; Juridical Society of Edinburgh, *Juridical Styles*, 6th edn (1908) Vol. II, 1360.

(c) Commentary

There was, though, some contrary opinion. In a double article of 1909–1910, A J P Menzies argued that a general non-possessory security was not foreign to Scots law, given the existence of, for example, the heritable creditor's right to poind the ground and the landlord's hypothec.[193] Of course, unlike floating charges, these were longstanding exceptions in Scots law to which a reasonable degree of certainty was attached and for which potential creditors could have notice due to the existence of, for example, a recorded heritable security (enabling poinding of the ground) or the debtor's possession of leased property (or registration of a tenancy for a long lease).[194] Menzies concluded, following a detailed examination of the Companies Consolidation Act 1908, that, on balance, the floating charge had been introduced into Scots law for companies.[195] His argument was founded on the statutory interpretation ground that an alternative conclusion would render certain provisions meaningless for Scotland and on the commercial policy ground that the floating charge was greatly valued by English companies and that prohibiting it 'would unfairly handicap the Scotch company in competition with its English rival'.[196] His suggestion that, by implication, certain sections enabled Scottish companies to grant floating charges, despite Scottish companies not being required to register such charges, is unconvincing on both strictly legal and policy grounds. Although there may have been certain commercial benefits for companies and particular creditors, there were also acknowledged drawbacks that rendered the floating charge controversial in England too. The non-applicability of the registration provisions that resolved some points of difficulty is a considerable negative point against

---

193 Menzies (n 184) at 159 and 160. He refers here to the poinding of the ground case of *Athole Hydropathic* (1886) 13 R 818 and compares Lord Shand's 'lament' in that case with Lord Macnaghten's in *Salomon* (n 134). See also Hardman, *Granting Corporate Security* (n 184) para. 6–03.

194 For details of the landlord's hypothec and poinding of the ground under the law at the time, see Gloag and Irvine, *Law of Rights in Security* (n 165) 105 onwards and 416 onwards, and the authorities cited there. Gloag and Irvine note (at 105) that an action for poinding of the ground could be brought by a superior for feuduty, by the creditor in a real burden or by the holder of a bond and disposition in security, but not by the assignee of a recorded lease nor by the holder of a disposition *ex facie* absolute with back-bond (as the latter is a proprietor of the land and not merely a creditor). See also Bell, *Principles*, § 699.

195 Menzies (n 184) at 168.

196 Menzies (n 184) at 168–169. He also refers to the disadvantages that would arise for the legal profession, by way of remuneration, if companies were to be registered in England rather than Scotland in order to grant floating charges (and thus English courts would hear matters that Scottish courts otherwise would).

Menzies' interpretation. The suggestion that Scottish companies would lose out to English companies may have had substance (and was influential later when the LRCS recommended the introduction of floating charges).[197] However, if this was to be addressed then the appropriate course would be for the legislature to build an acceptable regime for Scotland on the basis of demands made by stakeholders. As we shall see, widespread demands were not forthcoming at this point.

In a brief article written a short time later, J Burns stated that '[e]very practitioner is from time to time pressed as to whether it is not possible to obtain a security more or less on the lines of an English floating charge. The usual answer is *non possumus*'.[198] This suggests that there may have been some desire for a Scottish equivalent of the floating charge amongst clients of Scottish solicitors. However, as Burns acknowledged, the consensus was that such an equivalent was not available.[199] He did, though, note that the issue could be circumvented by, for example, incorporating an English company (to allow for the granting of a floating charge) or using a formal sale mechanism (for security purposes).[200] Given the problems with these alternative solutions and apparent interest in a floating charge-esque device, at least from some sections of the Scottish business community, it would not have been surprising for there to have been greater pressure for a non-possessory security as wide-ranging and flexible as the floating charge of English law.

(3) Opposition to floating charges

In reality, the voices in favour of introducing express non-possessory security such as a floating charge seem to have been in the minority well into the twentieth century. At various points, there were opportunities for interested parties in Scotland to press for the introduction of floating charges. For example, the views of a number of Scottish organisations including the Edinburgh and Glasgow Stock Exchanges and the Glasgow and Leith

---

197 See MacPherson, 'The Genesis of the Scottish Floating Charge', Chapter 3 for more details.

198 J Burns, 'Floating Charges in Scotland' 1910–1911 Jur Rev 260. The note principally focuses on the assignation of future book and bill debts for security purposes.

199 J Burns, 'Floating Charges in Scotland' (n 198).

200 He did though identify difficulties with using a formal sale, due to the Sale of Goods Act 1893 s. 61(4). Regarding this, and the successor s. 62(4) of the 1979 Act, see G L Gretton, 'The Concept of Security', in D J Cusine (ed), *A Scots Conveyancing Miscellany: Essays in Honour of Professor J M Halliday* (Edinburgh: W. Green, 1987) 126 at 135–138.

Chambers of Commerce were solicited for the *Davey Report* of 1895.[201] Despite responding to questions about the registration of security interests and whether or not the floating charge should be abolished, the Scottish parties did not express a wish to have floating charges made available in Scots law.[202] In addition, the Glasgow Chamber of Commerce stated that the floating charge should be abolished and that if Scots law was applied in the rest of the country 'with reasonable modification' then the law 'might without great difficulty be put on a proper basis'.[203] They stressed the importance of legal uniformity throughout the UK. Yet the prospect of the much larger English jurisdiction abandoning established practices and legal developments and adopting the Scottish approach was a forlorn hope.

The negativity towards, and lack of enthusiasm for, floating charges at this point is understandable when we consider that this was prior to the introduction of public registration for floating charges and a regime that would give priority to preferential creditors. As a result of the controversy stoked by the floating charge in England and the fact that organisations were expressly asked whether the floating charge should be abolished, the future of this security device may have seemed questionable. Consequently, pressing for its introduction in Scotland would have appeared unattractive and imprudent, even if legal uniformity was an apparent aim.

In the early years of the twentieth century, there was a belief, at least according to William Shaw, that the law had recently progressed 'in the direction of increasing the facilities for constituting security rights … ', by recognising and regulating mercantile customs and practice.[204] There was an apparent acknowledgment that the public interest supported the taking of steps 'to remove impediments to the growth of credit, and to encourage the confidence on which credit is based … '.[205] However, the recognition of the connection between commerce and the security rights regime, and the wish to liberalise credit, did not extend to any strong desire to provide for new security rights such as a floating charge. Another writer pointed to UK-wide

---

201 For details of stock exchanges in Scotland in the period, see R C Michie, *Money, Mania and Markets: Investment, Company Formation and the Stock Exchange in Nineteenth-Century Scotland* (Edinburgh: John Donaldson Publishers, 1981).

202 See e.g. the summary responses of certain Scottish organisations at *Davey Report*, Appendix, 97, 126 onwards and 146–147, where there are acknowledgments of the non-existence of floating charges in Scots law as well as an emphasis on the importance and desirability of public registration.

203 *Davey Report*, Appendix, 146.

204 W Shaw, *Securities over Moveables* (Edinburgh: W. Blackwood & Sons, 1903) 2.

205 Shaw, *Securities over Moveables*, 2.

statutory treatment of various legal areas in the Victorian period, as well as uniform consolidation and codification, but noted that the requirement for possession to create security over moveable property had 'maintained [its] place without discredit to the native jurisprudence' and stated that the rule 'had just been expressly kept alive for Scotland in the Companies Act, 1900'.[206]

Even after the remodelling of the floating charges regime in England, the orthodoxy in Scotland held sway. G W Wilton[207] referred to the fact that the floating charge had been 'judicially condemned' and added that 'there are not wanting signs of a serious movement for its abolition'.[208] He suggested that registration was 'no real protection' for creditors because, although they could determine that a floating charge existed, the creditors could not know the risks of what proportion of the assets would be affected until the security holder intervened.[209] Although this is true, a counter-argument is that the floating charge allows the debtor to continue to trade with their assets and thus means that they can generate income to fulfil obligations to their creditors.[210] With or without the floating charge there would be a risk of the debtor's insolvency (or creditors doing diligence) and consequent minimal debt recovery for unsecured creditors. In addition, some creditors can seek to factor the relevant risks into their transactions, albeit that this is unlikely to be straightforward.

In 1925, Wilton and Sir William McLintock,[211] a renowned Scottish accountant, were appointed to a Board of Trade committee to consider reforms to the Companies Acts. At one point, McLintock sought the views of a witness in relation to whether the floating charge ought to be abolished or

206 W C Smith, 'Scots Law in the Victorian Era' 1901 Jur Rev 152 at 162.
207 The works of Wilton (1862–1964) include *Company Law and Practice in Scotland* (n 113), *Company Liquidation Law and Practice* (Edinburgh: Hodge & Co, 1922), and *Company Law: Principal Distinctions* (n 101). For an obituary, see J A L, 'The Late Sheriff Wilton, QC' 1964 SLT (News) 73, within which reference is made to a humorous essay by Wilton entitled 'The Floating Charges'.
208 Wilton, *Company Law and Practice in Scotland* (n 113) 190. See also Wilton, *Company Law: Principal Distinctions* (n 101) 21 onwards where he outlines problems with floating charges and details some English opposition to them.
209 Wilton, *Company Law and Practice in Scotland* (n 113) at 190. See also Wilton, *Company Law: Principal Distinctions* (n 101) 24 where he states that registration of floating charges 'is no real protection' as, in practice, the register is rarely checked by those engaged in business and even if it was checked, the company could subsequently grant a floating charge. He adds that '[t]he true remedy is the complete abolition of the security'.
210 See Hardman, 'Law and Economics of the Floating Charge', Chapter 5 for more details.
211 For biographical details, see J R Edwards, 'McLintock, Sir William, first baronet (1873–1947)', *Oxford Dictionary of National Biography* (2004) available at *https://doi.org/10.1093/ref:odnb/34790* (last accessed 11 November 2021).

whether it should be subjected to further safeguards. In doing so, McLintock expressed his negativity towards the security and pointed out that in Scotland it did not exist. He stated that he had 'never heard any serious complaint that [large limited companies] were being deprived of the necessary trading facilities by being unable to pledge their floating assets'.[212]

In the subsequent *Company Law Amendment Committee Report* of 1926 it was noted that a questionnaire on specific Scottish matters was sent to various legal, business and other organisations in Scotland. The report mentioned that '[n]o desire has been expressed on behalf of any Scottish interest, professional, commercial or otherwise, for the introduction of [floating charges] into Scottish law and practice'.[213] Therefore, even in the 1920s there appears to have been a lack of appetite to bring floating charges into Scots law. It is almost certainly true that if various bodies had pressed for its introduction, the Company Law Amendment Committee would have been amenable to recommending such a change. In spite of the awareness of floating charges that many Scottish businesses must have had, due to the intertwining commerce and company law in Scotland and England, there was no real interest in pushing for them to be available to Scottish companies.

(4) Demand for floating charges?

It is surprising that certain commercial entities did not press for the introduction of non-possessory securities earlier. On a related note, regarding an earlier time period, Zwalve has pondered why banks and parts of the business community did not more strongly resist the abolition of non-possessory security rights in moveables[214] in various countries in the late eighteenth and early nineteenth centuries (Scots law, of course, already did not generally allow such security).[215] He explains that the banking world of that period 'was ... not structured to provide business capital to the industrial community

---

212 *Minutes of Evidence taken before the Departmental Committee Appointed by the Board of Trade to Consider and Report what Amendments are Desirable in the Companies Acts, 1908 to 1917* (1925) paras 1342 onwards.

213 *Company Law Amendment Committee (1925–26) Report* (Cmd 2657: 1926) 62. One change relating to the floating charge in England that was proposed in the Report was that the time period prior to commencement of winding up within which a floating charge could be void should be extended from three months to six. This was enacted by the Companies Act 1928 s. 43(3).

214 Given that the debtor would not be able to use the goods and the creditor would be required to store and maintain the goods without using them.

215 Zwalve (n 67) at 47–48.

on the basis of security interests in the stock-in-trade and machinery of its clients'.[216] Instead, they called upon personal security. Zwalve presumes that banks looked for non-personal forms of security following the emergence of modern business corporations. There is some logic to this; however, it does not explain why there was an absence of discernible demand for the reform of the Scots law of security rights to facilitate security over changing property in the period examined here.

The appearance of modern companies in the UK from the middle part of the nineteenth century was paralleled by the emergence of more flexible and liberal security rights, including the floating charge, in England. However, in Scotland, the security rights position was relatively static, despite significant economic and commercial developments, such as an increasingly sophisticated banking and finance system and the growing importance of moveable property in comparison to heritable property.[217] Bell could write in his *Principles of the Law of Scotland* that: 'In modern times, moveable property is frequently of much greater value than property in land. It is the part of the wealth of the people most generally diffused, and the most frequent subject of transaction and of transference … '.[218] Professor Kenneth Reid has written of the increased importance of corporeal and incorporeal moveable property as a result of the Industrial Revolution.[219] The significance and value of moveable property was later identified as a factor in the LRCS's recommendation for reforming security rights over such property by introducing the floating charge.[220] However, somewhat oddly, this growth in importance does not seem to have earlier led to a corresponding demand for security rights that would allow this property (especially corporeal moveables) to be utilised more economically. We are, to some degree, left guessing as to what methods of security were used in Scotland instead of the forms available in England: although considerable use of personal security (i.e. caution),[221] documents of title, assignation with intimation of incorporeal moveables, security over heritable property, the creation of trusts, *ex*

---

216 Zwalve (n 67) at 48.
217 The development of an efficient and well-functioning banking system has been viewed by a number of scholars as a crucial component in Scotland's economic transformation from the seventeenth century onwards – see e.g. Checkland, *Scottish Banking* (n 52); and Whyte, *Scotland before the Industrial Revolution* (n 159) at 307 onwards.
218 Bell, *Principles*, § 1283.
219 K Reid, 'Property Law: Sources and Doctrine', in K Reid and R Zimmermann (eds), *A History of Private Law in Scotland* (n 5) 209.
220 LRCS, *Eighth Report* (n 75) paras 5–6.
221 Gloag and Irvine, *Law of Rights in Security* (n 165), of course cover cautionary obligations alongside real security rights.

facie absolute sales[222] and even the establishment of companies in England to utilise the English regime of security rights, would have featured to varying degrees.[223]

Alongside industrial and commercial development, there was demand for, and moves towards, convergence of English and Scottish commercial law in the mid-to-late-nineteenth century, most notably by way of the Companies Acts, the Bills of Exchange Act 1882,[224] the Factors Act 1889 (applied to Scotland by the Factors (Scotland) Act 1890, the Partnership Act 1890, the Sale of Goods Act 1893 and the Patents Acts. Alan Rodger has correctly challenged any assumption that English law was imposed upon Scotland and has pointed to the role of Scottish businessmen and lawyers as 'enthusiastic supporters' of assimilation of the laws (particularly commercial laws) of England, Scotland and Ireland.[225] The growing convergence in commercial and corporate law matters in the later nineteenth and early twentieth centuries is also discussed by Lord Rodger elsewhere.[226]

Perhaps naturally, given the disparity in size of the jurisdictions joined in the Union, Scots commercial law principally converged to the English law position rather than the other way round.[227] Yet, with security rights, as we

---

222 Despite the introduction of the Sale of Goods Act 1893, delivery was still necessary in order to transfer ownership if the transaction was intended to operate by way of security (s. 61(4)).

223 A number of these are mentioned by Wilton, *Company Law: Principal Distinctions* (n 101) 26–27, within his discussion of floating charges being unnecessary in Scotland.

224 For details of the origin of the 1882 Act, see R G Anderson, 'Scots Law and the UK Codification of Bills of Exchange', in M Milo et al. (eds), *Tradition, Codification and Unification* (Cambridge: Intersentia Ltd, 2014).

225 A Rodger, 'The Codification of Commercial Law in Victorian Britain' (1991) 80 Proceedings of the British Academy 149 at 151 (also published at (1992) 108 LQR 570). Lord Rodger (at 153–154) discusses the involvement of organisations such as the Law Amendment Society and the Edinburgh Committee for the Amendment and Consolidation of Commercial Law. See also the following, which are cited by Lord Rodger: O Checkland and S Checkland, *Industry and Ethos Scotland 1832–1914*, 2nd edn (Edinburgh: Edinburgh University Press, 1989) Ch. 1 (on the development of industry); and I G C Hutchison, *A Political History of Scotland 1832–1924: Parties, Elections and Issues* (Edinburgh: John Donald, 1986) 93–95 (on the mid-nineteenth century demands of Scottish businessmen that their transactions should be governed by modern law). There were even calls for commercial law to apply uniformly not only within the UK but across the British Empire – see e.g. J Dove Wilson, *The Formation of a Code of Commercial Law for the United Kingdom: Why Not Begin Now?* (1884); J Dove Wilson, 'Proposed Imperial Code of Commercial Law – A Plea for Progress' 1896 Jur Rev 329; J E Hogg, 'The Unification of Commercial Law in the Empire' 1914 Jur Rev 154; and J E Hogg, 'A Commercial Code for the Empire' 1916 Jur Rev 246.

226 Rodger (n 159) at 16 onwards.

227 J W Cairns, 'Historical Introduction' in K Reid and R Zimmermann (eds), *A History of Private Law in Scotland* (n 5) 183, notes that: 'Given the dominance of England within the United Kingdom, the models for reform and development adopted in Scotland – as Goudy has pointed out [H Goudy, *An Inaugural Lecture on the Fate of Roman Law North and South of the Tweed*

have seen, this wish for assimilation was largely absent during the nineteenth and early twentieth centuries. The reasons for this are not entirely clear, but it may have been a combination of the following: that security rights were deemed too close to property law for convergence to be realisable (due to the markedly different systems in Scotland and England); that security rights in England were still in a state of flux, due to the identified controversies above, and were deemed undesirable to be introduced into Scots law[228]; that reform of the law would be too complex; that other areas of law more suitable for assimilation were to be focused upon first; and that the existing law was not considered sufficiently problematic. In any event, there was a lack of enthusiasm for introducing floating charges in this period as well as some outright opposition.

E. AGRICULTURAL CHARGES

(1) Nature and operation

One notable development in the Scots law of security rights in the late 1920s was the introduction of the agricultural charge to address a perceived need for short-term credit in the agricultural community. The agricultural charge shares characteristics with the floating charge. The Agricultural Credits (Scotland) Act 1929 (the 1929 Act) followed the Agricultural Credits Act 1928, which applies to England and Wales.[229] The 1928 Act enables 'farmers'[230] to grant 'agricultural charges' as security and such charges may be fixed, floating or both.[231] By contrast, the 1929 Act contains neither a distinction between fixed and floating charges nor does it use these terms. It limits the granting of 'agricultural charges' to certain cooperative societies[232]

(1894) 27] – tended to be those of English practice and law'. This was also true when the floating charge was identified as the model for Scots law to follow – see MacPherson, 'The Genesis of the Scottish Floating Charge', Chapter 3. Earlier in the nineteenth century, there was, however, a significant degree of English interest in adopting aspects of Scottish bankruptcy law – M Lobban, 'Reshaping Private Law in Victorian Britain: The View from Westminster', in H L MacQueen (ed), *The Stair Society Miscellany VII* (Edinburgh: The Stair Society, 2015) 337.

228 As we have seen, it was not even clear (at least for a time) whether the floating charge would remain available, or whether it would be abolished.

229 See also the Agricultural Marketing Act 1958 s. 15(6), which allows an agricultural board to grant an agricultural charge over agricultural produce in Scotland.

230 As defined in Agricultural Credits Act 1928 s. 5(7).

231 Agricultural Credits Act 1928 s. 5(1)–(2). The effects of the fixed charges and floating charges are outlined in ss. 6 and 7 respectively.

232 Namely, industrial and provident societies. See s. 9(1) for the full definition of the societies able to grant agricultural charges.

focused on agriculture that are registered in Scotland and these charges can only be granted in favour of 'banks'.[233]

The Scottish agricultural charge affects all or any part of the 'stocks of merchandise from time to time belonging to and in the possession of the society ...'[234] and is more influenced by an English floating charge than a fixed charge.[235] The agricultural charge is a right in security over the property affected by it and, on the occurrence of a specified event (outlined within the instrument creating the charge), the Act states that it can be enforced by the sequestration and sale of secured property 'in like manner in all respects as in the case of the hypothec of a landlord'.[236] This differs from the English position where the floating variant of the agricultural charge becomes a fixed charge upon the happening of certain events.[237] There was formerly a requirement for the Scottish agricultural charge to be registered within seven clear days after execution, otherwise it would be void against any party other than the granting society; however, this registration requirement has oddly, and unwarrantably, been abolished.[238]

Although the agricultural charge was seemingly original in Scots law, as an express, statutory, non-possessory hypothec over a changing body of assets, an attempt was made to tie it to existing law by reference to the

233 'Banks' are defined in s. 9(2). It is unclear whether the security can be assigned by a bank to another party. The equivalent security under the Agricultural Credits Act 1928 has been held to be assignable – *McLean v Berry* [2016] EWHC 2650 (Ch), [2017] Ch 422.

234 1929 Act s. 5(2).

235 For the equivalent provisions for the English fixed and floating agricultural charges see the Agricultural Credits Act 1928 s. 5(3) and 5(4).

236 1929 Act s. 6(1). In Scottish Law Commission, *Discussion Paper on Moveable Transactions* (Scot. Law Com. DP No. 151, 2011), it is stated that agricultural charges seem to no longer be enforceable outside insolvency as the 1929 Act only provides for enforcement using sequestration for rent, a process that has been abolished (see Bankruptcy and Diligence etc. (Scotland) Act 2007 s. 208) (para. 6.22). The Scottish Law Commission suggest that placing the debtor into insolvency seems a 'disproportionate' method of enforcement (para. 6.22).

237 Agricultural Credits Act 1928 s. 7(1)(a).

238 Agricultural Credits Act 1928 s. 8(1). The Assistant Registrar of Friendly Societies for Scotland was required to keep the register of agricultural charges. The registration requirement provision was repealed by the Financial Services and Markets Act 2000 (Consequential Amendments and Repeals) Order 2001, art. 216. Within the Scottish Law Commission, *Discussion Paper on Moveable Transactions* (n 236), para. 6.21 it is pointed out that this is contrary to the general legal policy that 'secret security rights are undesirable' (and see paras 16.80–16.81). Due to the rarity of such charges and the availability of floating charges instead, the Scottish Law Commission have proposed that it should no longer be competent to grant agricultural charges – see Scottish Law Commission, *Report on Moveable Transactions* (n 60) paras 38.13–38.15, and Draft Bill s. 115. Enquiries to the Bank of England and the Financial Conduct Authority, who now have responsibility for the Registry of Friendly Societies for Scotland, have proved fruitless in ascertaining how many agricultural charges have been granted and how many continue to exist.

(then applicable) enforcement procedure of the landlord's hypothec. The agricultural charge equivalent to 'attachment' involves the security becoming enforceable against the affected assets at the relevant time, rather than only having real effect at that point (as the floating charge does).[239] Instead, the agricultural charge operates as a real right in security upon its creation but no longer affects property where ownership or possession is lost by the chargor. This also appears to mean that possessory securities prevail over the agricultural charge (as the property would no longer be subject to the charge). In addition, the charge is expressly subordinated to the landlord's hypothec and (formerly) to the hypothec of the feudal superior.[240] Agricultural charges expressly rank against one another according to the dates of their registration – with earlier registered charges ranking ahead of those registered later.[241] The grantor is, however, obliged to pay to the bank proceeds of sale of property affected by the charge, with the sums to be applied towards discharge (unless there is contrary agreement).[242] Subject to this, the society can sell the charged property and the purchaser 'shall not be concerned to see that such obligation is complied with notwithstanding that he may be aware of the existence of the charge'.[243] The charge therefore loses real effect in relation to property that is sold, irrespective of whether the purchaser is in good faith. The narrow applicability of the agricultural charge and the general absence of reported cases mean that the 1929 Act provisions and the charge itself have been the subject of little analysis. However, its relevance to the topic of floating security justifies its consideration in some detail here.

(2) Contemporary commentary

Given the novelty of the agricultural charge in Scots law, it is not surprising that the Bill which became the 1929 Act provoked some controversy. At the Second Reading of the Bill in the House of Lords it was stated that the

---

239 For the nature of the floating charge before attachment, see MacPherson, *Floating Charge* (n 50) Ch. 2.

240 1929 Act s. 6(2). The superior's hypothec was repealed by the Abolition of Feudal Tenure etc. (Scotland) Act 2000 s. 13(3). Section 6(3) of the 1929 Act should also be noted, as it states that the charge 'shall be no protection in respect of the property affected by it against any process, execution, or diligences for recovery of taxes or rates'.

241 1929 Act s. 7(1). Given the abolition of the registration requirement, the position for agricultural charges ranking inter se is now uncertain.

242 1929 Act s. 6(4).

243 1929 Act s. 6(5). Regarding proceeds of sale, see s. 6(6).

government was of the view that in framing the Bill as they had done, they had 'gone as far as it is wise to go at the moment in Scotland'.[244] This was because the introduction of the 'chattel mortgage' system would be a 'very great innovation'. In addition, it was noted that 'the various legal bodies in Scotland are opposed to the 'chattel mortgage' system … '.[245] Apparently in order to address the criticisms, the ability to grant agricultural charges was limited to certain societies, and thereby excluded individual farmers, and an attempt was made to tie the proposed new security into the existing Scots law through its function and enforcement mechanism. Another peer suggested, however, that the effect of the planned move was 'to make a fundamental change in the law of Scotland by a side issue'.[246] He also noted that banks had indicated that the new security would benefit them but would damage the credit of farmers and therefore they were not in favour of the change.[247]

Within the agricultural community itself, there was some diversity of opinion. Seemingly, the 'Farmers' Union in Scotland'[248] was in favour of introducing the system of short-term credits and agricultural charges while the Chamber of Agriculture was against.[249] There was a degree of awareness among interested parties regarding the 'fundamental change' required for Scots law to accommodate the arrival of a 'chattel mortgage' or 'floating charge'.[250] It was also suggested that the demand in Scotland for a short-term credits Bill was much lower than in England.[251] By contrast, the Committee of the President of the National Farmers' Union of Scotland recommended that it should be competent for an individual farmer to grant a 'chattel mortgage' and proposed that it should also be grantable to any party. Furthermore, a member also apparently pointed out that Scotland was

244 HL Deb 28 Feb 1929, col 1196 (Earl of Airlie). For the Second Reading stage in the House of Commons, see HC Deb 30 Nov 1928, cols 788–804, at which A V Alexander MP stated that the Scottish Chamber of Agriculture had earlier disapproved of the application of the provisions of the English Bill regarding short-term credits (including agricultural charges) to Scotland and this was part of the reason why the provisions in the Scottish Bill were different from those in the English legislation (col 799).

245 HL Deb 28 Feb 1929, col 1196 (Earl of Airlie). The term 'chattel mortgage' is clearly being used here in a loose way to refer to non-possessory security over moveables.

246 HL Deb 28 Feb 1929, col 1201 (Viscount Novar).

247 Why the credit of farmers would be damaged is unclear.

248 Presumably the National Farmers' Union of Scotland.

249 As mentioned at HL Deb 28 Feb 1929, cols 1195–1196 (Earl of Airlie).

250 *The Scotsman*, 'Credits for Farmers – Scheme Criticised', 17 February 1926, 11. See also the comments of the directors of the Highland and Agricultural Society – *The Scotsman*, 10 January 1929, 13.

251 *The Scotsman*, 5 May 1928, 10.

'almost unique in not having a system of granting security over movables'.[252] It was suggested that the government should be pressed to amend the Bill to give Scottish farmers equal short-term credit facilities as English farmers and therefore they should be able to grant floating charges over their moveable assets.[253] As well as noting the proposed introduction of a 'novelty' in Scots law and expressing some doubts about the 'experiment', the directors of the Highland and Agricultural Society suggested that if the government was confident that a scheme would operate well in practice then it should be considered whether societies should be able to grant floating charges over all of their assets.[254]

Therefore, although there was recognition that the agricultural charge would represent a noteworthy change in Scots law, within some sections of the agricultural community there was willingness to embrace the change and even to go further than what was proposed. There does though seem to have been little support for agricultural charges outside the agricultural sector. In addition to the negative views of the legal profession (noted above), certain committees of the Glasgow Chamber of Commerce stated that something 'in the nature of a floating charge' for moveable assets was being proposed and this was 'quite unknown' and 'would cut deeply into one of the most cherished principles of Scottish law'.[255] They therefore recommended that it was not in the interests of trade and industry for Scots law to be altered in this way.

(3) Floating charges and agricultural charges

Despite certain contrary voices, it seems as if there continued to be fairly widespread dogmatic disapproval of the floating charge as a creation that would not appropriately fit within Scots law. For some, this view appears to have extended to the agricultural charge and may have been accompanied by a fear that this would represent the first assault upon the general Scots law position. Also, it seems as if, rather than pressing for a change in the law on commercial grounds, business organisations may have valued the certainty and stability of the existing legal position and were doubtful as to the commercial benefits that a floating security might confer.

---

252 *The Scotsman*, 8 December 1928, 10. By this, what is surely meant is the absence of a system of *non-possessory* security over moveables.
253 *The Scotsman*, 8 December 1928, 10.
254 *The Scotsman*, 10 January 1929, 13.
255 *The Scotsman*, 18 December 1928, 5.

Agricultural charges were followed by floating charges some thirty-two years later. The two types of security are related in a number of ways: they are both exceptions to the general position of Scots law regarding non-acceptance of voluntary hypothecs; only certain types of entity can create them; there is a registration requirement for floating charges to be fully effective and registration was also formerly needed for agricultural charges; and they were also both developed from an English model with some variation for integration into Scots law. Yet, the differences help us to identify why the agricultural charge could be introduced at this time while the floating charge only came later. The former was a much narrower exception to the general rule: the granting societies were far less commonplace than companies; the grantees were limited to banks; the charge was limited to one category of moveable property; and it was to be operated and enforced in a way that was more compatible with existing Scots law.

It is possible, of course, that the creation of one exception to the general rule made further exceptions seem more legitimate. The introduction of a principally English law concept and terminology by way of legislation, but with Scottish adaptations, can be seen as a precursor to the floating charge.[256] The considerable integration of England and Scotland also created demands for legal assimilation and this could lead to Scots property law, especially in commercial areas, becoming susceptible to changes based upon English foundations, such as the Sale of Goods Act 1893, the agricultural charge and, later, the floating charge.

Finally, there is also an interesting parallel between the introduction of the agricultural charge followed by the floating charge in Scots law and how the law developed in Roman law. The Roman hypothec seems to have first been utilised in relation to agricultural estates before being extended more broadly.[257] They are both examples of systems moving from the availability of non-possessory securities within a discrete context (specifically within agriculture) to such rights being made much more widely available.

---

256 With the agricultural charge the existing English legislation was modified, whereas with the floating charge there was an attempt to translate an institution of equity into legislation (albeit incorporating certain elements of existing English legislation such as for registration).

257 See e.g. Goebel (n 7) at 36. However, a key difference is that with the Roman law the same institution developed and expanded, whereas in Scotland the change is more correctly characterised as one type of security being followed sometime later by another similar one.

F. LATER DEVELOPMENTS

(1) Increasing support for floating charges?

Over time, some bodies do seem to have become more amenable towards non-possessory securities generally and floating charges more specifically. In 1943 the Glasgow Chamber of Commerce suggested that the Board of Trade committee reviewing the Companies Acts should consider differences between Scots law and English law in relation to the creation of securities over moveables, such as stock-in-trade and book debts.[258] It was believed that floating charges placed English businesses in a relatively more favourable position than Scottish companies regarding the obtaining of finance and it was requested that this should be investigated. However, the prominent businessman Sir George Mitchell[259] expressed his disapproval of the law of floating charges and stated that it would be preferable if the English law was assimilated to Scots law and not the other way round. It was therefore agreed to note that there was 'a considerable difference of opinion' in the committee.[260]

Even if there was growing support for floating charges in certain organisations, many continued to be resistant to introducing the security and, in any event, there does not seem to have been much willingness to press strongly for their introduction. Ultimately, the Board of Trade's *Report of the Committee on Company Law Amendment* (1945) did not contain any proposal for introducing a floating charge in Scotland nor was there any suggestion that this was something stakeholders were interested in.[261] And the subsequent Companies Act 1948 contained no provision for floating charges being made available in Scots law.[262]

(2) *Re Anchor Line*

A short time earlier, in 1937, the Chancery Division in *Re the Anchor Line (Henderson Brothers) Ltd*,[263] had to determine the validity of a floating

---

258 *The Scotsman*, 21 September 1943, 3.

259 Sir George Arthur Mitchell (1860–1948). For biographical details, see *http://www.universitys tory.gla.ac.uk/biography/?id=WH2009&type=P* (last accessed 21 October 2021).

260 *The Scotsman*, 21 September 1943, 3.

261 *Board of Trade. Report of the Committee on Company Law Amendment* (Cmd 6659: 1945).

262 As regards registration of charges, the Companies Act 1948 s. 95(1) was limited to companies registered in England and therefore impliedly excluded companies registered in Scotland.

263 [1937] Ch 483.

charge over property in Scotland. A company registered in England executed a charge, in Glasgow, in favour of a Scottish bank, by way of floating security on its undertaking and all its property and assets, present and future. Luxmoore J acknowledged that this type of charge was 'unknown to the law of Scotland' but that it was given by an English company and, although executed in Scotland, it had to be construed in accordance with English law.[264] He added that the Companies Act 1929 s. 270 did not place an English company's property in Scotland in a different position to property belonging to it in England or anywhere else.[265]

An English court therefore recognised the validity of a floating charge granted by an English company in relation to property, irrespective of the property's location. An alternative approach would have been to assess the security's validity according to the laws of the location of the 'charged' property. Given the range of property potentially covered by a floating charge and the fact that it is a form of security closely bound up with the person of the grantor, including with respect to enforcement processes, there is something to be said for an approach that depends upon where the grantor is registered.[266]

(3) *Carse v Coppen*

Re Anchor Line was a case before an English court involving the question of whether a floating charge created by an English company was effective over assets in Scotland. By contrast, *Carse v Coppen*[267] was decided by the First Division of the Inner House (in 1950 and reported in 1951) and concerned the validity of a purported floating charge by a Scottish company over assets in England, where the company had a place of business. The company had borrowed sums under two debentures executed in Scotland but in English form and, by virtue of these debentures, sought to create a floating charge over its whole undertaking, property

---

264 *Re Anchor Line* (n 263) at 487.
265 *Re Anchor Line* (n 263) at 489. See the alternative view of Lord Keith in his dissenting opinion in *Carse* (n 3) at 247–248.
266 There could, however, still be difficulties enforcing a floating charge in relation to assets in another jurisdiction that does not recognise floating charges – see e.g. Lord Collins of Mapesbury and J Harris (eds), *Dicey, Morris & Collins on the Conflict of Laws*, 15th edn (London: Sweet & Maxwell, 2018) paras 30–022, 30–134 onwards and 30–242 onwards. For discussion of floating charges (in Scots law) as patrimonial devices connected to the person of the grantor, see MacPherson, *Floating Charge* (n 50), especially Ch. 6.
267 *Carse* (n 3).

and assets.[268] It was conceded that a floating charge over Scottish assets could not be created by the debentures. However, the court had to decide whether a valid floating charge over the company's assets in England had been created. The court held (with Lord Keith dissenting) that an effectual floating charge was not created.

Lord President Cooper pointed out that there was no recorded decision indicating the 'feasibility' of a Scottish company creating a valid floating charge over its 'undertaking and assets' in England or anywhere else.[269] He therefore suggested that given the number of Scottish companies liquidated by the Scottish courts, and the fact that a number of them must have had assets in England, the 'silence of the reports is significant'. The Lord President referred to certain writings that speculated that it might be possible to create floating charges over English assets but noted that this seemed not to have been tried.[270] In speculating as to why this was so, he proceeded to give what has become the definitive Scots common law statement on floating charges:

> 'The explanation doubtless is that it is clear in principle and amply supported by authority that a floating charge is utterly repugnant to the principles of Scots law and is not recognised by us as creating a security at all. In Scotland the term "equitable security" is meaningless. Putting aside the rare and exceptional cases of hypothec, we require for the constitution of a security which will confer upon the holder rights over and above those which he enjoys in common with the general body of unsecured creditors of a debtor, (a) the transfer to the creditor of a real right in specific subjects by the method appropriate for the constitution of such rights in the particular classes of property in question, or (b) the creation of a nexus over specific property by the due use of the appropriate form of diligence. A floating charge, even after appointment of a receiver, satisfies none of these requirements.'[271]

In seeking to find a solution in the case, the Lord President interpreted the decision of Luxmoore J in *Re Anchor Line* as involving issues 'purely

---

268 The security was referred to by Lord President Cooper, arguably misleadingly, as a 'universal or general assignment' – *Carse* (n 3) at 241–242. Cf at 244–245 per Lord Keith.

269 *Carse* (n 3) at 239.

270 The writings referred to are Wilton, *Company Liquidation Law and Practice* (n 207) 38, and J A Lillie, *Encyclopaedia of the Laws of Scotland*, Supplementary Volume, Part I (1949) 307–308. Wilton, *Company Law: Principal Distinctions* (n 101) 26 and 28, also suggested that an alternative to a floating charge in Scots law would be where the parties agreed that the creditor could take possession of property under certain circumstances and acquiring possession would represent 'crystallisation' and render the security effective.

271 *Carse* (n 3) at 239. In addition to referring to general principles and rules of security rights in Scots law, the Lord President also used excerpts from *Ballachulish* (n 178) to support his assertions on floating charges.

domestic' to the Chancery Division, rather than having wider application.[272] Instead, he examined the provisions of the Companies Act 1948 relating to floating charges to determine the answer. As well as pointing out that there was no register of charges in Scotland he noted that certain provisions expressly only applied to English companies, while others impliedly did so, and therefore concluded that the only reasonable view was that Scottish companies could not grant floating charges.[273] He also interpreted certain legislative provisions, including provisions relating to receivers, as involving restrictive reforms to address 'the many criticisms which have been directed against the injustices capable of being inflicted on the trade creditors by the use of floating charges'.[274] The Lord President added that for Scottish courts to introduce unrestricted floating charges when Parliament had 'just subjected' floating charges of English companies to 'material restrictions' would be a 'remarkable effort in judicial legislation'.[275] He also stated that to hold that Scottish companies could grant floating charges, even if they were limited to English assets, 'would reduce company law and practice to chaos'.[276] His views on a Scottish company creating a floating charge specifically restricted to assets in England are, however, obiter and Lords Carmont and Russell reserved their opinions on this point.[277]

For Lord President Cooper then, the applicable law depended upon where the company was registered. This was consistent with the approach of the companies legislation, where various rules regarding floating charges applied if a company was registered in England and did not apply if a company was registered in Scotland. Deciding otherwise would have involved significant judicial activism, especially when floating charges granted by English companies had been subjected to substantial legislative limitation in order to make them widely acceptable in England. There is a lack of evidence to suggest that there was an intention for Scottish companies to be able to grant floating charges under the legislation, and the applicability of relevant provisions to companies registered in England supports this. Also, the close relationship between floating charges and liquidation, regarding enforcement and giving effect to floating charges, further justifies an

---

272 *Carse* (n 3) at 239–240.
273 *Carse* (n 3) at 240–241. He referred to Part III and ss. 94, 319(5)(b) and 372–376. Cf the comments of Lord Keith in his dissenting opinion at 246–247.
274 *Carse* (n 3) at 241.
275 *Carse* (n 3) at 242.
276 *Carse* (n 3) at 242.
277 *Carse* (n 3) at 242 per Lord President Cooper; at 243 per Lord Carmont; at 244 per Lord Russell.

approach that ties the issue of the effectiveness of the security to the granting company's place of registration, and to the chargor as a person (rather than simply to where its property is located).[278]

It is true that the court in *Carse* did not consider the economic merits of floating charges or how Scots law's objections, from a publicity standpoint and otherwise, could be overcome. In addition, the confirmed inability of a Scottish company to grant a floating charge over English assets would have diminished the attractiveness of Scottish registered companies as a vehicle for commerce, due to the difficulties that they might encounter acquiring finance compared to their English counterparts. Yet, it is clear that if floating charges were to be introduced into Scotland (including for assets outside Scotland), the more appropriate course was for this to be done through legislation. This would enable the creation or adoption of a suitable registration regime, provide an opportunity for interested parties to make representations, give some notice to potentially affected parties that such a substantial change was to be made, and would avoid some of the uncertainty that would arise from a court's decision. The courts were, after all, not well-placed to provide an adequate solution to the issue and the benefitting of a particular group of commercial entities at the expense of other parties would have been a controversial course to take.

The decision in *Carse v Coppen* has, however, been criticised. Lord Rodger refers to Lord President Cooper's 'curious reasoning' and states that it is unclear how Scots law could prevent Scottish companies creating floating charges over assets in England where the documents were signed in England, unless there was something in the companies' articles to prevent this.[279] According to David Edward, it was the view of Professor J D B Mitchell that 'Lord President Cooper's forthright rejection in 1951 of the floating charge, as being conceptually incompatible with Scots law, set back the post-war recovery of the Scottish economy by a vital ten years'.[280] This may overstate the value of floating charges in economic terms and

---

278 See MacPherson, *Floating Charge* (n 50) especially Ch. 6, for more details regarding a patrimonial view of the floating charge after it arrived in Scots law.

279 Lord Rodger of Earlsferry, '"Say Not the Struggle Naught Availeth": The Costs and Benefits of Mixed Legal Systems' (2003) 78 Tul L Rev 419 at 423. See also A E Anton, *Private International Law*, 3rd edn, by P R Beaumont and P E McEleavy (Edinburgh: W. Green, 2011) paras 25.69 onwards.

280 D Edward, 'The Scottish Reactions–An Epilogue', in B Markesinis (ed), *The Gradual Convergence: Foreign Ideas, Foreign Influences, and English Law on the Eve of the 21st Century* (Oxford: Clarendon Press, 1994) 264. On J D B Mitchell, see M Loughlin, 'Sitting on a Fence at Carter Bar: In Praise of J D B Mitchell' 1991 Jur Rev 135.

seems to unfairly blame Lord President Cooper.[281] *Carse v Coppen* was limited to whether or not a floating charge granted by a Scottish company over all of its property would be valid over assets in England. It was already well-established that floating charges could not be created in Scots law and allowing Scottish companies to grant floating charges over English assets would have been an uncertain course and one arguably unjustified by the companies legislation.

G. CONCLUSION

The judgments of the majority in *Carse v Coppen* (especially that of Lord President Cooper) re-emphasised Scots law's negativity towards floating charges and confirmed the general inability of Scottish companies to create such a security, including with respect to assets in England.[282] At the time, the prospect of a type of floating charge being introduced into Scots law a decade later would have seemed distinctly remote. Yet that is what happened. The arrival of the floating charge was facilitated by other developments and required implementation by legislation. Although it would be wrong to suggest that there was inevitability about the change, by the mid-twentieth century the landscape was more favourable than it had been in the past.

Scots law had rejected express hypothecs over moveables for a long time, with the institutional writers explaining that this was for reasons of commerce since there would be uncertainty as to whether a party had granted a security if there was no publicity, such as by way of possession. As time passed, however, the dogmatic adherence to the doctrine meant that the underlying rationale was obscured. Instead, the general rejection of hypothecs came to be presented, especially by the courts, as an immutable principle of Scots law. In addition, against the background of changing economic circumstances, other jurisdictions were changing their laws to become more favourable towards hypothecs. Scots law's stasis meant that it was becoming more unusual in its generally strict rejection of hypothecs.[283] The contrast of

---

281 See Hardman, 'Law and Economics of the Floating Charge', Chapter 5 for discussion of the economic value of floating charges.

282 However, the question of whether a floating charge specifically limited to English assets could be valid if granted by a Scottish company was left open, with Lords Carmont and Russell reserving their opinions.

283 The changes in other jurisdictions were later noted by T B Smith in his 'Historical Note' to LRCS, *Eighth Report* (n 75) Appendix I. See MacPherson, 'The Genesis of the Scottish Floating Charge', Chapter 3, for more details. As well as Scotland and England within the UK,

Scots law with English law was particularly sharp. From the mid-nineteenth century, English equity recognised floating charges for principally commercial reasons. Yet floating charges proved to be controversial and were often viewed as unfair to ordinary creditors. Even into the twentieth century, it was not entirely clear whether they would remain available. This helps explain why there was little appetite in Scotland for introducing floating charges, despite their widespread usage in England and the increasing economic and commercial unity of the two countries. It is true that certain businesses, especially those operating on a cross-border basis, would have preferred a uniform law across the UK and there was realisation that Scots law was less permissive than English law as far as the granting of security rights was concerned. But there was no widespread push for reform on the English model.

Nevertheless, mechanisms to facilitate floating security were emerging. The development of a registration system for floating charges was a key step for addressing some of the concerns about such charges in English law but also provided a model that could be adopted in Scotland, albeit through legislation rather than case law. The registration system could provide a level of compliance with the publicity principle of Scots law. This would, to some extent, meet the objections of the institutional writers and others regarding the absence of publicity and its consequent impact on commerce, albeit that using registration for the purposes of creation of the security (rather than it being a post-creation requirement) would have been more faithful to the publicity principle. The existence of a register corresponding to a legal person,[284] rather than to particular types of property, would also overcome the inability of a party at common law to create a security over multiple types of property due to the differing publicity requirements involved for different property. A security over all, or part, of a company's present and future property could be facilitated by a register of charges corresponding to that company. Other reforms to floating charges in the late nineteenth and early twentieth centuries, such as subordinating the chargeholder to preferential creditors and invalidating certain charges granted in close proximity to liquidation also made the floating charge less of a controversial proposition. Although there is perhaps a discernible increase in support for introducing floating charges towards the end of the period covered in this chapter, there was by no means a torrent of support for this. Even

other major industrial states, especially Germany and the US, adopted different approaches for non-possessory security rights in the period.

284 Which was facilitated by the development of modern companies.

the arrival of agricultural charges, as a narrow exception to the background Scots law, was divisive.

Of course, the Scottish courts also rejected the applicability of floating charges in Scots law. Yet, despite this, the steps mentioned above provided a platform upon which the law of floating charges could more appropriately be built by legislation. The desirability of a registration regime for floating security and the inability of judges to facilitate this, as well as difficulties they would encounter in weighing up commercial advantages and disadvantages that might arise from admitting floating security, meant that legislation was a preferable vehicle for reform. As will be seen in the Genesis of the Scottish Floating Charge chapter, further developments in the 1950s, such as a growing perception of the commercial value that floating charges could offer Scottish companies, and the reform conduit provided by the LRCS, ultimately led to the arrival of the Scottish floating charge.

2 Borrowing on the Undertaking: Scottish Statutory Companies

Ross G Anderson

A. INTRODUCTION
B. NINETEENTH CENTURY LEGAL PERSONS
    (1) Partnerships and common law companies
    (2) Charter companies and Letters Patent Acts
    (3) Statutory companies
    (4) Joint stock companies and the Companies Act 1862
    (5) Statutory companies and the Clauses Acts
C. THE CLAUSES ACTS
    (1) Pre-1845 Private Acts
    (2) Overview of Clauses Acts
    (3) Companies Clauses Consolidation (Scotland) Act 1845
    (4) Lands Clauses Consolidation (Scotland) Act 1845
    (5) Railways Clauses Acts
    (6) Tramways
    (7) Commissioners Clauses Act 1847: mortgages and receivers
    (8) Harbours, Docks and Piers Clauses Act 1847
    (9) Burgh Harbours (Scotland) Act 1853
D. BONDS, MORTGAGES AND DEBENTURE STOCK
    (1) Bonds
    (2) Statutory mortgages and assignations in security
    (3) Debenture stock
E. THE UNDERTAKING
F. PUBLIC PURPOSES AND PROFIT
G. ENFORCEMENT: JUDICIAL FACTORS AND RECEIVERS
    (1) Personal creditors: diligence
    (2) Judicial factors

(3) Management and moratorium: judicial factor for railway debenture holders

(4) A local Act example: the Greenock Harbour Trustees
    (a) Background
    (b) Priority and scope of the statutory assignments

(5) 'A little more intensity to the Conveyance': 'Property and Works'

(6) Receivers, managers and judicial factors

H. CONCLUSIONS

A. INTRODUCTION

'The whole method of creating a floating charge,' said Lord Dunedin in 1908, 'is absolutely foreign to our law.'[1] For Lord Cooper, the floating charge 'is utterly repugnant to the principles of Scots law and is not recognised by us as creating a security at all. In Scotland, "equitable security" is meaningless'.[2]

Floating charges were introduced into Scots law by the Companies (Floating Charges) (Scotland) Act 1961.[3] Prior to 1961, it is often said, it was impossible for a Scottish company to create a 'floating charge' over the whole or any part of its property and undertaking.[4] The purpose of this paper is to demonstrate that the quotable *dicta* from Lord Dunedin and Lord Cooper, though correct in relation to the 'equitable' aspect of floating charges, may otherwise be taken too far. The floating charge has a number of aspects. First, it may be (though it need not be) a universal

---

1 *Ballachulish Slate Quarries Company Ltd v Bruce* (1908) 16 SLT 48 at 51 per Lord President Dunedin.

2 *Carse (Liquidator of Shop Fronts (Great Britain) Ltd) v Coppen* 1951 SC 233 at 239. In addition to the writers cited to the court, the other significant author who had addressed the question of whether a Scottish company could grant an effectual floating charge was A J P Menzies, 'Is Creation of a Floating Charge Competent to a Limited Company Registered in Scotland?' (1909–1910) 21 Jur Rev 87 and 129.

3 The Companies (Floating Charges) (Scotland) Act 1961 s. 1; the Companies (Floating Charges and Receivers) (Scotland) Act 1972 s. 1; and the Companies Act 1985 ss. 462(1) and 486(1), conferred the power under the law of Scotland to grant floating charges on an incorporated company 'whether incorporated under the Companies Acts or not'. That would suggest that a company incorporated by Act of Parliament may grant a floating charge, though it would not appear to be subject to the registration requirements of Part 25 of the Companies Act 2006, as s. 859A(7) applies only to UK registered companies.

4 *Re Spectrum Plus Ltd (in liquidation)* [2005] 2 AC 680 at [49] per Lord Hope of Craighead. See also A D J MacPherson, 'The "Pre-History" of Floating Charges in Scots Law', Chapter 1 within this volume.

security: it may cover all of the granter's patrimonial rights. In the actual words of the statute, the company may grant a floating charge 'over all or any part of the property (including uncalled capital) which may from time to time be comprised in its property and undertaking'.[5] Secondly, it allows real subrogation: in commercial terms, the granter company can trade; the patrimonial rights covered by the charge may be transferred, discharged or varied, and the consideration for those transactions will in turn fall under the charge.[6] Thirdly, the floating charge covers future assets acquired after the creation of the charge.[7] Fourthly, it allows the creditors to exercise certain control over the granter company, because enforcement is normally by appointment of a court officer: a liquidator, a receiver,[8] an administrative receiver (until 2003 albeit with some ongoing exceptions) or administrator. In relation to some of these aspects, at least, Scottish statutory companies have had some of these powers since the first half of the nineteenth century.

In the nineteenth century, the number of companies incorporated in Scotland either under the Joint Stock Companies or the Companies Acts was relatively modest: between 1856 (when limited liability became available) and 1885 around 1,393.[9] Between 1800 and 1885, meanwhile, Parliament passed some 18,500 private Acts (compared to about 9,500 public Acts).[10] Many of these local Acts incorporated bodies corporate with borrowing powers. There appear to be no figures for the actual number of statutory companies incorporated, but the number appears to have been very significant. Unlike many of the companies incorporated under the Companies Acts that had no meaningful trade,[11] the considerable sums incurred to procure an Act of Parliament incorporating the statutory company normally meant that statutory companies did in fact trade.[12]

---

5 Companies (Floating Charges) (Scotland) Act 1961 s. 1(1); Companies Act 1985 s. 462(1).
6 *Ballachulish* (n 1) 51 per Lord McLaren.
7 *Ballachulish* (n 1).
8 Since the Companies (Floating Charges and Receivers) (Scotland) Act 1972.
9 P L Payne, *The Early Scottish Limited Companies 1856–1895* (Edinburgh: Scottish Academic Press, 1980) 19, Table 2. This represented about 5 per cent of the total UK companies incorporated over that period. To put the figures in perspective, in March 2020 there were some 4,350,913 entities registered at Companies House, of which 224,640 were registered in Scotland.
10 R Cunliffe, *A History of Private Bill Legislation* (London: Butterworths, 1885) Vol. I, vii.
11 Payne, *Early Scottish Limited Companies* (n 9) 26.
12 Return of the very significant deposits required to procure incorporation of a company by local Act was also regulated by statute and subject to extensive litigation.

Each statutory company was normally[13] incorporated by its own local or special Act of Parliament. Sometimes the special Act established bodies of commissioners. These special Acts drew on the various public general 'Clauses Acts', each reflecting the main sectors of practice required for industrial development: companies; land; harbours, docks and piers; railways; canals[14]; and, later, tramways, gas and lighting. These formed the bulwarks of a comprehensive, if light-touch, regulatory system that allowed court decisions under one Clauses Act to apply as an authority for another Clauses Act.[15] Monuments to Victorian aspiration as much as to Victorian engineering, the legal legacy of the Clauses Acts, and the Scottish statutory companies that incorporated their provisions, has not received the attention it deserves.[16]

Until around 1914, statutory companies were the vehicles for capital projects of unparalleled scale: they designed, constructed and operated the main pillars of UK domestic infrastructure. Ambition alone, however, does not bring such projects to fruition. They must be financed. And their financing required legal structures suitable for the industrial rather than feudal age. Often these companies borrowed sums that, if adjusted for inflation, were the equivalent of hundreds of millions of pounds today. In 1884, statutory companies continued to account for around three-quarters of the capital of UK corporations with securities quoted on a stock exchange.[17] In the UK as a whole, it was probably not until the eve of the Great War that the market capitalisation of companies incorporated under the Companies Acts exceeded the market capitalisation of statutory companies.[18] Well into the

13 Subsequent legislation delegated powers to the Board of Trade to incorporate, by certificate (incorporating extensive provisions of the Clauses Acts), companies as bodies corporate for those statutory purposes: Railway Companies Construction Facilities Act 1864 (27 & 28 Vict, c. 121) ss. 24–30. The certificate and any changes to it had to be published in the respective London, Edinburgh or Dublin *Gazettes*. Similar powers to incorporate companies on certification were conferred on the Secretary of State for Scotland under the Light Railways Act 1896 s. 11(e) (as read with s. 26).

14 The history of canals and the companies that worked them pre-dated the developments addressed in the present contribution and are thus not covered.

15 *Greenock Harbour Trustees v Judicial Factor on the Greenock Harbour Trust* 1908 SC 944 at 956 per Lord President Dunedin. W M Gloag and J M Irvine, *Law of Rights in Security Heritable and Moveable Including Cautionary Obligations* (Edinburgh: W. Green, 1897) 611 onwards refer to the Clauses Acts as the 'consolidating Statutes' or the 'general Statutes'.

16 Cf Gloag & Irvine, *Rights in Security* (n 15) Ch. 18.

17 J Foreman-Peck and L Hannah, 'UK Corporate Law and Corporate Governance before 1914: a Re-interpretation' European Historical Economics Society (EHES), EHES Working Paper No. 72 (2015) 7.

18 C Coyle et al., 'Law and Finance in Britain c 1900' (2019) *Financial History Review* 267 at 277, Table 2 and 279, Table 3.

twentieth century, therefore, references in the books to 'public companies' were references not to companies incorporated under the Companies Acts but to statutory companies.[19] Many of the foundational common law rules of modern company law – such as *Aberdeen Railway Co v Blaikie*[20] or the rule in *Foss v Harbottle*[21] – were decided in relation to companies incorporated by special Act of Parliament. Those authorities may be applied to companies incorporated under the Companies Acts because they too are creatures of statute.[22]

Very little consideration, however, has been given to the legal tools that were actually used in order to attract the 'colossal capital'[23] required to finance the industrialisation of modern Scotland. The wider failure to consider the terms of the Clauses Acts in relation to the development of company law more generally, such as director rights, has already been identified.[24] And although the link between the Clauses Acts and the power to grant security over the 'undertaking' in the development of the floating charge has been recognised in England,[25] the historical link in Scotland has been largely overlooked. Alisdair MacPherson's superb recent study of the floating charge has rightly recognised that there are, however, 'unmistakable analogies' to be drawn from the Clauses Acts provisions and the later floating charge.[26] For companies incorporated by statute, at least, non-possessory statutory mortgages over the company's 'undertaking' had already been in operation in Scotland since the first half of the nineteenth century.

---

19 J L Wark KC, 'Public Company' in Viscount Dunedin and J L Wark (eds), *Encyclopaedia of the Laws of Scotland* Vol. 12 (Edinburgh: W. Green, 1931). See too Gloag & Irvine, *Rights in Security* (n 15) 611. Companies incorporated under the Companies Acts were not divided between public and private companies until private companies were separately recognised in the Companies Act 1907 s. 37.

20 (1854) 17 D (HL) 20, (1854) 1 Macq 461.

21 (1843) 67 ER 189.

22 *Liquidator of the Garpel Hoematite Company Ltd v Andrew* (1866) 4 Macph 617 at 623 per Lord Curriehill. The winding-up of this company took an astonishing seventy years, being completed only in 1932: P Payne, *Early Scottish Limited Companies* (n 9) 5, n 2.

23 R Cunliffe, *Private Bill Legislation* (n 10) vi.

24 Foreman-Peck and Hannah (n 17).

25 C Stebbings, 'Statutory Railway Mortgage Debentures and the Courts in the Nineteenth Century' (1987) 8 *Journal of Legal History* 36; *Agnew v Commissioner of Inland Revenue* [2001] UKPC 28, [2001] 2 AC 710 at [5]–[6] per Lord Millet under reference to the first case in which the floating charge was recognised: *In re Panama, New Zealand and Australian Royal Mail Company* (1870) LR 5 Ch App 318; R C Nolan, 'Property in a Fund' (2004) 120 LQR 108 at 118.

26 A D J MacPherson, *The Floating Charge* (Edinburgh: Edinburgh Legal Education Trust, 2020) paras 4–30 and 4–31.

A history of the place of these statutory companies and their legal structures would require several PhDs. But the following elements may be highlighted:

1. Parliament provided what, until 1856, the general law did not, namely suitable corporate vehicles with perpetual succession, and limited liability, for shareholder investors.
2. The Clauses Acts allowed wholesale standardisation for many dozens of specialised undertakings; the conception of the 'undertaking' was central to each of the Clauses Acts.[27]
3. In granting minor monopolies to the companies thereby incorporated to charge fees and tolls in respect of the statutory undertaking, an asset – in the form of a future income stream – was immediately created and against which securities could be issued.
4. These statutory companies were empowered to grant universal securities ('mortgages' or 'assignations in security') over their entire undertaking; security was possible against future income streams. The effect of such mortgages depended on which Clauses Act provisions were incorporated.
5. Where the whole undertaking was mortgaged, creditors could not enforce against heritable property by sale or adjudication.
6. Registration of such mortgages was in the statutory registers of the issuer company itself; there was no comprehensive system of public registration.
7. The *prior tempore potior jure* principle did not generally apply to holders of secured debt of the same class.
8. In the case of default, the enforcement remedy was by appointment of a court officer; in Scotland this was normally the judicial factor but, on occasion, a statutory receiver.
9. Some judicial factors were pure receivers; others were managers more akin to modern administrators.
10. The judicial factor had to continue the undertaking as a going concern and pay the creditors from the revenue thus generated.

As will be seen, the financing of statutory companies granting statutory mortgages over the company's whole undertaking was a tried and tested

---

27 Cf R Kraakman, et al., *The Anatomy of Corporate Law*, 3rd edn (Oxford: Oxford University Press, 2017) para. 1.4.

security method, both legally (in the courts) and commercially (the infrastructure projects were, in the main, delivered).

B. NINETEENTH CENTURY LEGAL PERSONS

(1) Partnerships and common law companies

Most modern textbooks on company law are written from an English perspective.[28] A brief precis of the different vehicles in commercial life in nineteenth century Scotland may therefore be useful. Firms – partnerships – were long recognised as having separate legal personality.[29] Whereas in an ordinary partnership there was *delectus personae* amongst the partners, in practice 'joint stock companies' had operated at common law with tradeable stock in the form of private partnerships, where the contract of co-partnery envisaged, expressly or impliedly, that the partners would come and go. Some, such as banks, had many hundreds of 'partners'. The Royal Exchange and London Assurance Corporation Act 1719[30] – otherwise known as the 1720 Bubble Act – probably did not apply to Scotland, although it was only after its repeal that the point was authoritatively decided.[31] The winding-up of a firm could occur either consensually, where the firm was solvent; or by sequestration and/or the appointment of a judicial factor.

(2) Charter companies and Letters Patent Acts

Incorporation by Royal Charter continued to be attractive in Scotland. The prize was not just limited liability but the status of a body corporate with perpetual succession.[32] The Royal Bank of Scotland, for instance, had been

---

28 A difficulty highlighted by R H Campbell, 'The Law and the Joint Stock Company in Scotland' in P L Payne (ed), *Studies in Scottish Business History* (Oxford: Routledge, 1967) 136.

29 Bell, *Principles*, 4th edn (1839) § 357; *Forsyth v Hare & Co* (1834) 13 S 42 at 46 per Lord Medwyn; R C Michie, *Money, Mania and Markets* (Edinburgh: John Donald, 1981).

30 6 Geo I, c. 18.

31 *Albion Fire and Life Insurance Company v Mills* (1828) 3 W & S 218; *Muir v City of Glasgow Bank* (1879) 6 R 392 at 399. Cf Bubble Companies Act 1825 (6 Geo IV, c. 91).

32 M Freeman, R Pearson and J Taylor, '"Different and Better"? Scottish Joint Stock Companies and the Law, c. 1720–1845' (2007) 122 *English Historical Review* 61. But the analysis of partnerships in Scots law does not properly recognise the fundamental conceptual difference, which remains today, between separate legal personality and constitution as a body corporate with perpetual succession. Scottish partnerships and limited partnerships today have separate legal personality but not the perpetual succession of the body corporate, such as a company incorporated under the Companies Acts or a limited liability partnership.

incorporated by Royal Charter under the Great Seal of Scotland in 1727. The Letters Patent Act 1837[33] was a near dead letter in Scotland, the status of the letters patent being unclear and the common law already conferring legal personality. The Faculty of Advocates, in their response to the Royal Commission on Mercantile Laws in 1855, would describe the 1837 Act as having been 'wholly inoperative' in Scotland.[34] The Privy Council maintains a list of the bodies (many are not companies) – about 1,000 – incorporated by Royal Charter.[35]

(3) Statutory companies

Prior to 1707, two of the most well-known companies in Scottish history were incorporated by Acts of the Parliament of Scotland: the Company of Scotland trading to Africa and the Indies (the Darien company);[36] and the Governor and Company of the Bank of Scotland.[37] Following the Union, it was statutory companies – often enjoying monopolies – that dominated colonial and domestic commerce.[38] The Royal Bank of Scotland, incorporated by Royal Charter in 1727 under the Great Seal of Scotland (as amended by seven subsequent charters), was authorised to operate only in Scotland and thus required an Act of Parliament to establish a branch in the City of London.[39]

(4) Joint stock companies and the Companies Act 1862

As the history of the Scottish partnership demonstrates, it is possible to have a separate legal person the partners of which were also personally liable for the debts of the firm. Such Scottish firms often had capital divided into

---

33 1 Vict, c. 73.
34 *Second Report of the Commissioners on the Mercantile Laws and the Law of Partnership* (1855) 102: 'It is believed that no company in Scotland has obtained letters patent under it'.
35 The Privy Council Office, *List of Charters Granted*, *https://privycouncil.independent.gov.uk/ royal-charters/list-of-charters-granted/* (last accessed 21 October 2021).
36 Records of the Parliaments of Scotland to 1707, RPS 1695/5/104: *http://www.rps.ac.uk/ mss/1695/5/104* (last accessed 21 October 2021).
37 Records of the Parliaments of Scotland to 1707, RPS 1695/5/239. The Governor and Company of the Bank of Scotland came to be registered as a public limited company under the Companies Acts only in 2006 by virtue of a private Act of Parliament: HBOS Reorganisation Act 2006 (c. i).
38 See generally R Harris, *Industrializing English Law: Entrepreneurship and Business Organization 1720–1844* (Cambridge: Cambridge University Press, 2000).
39 The Royal Bank of Scotland Act 1873 (36 & 37 Vict, c. ccxvii) s. 2. By the Royal Bank of Scotland Act 1907 (7 Edw 7, c. xxi) s. 6 it was permitted to carry on the business of banking in any part of the UK.

shares transferable without the consent of the partners. These firms were sometimes known as 'joint stock' companies. Whether they were strictly bodies corporate was never authoritatively decided. The partners had a secondary liability for the firm's debts. While such firms could be established in Scotland without publicity, from 1844, such firms could be established elsewhere in the UK only by registration.[40] The Limited Liability Act 1855 did not apply to Scotland; it was extended to Scotland only with the Joint Stock Companies Act 1856. Even after its passing, however, and despite the collapse of the Western Bank, uptake was limited. Between 1856 and the end of the century, the numbers of privately incorporated Scottish companies was relatively modest.

The Joint Stock Companies Act 1856 had allowed companies of between seven and twenty members to be incorporated with limited liability. Implicit in incorporation was a power to borrow, the 1856 Act expressly providing for the 'obligations and undertakings' to be implied into bonds and dispositions in security (s. 45); the latter, somewhat superfluously, were expressly required to be registered in the General or Particular or Burgh Register of Sasines. The 1862 Act required the company to keep a register of mortgages and charges,[41] but otherwise no express provision was made in relation to the borrowing powers of the company, whether in the body of the Act or in Table A.

It is important to emphasise too that it was possible for common law partnerships to incorporate under the Companies Act 1862, s. 192, with unlimited liability; the City of Glasgow Bank being the most notorious example.[42] (It may be observed in passing that, even in the twenty-first century, some sophisticated banking structures continued to use unlimited companies, such as Lehman Brothers International (Europe).)[43] For insolvent firms with more than seven partners, winding-up as an unregistered company under the Companies Act 1862 became possible.[44] In the nineteenth

---

40 Joint Stock Companies Act 1844 (7 & 8 Vict, c. 110). It did not apply to Scotland: s. 2.
41 1862 Act s. 43. There was no time limit for registration.
42 *Muir v City of Glasgow Bank* (1879) 6 R (HL) 21 at 21 per Lord Cairns LC.
43 *Joint Administrators of Lehman Brothers International (Europe) (in administration)* [2008] EWHC 2869 (Ch) at [4].
44 1862 Act s. 199. Railway companies incorporated by Act of Parliament were excluded from the ambit of s. 199 as well as from the Companies (Consolidation) Act 1908 s. 267. But other statutory companies could be wound up under the 1862 Act as unregistered companies: see e.g. *Re Bradford Navigation Company* (1870) LR 10 Eq 331. According to G W Wilton, *Company Liquidation: Law and Practice* (Edinburgh: Hodge & Co, 1922) 53, the first winding-up of an unregistered joint-stock company in Scotland was the *Aberdeen Meal and Provision Society* (1863) 2 M 385, the report of which also refers to the procedure adopted by the First Division

century, the term 'corporation' was not always used consistently. But the modern usage is that a corporation is a body corporate.[45]

(5) Statutory companies and the Clauses Acts

It is against that background that we turn to consider what will be the focus of the present contribution: statutory companies. In the nineteenth century, very many companies were incorporated by private Acts of Parliament in order to carry out what, in general terms, were public works.[46] These companies were incorporated as bodies corporate, which could sue and be sued; and, importantly, with clear powers to issue shares and borrow money on the security of the 'undertaking'. The provisions of many of these local Acts were formulaic, so their provisions were consolidated in a comprehensive framework of pro forma legislation in the form of public general 'Clauses' Acts.

C. THE CLAUSES ACTS

(1) Pre-1845 Private Acts

The first railway company in Scotland was apparently the Kilmarnock and Troon Railway, incorporated by a special Act of 1808.[47] But the first railway in Scotland that was apparently not primarily concerned with the carriage of minerals was that laid down by the Dundee and Newtyle Railway Company, which was incorporated in 1826 as a body corporate with perpetual succession.[48] 'The making and maintaining a railway' from Dundee to the valley of Strathmore, and terminating at a point near the Miln of Newtyle, the preamble to the local Act recited, 'will be of great local and public utility.' The company could issue shares and the shareholders were not to be liable for the debts of the company beyond the amount of their shares in the company stock (s. 92). In addition, the company was able to borrow money on the credit of said undertaking; and, in security of which, it was authorised

on a petition for the winding-up of the 'Fraserburgh Arctic Company'. See now Insolvency Act 1986 s. 220 and n 179 below.

45 Companies Act 2006 s. 1173(1). For tax purposes, however, unincorporated associations fall within the definition of 'companies', but partnerships do not: Corporation Taxes Act 2010 s. 1121. For LLPs, see Income Tax (Trading and other Income) Act 2005 s. 863 onwards.

46 See the long title to the Companies Clauses Consolidation (Scotland) Act 1845 (n 50) below.

47 48 Geo III, c. xlvi.

48 7 Geo IV, c. ci. See W Vamplew, 'Sources of Scottish Railway Share Capital before 1860' (1970) 17 *Scottish Journal of Political Economy* 425 at 426.

to 'assign the property of the said company or the rates arising or to arise by virtue of this Act as a security for any such sum or sums of money to be borrowed as aforesaid' to such persons as shall advance the same. The Act provided for a style of assignation, a form that later came to be the default form applied to all statutory companies incorporated in Scotland. A second Act was procured in 1830 that increased the company's capital; authorised further borrowing; and authorised the company to 'assign and convey the said railway, and other works and property of the said company, and the rates arising or to arise thereon' to the persons making such advances.[49] The company defaulted. The story of its default, and the court's consideration of the meaning of 'undertaking', will be addressed below.

(2) Overview of Clauses Acts

In order to standardise the terms of private Acts, various Clauses Acts were passed. The Clauses Acts provided a sophisticated, off-the-shelf framework that could be incorporated by reference, in whole or in part, into special Acts of Parliament, many of which incorporated a statutory company. The framework had a number of pillars, starting with the formation of the vehicle, powers of borrowing and compulsory purchase of land in order to construct, maintain and run, in particular, harbours and railways. In outline the Clauses Acts were:

1. Companies Clauses Acts: Companies Clauses Consolidation (Scotland) Act 1845[50] (the 'CCCSA') and the Companies Clauses Act 1863 ('CCA 1863'),[51] Companies Clauses Act 1867 and 1869 ('CCA 1869').[52]
2. Lands Clauses Acts: Lands Clauses Consolidation (Scotland) Act 1845[53] and the Lands Clauses Consolidation Acts Amendment Act 1860[54] ('LCCSA').

---

49 Dundee and Newtyle Railway Act 1830 (11 Geo IV, c. lx) s. 5. By s. 11 it was deemed to be a public Act. There was another Act in 1836 (6 & 7 Will IV, c. cii) recording the success of the railway, increasing the authorised capital of the company and increasing the rates and tolls that could be charged. The Companies Clauses Consolidation (Scotland) Act 1845 was, in time, applied also to the Dundee and Newtyle Railway Company: Dundee and Newtyle Railway Improvement Act 1859 (22 & 23 Vict, c. xviii) s. 3.
50 8 & 9 Vict, c. 17. The long title was: 'An Act for consolidating in One Act certain Provisions usually inserted in Acts with respect to the Constitution of Companies incorporated for carrying on Undertakings of a public Nature in Scotland'.
51 26 & 27 Vict, c. 118.
52 32 & 33 Vict, c. 48.
53 8 & 9 Vict, c. 19.
54 23 & 24 Vict, c. 106.

3. Railway Clauses Acts: Railways Clauses Consolidation (Scotland) Act 1845 ('RCCSA')[55] and the Railway Companies (Scotland) Act 1867 ('RCSA 1867').[56]
4. Harbours, Docks and Piers Clauses Act 1847 ('HDPCA 1847').[57]
5. Commissioners Clauses Act 1847 (the 'CCA').[58]
6. Burgh Harbours (Scotland) Act 1853 (although not normally referred to as a Clauses Act, it was in substance).[59]

Certain other Clauses Acts can be mentioned though they will not be much further considered here: Markets and Fairs Clauses Act 1847[60]; the Gas Works Clauses Acts 1847[61]; and the Water Works Clauses Acts 1847.[62] The Tramways Act 1870,[63] though also not described as a Clauses Act, contained in Parts II and III provisions which functionally operated as such. Another was the Electric Lighting (Clauses) Act 1899.

(3) Companies Clauses Consolidation (Scotland) Act 1845

The CCCSA 1845, passed the same day as the equivalent English Act (the CCCA),[64] was a foundational statute. By s. 1 the CCCSA applied to:

'every joint stock company in Scotland which shall by any Act of Parliament which shall hereafter be passed be incorporated for the purpose of carrying on any undertaking; and this Act shall be incorporated with such Act, and all the clauses and provisions of this Act, save so far as they shall be varied or excepted by any such Act, shall apply to the company which shall be incorporated by any Act, and to the undertaking for carrying on which such company shall be incorporated, so far as the same shall be applicable thereto respectively; and such enactments and provisions, as well as the enactments and provisions of every other Act which shall be incorporated with such Act, shall, save as aforesaid, form part of such Act, and be construed together therewith as forming one Act'.

---

55 8 & 9 Vict, c. 33.
56 30 & 31 Vict, c. 126.
57 10 & 11 Vict, c. 27.
58 10 & 11 Vict, c. 16.
59 16 & 17 Vict, c. 93.
60 10 & 11 Vict. c. 14.
61 10 & 11 Vict, c. 15 as amended by the Gas Works Clauses Act 1863 (34 & 35 Vict, c. 41).
62 10 & 11 Vict, c. 17, as amended by Water-works Clauses Act 1863 (34 & 35 Vict, c. 93).
63 33 & 34 Vict, c. 78.
64 10 & 11 Vict, c. 16, for which see R J Sutcliffe, *Statutory Companies and the Companies Clauses Consolidation Acts* (1924).

'Undertaking' was defined as 'the undertaking or works, of whatever nature, which shall by the special Act be authorized to be executed'.[65] The liability of the shareholders of an incorporated undertaking was to be limited to their share in the capital of the company (s. 37).

Section 40 authorised borrowing of money 'on mortgage or bond' and 'for the securing the repayment of the money so borrowed, with interest, to mortgage the undertaking, and the future calls on the shareholders, or to give bonds in manner hereinafter mentioned'. Section 43 provides:

> 'Every mortgage and bond for securing money borrowed by the company shall be by deed under the common seal of the company, duly stamped, and wherein the consideration shall be truly stated; and every such mortgage deed or bond may be according to the form in the schedule (C) or (D) to this act annexed, or to the like effect and every such mortgage deed shall have the full effect of an assignation in security duly completed.'

The second part of s. 43 – 'every such mortgage deed shall have the full effect of an assignation in security duly completed' – has no equivalent in the CCCA. A form mortgage deed was provided in Schedule C:

> The [insert] Company
> Mortgage Number [insert] £ [insert]
> By virtue of [here name the Special Act], we 'The [insert] Company', in consideration of the Sum of [insert] Pounds paid to us by A.B. of [insert] do assign to the said A.B., his Executors, Administrators, and Assignees, the said Undertaking [and (in case such Loan shall be in anticipation of the Capital authorized to be raised) all future Calls on Shareholders], and all the Tolls and Sums of Money arising by virtue of the said Act, and all the Estate, Right, Title and Interest of the Company in the same, to hold unto the said A.B., his Executors, Administrators, and Assigns, until the said Sum of [insert] Pounds, together with the Interest for the same at the Rate of [insert] for every One Hundred Pounds by the Year, be satisfied [the Principal Sum to be repaid at the End of [insert] Years from the Date hereof … In witness whereof &c. [Here insert Testing Clauses of Deeds executed in Scotland].

The style provides an assignation in security over 'the Undertaking … and all the Tolls and Sums of Money arising', and without the need for intimation. Many of the statutory companies that would come to be incorporated would receive also minor monopoly rights to charge rates, tolls and other fees. The right to such future income stream was an obvious asset against which money could be borrowed; but in respect of which an effectual security could not practically be worked out at common law (no intimation could be made to future debtors). So useful was the idea of borrowing against future income

---

65 CCCA is in similar terms.

streams that it was extended to finance churches and schools.[66] Enforcement of such a mortgage was by way of appointment by the court of a judicial factor (s. 58). The powers of such a judicial factor will be examined below.

Much, however, was left unsaid. An assignation in security is an outright transfer to the creditor: *fiducia cum creditore*. But a mortgage deed in terms of s. 43 could not be such a transfer before the future income had come into existence. And the enforcement mechanism, appointment of a judicial factor to the company, rather presupposed that the company had not divested its rights to collect the tolls. Although some authorities proceed on the view that the mortgage was a limited security right, the nature of the right was never fully worked out. But as will be seen, s. 43 CCCSA was as fundamental to the history of Scots commercial law, as s. 1 of the 1961 Act introducing floating charges.

(4) Lands Clauses Consolidation (Scotland) Act 1845[67]

The LCCSA contains the core of the law of compulsory purchase for every undertaking in Scotland authorised by any Act of Parliament to take lands for such undertaking (s. 1). The LCCSA produced a vast volume of case law, but little more will be said about it in the present contribution other than in explaining the seminal decision of the House of Lords in *Ayr Harbour Trustees v Oswald*.[68]

(5) Railways Clauses Acts[69]

Railway companies were by some distance the most important statutory companies: it was the boom in railway stocks that led to the formation of the

---

66 Parochial Buildings (Scotland) Act 1862 s. 3 conferred on the heritors of a parish, to defray the expense of the erection, improvement or enlargement of parish buildings (i.e. church, manse, churchyard walls, schoolhouse and schoolmaster's house), the power to borrow money and, in security thereof, 'to charge and assign the said annual assessments by a bond and assignation'. The whole court in *Sir James Boswell v Duke of Portland, Heritors of Mauchline* (1834) 13 S 148 held the heritors of a parish were, for certain purposes, to be regarded as a 'corporation'.
67 As amended by the Lands Clauses Consolidation Acts Amendment Act 1860.
68 See n 107 below.
69 See generally R Perman, *The Rise and Fall of the City of Money: A Financial History of Edinburgh* (Edinburgh: Birlinn, 2019) 173–182. For the legislation, see: J Biggs (ed), *A Collection of the Public General Acts relating to Railways in Scotland, including the Companies, Lands, and Railways Clauses Consolidation (Scotland) Acts, 1830–1861*, 5th edn (1862).

stock exchanges in Glasgow and Edinburgh.[70] The Railways Clauses Acts defined the 'undertaking' as the 'railway and works, of whatever description, by the special Act authorised to be executed'. It conferred the power to levy and to vary the tolls (s. 83) that would normally be used as the security for borrowing.

The pre-eminent nineteenth century Scottish railway companies were the North British Railway Company (NBR)[71] and the Caledonian Railway Company.[72] The NBR having been incorporated in 1844, its special Act ran to some 134 pages; the Caledonian Railway Company's incorporating Act of 1845, in contrast, was able to incorporate various Clauses Acts, and thus required only fourteen pages. Many special Acts for each company would follow and the competition between these two companies would be the defining feature of the nineteenth century Scottish railway market.

In relation to financing, the Railway Mortgage Transfer (Scotland) Act 1861,[73] allowed any mortgage or bond that had been issued by a railway company and registered in the books of the company in terms of the CCCSA to be transferred by endorsement and without stamp duty; the endorsement of such a mortgage having the same effect as an assignation of a mortgage under the CCCSA.

The principal purpose of the Railway Companies (Scotland) Act 1867[74] was to introduce schemes of arrangement between a railway company and its creditors.[75] But it also contains three provisions of importance to the present discussion. First, it confers upon railway companies the remarkable privilege that their rolling stock and plant should not be liable to diligence (s. 4)[76]; and that a creditor holding a decree 'may obtain the appointment

---

70 Harris (n 38) 228; R W Kostal, *Law and English Railway Capitalism 1825–1875* (Oxford: Clarendon Press, 1998). The introduction to the *Records of the Glasgow Stock Exchange Association 1844–1898* (1898) traces share-trading in the city to 1830. There had already been a joint-stock mania in 1825–1826: see H Cockburn, *Memorials of His Time* (Edinburgh: Grant & Son, 1856) 432.

71 Incorporated by the North British Railway Act 1844 (8 & 9 Vict, c. xlvi) s. 1. Sections 41–43 authorised the granting of mortgage deeds of the tolls, sums and premises, which mortgages were to be registered in the company's own register within fourteen days.

72 Incorporated by the Caledonian Railway Act 1845 (8 & 9 Vict, c. clxii) s. 4. The Act incorporated the CCCSA, the RCCSA and the LCCSA.

73 24 & 25 Vict. c. 50.

74 30 & 31 Vict, c. 126.

75 Schemes were extended to non-railway companies by the Joint Stock Companies Arrangements Act 1870 (33 & 34 Vict, c. 104).

76 A provision initially enacted as a temporary measure, but which was extended and then made perpetual by the Railway Companies Act 1875 (38 & 39 Vict, c. 31) s. 1. A similar provision applies to 'franchise assets' under the modern railway franchising framework: Railways Act 1993 s. 27(7).

of a judicial factor on the Undertaking of the Company'. The provision, in amended form, remains in force. Secondly, s. 24 allowed a railway company to issue debenture stock in terms of the Companies Clauses Act 1863, but without any limitation on the rates that could be paid on the stock. Thirdly, s. 23 provided:

> 'All money borrowed or to be borrowed by a Company on Mortgage, Debenture, or Bond, or Debenture Stock, under the provisions of any Act authorizing the borrowing thereof, shall have priority against the Company and the property from Time to Time of the Company over all other Claims on account of any Debts incurred or Engagements entered into by them after the passing of this Act ... '

The section went on to provide that sums secured on land are exempted from the preference that would be granted to the holders of a statutory mortgage over the undertaking of a railway company. There were other Public General Acts that permitted extensions to the powers of railway companies without the need for still further private Acts of Parliament.[77]

(6) Tramways

The maps of the towns of Scotland as they developed through the nineteenth into the mid-twentieth century record the indelible impression of the tramway systems. Again, the finance required for such projects was considerable and Parliament provided the tools in the form of the Tramways Act 1870. The 1870 Act provided in Parts II and III clauses that were capable of incorporation in special Acts. Section 19 of the 1870 Act dealt with the financing of the expenses to be incurred and, in turn, incorporated the provisions of the Commissioners Clauses Acts 1847 dealing with 'mortgages'.

(7) Commissioners Clauses Act 1847: mortgages and receivers

The CCA 1847 consolidated in one Act the provisions usually contained in Acts with respect to the 'Constitution and Regulation of Bodies of Commissioners appointed for carrying on Undertakings of a public Nature'. These bodies of commissioners were often subject to election (s. 17 onwards). The commissioners had the power to contract and to bind their successors

---

77 See e.g. Railway Companies Powers Act 1864 (27 & 28 Vict, c. 120), Railway Companies Construction Facilities Act 1864 (n 13) and Railways (Powers and Construction) Acts 1864, Amendment Act 1870 (33 & 34 Vict, c. 19).

(s. 56); the 'Bodies or Goods or Lands' of the several commissioners were not liable to legal execution on contracts or instruments entered into by them in execution of their powers as commissioners (ss. 60 and 62); and they were to be indemnified out of the rates. The commissioners could be incorporated by special Act as a body corporate (s. 61); otherwise they could be sued in the names of any two commissioners.

Section 75 and following dealt with borrowing and right in security. Section 75 provided that 'every Mortgage or Assignation in Security of Rates or other Property' was to be executed in the form annexed to the CCA; and

> 'the respective Mortgagees or Assignees in Security shall be entitled one with another to their respective Proportions of the Rates and Assessments or other Property comprised in such Mortgages or Assignations respectively, according to the respective sums in such Mortgages and Assignations mentioned to be advanced by any Mortgagees or Assignees respectively, and to be repaid the sums so advanced, with Interest, without any Preference one above another by reasons of the Priority of advancing such Monies, or the dates of any such Mortgages or Assignations respectively'.

Such mortgages and 'assignations in security' were themselves assignable. Schedule B contained a single form to operate as the mortgage or assignation in security:

> 'By virtue of [*special Act*] we [*Commissioners*] appointed in pursuance of the said Act in consideration of the Sum of [*insert*] paid to the Treasurer of the said Commissioners by A.B. of [*insert*] for the Purposes of the said Act, do grant and assign unto the said A.B. his Executors, Administrators, and Assigns, such Proportion of the Rates, Rents, Profits and other Monies arising or accruing by virtue of the said Act from [*insert*] as the said Sum of [*insert*] doth or shall bear to the whole Sum which is or shall be borrowed upon the Credit of the said Rates, Profits or Monies to hold to the said A.B. his Executors, Administrators, and Assigns, from this Day until the said sum of [*insert*] with Interest at [*insert*] per annum for the same, shall be fully paid and satisfied (the Principal Sum to be repaid at the End of [*insert*] Years from the Date hereof [*if the Deed be granted in Scotland, insert the Testing Clause required by the Law of Scotland*].'

Schedule C contained a form of transfer of mortgage, which made certain modifications for Scotland. There was no provision in the CCA equivalent to s. 43 of the CCCSA 1845 deeming any assignation in that form to be an 'assignation in security duly completed'. As a result, the common law of intimation continued to apply to the constitution of such assignations in security. Enforcement of assignations in security granted under the CCA was, however, even in Scotland, by application to the sheriff for the appointment of a 'Receiver': s. 86.

(8) Harbours, Docks and Piers Clauses Act 1847

The law in the HDPCA 1847, mediated through the myriad of local enactments that incorporate it, continue to regulate much of modern harbour law throughout the UK; and the open harbour provision in s. 33, for an island nation, is perhaps one of those provisions that every law student ought to know.[78] For present purposes, although the HDPCA 1847 does not contain financing provisions, it does proceed on the same footing as the other Clauses Acts. Section 1 provides that all the clauses of the HDPCA 1847, save so far as they shall be expressly varied or excepted by the special Act, 'shall apply to the undertaking authorised thereby'; in s. 2 it provides that 'the undertakers' shall mean 'the persons by the special Act authorised to construct the harbour, dock, or pier, or otherwise carry into effect the purposes of the special Act with reference thereto' (s. 2).

(9) Burgh Harbours (Scotland) Act 1853

The corporate personality enjoyed by the Royal Burghs of Scotland has been the subject of scholarly analysis.[79] That they should be suitable vehicles to borrow the finance required for the construction of modern harbours is thus unsurprising. The Burgh Harbours (Scotland) Act 1853 was passed in the form of a Clauses Act: s. 1 provided that it could be adopted and applied in any Royal Burgh in Scotland that possessed a harbour but which was not otherwise regulated by a special Act of Parliament. The 1853 Act itself incorporated both the LCCSA 1845 (s. 4) and the HDPCA 1847 (s. 5); and, by s. 6, explained that the references to 'special Act' in those Clauses Act should be construed to mean the 1853 Act. The Act set the rates to be paid by Vessels entering the harbour and goods to be shipped. And having created a potential income stream from these rates, proceeded to set out, in Scottish form, a statutory 'Bond and Assignation' that Royal Burghs were entitled to grant over future income from harbour dues, in security of borrowing to be

78 For modern references, see: R (Newhaven Port & Properties Ltd) v East Sussex County Council [2015] UKSC 7, [2015] AC 1547 at [5] and [94] per Lord Neuberger and Lord Hodge. For its application in Scotland, see Petroineos Manufacturing Scotland Ltd v Clydeport Operations Ltd [2017] CSOH 49.

79 D Murray, Early Burgh Organisation in Scotland (Glasgow: Maclehose, Jackson & Co, 1924) 348–365; R L C Hunter, 'Corporate Personality and the Scottish Burgh' in G W S Barrow (ed), The Scottish Tradition Essays: in Honour of Ronald Gordon Cant (Edinburgh: Scottish Academic Press, 1974).

'applied and expended in the Extension and Improvement of the Harbour' (s. 18).[80] Because there were no identifiable debtors to whom intimation of an assignation of future income streams could be made, the 1853 Act provided for registration and that the effect of the registration was to create a 'lien' on the rates:

> 'XIX. The Bonds and Assignations to be granted for securing the Repayment of the Sums to be borrowed or advanced as aforesaid shall be in the Form of the Schedule (B.) hereunto annexed, or as near as may be, and shall be signed [officers recited] and such Bonds and Assignations shall be recorded in the Minute Books of the Town Council, and a Certificate of such Registration shall be indorsed on such Bonds and Assignations, and signed by the Town Clerk; and in case of Competition such Bonds and Assignations shall have Priority and Preference according to the Dates of such Registration; and until Repayment of the Sums so borrowed or advanced, and Interest thereon, such Sums, and the Bonds and Assignations granted therefor respectively, shall form a *Lien on the Rates* by this Act authorised to be levied preferable to all other Debts and Claims against the Burgh, and the Creditors in right of such Sums shall be entitled to *receive* the same from the Town Council and their Officers out of the first and readiest of such Rates.'

The form of the bond and assignation, creating a 'lien' on the income was contained in Schedule B and was in these terms:

> 'The Royal Burgh of [insert] has this Day borrowed the Sum of [insert] from A.B. [or has this Day obtained a Cash Credit to the Extent of [insert] Pounds with the [insert name of Bank] for the Extension and Improvement of the Harbour of the said Burgh, which Sum ... we hereby bind the said Burgh to pay to the said A.B. his Heirs, Executors and Assignees [or to the said Bank] at the Term of [insert] next, with Interest thereof [sic] at the Rate of [insert] per Centum per Annum from the Date hereof, payable ...; and we hereby assign to the said A.B. and his foresaids [or to the Bank] the Rates authorised to be levied at the said Harbour by the Act [specify this Act] in security of the Repayment of the foresaid Sums, Principal and Interest, which are hereby declared a Lien on the said Rates; and we consent &c [Registration and Testing Clause according to the Form of the Law of Scotland].'

Section 20 provided that such bonds and assignations were themselves assignable. The express reference to the effect of the bond and assignation creating a 'lien' on the rates, was almost certainly deliberate; the meaning of a lien on revenue had given rise to a difference of opinion between two judges of the First Division in an application by holders of certain

---

80 The Burgh remained personally liable to pay the sums borrowed if the rates were insufficient: *Haldane's Trs v Elgin and Lossiemouth Harbour Co* (1879) 6 R 987; *Royal Burgh of Renfrew v Murdoch* (1892) 19 R 822.

preferential stock in a railway company in 1850 and 1851.[81] But the juridical nature of this lien was never the subject of detailed analysis.

D. BONDS, MORTGAGES AND DEBENTURE STOCK

(1) Bonds

The CCCSA provided a standard form of bond in Sch. D. These were in orthodox form and assignable.

(2) Statutory mortgages and assignations in security

The statutory 'form of mortgage' provided for by CCCSA 1845, s. 43 has been set out above. The court, and counsel appearing before it, often used more recognisable synonyms for statutory mortgages, such as a 'deed of pledge'[82]; or in describing the effect of the statutory mortgage as being that 'it was only the nett receipts that were impignorated'.[83]

Section 43 CCCSA 1845 provided that 'every such mortgage deed shall have the full effect of an assignation in security duly completed'. Although describing the provisions as 'exceedingly vague', Gloag and Irvine accepted that the deemed assignation in security did 'not prevent the company dealing with, or even disposing of, that property in the ordinary course of their business'.[84] Extensive case law developed on the meaning of this statutory mortgage in relation to assets that were not incorporeal moveables. But it is important to recall that the classic decision of the Court in *Clark v West Calder Oil Co Ltd*,[85] holding that it was not possible to create security at common law over corporeal moveables *retenta possessione*, involved a company incorporated under the Companies Act 1862, and not a company incorporating the CCCSA 1845. Mortgages *retenta possessione* granted under the CCCSA, in contrast, were 'unquestionably preferential securities'.[86] As Lord Shand said:

---

81 *Baird v Caledonian Railway Company* (n 129); and *Primrose* (n 131) below.
82 *Howden v Elgin and Lossiemouth Harbour Company* (1879) 6 R 987 at 994 per Lord Gifford.
83 *Cotton (Judicial Factor on the Edinburgh Tramways Company) v Beattie* (1889) 17 R 262 at 265 *arguendo* by Graham Murray, later Lord Dunedin.
84 Gloag & Irvine, *Rights in Security* (n 15) 632; MacPherson, *Floating Charge* (n 26) para. 4–29.
85 (1882) 9 R 1017.
86 (1882) 9 R 1017 at 1023 per Lord President Inglis.

'We have statutes which do give that power [to create security over subjects without delivery]. The [CCCSA 1845], for example, carefully provides in its enactments, and in relative schedules appended to it, for the granting of mortgages and debentures. The statute authorises companies incorporated under any statute by which the clauses of that Act are incorporated to grant mortgages which shall affect their whole undertaking; so that companies which comes under that Act, such as railway companies and others, have power by statute to grant debentures by which the whole undertaking is affected, and the creditors without possession … acquire an effectual security over the whole property of the company.'[87]

So where a trustee, under an English trust, authorised to invest the trust funds on 'real security' invested in Scottish railway mortgages, there was a question of whether the trustee was in breach of trust. The Lord Ordinary, Lord Kinnear, in an opinion upheld by the Second Division, confirmed that a mortgage of the railway undertaking was a 'real security' and therefore the trustee had not breached his duties.[88] Certain general principles of the law of rights in security, such as the accessory principle, were applied without difficulty to such statutory mortgages.[89] And in a series of decisions the operation of the enforcement of mortgage holders over the undertaking was worked out. These are considered below.

(3) Debenture stock

Under the Companies Clauses Act 1863,[90] a statutory company whose special Act authorised it to borrow money on mortgage or bond, had the power, if 60 per cent of the shareholders in general meeting agreed, to issue 'debenture stock'. Sections 23 and 24 of the 1863 Act declared such stock to be 'a charge upon the undertaking prior to all shares or stock of the company' for the interest as a perpetual annuity, but with no right to repayment of principal. It was thus a hybrid instrument, preferable to equity, but not an orthodox secured bond. As under the CCCSA 1845, where the amounts of

---

87 (1882) 9 R 1017 at 1033.
88 *Breatcliffe v Bransby's Trs* (1887) 14 R 307 at 308 (mortgagee has a real security of the whole real and moveable property of the company; enforceable not by ordinary diligence but by appointment of a judicial factor). As Dean of Faculty, Kinnear had appeared (with Graham Murray as his junior) for the judicial factor, Haldane, in the *Girven Company* cases: see n 141 below.
89 *Howden v Elgin and Lossiemouth Harbour Company* (1879) 6 R 987 at 994 per Lord Gifford: 'A subsisting security for a debt implies a debt. If there was no debt there would be no security, and the subsistence of the debt may often be very well and very easily proved by the deed creating a security for it although that deed may contain no words of obligation whatever'.
90 26 & 27 Vict, c. 118.

interest on such debenture stock were not paid within thirty days, the holders of the stock could apply to the Court of Session for the appointment of a judicial factor; this officer being the equivalent of the 'receiver'.[91]

E. THE UNDERTAKING

Each of the Clauses Acts defined 'undertaking'.[92] It was the 'undertaking' that a body of persons was incorporated as a body corporate to pursue.[93] And it was over this 'undertaking' that mortgages could be granted.[94] The question thus arose as to what this term meant. The foundational Scottish case is that of *Dundee and Newtyle Railway Company*.[95] Its incorporating special Act has been referred to above.[96] Although the decision predated the Clauses Acts, it was always taken to apply to them. The company granted mortgages to the Dundee Union Bank, the operative terms of which were:

'do hereby assign unto the said [creditor] and to the assignees of the said trustees and trustee, the said Dundee and Newtyle Railway, and all the works and

---

91 CCA 1863 ss. 25 and 26. From 1869, Part III of the 1863 Act was applied to every company having the power to raise money on mortgage or bond, but not having the express power to issue debenture stock: Companies Clauses Act 1869 (32 & 33 Vict, c. 48) s. 3.

92 See generally MacPherson, *Floating Charge* (n 26) paras 4–07–4–33.

93 See e.g. Kilmarnock and Troon Railway Company Act 1808 (n 47): by s. 1 was incorporated 'one Body Politic and Corporate by the name of the "The Company of Proprietors of the Kilmarnock and Troon Railway" and by that Name have perpetual succession and a Common Seal, and by that Name shall or may sue and be sued, and shall have full Power to purchase Lands, Tenements, and Heritages, to them, their Successors and Assigns, for the Use of the said Undertaking, without incurring any of the Penalties or Forfeitures of the Statutes of Mortmain, and also to sell any of the Lands Tenements or Heritages so purchased, as shall not be necessary for the Purposes of this Act'. The reference to the English Statutes of Mortmain, which never applied in Scotland, suggests the copying of an English style. By s. 7 the company was given the power to raise money 'by Heritable Debt or by Mortgage of the said Undertaking ... and to assign the Property of the said Undertaking'.

94 See J Ferguson and F Deas, *The Law of Railways applicable to Scotland*, 2nd edn (Edinburgh: W. Green, 1897) 812–815. The volume is almost identical in size to another publication that year: Gloag and Irvine, *Law of Rights in Security and Cautionary Obligations* (Edinburgh: W. Green, 1897). Ferguson took silk in 1902 and was a sheriff in Argyll, Inverness and Forfar. He was a prolific writer. He also published: *Railway Rights and Duties: a summary of the law relating to a railway in operation* (1889); and *Ferguson's Five Years' Railway Cases 1889–1893, with Acts of Parliament and of Sederunt; and the Railway and Canal Commission Rules* (1894); *The Public Statutes relating to Railways in Scotland: with appendix containing the Act of Sederunt regulating appeals from the Railway Commission, the Railway and Canal Commission rules, and the rules regulating applications for light railways* (1898); together with his *Law of Roads, Streets and Rights of Way, Bridges and Ferries in Scotland* (1904); and *Law of Water and Water Rights in Scotland* (1907).

95 *Dundee Union Bank v Dundee and Newtyle Railway Company* (1844) 6 D 521.

96 See n 48 above.

property belonging to us; and generally all and whole the said undertaking, and all and singular the rates arising or to arise thereon by virtue of the said acts of Parliament ... '.[97]

The company defaulted and the Dundee Union Bank applied to the Court for warrant: (1) to sell the whole railway undertaking; (2) to have the company ordained to concur in the sale and for this purpose to grant a conveyance of the shares in the company; which failing (3) for the sale to be carried through judicially; and (4) for all rights and privileges under the Acts of Parliament to be conferred on the purchasers. It is obvious from the terms of the conclusions that there was not the clear division as there is today between an asset sale and an equity sale.

The court held that the statutory form permitted only an assignation of the undertaking, not specific conveyances; and that the term 'undertaking' was wholly insufficient to provide a proper description of heritable property. The words of the mortgage 'simply import a right to hold the railway and the rates as a security until payment, which is to be a burden on, not a transference of, the right in the Railway company'.[98] In the result, there was no basis for granting the conclusions[99]:

> 'It seems to be quite clear, that what was intended to be the subject of the security was to be the undertaking as it exists, and the rates arising therefrom, which are to be held in security; and that clearly implied that the undertaking is not to be dismantled, and all the moveable property sold, so that there shall only be rails, and nothing to run thereon. That would not be the undertaking, and would be inconsistent with holding the undertaking; for it would destroy it and put an end to the means of raising the rates which are contemplated as the important subject of the security, out of which repayment is to be obtained.'

So, as the court would confirm more than forty years later, although the proper object of the statutory mortgage was nonetheless the 'undertaking',[100] rights of enforcement were limited. Creditors could obtain payment under such a mortgage only from the income generated by the undertaking as a going concern. An asset sale – as often carried out by an administrator

---

97 *Dundee Union Bank v Dundee and Newtyle Railway Company* (n 95) at 523.

98 *Dundee Union Bank v Dundee and Newtyle Railway Company* (n 95) at 526.

99 *Dundee Union Bank v Dundee and Newtyle Railway Company* (n 95) at 527 per Lord Justice Clerk Hope. Cf G W Wilton, *Company Law: Principal Distinctions between the Laws of England and Scotland* (Edinburgh: Hodge & Co, 1923) 15–19, but no reference is made to the older Scottish authorities under the CCCSA.

100 *Cotton* (n 83) at 267–288 per Lord President Inglis: 'The undertaking, therefore, is the thing that is mortgaged, and of course with that undertaking is also assigned the income arising from the tolls and other sums of money'.

today – was thus not practically possible. Indeed, in 1845, a short public general Act expressly prohibited sales and leases of railways.[101]

Lord Justice Clerk Hope's opinion anticipated by more than twenty years the classic description of the 'undertaking' given by Sir Hugh Cairns, as he then was, in *Gardner v London Chatham Railway Company*[102]:

'Moneys are provided for, and various ingredients go to make up the undertaking; but the term "undertaking" is the proper style, not for the ingredients, but for the completed work, and it is from the completed work that any return of moneys or earnings can arise. It is in this sense, in my opinion, that the 'undertaking' is the subject of a mortgage … the undertaking, so far as these contracts of mortgage are concerned, is, in my opinion, made over as a thing complete or to be completed; as a going concern, with internal and parliamentary powers of management not to be interfered with; as a fruit-bearing tree, the produce of which is the fund dedicated to by the contract to secure payment of the debt. The living and going concern thus created by the Legislature must not, under a contract pledging it as security, be destroyed, broken up, or annihilated.'

In a later Court of Session decision, it was suggested *obiter* that a company incorporated by statute could exist but, if it had not actually acquired appliances and vehicles to run the line, it had no 'undertaking' to which a judicial factor could be appointed.[103] There has been subsequent discussion of whether, if the functions of a statutory undertaking have been transferred elsewhere, the statutory undertaking continues to exist in the absence of express statutory provision.[104] Today, for the purposes of the Companies Acts, undertaking is now identified with the body, in terms that rather reflect the modern EU understanding of the term,[105] and is defined as meaning: (a) a body corporate or partnership; or (b) an unincorporated association carrying on a trade or business, with or without a view of profit.[106] Standing those definitions, however, it is difficult to understand why the foundational provision for floating charges in Scots law, in s. 462 of the Companies Act 1985,

---

101 Railways (Sales and Leases) Act 1845 (8 & 9 Vict, c. 96).
102 (1867) 2 LR Ch App 201. It was only in 1870 in *Re Panama* (n 25) that the floating charge was recognised in English law.
103 *Paterson v Best* (1900) 2 F 1088. But it is difficult to square that dictum with the ratio of the decision, contained in the opinions of Lord Traynor and Lord Moncreiff, that the court could not grant the prayer of the petition to appoint a judicial factor because the estates of the company had already been sequestrated and a judicial factor appointed in the 1880; and that factory appeared never to have been formally concluded.
104 *County Council of the County of Angus v Provost, Magistrates and Councillors of the Royal Burgh of Montrose* 1933 SC 505 at 518–519 per Lord President Clyde (dissenting).
105 Cf *Unternehmen, entreprise*, or 'undertaking': e.g. arts 49, 101–102 and 106–107 Treaty on the Functioning of the European Union (TFEU).
106 Companies Act 2006, s. 1161(1). Cf n 45 above.

continues to refer to property comprised in the 'property and undertaking' of the company at all.

F. PUBLIC PURPOSES AND PROFIT

At this juncture it is necessary to say something of a distinction that became clear only as a result of the seminal decision in *Oswald v Ayr Harbour Trustees*.[107] The Ayr Harbour Trustees, were constituted as a body of trustees.[108] By a local Act of 1855, they were constituted in terms that incorporated the CCA and HDPCA.[109] By an amendment Act of 1866 passing reference was made to 'the Ayr Harbour Trustees' incorporated by this Act, but the framework for borrowing remained the CCA.[110] A further special Act of 1879 incorporated the LCCSA,[111] thus conferring the power of compulsory purchase. The question arose whether the trustees could bind themselves in perpetuity, whether by contract or servitude, not to build on land thus acquired. A bare majority of the judges of the Inner House of the Court of Session and the House of Lords held that the harbour trustees, in seeking to undertake by minute not to build on the ground acquired (and to reduce the compensation payable) acted *ultra vires* of their powers, creating a significant principle of modern administrative law, that public bodies could not fetter their discretion to exercise statutory powers.[112]

For present purposes, the point that Lord President Inglis made was that, while a wide 'business judgment' discretion was vested in the directors of companies incorporated by special Acts for profit, such as railway companies, the harbour trustees were rather a body of 'Parliamentary Commissioners' for managing and improving the harbour that, but for the special Acts, would, like other *res publicae*, be vested in the Crown for the benefit of the

---

107 *Oswald v Ayr Harbour Trustees* (1883) 10 R 472 affd (1883) 10 R (HL) 85, (1883) 8 App Cas 623. The *Appeal Cases* report is rather fuller.

108 Ayr Harbour Act 1772 (12 Geo III, c. xxii) continued by Ayr Harbour Act 1794 (34 Geo III, c. xcix); Ayr Harbour Act 1816 (57 Geo III, c. xx). By the Ayr Harbour Act 1835 (5 & 6 Will IV, c. lxxix) s. 56 the trustees were absolved of personal liability; and s. 70 made provision for how they were to be sued. Some of the private law history of the port is recounted in *Ayr Harbour Trustees v Weir* (1876) 4 R 79.

109 Ayr Harbour Act 1855 (18 & 19 Vict, c. cxix) s. 11.

110 Ayr Harbour Amendment Act 1866 (29 & 30 Vict, c. cviii) s. 4 and s. 5. This Act sought to link the harbour to the Glasgow and South Western Railway Company's lines, and incorporated, in addition to the LCCSA, the HDPCA the RCCSA and RCA 1863: ss. 2 and 3.

111 Ayr Harbour Act 1879 (42 & 43 Vict, c. cxl).

112 See n 117 below.

nation.[113] Such trustees, he considered, were to be distinguished from 'all statutory corporations constituted for the purpose of carrying on a trade'. The Lord President appeared to consider that a railway company incorporated by statute was nonetheless a form of partnership, on which Parliament conferred powers to carry out works that were deemed 'likely to be of public utility'; the directors of these companies were 'entitled to manage their affairs in the way they think best calculated to produce the greatest profit to themselves, which is the sole end and aim of the partnership'. 'Such an incorporated company', he held, 'is in no sense a trustee for the public.' The position of the harbour trustees, in contrast, was that[114]:

> 'They are entrusted with the management and improvement of a subject which is *inter res publicas*, and cannot be made the source of profit or patrimonial interest to any one. Their powers are strictly defined, and their revenues specially appropriated. In the exercise of their powers are merely the commissioners or agents of the Crown and Parliament, and the statutes constitute their mandate, the terms of which they implicitly follow. When, therefore, they have exercised any of the powers committed to them, they are not entitled to engraft on the simple exercise of the power something which limits or restricts the full operation and effect of what they have done, so as to convert it into the exercise of a power which the Legislature has not thought fit to confer upon them.'

Lords Shand, Craighill and Rutherford Clark, for their parts, could see no real distinction between the powers that should be accorded to commissioners and those accorded to statutory companies and were for adhering to the interlocutor of the Lord Ordinary, Lord Kinnear.[115]

On this point, in the House of Lords, Lord Blackburn held that there was no real distinction to be drawn between a body 'seeking to make profit for shareholders or, as in the present case, a body of trustees acting solely for the public good'. But he agreed with Lord President Inglis as to the effect of the purported agreement: 'in either case …. [a] contract purporting to bind them and their successors not to use those powers is void'.[116] A fundamental principle of administrative law was thus born.[117] In the context of statutory

---

113 (1883) 10 R 472 at 481.
114 (1883) 10 R 472 at 482. The Lord Justice Clerk and Lord Mure concurred. Lord Young wrote his own concurring opinion.
115 (1883) 10 R 472 at 486 (Lord Shand); 492 (Lord Craighill); 494 (Lord Rutherford Clark). Including the Lord Ordinary, therefore, the Court of Session was equally divided, 4:4.
116 (1883) 8 App Cas 623 at 634. The result, as Lord FitzGerald concluded, was that 'The minuters are not bound by their own minute' (640).
117 A W Bradley et al., *Constitutional and Administrative Law*, 17th edn (London: Pearson, 2018) 729; P Craig, *Administrative Law*, 8th edn (London: Sweet & Maxwell, 2016) para. 18–038, with some justification, concludes that the decision in *Ayr Harbour Trs* is 'unnecessarily draconian'. It must now be read in light of *Birkdale District Electricity Supply Company v Southport*

powers, Lord President Inglis' dictum,[118] that a statutory body established for a public purpose could alone carry on the undertaking (that could not, therefore, be sold without parliamentary authority), came to be extended also to statutory companies with shareholders.

G. ENFORCEMENT: JUDICIAL FACTORS AND RECEIVERS

(1) Personal creditors: diligence

Before turning to the position of secured creditors, it is worth saying something of ordinary unsecured creditors. As a matter of general principle, assets held by a statutory company were subject to diligence by personal creditors who obtained decrees.[119] As has been seen, certain statutory provisions in relation to railways expressly provided that rolling stock and plant was not liable to diligence. That principle was also applied to the solum of the lands on which the railway was constructed: 'It is the matured opinion of lawyers,' Lord President Inglis held, 'that the composite heritage called a railway is not subject to adjudication for debt'.[120]

(2) Judicial factors

Three classes of persons were, in general, entitled to appoint a judicial factor to collect and pay over the tolls and other income of the undertaking in satisfaction of arrears of debt:

(i)   statutory mortgagees under CCCSA 1845 s. 45;
(ii) holders of debenture stock issued in terms of the Companies Clauses Act 1863; and
(iii) ordinary creditors of railway companies holding decree for their debts in terms of the Railway Companies (Scotland) Act 1867.

Section 56 CCCSA 1845 confers on mortgagees, empowered by the special Act to enforce payment of arrears of principal or interest or both by

Corporation [1926] AC 355 at 371–372 per Lord Sumner; and *British Transport Commission v Westmorland County Council* [1958] AC 126 at 142–143 per Viscount Simonds, and 154–157 per Lord Radcliffe.

118 Which reflected pre-1870 English law: *Gardner* (n 102).
119 *Howden v Elgin and Lossiemouth Harbour Company* (1879) 6 R 987 at 993 per Lord Ormidale (undertaking as a whole could not be attached but 'it is scarcely conceivable that no such property or effects [subject to diligence] exists or may come to exist').
120 *Glover's Trs v City of Glasgow Union Railway Co* (1869) 7 Macph 338 at 340.

appointment of a judicial factor. A formal requisition by written demand is a condition precedent to the presentation of the petition for the appointment of a judicial factor.[121] Section 57 provides:

> 'Every application for a judicial factor in the cases aforesaid shall be made to the Court of Session, and on any such application so made, and after hearing the parties, it shall be lawful for the said court, by order in writing, to appoint some person to receive the whole or a competent part of the tolls or sums liable to the payment of such interest, or such principal and interest, as the case may be, until such interest, or until such principal and interest, as the case may be, together with all costs, including the charges of receiving the tolls or sums afore-said, be fully paid; and upon such appointment being made, all such tolls and sums of money as aforesaid shall be paid to and received by the person so to be appointed; and the money so to be received shall be so much money received by or to the use of the party to whom such interest, or such principal and interest, as the case may be, shall be then due, and on whose behalf such judicial factor shall have been appointed; and after such interest and costs, or such principal, interest, and costs, have been so received, the power of such judicial factor shall cease, and he shall be bound to account to the company for his intromissions, or the sums received by him, and to pay over to their treasurer any balance that may be in his hands.'

In 1850, there were a number of applications for judicial factors over the undertaking of various railway companies. The background lay in railway company amalgamations effected by schemes of arrangement contained in a series of private Acts of Parliament in the 1840s. These involved the statutory creation of new classes of securities – 'guaranteed stock' – in favour of the shareholders of the local railway companies that ceased to exist, their whole business and undertaking being transferred into the Caledonian Railway Company.[122] Each gave rise to subsequent court applications: the Wishaw and Coltness Railway Company[123]; the Glasgow, Garnkirk and Coatbridge Railway Company[124]; the Clydesdale Junction Railway Company; and the Polloc and Govan Railway Company.[125] The combined authorised capital of the Caledonian Railway Company, following the first amalgamation was

---

121 *Baird v Caledonian Railway Company* (1850) 13 D 36 at 38–39 per Lord President Boyle.
122 The Caledonian, Polloc and Govan and Clydesdale Junction Railways Amalgamation Act 1846 (9 & 10 Vict, c. 379); the Caledonian Railway (Wishaw and Coltness Railway Purchase) Act 1849 (12 & 13 Vict, c. 67).
123 *Wishaw and Coltness Railway Company v Caledonian Railway Company* (1850) 22 Sc Jur 541 (9 July 1850); *Primrose v Caledonian Railway Company* (1851) 23 Sc Jur 194 (14 January 1851); *Primrose v Caledonian Railway Company* (1851) 13 D 1214 (21 June 1851).
124 *The Glasgow, Garnkirk and Coatbridge Railway Company* (1850) 12 D 944 and 1014.
125 *Baird v Caledonian Railway Company* (1850) 13 D 36 and 795. Inglis was junior counsel for the Caledonian Railway Company.

to be some £2,550,000.[126] To put this in perspective, that sum, depending on the methods employed, would have an equivalent purchasing power of £150,000,000 in 2017[127] or, on an inflation basis, £300,000,000 in 2019.[128]

The cases are of interest for a number of reasons. First, in the *Wishaw and Coltness Railway* case, the court was required to wrestle with the question of whether shareholders in the Wishaw and Coltness Railway company who received guaranteed stock on conveying the property of that undertaking to the Caledonian Railway Company were properly to be considered as creditors or shareholders. The court held that they were creditors and appointed the judicial factor. Secondly, there are the observations of the judges on the meaning of a 'lien' on rates and tolls. In *Baird*, there was a divergence in opinion between Lord Mackenzie and the dissenting judge, Lord Cuninghame. Lord Mackenzie said this:

> 'It is said that … a lien over this part of the stock has been reserved to … the petitioners. I confess that I do not very well know what to make of the English term "lien", which has been a torment to our law. We cannot well tell what it is, and what it is not. It is not retention, that at least is settled. I wish the legislature had given us some explanation of the word in the interpretation clause. The statute says that the petitioners are to have a lien, but it does not tell us how this lien is to be worked. It is not said that the holders of this lien are entitled to apply for the appointment of a judicial factor, without averring that there has been any mismanagement. Even an heritable security has not that effect. I see nothing in the statute which makes the appointment of a judicial factor a necessary consequence of this right of lien.'[129]

Lord Cuninghame, for his part, took a fundamentally different approach; he considered that:

> 'on any legal or reasonable construction of the term *lien*, that the sellers should have, in addition to the obligation of the combined company, a preferable burden and real right, at least over the proceeds of their own railways'.[130]

In *Primrose*, Lord Fullerton (with whom Lord Cunninghame had concurred) observed that 'Whatever may be thought of the strict accuracy of the

---

126 1846 Act (n 122) s. 6. A further £240,000 was added on the amalgamation under the 1849 Act (n 122) s. 7. Figures for authorised share capital, of course, do not necessarily reflect what was actually issued or paid up: Perman (n 69) 181.

127 The National Archives, *Currency Converter: 1270–2017*, https://www.nationalarchives.gov.uk/currency-converter (last accessed 21 October 2021).

128 Bank of England, *Inflation Calculator*, https://www.bankofengland.co.uk/monetary-policy/inflation/inflation-calculator (last accessed 21 October 2021).

129 *Baird v Caledonian Railway Company* (1850) 13 D 795 at 798. Lord Fullerton concurred with Lord Mackenzie's opinion.

130 (1850) 13 D 795 at 802 (dissenting).

term *lien*, it can mean nothing but a real security'.[131] Despite the difficulties expressed about the terminology of lien, it was nonetheless employed, as has been seen, in the Burgh Harbours (Scotland) Act 1853. Finally, there is the strikingly modern approach of the court to construction of private Acts of Parliament implementing the amalgamations, drawing on commercial common sense, the purpose of the statute and the good faith of the transaction.[132]

In the event, in relation to the Wishaw and Coltness line, the court appointed a judicial factor. The interlocutor authorised the judicial factor:

> 'to collect and receive the whole tolls and revenues exigible, under statutory authority, over the whole length of the line of the Wishaw and Coltness Railway, and its branches, paying therefrom the sums necessary for the ordinary working of the said line, and other costs and charges as authorised by the provisions of the statutes, as the amount thereof shall be agreed on, or in the case of difference, shall be fixed by the Court … '.[133]

The principal discussion of the powers of a CCCSA judicial factor is, however, found in relation to Edinburgh Northern Tramways Company in 1888. The private Act[134] in question incorporating the company incorporated parts of the CCCSA and parts of the Tramways Act 1870. The company had granted statutory mortgages to creditors who sought the appointment of a judicial factor.[135] The court considered that a petition for the appointment of an interim judicial factor upon the undertaking and property of the company, under s. 57 CCCSA, to 'receive the whole or a competent part of the tolls or sums liable in the payment of the interest payable on the mortgages' was a form of diligence.[136] Lord President Inglis observed that the description of the officer appointed under CCCSA, s. 57 as 'judicial factor' was:

> 'a little misleading, because he is not clothed with the ordinary powers of a judicial factor … he is what is called in England a receiver … he was appointed

---

131 *Primrose v Caledonian Railway Company* (1851) 13 D 464 especially at 479.

132 (1851) 13 D 464 at 479 per Lord Fullerton; *Baird* at 802 per Lord Cunninghame (dissenting). Cf *Ashtead Plant Hire Co Ltd v Granton Central Developments Ltd* [2020] CSIH 2, 2020 SC 244.

133 *Primrose* (n 131) at 481.

134 Edinburgh Northern Tramways Act 1884 (47 & 48 Vict, c. ccxli) s. 2, incorporating: the CCCSA; the CCA 1863 Parts I & III; CCA 1869 Part II; Tramways Act 1870 Part III; and the LCCSA 1845 and 1860.

135 1884 Act (n 134), s. 43.

136 *Broad v Edinburgh Northern Tramways Company* (1888) 15 R 615 at 616 (20 March 1888).

to receive a portion of the income of the company sufficient to pay the overdue interest upon the petitioner's mortgages. That is the whole object and aim of the appointment'.[137]

In the event, despite the guidance from the court, and perhaps because the judicial factor had been appointed with the consent of the company, the factor in fact assumed management of the whole affairs of the company. When the judicial factor came to seek authority to pay the mortgagees and to obtain an exoneration and discharge in respect of his intromissions, the Lord President was somewhat scathing of the role the judicial factor had assumed for himself.[138] The factor's role was 'to pay over the money so received to the mortgagee to the extent of the mortgagee's claim as it stood as at the date of the factor's appointment, and to pay the balance to the company'.[139] Once that was done, his office was at an end. He was not 'a manager of the finances of the company' and the court therefore refused to consider the accounting provided by the judicial factor of his general intromissions with the finances of the company.

(3) Management and moratorium: judicial factor for railway debenture holders

The judicial factor appointed pursuant to a s. 43 CCCSA mortgage was essentially appointed to ingather the tolls and, as the interlocutor in *Primrose* set out[140] and the court in the *Edinburgh Northern Tramways* cases confirmed, after paying the ordinary expenses of the lines, to take the remaining revenues for the creditors. A judicial factor appointed under the Railway Companies (Scotland) Act 1867, s. 4 to the undertaking of a railway company, in contrast, was invested with the charge and management of the undertaking. Section 4 was essentially a prototype administration with a moratorium: it deprived the creditors of their right to do diligence against the company's moveables 'in the public interest, and for

---

137 *Broad v Edinburgh Northern Tramways Company* (1888) 15 R 641 at 643 per Lord President Inglis (19 May 1888). The Lord President's analysis is consistent with the Edinburgh Tramways Act 1871 (34 & 35 Vict, c. lxxxix), which incorporated the Edinburgh Street Tramway Company. Mortgagees of that company, holding not less that £3,000, had the remedy of appointing a 'receiver'.

138 In *Haldane* (n 141), in 1881, Lord Inglis had said that all judicial factors had powers of management.

139 *Cotton* (n 83) at 268 (Lord President Inglis) and at 271 per Lord McLaren (18 December 1889).

140 *Primrose* (n 131).

the sake of preventing a going railway from being stopped by a creditor using diligence against the plant'; having deprived the creditors of that right, therefore, it was, said Lord President Inglis, only to be expected that the creditors should get something in return; and the right that the creditors got in return – to appoint a judicial factor as manager – was itself a kind of diligence.[141]

Two other aspects of the Lord President's opinion are of interest. First, having held that a judicial factor appointed under the 1867 Act was 'a very different thing' from an appointment under the CCCSA, he nonetheless added that 'whenever a judicial factor is appointed on any estate or interest, the meaning is that he is to undertake the management of the estate or interest'; so when 'a factor is appointed on the undertaking of a company, that can mean nothing else than that he is thereby invested with the charge and management of the undertaking'.[142] Secondly, if a judicial factor was so appointed it could 'mean nothing less than that he is to have the entire control of its affairs under the supervision of the Court'. The control of the existing management was superseded. Thirdly, the court being alive to the practical challenges that may be presented to a judicial factor of managing 'a great railway concern'; if there was no objection to their appointment, then one or more of the existing directors or other officials could be chosen to undertake management under the control of the court.[143]

Having been so appointed, the factor did not require the authority of the court to enter into negotiations for the possible sale of the line, although before any sale could be concluded, the factor would require to seek the sanction of the court to apply for an Act of Parliament to obtain the powers to sell.[144] In the event, the factor received an offer for the line of some £200,000 subject to parliamentary approval, and he sought the sanction of the court to apply to Parliament for an Act to implement the agreement.[145] Meetings of the creditors had taken place that appeared to provide a narrow majority in favour of the factor's proposals. Various creditors, the company and the directors objected on the ground that a better price was likely to be capable of being obtained; moreover, when the case called, the offer of

141 *Haldane v Girvan and Portpatrick Junctions Railway Company* (1881) 8 R 669 at 673. As in *Broad* (n 136).
142 (1881) 8 R 669 at 674.
143 (1881) 8 R 669 at 674. A suggestion that appears never to have been taken up.
144 *Haldane, Judicial Factor v Girvan and Portpatrick Railway Company* (1881) 8 R 1003.
145 *Haldane v Rushton* (1881) 9 R 253.

the £200,000 that the factor thought he had, had been withdrawn. Lord President Inglis gave the respondents' arguments short shrift: 'from all I have seen in the course of the several discussions we have had it would be difficult to find any concern in a state of more utter and hopeless insolvency'; the 'sanguine picture drawn by the respondents' counsel of the company having turned the corner and being on the road to prosperity is a mere delusion. The line is hopelessly and irretrievably insolvent'.[146] The court granted to the factor the power to make the requisite application to Parliament for powers to sell, even in the absence of a firm offer.

Matters did not end there. The company had been obliged to contribute a proportion of the cost of the construction of Stranraer section of the line; and the Portpatrick Railway Company had obtained a decree-arbitral against the company for its share of the costs, which the Girvan company had not satisfied. Moreover, the judicial factor had repudiated an agreement in relation to the use of the section of the Portpatrick Company's line. The Portpatrick Company therefore sued the judicial factor for payment and, to boot, sought to interdict the Girvan Company, its factor and anyone claiming right through them from using that section of the line unless and until payment was made of the sums outstanding to them. The court granted the interdict.[147] Still further proceedings were required at the instance of the judicial factor to seek sanction for a revised scheme that was to be proposed to Parliament, which involved a reconstruction rather than a sale.[148]

The series of decisions by Lord President Inglis in the *Girvan and Portpatrick Railway* cases demonstrate the court's pragmatic approach to the carrying on by the judicial factor – under the supervision of the court – the business of the railway company as a going concern for as long as it could; followed by an insolvent restructuring; all while preserving the interests of creditors. Such tools would not become available to companies incorporated under the Companies Acts for another century.[149]

---

146 (1881) 9 R 253 at 255. Debenture debt was some £207,000 (c. £25m in 2020 if adjusted for inflation), plus £112,000 in unsecured debt (c £14m in 2020).

147 *The Portpatrick Railway Company v The Girvan and Portpatrick Junction Railway Company* (1882) 9 R 510.

148 *Haldane v Neilson* (1882) 9 R 854.

149 See further Coyle et al. (n 18) 273–274 observe that there were a number of other protections for shareholders and creditors of CCCA 1845 companies that would not be made available to shareholders of companies incorporated under the Companies Acts until 1980.

(4) A local Act example: the Greenock Harbour Trustees

(a) Background

The case of the Greenock Harbour Trustees may be taken as a paradigm example.[150] The harbours of Greenock had been originally constructed under a series of Acts of Parliament ending in 1817. There had been a local Act in 1842 authorising borrowing on the credit of the rates and duties of the harbour. Moving to the Greenock Port and Harbours Act 1866,[151] it well demonstrated how extensive concurrent use was made of the Clauses Acts. The 1866 Act incorporated four separate Clauses Acts: by s. 4, both the LCCSA and the CCA 1847; by s. 5, the HDPA 1847; and, by s. 50, the Railways Clauses Act 1863. The 1866 Act further provided that the trustees were incorporated and the whole undertaking was to be vested in those trustees.[152] The trustees initially had the power to borrow £650,000 (s. 66), raised within a year to £750,000[153]; to £1m in 1872[154]; and, by 1884, to £1.8m.[155] To put these figures in perspective, £1.8m in 1884, depending on the method, had a purchasing power of around £120,000,000 in 2017[156] or, adjusted for inflation, some £225,000,000 in 2019.[157] In security of such borrowing, s. 66 of the 1866 Act provided that:

> 'and for the securing the Repayment of the Money so borrowed, with Interest, the Trustees, or any Three or more of them, may assign over the said Rates and Duties or other Revenue, or any Part thereof, to the Person who shall advance or lend such Money, as a Security for the Payment of the Money so to be borrowed, together with Interest for the same'.

Section 67 provided a style 'Assignment' in Schedule A; and expressly provided that the trustees and their clerk 'shall not be personally liable, by reason of having signed such assignments, for the Repayment of the money

---

150 W W McBryde, *The Law of Contract in Scotland*, 3rd edn (Edinburgh: W. Green, 2007) para. 12–63 cites the local Acts applicable to Greenock Harbour as requiring particular forms of assignation. In fact, as can be seen, these forms come from the CCCSA 1845 and applied to most Scottish statutory companies.
151 29 & 30 Vict, c. clvi.
152 1866 Act (n 151), s. 2 and s. 36.
153 Greenock Port and Harbours Act 1867 (30 Vict, c. xxxv) s. 5. The 1867 Act also incorporated the Clauses Acts provisions: s. 4.
154 Greenock Harbour Act 1872 (35 & 36 Vict, c. clvi) s. 34.
155 Greenock Harbour Act 1884 (47 Vict, c. xvi) s. 9.
156 The National Archives, *Currency Converter: 1270–2017, https://www.nationalarchives.gov.uk/ currency-converter* (last accessed 21 October 2021).
157 Bank of England, *Inflation Calculator, https://www.bankofengland.co.uk/monetary-policy/ inflation/inflation-calculator* (last accessed 21 October 2021).

borrowed, or interest thereon' that they shall not have bound themselves personally to pay as individuals independent of their office. The clerk to the trustees was to keep a register of such assignments made by the trustees (s. 68). A creditor holding such an assignment was able to transfer the assignment (s. 69); and any such transfers of the assignments, were to be registered with the trustees within twenty-one days: s. 70. Similar provisions were made in the Greenock Harbour Acts of 1872,[158] 1880[159] and 1884.[160]

Section 72 of the 1866 Act had provided that:

'All assignments or mortgages for money borrowed under the authority of the recited Acts, and which shall be in force at the time of the passing of this Act, shall, during the continuance thereof, have priority over any assignments or mortgages for money borrowed by virtue of this Act, and the several holders of the assignments or mortgages first mentioned shall have the same priority among themselves in respect thereof as they would have had if this Act had not been passed.'

(b) Priority and scope of the statutory assignments

In 1887 the trustees found that they were unable to meet their liabilities. A special case was presented to the First Division to address fifteen detailed questions relating to the preferences and priorities of the various classes of creditors.[161] In particular, questions arose as to whether creditors who held only interim receipts and not formal 'Assignments' entered in the company's register were entitled to be ranked as preferential creditors; and whether the words 'works and property' used in the form of assignment contained in a Schedule to the 1872 Act (but not in the 1842 or 1866 Acts) extended the scope of the security held by the creditors holding those 1872 Act Assignments.

Lord President Inglis at first appeared to hold that the statutory assignments of the harbour rates and duties were not 'real securities in any proper sense of the term':

'There is nothing done by that Act to confer or make a real security. To do so in the case of ordinary securities in our law we know that in the case of heritable securities there must be infeftment or its equivalent, in the case of moveables there must be delivery, and in the case of incorporeal moveables there must be an intimated assignation. But none of these things was done, or could be done, in the case of the statutory assignments with which we are here dealing, and

158 35 & 36 Vict, c. lxxi.
159 43 & 44 Vict, c. clxx.
160 47 Vict, c. xvi.
161 *The Greenock Harbour Trustees v The Brown Society* (1888) 15 R 343.

therefore it follows of necessity that for one thing there was no priority of time under this Act of Parliament, and for another there was under it no priority in point of preference.'[162]

The Lord President's point was that the statutory assignments could not amount to effectual security over corporeal moveable or heritable property. No doubt it was the case that there had been no intimation of the statutory assignments so as to render them effectual as intimated assignations at common law. The 1866 Act did not incorporate the CCCSA 1845, s. 43[163]; the 1866 Act had, instead, incorporated the Commissioners Clauses Act (CCA) and the Railways Clauses Act 1863. As we have seen, the provisions of the CCA in relation to statutory 'mortgages or assignations in security' did not innovate on the common law requirement for intimation.

Lord President Inglis' references to there being no priority among the creditors must be understood in its context; as is clear from the rest of his opinion, his Lordship was saying that there being no priority *among creditors in the same class*.[164] Indeed, the Lord President proceeded to rank the various holders of the statutory assignments in their order; as the Lord President held, s. 72 of the 1866 Act 'makes it quite plain that the creditors under the Act of 1842 have a priority over the creditors under the Act of 1866' and proceeded to describe the statutory assignments he was considering as 'assignments in security' of the harbour dues.[165]

(5) 'A little more intensity to the Conveyance': 'Property and Works'

In *The Greenock Harbour Trustees* special case, one of the general questions that was raised related to the wording of the provision of the 1872 Act dealing with the assignments of the harbour duties. The 1872 Act provided that the trustees could borrow on the security of 'the rates, duties, and other revenues of the trust, and of the works and property of the trust'. The fundamental question was therefore asked whether the statutory assignment or mortgage that was capable of covering future income streams could cover also other property.

---

162 (1888) 15 R 343 at 350–351.
163 See too *Clark v West Calder Oil Co Ltd* (n 85) above.
164 This is consistent with the approach adopted by Lord President Inglis in *Cotton* (n 83) at 269.
165 *Greenock Harbour Trustees v The Brown Society* (n 161) at 354: 'the lapse of the period of payment prescribed in the assignment does not put an end to the effect of the assignment in security'.

'I think this only leads to one to the conclusion that the insertion of these words, "works and property of the trust," was really not meant to have any practical effect at all. The meaning of inserting these words at all was just to give a little more intensity to the conveyance. The works and property of the trust are revenue-producing subjects, and it is quite obvious that in no event under these Act of Parliament was it ever contemplated that a security should be created over the property and works of any efficacy, which could not be made effectual without doing real diligence against the property and works; and it is almost needless to say that there is not the smallest appearance of any such intention in the statutes. I do not suppose any your Lordships would have the slightest hesitation in saying that an adjudication led by one of the creditors under the Act of 1872, to carry off the harbour works from the statutory trustees would be an utterly absurd and ineffectual proceeding, and yet unless this to be the effect of this assignment of the property and works I do not see very well what the creditors can get by it except the revenue derived from the works and property.'[166]

There is much that could be said about this passage; the emphatic style tends rather to dilute the force of the argument. If the assignments were ineffectual as a conveyance, it is rather unsatisfactory to try to explain away the words, 'works and property of the trust' as words that were meant only to 'give a little more intensity *to the conveyance*'. But few would doubt correctness of the decision[167]: the idea of a generic mortgage of all 'property and works', not registered in the GRS, somehow covering heritable as well as moveable property, seemed a little too revolutionary. Of equal interest, however, is the recognition of a sophisticated package of debt instruments, with different rankings, secured against a future income stream, without any need to complicate matters by reference to 'real securities'. The income stream formed a fund from which the undertaking had to be operated (in order to generate further funds) and from this surplus the creditors would be paid according to their ranking.

(6) Receivers, managers and judicial factors

In England, mortgagees of the undertaking of statutory companies normally had the right to appoint either a receiver or a manager. In Scotland, the remedy was normally the power to appoint a judicial factor. Sometimes such a judicial factor was considered to have limited powers to act as a receiver[168]; sometimes to have the wider powers of a manager. The special

---

166 (1888) 15 R 343 at 357 per Lord President Inglis.
167 Cf Gloag & Irvine, *Rights in Security* (n 15) 627: 'this conveyance meant nothing and could have no effect'.
168 *Howden v Elgin and Lossiemouth Harbour Company* (1879) 6 R 987 at 995 per Lord Gifford.

case presented to the First Division by the *Greenock Harbour Trustees* in 1888 was not the end of the problems for the trustees. The creditors, having been ranked on the undertaking, had no ready means of obtaining payment.

'They [the creditors] were, however, in this unfortunate position that, although their rights of priority had been determined, they were practically powerless as to making their securities available, because the harbour could not be sold, and there was, to say the least of it, not much to take in the way of moveable property.'[169]

As a result, yet another Act of Parliament was obtained – the Greenock Harbour Act of 1888 – which swept away all that had gone before it and restructured all the debt into two classes of stock: A debentures and B debentures. According to the Lord President the effect of the statutory scheme was to change the position of the creditors of the Greenock Harbour Trust who held 'mortgages' (i.e. statutory assignments) into shareholders. At common law, a shareholder, said the Lord President, could seek to appoint a judicial factor. But this right was taken away by the 1888 Act and replaced with a limited statutory right.

The next question was the position of a judicial factor so appointed under s. 70 of the 1888 Act. 'He is a person appointed,' said Lord President Dunedin, 'and he is to receive the whole or a competent part of the rates and duties and other revenues of the Trust.' He considered the provisions under the different Clauses Acts to be practically identical, so as to make authority on one Act an authority upon the other.[170]

The creditors never having been paid from the income from harbour dues, they decided to exercise their remedy to appoint a judicial factor to take control of the undertaking. The question arose whether the judicial factor could exercise the powers of the trustees to increase the harbour dues. The House of Lords, as a matter of narrow statutory construction, held that he could not. But Lord Atkinson explained also the duty of the judicial factor:

'the judicial factor must not starve the undertaking. He must, out of the income he receives, make, as far as possible, adequate provision for the carrying on of the undertaking as a going concern. He is then free to divide such surplus as may remain amongst the incumbrancers according to the priority of their respective claims'.[171]

---

169 *Carmichael v Greenock Harbour Trustees* 1908 SC 944 at 954.
170 1908 SC 944 at 956.
171 *Greenock Harbour Trustees v Judicial Factor of Greenock Harbour Trust* 1910 SC (HL) 32 at 34 per Lord Atkinson. The history of the Greenock Harbour was reviewed by the Inner House in *Wilson v Inverclyde Council* 2003 SC 366.

In this, Lord Atkinson was echoing Lord McLaren's opinion in *Cotton v Beattie*.[172] Despite the apparent UK-wide nature of the issues, many of the statutory provisions relating to statutory mortgages were Scotland-specific. And although the courts were referred to English authorities, generally decisions were taken on the basis of the decisions of the Court of Session.[173]

H. CONCLUSIONS

The juridical nature of a statutory mortgage of the undertaking under CCCSA s. 43 was never properly clarified. It does appear to have allowed security over future assets and to allow the company to dispose of the very assets secured. An examination of these provisions and the extensive decisions of the court under them demonstrates that security over future income streams and receivership or management of undertakings for creditors by a court officer have been part of Scots law for almost two centuries. Lord President Cooper's dictum in *Carse v Coppen* that '[t]he law of Scotland does not empower Scottish corporations to create such securities [i.e. "universal assignments"] by such methods'[174] was inaccurate: Scottish corporations incorporated by Act of Parliament incorporating the CCCSA s. 43 were expressly authorised by primary legislation to do just that, albeit in the absence of much juridical analysis as to the nature of the security rights thus created. What is striking is that, despite the extensive case law, it was never seriously suggested that s. 43 CCCSA securities should be juridically characterised as 'floating charges'. But the detail of their operation on insolvency was not fully worked out.

Many of the provisions of the Clauses Acts – incorporated into thousands of pieces of local legislation – are still in force. No doubt many of the statutory companies that provided public utilities such as railways,[175] gas and water are no longer relevant.[176] In the case of harbours, however, many

---

172 *Cotton* (n 83) at 271.

173 *Carmichael* (n 169) 952 per Lord Dundas (Ordinary). His decision was upheld on appeal: see *Greenock Harbour Trustees v Judicial Factor of Greenock Harbour Trust* (n 171).

174 Carse (n 2) at 242. Cf Lord Rodger of Earlsferry, '"Say not the struggle naught availeth": the Costs and Benefits of Mixed Legal Systems' (2003) 78 Tul L Rev 419 at 423.

175 The Railways Act 1921 amalgamated many of the Scottish companies, including the Caledonian, into the London, Midland and Scottish Railway. See now Railways Act 1993 and associated regulations.

176 N M L Walker, *Judicial Factors* (Edinburgh: W. Green, 1974) 58 considered the right to appoint a judicial factor to a 'public utility company' in the past tense. But as Lord President Inglis pointed out, the appointment of a judicial factor over any estate, including the estate of a company, is possible: *Haldane* (n 141) 673. For modern examples, see: *Fraser, Petitioner*

of the statutes remain in force. The law on judicial factors is often seen as archaic, as perhaps it sometimes is.[177] But it was not always so.

The law has clearly moved on: the ability of a receiver or administrator to sell the business and assets of a company as a going concern was a significant development. Some statutory companies may register under the Companies Acts[178]; others will be subject to some of the provisions of the Companies Acts.[179] It can be seen that, from a Scottish perspective, perhaps the major innovation of the floating charge was its extension to heritable property and corporeal moveables.

Two wider points emerge from this superficial study. First, statute law, it need hardly be said, is the principal source of law; yet, in the UK, the study of statutes is normally relegated behind the study of the common law. One reason for its lack of study may be the outrageous inaccessibility of UK legislation.[180] Secondly, there is a tendency to think that company law is not really Scots law, and not worthy of study other than as a footnote to English law; English books on company law, for their part, unsurprisingly only rarely consider the Scottish cases. But there is a significant body of Court of Session case law that laid the commercial foundations of modern Scotland. The idea of a universal security, covering in particular future income streams, and enforced by a court officer continuing the business of the undertaking as a going concern to trade its way out of difficulty, is as old as the modern company itself. And it was that tool, suitably modified, that came to represent, a century and a half later, the benchmark restructuring tool for companies incorporated under the Companies Acts.

1971 SLT 146, approved in *Weir v Rees* 1991 SLT 345 (which involved a public company); and *McGuiness v Black (No. 2)* 1990 SC 21, in which Lord McCluskey appointed a judicial factor *ad interim* in order to allow the affairs of a company, in respect of which an unfair prejudice petition had been presented, to continue as a going concern.

177 Cf Scottish Law Commission, *Discussion Paper on Judicial Factors* (Scot. Law Com. DP No. 146, 2010) and the *Report on Judicial Factors* (Scot. Law Com. No. 233, 2013).

178 Companies Act 2006 ss. 1040–1043.

179 Unregistered Companies Regulations 2009 (SI 2009/2436).

180 *https://www.legislation.gov.uk/* (last accessed 22 October 2021) is notoriously unreliable and incomplete; almost none of the private legislation mentioned in this chapter is available on it (February 2021). Compare and contrast: Eurlex, *https://eur-lex.europa.eu* (last accessed 22 October 2021); and the Swiss law portal, *https://www.admin.ch/gov/de/start/bundesrecht/systematische-sammlung.html* (last accessed 22 October 2021). Each of these portals (dealing with multilingual legal orders) is both reliable and user friendly.

3 The Genesis of the Scottish Floating Charge[1]

Alisdair D J MacPherson[*]

A. INTRODUCTION

B. THE ROAD TO REFORM
    (1) Growing support for reform
    (2) A response to economic problems

C. THE LAW REFORM COMMITTEE FOR SCOTLAND PROJECT
    (1) The LRCS remit
    (2) Problems and a solution
    (3) Comparative law
        (a) England
        (b) USA
        (c) Germany
        (d) Other Civilian jurisdictions
        (e) Lessons learnt
    (4) The scope of the floating charge
    (5) Reactions to the *Eighth Report*

D. THE LEGISLATIVE PROCESS
    (1) Departmental disputes
    (2) Pressures
    (3) Forbes Hendry's Bill
    (4) Passage of the Companies (Floating Charges) (Scotland) Bill

[*] I am grateful for the financial assistance provided by the Clark Foundation for Legal Education (*https://www.clarkfoundation.org.uk/* (last accessed 22 October 2021)), which enabled the archival research featured in this chapter to be completed. I would also like to thank George Gretton, Scott Wortley and my co-editor for their comments on earlier drafts of this chapter. Any errors are, however, mine alone.

1 The title of this chapter makes reference to R R Pennington, 'The Genesis of the Floating Charge' (1960) 23 *Modern Law Review* 630. Given that the Scottish floating charge is statutory, the present chapter has a legislative focus. By contrast, Pennington's article considers the English floating charge's origins in legal practice and equity; however, he does also discuss the relevance of security rights similar to floating charges that could be granted by statutory companies.

E. PROVISIONS OF THE COMPANIES (FLOATING CHARGES)
    (SCOTLAND) ACT 1961

    (1) 'Definition' of floating charge
    (2) Attachment
    (3) Definition of 'fixed security'
    (4) Ranking
    (5) Diligence
    (6) Registration of charges
    (7) Assignation of floating charges
    (8) Receivers

F. CONCLUSION

A. INTRODUCTION

The introduction of the floating charge was a watershed moment for Scots
commercial law. It represented a significant departure from the pre-existing
law of security rights,[2] and involved a conscious attempt to more closely
align Scots law with English law. There were only ten years between the
expression of judicial antipathy to floating charges in *Carse v Coppen*[3] and
an adapted version of the English floating charge being introduced by the
Companies (Floating Charges) (Scotland) Act 1961 (the 1961 Act). The
following decades have, however, witnessed much uncertainty and litigation regarding the operation of floating charges. On this point, the drafting
of relevant legislation has often been criticised as ambiguous and unclear.[4]
This has hindered the development of a coherent law of floating charges in
Scotland. The genesis of various important provisions that remain applicable within the Companies Act 1985 and Insolvency Act 1986 can be traced

---

2 As specified in A D J MacPherson, 'The "Pre-History" of Floating Charges in Scots Law',
  Chapter 1 within this volume.
3 1951 SC 233. And see MacPherson, 'The "Pre-History" of Floating Charges in Scots Law',
  Chapter 1.
4 See e.g. G L Gretton, 'What Went Wrong with Floating Charges?' 1984 SLT (News) 172; see
  also Lord Cameron (on the Companies (Floating Charges and Receivers) (Scotland) Act 1972)
  in *Lord Advocate v Royal Bank of Scotland* 1977 SC 155 at 173 where he states: 'The language
  and structure of this statute are of considerable obscurity. It is by no means easy to relate with
  accuracy and certainty the various provisions designed to fit the introduction of the device of a
  receivership into the Scottish law of diligence. It was said of the Treaty of Versailles of 1919 that
  it "contained all the seeds of a just and durable war." It could readily be said of this statute that
  its provisions are well designed to provide a rich variety of issues for decision in delicate and prolonged litigation'. And see the remaining chapters of this book, especially J Hardman, 'Hohfeld
  and the Scots Law Floating Charge', Chapter 7 and J Hardman and A D J MacPherson, 'The
  Ranking of Floating Charges', Chapter 9.

to the 1961 Act, as can the registration of charges regime which is now found within the Companies Act 2006 in altered form.[5] Consequently, an enhanced awareness of the origins of legislative provisions and their original intended purpose may be useful for the future progress of the law.

Some commentators have reflected upon the arrival of the floating charge and discussed provisions of the 1961 Act, while also commenting on the Report by the Law Reform Committee for Scotland (LRCS)[6] that preceded and precipitated that legislation.[7] However, there has been little examination of the circumstances and process(es) that culminated in the enactment of the 1961 Act as well as the origins of its provisions.[8] The present chapter seeks to remedy this by examining Hansard records and National Records of Scotland (NRS) material (comprising documents from a number of government departments) and other sources relating to the 1961 Act.[9] This enables a better understanding of the intended meaning of certain statutory provisions, as well as how and why the floating charge took the form that it did and why the introduced registration of charges regime extended beyond floating charges. The chapter therefore helps to answer long-standing questions regarding floating charges in Scots law.[10] In order to reach conclusions in relation to all of these matters, the following will be considered in turn: the growing support for reform in the lead up to the remitting of the reform

5 The Companies Act 1985, Insolvency Act 1986 and Companies Act 2006 are the three principal pieces of legislation for floating charges under the current law. For the present registration of charges regime, see the Companies Act 2006 Part 25, Ch. A1 (ss. 859A–859Q).

6 Law Reform Committee for Scotland, *Eighth Report of the Law Reform Committee for Scotland: The Constitution of Security over Moveable Property; and Floating Charges* (Cmnd 1017: 1960). The LRCS is sometimes referred to as the Scottish Law Reform Committee.

7 See, most notably, R B Jack, 'The Coming of the Floating Charge to Scotland: An Account and an Assessment' in D J Cusine (ed), *A Scots Conveyancing Miscellany* (Edinburgh: W. Green, 1987) 33.

8 For exceptions, see e.g. the discussion of particular provisions at A D J MacPherson, *The Floating Charge* (Edinburgh: Edinburgh Legal Education Trust, 2020) paras 4–16 onwards and 5–03 onwards; and S Wortley, 'Squaring the Circle: Revisiting the Receiver and "Effectually Executed Diligence"' (2000) Jur Rev 325.

9 It should be noted that although considerable care has been taken to refer to the details and content of NRS materials precisely, some of the handwritten text is difficult to read or indecipherable and correspondence often does not provide complete information, for example with respect to names of correspondents. References are made as accurately as possible using the information available. Where documents referred to are copies, rather than originals, this is acknowledged. A further point is that the term 'memorandum' used in references in this chapter covers different forms of communication, including internal typed and handwritten messages, minutes between colleagues and teleprinter messages.

10 See e.g. G L Gretton, 'Reception without Integration? Floating Charges and Mixed Systems' (2003) 78 Tul L Rev 307 at 316 onward; G L Gretton, 'Registration of Company Charges' (2002) 6 Edin L Rev 146 at 149.

of security rights to the LRCS; the LRCS project and report; the legislative process for what was to become the 1961 Act; and substantive provisions of that legislation, such as those dealing with the concepts of floating charges and fixed securities, ranking and registration of charges.

B. THE ROAD TO REFORM

(1) Growing support for reform

The background Scots law position regarding floating charges was outlined in detail in an earlier chapter.[11] As has been noted, *Carse v Coppen* provided a powerful statement on the subject and was a (further) judicial rejection of floating charges. Prior to that case, there was little sign of widespread support for introducing floating charges into Scots law. Yet, as the 1950s progressed, there was increasing pressure to reform the law.

In 1953, Douglas Johnston MP[12] suggested during a House of Commons debate on industry and unemployment in Scotland that the introduction of 'something equivalent to the floating charge' of English law should be considered.[13] The comment and its context demonstrate a belief that allowing for the granting of floating charges could be economically beneficial to Scotland and Scottish enterprises. The suggestion by Johnston was privately rejected by the Lord Advocate's Department.[14] This was on the basis of the judiciary's apparent negativity towards floating charges, as evidenced by the critical remarks of Lord President Cooper in *Carse v Coppen* and the alleged incompatibility of floating charges with the principles of Scots law. It was concluded that the matter should not be pursued 'unless there is evidence of any strong desire for a change in the law'.[15] The possibility of

11 MacPherson, 'The "Pre-History" of Floating Charges in Scots Law', Chapter 1.
12 Labour MP for Paisley, who later became Lord Johnston. For brief biographical details of Johnston (1907–1985), see *The Times*, 21 February 1985, 14.
13 HC Deb 15 July 1953, col 2073.
14 National Records of Scotland (NRS) AD61/55: Copy Letter from A L Innes, Lord Advocate's Department, to R H Law, Scottish Home Department, 17 August 1953. Innes added that he had never heard a complaint regarding the need for the introduction of floating charges. In seeking to explain Johnston's position, Innes stated: 'I fear that Mr Johnston has been corrupted by his association with English law as a result of his being a member of the English Bar, as well as of the Scots Bar'. For the previous piece of correspondence, see NRS AD61/55: Copy Letter from R H Law, Scottish Home Department, to A L Innes, Lord Advocate's Department, 14 August 1953. As noted later, NRS AD61/55: Letter from J M Fearn, Scottish Home Department, to J H Gibson, Lord Advocate's Department, 17 September 1958, the views of Innes were submitted to ministers and no further action was taken.
15 NRS AD61/55: Copy Letter from Innes, 17 August 1953 (n 14).

amending the Scots law of security over moveables had also similarly been rejected in the previous decade.[16]

Momentum for the reform of rights in security over moveable property grew in the mid-to-late 1950s. For example, the Scottish Council for Development and Industry sought such reform to bring Scots law more into line with English law and made representations to this effect to the Radcliffe Committee on the Working of the Monetary System on 29 January 1958.[17] This committee considered that it was a matter that could most appropriately be dealt with by the LRCS.[18]

A notable part of the growing momentum for change was the perception that Scottish companies were at a disadvantage compared to their English counterparts.[19] This was due to problems granting rights in security in Scots law; in particular, the requirement for delivery of corporeal moveables to constitute a valid security (of pledge). An especially significant example involved an Aberdeen company that had sought to borrow money from the White Fish Authority[20] to fund installation costs for a fish refrigeration business. However, the company was only offered loans amounting to half of the required costs (rather than the maximum 80 per cent that the

16 NRS AD61/55: Letter from Fearn, 17 September 1958 (n 14). This letter refers to sources from 1942 (as well as in 1955) in which the possibility of amending the Scots law of security over moveables had been contemplated but rejected. Sir Charles Cunningham had apparently minuted in 1942 that legislation providing for the granting of 'mortgages' over changing assets and machinery 'would inevitably be controversial on the ground that it contravened the accepted principles of Scots law' and that before further considering such legislation, they should see how far they could proceed with other administrative improvements in the financing of Scottish industry.

17 NRS AD61/55: The Scottish Council (Development and Industry) Executive Committee Memorandum submitted to the Radcliffe Committee on the Working of the Monetary System, enclosed with Letter from W S Robertson, Chief Executive Officer, The Scottish Council (Development and Industry), to J H Gibson, Lord Advocate's Department, 22 August 1958. The Radcliffe Committee produced its report in 1959, see *Committee on the Working of the Monetary System Report* (Cmnd 827: 1959).

18 NRS AD61/55: Letter from R T Armstrong, Secretary to the Committee, Committee on the Working of the Monetary System, to N J P Hutchison, Scottish Office, 17 February 1958; NRS AD61/55: Memorandum from N J P Hutchison, Scottish Office, to J H Gibson, Lord Advocate's Department, 21 February 1958; NRS AD61/55: Memorandum from J H Gibson, Lord Advocate's Department, to R T Armstrong, Committee on the Working of the Monetary System, 3 March 1958; NRS AD61/55: Letter from R T Armstrong, Committee on the Working of the Monetary System, to J H Gibson, Lord Advocate's Department, 5 March 1958; NRS AD61/55: Letter from N J P Hutchison, Scottish Home Department, to J H Gibson, Lord Advocate's Department, 21 March 1958.

19 Due to the significant overlap between companies incorporated in Scotland and companies operating in Scotland, the difficulties in creating security over assets in Scots law were, and are, likely to have greatest impact on companies incorporated in Scotland.

20 Which was established under the Sea Fish Industry Act 1951.

White Fish Authority was empowered to grant). This was because of the company's inability to feasibly grant security over its moveable property, due to the need under Scots law to deliver the security property to the creditor.[21] Companies operating in England had apparently been offered the maximum amount, seemingly because they could give greater security, including security over moveables without the transfer of possession. This example was later used by the LRCS in its report as a justification for introducing the floating charge.[22] The LRCS also referred to the fact that the Industrial and Commercial Finance Corporation Ltd, which was formed in 1945 to provide long-term share and loan capital for small and medium sized companies in Great Britain,[23] had drawn attention to 'the failure of Scottish companies to take full advantage of the facilities it provide[d]', and had confirmed that the inability of Scottish companies to grant (non-possessory) security over their moveable assets had 'contributed to this difficulty'.[24] In addition, when the LRCS was considering reform of the law, the then Secretary of State for Scotland[25] apparently expressed a fear that another organisation could refuse a loan to a Scottish business and that it would be 'very difficult to defend a situation in which a Scottish firm would be at a disadvantage by comparison with an English firm in the same circumstances'.[26]

The White Fish Authority example was important as it provided a scenario in which the respective laws of rights in security of England and Scotland could be directly compared and contrasted within the context of companies seeking to acquire debt finance from the same entity. The growth of UK-wide bodies created by the state in the wake of the Second World War therefore highlighted the issue. In this context, it is perhaps understandable

---

21 For difficulties granting security under Scots law, see MacPherson, 'The "Pre-History" of Floating Charges in Scots Law', Chapter 1.

22 LRCS, *Eighth Report* (n 6) para. 12. One of the individuals who established the company had written to the Secretary of State providing details and his solicitors sent a letter to the LRCS with further information: NRS AD61/55: Copy Letter from B S Bellamy, Byron S Bellamy Ltd, to Secretary of State for Scotland, 8 August 1958; NRS AD61/55: Letter from Brander & Cruickshank, Advocates in Aberdeen (Solicitors), to the Secretary of the LRCS, 6 September 1958.

23 The company's share capital was subscribed for by the Bank of England and major clearing banks.

24 LRCS, *Eighth Report* (n 6) para. 10.

25 John Scott Maclay (1905–1992), later Viscount Muirshiel, was Secretary of State for Scotland from 1957 until 1962. See C Harvie, 'Maclay, John Scott, Viscount Muirshiel (1905–1992)', *Oxford Dictionary of National Biography* (2004) (online edition, 2009).

26 NRS AD61/55: Memorandum from A Mitchell to N E Sharp, Scottish Home Department, 5 February 1959.

if there was demand for more uniformity of laws across the UK, especially when businesses were in competition to obtain funding from state bodies. The situation demonstrated that the Scots law position was comparatively disadvantageous. Given that the example involved a company, the decision to ultimately allow floating charges to be granted by such entities would help resolve this particular problem in future.[27]

The situation involving the White Fish Authority certainly led to parliamentary pressure for reform. Lady Tweedsmuir,[28] MP for Aberdeen South, sought the resolution of the issue and also pressed more generally for the removal of obstacles to the formation of rights in security over moveables. She wrote privately to the Secretary of State for Scotland and also posed parliamentary questions regarding the matter.[29] Douglas Johnston MP[30] followed up one such question from Lady Tweedsmuir by referring to floating charges and he suggested that the Secretary of State should consider remitting the issue of floating charges to the LRCS.[31]

Despite the increasing appetite for reform, there continued to be dissenting voices. Upon reviewing a note that suggested reform of security over moveables was one possible means of addressing unemployment problems in Scotland, the Minister of State for Scotland[32] apparently minuted on 24 February 1958:

'I cannot think of anything I would like to see less than our coming into line with English law and granting security for advances over moveables. It is a vicious and most unfair system and when I say that I speak from years of experience. If

27 Albeit that under English law companies can grant non-possessory *fixed* securities too, whereas Scots law still does not generally allow for this form of security over corporeal moveables. See A J M Steven, 'Reform of the Scottish Floating Charge', Chapter 12 within this volume, for potential changes to Scots law in this area.

28 Priscilla Buchan (*née* Thomson) was a Unionist and Conservative MP for Aberdeen South between 1946 and 1966 and became Lady Tweedsmuir upon her marriage to John Buchan, second Baron Tweedsmuir, the son of the renowned author and politician John Buchan – see G E Maguire, 'Buchan, Priscilla Jean Fortescue, Lady Tweedsmuir and Baroness Tweedsmuir of Belhelvie (1915–1978)', *Oxford Dictionary of National Biography* (2004) (online edition, 2009).

29 NRS AD61/55: Copy Letter from J S Maclay, Secretary of State for Scotland, to Lady Tweedsmuir MP, 17 December 1957 in response to her letter of 28 November 1957 about the problem concerning the provision of loan capital by the White Fish Authority, which had been brought to her notice by Byron Bellamy (see above); HC Deb 17 December 1957, cols 185–186; HC Deb 4 March 1958, col 953.

30 Who, as noted above, had asked in 1953 for consideration to be given to introducing floating charges.

31 HC Deb 17 December 1957, col 187.

32 Thomas Galbraith (1891–1985), First Baron Strathclyde, who was a chartered accountant by profession. See *The Times*, 15 July 1985, 10, for biographical information.

a change is contemplated I suggest the Institute of Chartered Accountants be consulted.'[33]

Which particular aspect of the English system he considered to be so inequitable is unclear, but it may have been the disadvantageous treatment of ordinary unsecured creditors, who rank behind floating charge holders.[34] If, however, he believed that the Institute of Chartered Accountants of Scotland (ICAS) would not favour the change, he was mistaken. In its later submission to the LRCS, ICAS supported the introduction of floating charges (but advised against the introduction of receivership).[35]

(2) A response to economic problems

The economic position in Scotland was of significant concern for ministers and was a motivating factor in the referral of the reform of security rights to the LRCS. One particularly worrying piece of information was that the post-Second World War level of unemployment in Scotland was around double the average level in the UK as a whole, even in early 1958, and there were additional adverse features relating to unemployment in Scotland.[36] A number of solutions to the problems within Scotland were proposed, including the reform of security over moveables, given that Scottish industrialists were at an 'appreciable disadvantage' compared with their English

33 NRS AD61/55: Letter from Fearn, 17 September 1958 (n 14). See also NRS AD61/55: Memorandum from E Gillett to Mackay, Scottish Home Department, 24 February 1958; and NRS AD61/55: Letter from Hutchison, 21 March 1958 (n 18).

34 See MacPherson, 'The "Pre-History" of Floating Charges in Scots Law', Chapter 1, for more details.

35 LRCS, *Eighth Report* (n 6) paras 9, 26 and 40.

36 NRS AD61/55: 'Scottish Unemployment' Note for Meeting between the Secretary of State, the President of the Board of Trade, the Minister of Housing and Local Government, the Minister of Labour and the Postmaster General on 24 February 1958. For discussion of unemployment and other economic problems in Scotland compared to the UK as a whole in this period, including a graph showing the respective levels of unemployment, see G C Peden, 'The Managed Economy: Scotland, 1919–2000' in T M Devine, C H Lee and G C Peden (eds), *The Transformation of Scotland: The Economy Since 1700* (Edinburgh: Edinburgh University Press, 2005) 233 at 247 onwards. Peden states that by 1958 the comparatively higher level of unemployment in Scotland had come to be seen by Prime Minister Harold MacMillan 'as a political problem' (247). The unemployment rate in Scotland was also referred to as a factor justifying reform in later documentation produced prior to the passing of the floating charges legislation: see e.g. NRS HH41/1434: Draft Note by President of the Board of Trade and the Secretary of State for Scotland, Security over Moveable Property and Floating Charges in Scotland, enclosed with Copy Letter from Secretary of State for Scotland to President of the Board of Trade, 9 November 1960.

and Welsh counterparts in raising finance.[37] In addition, moveable property, such as plant and machinery, was becoming more costly and important relative to heritable property and was therefore of increasing worth as potential collateral.[38] It was therefore realised within the Government that 'whatever may have been the situation earlier, there is now a good deal of agitation for a change'.[39]

The political pressure to make the Scots law of rights in security more business-friendly and to address disadvantages suffered by Scottish businesses in comparison to their English counterparts intensified.[40] Following initial hesitation by the Secretary of State to commit to remitting the question of reforming security over moveables to the LRCS,[41] the Lord Advocate,[42] in response to a written question from Lady Tweedsmuir, agreed to refer the matter to the LRCS for their consideration as soon as possible.[43] Some further parliamentary questioning of ministers by Lady Tweedsmuir and Hector Hughes MP took place before the matter was formally remitted.[44] Following the referral, Lady Tweedsmuir enquired about the status of the LRCS's work.[45]

---

37 NRS AD61/55: 'Scottish Unemployment': Note for Meeting on 24 February 1958 (n 36).
38 NRS AD61/55: Letter from Fearn, 17 September 1958 (n 14). It was noted that 'the relative importance (and cost) of machinery and plant, compared with actual factory building, is obviously increasing year by year'.
39 NRS AD61/55: Letter from Fearn, 17 September 1958.
40 NRS AD61/55: Memorandum from J A M Mitchell, Scottish Office, to M K Howat, Lord Advocate's Department, 5 March 1958 – in the face of multiple parliamentary questions from Lady Tweedsmuir and others, the Secretary of State for Scotland apparently stated that 'Ministers are likely to be pressed hard on this subject'.
41 HC Deb 17 December 1957, col 187.
42 William Rankine Milligan (1898–1975), later Lord Milligan, who was Lord Advocate from 1955 until 1960, see *The Times*, 29 July 1975, 14; and *The Edinburgh Gazette*, 11 January 1955, 13. In March 1960 he was replaced by William Grant (1909–1972), later Lord Grant, who would remain Lord Advocate until 1962, see *The Times*, 21 November 1972, 17; and *The Edinburgh Gazette*, 12 April 1960, 221.
43 HC Deb 4 February 1958, col 160W.
44 Hughes (Aberdeen North, Labour) and Lady Tweedsmuir asked the Secretary of State about the remitting of the issue and he said he would need to speak to the Lord Advocate – HC Deb 4 March 1958, col 953. Hughes asked a similar parliamentary question (written), which was responded to by Lord John Hope, Parliamentary Under-Secretary of State for Scotland, on 11 March 1958 (HC Deb 11 March 1958, col 23W), who said he had nothing to add to what the Lord Advocate said in reply to Lady Tweedsmuir on 4 February 1958.
45 See HC Deb 10 July 1958, col 631. She also continued to privately correspond on the matter: see NRS AD61/55: Copy Letter from J S Maclay, Secretary of State for Scotland, to Lady Tweedsmuir MP, 31 July 1958 in response to a letter from Lady Tweedsmuir MP, 22 July 1958. Maclay noted that the subject had been remitted to the LRCS for consideration, they had begun their work and had advertised the remit. Lady Tweedsmuir responded, stating her interest in knowing when the report was expected: NRS AD61/55: – Copy Letter from Lady Tweedsmuir MP to J S Maclay, Secretary of State for Scotland, 4 August 1958.

C. THE LAW REFORM COMMITTEE FOR SCOTLAND PROJECT

The LRCS was established in 1954 by the then Lord Advocate, Lord Clyde, succeeding a Legal Reform Committee that had been set up in 1936. It was the predecessor of the Scottish Law Commission but its structure and work was less formalised than the Scottish Law Commission and it had much more limited resources.[46] The LRCS reviewed legal issues that were referred to it and made recommendations for reform.

(1) The LRCS remit

In May 1958 the LRCS received a remit from the Lord Advocate to consider 'the law relating to the restrictions imposed in Scotland on the constitution of security over moveable property'.[47] A variety of organisations perceived to have an interest in the matter were notified and representations were invited from them.[48] These organisations included the Faculty of Advocates, the Law Society of Scotland, the Institute of Bankers, the Scottish Trades Union Congress, the Board of Trade and the Council of Scottish Chambers of Commerce.

The LRCS was only established a few years previously but represented an appropriate forum for the consideration of the remitted issue. Despite its limitations,[49] the LRCS brought to bear considerable expertise. Its personnel included judges, professors, advocates and solicitors.[50] The members working on the security over moveables project formed a sub-committee consisting of: Professor T B Smith, then Professor of Civil Law at the University of Edinburgh[51]; W A Cook, a solicitor with a Glasgow law firm, who was

---

46 See G L Gretton, 'Of Law Commissioning' (2013) 17 Edin L Rev 119 at 121–122. See also S W Stark, 'The Longer you can Look Back, the Further you can Look Forward: The Origins of the Scottish Law Commission' (2014) 18 Edin L Rev 59 at 61; Lord Hope of Craighead, 'Do we Still Need a Scottish Law Commission?' (2006) 10 Edin L Rev 10 at 12–16; and, for an announcement of the creation of the LRCS, see 1954 SLT (News) 221.

47 LRCS, *Eighth Report* (n 6) para. 1. And see NRS AD61/55: Note by Secretary (J H Gibson) of Law Reform Committee (Scotland) – Sub-Committee on Remitted Subject No. 10 (Security over Moveables), 1 October 1958. The LRCS's remit was announced in various publications: *The Scotsman*, 15 May 1958; *Glasgow Herald*, 15 May 1958, 1; *Scots Law Times (News)* (24 May 1958) 108; and *Scottish Law Review* (May 1958) 87.

48 NRS AD61/55: Note by Secretary (Gibson), 1 October 1958 (n 47).

49 See Gretton (n 46) at 122.

50 See LRCS, *Eighth Report* (n 6) ii, for a full list of members of the LRCS at that time.

51 For discussion of T B Smith (1915–1988) and his legacy, see e.g. E Reid and D L Carey Miller (eds), *A Mixed Legal System in Transition: T B Smith and the Progress of Scots Law* (Edinburgh: Edinburgh University Press, 2005).

later described as the 'father' of the LRCS report[52]; and Peter Maxwell, an advocate who would later become Lord Maxwell.[53] They were joined by J H Gibson, advocate and secretary of the committee who subsequently worked as draftsman on the Companies (Floating Charges) (Scotland) Bill.[54] Professor J M Halliday, who held the part-time chair of conveyancing at the University of Glasgow, was later co-opted to the sub-committee to give consideration to conveyancing difficulties that would arise from allowing floating charges to also apply to heritable property.[55]

The representations received by the LRCS led them to consider the introduction of floating charges based upon the English model.[56] ICAS pointed to the greater ease in granting security over moveables in English law and suggested that due to Scotland's unemployment problems it was 'of the first importance to remove any unnecessary barrier to successful economic activity in Scotland'.[57] The LRCS was informed by another organisation that the inability of Scottish companies to create a floating charge had contributed to difficulties in generating an 'adequate volume of business in Scotland'.[58]

52 NRS AD63/481/1: Handwritten Memorandum from J H Gibson, Lord Advocate's Department to Lord Advocate, 16 January 1961.
53 And would subsequently become the chairman of the Scottish Law Commission between 1981 and 1988. For brief biographical details, see e.g. *The Herald*, 5 January 1994.
54 See LRCS, *Eighth Report* (n 6) 12, and see below for his role in drafting the 1961 Act. See also the references to Gibson in G Stott, *Lord Advocate's Diary 1961–1966* (Edinburgh: Mercat Press, 1991).
55 NRS AD61/55: Letter from W A Cook, Biggart, Lumsden & Co, to J H Gibson, Lord Advocate's Department, 10 March 1959. For details about Halliday (1909–1988) and his career, see e.g. D J Cusine (ed), *A Scots Conveyancing Miscellany* (n 7); and D J Cusine, 'Halliday, John Menzies (1909–1988), jurist', *Oxford Dictionary of National Biography* (2004) (online edition, 2004). Halliday was later chairman of a working group that examined the Companies (Floating Charges) (Scotland) Act 1961, and this was followed by Scottish Law Commission, *Report on the Companies (Floating Charges) (Scotland) Act 1961* (Cmnd 4336: 1970), which in turn led to the Companies (Floating Charges and Receivers) (Scotland) Act 1972. See also MacPherson, *Floating Charge* (n 8) para. 7–89.
56 LRCS, *Eighth Report* (n 6) para. 3 provides details of the organisations from whom the LRCS received memoranda or letters. This included the Federation of British Industries Scottish Council, the Council of the Scottish Chambers of Commerce, the Faculty of Advocates and the Law Society of Scotland.
57 'The Restrictions Imposed on the Constitution of Security over Moveable Property and Other Matters: Memorandum of Evidence from the Institute of Chartered Accountants of Scotland to the Law Reform Committee (Scotland)' (1960) 64 *The Accountants' Magazine* 118 at 122 (available at NRS AD61/55). The memorandum was submitted on 22 May 1959 and the views of ICAS were reported in LRCS, *Eighth Report* (n 6) paras 9 and 40.
58 NRS AD61/55: Letter from Lord Piercy, Chairman, Industrial and Commercial Finance Corporation Ltd, to J H Gibson, Lord Advocate's Department, 10 September 1959. See LRCS, *Eighth Report* (n 6) para. 10.

On the basis of submissions received, the LRCS's remit was widened to read as follows:

> 'To consider the law relating to the restrictions imposed on the constitution of security over moveable property; whether a security on the lines of the English floating charge should be introduced into the law of Scotland; and, if so, over what property it should be competent to constitute such a security; and to report whether any changes in the law are desirable.'[59]

According to the LRCS report, every organisation that provided a submission favoured a legal change to 'permit ... the creation of some form of security over moveables'.[60] And, in the view of the LRCS, all of these bodies 'expressly or by implication' favoured the introduction of floating charges and this was recommended accordingly.[61] The LRCS's starting point had been consideration of security over moveables; however, once representations were made regarding the adoption of a floating charge comparable to the English version, this caused them to also examine the applicability of floating charges to heritable property, in line with the English model. The difficulties of limiting a security that encompasses circulating assets to only certain types of property was also acknowledged by the LRCS in its report.[62] The scope of the proposed floating charge is discussed further below.

(2) Problems and a solution

Economic and financial considerations were central to the LRCS's desire to reform the Scots law of security over moveables and to introduce the floating charge.[63] A number of the economic problems already referred to above were drawn upon in the report and the difficulties in creating security over moveables and the identified economic and financial issues were expressly linked. The inability of a party to grant security over corporeal moveable property in their possession and the necessity of assignation and intimation to create a security over book debts was described as 'troublesome'.[64]

---

59 See LRCS, *Eighth Report* (n 6) para. 1. For correspondence regarding the change of the remit see NRS AD61/55: Copy Letter from J H Gibson, Lord Advocate's Department, to W A Cook, Biggart, Lumsden & Co, 9 April 1959; NRS AD61/55: Memorandum from J H Gibson, Lord Advocate's Department, to Lord Advocate, 2 March 1960.

60 LRCS, *Eighth Report* (n 6) para. 4. Presumably what was meant was the creation of non-possessory security.

61 LRCS, *Eighth Report* (n 6) para. 26.

62 LRCS, *Eighth Report* (n 6) paras 27–31.

63 LRCS, *Eighth Report* (n 6) paras 5–12.

64 LRCS, *Eighth Report* (n 6) para. 5.

Therefore, in practice, the only assets over which security could ordinarily be granted by Scottish businesses to obtain loans, according to the report, were heritable property and investments. The LRCS report referred to evidence from the Scottish Council (Development and Industry) that there were 'numerous American concerns who planned expansion in the United Kingdom' and wished to borrow for this purpose but considered 'the restrictions in Scotland in the granting of security over moveables to be a discouraging factor to these potential investors in Scottish industry'.[65]

The LRCS recognised that unsecured creditors could be harmed by allowing for the creation of security over moveable property without delivery but suggested that they would be able to satisfy themselves as to creditworthiness of a company by checking the charges register. In addition, the LRCS believed, based on evidence from England, that the ability of a company to grant a floating charge could actually benefit unsecured creditors by enabling companies to overcome financial difficulties.[66] As a result, they were of the opinion that it should be made possible in Scotland for companies to create some form of security over moveables without, in the case of corporeal moveables, the necessity of delivery.[67]

The LRCS report noted that despite the development of hire purchase, which had met some of the difficulties of the inability to create security over moveables without delivery, there existed no legal device that 'compensates for the legal impossibility of creating a floating charge'.[68] The LRCS ultimately preferred the creation of a floating security over a fixed security on the basis that a floating security automatically covering after-acquired property would be more effective than a fixed security over moveables that they believed would require to be 'renewed' frequently.[69] The meaning of renewal in this context is unclear. Fixed charges in English law can cover future acquired property but disposing of charged property unaffected by the charge would ordinarily need the chargee's consent, which can prove inconvenient.[70]

---

65 LRCS, *Eighth Report* (n 6) para. 11.
66 LRCS, *Eighth Report* (n 6) paras 13–15.
67 LRCS, *Eighth Report* (n 6) para. 16. And without intimation for incorporeal property, specifically claim rights.
68 LRCS, *Eighth Report* (n 6) para. 2.
69 LRCS, *Eighth Report* (n 6) para. 22.
70 See *Holroyd v Marshall* (1862) 10 HL Cas 191; L Gullifer and J Payne, *Corporate Finance Law: Principles and Policy*, 3rd edn (London: Bloomsbury, 2020) 293 onwards. See also Scottish Law Commission, *Report on Moveable Transactions* (Scot. Law Com. No. 249, 2017) paras 20.11 onwards.

(3) Comparative law

In reaching the conclusion that a floating security would be preferable to a new type of fixed security, the LRCS relied upon information regarding other jurisdictions. Comparative legal analysis was also used for other points, such as the broader issue of whether to introduce a non-possessory security and to determine applicable features of the proposed floating charge. The comparative analysis arose from input received by a network of experts for a number of jurisdictions: Dr Ernst von Caemmerer of Freiburg (Germany); Professor Réné David of Paris (France); Professors Allison Dunham and Max Rheinstein of Chicago (USA); Professor Vinding Kruse of Copenhagen (Denmark); and Professor L C B Gower of London (England).[71] The references to such a range of jurisdictions for this project was unusual for the time but later became commonplace in the work of the Scottish Law Commission.

(a) England

Given that the contrast between Scots law and English law in the area of security rights was a motivating factor for considering the reform of security rights over moveables in Scots law, it is unsurprising that English law was examined to establish what made it apparently more attractive to businesses. In correspondence, T B Smith was cautious regarding the imitation of English law but was keen to have a critical analysis of the English position from Gower.[72] Smith suggested that 'a codification' of the English law of floating charges should be avoided and instead they should seek the 'codification of what would become the Scottish Law of floating charges'.[73] He identified potential 'complications' due to the English division of law and equity yet acknowledged that they should utilise English experience as much as possible.

71 See LRCS, *Eighth Report* (n 6) para. 3.
72 Professor Gower (1913–1997) is well known as the author of *Gower's Principles of Modern Company Law* (now in its 11th edition (London: Sweet & Maxwell, 2021)). See *The Times*, 5 January 1998, 23, for biographical details. Given Gower's involvement in the drafting of the Ghanaian Companies Code, the draft legislation for Ghana was also distributed to members of the sub-committee for consideration – see e.g. NRS AD61/55: Copy Letter from J H Gibson, Lord Advocate's Department, to L C B Gower, London School of Economics and Political Science, 30 July 1959; and NRS AD61/55: Letter from W A Cook, Biggart, Lumsden & Co, to J H Gibson, Lord Advocate's Department, 12 May 1959.
73 NRS AD61/55: Copy Letter from T B Smith, University of Edinburgh, to W A Cook, Biggart, Lumsden & Co, 12 March 1959. In a letter dated 6 October 1958 (NRS AD61/55) Smith wrote to J H Gibson, Lord Advocate's Department, that even if there was dissatisfaction with Scottish practice 'it by no means follows that we should adopt the English practice'.

Due to Smith's general views regarding the influence of English law, his support for introducing the floating charge may be surprising.[74] However, his position in relation to the floating charge is more nuanced than may be thought. He supported looking to English law to identify how the Scots law of security rights could be made more effective, including by learning from difficulties encountered in England, but was keen on the creation of a law of floating charges specific to Scotland that could fit with the rest of the legal system.

Gower recommended that consideration should be given to introducing floating charges that could be granted by companies (by simply amending the Companies Act 1948), stating that floating charges had 'proved of immense importance' and had 'come to perform a very valuable economic function' in England.[75] He also suggested that in Scotland thought should be given to allowing partnerships to grant floating charges, due to partnerships' separate legal personality (unlike under English law). Partnerships in Scotland have, however, never been given such a power.[76]

The Board of Trade was also involved in correspondence with the LRCS regarding the creation of security over movables in English law. Their memorandum included discussion of the Bills of Sales Acts,[77] recognition of some criticism of the Acts[78] and references to the types of case to which the provisions of the Acts did not apply.[79] Gower was highly critical of the Bills of Sale Acts in English law but also noted that, in any event, the difficulty of distinguishing personal from business assets meant that using floating charges for individuals was somewhat impractical.[80] Yet, in his view, this was not a significant issue as an individual could simply incorporate a company.[81] These views were largely adopted in the LRCS report, in which

---

74 For discussion of this, see e.g. G L Gretton, 'The Rational and the National: Thomas Broun Smith' in E Reid and D Carey Miller (eds), *A Mixed Legal System in Transition* (n 51) 30 at 39 onwards.

75 NRS AD61/55: Letter from L C B Gower, London School of Economics and Political Science, to J H Gibson, Lord Advocate's Department, 20 November 1958.

76 By contrast, limited liability partnerships (LLPs) are able to grant floating charges.

77 See MacPherson, 'The "Pre-History" of Floating Charges in Scots Law', Chapter 1, regarding this legislation.

78 Particularly criticism of the Bills of Sale Act 1882 by Lord Chancellor Halsbury and Lord Macnaghten in *Thomas v Kelly* (1888) 13 App Cas 506 at 510 and 517.

79 NRS AD61/55: Memorandum on the Mortgaging of Movables in English Law – referred to and enclosed with Letter from R Speed, Board of Trade, to J H Gibson, Lord Advocate's Department, 8 August 1958.

80 The Bills of Sale legislation remains controversial. See e.g. Law Commission, *Bills of Sale* (Law Com. No. 369, 2016).

81 NRS AD61/55: Letter from Gower, 20 November 1958 (n 75).

it was concluded that in English law it appeared that the 'only practicable method' by which an industrialist or trader could grant a security over moveables was by floating charge (presumably because of the revolving nature of the assets to be covered) and this method was only open to incorporated companies.[82]

(b) USA

The laws of the USA were also given attention by the LRCS.[83] Dunham stated that although the states of the USA did not have precise equivalents of the floating charge[84] there were certain security devices that allowed the debtor to remain in possession.[85] And on the basis of the material provided by Dunham, the LRCS report later noted that 'elaborate arrangements' such as revolving loan facilities were utilised in the USA to achieve a security right 'substantially similar' to the floating charge.[86]

Dunham also referred to the then (relatively) new Uniform Commercial Code (UCC) art. 9, which only applied in a proportion of the US states at the time. He noted that an after-acquired property clause plus a future advance clause (allowing the security interest to affect property upon its acquisition and to allow further loans by the lender to be secured by the original security) were 'the essence of the English floating charge' and could be used under UCC art. 9.[87] In addition, Dunham stated that UCC art. 9 generally required public recording of the relevant security agreement or of a notice or caveat of the existence of the security interest. The importance of

---

82 LRCS, *Eighth Report* (n 6) para. 21. See also paras 20 and 32.

83 For further details about the LRCS's acquisition of information about the law of the USA (and other jurisdictions) in this context, see A D J MacPherson, 'T B Smith and Max Rheinstein: Letters from America' (2016) 20 Edin L Rev 42 at 51 onwards.

84 In fact, floating charges were rejected in the USA, see *Benedict v Ratner* 268 US 353 (1925), which was a US Supreme Court decision regarding the law of New York but was also considered to reflect the law in other states. And see generally G Gilmore, *Security Interests in Personal Property* (Boston: Little, Brown & Co, 1965).

85 In NRS AD61/55: Letter from T B Smith, University of Edinburgh, to J H Gibson, Lord Advocate's Department, 7 January 1959 (the letter erroneously gives the date as 7 January 1958), Smith stated that he had received an enclosed memorandum from Professor Dunham of Chicago and this was to be distributed to the LRCS members – A Dunham, 'Security Interests Over Commercial Chattels in the United States'.

86 See LRCS, *Eighth Report* (n 6) para. 24 for further details.

87 NRS AD61/55: Dunham, 'Security Interests Over Commercial Chattels in the United States', enclosed with Letter from Smith, 7 January 1959 (n 85). UCC art. 9 permits the creation of security over after-acquired assets and this is known as a 'floating lien'. For consideration of this from a Scots law perspective, see Scottish Law Commission, *Discussion Paper on Moveable Transactions* (Scot. Law Com. DP No. 151) (2011) para. 13.37 and Ch. 22.

registration for such rights to be effective was therefore no doubt reinforced from the perspective of the members of the LRCS.

(c) Germany

The LRCS (especially T B Smith), was keen to give consideration to the law in Civilian jurisdictions, due to Scots law's Civilian roots in property law (including for security rights).[88] One such jurisdiction that was considered was Germany. The LRCS was informed by von Caemmerer that the German legislature had refused to recognise any form of security over moveable property without possession by the creditor (i.e. a *Hypothek*).[89] In the German Civil Code, the Bürgerliches Gesetzbuch, a *Pfandrecht* (pledge) could only be based upon transfer of possession.[90] However, in practice, a security transfer of property, known as a *Sicherungsübereignung*, allowed (and still allows) a borrower to retain possession of property utilised as security collateral and this was recognised by the courts. Likewise, a security transfer of a claim right, a *Sicherungszession* (otherwise known as *Sicherungsabtretung*), could take place by way of secret assignment between cedent and assignee, i.e. without notice to the debtor. The courts recognised these security rights due to mercantile needs. By means of 'nice legal distinctions' such as the 'anticipatory agreement as to possession' it had become possible for constantly changing stock to be used as security collateral so that goods coming in to replace those disposed of in the normal course of business could, in advance, equally be pledged for security purposes.[91] *Sicherungsübereignung* (as well as reservation of ownership) could extend to the substitutes for goods serving as collateral.

On the basis of information provided by von Caemmerer, Smith considered that the 'great defect' of the German system was the absence of

---

88 See e.g. NRS AD61/55: Letter from T B Smith, University of Edinburgh, to J H Gibson, Lord Advocate's Department, 6 October 1958. This is not surprising given Smith's preference for, and promotion of, Civilian elements of Scots law – see e.g. T B Smith, *Studies Critical and Comparative* (Edinburgh: W. Green, 1962) 72 onwards; and see e.g. K G C Reid, 'The Idea of Mixed Legal Systems' (2003–2004) 78 Tul L Rev 5 at 11 onwards and the sources cited there.

89 NRS AD61/55: Letter from E von Caemmerer, University of Freiburg, to T B Smith, University of Edinburgh, 17 December 1958 (trans by I Vair-Turnbull, Foreign Office). Von Caemmerer also referred to German courts giving protection to unsecured creditors by regarding as contrary to public policy and void any agreement for security that was unnecessarily wide and which resulted in leaving no property available to satisfy unsecured creditors. .

90 Bürgerliches Gesetzbuch s. 1205.

91 NRS AD61/55: Letter from von Caemmerer, 17 December 1958 (n 89). And see LRCS, *Eighth Report* (n 6) para. 25, which also seems to be referring to the German position.

machinery providing adequate publicity.[92] Von Caemmerer noted that German jurists had sought legislative recognition of non-possessory security over moveables but with the requirement of registration.[93] However, there has never been such legislative intervention. In the present day, the German position is considered to work in practice but is not without criticism from a publicity point of view.[94]

(d) Other Civilian jurisdictions

T B Smith's 'Historical Note' at Appendix I of the LRCS's report also considers other jurisdictions for which information was provided to the LRCS.[95] As well as historical considerations, the note details the then applicable law in other systems. Smith sought to justify the introduction of the floating charge to Scots law by demonstrating that it would not be inconsistent with the Civilian tradition.[96] He referred to the extensive use of non-possessory *hypotheca* in many forms in Roman law but because these might 'constitute embarrassing and unreasonable clogs upon property' they seemed to have disappeared in the 'Barbarian Kingdoms' and 'revived in Europe only to a certain extent with the renewed interest in Roman legal studies' from the twelfth century onwards.[97] For moveables, unlike land, there was, however, resistance to the re-emergence of conventional hypothecs. Yet, Smith suggested, in certain jurisdictions like the Netherlands such security rights could be made binding on third parties if executed with the necessary notarial formalities, and this practice was also received in South Africa.[98]

It was stated by Smith that, prior to the French Revolution, France recognised general hypothecs derived from Roman law over moveables but the absence of a means by which the security could be publicised meant

---

92 LRCS, *Eighth Report* (n 6) 14 (Appendix I).

93 NRS AD61/55: Letter from von Caemmerer, 17 December 1958 (n 89).

94 See M Brinkmann, 'The Peculiar Approach of German Law in the Field of Secured Transactions and Why It Has Worked (So Far)', in L Gullifer and O Akseli (eds), *Secured Transactions Law Reform: Principles, Policies and Practice* (London: Bloomsbury, 2016) 339. For discussion of the German law from a Scottish perspective, see Scottish Law Commission, *Discussion Paper on Moveable Transactions* (n 87) paras 12.17, 16.6, 18.15, 22.1 and Appendix B paras 20 onwards. See also MacPherson, *Floating Charge* (n 8) paras 9–60–9–61.

95 LRCS, *Eighth Report* (n 6) 13–14.

96 See MacPherson, 'The "Pre-History" of Floating Charges in Scots Law', Chapter 1, and the sources cited there for further discussion of the relevant law in the Civilian tradition.

97 LRCS, *Eighth Report* (n 6) 13 (Appendix I).

98 LRCS, *Eighth Report* (n 6) 13 (Appendix I).

that such securities were later rejected.[99] However, this was found to be impracticable and *gage sans dessaisissement* (non-possessory pledge) had been accepted over certain property since the early twentieth century.[100] Smith also referred to Danish law, which had long allowed hypothecs over moveable property as long as particular formalities were complied with.[101]

(e) Lessons learnt

Comparative analysis provided the LRCS with lessons as to how the law of security rights should be reformed. The differing laws in Scotland and England were one perceived factor to explain economic disparities between the countries. The latter's floating charge was pointed to by organisations responding to the LRCS and by Gower as conferring significant advantages on companies operating in England. As such, the LRCS considered that it might be appropriate to emulate it. As well as this business-oriented push towards greater conformity with English law, there was a desire for an introduced security to be compatible with existing Scots law.

The rejection of conventional hypothecs over moveables in Scotland was referred to by Smith in his 'Historical Note'. He suggested, however, that 'it does not necessarily represent an absolute principle of justice valid for all times and circumstances'.[102] The law of other Civilian systems indicated that introducing a form of non-possessory security right over corporeal moveables (and other property) would not automatically be incompatible with Scots law. On the basis of Roman law and modern systems, which allowed hypothecs over moveable property to a lesser or greater extent, it was suggested by Smith that introducing this type of security in Scotland would be 'consistent with' the Civilian principles Scots law had 'inherited'.[103]

The modern systems referred to by the LRCS showed that there was a general trend towards a more liberal approach to creating non-possessory security rights, which could encompass future property acquired by the grantor. Yet, the position in the USA and the identified 'defect' of German law highlighted the significance of registration as a means of publicity (in the

---

99 LRCS, *Eighth Report* (n 6) 13 (Appendix I). Smith made reference to 'two celebrated Revolutionary laws' that preceded the Code Civil.
100 LRCS, *Eighth Report* (n 6) 13 (Appendix I).
101 LRCS, *Eighth Report* (n 6) 13 (Appendix I).
102 LRCS, *Eighth Report* (n 6) 14. Smith referred to Stair, *Institutions* I, 13, 14 and W M Gloag and J M Irvine, *Law of Rights in Security, Heritable and Moveable Including Cautionary Obligations* (Edinburgh: W. Green, 1897) 188, as authority for the Scots common law position.
103 LRCS, *Eighth Report* (n 6) 14 (Appendix I).

absence of possession). The mechanism for securing publicity had considerably improved over time and there was already a registration regime for charges (granted by English companies) by virtue of the Companies Act that could be extended to enable the creation of floating charges in Scots law. Fulfilment of publicity to third parties was particularly important within the Scots law of security rights and remains so.[104]

The importance of balancing closer alignment with English law (by adopting the floating charge) with Scots property law's Civilian heritage was recognised. Smith stated that introducing a floating charge would not be inconsistent with the Civilian tradition 'provided no attempt were made to import the technicalities of English Equity jurisprudence'.[105] In light of later difficulties, this is a perceptive caveat.[106]

(4) The scope of the floating charge

As regards the precise scope of the proposed floating charge, there was an absence of consensus among respondents to the LRCS. The Society of Writers to Her Majesty's Signet recommended that the floating charge should be restricted to assets not capable of being validly conveyed in security without delivery, and that it should not include heritable property, cash, book debts, investments, uncalled capital or ships for which statutory mortgages were available.[107] Meanwhile, the Law Society of Scotland proposed that heritable property, stocks and shares quoted on a recognised stock exchange, policies of assurance and ships should be excluded.[108] Other bodies did not recommend restrictions and certain organisations expressed a desire for Scots law to follow the scope of the floating charge in English law (i.e. to potentially cover all or any part of a company's property).[109]

The LRCS viewed book debts and cash as part of an ongoing business cycle also involving corporeal moveable items, whereby one form of asset led to the obtaining of another type of asset and so on.[110] Thus, eliminating any one of these would diminish the worth of floating charges. It was

---

104 See e.g. G L Gretton and A J M Steven, *Property, Trusts and Succession*, 4th edn (London: Bloomsbury Professional, 2021) paras 21.8–21.9.
105 LRCS, *Eighth Report* (n 6) 14 (Appendix I).
106 Unfortunately, this was not heeded in later cases such as *Sharp v Thomson* 1997 SC (HL) 66; see MacPherson, *Floating Charge* (n 8) paras 7–14 onwards, for discussion.
107 LRCS, *Eighth Report* (n 6) para. 27.
108 LRCS, *Eighth Report* (n 6) para. 27.
109 LRCS, *Eighth Report* (n 6) paras 28–29.
110 LRCS, *Eighth Report* (n 6) para. 30.

also pointed out by the LRCS that cash could instead be invested in the purchase of shares, heritable property or other assets and therefore the value of the floating charge would be 'much reduced' if a grantor could use charged property such as cash to obtain property that was not covered by the charge.[111] The LRCS added that in commercial law, 'unless there is good reason to the contrary, it is desirable that the law of England and Scotland should be the same'.[112] This again reinforces a guiding notion of closer alignment with English law, motivated by economic concerns. Consequently, it was recommended that it should be competent for a company to grant a floating charge over all or any part of its property, heritable and moveable.

With respect to the parties that could grant the floating charge, the LRCS concluded that only incorporated companies should be able to do so.[113] It was considered undesirable to be able to grant a floating charge over 'private' assets rather than business assets, and for partnerships or individuals carrying on trade it would be difficult, if not impossible, to distinguish between business assets and private (personal) assets. Furthermore, there was no evidence suggesting a 'real demand' for individuals or partnerships to be able to grant floating charges.[114] If parties wished to utilise a floating charge they could incorporate a company. The recommendation not to allow individuals and partnerships to create floating charges may also be explained by the willingness to follow the English law position and the impossibility or impracticality of partnerships and individuals granting valid and effective floating charges in England. Furthermore, the existence of the charges register for companies would be a ready-made mechanism for publicity that did not exist for individuals or partnerships.[115]

As regards enforcement of the floating charge, the LRCS rejected the introduction of receivership and considered that the holder of a floating charge would be adequately protected if their security 'crystallized' only on liquidation.[116] The LRCS suggested that introducing receivers would

---

111 LRCS, *Eighth Report* (n 6) para. 30.
112 LRCS, *Eighth Report* (n 6) para. 30. The LRCS also did not recommend the restriction of floating charges to securing cash advances made on or after the date of the charge rather than prior indebtedness (para. 31).
113 LRCS, *Eighth Report* (n 6) para. 32.
114 LRCS, *Eighth Report* (n 6) para. 32.
115 See further MacPherson, 'The "Pre-History" of Floating Charges in Scots Law', Chapter 1.
116 LRCS, *Eighth Report* (n 6) paras 33–40. Before preparing the report, the LRCS sub-committee had sought more information on certain issues such as whether the creation of a floating charge over heritable property would cause any conveyancing difficulties and whether provision for the appointment of receivers should be included: NRS AD61/55: Letter from Cook, 10 March 1959 (n 55).

require codification of the law of receivership in England or detailed legislation to enable judicial factors to serve a similar purpose. And this was something for which there was little enthusiasm. In addition, the only body that directly dealt with receivers in their response (ICAS) suggested it would be unwise to introduce receivership.[117]

(5) Reactions to the *Eighth Report*

The *Eighth Report* of the LRCS was completed in May 1960 and presented to Parliament by the Lord Advocate in June 1960. In comparison to recent Scottish Law Commission reports,[118] the *Eighth Report* is brief, amounting to only twelve substantive pages plus two appendices covering a further five pages. One cause (and possible consequence) of the brevity was no doubt that various complex issues were not explored in the depth that they might have been. In any event, shortly prior to the report being laid before parliament, the Lord Advocate wrote privately of his agreement with its recommendations and his expectation that the Government would, in principle at least, accept them. He also expressed his view that for a long time Scots law had 'lagged behind that of England' and that Scotland was consequently 'suffering financially and industrially'.[119] The responses of other figures in Government are outlined in the next section.

Upon the report being made public, one writer considered that the LRCS had generally followed English law and practice in its recommendations.[120] He also wrote that it was 'regrettable' that the LRCS had not recommended introducing an officer with powers analogous to a receiver and manager, as there would undoubtedly be cases where companies in difficulty could be saved with careful management, without the necessity of liquidation.[121] While there may be some truth that businesses (if not the companies themselves) could have been saved by this, the introduction of receivers to Scots law did not take place at this stage (as discussed

---

117 LRCS, *Eighth Report* (n 6) paras 33–40.
118 For example, Scottish Law Commission, *Report on Moveable Transactions* (n 70), which encompasses three volumes and is over 600 pages long (including a draft Bill).
119 NRS AD61/55: Letter from the Lord Advocate to J H Gibson, Lord Advocate's Department, 31 May 1960. See also NRS HH41/1434: Copy Letter from J H Gibson, Lord Advocate's Department, to R J W Stacy, Board of Trade, 2 June 1960, enclosing an advance copy of the LRCS report.
120 A C B, 'Constitution of Security over Moveable Property' 1960 SLT (News) 137.
121 A C B, 'Constitution of Security over Moveable Property'. For details of what is meant by a receiver and manager, see e.g. T Robinson and P Walton (eds), *Kerr & Hunter on Receivership and Administration*, 21st edn (London: Sweet & Maxwell, 2020) Ch. 11.

below) and had to await the Companies (Floating Charges and Receivers) (Scotland) Act 1972.[122]

Another commentator noted the Scottish courts' previous interactions with 'floating charges' and outlined the history of the floating charge in England, highlighting its mixed history including judicial criticism.[123] There was also reference to English courts having been preoccupied by the potential prejudice that ordinary creditors would suffer where a chargor enters liquidation, a problem identified by the LRCS.[124] It was added that while the LRCS accepted a new principle in the floating charge they 'did not feel disposed to take it to its logical conclusion' in altering the general law that rights in security cannot be created over specific moveables without delivery. This illustrated a 'cautious approach' by the LRCS that 'may well prove to have recommended an extremely useful addition to our commercial law'.[125] David Antonio, a lawyer with the British Linen Bank, was even more enthusiastic, stating that the LRCS could not have 'recommended any other single change in our law which would have been so rich in the promise of future benefits'.[126]

Various newspapers reported upon the contents of the LRCS report and some, like the *Glasgow Herald*, openly expressed their support.[127] Organisations such as the Scottish Board for Industry enquired with the Government as to whether there was an intention to effect the

---

122 For archival materials relating to the 1972 Act, see e.g. NRS AD63/996/1; NRS AD63/996/2; NRS AD63/996/3; NRS AD63/996/4; NRS AD63/996/5; NRS AD63/996/6; and NRS SEP4/59. As discussed in G L Gretton, 'The Story of the Scots Law Floating Charge: 1961 to Date', Chapter 4 within this volume, receivership would cause substantial problems in Scots law following its introduction.

123 H McL, 'Floating Charges' 1960 5 JLSS 178 at 178.

124 H McL, 'Floating Charges' at 179.

125 H McL, 'Floating Charges' at 180.

126 D G Antonio, 'A Further Step Towards Floating Charges' (1960) 52 *The Scottish Bankers Magazine* 104 at 104, a copy of which is held at NRS HH41/1434. He also stated in correspondence with Gibson: 'I can think of no single change in the law which would hold out the promise of greater benefits to Scotland than that which the Committee have recommended': NRS AD61/55: Letter from D G Antonio, British Linen Bank, to J H Gibson, Lord Advocate's Department, 8 July 1960. An earlier article by Antonio had been of assistance to the LRCS, as acknowledged within their report (LRCS, *Eighth Report* (n 6) para. 3). Antonio went on to author *Scots Law for Administrative, Commercial and Professional Students* (Glasgow: Collins, 1968) (and a second edition in 1971) and was a member of the working party for the Scottish Law Commission, *Report on the 1961 Act* (n 55).

127 *Glasgow Herald*, 29 June 1960, 6, where the report was described as 'timely as well as significant' and hope was expressed that the change in the law would 'not be long delayed'; *Evening Times*, 29 June 1960, 4, in which it was suggested that Scotland had not been getting a 'fair deal' since the war and that the proposed change could 'lift us to real prosperity'; *The Scotsman*, 29 June 1960. Extracts of these reports are available at NRS HH41/1434.

recommendations in the report and when this would take place.[128] As detailed in the next section, parliamentary questions were being asked in similar terms.

D. THE LEGISLATIVE PROCESS

The period between the laying of the LRCS report before Parliament and Royal Assent being given to the Companies (Floating Charges) (Scotland) Bill on 27 July 1961 was remarkably short. One commentator suggested, in February 1961, that the Bill (which became the 1961 Act) had followed the LRCS report 'with almost unheard-of speed' due to the 'initiative' of Forbes Hendry and other MPs who had introduced it as a Private Members' Bill.[129] The Bill's progression was largely the result of a fortuitous convergence of circumstances rather than design. However, some of the deficiencies in the resulting legislation may be blamed on the way the legislation was drafted and how it proceeded through Parliament.

(1) Departmental disputes

Even before the publication of the LRCS report there were internal disputes between the Board of Trade and the Scottish Home Department regarding responsibility for appropriate implementing legislation, and these disputes continued after publication of the LRCS report.[130] The Scottish Home Department argued that because legislation was to take the form of additions and amendments to the Companies Act 1948, as recommended by the LRCS, it would be a matter for the Board of Trade as the Secretary of State for Scotland had no responsibility for that legislation.[131] However, it

---

128 See e.g. NRS HH41/1434: Letter from J Lang, Chairman of Scottish Board for Industry, to President of the Board of Trade, 27 September 1960, enclosed with Letter from V A Winch, Private Secretary, Board of Trade, to J Glendinning, 10 October 1960.

129 D Antonio, 'Companies (Floating Charges) (Scotland) Bill' (1961) 65 *The Accountants' Magazine* 172 at 172. A copy of the article is available at NRS AD63/481/1.

130 See e.g. NRS HH41/1434: Memorandum from Unknown Author to H H A Whitworth, Scottish Home Department, 10 June 1960. For details about the Scottish Home Department and the Scottish Office more broadly, see J S Gibson, *The Thistle and the Crown: A History of the Scottish Office* (Edinburgh: HMSO, 1985).

131 See e.g. NRS AD61/55: Copy Letter from J H Gibson, Lord Advocate's Department, to J M Fearn, Scottish Home Department, 12 February 1960. The LRCS had recommended that the proposed changes be effected by amendment of the Companies Act 1948 – LRCS, *Eighth Report* (n 6) para. 41 and Appendix II. This was also suggested by Gower in his correspondence with the LRCS – see above (n 75).

was acknowledged that the Secretary of State would be subjected to 'political pressure' in Scotland if legislation was not 'speedily' introduced. It was also suggested that once the report from the LRCS was published various bodies would press strongly for implementing legislation.[132]

The Board of Trade wished to take an interest in any amendments to be made to the Companies Act 1948 but were of the view that the change was not so urgent and necessary to justify immediate government approval for initiating legislation. They also considered the reform to relate to the general law of Scotland.[133] As such, it was the responsibility of the Secretary of State for Scotland to obtain a place in the legislative programme for the Bill and it would be for him and the Lord Advocate to bring the matter before Ministers collectively. The President of the Board of Trade repeated his department's position and expressed some doubt over whether there existed a 'barrier to successful economic development' that should be removed, particularly in the absence of introducing receivers and managers.[134]

In the early part of the disputes, it was undecided whether the change would be made by amending the Scots law of rights in security over moveables with the necessary consequential changes in the Companies Act 1948 or simply by introducing a piece of amending companies legislation, as the LRCS had recommended.[135] Ultimately, an approach more aligned with the former was adopted, with the 1961 Act introducing the floating charge to Scots law but with a Schedule containing amendments to the Companies Act 1948, in relation to registration of charges. The long title of the Act referred to the amendment being made to Scots law: 'An Act to amend the law of Scotland so as to empower companies to give security by way of floating charges; and for purposes connected herewith'. The debate regarding how the floating charge should be introduced demonstrates uncertainty

---

132 See e.g. NRS AD61/55: Copy Letter from Gibson, 12 February 1960 (n 131).
133 NRS HH41/1434: Letter from P J Mantle, Board of Trade, to H H A Whitworth, Scottish Home Department, 7 October 1960. For discussion of the Board of Trade's claims by the Lord Advocate's Department and the Scottish Home Department see e.g. NRS HH41/1434: Letter from J H Gibson, Lord Advocate's Department, to H H A Whitworth, Scottish Home Department, 25 October 1960; and NRS HH41/1434: Paper by Scottish Home Department to R Brooman-White, Minister of State, and the Secretary of State, 8 November 1960.
134 NRS HH41/1434: Letter from President of Board of Trade to Secretary of State for Scotland, 17 November 1960. See also NRS HH41/1434: Letter from Secretary of State for Scotland to President of the Board of Trade, 9 November 1960. The President of the Board of Trade at this time (1959–1961) was Reginald Maudling, a future Chancellor of the Exchequer and Home Secretary: R Shepherd, 'Maudling, Reginald (1917–1979)', Oxford Dictionary of National Biography (2004) (online edition, 2008).
135 NRS HH41/1434: HC 14 November 1960 – Written Answer. This is according to a supplementary handwritten note to the written answer document in the archive file.

regarding precisely how the floating charge was to fit in with company law and the law of rights in security. It also highlights doubt regarding whether the floating charge should primarily be a matter for the law of rights in security or company law.

(2) Pressures

As noted above, the publication of the LRCS report brought pressure upon the government to implement its recommendations.[136] The pressure came from various quarters. This extended to parliamentary questions, with Anthony Stodart MP and Lady Tweedsmuir asking what action was to be taken to implement the recommendations in the *Eighth Report*, accompanied by a plea for the speedy introduction of appropriate provisions.[137]

Doubts were raised internally about whether there was sufficient time within the 1960–1961 parliamentary session to introduce implementing legislation. In the absence of sufficient government time it was suggested that there was a remote possibility that a private member (high enough in the relevant ballot) could introduce legislation but this would probably only be suitable if they were legally qualified.[138]

Despite the pressure for implementation there also seems to have been some hesitation given that the committee chaired by Lord Justice Jenkins was simultaneously examining company law. In November 1960 the expectation was that the Jenkins Committee was unlikely to report before the end of 1961 with legislation possibly following in 1962–1963.[139] Another difficulty with a separate Scottish Bill was noted to be that the Jenkins Committee

136 See also NRS HH41/1434: Paper HA(60)155, 'Security over Moveable Property and Floating Charges in Scotland: Memorandum by the Secretary of State for Scotland' for some details regarding pressure being placed upon the Government. It was also stated that 'clearly pressure for Government action will build up both inside and outside Parliament'.

137 HC Deb 19 July 1960, cols 232–233. Stodart (Edinburgh West, Unionist/Conservative) asked the initial question and Lady Tweedsmuir asked a supplementary question. It was responded on behalf of the President of the Board of Trade that he was considering the matter in conjunction with the Secretary of State for Scotland. See also HC Deb 14 November 1960, col 12W – Stodart asked the President of the Board of Trade what progress he had made in considering, with the Secretary of State for Scotland, the recommendations of the LRCS regarding reform of the existing law of security over moveables and whether he proposed to amend the Companies Act 1948 to effect this. In response, the matter was said to still be under consideration.

138 See e.g. NRS HH41/1434: Memorandum from R Brooman-White to Secretary of State, 8 November 1960. NRS HH41/1434: Paper by Scottish Home Department, 8 November 1960 (n 133). See also NRS HH41/1434: Memorandum by Unknown Author, 7 November 1960. And see NRS HH41/1434: Paper HA(60)155 (n 136), regarding a suggestion for the preparation of a Bill to be handed to a private member.

139 On this see also HH41/1434: Paper HA(60)155 (n 136).

were seemingly considering the amendment of the law of floating charges in England so if the Scottish system was to replicate the English system the former would perhaps need to be altered soon after introduction.[140] While the Bill on floating charges was making its parliamentary progress, the Jenkins Committee received evidence in favour of the introduction of receivers from the Committee of Scottish Bank General Managers.[141]

If there was to be delay in introducing the floating charge, it was suggested that the matter could be dealt with in the amendment of the Companies Act 1948 that was considered likely to follow the Jenkins Report. However, this was not deemed desirable given that delay in removing an apparent obstacle to potential investors in Scotland would be heavily criticised, while taking swift steps to implement the LRCS's recommendations would be politically advantageous.[142] It was also noted within the Scottish Home Department that with an 'innovation' like the floating charge 'some experience may be necessary before we get everything right' and that there would probably be a reasonably early opportunity of making amendments due to the anticipated Jenkins Report.[143] The *Report of the Company Law Committee* (Jenkins Committee) was presented to Parliament in June 1962 but did not directly lead to changes to the Scots law of floating charges.[144]

(3) Forbes Hendry's Bill

The lack of immediate governmental progress in producing implementing legislation allowed Forbes Hendry, a legally qualified Scottish MP,[145] to step into the gap with a pre-prepared draft Bill.[146] Hendry was reported

---

140 NRS HH41/1434: Memorandum from N E Sharp, Scottish Home Department, to H H A Whitworth, Scottish Home Department, 21 June 1960.

141 NRS HH41/1434: Letter from N J P Hutchison, Scottish Home Department, to D Oulton, Lord Chancellor's Office, 17 January 1961 (the letter erroneously gives the date as 17 January 1960). An enquiry was made as to whether there was any likelihood of codification of the English law of receivers in the foreseeable future.

142 NRS HH41/1434: Paper by Scottish Home Department, 8 November 1960 (n 133).

143 NRS HH41/1434: Scottish Home Department Notes, 'LC(61)9 Companies Floating Charges (Scotland) Bill', 18 January 1961.

144 Board of Trade, *Report of the Company Law Committee* (Cmnd 1749: 1962). Some of the report's recommendations were introduced by the Companies Act 1967, which amended existing companies legislation.

145 Lt Col Alexander Forbes Hendry (1908–1980) was a Unionist/Conservative MP for the Aberdeenshire West constituency from 1959 until 1966. He practised law in Stirlingshire. See *The Times*, 22 November 1980, 14, for biographical details.

146 This development may have been attractive to the Lord Advocate's department and the Scottish Home Department given the difficulties encountered with the Board of Trade.

to have had private help preparing the Bill (although it is unclear from whom) and was said to have 'put in three or four days hard work on it'.[147] He informed the Lord Advocate of his intention to introduce the Bill under the ten-minute rule procedure,[148] and declared the existence of his draft Bill publicly by way of a parliamentary question on 29 November 1960.[149]

Newspapers reported that the private member's Bill was to be introduced under the ten-minute rule in the House of Commons.[150] At this stage, the short title of the Bill was the Security over Moveables (Scotland) Bill; however, this was changed prior to the Bill's introduction to the 'Companies (Floating Charges) (Scotland) Bill' seemingly on the basis that it did not enact a general change in the law to enable security rights to be created over specific moveables without delivery.[151] The inclusion of heritable property within the potential scope of the floating charge also made the original title inaccurate.

The Bill largely followed the suggestions of the LRCS and various provisions in the Bill were in similar terms to the ensuing Act, for example in relation to ranking.[152] The attempted implementation of the LRCS recommendations was acknowledged by Hendry in a letter that he sent to every Scottish MP which outlined economic problems he claimed were contributed to by the requirement for delivery of moveables (to create security).[153] Later, within the discussion of the Bill at the Scottish Standing Committee stage,[154] there were references to parties in Scotland not being able to give security over stock-in-trade, vehicles and plant and equipment, which

---

147 NRS HH41/1434: Memorandum from A Macpherson to J J McCabe, Scottish Home Department, 25 November 1960, referring to a minute of R Brooman-White that reported Hendry's comments.

148 NRS HH41/1434: Memoranda from J Glendinning to J J McCabe, Scottish Home Department, 25 November 1960; and see NRS HH41/1434: Copy Letter from F Hendry to Lord Advocate, 26 November 1960, enclosing draft Bill. For details of the ten-minute rule, see M Hutton et al. (eds), *Erskine May: Parliamentary Practice*, 25th edn (London: LexisNexis, 2019) para. 28.4.

149 HC Deb 29 November 1960, col 175.

150 *Glasgow Herald*, 'Private Bill to Help Business Men', 26 November 1960; and *Glasgow Herald*, 'Scots Law Reform: Private Member's Bill', 17 December 1960. Extracts of these are available at NRS HH41/1434.

151 NRS HH41/1434: 'Floating Charges in Scotland: Memorandum by the Secretary of State for Scotland', 8 December 1960.

152 NRS HH41/1434: Draft Bill, enclosed with Copy Letter from Hendry, 26 November 1960 (n 148).

153 NRS HH41/1434: Letter from F Hendry, 10 December 1960.

154 For details of the Scottish Standing Committee, see e.g. J G Kellas, *The Scottish Political System*, 4th edn (Cambridge: Cambridge University Press, 1989) 85–95.

should be read to mean the giving of non-possessory security.[155] This emphasises that the reform of the law of rights in security over corporeal moveables was the principal focus of the legislation, and the existing law was believed to be a cause of relative economic disadvantage for Scottish businesses.

(4) Passage of the Companies (Floating Charges) (Scotland) Bill

Approval for leave to introduce the Bill under the ten-minute rule was given to Hendry by the Legislation Committee on 13 December 1960 and the Bill was introduced on 20 December 1960.[156] Hendry referred to the negative economic consequences of requiring the delivery of corporeal moveable property to a creditor in order to constitute a valid security. He suggested that it was the 'duty of every patriotic Scot' to address the economic disparity between England and Scotland and that the Bill would be a 'modest step in the right direction'.[157] He also stated that the Bill was not an attempt to alter company law[158] and that it was designed to amend the law of Scotland and did not affect English law in any way.[159] Shortly prior to this, the Lord Advocate introduced Hendry to Gibson, who was to be the draftsman for the Bill thereafter.[160] Hendry had apparently secured a broad basis of support for the Bill from opinion in Scotland and backers in the House.[161] The publication of Hendry's Bill was reported in passing in *The Scotsman* at the end of January 1961.[162]

---

155 HC Deb, Scottish Standing Committee, 20 June 1961, cols 10–11. Indeed, Hendry later, at col 51, noted that as matters stood the only way to give security over corporeal moveables was to 'put them in a pawn shop or something similar'.

156 See HC Deb 20 December 1960, cols 1118–1120. For details of the legislation committee's consideration of and decision to approve the proposal (including giving approval to parliamentary counsel's provision of assistance to Hendry in preparing the Bill), see NRS HH41/1434: Copy Legislation Committee Record – 13 December 1960. See also NRS HH41/1434: Paper by the Scottish Home Department, 12 December 1960.

157 See HC Deb 20 December 1960, cols 1118–1120.

158 Of course, the legislation would make some changes to company law in Scotland; however, the comment should be read as meaning that substantive company law was not going to be altered in a more general way.

159 See HC Deb 20 December 1960, col 1118.

160 NRS HH41/1434: Copy Letter from N J P Hutchison, Scottish Home Department, to P J Mantle, Board of Trade, 15 December 1960.

161 NRS HH41/1434: Scottish Home Department Notes, 18 January 1961 (n 143). The following names were given as supporters of the Bill in the House of Commons: Sir J Henderson-Stewart, Mr Lawson, Mr McArthur, Mr John MacLeod, Mr Millan, Sir D Robertson, Mr Stodart, and Sir M Galpern.

162 *The Scotsman*, 'Company Law Bill', 31 January 1961, noting that the text of the Bill was issued that day. An extract is available at NRS HH41/1434.

The second reading of the Bill was originally scheduled for 10 February 1961 but was delayed until 24 February 1961 and then further postponed.[163] Hendry understood that its subsequent progress in the Scottish Standing Committee was subject to the priority status of Government Bills but he was aware that it could still be possible to fit in consideration of his Bill.[164] There was considerable doubt though as to whether there was enough space in the legislative programme. The committee stages of various Bills such as the Sheriffs' Pensions and Crofters Bills[165] were to take priority over Hendry's Bill.[166] However, space did become available allowing Hendry's Bill to make further progress. The pressing need to utilise the opportunities that arose partly explains the speed of the Bill's passage.

On 10 March 1961 the Bill was read a second time and committed to a standing committee.[167] The Scottish Standing Committee considered the Bill on 20 June 1961.[168] There was some criticism of the large volume of amendments moved at that stage. One MP suggested that Hendry 'must have prepared the Bill very hurriedly and that it must have been ill-considered …'.[169] The Lord Advocate and Hendry sought to defend the changes on the basis that the Bill was prepared shortly after the publication of the LRCS report and that subsequently a range of organisations had provided representations that they had sought to give effect to within the Bill.[170] The contents of the Bill including amendments combined with the haste with which it proceeded were to store up later problems with the legislation (and successor legislation).

In any event, the Bill received its third reading and passed the House of Commons on 23 June 1961.[171] A few days later, on 26 June 1961, the Bill was brought from the Commons to the House of Lords and was read for the first time.[172] The Bill was promoted in the House of Lords by Viscount

---

163 On the first date there appears to have been an objection taken by another MP upon grounds unrelated to the Bill itself: NRS AD63/481/1: Memorandum from N J P Hutchison, Scottish Home Department, to H H A Whitworth, Scottish Home Department, 15 February 1961.
164 NRS HH41/1434: Memorandum by the Secretary of State for Scotland, 16 January 1961.
165 Which became the Sheriffs' Pensions (Scotland) Act 1961 and the Crofters (Scotland) Act 1961 respectively.
166 NRS HH41/1434: Memorandum from J Glendinning to J J McCabe, Scottish Home Department, 22 December 1960.
167 HC Deb 10 March 1961, col 943.
168 HC Deb, Scottish Standing Committee, 20 June 1961, cols 3–52.
169 HC Deb, Scottish Standing Committee, col 4, per E G Willis MP (Edinburgh East, Labour).
170 HC Deb, Scottish Standing Committee, cols 4–5.
171 HC Deb 23 June 1961, col 1933.
172 HL Deb 26 June 1961, col 815.

Colville of Culross.[173] At the second reading stage in the House of Lords, on 5 July 1961, Lord Strathclyde expressed some misgivings about the Bill.[174] He stated that it would be 'not welcome' in certain quarters and that one of the 'great advantages' of Scots law over English law was not having the floating charge, as it was 'an unfair method of getting a preference in the case of liquidation'.[175] He considered it to be a negative point that Scots law in this area was becoming more like English law.[176] This, however, was the only dissenting opinion at this time and Lord Craigton stated that the Bill was 'welcomed by the Government', 'all political parties' and, according to his sources, 'all the learned and commercial interests in Scotland who will be concerned in its operation'.[177] He added that Lord Strathclyde's was the 'first unwelcoming voice' he had heard in relation to the Bill.[178] Certainly, very few negative views were expressed regarding the introduction of the floating charge itself (rather than specific details about the legislative provisions) as the legislation proceeded through Parliament.

After the second reading in the House of Lords the Bill proceeded to a Committee of the Whole House.[179] On 20 July 1961, with the House in Committee, the Bill was reported without amendment and the Bill was read a third time and passed.[180] The Bill received Royal Assent on 27 July 1961.[181] In doing so, it joined a limited number of Private Member Bills introduced by way of the ten-minute rule to have become Acts of Parliament.[182] The Act came into force on 27 October 1961.

173　Mark Colville, 4th Viscount Colville of Culross (1933–2010). For biographical details, see *The Times*, 30 April 2010, 72.

174　HL Deb 5 July 1961, cols 1434–1443.

175　This reflects some of the more 'traditional' Scottish views alluded to above and discussed in MacPherson, 'The "Pre-History" of Floating Charges in Scots Law', Chapter 1.

176　HL Deb 5 July 1961, col 1441. At the earlier Scottish Standing Committee stage, one of the MPs (J A Stodart: Edinburgh West, Unionist/Conservative) was also critical of English law, stating (perhaps mischievously): 'One of the things of which the Scottish legal system is proud is that it is based on Roman law as opposed to the much inferior system operating in this country, which is based on Saxon law' (HC Deb, Scottish Standing Committee, 20 June 1961, col 30).

177　HL Deb 5 July 1961, col 1442. The Earl of Lucan referred to the Bill as 'excellent' (col 1442).

178　HL Deb 5 July 1961, col 1442.

179　HL Deb 5 July 1961, col 1443.

180　HL Deb 20 July 1961, col 814.

181　HL Deb 27 July 1961, col 1149; HC Deb 27 July 1961, col 672.

182　For ten-minute rule Bills achieving Royal Assent between 1945 and 2010, see House of Commons Information Office, *The Success of Private Members' Bills* (2010), available at: *https://www.parliament.uk/globalassets/documents/commons-information-office/l03.pdf* (last accessed 25 October 2021).

E. PROVISIONS OF THE COMPANIES (FLOATING CHARGES) (SCOTLAND) ACT 1961

It is useful to consider how provisions of the 1961 Act developed from the recommendations of the LRCS through the passage of the Bill into the Act itself. By doing so, we can better comprehend the intended purpose and scope of particular statutory provisions and also identify key concerns for parties involved in the legislative process. This in turn can help us to have a deeper and more accurate understanding of not only the 1961 Act but also the current law, since successor legislation has inherited some of the earlier Act's content. It is not possible here to consider each and every provision of the 1961 Act. Instead, the focus will be upon selected key aspects of the floating charge, as outlined below.

(1) 'Definition' of floating charge

The LRCS report recommended that a 'definition' of the floating charge be included in any legislation and suggested the following:

> 'A security over the whole or a specified part of a company's undertaking and assets which shall not preclude the company from selling or otherwise dealing with such assets in the ordinary course of business until the company goes into liquidation, when the charge shall crystallize and become a fixed security over such of the company's assets as are subject to the charge.'[183]

There are a few notable aspects of this proposed definition. First, the scope of the proposed charge as regards property to be affected is familiar, given the form that the introduced floating charge took, yet the term 'company's undertaking and assets' was changed for the legislation (see further below). Secondly, the company's ability to sell or otherwise deal with assets subject to a floating charge was expressly stated to be limited to dealings in the ordinary course of the company's business. This is the position in English law and may represent the current position in Scots law by implication, but this is debatable.[184] Thirdly, the definition used the term 'crystallize' derived from English law, rather than 'attach' (which was used in the legislation that would follow), and stated expressly that the charge would 'become a fixed security' over charged property in the event of the chargor's liquidation.[185]

---

183 LRCS, *Eighth Report* (n 6) Appendix II, para. 1. See also para. 42 of the main part of the report.
184 See MacPherson, *Floating Charge* (n 8) para. 2–03.
185 See the next two sub-sections for further details.

As Professor Jack notes, the 1961 Act[186] did not ultimately contain a definition of the floating charge.[187] Instead, it referred to the effects of the floating charge largely based upon the English model. Hendry, at the Scottish Standing Committee stage, had noted that instead of defining 'floating charge' the amended Bill explained what a floating charge could do.[188] The 1961 Act stated that it was competent in Scots law to create a floating charge in favour of a creditor 'over all or any of the property, heritable and moveable, which may from time to time be comprised in its property and undertaking'.[189] It made clear that the floating charge would not affect any property that 'ceases prior to the commencement of the winding up of the company to be comprised in, and remains outwith, the company's property and undertaking'.[190] There have been some changes to the wording in the equivalent provisions in subsequent floating charges legislation, yet the substance is generally the same. It should be noted, however, that the 1961 Act required the use of an instrument of (floating) charge 'as nearly as practicable' to the form contained in the First Schedule to the Act or a bond or other written acknowledgment of debt 'incorporating words to the like effect'.[191] The restrictiveness of this was criticised and the Scottish Law Commission proposed a more flexible approach in line with the English law position, which led to the form being omitted from later legislation on floating charges.[192]

Returning to the 1961 Act, within the notes on clauses of the Bill in the House of Lords it was suggested that a floating charge is 'analogous in principle to a hypothec', and that some examples of hypothecs already existed in Scots law: the landlord's hypothec and the maritime hypothec.[193] It is certainly true that a floating charge is a hypothec in the general sense of the term, i.e. a security that does not depend upon the security holder's possession of the collateral property in order for the security to exist. However,

---

186 With the same being true of the successor Companies (Floating Charges and Receivers) (Scotland) Act 1972 and (the currently applicable) Companies Act 1985.

187 Jack (n 7) 36–37.

188 HC Deb, Scottish Standing Committee, 20 June 1961, col 7.

189 Companies (Floating Charges) (Scotland) Act 1961 s. 1(1).

190 Companies (Floating Charges) (Scotland) Act 1961 s. 1(2).

191 Companies (Floating Charges) (Scotland) Act 1961 s. 2.

192 Scottish Law Commission, *Report on the 1961 Act* (n 55) para. 13; Companies (Floating Charges and Receivers) (Scotland) Act 1972 s. 2; Companies Act 1985 s. 462.

193 NRS AD63/481/2: Revised Note (HL) on Bill: Notes on Clauses, Clause 1(1); and see accompanying Letter from N J P Hutchison, Scottish Home Department, to J H Gibson, Lord Advocate's Department, 29 June 1961. Notes on clauses can be considered the equivalent of explanatory notes that accompany present-day legislation.

it was a departure from existing hypothecs in Scots law due to its 'floating nature', which meant it did not, and does not, affect specific property until a later attachment event.[194]

(2) Attachment

As detailed above, the (proposed) definition of a floating charge in the LRCS report provided that it was a security over the 'undertaking and assets' of a company. Yet, under that definition, it was to crystallise and become a fixed security only over the company's assets (i.e. not 'undertaking and assets').[195] Archived correspondence highlights uncertainty about the meaning of the term 'undertaking and assets'. The decision was taken to adopt the term 'property and undertaking' in relation to the floating charge's creation and attachment during the Bill's progress, in order to reflect English practice and the existing use of the terminology for English law under the Companies Act 1948.[196] This has been discussed in more detail elsewhere.[197]

The 1961 Act specified that a floating charge would 'attach' to the property 'comprised in the company's property and undertaking not being excepted property' at the commencement of winding up.[198] The term 'property and undertaking' has persisted in the attachment provisions of later legislation. And, of course, the meaning of the term has proved to be highly controversial and is particularly unclear due to the decision in *Sharp v Thomson*,

---

194 For the nature of the floating charge before attachment, see MacPherson, *Floating Charge* (n 8) Ch. 2. The nature of the landlord's hypothec has been a matter of some debate, but it is better characterised as a fixed security arising by operation of law. See below and the discussion in MacPherson, *Floating Charge* (n 8) paras 8–61–8–62 and A Sweeney, *The Landlord's Hypothec* (Edinburgh: Edinburgh Legal Education Trust, 2021) paras 11–29 onwards. For details of the maritime hypothec (lien), see e.g. A J M Steven, *Pledge and Lien* (Edinburgh: Edinburgh Legal Education Trust, 2008) paras 9–05 and 10–55. A floating charge also differs from the landlord's hypothec and maritime hypothec because it is a voluntary security, whereas those other security rights arise by operation of law. It should be noted too that there is a lengthy history of voluntary hypothecs for heritable property in Scots law and the modern standard security is such a security – these are, however, fixed securities.

195 As well as being used in this context, the term 'assets' rather than 'property' was used elsewhere within Appendix II of the LRCS report – see e.g. the ranking provisions suggestions in para. 4; paras 6 and 7 regarding winding up by the court if the interests of the floating charge creditor were in jeopardy (this enforcement method was included in the 1961 Act and in subsequent legislation – see now Insolvency Act 1986 s. 122(2)); and paras 8–10.

196 NRS AD61/55: Note on Draft Appendix II to Report to the Lord Advocate on Remitted Subject No. 10, enclosed with Copy Letter from J H Gibson, Lord Advocate's Department, to W A Cook, Biggart, Lumsden & Co, 10 March 1960; NRS AD61/55: Letter from W A Cook, Biggart, Lumsden & Co, to J H Gibson, Lord Advocate's Department, 14 March 1960.

197 MacPherson, *Floating Charge* (n 8) paras 4–16 onwards.

198 Companies (Floating Charges) (Scotland) Act 1961 s. 1(2).

which was facilitated by the term's ambiguity.[199] In attempting to imitate English law and usage there appears to have been inadequate consideration given to the potential meaning of the term within Scots law. The decision to include the term 'property and undertaking' without further explanation has had significant repercussions that still reverberate in the present day.[200]

During the course of the Bill, some attention was given to when property would cease to be subject to the floating charge and therefore become incapable of being attached by it. Yet little clarity is provided. In one document, it was stated that when heritage was sold or goods delivered the property had ceased to be part of the company's property and undertaking and therefore the floating charge could not affect them.[201] Unfortunately, there was no suggestion as to the precise point at which heritable property was considered 'sold'. In another context relating to the Bill,[202] and following a query from the Professor's Committee to the Council of the WS Society,[203] W A Cook considered it to be clear that the date that 'acquisition' of heritable property was completed was when the price was paid in exchange for the disposition.[204] But this was expressly equated to the Scottish term 'settlement', which Cook suggested should be used instead.[205] Consequently, the intended meaning here is unclear. For goods, although the common law requires delivery for the transfer of ownership, the then applicable Sale of Goods Act 1893 allowed for ownership of sold goods to pass when the parties intended it to do so.[206] This is also true under the currently applicable Sale of Goods Act 1979.[207] Points made by the Lord Advocate at the standing committee stage regarding when goods sold in a shop would no longer be

---

199 *Sharp* (n 106). See the discussion and sources cited in MacPherson, *Floating Charge* (n 8) paras 7–14 onwards.

200 See MacPherson, *Floating Charge* (n 8) paras 4–07 onwards for detailed analysis of the terminology.

201 NRS AD63/481/2: Revised Note (HL) on Bill: Notes on Clauses, Clause 1(2).

202 The new s. 106C(1) of the Companies Act 1948, as it then stood in the Bill.

203 NRS AD63/481/1: Report by the Professor's [sic] Committee to the Council of the Society of Writers to Her Majesty's Signet on The Companies (Floating Charges) (Scotland) Bill, para. 21(b), enclosed with Letter from R C Notman, Society of Writers to HM Signet, to Lord Advocate, 22 March 1961. It was queried whether it was the date of the missives, the date of the disposition, the date of entry, the date when the price was exchanged or the date of recording in the Sasine Register.

204 NRS AD63/481/1: Letter from W A Cook, Biggart, Lumsden & Co, to J H Gibson, Lord Advocate's Department, 10 April 1961.

205 This was included in s. 106C(1) of the provisions to be inserted into the Companies Act 1948, although only in relation to property situated, and the charge being created, outside Great Britain.

206 Sale of Goods Act 1893 ss. 17(1) and 19(1).

207 The equivalent provision is now contained in Sale of Goods Act 1979 ss. 17(1) and 19(1).

subject to the floating charge are not fully explained, lack nuance and shed little light on the subject.[208]

All of this material seems to raise more questions than answers as to when property was intended to leave the ambit of a floating charge. Again, more time could have been expended exploring the issues and considering the consequences of the wording chosen but time was deemed to be of the essence in passing the legislation. Furthermore, the uncertainty that arose from the ambiguity of terms such as property and undertaking is also a reflection of the condition of Scots property law in the 1960s and in the following few decades.

Also of key relevance to the attachment of the floating charge under the 1961 Act was the statement within s. 1(2) that the provisions of the Companies Act 1948 relating to winding up, except s. 327(1)(c),[209] would have effect 'as if the charge were a fixed security over the property to which it has attached … '. This is the initial usage of what Professor Bill Wilson referred to as the 'statutory hypothesis'.[210] The wording in the 1961 Act indicates that the floating charge was intended to only have the effect of a fixed security within the confines of the liquidation statutory provisions. This seems to be narrower than the fixed security effect often ascribed to the floating charge, whereby it takes on the characteristics of the fixed security applicable to the property attached. For example, in *Forth & Clyde Construction Co Ltd v Trinity Timber & Plywood Co Ltd*,[211] the floating charge was deemed to attach to book debts (receivables) as if it were an intimated assignation in security.[212]

Substantially the same statutory wording has been used in later legislation for liquidation, while the equivalent wording for receivership and administration does not expressly state that the fixed security effect is limited to the application of particular provisions.[213] It could therefore be argued that

---

208 See MacPherson, *Floating Charge* (n 8) paras 8–09 onwards, for details.
209 This is a provision relating *inter alia* to the sale by a secured creditor of the heritable property over which they held security.
210 See W A Wilson, 'The Receiver and Book Debts' 1982 SLT (News) 129; and W A Wilson, *The Scottish Law of Debt*, 2nd edn (Edinburgh: W. Green, 1991). And see MacPherson, *Floating Charge* (n 8) paras 5–12 onwards for discussion.
211 *Forth & Clyde Construction Co Ltd v Trinity Timber & Plywood Co Ltd* 1984 SC 1.
212 Albeit that it was not considered to take on all of the characteristics of the security, e.g. there was not considered to be an actual transfer and the common law rules of catholic and secondary security were held not to apply. See Hardman and MacPherson, 'The Ranking of Floating Charges', Chapter 9 for more details.
213 For liquidation, Companies Act 1985 s. 463(2); for receivership, Insolvency Act 1986 ss. 53(7) and 54(6); and for administration, Insolvency Act 1986 Sch. B1, para. 115(4).

the effect of the statutory hypothesis in receivership and administration is broader than in liquidation, thus justifying the decision in *Forth & Clyde*, but this approach is problematic in other respects and the decision in *Forth & Clyde* is certainly questionable.[214]

(3) Definition of 'fixed security'

The contrast between the floating charge and fixed security was expressly drawn out within the 1961 Act, s. 8(1)(c), which contained a definition of the latter term:

> '"fixed security" in relation to any property of a company means any security, other than a floating charge or a charge having the nature of a floating charge, which on the winding-up of the company in Scotland would be treated as an effective security over that property, and (without prejudice to that generality) includes a security over that property created by way of an *ex facie* absolute disposition or assignation qualified by a back letter';

The LRCS report did not contain a definition of fixed security and neither did the early drafts of the Bill. When a definition was first inserted it only mentioned that the term included, for heritable property, a security created by way of *ex facie* absolute disposition and back letter, but this was replaced with a definition that provided more clarity as to the securities that were generally to have priority over the floating charge.[215] According to Hendry at the Scottish Standing Committee stage, critical comments by the Royal Faculty of Procurators in Glasgow led to the addition of the definition.[216] And the Professor's Committee to the Council of the WS Society had suggested that if the original definition of 'fixed security' was to remain it should be extended to include an *ex facie* absolute assignation and back letter in relation to moveable property.[217] Cook agreed with this proposal and the reference to such a security right was ultimately included in the

---

214 This is discussed in more detail in MacPherson, *Floating Charge* (n 8) paras 5–21 onwards.

215 See NRS AD63/481/2: Revised Note (HL) on Bill: Notes on Clauses, Clause 8.

216 HC Deb, Scottish Standing Committee, 20 June 1961, col 31; NRS AD63/481/1: Letter from Royal Faculty of Procurators in Glasgow to Secretary, Lord Advocate's Department, 28 April 1961 enclosing Memorandum on the Bill, para. 7. They suggested a definition in broad terms: 'any security or preferential right duly constituted (otherwise than by way of floating charge) including deposit, hypothec, completed diligence, lien, retention and security created by way of an *ex facie* absolute disposition whether or not qualified by a back letter'. They also stated that reference could be made to definitions in the Titles to Land Consolidation (Scotland) Act 1868 and the Conveyancing (Scotland) Act 1924.

217 NRS AD63/481/1: Report by the Professor's Committee (n 203) para. 18.

definition of 'fixed security' in s. 8(1)(c) of the 1961 Act, but without it being limited to the assignation of moveable property.[218]

Standard securities were introduced to Scots law by the Conveyancing and Feudal Reform (Scotland) Act 1970 and that Act specifies that they are the only heritable security that can be granted over land.[219] On the back of this, the definition of fixed security in the Companies (Floating Charges and Receivers) (Scotland) Act 1972 replaced the references to *ex facie* absolute dispositions and *ex facie* absolute assignations qualified by back letter with reference to security granted under the 1970 Act. Given that *ex facie* absolute assignations qualified by back letter remain possible for various types of property, such as incorporeal moveable property and short leases, the removal of express reference to this form of security from the definition of fixed security is highly questionable.[220] It shows that those involved with later floating charges legislation could (also) be criticised for exercising insufficient care regarding the content of the legislation.

(4) Ranking

The definition of fixed security is of significance within the context of ranking.[221] In the LRCS report, suggestions were made as to how the floating charge should rank against other security rights. It was proposed that if any assets were subject to: (1) a floating charge; and (2) a landlord's hypothec or a fixed security, then the hypothec or fixed security should have priority.[222] This was therefore to be the default ranking rule. At that stage, the landlord's hypothec was apparently not considered to be a fixed security but there was no further reference to other security rights arising by operation of law.

218 NRS AD63/481/1: Letter from Cook, 10 April 1961 (n 204); and see NRS AD63/481/1: Letter from W A Cook, Biggart, Lumsden & Co, to J H Gibson, Lord Advocate's Department, 2 March 1961.

219 1970 Act s. 9. More specifically, they are the only voluntary heritable security available over land or a real right in land that is capable of being recorded in the Register of Sasines and now registered in the Land Register. Consequently, there is non-registrable heritable property, such as a short lease, over which standard securities cannot be granted, and for which alternative security is used. Floating charges are, of course, voluntary securities that encompass heritable property; however, they are not technically heritable securities as they cannot be registered in the Register of Sasines or Land Register.

220 See MacPherson, *Floating Charge* (n 8) paras 7–93 onwards and 9–34 onwards for further discussion.

221 See Hardman and MacPherson, 'The Ranking of Floating Charges', Chapter 9 for detailed consideration of ranking.

222 LRCS, *Eighth Report* (n 6) Appendix II, para. 4.

The default rule for fixed securities and floating charges remained essentially the same in the 1961 Act as had been proposed by the LRCS.[223] However, the reference to landlord's hypothec was replaced with the wider term 'fixed security arising by operation of law'.[224] Hendry said in the Scottish Standing Committee that by this latter term he principally meant the landlord's hypothec but that it also included the solicitor's hypothec and the repairer's lien.[225] Viscount Colville similarly referred to the landlord's hypothec but also mentioned maritime hypothecs.[226] Fixed security arising by operation of law was therefore intended to be wide-ranging and inclusive of various implied (or tacit) security rights.[227] Knowledge of this information may have helped avoid some of the later uncertainty regarding the status of the landlord's hypothec in competition with a floating charge.[228]

In the LRCS report it was suggested that there should be an exception to the default ranking rule, allowing a floating charge to rank ahead of fixed securities, but not the landlord's hypothec, where certain conditions were met. These conditions were that: (i) the terms on which the floating charge was created prohibited the company from creating any later fixed security having priority over, or ranking *pari passu* with, the floating charge[229]; and (ii) the person in whose favour the later fixed security was created had 'actual notice' of the prohibition when their security was created.[230] Registration (in the register of charges) of the particulars of any restriction on the power of a company to grant additional securities ranking ahead of, or *pari passu* with, a floating charge would constitute actual notice of such particulars from the date of registration.[231]

The inclusion of the actual notice condition was intended to be a reflection of English law.[232] The LRCS report also stated that although in England

---

223 Companies (Floating Charges) (Scotland) Act 1961 s. 5(2).
224 Companies (Floating Charges) (Scotland) Act 1961 s. 5(1).
225 HC Deb, Scottish Standing Committee, 20 June 1961, cols 24–25.
226 HL Deb 5 July 1961, col 1439.
227 See also NRS AD63/481/2: Revised Note (HL) on Bill: Notes on Clauses, Clause 5, albeit that there is apparent misunderstanding about the role of possession in the context of tacit securities.
228 See the discussion in MacPherson, *Floating Charge* (n 8) paras 8–61 onwards.
229 This type of restriction is known as a negative pledge. For more details, regarding negative pledges and their effects under the current law, see Hardman and MacPherson, 'The Ranking of Floating Charges', Chapter 9.
230 LRCS, *Eighth Report* (n 6) Appendix II, para. 4(a) and (b). See NRS AD63/481/1: Letter from Cook, 10 April 1961 (n 204) for some discussion of when the fixed security holder could be considered to have actual notice.
231 LRCS, *Eighth Report* (n 6) Appendix II, para. 5. And see Appendix II, para. 15.
232 LRCS, *Eighth Report* (n 6) para. 46.

registration of a floating charge constituted actual notice of the charge to all persons, it was uncertain whether such registration would operate as notice of any restriction accompanying the charge, even if the relevant particulars of the restriction were registered.[233] The recommendation by the LRCS regarding the actual notice effect of registration of particulars of a restriction was included to avoid any such uncertainty.

By the time the 1961 Act was passed, however, the reference to 'actual notice' had been dropped. For a floating charge to rank ahead of a voluntary fixed security, the following conditions required to be met: (i) the contract or undertaking 'creating'[234] the fixed security was made or granted after the Act's commencement; (ii) the floating charge was registered before the right of the creditor in the fixed security was constituted as a real right; and (iii) the floating charge instrument prohibited the company from 'subsequently creating any fixed security having priority over, or ranking equally with, the floating charge'.[235] It should be noted that publicity through registration in the charges register was a requirement for a floating charge with negative pledge to rank ahead of a later fixed security.

During discussions regarding the Bill, it was stated that for floating charges the date of registration in the charges register was the crucial date for ranking competitions, while for other rights in security it was the date of becoming a real right, and this was all 'more in accordance with Scottish practice'.[236] Despite this recognition that ranking a floating charge with negative pledge from its registration date against fixed securities aligns more favourably with Scots law, due to its compliance with the publicity principle and reliance on the register, it is no longer the case. Since the Companies (Floating Charges) (Scotland) Act 1972, registration has not been the priority point for a floating charge to rank ahead of fixed securities.[237] The rule was omitted from that Act without explanation, which again indicates inattention or inadequate

---

233 LRCS, *Eighth Report* (n 6) para. 51; the cases of *Re Standard Rotary Machine Co* (1906) 95 LT 829 and *Wilson v Kelland* [1910] 2 Ch 306 were cited in support of this assertion. Under the current law, it is more likely that a party will be considered to have notice of a negative pledge due to registration in the charges register, see e.g. E McKendrick, *Goode and McKendrick on Commercial Law*, 6th edn (London: LexisNexis, 2020) paras 24.42 onwards.

234 The term 'to create' would have been more technically correct here, as the contract or undertaking does not itself create the security.

235 Companies (Floating Charges) (Scotland) Act 1961 s. 5(2)(a), (b) and (c).

236 NRS AD63/481/1: Letter from W A Cook, Biggart, Lumsden & Co, to J H Gibson, Lord Advocate's Department, 31 May 1961. See also NRS AD63/481/1: Copy Letter from J H Gibson, Lord Advocate's Department, to W A Cook, Biggart, Lumsden & Co, 18 May 1961.

237 For the equivalent ranking provisions within the 1972 Act see s. 5(1). For the current provisions, see Companies Act 1985 s. 464(1).

explanation as well as a departure from an approach better suited to integrating the floating charge into the law of security rights in Scotland. The ability of a floating charge to affect third parties, including those with real rights in property covered by the charge, supports a requirement that those parties are entitled to publicity of the existence of the floating security.

With respect to floating charges ranking *inter se*, the LRCS report recommended that floating charges securing debentures should rank in accordance with the dates of the debentures with the earlier having priority over those that were later.[238] The LRCS proposed that floating charges should rank according to the dates of the relevant instruments (and not according to registration dates) in order to follow English law.[239] The recommendation was initially adopted in the Bill but this was criticised. One of the grounds of objection was that there would be a period of up to twenty-one days within which a floating charge creditor would not know if another party had already been granted a floating charge, with such earlier charge not being registered until after the granting of the second floating charge.[240] If this were the case, the earlier granted charge would still rank ahead.

During the Bill's passage, Hendry briefly discussed the change from using the date of execution of the deed as the effective date for the ranking of floating charges, to using the date of registration, which was to apply to competitions between multiple floating charges and between floating charges with negative pledges and voluntary fixed securities.[241] It was stated that this change caused the removal of the provision regarding 'actual notice' as parties should be able to just check the charges register to determine if a floating charge prohibiting subsequent securities already existed.[242] The

---

238 LRCS, *Eighth Report* (n 6) Appendix II, para. 10. See para. 11 for the suggested definition of 'debenture' in this context.

239 NRS AD63/481/1: Letter from Cook, 10 April 1961 (n 204). Even though it was acknowledged that the ranking of charges according to their registration dates could be considered more in accordance with Scottish practice, Cook, at this stage, remained in favour of leaving the Bill as it was and thereby ranking floating charges according to the dates when they were granted.

240 NRS AD63/481/1: Report by the Professor's Committee (n 203) para. 7. See also NRS AD63/481/1: Letter from Cook, 10 April 1961 (n 204) – where it was stated that anyone lending money on security of the floating charge would require assurance from the company that no earlier floating charge had been granted and if such an assurance was given wrongfully that could constitute a criminal offence. The possibility of a creditor being defrauded in this way was, however, not considered to be a major risk.

241 HC Deb, Scottish Standing Committee, 20 June 1961, cols 25–27. See also NRS AD63/481/1: Report by the Professor's Committee (n 203) paras 7–14, who had suggested ranking floating charges from the date of registration as it would involve a public element, and that other security rights should rank from when they became real rights.

242 HC Deb, Scottish Standing Committee, 20 June 1961, col 27.

use of registration as a priority point, rather than notice, meant that the same ranking rule could apply to all parties holding later-created voluntary securities.[243]

The 1961 Act, therefore, ranked floating charges against one another on the basis of when they were registered, although floating charges received by the registrar for registration by the same postal delivery were to rank equally.[244] These continue to be the default rules for the inter-ranking of floating charges (i.e. where there is no negative pledge or ranking agreement). Given that the default ranking of floating charges (without negative pledges) depends on registration, the potential twenty-one-day blind period noted above does not apply. However, it is a well-known risk in relation to the (far more common) floating charge with negative pledge. This is because, since the Companies (Floating Charges and Receivers) (Scotland) Act 1972 (as discussed above), such a floating charge does not rank from its date of registration but from an earlier creation date against other floating charges and voluntary fixed securities, which is not publicly available information. It means that a party checking the charges register cannot be sure whether or not a (potentially prior-ranking) floating charge was created within the preceding twenty-one days,[245] and this could affect their decision-making or require them to obtain further information and/or assurances.

Within the LRCS report, an exception to the proposed rule regarding the ranking of floating charges *inter se* was that if two or more debentures provided that they would rank *pari passu* this would be given effect to.[246] The 1961 Act followed suit allowing agreements to rank floating charges in such a way, although the reference to *pari passu* was replaced with the

---

243 The application of a notice system, by contrast, could lead to inconsistent ranking outcomes. For example, A grants a floating charge with negative pledge to B, but before B registers, A grants fixed securities to C and D in turn, who each obtain real security rights and register in the charges register. If C had notice of B's floating charge and negative pledge but D did not, then the ranking relationship would appear to be a circle of priority (B > C; C > D; D > B) if there was a competition over the same property. This is a potential risk under English law. For further discussion of circles of priority, see Hardman and MacPherson, 'The Ranking of Floating Charges', Chapter 9.

244 Companies (Floating Charges) (Scotland) Act 1961 s. 5(3)–(4). The requirement for a specific ranking rule for floating charges received in the same postal delivery, if floating charges were to rank according to their date of registration, was suggested in NRS AD63/481/1: Report by the Professor's Committee (n 203) para. 7; and agreed with in NRS AD63/481/1: Letter from Cook, 10 April 1961 (n 204).

245 See e.g. Scottish Law Commission, *Report on Registration of Rights in Security by Companies* (Scot. Law Com. No. 197, 2004) para. 1.14.

246 LRCS, *Eighth Report* (n 6) Appendix II, para. 10.

term 'equally'.[247] During the Bill's progress, one organisation had, however, recommended that provision should be made for the extension of ranking agreements to allow for postponed or preferred ranking.[248] This was privately rejected by Cook on the basis that it would be an unnecessary complication and it was considered doubtful whether this was competent in England.[249] Provision for agreements enabling prior or postponed ranking was, however, made in the Companies (Floating Charges and Receivers) (Scotland) Act 1972[250] (in part to reflect the actual position in England)[251] and the current ranking rules also give effect to such agreements.[252]

(5) Diligence

The LRCS report did not expressly refer to the intended ranking relationship between floating charges and diligence. However, a provision dealing with the relationship was added to the Bill during its progress. Hendry noted during the Scottish Standing Committee stage that the priority of the floating charge holder was subject to a party who had exercised diligence, this being 'a creditor who has gone to the courts and has got a decree and has poinded certain assets'.[253] He explained that a party who had already executed diligence competently had priority over a charge holder. Hendry also stated that the floating charge 'does not come into effect until the beginning of the winding-up and the beginning of the winding-up has an equalising effect on diligences' and so, at an earlier stage, diligence could be validly executed over property that was subject to a floating charge.[254] He elaborated upon this by stating that 'if one has done one's diligence more than 60 days before liquidation, one very properly stands to benefit, but if one ... has done one's diligence within the 60 days, one ranks equally with other creditors'.[255] The

---

247 Companies (Floating Charges) (Scotland) Act 1961 s. 5(3).
248 NRS AD63/481/1: NRS AD63/481/1: Report by the Professor's Committee (n 203) paras 7–14.
249 NRS AD63/481/1: Letter from Cook, 10 April 1961 (n 204), citing *Re Benjamin Cope & Sons* (1914) 1 Ch 800 and *Re Automatic Bottle Makers Ltd* (1926) 1 Ch 412.
250 Companies (Floating Charges and Receivers) (Scotland) Act 1972 at s. 5(1).
251 Scottish Law Commission, *Report on the 1961 Act* (n 55) para. 16.
252 Companies Act 1985 s. 464(1). See Hardman and MacPherson, 'The Ranking of Floating Charges', Chapter 9.
253 HC Deb, Scottish Standing Committee, 20 June 1961, cols 12–13. Given the context and further statements, it seems safe to assume that he also intended to include equivalent diligences for other types of property, such as arrestment for incorporeal moveable property.
254 HC Deb, Scottish Standing Committee, 20 June 1961, col 15.
255 HC Deb, Scottish Standing Committee, 20 June 1961, cols 15–16.

reference to 'creditors' here seems to refer to unsecured creditors, who rank behind floating charge holders.[256]

Hansard records have been drawn upon by Wortley to show that the intended meaning of 'effectually executed diligence', referred to within the 1961 Act s. 1(2)(a) as having priority over a floating charge, was any diligence not made ineffectual by virtue of it having been executed within sixty days prior to liquidation.[257] The same term has been used in later legislation, including the Companies Act 1985 and the Insolvency Act 1986.[258]

A note accompanying the Bill in its passage through the House of Lords also supports the above-noted analysis based upon the Hansard material. In explaining what was meant by 'effectually executed diligence', reference was made to s. 327 of the Companies Act 1948.[259] This section specified that an arrestment or poinding of a company's property within sixty days of its winding up was ineffective. Consequently, any arrestment or poinding not rendered invalid in this way could be effectually executed diligence.[260] In addition, Cook had earlier queried whether floating charges ought to be made subject to rights of creditors who had executed arrestment or poinding more than sixty days prior to the commencement of the winding up.[261] The insertion of the 'effectually executed diligence' priority provision should be seen within this context.

Of course, a different and controversial meaning was given to the term in *Lord Advocate v Royal Bank of Scotland*,[262] where an arrestment without furthcoming was held not to be effectually executed diligence (despite its execution not being within sixty days of the commencement of the company's liquidation). Even a brief definition of the term in the 1961 Act, and repeated in later legislation, would have negated such a possibility. The

256 With the exception of the prescribed part, which has only existed since the Enterprise Act 2002. See Hardman and MacPherson, 'The Ranking of Floating Charges', Chapter 9 for more details.
257 Wortley (n 8) at 337–340.
258 Companies Act 1985 s. 463(1)(a); and Insolvency Act 1986 ss. 55(3)(a) and 60(1)(b). The term was also previously used in the Companies (Floating Charges and Receivers) (Scotland) Act 1972 ss. 1(2)(a), 15(2)(a) and 20(1)(b). For the sixty-day rule under the current law, see Insolvency Act 1986 s. 185(1)(a) applying Bankruptcy (Scotland) Act 2016 s. 24(6), (7), with adjustments. See also the 2016 Act s. 24(2), (3), the latter of which (combined with Insolvency Act 1986 s. 185(1)(a)) provides a similar sixty-day rule for the vesting of an inhibitor's rights of challenge in the liquidator.
259 AD63/481/2: Revised Note (HL) on Bill: Notes on Clauses, Clause 1(2).
260 Companies Act 1948 s. 327(1)(a). It also included an equivalent rule for poinding of the ground (s. 327(1)(d)).
261 NRS AD63/481/1: Letter from Cook, 2 March 1961 (n 218). See also D G Antonio, 'Correspondence' (1961) 65 *The Accountants' Magazine* 942.
262 *Lord Advocate v RBS* (n 4).

recent Inner House decision in *MacMillan v T Leith Developments Ltd*[263] has, however, overturned the decision in *Lord Advocate v RBS*. The court in *MacMillan* adopted an interpretation in line with what was originally intended.[264] As acknowledged by Lord President Carloway, the Hansard material supported the decision reached in *MacMillan*, albeit that he did not consider the criteria from *Pepper v Hart*[265] to have been met and so could not rely on that material.[266]

(6) Registration of charges

As well as allowing for companies to grant a floating charge, the 1961 Act introduced to Scots law the registration of charges regime for floating charges and other types of security right. Given the potential impact of floating charges on third party creditors, it was considered necessary to introduce some form of registration to provide publicity to others. The absence of machinery that could provide the necessary publicity for the granting of non-possessory security over corporeal moveables had caused such securities to be historically rejected in Scots law, as discussed in the Pre-History of Floating Charges in Scots Law chapter. The registration of charges mechanism was believed to overcome this obstacle.[267]

Due to identified difficulties with registering floating charges in the Register of Sasines and the Register of Inhibitions and Adjudications,[268] the LRCS had proposed the use of a register of charges based upon the English model. It was recommended that the English system should be adopted not only for floating charges but for a whole range of fixed securities, as was

---

263 [2017] CSIH 23, 2017 SC 642.
264 For discussion of the relationship between floating charges and diligence now, see A D J MacPherson, 'The Circle Squared? Floating Charges and Diligence after *MacMillan v T Leith Developments Ltd*' (2018) Juridical Review 230.
265 [1993] AC 593. As per Lord Browne-Wilkinson at 634, 'reference to Parliamentary material should be permitted as an aid to the construction of legislation which is ambiguous or obscure or the literal meaning of which leads to an absurdity. Even in such cases references in court to Parliamentary material should only be permitted where such material clearly discloses the mischief aimed at or the legislative intention lying behind the ambiguous or obscure words. In the case of statements made in Parliament, as at present advised I cannot foresee that any statement other than the statement of the Minister or other promoter of the Bill is likely to meet these criteria'.
266 *MacMillan* (n 263) para. [56]. He did not consider the wording to be sufficiently ambiguous. Cf Lord Drummond Young in *MacMillan* at paras [98]–[102] who believed the wording to be ambiguous or obscure enough to rely upon parliamentary material.
267 NRS AD63/481/2: Revised Note (HL) on Bill: Notes on Clauses, Clause 6.
268 See MacPherson, *Floating Charge* (n 8) paras 7–06 onwards for further details.

also the case in England.[269] In the report it was suggested that the relevant provisions of the Companies Act 1948 regarding the registration of charges should be applied to certain 'charges' granted by companies registered in Scotland. These included 'heritable security', 'security over incorporeal moveable property' and 'floating charge[s]'.[270]

Provisions for registration were included within the Bill. It was noted internally during the Bill's progress that the registration of charges provisions were included for security rights beyond the floating charge 'so that the Scottish register may be as fully informative to potential debenture-holders as the English, and because it might otherwise mislead' regarding existing security rights granted by the company.[271] This sentiment was eventually reflected in the legislation, as s. 6 of the 1961 Act stated that the registration of charges regime was to apply to Scottish companies: 'For the purpose of securing the publication of floating charges created by companies and other charges so created which ought to be published for the information of persons considering taking security from such companies by way of floating charge'. In addition, Cook stated in a letter to Gibson that 'the recommendations of the [LRCS] about the registration of fixed securities were incidental to the requirement that floating charges had to be registered' and that he did not think 'the Committee considered whether their recommendations went further than the obligations imposed on companies in England'.[272] He also added, '[t]heoretically it seems right that all fixed securities should be registered and this has the advantage that the Company's file would then disclose the true position' but if the provisions differed from England and gave rise to 'practical difficulties' he did not object to their modification.[273]

The particular security rights requiring registration were refined during the course of the Bill's passage through Parliament. In a letter regarding the Bill, Cook wrote that for practical purposes the categories of incorporeal moveable property over which security rights did not need to be registered appeared to comprise: stocks and shares, insurance policies and ('possibly') interests under a contract (but obviously excluding book debts, due to express provision regarding registration of security over such property).[274]

269 LRCS, *Eighth Report* (n 6) paras 48–50.
270 LRCS, *Eighth Report* (n 6) Appendix II, paras 12–13, regarding the application of s. 95(1) and (2) of the Companies Act 1948. The particulars of prohibition of subsequent fixed securities were also to be registered – see above.
271 NRS HH41/1434: Memorandum by the Secretary of State for Scotland, 16 January 1961.
272 NRS AD63/481/1: Letter from Cook, 2 March 1961 (n 218).
273 NRS AD63/481/1: Letter from Cook, 2 March 1961 (n 218).
274 NRS AD63/481/1: Letter from Cook, 31 May 1961 (n 236).

Hendry acknowledged that security over stocks and shares and investments had been omitted from the registration requirements within the Bill on the basis of representations regarding the impracticability of registering securities over such property.[275] Requiring registration of security over those property types would also mean that the requirements were more onerous than in England, which was not considered desirable, and so it was decided that the categories included for incorporeal property were to correspond with those in English law.[276]

The inclusion of charges over certain types of property provoked debate. For example, in the context of discussing the inclusion of security over 'goodwill' (which ultimately made it into the 1961 Act),[277] one MP in the Scottish Standing Committee stated: '[i]t is just not good enough to tell the Committee that we should include certain legal terminology in a Scottish Statute just because it appears in an English Act. That does not always work out satisfactorily'.[278] Due to subsequent problems with the floating charge in other areas, including as a result of using terms such as 'property and undertaking' in imitation of the English position, these comments seem prescient.[279]

The 1961 Act provided that *inter alia* a 'charge on land wherever situated' (with further detailed description about what was and was not included), a security over certain specified types of incorporeal moveable property (including book debts, various types of intellectual property and calls made but not paid), and a floating charge were all to be registered within twenty-one days of their creation, otherwise they would be void against the liquidator

275 HC Deb, Scottish Standing Committee, 20 June 1961, cols 43–45; AD63/481/2: Revised Note (HL) on Bill: Notes on Schedules – s. 106A of the Companies Act 1948. For example, see NRS AD63/481/1: Memorandum by the Committee of Scottish Bank General Managers on Companies (Floating Charges) (Scotland) Bill, where it was stated that to require registration of all securities over incorporeal moveable property, including every transfer in security of a stock exchange investment, 'would be impracticable and create an amount of work quite out of proportion to any advantage gained'. NRS AD63/481/1: Letter from Cook, 2 March 1961 (n 218) – Cook noted that he had spoken to the secretary of one of the Scottish banks and he had confirmed that the requirements for registration of charges 'would cause a considerable amount of work' in relation to, for example, investment trust companies and companies trading shares.

276 Corresponding to s. 95(2)(e), (g) and (i) of the Companies Act 1948: AD63/481/2: Revised Note (HL) on Bill: Notes on Schedules – s. 106A of the Companies Act 1948.

277 Companies (Floating Charges) (Scotland) Act 1961 Second Schedule, inserting s. 106A(2)(c) (iii) into the Companies Act 1948.

278 HC Deb, Scottish Standing Committee, 20 June 1961, col 47 per J McInnes MP (Glasgow Central, Labour).

279 See MacPherson, *Floating Charge* (n 8) paras 4–07 onwards.

and any creditor of the company.[280] Various particulars of charges required to be registered under the 1961 Act and these included, for a floating charge, a statement of any restrictions on the power of the company to grant additional securities ranking in priority to, or *pari passu* with, the floating charge (i.e. a negative pledge).[281]

Following some doubt being cast upon the meaning of the date of a creation of a charge it was decided that this should be made clear.[282] It was expressly stated in the 1961 Act that, within the context of the inserted Part IIIA of the Companies Act 1948, the date of creation of a floating charge was 'the date on which the instrument creating the floating charge was executed by the company creating the charge', while for other charges (i.e. security rights other than floating charges) it was 'the date on which the right of the person entitled to the benefit of the charge was constituted as a real right'.[283] These creation dates, following their repetition within later legislation, would also be used to interpret the meaning of the ranking provisions within the Companies Act 1985 s. 464.[284] A floating charge with negative pledge was thereby held to rank from the date of its execution even if it was registered after a fixed security became a real right. This would not have been possible under the 1961 Act as a floating charge could only rank ahead of a fixed security if it was registered before the fixed security became a real right.[285]

It should be noted that certain fears were raised regarding the requirement to register an *ex facie* absolute disposition of heritage or *ex facie* absolute assignation of a long lease or of incorporeal moveable property. This was, in part, because it would constitute evidence in a public register that the deed was in security and not *ex facie* absolute, so future advances

---

280 Companies (Floating Charges) (Scotland) Act 1961 Second Schedule, inserting s. 106A(1)–(2) into the Companies Act 1948.
281 Companies (Floating Charges) (Scotland) Act 1961 Second Schedule, inserting s. 106D(1) into the Companies Act 1948 (in particular regarding the restriction – s. 106D(1)(b)(v)).
282 See e.g. NRS AD63/481/1: Royal Faculty of Procurators in Glasgow Memorandum (n 216) para. 8, for problems raised; and NRS AD63/481/1: Report by the Professor's Committee (n 203) para. 21(c); NRS AD63/481/1: Letter from Cook, 10 April 1961 (n 204).
283 Companies (Floating Charges) (Scotland) Act 1961 Second Schedule, inserting s. 106A(10) into the Companies Act 1948. See also NRS AD63/481/1: Letter from Cook, 2 March 1961 (n 218), in which it was stated that a heritable security was probably not created until it was recorded in the Sasine Register and that a security over debt was not created until intimated to the debtor and 'it might therefore be desirable to make it clear' that a floating charge would be created on the date of its execution by the company.
284 See *AIB Finance Ltd v Bank of Scotland* 1993 SC 588.
285 See above in section E(4) on ranking.

by the creditor after registration would not be secured.[286] Cook disagreed that disclosing the security nature of the transaction, by virtue of registration, would mean that future advances by the creditor after registration would not be secured.[287] He did suggest, though, that the Bill should provide certainty in this regard.[288] Such a change was made and referred to by Hendry during the Scottish Standing Committee stage.[289] The 1961 Act provided (in what became s. 106A(9) of the Companies Act 1948) that, for the avoidance of doubt, for a charge created by way of *ex facie* absolute disposition or assignation qualified by back letter, compliance with the registration requirements of s. 106A(1) would not 'of itself render the charge unavailable as security for indebtedness incurred after the date of the compliance'.

A further registration issue related to the Sasine Register. During the passage of the Bill, the Keeper of the Registers of Scotland expressed concern regarding the creation of a floating charge over heritable property without recording the charge in the General Register of Sasines.[290] This was rejected and is discussed elsewhere.[291] The 1961 Act contained a provision that stated that a floating charge would have effect in relation to any heritable property in Scotland notwithstanding that the floating charge was not recorded in the Register of Sasines.[292] There is an equivalent provision, noting the effectiveness of a floating charge despite the absence of registration in the Land Register, in the currently applicable Companies Act 1985 s. 462(5).

(7) Assignation of floating charges

It was pointed out by the Professor's Committee to the Council of the WS Society that there was no provision in the Bill for a party to assign a floating

---

286 NRS AD63/481/1: Report by the Professor's Committee (n 203) paras 15–17.
287 NRS AD63/481/1: Letter from Cook, 10 April 1961 (n 204). In support, he cited the article on 'absolute dispositions' in Viscount Dunedin et al. (eds), *Encyclopaedia of the Laws of Scotland* Vol. I (1926) 14 and the Lord Justice Clerk's opinion in *National Bank of Scotland v Union Bank of Scotland* (1885) 13 R 380 at 390.
288 NRS AD63/481/1: Letter from Cook, 10 April 1961 (n 204). On a similar note, in NRS AD63/481/1: Memorandum by the Committee of Scottish Bank General Managers (n 275), it was stated, with respect to s. 106D(1)(b)(ii), that it should be declared competent to register a charge securing all money due and to become due.
289 HC Deb, Scottish Standing Committee, 20 June 1961, col 49.
290 NRS HH41/1434: Letter from G Black, Keeper of the Registers of Scotland, to N E Sharp, Scottish Home Department, 11 January 1961.
291 MacPherson, *Floating Charge* (n 8) paras 7–06 onwards.
292 Companies (Floating Charges) (Scotland) Act 1961 s. 3.

charge and it was suggested that there should be provision for this and for the registration of an assignation to identify the assignee.[293] In correspondence referring to this criticism, Cook stated that he did not think it was necessary to provide a form of assignation of a floating charge.[294] He wrote that the proposed s. 106D(1)(b)(iv) of the Companies Act 1948 was identical with s. 98(1)(b)(iv) that applied in English law (the relevant sections stating that the details of the persons entitled to the charge required to be registered with the charge). Cook added that he did not know whether assignments of charges were registered in England but (rightly) surmised that only the name(s) of the person(s) originally entitled to the charge would be entered in the charges register.[295] Again, there was an apparent urge to replicate the English position but while a requirement to register an assignation may have been deemed too onerous in comparison to English law, this was never properly examined.

The 1961 Act contained no provision for assignation of floating charges and this is also true of later legislation.[296] Nevertheless, it has been judicially held that floating charges are assignable.[297] This seems to be in line with what was intended by those involved with the original floating charges legislation and is plainly commercially desirable. However, further certainty could have been provided by stating within the Act that floating charges could be assigned and outlining how this could be achieved, e.g. if intimation to the chargor in the same way as for claims is required and whether a charge can be assigned separately from an underlying secured debt claim.[298]

(8) Receivers

There was some pressure during the Bill's progress for the inclusion of provisions for the appointment of a receiver and manager to enforce a floating

293 NRS AD63/481/1: Report by the Professor's Committee (n 203) para. 19.
294 NRS AD63/481/1: Letter from Cook, 10 April 1961 (n 204).
295 NRS AD63/481/1: Letter from Cook, 10 April 1961 (n 204).
296 Bankruptcy and Diligence etc. (Scotland) Act 2007 s. 42, does provide for assignation of floating charges by registration in the Register of Floating Charges. However, that provision, along with the rest of Part 2 of the Act, has never been brought into force. See A J M Steven and H Patrick, 'Reforming the Law of Secured Transactions in Scotland', in L Gullifer and O Akseli (eds), *Secured Transactions Law Reform: Principles, Policies and Practice* (London: Bloomsbury, 2016) 253 at 262–263.
297 *Libertas-Kommerz GmbH v Johnson* 1977 SC 191; cf W Lucas, 'The Assignation of Floating Charges' 1996 SLT (News) 203.
298 See MacPherson *Floating Charge* (n 8) para. 2–24 n 74 for some discussion.

charge. The Committee of the Scottish Bank General Managers stated that they were 'disappointed and perturbed' that the Bill omitted any such provision and criticised the consequent necessity of liquidation for a creditor to enforce their security.[299] They expressed their view that Scots and English law in the area should be the same and that the advantages of the floating charge would not be fully achieved unless there was a power to appoint a receiver and manager.[300] The Professor's Committee to the Council of the WS Society suggested the facility to appoint a receiver should be introduced so that a floating charge creditor would have an alternative offering better prospects than placing a party into liquidation.[301] They stated that the full benefit of the floating charge could be lost if receivership in some form was not introduced.

In the House of Lords, Viscount Colville pointed out that although there was no provision for the appointment of a receiver, a floating charge holder had a safeguard if they thought their interest was going to be in jeopardy, as they could go to court and ask for a winding up (which would cause the floating charge to attach).[302] As well as being included in the 1961 Act, such a provision has appeared in subsequent legislation, despite the introduction of other enforcement methods, namely receivership and administration.[303]

Hendry stated in correspondence that it was not practicable to include receivers and managers, or the appointment of judicial factors (as an equivalent) in the Bill in 1961, as there was insufficient time remaining in the session and it would not be possible to pass the Bill in the time available if various interested parties had to be consulted.[304] As such, time pressures again played a role in the final form taken by the 1961 Act. Hendry also referred to the conclusion in the LRCS report that receivers should not

---

299 NRS AD63/481/1: Memorandum by the Committee of Scottish Bank General Managers (n 275). See also NRS HH41/1434: Letter from Companies Registration Office, Edinburgh, to H H A Whitworth, Scottish Home Department, 5 December 1960. For some comments on the omission of receivers, see AD63/481/2: Revised Note (HL) on Bill: Notes on Clauses, Annex: Omission of Provision for Receivers.

300 NRS AD63/481/1: Memorandum by the Committee of Scottish Bank General Managers (n 275).

301 NRS AD63/481/1: Report by the Professor's Committee (n 203) paras 3–6.

302 HL Deb 5 July 1961, cols 1438–1439.

303 1961 Act at s. 4. This was followed by the Companies (Floating Charges and Receivers) (Scotland) Act 1972 s. 4. For the provision under the current legislation, see Insolvency Act 1986 s. 122(2).

304 NRS AD63/481/1: Copy Letter from F Hendry MP to J O Leslie, Secretary, the Committee of Scottish Bank General Managers, 27 April 1961, enclosed with Letter from F Hendry MP to J H Gibson, Lord Advocate's Department, 27 April 1961.

be introduced and added that recommendations to the contrary had been too late. The principal perceived problem was that there was no codified English statute on the matter and codification would be a 'monumental task'.[305] Another (internal) correspondent suggested that:

> 'Even if the absence of any remedy other than compulsory winding up limits severely the number of cases in which advantage is taken of the new powers it should not act as an absolute deterrent: in other words we should expect many companies in good standing to benefit.'[306]

This was a view broadly shared by others.[307]

Of course, it was not long before the issue was revisited and receivers were introduced by the Companies (Floating Charges and Receivers) (Scotland) Act 1972. In the Scottish Law Commission Report preceding the legislation, the necessity of 'codifying' the English law of receivers was rejected and the merits of receivership were identified.[308] These merits included the possibility of 'reviv[ing] the fortunes of a company and prevent[ing] unnecessary liquidation', the fact that a floating charge holder's powers were 'weakened by his inability' to enforce the security other than by liquidation, as well as the disparity between English law and Scots law, which was viewed as particularly problematic for corporate groups containing Scottish and English companies.[309] As demonstrated by later case law, however, fitting floating charges and receivership into Scots law produced considerable difficulties.[310]

F. CONCLUSION

There were a number of crucial factors that led to the introduction of the Scottish floating charge. The rejection of floating charges at common law in combination with the commercial impracticality of transferring possession to constitute security over corporeal moveable property made Scots law

---

305 NRS AD63/481/1: Copy Letter from Hendry, 27 April 1961 (n 304). See also AD63/481/2: Revised Note (HL) on Bill: Notes on Clauses, Annex: Omission of Provision for Receivers.

306 NRS AD63/481/1: Letter from N J P Hutchison, Scottish Home Department, to J H Gibson, Lord Advocate's Department, 27 February 1961.

307 See e.g. Antonio (n 129) at 173 onwards, reflecting on his earlier article D G Antonio, 'A Plea for Receiverships under Scottish Floating Charges' (1960) 64 *The Accountants' Magazine* 731.

308 Scottish Law Commission, *Report on the 1961 Act* (n 55) paras 36 onwards.

309 Scottish Law Commission, *Report on the 1961 Act* (n 55) paras 36 onwards.

310 See e.g. *Lord Advocate v RBS* (n 4); *Forth & Clyde* (n 211); *Ross v Taylor* 1985 SC 156; *Sharp* (n 106). And see G L Gretton, 'The Story of the Scots Law Floating Charge: 1961 to Date', Chapter 4.

seem unresponsive to modern business needs.[311] Meanwhile, the relative economic problems faced by Scotland in the post-war period helped to create demand for the reform of the law of rights in security to support economic activity. English law already offered security rights that were considered commerce friendly, particularly the floating charge, and this provided an example as to how Scots law could be reformed.

The differences in the laws of rights in security between Scotland and England were highlighted by scenarios in which bodies, such as the White Fish Authority, offered loans to companies in both countries but demanded security. Businesses operating in Scotland were disadvantaged by their general inability to offer non-possessory security over their corporeal moveables. This, along with some pressure from parliamentarians, led to the issue of security over moveables being remitted to the Law Reform Committee for Scotland, which proved to be a focal point for various organisations to press the case for reform.

Given that the LRCS were required to consider the reform of security over moveables in part because of the differences between Scots law and English law, it is unsurprising that they recommended the introduction of an adapted version of the English floating charge, a security that was flexible and commercially attractive to lenders. This position seemed to be supported by a general move in other jurisdictions away from the rejection of non-possessory security rights, including in systems sharing Scots law's Civilian property law heritage. Instead, registration could be used as an alternative to possession to provide publicity to third parties.

The existence of a registration of charges regime for England that could be adopted readily for Scottish companies facilitated the introduction of a floating charge, especially since the entries corresponded to legal persons rather than specific items of property.[312] The position in England and identified impracticalities and drawbacks of limiting the floating charge to only certain types of property were also influential in supporting the recommendation to allow a floating charge to cover all property of a company,

---

311 This is arguably an example of the dysfunctionality of law discussed by A Watson, *Society and Legal Change*, 2nd edn (Philadelphia, Temple University Press, 2001) 4 onwards in so far as the existing law did not respond adequately to societal requirements, or at least the 'requirements' of certain key groups within society. Related to this, Gretton, 'Registration of Company Charges' (n 10) at 150 has suggested that the continued existence of the registration of charges regime, originally introduced to Scots law by the 1961 Act, may itself be an example of such 'dysfunctionality'.

312 Floating charges are closely tied to the grantor's patrimony – see MacPherson, *Floating Charge* (n 8) for detailed discussion of this.

including heritable property. Applying the charges regime to security rights other than floating charges would also align the Scottish position more with English law and allow the register to give a more complete picture of security rights affecting the company's property. By shedding further light on these issues and others, the chapter has given at least partial answers to some of the previously unanswered questions regarding the Scots law floating charge.

The agitation for reform which had already built up in parliament and elsewhere continued after the publication of the LRCS report. In the absence of governmental agreement as to which department should have responsibility for implementing legislation, Forbes Hendry MP appeared with a draft Bill. With assistance from the Scottish Home Department and the Lord Advocate's Department, Hendry's Private Member's Bill introduced by way of the ten-minute rule progressed through Parliament quickly and received Royal Assent. The importance of 'background' figures, such as W A Cook and J H Gibson, in progressing the legislation and shaping the form that the legislation took is clear from the material discussed in this chapter.

The examination of certain provisions of the 1961 Act above has shown that there were a number of alterations prior to the legislation's passing, often in response to suggestions made by interested parties or resulting from discussions of individuals involved in drafting the statute. Various provisions were, however, included without full consideration of their implications, while other relevant issues were simply overlooked or ignored. Analysis of the 1961 Act remains instructive with respect to the current version of the floating charge, as regards matters such as the charge's definition, the meaning of fixed security and the charge's ranking against other rights, albeit that there have been subsequent changes in these areas (and not always positive ones). The introduction of the floating charge into Scots law would perhaps have been smoother and ultimately less problematic had the starting point for each issue been how the floating charge could be integrated into Scots law rather than identifying what the position in England was. Nevertheless, there were and are clear commercial advantages in adopting solutions that align with the English position.

The reforms brought about by the 1961 Act were quickly acknowledged as significant commercial developments but there was some wariness as to how well the floating charge would fit with Scots law. One generally positive commentator noted that the charge was 'a bold break with tradition' and perceived that it 'may not be universally acclaimed'.[313] His sentiments and those expressed by writers such as Bill Wilson, who queried whether the legislation took proper account of aspects of property law and conveyancing,[314] foreshadow the battles involving the floating charge in Scots law in the following decades, which still resonate today.

---

313 D G Antonio, 'Companies (Floating Charges) (Scotland) Act, 1961' (1961) 6 JLSS 241 at 241. See also D G Antonio, 'Companies (Floating Charges) (Scotland) Act, 1961' (1961) 65 *The Accountants' Magazine* 647.
314 W A Wilson, 'Floating Charges' 1962 SLT (News) 53 at 55; W A Wilson, 'The Companies (Floating Charges) (Scotland) Act 1961' [1962] JBL 65 at 66; W A Wilson, 'The Companies (Floating Charges) (Scotland) Act, 1961' (1962) 25 MLR 445 at 448.

4 The Story of the Scots Law Floating Charge: 1961 to Date

George L Gretton

A. INTRODUCTION
B. LEGISLATION: A BIRD'S EYE VIEW
C. CONSULTATIONS AND REPORTS
    (1) Introduction
    (2) The consultations and reports
D. SOME PARTICULAR TOPICS
    (1) The literature
    (2) Enforcement – attachment – crystallisation – liquidation –
         receivership – administration
    (3) Ranking and diligence
    (4) *Sharp v Thomson*
    (5) Publicity/registration
         (a) Crystallisation
         (b) The central bank exemption
         (c) The strange tale of Part 2 of the 2007 Act
E. PERSONAL REFLECTIONS

A. INTRODUCTION

Three score years have passed, during which the floater has changed (one hesitates to write 'developed'). Most of the changes have been in matters of detail, but there have been two major exceptions: enforcement, and ranking. As to the first there was the introduction of receivership by the Companies (Floating Charges and Receivers) (Scotland) Act 1972 (the 1972 Act) and its replacement, by the Enterprise Act 2002, by administration.[1] As to the second, ranking, there have been two major changes, in

---

1 Administration dates to the Insolvency Act 1985, but its displacement of receivership came from the Enterprise Act 2002 s. 242 onwards.

2002 and in 2020. The Enterprise Act 2002 effected: (a) a ranking down-grade, through the introduction of the 'prescribed part'[2]; and (b) a ranking upgrade through the abolition of Crown preference.[3] This abolition was, however, reversed by the Finance Act 2020,[4] so that the ranking of the floater is, from 2020, lower than it has ever been. In addition to these actual changes there have been some unimplemented changes and these too will be mentioned.

To list every actual or proposed change, however minor, would make dull reading, so what follows is selective, but, even with selection, a connected and engaging narrative is hardly possible. One of the difficulties (and not only a difficulty confronting the historian) is that the floater is not a neatly demarcated topic. It is an area of land[5] co-owned by three neighbouring proprietors, all strong-willed, namely (in alphabetical order, so as to upset nobody) the Laird of Company Law, the Laird of Insolvency Law and the Laird of Property Law. And between this co-owned area of land and the estates of those three lairds can be found no stockproof dykes, hedges or fences.

Critics of the floater will find in this history not much of comfort; perhaps they will opine that after sixty years the floater is not much better than it was in 1961. The editors have asked me to include, in this account, something about my own criticisms, made chiefly in the 1980s, perhaps on the footing that I myself was, to a tiny extent, part of the history and that my thoughts might be worth recording before I have ceased to float. I do so in the final part of this chapter.

Unsurprisingly, key litigation about floating charges took place predomi-nantly in the first half of its history, those decisions resulting in answers (good or bad) to many questions. Of course there is no clear break at the thirty-year mark, significant cases in the second thirty years including *Sharp v Thomson*[6] and *MacMillan v T Leith Developments Ltd*.[7] The former was about the interaction of the floater with the law of property, the latter about its interaction with the law of diligence. They are thus typical, for much of

2 Enterprise Act 2002 s. 252.

3 Enterprise Act 2002 s. 251.

4 Finance Act 2020 ss. 98 and 99.

5 This metaphor does not fit 'floating' but I am unabashed. 'The pot-pourri of metaphors is enter-taining. It floats, sleeps, shifts, hovers, swoops, and finally crystallises,' G W Wilton, *Company Law: Principal Distinctions between the Laws of England and Scotland* (Edinburgh: Hodge & Co, 1923) 15.

6 1994 SC 503, affd 1995 SC 45, rev 1997 SC (HL) 66.

7 [2017] CSIH 23, 2017 SC 642.

the history of the floating charge has been the history of collision – collisions with the rest of the law. So violent was the collision in *Sharp* that it came near to sinking property law. Dr MacPherson has suggested that around the thirty-year mark there took place a shift in judicial attitudes, with decisions in the earlier period being more favourable to floating charge holders than in the later period.[8]

One more preliminary matter, not about the history of the floater as such but about the way it functions in Scots law as opposed to English law. This question of function is a background to the history. It can be put in a nutshell: *the floating charge is more important in Scotland than it is in England*. In England there can be *fixed equitable* charges over property of any kind, moveable and immoveable. Such charges 'in equity' need not conform to the requirements imposed on securities 'at law'. For example, an equitable charge on land granted by a company, though it must be registered in the Companies Register, does not have to be registered in the Land Registry. So flexible and useful are such fixed charges – whether over realty or personalty – that an equitable charge that floats has, consequentially, a rather limited function.[9] (It acts as a long-stop, to catch what the fixed charges may miss and it gives some power of control.) There is nothing equivalent in Scots law to fixed equitable charges. Hence in Scotland the floater does the job *not only* of the English floater *but also* (to a large extent) the job of the English fixed equitable change. This is one of the reasons why the present chapter gives some space to the various projects for the reform of the law of moveable security, because the effect of such reform would be to introduce to Scotland something parallel to – though by no means the same as – English fixed equitable charges, the effect of such reform being to reduce substantially the significance of the floating charge, as far as moveable property is concerned. Indeed, they might even lead to the eventual disappearance of the floater.[10] As for immoveable property, nobody suggests that it should be possible (as it is possible in England) for there to be a fixed security that is not registered in the Land Register, and so in Scots law the floating charge over land has, and is likely to continue to have, a significance it does not have in English law.

8 A D J MacPherson, *The Floating Charge* (Edinburgh: Edinburgh Legal Education Trust, 2020) para. 7–52.
9 Though here one must mention *Re Spectrum Plus Ltd* [2005] 2 AC 680, which to some extent restricted the scope of fixed equitable charges.
10 Cf what has happened to the floater in New Zealand, Australia, most of Canada and so on as a result of legislation based on art. 9 of the Uniform Commercial Code.

The temptation to compare and contrast the Scottish and English floating charge must not be further indulged in a historical chapter[11] – except for one last point, which, again, though not historical in itself, must be mentioned as a background to the history, not least for any non-Scottish reader. In England the equitable charge is a single species, with two subspecies: fixed and floating. Thus fixed and floating equitable charges are not to be seen as separate institutions but rather two forms in which a single institution may manifest itself. It can indeed be uncertain whether a given charge is fixed or floating, rather as it can be hard to distinguish different botanical subspecies. Because in Scots law there is no such thing as the equitable charge, when, in 1961, the floating charge was introduced, it was as a standalone institution. This conceptual point parallels the more functionalist point made in the preceding paragraph.

After this introduction, there is a second part (Part B) outlining the legislative changes since 1961. Part C then recounts the numerous consultations and reports relevant to the floating charge, some of them implemented, others not. Part D picks up some particular topics and Part E contains some personal reflections. To some extent these parts overlap.

B. LEGISLATION: A BIRD'S EYE VIEW

This part summarises the legislative developments – or at least changes. Some minor items have been omitted.

Companies (Floating Charges) (Scotland) Act 1961

The floating charge originated with the Companies (Floating Charges) (Scotland) Act 1961 (the 1961 Act).[12] This did two things: (i) first, it introduced the floating charge as a juridical institution into Scots law; (ii) secondly, it introduced a registration system. That floaters should be registered was obvious enough,[13] but the 1961 Act not only provided for *their* registration, but also for the registration, in the Companies Register, of most

---

11 Instead, see M Raczynska, 'The Species and Structure(s) of the Floating Charge: The English Law Perspective on the Scottish Floating Charge', Chapter 8 within this volume.

12 See A D J MacPherson, 'The Genesis of the Scottish Floating Charge', Chapter 3 within this volume for further discussion of the origins of the floating charge.

13 Or, alternatively, not obvious. In England, floaters did not have to be registered until the Companies Act 1900 (s. 14). For some of the history see J de Lacy, 'The evolution and registration of security interests over personal property in English law' in J de Lacy (ed), *The Reform of UK Personal Property Security Law* (Oxford: Routledge, 2010).

other types of security right granted by companies, even though such other securities *already* had their own way of satisfying the publicity principle. (For instance, a heritable security granted by a company in 1960 had to be registered in the Register of Sasines; one granted in 1962 had to be registered both in the Register of Sasines and in the Companies Register.) Thus were born the problems of double publicity,[14] problems that remain with us. (Though for floaters themselves the Act did not mean double publicity, since for them no other publicity existed.[15]) To that extent, therefore, the statute's title was misleading, because its scope went well beyond floating charges. The home of this new registration regime was the Companies Register.[16]

Whilst the 1961 Act has long since been repealed[17] in substance it lives on, its provisions re-enacted, albeit with changes, over the years: see below. And whatever criticisms might be offered, it did do something technically notable, which was to put into statutory form an institution that in its home country was not in such form, being solely (except for the registration rules[18]) the creation of case law. The same was to happen eleven years later when receivership was introduced by the 1972 Act, for receivership too was in England a non-statutory institution. Indeed, the latter was particularly remarkable, in that the Scottish statutory version came to be adopted, as far as the powers are concerned, in English law itself, for receivership, and also for the whole of the UK for administration.[19] The powers set out in the 1972 Act themselves were of English origin, based on the standard documentation used in England at that time[20]: a cross-border shuttle. No such story can be told for the floater itself, which remains, in the land of its birth, based on case law, not statute.

In 1961 the chief company law enactment was the Companies Act 1948; the 1961 Act inserted into that Act provisions[21] about registration, these

---

14 Double publicity is a vast subject, touched on below in connection with registration.
15 Had Part 2 of the Bankruptcy and Diligence etc. (Scotland) Act 2007 come into force (see below) then the double publicity issue would have arisen also for floating charges.
16 As it is not called. It has no name.
17 By the Companies (Floating Charges and Receivers) (Scotland) Act 1972.
18 Which originated in s. 14 of the Companies Act 1900, and which by 1961 were in Part III of the Companies Act 1948.
19 Insolvency Act 1986 Sch. 1 (previously Insolvency Act 1985 Sch. 3). This sets out the powers of: (i) administrators; and (ii) English receivers. The powers of Scottish receivers are set out in Sch. 2 to the 1986 Act: the likeness of Sch. 1 to Sch. 2 is obvious, Sch. 2 itself deriving from the Companies (Floating Charges and Receivers) (Scotland) Act 1972.
20 See Scottish Law Commission, *Report on the Companies (Floating Charges) (Scotland) Act 1961* (Cmnd 4336: 1970) paras 55–56.
21 Companies Act 1948 s. 106A–s. 106K, as inserted by s. 6 and Sch. 2 of the 1961 Act.

provisions being based on the existing provisions of English law, though not quite identical with them.

Thus initially the law was to be found in two places: (i) mainly in the 1961 Act; but (ii) partly (as to registration) in the 1948 Act as amended by the 1961 Act. (And the latter also covered security rights other than floating charges.) This state of affairs lasted from 1961 until 1972.

Companies (Floating Charges and Receivers) (Scotland) Act 1972

The 1961 Act was replaced by the Companies (Floating Charges and Receivers) (Scotland) Act 1972.[22] This re-enacted, with certain changes, the provisions of the 1961 Act, the changes including the registration provisions, so that a new set of sections (106A–106K) in the 1948 Act were substituted for the previous ones. There were some other changes too.[23]

The most important change effected by the 1972 Act was the introduction of receivership. It was, at least in principle, not an insolvency process but a mechanism for the enforcement of a floating charge.[24] As an enforcement mechanism it existed in parallel with liquidation but, in practice, a floating charge holder who wished to enforce would opt for receivership.

The introduction of receivership was not done by amending the 1948 Act but was contained within the 1972 Act itself.[25] Thus after the 1972 Act the law was to be found in two places: (i) the 1972 Act (including the law of receivership); and (ii) in the new provisions about registration, which were in the 1948 Act.

22 As with the 1961 Act its title was inaccurate, since it covered more than floating charges and receivers.

23 One change was that under the 1961 Act (s. 1(1)) a floater could secure 'any debt incurred or to be incurred by it'. So it could not secure a third-party debt (except by granting caution and then granting a floater to secure the caution). An example of over-drafting: had the sentence stopped after 'debt' there would have been no problem, given that at common law a security can be granted for the obligation of a third party. The 1972 Act s. 1(1) said that a floater could secure 'any debt or other obligation (including a cautionary obligation) incurred or to be incurred by, or binding upon, the company or any other person'. That cured the problem of too many words by adding even more words. The text remains in current law: Companies Act 1986 s. 462(1).

24 For more details, see D McKenzie Skene, 'The Floating Charge and Insolvency Law', Chapter 10 within this volume.

25 Today the legislation on company insolvency is separate from the general legislation about companies, and receivership is covered by the former. But previously it was not so: the Companies Act 1948, like its predecessors, included company insolvency. So one might perhaps have expected this new law of receivership to have been inserted into the 1948 Act. That was not the decision.

Companies Act 1985

Then the Companies Act 1985 repealed both the 1972 Act and the 1948 Act, all the legislation being brought under one roof, namely the 1985 Act itself. Never before, and never since, has all the legislation on floating charges been in a single statute.[26] No substantive alterations were made.

Insolvency Act 1986

The phase just mentioned was short-lived, for in the following year, 1986, things changed again. The Insolvency Act 1986 absorbed the provisions about receivership from the 1985 Act, making no significant changes.[27] So after 1986 the legislation about floating charges was, once again, to be found in two places, though the new twofold division was different from the earlier twofold division. From 1972 to 1985 the division had been between the main provisions, including receivership, which were in the 1972 Act, and the registration provisions, which were in the 1948 Act, whereas from 1986 both the main provisions and the registration provisions were in the 1985 Act but receivership was in the 1986 Act. (I hope everyone is *concentrating*.)

Companies Act 1989

The Companies Act 1989[28] provided for a new system of registration of company charges. For the first time this was a unitary system applicable equally on both sides of the border. But it was never brought into force. (History was to repeat itself: in 2007 another reform of the law of registration was enacted, but never came into force – see below.)

Enterprise Act 2002[29]

The Enterprise Act 2002 made three major changes, all effected by amending the 1986 Act. First, it made receivership incompetent in most cases,

---

26 The provisions about floating charges and receivers were in Part XVIII, i.e. ss. 462–487, while the registration provisions were in ss. 410–424. As will be seen, five of these sections, ss. 462–466, remain in force today, with some amendments. These five sections are the core of the floating charge.

27 Insolvency Act 1986 ss. 50–71.

28 Companies Act 1989 Part IV.

29 S Frisby, 'In Search of a Rescue Regime: The Enterprise Act 2002' (2004) 67 MLR 247 gives a good account of the legislation.

generally replacing it with administration.[30] Secondly, it introduced the 'prescribed part' whereby a floating charge, which had always been postponed to preferred creditors, was now also postponed, to a limited extent, to ordinary unsecured creditors, but retaining priority over others.[31] That impaired the rights of the floating charge holder, but – and this was the third major change – it was balanced by the abolition of 'Crown preference' under which Crown claims had enjoyed priority over floaters.[32]

After the 2002 Act the law was still to be found in two places, namely the 1985 Act and the amended 1986 Act. This phase lasted from 2002 to 2006.

Companies Act 2006

In 2006 the 1985 Act was for the most part repealed and replaced by the Companies Act 2006. But the core provisions about floating charges were left in the 1985 Act[33] – an island, all that remained of a drowned continent. The reason why they were left there, and not taken into the 2006 Act, is that at that time the Bill that was to become the Bankruptcy and Diligence etc. (Scotland) Act 2007 was making its way through the Scottish Parliament and was intended to replace those provisions. That being the case, there was – it seemed at the time – no point in re-enacting them in the 2006 Act.

The position following the 2006 Act has thus been that the law is to be found in three places: (i) the core provisions are to be found in the 1985 Act[34]; (ii) the provisions about receivership (in so far as receivership is still competent) and administration are to be found in the much-amended 1986 Act[35]; and (iii) the provisions about registration are to be found in the 2006 Act.[36]

---

30 Section 248 of the 2002 Act inserted a new Sch. B1 into the 1986 Act. This replaced the existing administration system with a new one – that is currently in force. (But the powers of an administrator, set out in Sch. 1 to the 1986 Act, remained unaltered.) Section 250 of the 2002 Act inserted new sections 72A–72H and a new Sch. 2A into the 1986 providing that receivership would no longer be competent to enforce floaters granted after the 2002 Act, with certain exceptions. See further below.
31 2002 Act s. 252.
32 2002 Act s. 251.
33 1985 Act ss. 462–466.
34 1985 Act ss. 462–464.
35 Insolvency Act 1986 Part III (receivership) and Part II and Sch. B1 (administration).
36 Companies Act 2006 Part 25.

Bankruptcy and Diligence etc. (Scotland) Act 2007

Part 2 of the Bankruptcy and Diligence etc. (Scotland) Act 2007 prospectively established a new register, the Register of Floating Charges, registration in that register being a necessary condition for the creation of a floating charge. Part 2 made various other reforms, for instance as to ranking and as to assignation. It never came into force.[37] More of this is said below.

Companies Act 2006 (Amendment of Part 25) Regulations 2013

By the 2013 regulations, the registration provisions, applicable of course to company charges in general, not only to floaters, were reformed in matters of detail, and moreover instead of two sets of rules, one for England and Wales and one for Scotland, there was henceforth one set of rules only.[38] The new rules represented many changes in points of detail but no change in matters of principle. In particular, the twenty-one-day invisibility period (discussed further below) was preserved.

Small Business, Enterprise and Employment Act 2015

This Act changed the rules about when a floating charge crystallises in the event of administration.[39] It also provided that assets recovered under the law relating to gratuitous alienations and unfair preferences are for the benefit of creditors in general and not for the benefit of a floating charge holder – a point on which there was previously some uncertainty.[40]

---

37 But remains unrepealed, a trap, luring to their perdition those trusting to the efficiency of government. It is common to leave on the statute book legislation that the Government intends never to commence. The favourite example of my predecessor in the Lord President Reid chair, Bill Wilson, was the Easter Act 1928. Bill passed away in 1994. He would be amused to know that more than twenty-five years later the 1928 Act still remains, neither commenced nor repealed. Above was mentioned the Companies Act 1989 with its uncommenced reform of registration. It took twenty years to repeal: Companies Act 2006 (Commencement No. 8, Transitional Provisions and Savings) Order 2008 (in force 2009).

38 Companies Act 2006 (Amendment of Part 25) Regulations 2013.

39 Small Business, Enterprise and Employment Act 2015 s. 130, amending para. 115 of Sch. B1 to the Insolvency Act 1986. Both in its original and amended form para. 115 is hard to make sense of.

40 Section 119, inserting s. 176ZB into the Insolvency Act 1986. For the previous uncertainty see the discussion, below, of the Scottish Law Commission's 1986 Discussion Paper.

Not only companies but also ...

Finally, a set of closely-connected changes that happened, however, at different times. Under the 1961 Act, a floater could be granted by 'an incorporated company (whether a company within the meaning of the Act of 1948 or not)'.[41] That wording was repeated in the 1972 Act[42] and also in the current legislation.[43] The power to grant floating charges has since been extended to certain other specific entities, the provisions being contained in legislation outwith the companies legislation. In 1967 industrial and provident societies were empowered to grant floating charges.[44] In 1989 the power was extended to European economic interest groupings.[45] These were joined in 2001 by limited liability partnerships.[46] Turning, finally, to building societies, in 1997 it was enacted that they could *not* grant floaters,[47] though what debate there had previously been on this point I have not ascertained. The prohibition was partly lifted in 2012[48] and wholly lifted in the following year.[49]

The prohibition raises the broader question of what is meant by (to quote the Companies Act 1985[50]) 'an incorporated company (whether a company within the meaning of this Act or not)'. All three types of entity mentioned above are, in the applicable legislation, expressly said to be 'incorporated'. Are they 'companies'? If that word means a for-profit incorporated entity,[51] then LLPs qualify, but not the other two. But having said that, in UK legislation the word 'company' is in fact not so limited. An example is the company

---

41 1961 Act s. 1(1). The '1948 Act' meant the Companies Act 1948.

42 Companies (Floating Charges and Receivers) (Scotland) Act 1972 s. 1(1).

43 Companies Act 1985 s. 462: ' ... an incorporated company (whether a company within the meaning of this Act or not)'.

44 Industrial and Provident Societies Act 1967 s. 3, and now Co-operative and Community Benefit Societies Act 2014 s. 62.

45 European Economic Interest Grouping Regulations 1989 (SI 1989/638). UK-registered EEIGs are converted into 'UK Economic Interest Groupings' (UKEIGs) under the European Economic Interest Grouping (Amendment) (EU Exit) Regulations 2018 (SI 2018/1299).

46 Limited Liability Partnerships (Scotland) Regulations 2001 (SSI 2001/128) reg. 3. How the Scottish Ministers had power to make these regulations I have not fathomed. The SSI's preamble cites 'ss 14(1) and (2), 15, 16 and 17(1) and (3) of the Limited Liability Partnerships Act 2000'. Hmm.

47 Building Societies Act 1997 s. 11 inserting a new s. 9B into the Building Societies Act 1986.

48 Financial Services Act 2012 s. 55.

49 Financial Services (Banking Reform) Act 2013 s. 138 and Sch. 9 para. 4.

50 Companies Act 1985 s. 462.

51 The common law meaning is less demanding, the term including ordinary partnerships. The fact that the legislation uses the term *incorporated* company' suggests that 'company' is being used in its common law sense.

limited by guarantee. There are also international private law questions. But I stray from the path of historiography.

C. CONSULTATIONS AND REPORTS

(1) Introduction

Since 1961 there have been many consultations and reports; few leading to legislation.[52] (Often, alas, are public funds thus wasted.) Two were specifically on floating charges, namely the Scottish Law Commission's (SLC) 1970 report,[53] which led to the 1972 Act, and its 1986 consultative memorandum,[54] which was never followed by a report.[55] Some others have been on registration of company charges (and therefore not *only* about floating charges).

Some were about introducing a system of security over moveable property based loosely on art. 9 of the Uniform Commercial Code (UCC) of the US. There is, it is true, a gap between that idea and the floating charge, partly because the floater covers not only moveable but also immoveable property and partly because the conceptual foundation of art. 9 differs from that of the floating charge. Nevertheless the two (reform of the floating charge, and a new system based to some extent on UCC art. 9) cannot be wholly separated, and so something should be said of these proposals, albeit briefly, in a history of the floating charge. In this connection it should be noted that the introduction of systems deriving from art. 9 has resulted in the disappearance of the floater in other places such as Australia, Canada and New Zealand.[56] If the proposals in the Halliday Report, or in the Diamond Report, or in the Murray Report (discussed below) had been implemented, the importance of the floating charge would have been much diminished. The same will be the case if the recommendations of the SLC about moveable transactions are implemented.[57]

---

52 Some of this material is also considered from a reform perspective in A J M Steven, 'Reform of the Scottish Floating Charge', Chapter 12 within this volume.
53 Scottish Law Commission, *Report on the 1961 Act* (n 20).
54 What would today be called a discussion paper (DP), and that term will be used here.
55 Scottish Law Commission, *Consultative Memorandum on Floating Charges and Receivers* (Scot. Law Com. DP No. 72, 1986).
56 This is true in a practical sense. Whether the floater still exists in theory is another matter.
57 Scottish Law Commission, *Report on Moveable Transactions* (Scot. Law Com. No. 249, 2017).

(2) The consultations and reports

The SLC's 1970 report: receivership, etc.

In 1970 the SLC published its *Report on the Companies (Floating Charges) Act 1961*.[58] Its recommendations were fully implemented by the 1972 Act (for which see above).

The Crowther Report (1971)

The *Report of the Committee on Consumer Credit*, chaired by Geoffrey Crowther, appeared in 1971.[59] It was UK-wide in its scope. It was partially implemented by the Consumer Credit Act 1974. Part 5 of the report recommended a system based on art. 9 of the UCC. Had it been implemented the floater would not have survived, at least in anything like its present form, and perhaps not at all, though little about floaters was said in the report. It was not implemented, but neither did it ever quite go away: fifty years later, Part 5 of the Crowther Report remains conspicuous in the landscape, on both sides of the border.

The SLC 1976 Registration Discussion Paper

In 1976 the SLC issued a consultative memorandum on the registration of company charges. (Not only of floating charges, since, as already mentioned, there was and is a general scheme for the registration of 'charges' granted by companies.) At twenty-two pages it was not a major piece of work and considered only certain points of detail. The SLC's *Twelfth Annual Report* (1978) said that 'in due course we shall submit a report'.[60] That never happened. Although occasionally mentioned in subsequent annual reports, the project eventually perished: the *Twenty-First Annual Report* (1986) said that

'the topic of company charge registration has been omitted from the consultative memorandum[61] at the request of the Department of Trade and Industry which has included this subject in its general review for Great Britain of the law relating to security over moveable property'.[62]

---

58 Report 14. It was preceded by a discussion paper, *Examination of the Companies (Floating Charges) (Scotland) Act 1961* (1969).
59 (Cmnd 4596: 1971).
60 Scottish Law Commission, *Twelfth Annual Report 1976–1977* (Scot. Law Com. No. 47, 1978) para. 77.
61 Scottish Law Commission, *Floating Charges and Receivers* (n 55).
62 Scottish Law Commission, *Twenty-First Annual Report 1985–1986* (Scot. Law Com. No. 101, 1986) para. 2.59.

The reference to the Department of Trade and Industry review was a reference to the Diamond project (see below), which turned out to be another initiative that led to nothing.

The SLC Moveable Security Project (1974–1986) and the Halliday Report

In 1974 the SLC decided to begin work on security over moveable property. The decision was taken expressly on the basis of the ideas in the Crowther Report,[63] themselves based on art. 9 of the UCC. The first step was the setting up of a working party of experts,[64] chaired by Professor Halliday.[65] The report was submitted to the SLC in 1983, which published it three years later.[66] It set out a scheme for security over moveable property, both corporeal and incorporeal, based in broad terms on art. 9 of the UCC. It did not contain a draft Bill. It was never implemented. Nothing was said in the report about what the effects of the proposals would be on the floating charge, but it seems to have been taken for granted that it would continue to be competent.

The SLC's *Nineteenth Annual Report* (1984) said[67]:

'In recent months we have been considering a paper prepared within the Commission with a view to consultation in the fairly near future on a wide range of issues concerned with rights in security. Because of the clear connection between these issues and certain of the issues raised by our exercise on the Companies

63 See Scottish Law Commission, *Tenth Annual Report 1974–1975* (Scot. Law Com. No. 41, 1976) para. 21.
64 This was something the SLC did quite commonly at the time. For instance the *Eleventh Annual Report 1975–1976* (Scot. Law Com. No. 43, 1977) lists (Appendix I) eight such groups: (i) Working Party on Security over Moveable Property; (ii) Working Party on Diligence; (iii) Steering Committee on Private International Law; (iv) Joint Working Party on Private International Law (Conflicts of Laws in Respect of Marriage); (v) Joint Working Party on Private International Law (Matrimonial Property); (vi) Joint Working Party on Conflicts of Jurisdiction affecting the Custody of Children; (vii) Working Party to Examine Law Commission Working Papers on Criminal Law; (viii) Working Party to Examine Law Commission Working Papers on the Law of Contract. In some cases a commissioner was a member of the group; for instance T B (Tom) Smith was a member of the contract group, and A E (Sandy) Anton was a member of all four groups looking at international private law.
65 John (Jack) Halliday had been a Scottish Law Commissioner from 1965 to 1974. Other members included R B (Bob) Jack, later chair of the Jack Committee (*Banking Services: Law and Practice* (Cm 622: 1989)), Alexander (Alistair) Hamilton of Messrs McGrigor Donald, also a banking lawyer, and W A (Bill) Wilson, of Edinburgh University.
66 Scottish Law Commission, *Report by Working Party on Security Over Moveable Property* (SLC, 1986) (Halliday Report). I do not know the reason for the delay, but the more interesting point is that it was published at all. I do not think that the reports of any other working groups were published.
67 Scottish Law Commission, *Nineteenth Annual Report 1983–1984* (Scot. Law Com. No. 89, 1984) para. 3.22. And see para. 3.55.

(Floating Charges and Receivers) (Scotland) Act 1972, we have decided that the two projects should be combined.'

If that merger did in fact happen, it was short-lived. No paper 'in the fairly near future' or otherwise appeared. The floating charges Discussion Paper went ahead on its own, being published in 1986: see below. The SLC's *Twenty-First Annual Report* (1986) announced that work on the project on moveable security had been 'suspended' because of the Diamond project.[68]

The SLC's 1986 Discussion Paper

The SLC's *Twelfth Annual Report* (1977), as well as promising a report on registration, added that 'there have been drawn to our attention a number of other points affecting the operation of the Act [the 1972 Act] and we propose to examine these in a future memorandum'.[69] This was the beginning of a project that took several years to reach the stage of a discussion paper, the 1986 *Consultative Memorandum on Floating Charges and Receivers*.[70] That too never proceeded to a report. It is worth spending a little time on it, though such examination can only be selective. Its length – 151 pages – is already suggestive of its significance. And, on a personal note, it was in some respects a response to my own criticisms. Despite certain imperfections, there has been nothing quite like it before or since.

Beginning with a ten-page introduction (Part I), there were then two major sections (Parts II and III), which were about the floating charge itself and receivership respectively. The overall approach was that the floating charge and receivership were essentially sound and were in need only of some reform in matters of detail.[71] This approval had two aspects, the first being that the basic policy of the law – the floating charge itself and its enforceability via receivership – was right, and the second being that that basic policy was given effect to by the legislation in a way that was workable and coherent with the general body of Scots law. As to the first aspect, this passage is indicative: 'We have ... approached the reform of the present

---

68 Scottish Law Commission, *Twenty-First Annual Report* (n 62) para. 2.21. For the Diamond project see below.
69 Scottish Law Commission, *Twelfth Annual Report* (n 60) para. 77.
70 The lead commissioner was, I believe, R D D ('Bobby') Bertram.
71 Despite the SLC paper's approval of receivership, it may be worth noting that in 1973 it had been said that 'the power to appoint receivers ... introduced by the Companies (Floating Charges and Receivers) (Scotland) Act 1972, has not been welcomed by all members of the profession' (Anon, 'Introduction of Receivers into Scotland' 1973 (18) JLSS 248 (this was a report of a conference on the subject)).

statutory provisions on the basis that the concept of the floating charge as such should be retained and that the particular mechanism of receivership should similarly be retained'.[72]

As to the second aspect, namely whether the floating charge coheres with the general body of the law, I would quote – if I may – the following: 'Commentators such as Mr G L Gretton have argued with some trenchancy that the present legislation does not provide a satisfactory basis for the co-existence of floating charges with the general law'.[73] But the Discussion Paper did not agree. After discussing certain cases and in particular *Ross v Taylor*[74] and *Forth & Clyde Construction Co Ltd v Trinity Timber & Plywood Co Ltd*[75] the Discussion Paper said:

> 'We do not think that there is evidence of any fundamental problem as regards the ability of the legislative techniques to co-exist with the surrounding law and we think that the courts have been able to provide a robust and workmanlike explanation of the legislation where it confronts this problem.'[76]

Part II, dealing with the floating charge, had a wide-ranging discussion of 'the effect of attachment'. One issue was about what happens when a company acquires assets after the floater has crystallised. Do they fall under the charge? It was a topical question.[77] The discussion in the Discussion Paper was limited to two types of case: reduction of unfair preferences[78];

---

72 Scottish Law Commission, *Floating Charges and Receivers* (n 55) para. 1.1.
73 Scottish Law Commission, *Floating Charges and Receivers* (n 55) para. 2.11. The footnote here is: 'See for example Mr Gretton's articles in 1984 SLT (News) 172 (where he refers to 'genetic incompatibility') and in 1984 JBL 344'.
74 1985 SC 156. The case was a dispute between a company's receiver and its liquidator about property that had been returned to the company after the opening of the receivership. Did it fall under the charge? (The ratio of the decision seems to me open to debate, but this is not the place for discussion. I might add, though again this is not the place for discussion, that if one had to explain to the intelligent jurist visiting from the Andromeda galaxy why and how a company can be at one and the same time in receivership and in liquidation one might not find the task easy.)
75 1984 SC 1. This held (though I would hesitate to enunciate the ratio) that an arrestment used after the opening of the receivership was not merely postponed to the charge but wholly invalid.
76 Scottish Law Commission, *Floating Charges and Receivers* (n 55) para. 2.12. I am not clear quite what is meant here by 'this problem', since the sentence has just said that there is no evidence of any problem. Probably by 'this problem' is meant 'the issue of the coherence of floating charges and receivership with the general body of Scots law' – i.e. that issue ('problem') was not a problem.
77 See e.g. D P Sellar, 'Floating Charges and Fraudulent Preferences' 1983 SLT (News) 253 and the same author's 'Future Assets and Double Attachments' (1985) 30 JLSS 242. The central case was *Ross* (n 74).
78 The DP used the older term 'fraudulent preference'. The modern term is preferable because transactions falling under this heading are not necessarily, and indeed seldom are, fraudulent in the ordinary sense.

and diligence struck down by the sixty-day rule.[79] One might have thought that gratuitous alienations would also have been discussed, but they were not.[80] Nor was the question of assets acquired, after crystallisation, in other ways.

Another major issue in this sub-part of the Discussion Paper, also topical at the time, was the competition between a floating charge and diligence. The decision of the Inner House in *Lord Advocate v Royal Bank of Scotland*[81] was approved.[82] In 1986 some important floater v diligence cases still lay in the future, such as *Iona Hotels Ltd (In Receivership) v Craig*,[83] and the 2017 decision that overruled *Lord Advocate v Royal Bank of Scotland*, namely *MacMillan v T Leith Developments Ltd*.[84] After looking at diligence, the Discussion Paper discussed set-off, also a topical issue, for there was uncertainty as to the effect of attachment over a debt owed to a company where there was also a debt owed by that company to that same party.[85]

There was a substantial discussion[86] of the ranking rules set out in s. 464 of the Companies Act 1985. Connected with this, though at a different place in the Discussion Paper,[87] was the proposal that a floating charge should come into being at the time of registration, rather than the rule – still in force – that a floater can exist for up to twenty-one days prior to registration.[88] This

---

79 That rule, modified in certain respects since 1986, is now to be found in s. 185, as amended, of the Insolvency Act 1986.

80 Insolvency Act 1986 s. 176ZB as inserted by s. 119 of the Small Business, Enterprise and Employment Act 2015 made express provision, for the first time, in connection with unfair preferences and gratuitous alienations. It says that assets recovered under these branches of the law do not fall under a floating charge.

81 1977 SC 155, holding that an arrestment not completed by furthcoming, and executed after the creation of a floating charge but before its crystallisation, was not 'effectually executed diligence' and so was subject to the charge.

82 The decision was controversial: see, *inter alia*, A J Sim, 'The Receiver and Effectually Executed Diligence' 1984 SLT (News) 25. (See also, though of course much later than the 1986 DP, S Wortley, 'Squaring the Circle: Revisiting the Receiver and "Effectually Executed Diligence".' (2000) Jur Rev 325.)

83 1990 SC 330, holding that a floating charge granted by a debtor company after an arrestment against it had been executed was subject to the arrestment.

84 *MacMillan* (n 7).

85 The cases discussed were *McPhail v Lothian Regional Council* 1981 SC 119, *Taylor v Scottish and Universal Newspapers Ltd* 1981 SC 408 and *McPhail v Cunninghame District Council* 1983 SC 246. Another set-off case was decided soon after the appearance of the DP: *Myles J Callaghan Ltd (In Receivership) v Glasgow DC* 1987 SC 171.

86 Scottish Law Commission, *Floating Charges and Receivers* (n 55) paras 2.96–2.130.

87 Scottish Law Commission, *Floating Charges and Receivers* (n 55) para. 2.139.

88 This was formulated (ibid) as 'registration in the company's register of charges'. Read literally this meant registration in the 'company's register of charges' under s. 422 of the Companies Act 1985 (now s. 859P of the Companies Act 2006, as amended, in which, it may be noted, the terminology has changed), which refers to the company's own *internal* records. From context, there

is, it hardly needs to be said, one of the best-known issues about floating charges. In 1986 *AIB Finance Ltd v Bank of Scotland*[89] still lay in the future. Something more about registration is said below.[90]

One other thing worth noting is that the Discussion Paper observed that in English law a disposal frees an asset from the ambit of a floater only if it is done in the ordinary course of business, something on which the Scottish legislation was (and remains) silent. The Discussion Paper contained a brief – too brief – discussion of this issue.[91] It appeared to regard the point as being uncertain in Scots law, and asked consultees 'whether legislation should specifically provide' that the English rule should apply.

The last part of the Discussion Paper was about receivers. Given that receivership is now rare – see further below – this part is of less interest to the modern reader. There were sections on the duties of a receiver, and on the powers of a receiver. The latter covered the problems of the interaction of the powers of the receiver with those of the board of directors and also those of a liquidator, in the event of a concurrent winding up.[92] The intractability of these problems might suggest that receivership was an incoherent institution. That conclusion was not drawn.

Extensive though the Discussion Paper was, it is understandable that by no means every aspect of the floater was covered. For instance, about the international private law aspects little was said,[93] perhaps wisely, because

can be little doubt that this was mis-expressed and that the intention was to refer to registration in the Companies Register.

89 1993 SC 588. A company executed a standard security on 19 December 1986. It was registered in the Register of Sasines on 30 December and registered in the Companies Register on 9 January. Also on 19 December it executed a floating charge in favour of another lender, this being registered in the Companies Register on 30 December. Briefly stated, it was held that the floater trumped the standard security because the floater was created on 19 December while the standard security was created on 30 December.

90 The DP cites English sources criticising the '21 day rule' (see Scottish Law Commission, *Floating Charges and Receivers* (n 55) para. 2.112) but not Scottish sources, notably W W McBryde and D M Allan, 'The Registration of Charges' 1982 SLT (News) 177 and my own article at 1984 SLT (News) 172 (though the DP cites that article elsewhere). This is for the pot to call the kettle black, because when myself a commissioner I occasionally failed to cite what should have been cited and, moreover, when writing my 1984 article I myself overlooked the McBryde/Allan piece.

91 Scottish Law Commission, *Floating Charges and Receivers* (n 55) paras 2.93–2.95.

92 Not only could there be a receiver and a liquidator concurrently in the saddle, but there could be two – or indeed indefinitely many – receivers in the saddle at the same time, with or without a liquidator. This passed for rationality.

93 See Scottish Law Commission, *Floating Charges and Receivers* (n 55) paras 3.97–3.104, where there is discussion of some intra-UK issues.

they are insoluble. (The underlying problem is the floater's purported extraterritorial operation.)[94]

The Diamond Report (1989)

In 1985 the Department of Trade and Industry commissioned Professor Aubrey Diamond to report on security over personal/moveable property. It was a one-person commission. He reported in 1989,[95] recommending the introduction of legislation based on art. 9 of the UCC. Like the Crowther Report, and unlike the other consultations and reports mentioned in this chapter, it was UK-wide. 'If the parties purport to create an 'old-style' floating charge after the new scheme is introduced it would take effect as a security interest under the new scheme.'[96] The report was not implemented.

The Murray Report (1994)

Early in 1994 the Department that Keeps Changing its Name, at that particular time in world history called the Department of Trade and Industry, commissioned a study by a working party chaired by John Murray QC[97] to consider the reform of the law of moveable security in Scotland. It did its work with remarkable speed, submitting its report in the autumn of the same year.[98] Perhaps the speed was too great, because the issues were not (in my view) sufficiently thought through. But it was a valuable and pioneering piece of work, in some ways anticipating two SLC reports, that of 2004 on registration of company charges and that of 2017 on moveable transactions.

It proposed the introduction of a new 'moveable security'. Unlike the earlier Crowther, Diamond and Halliday reports, it had a good deal about floating charges. They would not be abolished but the possibility that they should

---

94 The only discussion that I can recall is Part 5 of the Scottish Law Commission, *Report on Registration of Rights in Security by Companies* (Scot. Law Com. No. 197, 2004).
95 A L Diamond, *A Review of Security Interests in Property* (Department of Trade and Industry, 1989).
96 A L Diamond, *A Review of Security Interests in Property* para. 16.12.
97 He had been a Scottish Law Commissioner from 1977 to 1988. During his brief tenure on the Court of Session bench he took the title of Lord Dervaird. In 1994 he was the Professor of Commercial Law at the University of Edinburgh. The other members were James Birrell of Messrs Dickson Minto, Professor W W McBryde, at that time Professor of Scots Law at Dundee, Jane Ryder, then a consultant with Messrs Davidson Chalmers and Kevin Sweeney of Messrs McGrigor Donald.
98 Strictly it was a consultation paper rather than a report, but it became known as the Murray Report, perhaps because it had a draft Bill.

be restricted to moveable property was discussed.[99] They would be given their own register and they would come into effect only upon registration.

The 'Second Chance' Report (2001)

In 2001 a paper was published, *Insolvency – A Second Chance*, by what was at that particular moment called the Department of Trade and Industry, Productivity and Enterprise.[100] This recommended the changes that were enacted by the Enterprise Act 2002.[101] Receivership, which had in the SLC 1986 Discussion Paper been regarded as unimpeachable, was now impeached. The paper is so cursory that the reasons are less than clear, but one passage may be quoted:

> 'There has also been widespread concern as to the extent to which administrative receivership as a procedure provides adequate incentives to maximise economic value. There has, equally importantly, been concern about whether it provides an acceptable level of transparency and accountability to the range of stakeholders with an interest in a company's affairs, particularly creditors.'[102]

The paper also said that in certain types of case receivership would continue to be allowed, as the Enterprise Act 2002 in due course provided, but it did not explain why:

> 'The Government recognises that the floating charge and the right to appoint an administrative receiver plays[103] an important role in certain transactions in the capital markets. We will allow the right to appoint an administrative receiver to continue where floating charges are granted in relation to such transactions. Situations identified in Part VII of the Companies Act 1989 will fall outside the scope of our proposals.'[104]

Business Finance and Security over Moveable Property Report (2002)

This was a report prepared by J Hamilton, A Coulson, S Wortley and D Ingram for the Scottish Executive Central Research Unit.[105] It provided valuable empirical background information.

---

99 Department of Trade and Industry, *Security over Moveable Property in Scotland: a Consultation Paper* (DTI, 1994) (Murray Report) paras 4.15–4.18.
100 Department of Trade and Industry, *Insolvency – A Second Chance* (Cm 5234: 2001).
101 For which see above.
102 Department of Trade and Industry, *Insolvency – A Second Chance* (n 100) para. 2.2.
103 A typo for 'play'.
104 Department of Trade and Industry, *Insolvency – A Second Chance* (n 100) para. 2.18.
105 J Hamilton, A Coulson, S Wortley and D Ingram, *Business Finance and Security over Moveable Property* (2002).

The SLC Report on Registration of Company Charges (2004)

In 1998 the Department for Trade and Industry set up a 'steering group' to carry out a wide-ranging review of company law. In the final report, which appeared in 2001,[106] there was a chapter about 'the registration of company charges',[107] which was to lead to proposals more extensive than that description would suggest. The report said that there had not been enough time to consider possible reform in detail and recommended that the matter be referred to the two law commissions 'to examine the system for registering company charges and security and "quasi-security" generally over property other than land in both England and Wales and in Scotland'.[108] The initial plan was for this to be a joint project between the two commissions, but the SLC, though at first going along with that idea,[109] finally came to the view that this would be unlikely to work well and discussions between the commissions and the DTI eventually led to two separate references. The reference to the SLC was:

> 'To examine the present scheme on the registration and priority of rights in security granted by companies and to make recommendations for its reform as it applies to (a) companies having their registered office in Scotland wherever the assets are located; (b) security granted under Scots law by oversea companies and companies having their registered office in England and Wales.'[110]

The result was the SLC's *Report on Registration of Rights in Security by Companies* (2004).[111]

It recommended that security rights – including floaters – granted by companies should no longer have to be registered in the Companies Register.[112] Floaters would be registrable in a new register, the Register of Floating Charges (RoFC), to be kept by the Keeper of the Registers of Scotland.[113] Creation would happen on registration in the RoFC, not

---

106 Company Law Review Steering Group, *Modern Company Law for a Competitive Economy: Final Report* (DTI, 2001).

107 Company Law Review Steering Group, *Modern Company Law for a Competitive Economy: Final Report* Ch. 12.

108 Company Law Review Steering Group, *Modern Company Law for a Competitive Economy: Final Report* para. 12.8.

109 Indeed, a draft joint discussion paper, to which David Guild (formerly of Messrs Brodies, but by this time advocate) made a major contribution, reached a fairly advanced stage of development.

110 Scottish Law Commission, *Discussion Paper on Registration of Rights in Security by Companies* (Scot. Law Com. DP No. 121, 2002) para. 1.1.

111 Scottish Law Commission, *Report on Registration of Rights in Security* (n 94).

112 Scottish Law Commission, *Report on Registration of Rights in Security* (n 94) para. 3.25.

113 Scottish Law Commission, *Report on Registration of Rights in Security* (n 94) para. 2.7.

before.[114] The ranking rules would be rationalised.[115] It would be possible to enter an advance notice of a floating charge. Various other recommendations were made. These recommendations were implemented by Part 2 of the Bankruptcy and Diligence etc. (Scotland) Act 2007, with one main exception, namely that company security rights should cease to be registrable in the Companies Register. For Part 2 of the 2007 Act, see below.

The reference to the Law Commission for England and Wales was broader, and too long to quote here.[116] What happened to the English project? That was a convoluted story that cannot be told here.[117] One thing that both projects had in common was failure. No legislation followed from the English project, and while legislation did follow from the Scottish one, namely Part 2 of the Bankruptcy and Diligence etc. (Scotland) Act 2007, outlined above, that never came into force.

The SLC's *Sharp v Thomson* Report (2007)

In *Sharp v Thomson*[118] a floater that had been granted by a selling company came into collision with the buyers from the company, the charge crystallising after the disposition to the buyers had been delivered but before it had been registered. Something more about this case will be said below. In 2000 the SLC received the following remit from the Scottish Justice Minister: 'To consider the implications of the decision of the House of Lords in *Sharp v Thomson*, 1997 SC (HL) 66 and to make recommendations as to possible reform of the law'. The SLC issued a discussion paper in 2001[119] and in 2007 issued a report.[120] The report was never implemented,[121] though some of the changes proposed in the Discussion Paper were enacted in the Bankruptcy and Diligence etc. (Scotland) Act

114 Scottish Law Commission, *Report on Registration of Rights in Security* (n 94) para. 2.5.
115 Scottish Law Commission, *Report on Registration of Rights in Security* (n 94) para. 2.19.
116 It will be found in Law Commission, *Registration of Security Interests: Company Charges and Property other than Land* (Law Com. CP No. 164, 2002) para. 1.16.
117 First there was, in 2002, a consultation paper (CP No. 164), mentioned above, and then in 2004 a 'consultative report' (CP No. 176). Finally, in 2005 there was a report (Law Com No. 296). The story does not reflect well on the DTI.
118 *Sharp* (n 6).
119 Scottish Law Commission, *Discussion Paper on Sharp v Thomson* (Scot. Law Com. DP No. 114, 2001).
120 Scottish Law Commission, *Report on Sharp v Thomson* (Scot. Law Com. No. 208, 2007). Kenneth Reid was responsible for the DP but other commitments prevented him from preparing the report, which thus fell to me to do.
121 With apologies to readers who are by now weary of the phrase 'never implemented'.

2007. These changes did not concern floating charges and nothing more will be said about them here.[122]

The Discussion Paper's first proposal was that 'the decision of the House of Lords in *Sharp v Thomson* should be reversed by statute', but by the time of the report in 2007 the scope of that decision had been radically cut back by *Burnett's Trustee v Grainger*,[123] so that the 2007 report did not recommend legislative reversal. More will be said below about *Sharp*; here something must be said about the recommendations in the report bearing on floating charges.

The legislation's inconsistency with the publicity principle in relation to the creation of floating charges is a familiar issue, criticised by numerous commentators and reports, and mentioned more than once in the present chapter. Less attention has been devoted to the legislation's inconsistency with the publicity principle at the opposite end – not creation, but crystallisation, in other words, the problem that crystallisation happens with no publicity at the time, but only later, and with plenty of scope for non-publicity even then. This problem was a major theme of the 2007 report and the core of its recommendations was that the crystallisation of a floating charge should happen upon, not before, registration. Registration was to be made in the Register of Floating Charges established under Part 2 of the Bankruptcy and Diligence etc. (Scotland) Act 2007. As already mentioned, Part 2 never came into force. But the 'no crystallisation without registration' principle could equally well be effected via registration in the Companies Register.

The SLC's Moveable Transactions Report (2017)

The SLC's project on moveable transactions had three strands: (i) transfer of incorporeal moveable property; (ii) security over incorporeal moveable property; and (iii) security over corporeal moveable property. The inclusion of (i) meant that it was broader in scope than the other projects discussed above. It began, as always with the SLC, with a discussion paper, which

---

122 Proposal 4 (para. 4.10) of the DP was implemented, subject to certain modifications, by s. 17 of the Bankruptcy and Diligence etc. (Scotland) Act 2007 (now ss. 78 and 87 of the Bankruptcy (Scotland) Act 2016). In my early months as a commissioner, much of my time was devoted to certain aspects of the Bill that became the 2007 Act, s. 17 among them.
123 2002 SC 580 affd [2004] UKHL 8, 2004 SC (HL) 19.

appeared in 2011,[124] and culminated in a report in 2017.[125] What would be its effect on floating charges? The answer here is the same as for the Halliday report and the Murray report: floaters would remain competent but their practical significance would be substantially reduced, the reason being that the proposed 'statutory pledge', available for most types of moveable property, would prove attractive to lenders.

D. SOME PARTICULAR TOPICS

In this part some particular topics are looked at, all them at least already mentioned. These topics are: (1) the literature from 1961 to the present; (2) enforcement; (3) ranking and diligence; (4) *Sharp v Thomson*; and (5) registration including the strange tale of Part 2 of the Bankruptcy and Diligence etc. (Scotland) Act 2007.

(1) The literature

The following is a list of significant publications – chiefly articles – about the floating charge in Scots law. It is intended not only as a bibliography, but also as an indication of the variations over time in scholarly interest. It will be seen that the period from the late 1970s to the late 1980s was one of particular activity. I have not included books on broader subjects, though they have material on floaters.[126] Articles on the registration of company charges are included, because although they deal with company charges in general, not only floating charges, the question of registration has always been a particularly important question for floaters.

No attempt has been made to list the publications on *Sharp v Thomson*,[127] in part because that cargo would sink the ship, in part because the *Sharp* literature generally has had property law as its focus, and in part (and this links to the previous point) because the literature merges into *Burnett's Tr*

---

124 Scottish Law Commission, *Discussion Paper on Moveable Transactions* (Scot. Law Com. DP No. 151, 2011).

125 Scottish Law Commission, *Report on Moveable Transactions* (n 57).

126 For example W A Wilson, *The Law of Scotland relating to Debt* (1982, 2nd edn in 1991 under the title *The Scottish Law of Debt* (Edinburgh: W. Green, both)) and J St Clair and J Drummond Young, *The Law of Corporate Insolvency in Scotland* (1988, subsequent editions in 1992, 2004 and 2011 (Edinburgh: W. Green, all)), and J Hardman, *A Practical Guide to Granting Corporate Security in Scotland* (Edinburgh: W. Green, 2018).

127 *Sharp* (n 6).

v Grainger,[128] a non-floater case. A fairly full catalogue of the literature can be found in the SLC's *Report on Sharp v Thomson*.[129] It remains to add that something about *Sharp* is said below.

1960s

- D G Antonio, 'The Companies (Floating Charges) (Scotland) Act 1961' (1961) 6 JLSS 241.
- W A Wilson, 'Floating Charges' 1962 SLT (News) 53.
- G L F Henry, 'Some Problems Arising out of the Companies (Floating Charges) (Scotland) Act 1961' (1962) 7 JLSS 111.
- D G Antonio, 'Floating Charges: A Plea for Reform' (1965) 10 JLSS 296.
- D Bennett, 'A Judicial Wet Blanket upon the Register of Charges' 1967 SLT (News) 153.

1970s

- E A Marshall, 'Floating Charges and Receivers' 1970 SLT (News) 109.
- E A Marshall, 'Companies (Floating Charges and Receivers) (Scotland) Bill' 1972 SLT (News) 93.
- E A Marshall, *The Companies (Floating Charges and Receivers) (Scotland) Act 1972* (1972).[130]
- W A Wilson, 'Effectively[131] Executed Diligence' (1978) Jur Rev 253.
- J R Campbell, 'Receivers' Powers' (1978) JLSS 275.

1980s

- G L Gretton, 'Diligence, Trusts and Floating Charges' (1981) JLSS 57.
- W A Wilson, 'The Receiver and Book Debts' 1982 SLT (News) 129.
- W W McBryde and D M Allan, 'The Registration of Charges' 1982 SLT (News) 177.
- G L Gretton, 'Inhibitions and Company Insolvencies' 1983 SLT (News) 145.
- W Simmons, 'A Legal Black Hole' (1983) JLSS 352.

---

128 *Burnett's Tr* (n 123).
129 Scottish Law Commission, *Report on Sharp* (n 120) appendix B.
130 The format was that of a book, but in fact its significance was less than that might suggest. Running to v + 42 pages, it was a reprint of the material in the *Current Law Statutes Annotated* series.
131 A typo: the term used in the legislation is 'effectually'.

- R J Reed, 'Aspects of the Law of Receivers in Scotland'. This appeared in three parts: 1983 SLT (News) 229, 1983 SLT (News) 237 and 1983 SLT (News) 261.
- D P Sellar, 'Floating Charges and Fraudulent Preferences' 1983 SLT (News) 253.
- G L Gretton, 'Receivership and Sequestration for Rent' 1983 SLT (News) 277.
- A J Sim, 'The Receiver and Effectually Executed Diligence' 1984 SLT (News) 25.
- W A Wilson, 'The Nature of Receivership' 1984 SLT (News) 105.
- G L Gretton, 'What Went Wrong with Floating Charges?' 1984 SLT (News) 172.
- G L Gretton, 'Receivers and Arresters' 1984 SLT (News) 177.
- D P Sellar, 'Future Assets and Double Attachments: *Ross v Taylor*' (1985) JLSS 242.
- G L Gretton, 'Should Floating Charges and Receivership Be Abolished?' 1986 SLT (News) 325.
- R B Jack, 'The Coming of the Floating Charge to Scotland' in D J Cusine (ed), *A Scots Conveyancing Miscellany: Essays in Honour of Professor JM Halliday* (Edinburgh: W. Green, 1987).
- K G C Reid, 'Trusts and Floating Charges' 1987 SLT (News) 113.
- J H Greene and I M Fletcher, *The Law and Practice of Receivership in Scotland* (Edinburgh: Butterworths Scotland, 1987, second edition 1992, third and last edition 2005).

1990s

- W Lucas, 'The Assignation of Floating Charges' 1996 SLT (News) 203.
- R Rennie, 'The Tragedy of the Floating Charge in Scots Law' (1998) SLPQ 169.
- S C Styles, 'The Two Types of Floating Charge: The English and the Scots' (1999) SLPQ 235.

2000s

- S Wortley, 'Squaring the Circle: Revisiting the Receiver and 'Effectually Executed Diligence" (2000) Jur Rev 325.
- S C Styles, 'Floating Charges and Subsequent Securities' 2001 SLPQ 73.

- G L Gretton, 'Registration of Company Charges' (2002) Edin L Rev 146.
- D Guild, 'The Registration of Rights in Security by Companies' 2002 SLT (News) 289.
- C Bisping, 'The Classification of Floating Charges in International Private Law' (2002) Jur Rev 195.
- G L Gretton, 'Reception without Integration? Floating Charges and Mixed Systems' (2003) Tul L Rev 307.
- D Cabrelli, 'The Curious Case of the "Unreal" Floating Charge' 2005 SLT (News) 127.
- D Cabrelli, 'The Case against the Floating Charge in Scotland' (2005) Edin L Rev 407.

2010s

- H Patrick, 'Receivership of Foreign-Based Companies: Scottish Government Consults' 2010 SLT (News) 177.
- H Patrick, 'Receivership of Foreign-Based Companies: Scottish Government Acts' 2011 SLT (News) 213.
- A D J MacPherson, 'In the Twilight Hour: The Ranking of Floating Charges and Inhibitions' (2016) Edin L Rev 353.
- A D J MacPherson, 'Floating Charges and Trust Property in Scots Law: A Tale of Two Patrimonies?' (2018) Edin L Rev 1.
- A D J MacPherson, 'The Circle Squared? Floating Charges and Diligence after *MacMillan v T Leith Developments Ltd*' (2018) Jur Rev 230.
- A D J MacPherson, 'Registration of Company Charges Revisited: New and Familiar Problems' (2019) Edin L Rev 153.
- R Caldwell, 'Enterprise Goes into Reverse for Floating Charge-holders' (2019) Jur Rev 103.

2020s

- A D J MacPherson, *The Floating Charge* (Edinburgh: Edinburgh Legal Education Trust, 2020).
- S Wortley, 'When is a Prior Ranking Floating Charge not a Prior Ranking Floating Charge?' 2020 SLT (News) 191.
- And finally, the present volume!

(2) Enforcement – attachment – crystallisation – liquidation – receivership – administration

The lawyer of 1961 reading the new statute for the first time might not have immediately understood how this new-fangled security right was enforceable. Perhaps they would have looked for at least one section devoted to the subject. In fact enforcement was merely mentioned *en passant* within a rambling 270-word sentence, itself submerged within a section headed 'Power of incorporated companies to create floating charges',[132] The text was:

> 'A floating charge ... shall on the commencement of the winding up of the company ... attach to the property then comprised in the company's property and undertaking ... and ... shall have effect as if the charge were a fixed security over the property to which it has attached ... '[133]

This wording remains virtually unaltered to this day, though the Companies Act 1985 dignified it with its own section, headed 'Effect of floating charge in winding up'.[134]

Thus initially (from 1961–1972) the floater had no specific enforcement mechanism. The benefit of the charge emerged in the way the liquidator distributed the proceeds of realisation. And something rather like that exists today, via administration as well as liquidation. But after 1972 and for many years, there was a specific enforcement mechanism, namely receivership. (Which indeed can still happen, exceptionally, even today, though it is rare.)

Receivership was introduced by the 1972 Act. It was adopted from England, and, as already mentioned, the draftsman had the task of putting into statutory form something that in its home country was, and is, non-statutory, being, like the floating charge itself, a creature of the common law.[135]

Immediately upon its introduction, receivership became the favoured means of enforcement and, since many companies that became insolvent had granted at least one floater, many company insolvencies involved receivership. Enforcement via liquidation, the sole means of enforcement from 1961 to 1972, became of only limited practical importance, as indeed is still the case today, though with administration playing the part once played

---

132 Companies (Floating Charges) (Scotland) Act 1961 s. 1.
133 Companies (Floating Charges) (Scotland) Act 1961 s. 1(2).
134 Companies Act 1985 s. 463, still in force.
135 Or to be exact, the creature of 'equity' rather than of 'law', for just as security rights can be legal or equitable, so enforcement processes can be legal or equitable. Thus the equitable security was equitably enforceable.

by receivership. From 1972 onwards, floating charge litigation was mainly receivership litigation, examples of standout cases being *Lord Advocate v Royal Bank of Scotland*,[136] *McPhail v Lothian Regional Council*,[137] *Taylor v Scottish and Universal Newspapers Ltd*,[138] *Forth & Clyde Construction Co Ltd v Trinity Timber & Plywood Co Ltd*,[139] *Ross v Taylor*,[140] *McPhail v Cunninghame District Council*,[141] *Tay Valley Joinery Ltd v C F Financial Services Ltd*,[142] *Iona Hotels Ltd v Craig*[143] and *AIB Finance Ltd v Bank of Scotland*[144] and, in receivership's long dusk, *MacMillan v T Leith Developments Ltd*.[145] To what extent decisions such as these – and of course others too – are decisions about the floating charge *as such*, as opposed to decisions about the floating charge in the context of receivership, is a large question that cannot be discussed here.

That the reign of receivership should ever end seemed impossible. But in a lifetime in law one learns that what seems impossible sometimes happens. The Enterprise Act 2002 provided that receivership would disappear,[146] being replaced by administration, an insolvency process that had been introduced by the Insolvency Act 1985[147] but which was remodelled by the 2002 Act.[148] Unlike receivership, administration is a true insolvency process but nevertheless has much in common with receivership, including the fact that a floating charge holder can appoint an administrator.[149] In some respects, but not all, administration is the new receivership.

In conformity with the longstanding and well-respected tradition of making corporate insolvency law as complex and incoherent as possible, the 2002 Act did not fully abolish receivership. In the first place, existing floaters were exempt,[150] leaving their eventual disappearance in the hands of

136 *Lord Advocate v RBS* (n 81).
137 *McPhail v LRC* (n 85).
138 *Taylor* (n 85).
139 *Forth & Clyde* (n 75).
140 *Ross* (n 74).
141 *Cunninghame District Council* (n 85).
142 1987 SLT 207.
143 *Iona Hotels Ltd* (n 83).
144 *AIB Finance Ltd* (n 89).
145 *MacMillan* (n 7).
146 Section 250 of the Enterprise Act 2002 inserting new sections 72A–72H and new Sch. 2A into the Insolvency Act 1986.
147 Insolvency Act 1985 ss. 27 onwards. These provisions were almost immediately repealed and re-enacted by the Insolvency Act 1986.
148 Section 248 of the Enterprise Act 2002 inserted a new Sch. B1 into the Insolvency Act 1986.
149 Insolvency Act 1986 Sch. B1 para. 14.
150 Defined as those created before 15 September 2003.

Old Father Time. In the second place, Sch. 2A to the Insolvency Act 1986, as inserted by s. 250 of the 2002 Act, listed certain cases where receivership would still be competent even for new floaters.[151] In the third place, the prohibition of receivership applies only to 'qualifying floating charges', which means one that 'relates to the whole or substantially the whole of the company's property'.[152] (This dovetails with the 'administration is the new receivership' idea, because it is only the holder of a *qualifying* floater who can appoint an administrator.) These 'limited asset floaters' are uncommon but not unknown.

The attachment provision, as applicable to liquidation, was quoted above, and a similar provision applies to receivership.[153] It might be supposed that there would be a similar rule for administration, i.e. that the process would at once trigger attachment. That is not so. The legislation says that the floater may or may not attach according to circumstances.[154] The rules here are – unsurprisingly – complex and (it seems to me) unsatisfactory. The fact that attachment can depend on the discretion of the administrator seems particularly odd.[155]

(3) Ranking and diligence

There have been two main statutory changes, both effected by the Enterprise Act 2002. In the first place, this statute abolished 'Crown preference' under which claims by the Crown had trumped not only the claims of ordinary creditors but also the claims of a floating charge holder.[156] (But the rights of other preferential creditors over the floater remained and remain intact.[157]) That change favoured floating charges. The other change had the opposite

---

151 See Department of Trade and Industry, *Insolvency – A Second Chance* (n 100). Since 2002 the list has been expanded by the Insolvency Act 1986 (Amendment) (Administrative Receivership and Urban Regeneration etc.) Order 2003.
152 Insolvency Act 1986 Sch. B1 para. 14, as applied by s. 72A(3).
153 Insolvency Act 1986 s. 52(7) and s. 54(4).
154 Insolvency Act 1986 Sch. B1 para. 115, as inserted by the Enterprise Act 2002, and as amended by the Small Business, Enterprise and Employment Act 2015 s. 130.
155 For discussion see D Cabrelli, 'The Curious Case of the "Unreal" Floating Charge in Scotland' 2005 SLT (News) 127.
156 For the Crown preference over the floating charge, see s. 5(5) of the Companies (Floating Charges) Scotland) Act 1961 read with Companies Act 1948 s. 319, thereafter s. 5(6) of the Companies (Floating Charges and Receivers) Scotland) Act 1972, and thereafter s. 464(6) of the Companies Act 1985, read with Insolvency Act 1986 s. 175 (as originally enacted).
157 See the Insolvency Act 1986 s. 464(6). This has been the law since the beginning (see s. 5(5) of the 1961 Act), and is the most important difference, as to ranking, between floaters and ordinary security rights.

effect. The Enterprise Act 2002 introduced the 'prescribed part' whereby a certain sum should be taken from the clutch of the floating charge holder and given to the ordinary unsecured creditors.[158]

The Finance Act 2020 provided for the reintroduction of Crown preference,[159] thus bringing about a major downgrade in the ranking of floaters. Its effect will be greater in Scotland than in England, where equitable fixed charges, unavailable in Scotland, will continue to rank ahead of Crown preference.

The 1961 Act provided that a crystallised floater was 'subject to the rights of any person who has effectually executed diligence on the property'[160] and similar provisions are to be found in the subsequent legislation about liquidation and receivership.[161] As for administration, the position is impenetrable: see above.

The case law on the floating charge in relation to ranking and diligence – in other words, in relation to the rights of other creditors – cannot be dealt with here, because of its bulk, and because it is dealt with elsewhere in this volume, and in Dr MacPherson's recent monograph. But something – albeit a very little – must be said of *Sharp v Thomson*. However, before that, one final note about ranking. There is a section headed 'ranking of floating charges' that began as s. 5 of the 1961 Act, was thereafter s. 5 of the 1972 Act and is now s. 464 of the Companies Act 1985. In each incarnation the wording has changed. The level of intelligibility has not.

(4) *Sharp v Thomson*

Many have been the collisions between floaters and other rights; of these none triggered more debate than *Sharp v Thomson*.[162] The facts were

---

158 Enterprise Act 2002 s. 252 inserting into the 1986 Act a new s. 172A. (Pub quiz question on legislative mess: what is s. 176A preceded by? [Answer: by s. 176ZA.]) For the calculation of the prescribed part see the Insolvency Act 1986 (Prescribed Part) Order 2003 as amended by the Insolvency Act 1986 (Prescribed Part) (Amendment) Order 2020.

159 Finance Act 2020 ss. 98 and 99. For the background see HM Revenue and Customs, *Protecting your Taxes in Insolvency* (26 February 2019). Only a consultation paper, and no final report, was published.

160 1961 Act s. 1(2).

161 Companies (Floating Charges and Receivers) (Scotland) Act 1972 s. 1(2) (liquidation) and s. 15(2) (receivership); Insolvency Act 1986 s. 463(1) (liquidation) and s. 55(3) (receivership). Curiously, this 'subject to' provision is, for liquidation, made a limitation to *attachment*, but for receivership it is not connected to *attachment*, but rather to the *powers* of a receiver. The reason for this difference is not one that the writer understands.

162 *Sharp* (n 6).

unusual, and thus unlikely to recur, so the significance of the case is in that sense surprising. But significant it was, because, to protect buyers from a floater previously granted by the seller, the House of Lords introduced (on one interpretation) equitable ownership. (Though not the same as the English system of equity.) That is why, as mentioned earlier, most of the large literature on the case had as its focus property law rather than the law of floating charges.[163] And as already mentioned, such was the unease created by the decision that the Scottish Government asked the SLC to review it.[164] But in the event the House of Lords did the job itself, in a non-floater case, *Burnett's Tr v Grainger*.[165] The result was that *Sharp* was shorn of its possible implications for property law in general and became a decision of narrow application. So near did the floating charge come to capsizing property law.[166]

(5) Publicity/registration

The topic of publicity – via registration – is here mentioned in three divisions, the first two very short: (a) crystallisation; (b) the central bank exemption; and (c) the strange tale of Part 2 of the Bankruptcy and Diligence etc. (Scotland) Act 2007.

(a) Crystallisation

Crystallisation happens without registration, though registration is supposed to happen – later. The SLC in its report on *Sharp v Thomson*[167] recommended that this breach of the publicity principle should be corrected (see above). The recommendation remains unimplemented.

(b) The central bank exemption

Certain floating charges nowadays do not have to be registered *at all*. They are absolutely secret. Section 252 of the Banking Act 2009 says that:

---

163 As mentioned above, most of the literature is listed in Scottish Law Commission, *Report on Sharp* (n 120) appendix B.
164 See above.
165 *Burnett's Tr* (n 123).
166 Though this is to stray from the history of the floater, *Gibson v Hunter Home Designs Ltd* 1976 SC 23, had it gone the other way, which easily might have happened, would also have capsized property law.
167 Scottish Law Commission, *Report on Sharp* (n 120).

'Part 25 of the Companies Act 2006 ... does not apply to a charge if the person interested in it[168] is— (a) the Bank of England, (b) the central bank of a country or territory outside the United Kingdom, or (c) the European Central Bank.'

Paragraph 564 of the Explanatory Notes gave the reason in one sentence, which might be characterised in many ways, but which I shall refrain from characterising: 'This is because registration could otherwise lead to early disclosure of liquidity support'. (Secrecy is always beneficial to some. And harmful to others.)

(c) The strange tale of Part 2 of the 2007 Act

One would have expected that the rule for creating floaters would have been essentially what it is for heritable security, namely that: (i) the security comes into existence on registration, so that an unregistered security has no third-party effect; and (ii) because of that basic rule there does not need to be a time limit for registration. But that was not the approach of the 1961 Act, which instead adopted the English rule, namely that a floater is created by the private act of the parties, but has to be registered in the Companies Register within twenty-one days, on pain of qualified invalidity. This was not a special rule for floaters, but merely part of the general rule for company charges and, as was seen above, when floaters were introduced in 1961 the legislation brought in the 'thou shalt register in the Companies Register within twenty-one days' commandment for almost all types of security granted by companies, so that the 1961 Act was, despite its name, not only about floaters.[169] But the rule worked differently for floaters than for other types of security, which all had their own publicity mechanism (e.g. recording in the Register of Sasines for heritable securities), so that registration in the Companies Register was always an *additional* publicity requirement. For those other types of security, the twenty-one-day period was not an 'invisibility period'. But for floaters the effect was inconsistent with the publicity principle, for they could exist for up to twenty-one days, unknown to third parties. This looked odder to Scottish eyes than to English eyes, for in Scotland the publicity principle has always had much weight, whereas in England that is not

---

168 Not 'the holder of it'. One is tempted to remark that many people might be interested in such a charge – if only they were allowed to know of its existence.

169 This is not the place to discuss this policy as to company charges, but on a historical note it may be mentioned that it has always had its critics. For instance in 1967 David Bennett had written that '[t]his was a thoughtless and unnecessary imitation of English provisions' (D Bennett, 'A Judicial Wet Blanket upon the Register of Charges' 1967 SLT (News) 153).

so.[170] That the drafters of the 1961 Act did it this way is understandable, for they were seeking substantive uniformity with English law, but the result has always rankled.[171] The rankling culminated in the SLC 2004 Report,[172] leading to Part 2 of the Bankruptcy and Diligence etc. (Scotland) Act 2007. Part 2 generally adopted the recommendations of the SLC's 2004 report, but it did not adopt the recommendation that security rights granted by companies should no longer have to be registered in the Companies Register. This was not a question of policy, but rather a question of legislative competence. The law of rights in security is devolved, but company law is reserved. The general view is that the registration of company security rights, under what is now Part 25 of the Companies Act 2006, is reserved, so that this aspect of the 2004 report could not be included in the 2007 Act.

The Caledonian uprising enjoyed quick and remarkable success, caused alarm in London, and ended in complete suppression. Ten years it took, five years of advance and five years of retreat, the beginning having been in 2002 with the publication of the SLC's Discussion Paper on *Registration of Rights in Security by Companies,* the high point of success being 15 January 2007 with Royal Assent, and the end coming in 2012. Part 2, though not repealed, was never commenced. The Scottish Government never actually announced its abandonment but by the end of 2012 the will to bring it into force had gone.

I am not able to give the full story but I can offer some of it, having been to some extent involved. In brief: the UK organisations, public and private, involved in questions of corporate finance, including the banks, the Bank of England, the remarkably powerful City of London Law Society, the Department of Trade and Industry[173] and Companies House[174] did not like the reform but seem to have been half-asleep during the first five years (2002–2007), waking up only after (indeed some time after) the legislation had been passed.

---

170 Though there is an essay to be written on the gradual, but imperfect, growth of the publicity principle in English private law beginning about the third quarter of the nineteenth century.
171 The list of publications above contains some illustrations.
172 Scottish Law Commission, *Report on Registration of Rights in Security* (n 94).
173 As it was to 2007, then becoming the Department for Business, Enterprise and Regulatory Reform, which in 2009 became the Department for Business, Innovation and Skills. Today and for the next several minutes it is the Department for Business, Energy and Industrial Strategy. In the days of yore it was the Board of Trade.
174 Nominally there are two registrars of companies, one in Cardiff and one in Edinburgh (not to mention Belfast), but in substance they are unified.

The two main issues[175] both concerned 'double registration', but of quite different types. The first was that a floater, once registered in the RoFC, would have to be registered again in the Companies Register. The other was that a floater by a non-Scottish company, although already registered outwith Scotland, would have to be registered again in the RoFC to ensure effectiveness in Scotland. In what follows something will be said of both issues.

First, the first issue. Double registration was and is a familiar problem: for instance, standard securities granted by companies have to be registered first in the Land Register and thereafter in the Companies Register. The SLC's 2004 report recommended abolition of that rule, i.e. it recommended that registration in the Companies Register should no longer be required for any type of security. Thus a standard security granted by a company would need to be registered only in the Land Register. As applied to floaters that would mean registration only in the RoFC. This recommendation could not be included in the 2007 Act because (see above) it would have been outwith legislative competence. Westminster legislation was equally out of the question because the change was opposed by the DTI. But an interesting idea – a sort of compromise – emerged. It was that once a security right was registered in a 'special' register,[176] such as the RoFC, that registration would automatically *also* enter the Companies Register – a ping-through. So double registration would be achieved but the bank, or other secured party, would no longer have to carry out an *actual* second registration. This idea was added to the Bill that became Companies Act 2006 as it progressed through Parliament, ending up as s. 893.

But s. 893 required activation on a register-by-register basis, a UK order being needed for each 'special' register. The DTI committed itself to making the necessary s. 893 order for the RoFC.[177] But Companies House raised difficulties. These on their own had the capacity to sink Part 2 because it was a matter of general acceptance that commencement of Part 2 would not happen unless a s. 893 order could be made. What were these difficulties? They concerned IT development costs and the question of whether those costs would be borne by Companies House or by the

---

175 There were others as well (such as s. 51(1) of the Insolvency Act 1986) but space precludes exhaustive discussion here.

176 *Every* register is special, *very* special.

177 HL Deb 2 Nov 2006 col 480. The commitment had a proviso, namely that the necessary 'information sharing arrangements' could be made. Perhaps this was merely an ordinary precaution. Or perhaps the DTI already knew of the attitude of Companies House.

'special' registers, there were problems about matching up data formats, and so on.[178] It seemed to me at the time that the problems were soluble, and that the real problem was one of attitude. That was a matter of impression and possibly I was wrong. It may be noted that in the event not only was no s. 893 order made for the RoFC, but no such order has ever been made for any 'special' register. Thus double registration is still with us for standard securities and so on.

The other 'double registration' problem was different. It was that where a non-Scottish company granted a floating charge, that would need (it was said) to be registered in the RoFC to have effect in Scotland, in addition to any other registration. So if Zykkzyn Ltd, incorporated in England/Wales, granted a floating charge to its bank, the charge being duly registered in the Companies Register in Cardiff, it would also need (it was said) to be registered in Edinburgh to have effect over Scottish assets.[179] Thus Part 2 would change things not only for Scottish companies but also for English (etc.) companies. This was an issue that s. 893 did not touch. This was the issue, above all, that really sank Part 2.

The banks, silent hitherto, began to mobilise in 2008. Perhaps the key moment was a letter of 2 September of that year from the Committee of Scottish Clearing Bankers to Kenneth MacAskill, Cabinet Secretary for Justice, objecting to Part 2 on the basis of this second 'double registration' issue. From that moment the implementation of Part 2 of the 2007 Act moved from 'probably yes' to 'probably no'.

Late in 2009 the Scottish Government decided to ask the Keeper of the Registers of Scotland to establish a 'Register of Floating Charges Technical Working Group' to thrash out the issues. Membership was large. It included two from the Bank of England's Financial Markets Law Committee, two from the Department for Business, Innovation and Skills, two from Companies House, two from the Committee of Scottish Clearing Bankers, two from the City of London Law Society and some others, of whom I was one. The only thing I will say about the meetings is that I found them depressing.

---

178 Some of these difficulties are mentioned in the Register of Floating Charges Technical Working Group, *Report to Scottish Government* (2011) available at *https://www.cicm.com/ wp-content/uploads/2013/07/Resources_GovCon_2012_ReportToScottishGovernment_ RegisterofFloatingChargesTechnicalWorkingGroup.pdf* (last accessed 26 October 2021), referred to below.

179 During the debates, curiously little was said about the fact that an English floating charge – being 'equitable' – operates extraterritorially regardless of what the law of the situs may say: *Re Anchor Line* [1937] Ch 483.

The final *Report to Scottish Government* was submitted in August 2011.[180] It did not, needless to say, achieve a consensus view, but presented three options: (i) to commence Part 2 of the 2007 Act without amendment; (ii) to commence it subject to amendment by subordinate legislation; and (iii) not to commence it. On 14 March the Scottish Government sent a letter to a wide variety of institutions and individuals asking which of the three options they supported. Thus when opposition arose the Scottish Government could not decide what was to be done. It remitted to a working group. The working group could not decide what was to be done. On receiving the report, the Scottish Government could not decide what was to be done. It then asked stakeholders what was to be done. The rest is silence.

On 25 June 2012 the Bank of England's Financial Markets Law Committee wrote to the Scottish Government's Law Reform Division objecting to Part 2. The letter was signed by Lord Hoffmann. By then Part 2 was barely twitching, but if there was a moment of *finis* this was it.[181]

E. PERSONAL REFLECTIONS

The editors invited me to include something about my own 'ardent criticisms' of the floating charge. In the preparation of this chapter I have asked myself whether those criticisms were just. Their expression was sometimes too ardent. That I regret. What of the substance?

First, there is the question of high-level policy, in the sense of whether it should be easy for any business asset (at least, any transferable business asset) to be collateralisable – whether it should be easy for a business to grant security over its assets, corporeal and incorporeal, moveable and immoveable. This is not an easy question. In the 1980s I was doubtful whether easy collateralisation would induce banks to lend more to businesses, as opposed to being better secured for what they did lend; moreover it would harm ordinary unsecured creditors; it would, on insolvency, transfer loss from the backs of the stronger creditors to the backs of the weaker. So the balance was, for me, negative: no real benefit, but some real harm: no positive *utilitas*, combined with negative *aequitas*.

My views have changed somewhat. In the first place, it now seems to me that regardless of one's assessment, the demand for easy collateralisation

---

180 Register of Floating Charges Technical Working Group, *Report* (n 178).
181 I have not carried out archival research: I have a copy of this letter, and also a copy of that of the Committee of Scottish Clearing Bankers of 2008 (above), as a result of my involvement throughout the debates.

cannot be resisted, though it can be and should be shaped. If the floater had not arrived in 1961, then either it would have arrived fairly soon after, or some other system would have been created. In the second place, the argument about free collateralisation being supportive of business finance now seems to me rather stronger than it did. The benefits can easily be overstated but I think that they exist, albeit that the law-and-economics issues are unfathomable.[182] The Modigliani–Miller theorem seemingly implies that a jurisdiction that does not readily facilitate secured business finance should not fare the worse, because equity finance will work as well as debt finance. But that approach now seems to me subject to many qualifications. Easy collateralisation of business assets has, it seems to me, real value. Whether the floater is the right way to do it is another matter. As for *aequitas*, that is a matter for insolvency law.

General policy is one thing, detailed implementation another. The 1960 committee could have opted for a system based, closely or not so closely, on art. 9 of the UCC.[183] Or it could have opted for the German system.[184] Less radically, the policy could have been implemented by a floating charge that covered moveables but not immoveables. Indeed the remit to the 1960 committee was limited to moveables.[185] (It is common internationally for immoveables to be excluded from the scope of business security arrangements.) But the English floater was not so limited. 'In the field of commercial law, unless there is good reason to the contrary, it is desirable that the law of England and Scotland should be the same.'[186] For that view there is much to be said. But, whatever its merits, it is not a principle to be applied unthinkingly. Thinking was sparse in the 1960 report[187] and the resulting legislation was incoherent. Judges often carp at legislation, not always fairly, but Lord Cameron was right when he said in 1978 that 'the language and structure of this statute are of considerable obscurity … its provisions are well designed to provide a rich variety of issues for decision in delicate and

---

182 On the whole subject see Dr Hardman's chapter in this volume on the economic issues, J Hardman, 'Law and Economics of the Floating Charge', Chapter 5.

183 In other words, something broadly like what was proposed by the SLC in its 2017 report.

184 Though I hasten to say that the German system (a combination of *Sicherungsabtretung* for incorporeal moveables and *Sicherungsübereignung* for corporeal moveables) seems to me unsatisfactory.

185 Law Reform Committee for Scotland, *Eighth Report of the Law Reform Committee for Scotland: The Constitution of Security over Moveable Property; and Floating Charges* (Cmnd 1017: 1960). See p. 1 for the remit.

186 Law Reform Committee for Scotland, *Eighth Report*, p. 6.

187 I say this with reluctance since some members of the 1960 committee were of the highest calibre. This was not their finest hour.

prolonged litigation'.[188] The legislation was a handful of rules, without structure or principle. 'As soon as one steps off the narrow path of specific rules, one finds oneself in a trackless and unknown country.'[189] And there was the connected point that 'the legislation fails to integrate with the general law. At times it seems even to go out of its way to avoid integration. The result is that the floating charge exists in a sort of conceptual vacuum'.[190] Should floating charges be abolished? 'The critic ... would argue that floating charges and receivership should be abolished, though such abolition would have to be accompanied by appropriate reforms of the general law of security over moveables, both corporeal and incorporeal. I suspect that he is right.'[191] My view is unchanged.

188 *Lord Advocate v RBS* (n 81) at 173.
189 G L Gretton, 'What Went Wrong with Floating Charges?' 1984 SLT (News) 172 at 173. A qualification: the words 'as if the charge were a fixed security' – what Bill Wilson dubbed the 'statutory hypothesis' – was some sort of an attempt at principle. It was a failure.
190 G L Gretton, 'What Went Wrong with Floating Charges?' at 173.
191 G L Gretton, 'Should Floating Charges and Receivership be abolished?' 1986 SLT (News) 325.

PART 2
THEORETICAL, COMPARATIVE AND POLICY PERSPECTIVES

5 Law and Economics of the Floating Charge

Jonathan Hardman

A. THE CHALLENGE
    (1) Introduction
    (2) Scots law's justifications
    (3) Law and economics and security
B. EFFICIENCY
    (1) Efficiency generally
    (2) Efficiency and law
    (3) Measuring efficiency
C. THE PARETO SUPERIORITY OF THE SCOTS LAW FLOATING CHARGE
    (1) Position without floating charge
    (2) Effect on debtor
    (3) Effect on the secured creditor
    (4) Effect on adjusting creditors
    (5) Effect on non-adjusting creditors
D. CRITIQUE AND CONCLUSION
    (1) Critique
    (2) Conclusion

A. THE CHALLENGE

(1) Introduction

'Much, and perhaps most, legal scholarship has been stamp collecting. Law and economics, however, is likely to change all that and, in fact, has begun to do so.'[1]

---

1 R H Coase, 'Law and Economics at Chicago' (1993) 36 *Journal of Law and Economics* 239 at 254.

The structure of this chapter arose following a discussion between the author and Professor Hector MacQueen in which Professor MacQueen provided a challenge to the author. Defenders of the floating charge in Scotland, said Professor MacQueen, had always asserted the horrors that would arise if the floating charge was suddenly removed from Scots law without being replaced by any functional equivalent. However, they had never demonstrated any advantages that the floating charge provided to Scots law. The Professor's challenge to the author was, therefore, to use this chapter to demonstrate the economic advantage to market participants of the floating charge under Scots law.

To meet this 'Challenge', this chapter is split into four parts. This first part (Part A) will explore the Challenge in further detail. It will review existing Scottish defences of the floating charge to examine whether the Challenge remains unanswered, and explore the general law and economics approach to security rights. The second part (Part B) will then examine the concept of efficiency and its use in law and economics. Having identified the strengths and weaknesses of different measurements of efficiency, the third part (Part C) will make the most ambitious claim of this chapter: that the floating charge under Scots law reflects a Pareto improvement: it makes at least one participant better off without making anyone worse off. It shall review this from the position of the debtor, the creditor and third parties. The fourth part (Part D) critiques these findings.

The economic issues outlined point to a clear conclusion: the Scots law floating charge provides a clear economic advantage to companies in Scotland. It is important to flag in advance the limitations of this analysis. This chapter will not argue that the current form of the floating charge is the optimal position for Scots law. Indeed, throughout the chapter there will be slight inefficiencies in the current framework that will be highlighted as potential areas for future reform. Instead, to meet the Challenge we shall adopt a slightly less difficult approach – our aim is to demonstrate that the world in which the current floating charge is contained in Scots law is economically superior to the world in which Scots law did not recognise a floating charge, or any functional equivalents, at all.

(2) Scots law's justifications

Our first question, therefore, must be to establish whether Scots law commentators have provided an adequate economic defence for the floating charge. If there is an adequate existing defence, then the Challenge is already solved. The initial response to the introduction of the floating charge was positive. This is because the ability to create valid security without the formalities of creation (recording at the Register of Sasines for heritable property, delivery for corporeal moveables and intimation for incorporeal moveables) provided increased flexibility to Scottish companies.[2] From then on, defence of the floating charge has, as would be expected, arisen as a response to criticism of the floating charge. Thus when Professor Gretton was launching his attacks on the floating charge in the 1980s,[3] Professor Jack responded with: 'To put the clock back to the pre-1961 position might easily have harmful consequences for the fragile Scottish economy dependent as it must continue to be on the attraction of business from other legal jurisdictions'.[4]

There are two key issues arising with this. First, Professor Jack's analysis appears in an epilogue to his main chapter and is therefore presented as an under-analysed assertion. Secondly, whilst this is a powerful, economics-driven response it is also negative in its nature – removing the floating charge would be harmful to Scotland. Unfortunately, this contains no analysis of the harms that would be caused, nor of the converse argument (the advantages provided to Scots law of the floating charge). Rather unfortunately, the argument rests on the idea that there would be harm to business if the floating charge were removed. Whilst an argument that this is the case can be extrapolated from the removal of flexibility arising from the disregard of formalities of creation, Professor Jack does not make it. Further attacks on the floating charge have been undertaken since by Professor Cabrelli.[5] Whilst Professor Cabrelli does deal with some economic concepts, he does not do so in a systematic way.

More recently, the author has undertaken his own economic analysis of security rights under Scots law.[6] Drawing on econometric analysis, the author has argued for reforms of various types of security, including the floating charge. This is based on the logic that, empirically, there are certain

---

2 W A Wilson, 'Floating Charges' 1962 SLT (News) 53.
3 For example, G L Gretton, 'What Went Wrong with Floating Charges?' 1984 SLT (News) 172 and G L Gretton, 'Should Floating Charges and Receivership be Abolished?' 1986 SLT (News) 325.
4 R B Jack, 'The Coming of the Floating Charge to Scotland: an Account and an Assessment', in D J Cusine (ed), *A Scots Conveyancing Miscellany: Essays in Honour of Professor J M Halliday* (Edinburgh: W. Green, 1987) 33 at 45–46.
5 D Cabrelli, 'The Case against the Floating Charge in Scotland' (2005) 9 Edin L Rev 407.
6 J Hardman, 'Some Legal Determinants of External Finance in Scotland: A Response to Lord Hodge' (2017) 21(1) Edin L Rev 30.

security rules that are associated with attraction of debt capital into a juris-diction.[7] These rules can be split into 'collateral' rules that enable enforce-ment of security outside insolvency, and 'bankruptcy' rules that require an insolvency process as part of the security enforcement mechanism.[8] The current attachment rules of the Scottish floating charge[9] mean that the float-ing charge currently only operates for Scottish companies as a bankruptcy rule rather than a collateral rule.[10] Enforcement of the floating charge may, of course, commence prior to the insolvency of the debtor, but it only attaches upon events that are fundamentally connected to bankruptcy. Creditors value collateral rules more than they value bankruptcy rules.[11] The author therefore pushed for reform of the floating charge in accordance with English law, to allow for variation of the point in time at which the float-ing charge attaches.[12]

This would seem to provide an adequate economic justification for the floating charge. However, the author commenced that argument with: 'Given the methodology employed, policy questions about the desirability of proposals such as fixed security over moveable assets and the existence of floating charges are ignored in the analysis of this paper'.[13]

By avoiding such analysis, the author also side-stepped the issue of the economic advantage of the floating charge to Scots law. However, the author did provide some argumentation in respect of rights in security converging in certain circumstances: transaction costs of differences between English and Scots law can be high and should be minimised wherever possible to maximise efficiency.[14] Somehow, however, it seems as if the argument that 'English law has it and so Scots law would be harmed without it' would not quite satisfy the Challenge.

---

7 R Haslemann, K Pistor and V Vig, 'How Law Affects Lending' (2010) 23(2) *The Review of Financial Studies* 549.

8 R Haslemann, K Pistor and V Vig, 'How Law Affects Lending' at 550.

9 Companies Act 1985 s. 463 (liquidation); Insolvency Act 1986 ss. 53(7) and 54(6) (receivership); and Insolvency Act 1986 Sch. B1 para. 115(1B), (3) and (4) (administration).

10 Hardman (n 6) at 49–50.

11 Haslemann, Pistor and Vig (n 7) at 551.

12 Hardman (n 6) at 50.

13 Hardman (n 6) at 31.

14 Hardman (n 6) at 39–42.

(3) Law and economics and security

Perhaps the answer to the Challenge can be borrowed from previous non-Scottish law and economics arguments. Real rights in security have been a difficult subject for law and economics thinkers since 1981, when Alan Schwartz challenged the view that:

> 'the institution of security is efficient. Lawyers commonly make this claim in a slightly different form, asserting that the ability of firms to give security increases the amount of credit available to the firms, but the implicit premise is that the gains to firms and secured creditors from additional credit exceed the costs that security may occasionally impose on priority and general creditors'.[15]

There are therefore two interlinked issues – why a chargor and creditor should make the private bargain to grant security, and why society should accept the concept of one creditor receiving a preferential return as a result of this private bargain.

The advantage to the creditor under the first question is, of course, simple – at the very least they receive an advantageous return on the insolvency of the debtor than they would in the absence of security.[16] In addition, security generally provides the ability to link specified assets to the repayment obligation, which can provide advantageous non-insolvency enforcement and debt recovery mechanisms.[17] Apart from the need to publicise the presence of debt relationship, it seems as if there are no disadvantages to a specific creditor in becoming the recipient of security.

From the granter's perspective Schwartz raised a simple concern – if granting security to a creditor reduces the cost of debt from that creditor, it will increase the cost of debt from other creditors who are not protected: 'the debtor's total interest bill is thus unaffected by the existence of security'.[18] This approach is reminiscent of the Modigliani-Miller hypothesis of capital structures: that the capital structure of a firm (i.e. its balance between debt and equity) cannot have an impact on the value of the firm, as debt will be priced into the purchase price of any acquisition of such firm.[19] When one

---

15 A Schwartz, 'Security Interests and Bankruptcy Priorities: A Review of Current Theories' (1981) 10 *Journal of Legal Studies* 1 at 2.
16 See e.g. Insolvency Act 1986 Sch. B1 para. 116(a).
17 In other words, the creditor is able (mostly) to enforce their security over specified assets without causing the bankruptcy of the debtor.
18 Schwartz (n 15) at 7–8.
19 F Modigliani and M H Miller, 'The Cost of Capital, Corporation Finance and the Theory of Investment' (1958) 48 *American Economic Review* 261.

factors in transaction costs of granting security,[20] there is no point in doing so. From a debtor's perspective, therefore, there are no advantages to agreeing to grant security as it will receive no benefits but incur minor costs. There are counterarguments to this analysis. It has been argued that the amount by which unsecured creditors' interest costs rise will be less than the drop in the interest rates in respect of the secured debt, as secured creditors have more of an incentive to monitor companies, and unsecured creditors are able to free-ride on this and so not have as much of an increase.[21] As a result, there may be net benefits to the blended interest rate payable.

In addition, it is argued that the presence of security provides a signal to unsecured creditors that the restrictions of the security are justified by the benefits that will be obtained by the secured debt.[22] In other words, it is possible that the grant of security reflects a signal by the managers and owners of the company that they believe they can use the funds secured to make sufficient profit to justify the return and inconvenience of the presence of security. This is, of course, not clear cut as the grant of security may also be a signal that the debtor is not as creditworthy, and instead may be a signal if the creditor will *only* extend credit if they obtain some form of security for repayment, in addition to the mere payment obligation. It is also possible that the grant of security could be associated with the incurrence of more debt as a way to push risk from the owners to the creditors, in the knowledge that creditors will bear the risk of failure but the owners will obtain the benefits of success.[23]

White has argued that credit support provided by security helps avoid inefficiencies of unnecessary risk aversion caused by banks.[24] This logic states that banks would normally behave inefficiently, either by refusing to lend or by charging higher interest rates than objectively justifiable. Borrowers grant security because it enables them to secure an efficient loan or lower the interest rates in a beneficial manner. It is certainly the case that security lowers interest rates.[25] It therefore may make sense to grant security

20 Schwartz (n 15) at 10.
21 T H Jackson and A T Kronman, 'Secured Financing and Priorities Among Creditors' (1979) 88 Yale LJ 1143; S Levmore, 'Monitors and Freeriders in Commercial and Corporate Settings' (1982) 92 Yale LJ 49.
22 Schwartz (n 15) at 15–17.
23 See J Hardman, 'The Moral Hazard of Limited Liability: An Empirical Scottish Study' (2018) 6 *Nottingham Insolvency and Business Law eJournal* 3.
24 J J White, 'Efficiency Justifications for Personal Property Security' (1984) 37 VandLRev 473.
25 J Qian and P E Strahan, 'How Laws and Institutions Shape Financial Contracts: The Case of Bank Loans' (2007) 62(6) *The Journal of Finance* 2803.

in order to lower your interest rate, if the benefit outweighs increases in interest rate from other debtors. However, this is more likely to be driven by a requirement for cheaper debt rather than by hopes of wider gains in efficiency.[26] Nonetheless, it presents a clear picture of why a granter will be keen to grant security.

Why, then, does society allow secured claims to be paid prior to unsecured claims? After all, this effectively allows for a private contract to have third party effect to the detriment of third parties, which is generally not accepted. This is an issue that Bebchuk and Fried have grappled with. They consider that the precise issue that means that it is efficient for a granter to grant security (namely that unsecured creditors may not adjust their prices accordingly) can make security inefficient from the perspective of the creditors.[27] This is not the case if an unsecured creditor has taken the informed decision to free-ride on the monitoring of the debtor by the secured creditor, as in those circumstances it is a deliberate decision by the unsecured creditor to not make any price adjustment. Such a creditor could adjust but chose not to. The issue, instead, arises from creditors who cannot make such adjustments. The key categories of such creditors are involuntary creditors, which is the law and economics terminology for those who do not choose to interact with the company – for example, delict sufferers and the state as tax creditor.[28] These creditors cannot adjust their prices to reflect for the increased risk of a prior ranking claim as they have no control over, and sometimes no awareness of, whether they have a claim or not. Similarly, there are those creditors whose claims are too small to justify them monitoring the debtor's financial standing and/or whose bargaining strength is not strong enough for them to successfully make any price adjustments.

It is tempting to dismiss the claims of non-adjusting creditors as irrelevant but, actually, they are a key and core element of any trading company as they normally include suppliers, customers and employees.[29] These key categories may be unable to adjust their terms at all, even with the grant of security by the debtor. The result is that security rules can encourage the inefficient grant of security, as certain creditors become over-protected and

---

26 A Schwartz, 'The Continuing Puzzle of Secured Debt' (1984) 37 VandLRev 1051.
27 L A Bebchuk and J M Fried, 'The Uneasy Case for the Priority of Secured Claims in Bankruptcy' (1996) 105 Yale LJ 857.
28 L A Bebchuk and J M Fried, 'The Uneasy Case for the Priority of Secured Claims in Bankruptcy' (n 27) at 882–883.
29 L A Bebchuk and J M Fried, 'The Uneasy Case for the Priority of Secured Claims in Bankruptcy' (n 27) at 885–887.

others exposed when they are not happy to be so.[30] To avoid this, Bebchuk and Fried propose a modified set of priority rules: secured creditors should obtain priority over adjusting non-secured creditors but not over non-adjusting non-secured creditors. Such framework would, they posit, be economically efficient. This article was subject to some debate,[31] leading the authors to provide a subsequent response to address the practical implications of their proposal.[32] Zhang points out some benefits to non-adjusting creditors of security: the interest rate burden of the debtor falls to secured parties, resulting in the debtor paying less interest, which results in the debtor having more funds to pay, *inter alia*, non-adjusting creditors.[33]

The result is clear: security provides benefits for the debtor, the creditor and adjusting third party creditors. Whether it is efficient from the perspective of non-adjusting third parties is debatable. Nonetheless, the structure to answer the Challenge exists, as does pre-existing analysis that the author can successfully crib to do so. The thorny issue remains, however, of how best to apply this to the case of the floating charge in Scots law. Unfortunately, the foregoing analysis is based on US law and concepts and is rather general: it draws no distinctions between the floating charge and fixed charges. It therefore may be that the analysis does not apply to floating charges. Certainly, a large section of the analysis defending security does so on the basis that security prevents the debtor from substituting assets from the secured pool without the prior approval of the creditors,[34] which is evidently not appropriate for the Scottish floating charge. Most of the above analysis is linked to the US Uniform Commercial Code notice-based system of security,[35] a system that Scots law has eschewed.[36] There have been two key applications

---

30 L A Bebchuk and J M Fried, 'The Uneasy Case for the Priority of Secured Claims in Bankruptcy' (n 27) at 896–897.

31 For example, S L Harris and C W Mooney, 'Measuring the Social Costs and Benefits and Identifying the Victims of Subordinating Security Interests in Bankruptcy' (1997) 82 Cornell LRev 1349 and R J Mann, 'The First Shall be Last: A Contextual Argument for Abandoning Temporal Rules of Lien Priority' (1996) 75 TexLRev 11.

32 L A Bebchuk and J M Fried, 'The Uneasy Case for the Priority of Secured Claims in Bankruptcy: Further Thoughts and a Reply to Critics' (1997) 82 Cornell LRev 1279.

33 W Zhang, 'The Paradoxes of Secured Lending: Is There a Less Uneasy Case for the Priority of Secured Claims in Bankruptcy' (2011) 16 *University of Pennsylvania Journal of Business Law* 789 at 815.

34 See J Bigus, 'Bankruptcy Law, Asset Substitution Problem, and Creditor Conflicts' (2002) 22 *International Review of Law & Economics* 109.

35 For a discussion, see M Schinner, 'Examining the integrity of a Notice-Filing System: Are Financial Statements Filed Solely Under a Debtor's Trade Name Sufficient to Perfect a Security Interest under UCC Section 9–402?' (1989) 94 *Commercial Law Journal* 175.

36 See Scottish Law Commission, *Report on Moveable Transactions* (Scot. Law Com. No. 249, 2017) para. 18.44.

of these theories to English law. However, the first looks at the subject holistically rather than split into its application to floating charges.[37] The second concluded in 2005 that, whilst the floating charge may have performed an important function, since the implementation of the Enterprise Act 2002 this has been redundant and that the floating charge should be abolished.[38] This means that there is not even an English law element to the analysis that can be borrowed for this chapter to meet the Challenge. The existing literature, therefore, does not resolve the Challenge, but it does give some basic arguments that can provide a backdrop to provide ammunition to the author to meet the Challenge. To do so, we will review the concept of economic efficiency and see whether the Scots floating charge can be considered to be economically efficient in light of the foregoing.

B. EFFICIENCY

(1) Efficiency generally

The first step in the analysis is to establish what we mean by 'efficiency'. In its widest sense, a transaction is 'efficient' if people feel that they are better off as a result of it. Thus if I buy something for £10 that I value at £12 the purchase is, from my perspective, efficient. The fact that the shop I bought it from was willing to put it up for sale for £10 demonstrates that, generally, they valued the item for less than £10. Accordingly, the transaction is 'efficient' from the perspective of the buyer and the seller. It seems intuitively difficult to apply this to a loan by a bank, as the bank lends £10 and receives an obligation to be repaid £10 (plus interest), whereas the debtor borrows £10 in exchange for an obligation to repay £10 (plus interest). However, by factoring liquidity into the position the analysis is clarified: the borrower values the liquidity acquired by obtaining £10 today more highly then the obligation to pay back £10 plus interest at some point in the future. Conversely, the bank values the fees and interests it gains in the future over the loss of liquidity today. Accordingly, a loan only will be made if it is efficient from the perspective of the borrower and the lender.

A complication arises when the actions of A and B affect a third party. This gives rise to an 'externality'. Pigou describes externalities as:

---

37 See L Gullifer and J Payne, *Corporate Finance Law: Principle and Policy*, 3rd edn (Oxford: Hart Publishing, 2020) para. 7.6.
38 R J Mokal, *Corporate Insolvency Law: Theory and Application* (Oxford: Oxford University Press, 2005) Ch. 6.

'The essence of the matter is that one person, A, in the course of rendering services, for which payment is made, to a second person, B, incidentally also renders services or disservices to other persons (not producers of like services) of such assort that payment cannot be exacted from the benefited parties or compensation enforced on behalf of the injured parties.'[39]

Externalities can be negative or positive. This means that third parties need to be included in the 'efficiency' analysis: they do not input into the contract, but they either benefit or are harmed by it (or, more likely, both). Consider a contract between a manufacturer and its customer that is efficient for both parties. There are a number of externalities that will be created by it: it may require additional employees to fulfil it, which will provide a positive externality to the community and the staff hired. It may also result in increased levels of pollution, which results in a negative externality for the community and the neighbours of the manufacturer. Pigou concludes that state action is required to mitigate negative externalities on the grounds that the sufferer cannot prevent them and suffers a harm from them.[40] This approach, however, is disputed by Coase.[41] Coase's argument is that Pigou's approach is based on an overly simplistic and unilateral model – the state must stop A doing harm to C. However, the way in which it would do so would be to make A worse off than they would otherwise be, and therefore there is a reciprocity of harm to consider.[42] He uses the following argument:

'Let us suppose that a farmer and a cattle-raiser are operating on neighbouring properties. Let us further suppose that, without any fencing between the properties, an increase in the size of the cattle-raiser's herd increases the total damage to the farmer's crops.'[43]

Coase argues, in what would famously become known as the 'Coase Theorem',[44] that in a frictionless world, the rancher and the farmer would come to an agreement to produce the optimal outcome. The argument is best illustrated by Coleman, who uses an example where the advantage to the rancher getting another cow is $50 and the damage to the crops of getting that cow is either $25 or $75. The default rule either benefits the farmer

---

39 A C Pigou, *The Economics of Welfare*, 4th edn (London: Macmillan & Co, 1932) 184.
40 A C Pigou, *The Economics of Welfare* 127–130.
41 R H Coase, 'The Problem of Social Cost' (1960) 3 *Journal of Law and Economics* 1.
42 R H Coase, 'The Problem of Social Cost' at 2.
43 R H Coase, 'The Problem of Social Cost' at 2–3.
44 Coase states that this phrase was initially formulated by Stigler – see S Schwab, 'Coase Defends Coase: Why Lawyers Listen and Economists Do Not' (1989) 87 MichLRev 1171 at 1173. See also S G Medema, 'A Case of Mistaken Identity: George Stigler, 'The Problem of Social Cost,' and the Coase Theorem' (2011) 31 *European Journal of Law and Economics* 11.

Table 5.1

	Crop damage $25	Crop damage $75
Default rule in favour of rancher	No transaction: the rancher is able to buy the cow and it is not worthwhile for the farmer to pay to prevent it.	Transaction: the farmer will bribe[1] the rancher between $50 and $75 to prevent the cow being acquired (i.e. between the benefit of doing the damage and the damage done).
Default rule in favour of farmer	Transaction: the rancher will pay the farmer between $25 and $50 for the right to buy the cow (i.e. between the damage done and the benefit of doing the damage).	No transaction: it is not worthwhile for the rancher to pay the farmer to be able to do so.

[1] The use of bribes to not be harmed produces the potential for the use of threats of harm to generate profit in and of itself, which result can result in resource misallocation – G A Mumey, 'The "Coase Theorem": A Re-examination' (1971) 85(4) *Quarterly Journal of Law and Economics* 718, but once more we will concentrate on the specific transactional effect.

(the rancher has to pay for the damage) or the rancher (the farmer has to absorb the cost of the damage). Depending on the default allocation of risk, we can see the four possibilities in Table 5.1.[45]

The result is therefore that the rancher and the farmer will negotiate together to produce an efficient result. Coase used this to repudiate Pigou on the grounds that no state action is necessary to resolve externalities as they will be internalised within the bargain.[46] This is, however, only the case if transaction costs are zero,[47] which they are unlikely to be.[48] However, the Coase Theorem goes much further than this and stipulates that this is the case *regardless of legal allocation of rules*.[49] It therefore appears as if rules have no place in deciding the efficiency of transactions, which would mean that the presence (or absence) of the floating charge would be irrelevant for efficiency. However, the above simple example shows us that the default

45 J L Coleman, 'Efficiency, Exchange, and Auction: Philosophic Aspects of the Economic Approach to Law' (1980) 68(2) CalLRev 221.

46 Coase (n 41) at 34.

47 See P Schlag, 'Coase Minus the Coase Theory – Some Problems with Chicago Transaction Costs Analysis' (2013) 99(1) Iowa LRev 175 at 193.

48 For example, R C Ellickson, *Order without Law: How Neighbors Settle Disputes* (Harvard: Harvard University Press, 1991).

49 This can be split into a 'strong' version – that parties will make efficient bargains regardless of the legal allocation of risk, and a 'weak' version – that the legal allocation of risk will not alter the efficiency of transactions concluded between parties. See S Schwab, 'A Coasean Experiment on Contract Presumptions' (1988) 17 *Journal of Legal Studies* 237 at 242–243.

allocation of rules (i.e. the default rules that apply) results in a variety of different transactional outcomes. In the example of the cow causing $25 crop damage, if the default rule is in favour of the rancher then the farmer has to suffer $25 damage and there will be no transaction, whereas if the default rule is in favour of the farmer then there will be a transaction as the rancher will pay the farmer between $25 (the cost to the farmer of the damage of an extra cow) and $50 (the advantage to the rancher of having an extra cow) to allow the rancher to have the extra cow. Whilst under either the cow will be bought, the steps required to effect it, and thus produce the efficient outcome, are different. In the example of the cow causing crop damage of $75, if the default rule is in favour of the rancher then the farmer will pay the rancher between $50 (the advantage to the rancher of having an extra cow) and $75 (the cost to the farmer of there being an extra cow) to avoid the damage. If the default rule is in favour of the farmer then there is no transaction. Once again, the efficient outcome will be achieved either way (the cow will not be bought) but the steps to achieve it vary. We can therefore see two different types of change that the legal rules have on any given transaction:

i.   They affect the *type of transaction* required to achieve an efficient end – whether a transaction is required at all or whether it is a payment of a bribe not to do something or a payment to obtain permission to injure.

ii.   They affect the *distribution of benefits* between the parties.[50] In the four outcomes the net position of each of the parties is provided in Table 5.2 opposite.

This example shows that if the default rule is in favour of the rancher then they will receive between $50 and $75, regardless of crop damage, whereas the farmer will lose between $25 and $75. If, however, the default rule is in favour of the farmer then the rancher will gain between $0 and $25 whilst the farmer will gain between $0 and $25: whilst all efficient overall, the transactions involved dramatically vary. Hale established that apparent neutrality of the law is never actually neutral[51] – a series of mandatory rules exist that provide bargaining chills to certain parties and bargaining boosts to others: for example, tort law provides a bargaining boost to factory owners and a bargaining chill to striking employees. This analysis can be easily

---

50   This applies in the long term as well as the short term – D H Regan, 'The Problem of Social Cost Revisited' (1972) 15 *Journal of Law & Economics* 427 at 432.

51   See R L Hale, 'Bargaining, Duress and Economic Liberty' (1943) 43 ColumLRev 603.

Table 5.2

	Crop damage $25	Crop damage $75
Default rule in favour of rancher	Rancher: +$50	Rancher: + between $50 and $75
	(+$50 for the cow, –$0 for permission to injure).	(as will receive between $50 and $75 in a bribe to not get the cow).
	Farmer: –$25	Farmer: – between $50 and $75
	(–$25 for the damage).	(as will suffer no damage but have to pay between $50 and $75 bribe for the rancher to not get the cow).
Default rule in favour of farmer	Rancher: +between $25 and $0	Rancher: $0 (as will not acquire cow).
	(+$50 for the cow, – between $50 and $25 for permission to injure).	
	Farmer: + between $25 and $0.	Farmer: $0 (as no damage done).
	(+ between $25 and $50 for permission to injure, –$25 for the damage).	

extended to default rules[52]: if all default rules are in my favour when I come to sell my company, it is easy to envisage me getting more from a buyer than were they not. Accordingly, default rules have a distributive impact that, in turn, affects the transaction to be undertaken. This means that the presence (or absence) of a floating charge available under the legal system would affect the 'efficiency' of debt transactions.

Indeed, it is possible that one of the parties is fundamentally better suited to pay certain types of costs than the other, even if they are recompensed for it by the other[53] – this, in turn, will affect the nature of transaction to be undertaken.

(2) Efficiency and law

What does the foregoing have to do with the floating charge? It shows us that the legal landscape matters for transactional purposes – at least for transaction structure. More than this, we live in a world that has transaction costs,

---

52 D Kennedy, *Sexy Dressing etc. Essays in the Power and Politics of Cultural Identity* (Harvard: Harvard University Press, 1993) 89.
53 See D W Carlton and A S Frankel, 'Transaction Costs, Externalities and "Two-Sided" Payment Markets' [2005] ColumBusLRev 617.

which provides a corollary of the Coase Theorem: in a world with transaction costs (i.e. the real world), legal allocation of risk by default rules affects the efficiency of the ultimate bargains struck between the parties.[54] Indeed, there has been considerable debate about whether Pigou is right (and unmitigated negative externalities should be mitigated by the state) or Coase is right (and unmitigated negative externalities should not be mitigated by the state as their very presence tells us that their presence is efficient as they have not been bargained away). The result is:

> 'What is involved is a value judgment: if you believe that markets internalize everything, you will believe that externalities do not exist; on the other hand, if you believe that markets do not internalize side effects, you will believe in the persistence of externalities as deviations from an attainable optimum ... it is thus doubtful whether the term 'externality' has any meaningful interpretation, except as an indicator of the political beliefs and value judgments of the person who uses (or avoids using) the term.'[55]

However, this value judgement can be resolved by considering the foregoing analysis: adjusting creditors will fit into the Coase model, whereas non-adjusting creditors will fit into the Pigou model. Accordingly, there may not be such a conflict after all.

This analysis shows us that laws affect efficiency. It provides a link for us to analyse the introduction of a law's effect on overall efficiency within the marketplace. Thus we can move from judging the efficiency of transactions to judging the efficiency of laws.[56] A law that gives everyone with the initials 'JH' £10 is clearly efficient from the perspective of the author. However, the classic economic problem is that resources are finite, which means that this £10 must come from somewhere. It is unlikely that the person who has lost £10 would consider this law to be efficient. This can be seen by the rancher/farmer example: default rules in favour of the rancher result in them gaining between $50 and $75 and the farmer losing between $25 and $75, whereas default rules in favour of the farmer result in the rancher gaining between $0 and $25, and the farmer gaining between $0 and $25. All are ostensibly efficient overall, but there are a wide variety of gains and losses suffered between the parties. We therefore need to consider how best to measure efficiency when we consider more than just two voluntarily contracting parties.

---

54 See H Demetz, 'When Does the Rule of Liability Matter?' (1972) 1 *Journal of Legal Studies* 13 at 26.

55 C J Dahlman, 'The Problem of Externality' (1979) 22 *Journal of Law and Economics* 141 at 156.

56 M Pacces and L Visscher, 'Methodology of Law and Economics' in B van Klink and S Taekema (eds), *Law and Method. Interdisciplinary Research into Law* (Tubingen: Mohr Siebeck, 2011) 85, 107.

(3) Measuring efficiency

There are several measurements of efficiency. The simplest test for a transaction to be 'efficient' is that everyone involved in the transaction has an improvement in their position: the direct parties to the arrangement consider it to be beneficial to themselves and the only externalities that are not internalised into the bargain are positive externalities. This results in everyone having a gain on their position. For each move taken that achieves this, the end state is said to be 'Pareto superior' to the start state.[57] Thus consider an example whereby I have £10 in my pocket that I value at £10, and there is a good for sale for £10 that I value at £12 but the seller considers to be worth £8 to them. Let us imagine there are no externalities. By completing that trade I lose £10 but gain £12, and the seller loses £8 but gains £10. Thus both of us makes a net gain on our position. Similarly in the situation of our manufacturer contract – so long as there are no negative externalities, then entering into the contract is Pareto superior to the position before the contract was entered into. When all Pareto superior moves have been made, we reach a position of Pareto optimality. Thus my purchase of one good for £10 is a Pareto superior position. But if I have £30 in my pocket[58] and there are three such items for sale, it is not Pareto optimal until I have purchased all three items. When I have purchased one item, each of myself and the seller have experienced a gain of £2 but can experience further gains of £4 – optimality is not reached until all potential gains are exhausted and it is not possible to make any further gains.

The cattle rancher and farmer outcomes noted above where the default rules were in favour of the farmer were Pareto superior as, whilst the farmer suffered damage, they experienced a net gain on their position. Indeed, it has been argued that the Coase Theorem is merely the tautological result of Pareto optimality.[59] Nevertheless, the losses that each party nets off must be their own: each participant must make a net gain from a transaction for it to be a Pareto superior transaction, or everyone affected must make a net gain from the introduction of a law for it to be Pareto superior. This is an

---

57 A M Feldman, 'Pareto Optimality' in P Newman (ed), *The New Palgrave Dictionary of Economics and the Law* Vol. 3 (London: Palgrave Macmillan, 1998) 8.
58 Assuming, for the sake of argument, there is no marginal change in my value of these purchases: I value the third purchased item the same as I value the first purchased item and I value the third and final £10 the same as I do the first £10, which would leave me with £20 left over.
59 G Calabresi and A D Melamed, 'Property Rules, Liability Rules, and Inalienability: One View of the Cathedral' (1972) 85 HarvLRev 1089 at 1095.

incredibly high bar to meet and 'in the world of government policy choices, or choices of law, almost every move makes someone worse off'.[60] This has resulted in an alternative measure of efficiency being utilised: Kaldor-Hicks efficiency. This measures the net result of a transaction: if in aggregate the participants are better off by the transaction then it is Kaldor-Hicks efficient – allowing individual parties to a transaction to be 'worse off'.[61] Thus the cattle rancher and farmer outcomes are all Kaldor-Hicks efficient and would be even if the farmer were not compensated: a transaction in which the rancher gained $50 for an additional cow that caused $25 of damage to the farmer would be efficient regardless of whether the farmer were indeed compensated.

Kaldor-Hicks efficiency is the dominant metric of efficiency in law and economics[62] and yet remains a fundamentally flawed metric. It only examines the ability for the loss sufferer to be adequately compensated, not whether the loss sufferer has actually been compensated.[63] Accordingly it ignores systemic and structural harm suffered by categories of market participants. Consider a world in which those with the initials JH valued each widget at £10, whereas those with the initials AM valued each widget at £8. A law that obliged everyone with the initials AM to hand over all of their widgets to someone with the initials JH would be Kaldor-Hicks efficient, as the result would be a net gain in 'value' across the economy: each expropriation of a widget would cost an AM £8 but provide a benefit to a JH of £10 – providing a net gain of £2 per expropriation. However, such analysis would be fundamentally flawed as it would ignore the distributive impact of such a law on those with the initials AM.[64] Accordingly, the ability to net aggregate losses against aggregate gains acts to disguise structural harm caused in the marketplace by an ostensibly efficient law.[65] There are other flaws within Kaldor-Hicks efficiency. Primarily, it is subject to a phenomenon known as the Scitovsky paradox[66]: which is that its analysis can be used to show, at the same time, that a move from position one to position two is more efficient

60 Feldman (n 57) 8. For a discussion of efficiency in a normative sense, see Hardman (n 6).
61 A M Feldman, 'Kaldor-Hicks Compensation' in P Newman (ed), *The New Palgrave Dictionary of Economics and the Law* Vol. 2 (London: Palgrave Macmillan, 1998) 417–421.
62 R A Posner, 'The Ethical and Political Basis of the Efficiency Norm in Common Law Adjudication' (1980) 8 Hofstra LRev 487.
63 Feldman (n 61).
64 Hale (n 51).
65 Kennedy (n 52) 89.
66 T Scitovsky, 'A Note on Welfare Propositions in Economics' (1941) 9 *Review of Economic Studies* 77.

and that a move from position two to position one is also more efficient.[67] Scitovsky provides a mathematical proof for this but also provides the example of trade imports: it can be shown to be Kaldor-Hicks efficient for trade imports to be put in place (as then the state has more money) and to be removed (as then the trader will receive more income).[68] This is especially the case when the act of change is the transformative element rather than what it is changed to. If, conversely, people value maintaining what they have rather than pushing for a gain the Kaldor-Hicks will value the status quo.[69] As a result, it is impossible to use Kaldor-Hicks to identify whether position one or position two should be adopted. We therefore cannot use Kaldor-Hicks to definitively state whether a policy move was correct.

As a result, despite its higher bar, in order to meet the Challenge it is necessary for us to argue that the introduction of the floating charge in Scotland was Pareto superior. In order to measure this, we need to identify two fixed positions. We will call the world in which Scots law does not acknowledge the floating charge or any functional equivalent 'Position one' and the world in which Scots law does acknowledge the floating charge 'Position two'. The next section will analyse whether a move from Position one to Position two is Pareto superior. To do so, it outlines whether the floating charge in Scotland leaves every category of market participant better off without any uninternalised negative externalities arising.

C. THE PARETO SUPERIORITY OF THE SCOTS LAW FLOATING CHARGE

(1) Position without floating charge

In order to establish whether a move to Position two is a Pareto superior move, we need to establish what Position one is. The present tense is important – our study is not whether the original introduction of the floating charge was a Pareto superior move but whether the current legal regime represents an improvement on a putative modern world without the floating charge.

---

67 J L Coleman, 'Economics and the Law: A Critical Review of the Foundations of the Economic Approach to Law' (1984) 94(4) *Ethics* 649 at 670–671.

68 Scitovsky (n 66) at 88.

69 R S Markovits, 'A Constructive Critique of the Traditional Definition and Use of the Concept of the Effect of a Choice on Allocative (Economic) Efficiency: Why the Kaldor-Hicks Test, the Coase Theorem and Virtually all Law-and-Economics Welfare Arguments are Wrong' [1993] *University of Illinois Law Review* 485.

Position one therefore, is the position detailed throughout this book but without the ability to grant a floating charge. As such, it represents a Scottish market where the flexibility of a debtor to grant security is limited. True security, being a subordinate real right in an asset,[70] is limited to two categories of property. Heritable property can be subject to a standard security,[71] noted on the title of the property.[72] The standard security provides some fundamental restrictions on major changes to the heritable property itself,[73] but the granter remains fundamentally free to use the property – not least to occupy it themselves. It is therefore possible to use heritable property as a way to obtain secured finance that delivers the theoretical benefits of granting security noted above. However, there are downsides. The method of enforcing a standard security is onerous and takes a long time.[74] More than this, however, this procedure (known as the 'calling up' procedure[75]) requires the creditor to actually undertake action in respect of the property in their own name.[76] Thus the serving of a calling up notice (and expiry of notice periods) enables the creditor to sell the property. The creditor is not able to use the standard security to contract in the name of the granter but must instead contract in their own name.[77] This exposes the creditor unnecessarily as they become the contractual counterparty to whom a purchaser would direct any recourse. Standard securities can only secure existing properties, not future properties to be owned by the debtor.[78]

True security can also be granted over corporeal moveables by way of pledge.[79] Thus a valuable watch can be pledged as a way of obtaining finance.

---

70 See A J M Steven and H Patrick, 'Reforming the Law of Secured Transactions in Scotland', in L Gullifer and O Akseli (eds), *Secured Transactions Law Reform: Principles, Policies and Practice* (London: Bloomsbury, 2016) 253 at 255–257.

71 Conveyancing and Feudal Reform (Scotland) Act 1970 s. 9.

72 Conveyancing and Feudal Reform (Scotland) Act 1970 s. 9(2).

73 For example, see the default position on granting new leases contained in Conveyancing and Feudal Reform (Scotland) Act 1970 Sch. 3 para. 6.

74 Conveyancing and Feudal Reform (Scotland) Act 1970 Form A of Sch. 6. Standard securities generally are being examined by the Scottish Law Commission, with their next discussion paper due to include enforcement of standard securities – see Scottish Law Commission, *Heritable Securities*, available at *https://www.scotlawcom.gov.uk/law-reform/law-reform-projects/herita ble-securities/* (last accessed 27 October 2021).

75 Conveyancing and Feudal Reform (Scotland) Act 1970 s. 19.

76 Conveyancing and Feudal Reform (Scotland) Act 1970 s. 26.

77 See J MacLeod, 'Research Paper on Enforcement of Standard Securities' para. 4–71, available at *https://www.scotlawcom.gov.uk/files/8315/3501/3935/FINAL_Paper_on_Enforcement_of_ Standard_Securities_by_Dr_John_MacLeod.pdf* (last accessed 27 October 2021).

78 Conveyancing and Feudal Reform (Scotland) Act 1970 s. 9(2) states that the standard security is only created when registered against property owned by the granter.

79 See A J M Steven, *Pledge and Lien* (Edinburgh: Edinburgh Legal Education Trust, 2008).

However, there are fundamental limitations to this. First, the pledged item must be actually delivered to the beneficiary of the pledge.[80] Any return of the pledged item results in the pledge falling away.[81] Similarly, any 'fruits' (i.e. profits) of the pledged items must sit with the beneficiary of the pledge rather than the pledgor.[82] As a result, the immediate practical effect of the pledge for the granter is more equivalent to a sale with an optional repurchase – whilst they retain formal ownership, they exchange possession for funds. Upon repayment of those funds (together with a premium) then possession will be returned. It is therefore possible to use the pledge to raise finance for something unconnected to the pledged item: I can pledge my watch to purchase a new kitchen. Similarly, a business can pledge their corporeal moveable property so long as they do not intend to use it. This therefore causes an issue in the business context as it becomes impossible to pledge moveable property that is intended to be used. Thus a widget manufacturer who owns only a widget-making machine cannot pledge that machine in order to provide working capital to put through the widget-making machine. The dispossession of the granter in the pledge directly causes an inability to use the business' main methods of generating sufficient profit to repay the debt secured. It is therefore not generally of use in a business context.[83]

It is not possible to create true security over incorporeal moveable property.[84] As a result a 'functional equivalent'[85] has developed in the marketplace: an assignation in security. The assignation in security involves assigning the incorporeal moveable property to the creditor and intimating the assignation to the debtor.[86] In the case of a monetary claim, this

---

80 See discussion in *Hamilton v Western Bank of Scotland* (1856) 19 D 152. Whether this remains the current law is debated – see Scottish Law Commission, *Report on Moveable Transactions* (n 36) paras 16.31, 17.18 and 25.4. The lack of clarity over this issue is, of course, less than ideal (and is the subject of a proposal to clarify this by overturning the rule in *Hamilton v Western Bank of Scotland* – see Scottish Law Commission, *Report on Moveable Transactions* (n 36) para. 25.10).

81 *Mackinnon v Max Nanson & Co* (1868) 6 M 974.

82 *Kirkwood and Pattison v Brown* (1877) 1 Guth Sh Cas 395. See also Steven, *Pledge and Lien* (n 79) para. 7–10.

83 Although may be if the product in question does not need to be used, but simply mature such as whisky or brandy. Similarly, a business that only used its machinery seasonally could, technically, deliver their machinery to the creditor when they are not using it. For obvious reasons this remains suboptimal.

84 See J Hardman, *A Practical Guide to Granting Corporate Security in Scotland* (Edinburgh: W. Green, 2018) para. 7–20.

85 Steven and Patrick (n 70) 255–257.

86 See generally R G Anderson, *Assignation* (Edinburgh: Edinburgh Legal Education Trust, 2008).

involves telling the payer to pay such amounts to the creditor instead. It is unclear whether a notice can be intimated confirming that the transfer has taken place but entitling the debtor to still pay amounts to the security provider.[87] Even if such a mechanic were to be held to be valid, the effect of an assignation in security remains that ownership of the asset transfers from the granter to the recipient.[88] Thus assignations in security of shares require the register of members of the company whose shares are subject to such security to be written up to reflect the ownership by the creditor.[89] Assignations in security cannot apply to future rights,[90] meaning that all that can be assigned are any current rights of the granter, with an agreement to grant security over future assets – an agreement that will not survive the insolvency of the granter.[91] This therefore limits the utility of this functional security to the creditor. There is some authority that provides an obligation on the recipient to return the assigned property if the debt is repaid[92] but the ambit of this right is not clear. Similarly, it is unclear what would happen to the assigned asset on the insolvency of the creditor – the author believes that common sense dictates that it should be excluded from the assets of the insolvent creditor and not open to be realised for distribution, but there is little authority for this analysis.[93] However, this application of 'common sense' is open to dispute: such an interpretation would result in the personal right of retrocession being prioritised over other personal rights owed by the assignee. This would result in the assigned property not being included within the assignee's estate. Upholding the clear distinction between real and personal rights in the insolvency context may be a preferred 'common sense' interpretation.

---

87 See discussion in Hardman, *Granting Corporate Security* (n 84) para. 7–30 outlining a disagreement between the author and the Scottish Law Commission in approach.

88 W M Gloag and J M Irvine, *Law of Rights in Security: Heritable and Moveable Including Cautionary Obligations* (Edinburgh: W. Green, 1897) 490.

89 See J Hardman, 'Scottish Share Pledges and Recent Legislative Developments: Lessons for the Great Repeal Bill' (2018) Jur Rev 64.

90 See *Bank of Scotland Cashflow Finance v Heritage International Transport Ltd* 2003 SLT (Sh Ct) 107, discussed in Hardman, *Granting Corporate Security* (n 84) para. 7–34. The definition of 'future rights' is a difficult one and can arise under different circumstances. In particular, a future right can be a contingent claim that arises in the future, or a currently-unknown claim without a known debtor – see discussion in Scottish Law Commission, *Report on Moveable Transactions* (n 36) paras 5.81–5.87.

91 As, on insolvency, the assets will be part of the insolvent granter's estate rather than the subject of the assignation. This does not apply if the accretion applies. It is unclear whether accretion applies to moveables – see the discussion in Anderson, *Assignation* (n 86) paras 11.46–11.47.

92 *Crerar v Bank of Scotland* 1921 SC 736.

93 See *Purnell v Shannon* (1894) 22 R 74.

Ultimately, therefore, Position one provides a limited comfort for the granters of or recipients of security – only over heritable property can a true security be granted under which the granter can retain the enjoyment of the asset in question. Position two reflects a movement from this to a position whereby all categories of assets owned by an incorporated vehicle can become subject to the floating charge. Examining the transition from Position one to Position two thus narrows the scope of the enquiry: we do not have to establish whether Position two could be improved upon, or any questions as to whether the categories of entities able to grant a floating charge should be extended.[94] Instead, our analysis must simply examine whether Position two represents an improvement for all relevant parties from Position one.

(2) Effect on debtor

First, we can analyse the effect of moving to Position two on the debtor. Position two enables the debtor to grant security over its assets without losing possession or control. This increases the pool of assets over which the debtor can grant security whilst also using the assets in its ordinary business. We have seen above that this is likely to produce a reduction of the costs of debt for the debtor: the secured creditor will reduce their interest costs, some adjusting creditors will increase their interest costs but some adjusting creditors may chose not to adjust and non-adjusting creditors will not adjust. This means that the borrower's interest bill will decrease.

Moving to Position two enables debtors to disassociate the individual assets from the provision of finance. This has twin benefits to the debtor. First, the debtor is able to obtain finance by securing its future assets and business. In other words, the provision of debt finance ceases to be linked to the presence of specific assets or the purchase of specific assets. This enables debtors working in structurally 'asset light' industries, such as businesses that rely on human capital, to obtain finance or better prices to their finance. It also enables growing businesses, with strong management and/ or business plans but without established assets or identified targets, an opportunity to obtain preferential terms to debt finance that is denied to them under Position one. Secondly, it enables debtors to substitute the assets that are subject to security. Under Position one, every security other than the passive holding of heritable property requires interaction with the

94 For example, to unincorporated partnerships or individuals.

secured creditor to dispose of assets, deal in assets in any way or obtain the advantage of assets. Position two removes the secured creditor's effective control[95] and returns it to the debtor. This is unlikely to matter if the debtor's business is the ownership of a single shop leased on a long-term lease to a tenant. However, the more active the debtor is in their business, the more important this substitution becomes. Consider any example whereby the business of the entity was the buying of assets and their sale for profit – any shop, securities speculator or arbitrage business. The business that the creditor intends to lend against is the business of constant substitution of assets for profit. Position one therefore presents a nonsensical position for such a debtor (and, we shall see, the relevant creditor) as the very act that the debtor relies on to service the debt, profit from the constant purchase and sale of assets, is precluded by the presence of security. It is, theoretically, possible under Position one for such a business to grant security – but they would need such constant releases from the secured creditor that the cost to the creditor and the debtor of spending time and resources on such releases would quickly outweigh any advantages of the grant of security in the first event.

Thus we can see that, from the perspective of a debtor, a move from Position one to Position two is Pareto superior: it decreases their interest bill whilst allowing them substitutability of assets.

(3) Effect on the secured creditor

What, then, is the effect on the secured creditor? The first thing to state is that the secured creditor does not lose anything by moving from Position one to Position two, it merely gains another option. Position two does not compel the secured creditor to eschew a standard security for a floating charge, indeed it is frequent for a floating charge to supplement other security taken by the creditor.[96] It is possible that debtors with strong covenants may require, through bargaining, the grant of a floating charge rather than, say, an assignation in security. However, it is likely that even under Position

---

95 Control has a particular meaning under the English law of fixed securities (*Re Spectrum Plus Ltd (in liquidation)* [2005] UKHL 41), but it is unclear whether Scots law adopts any similar position (see J Hardman, 'Three Steps Forward, Two Steps Back: A View from Corporate Security Practice of the Moveable Transactions (Scotland) Bill' (2018) 22 Edin L Rev 266). Instead, we refer for these purposes to the inherent involvement of the secured creditor and substitutability of the assets.

96 Hardman, *Granting Corporate Security* (n 84) para. 1–05.

one this debtor would be unwilling to grant such assignation, meaning that the move to Position two may result in the secured creditor obtaining security where otherwise they would not.

If the secured creditor does not lose options by a move to Position two, what does it gain? Under Position one, the creditor's interests are inextricably bound in the assets over which it has security. Thus the creditor has no recourse to other assets and they are merely an unsecured creditor in respect of any amount of their debt that remains unsatisfied following the realisation of their security. Whilst English law has long acknowledged the equitable concept that if the perfection formalities of a fixed charge are not carried out then it will constitute a floating charge,[97] under Scots law a creditor who has failed to perfect their fixed security obtains no security right at all (other than, potentially, contractually).[98] As we have seen, fixed security under Scots law can, arguably, only be granted over known current assets of the debtor, which means that a secured creditor will be unsecured for future assets. The floating charge under Scots law enables a grant of some form of security over future assets and unspecified categories of assets.[99] Taking a floating charge therefore provides the creditor with a 'sweeper' function that is denied to the security creditor in Position one. This accordingly represents a gain for the secured creditor.

Whilst obtaining the benefit of a floating charge is not as advantageous to the creditor as obtaining the benefit of a fixed security,[100] nonetheless the presence of a negative pledge can preclude other creditors receiving prior ranking security over the assets in question.[101] This therefore provides the floating charge holder with a form of negative control over the assets of the debtor (including future assets). This means that, whilst taking a floating charge instead of a fixed security involves the creditor forgoing possession or control of the asset in question, other creditors are precluded from obtaining a preferential right.

---

97 See the difference between the English *Re Spectrum Plus* (n 95) (which characterised a purportedly fixed charge without control as a floating charge) and the Scottish case of *Clark v West Calder Oil Co* (1882) 9 R 1017, which characterised a putative pledge without delivery as providing no security right.

98 See discussion in J Hardman, 'Hohfeld and the Scots Law Floating Charge', Chapter 7 within this volume.

99 Companies Act 1985 s. 464.

100 The recipient must use an insolvency process rather than a collateral process and their recovery will be net of the prescribed part. See discussion in this book contained in D W McKenzie Skene, 'The Floating Charge and Insolvency Law', Chapter 10 and J Hardman and A MacPherson, 'The Ranking of Floating Charges', Chapter 9.

101 Companies Act 1985 s. 464(1).

The main advantages that the floating charge offers to secured creditors relate to insolvency. Thus we have seen that Position one involves creditors being linked to specific assets, whereas Position two enables a 'catch all' position including future assets as well. Under modern UK law,[102] the holder of a floating charge that is a 'qualifying floating charge'[103] (most commonly achieved by stating that the relevant statutory provision applies to the floating charge[104]) over all or substantially all the assets of the company[105] is able to, out of court,[106] appoint their own insolvency practitioner to the creditor.[107] In order to do so, the granter does not need to be insolvent but the floating charge itself must, in accordance with its terms, be enforceable and the relevant insolvency practitioner must consider that the aims of administration are likely to be met: these are (in order) rescuing the company as a going concern, providing a better return for the company's creditors as a whole than they would get on a winding up, and realising property to distribute to secured/preferential creditors.[108] More than this, no other party can appoint an insolvency practitioner to the debtor without prior notice to the qualifying floating charge holder. Thus, by obtaining a floating charge over all or substantially all the assets of the debtor, a creditor is able to obtain prior warning of appointment of an insolvency practitioner in respect of that debtor and, in the notice period provided, 'trump' the appointment with their preferred insolvency practitioner.[109] Position two therefore provides the secured creditor with a form of control over when and how the debtor enters an insolvency process: both in terms of its ability to appoint itself and also in terms of its ability to prevent others from doing so.

The second insolvency-based benefit that Position two offers the secured creditor is a preferential return in the insolvency ranking. Whilst holders of fixed securities have always been able to obtain recourse to the specifically secured assets on the insolvency of the debtor, should these be insufficient

---

102 It was not always thus – the change was introduced by the Enterprise Act 2002.
103 Insolvency Act 1986 Sch. B1 para. 14.
104 Hardman, *Granting Corporate Security* (n 84) para. 6–11.
105 Insolvency Act 1986 Sch. B1 para. 14.
106 Any creditor is able to petition to the court for the court to appoint an administrator – but again control of the process is lost through this method.
107 Most commonly an administrator – see Hardman, *Granting Corporate Security* (n 84) para. 6–10. Historically, the creditor had an ability to appoint a receiver – see Companies (Floating Charges and Receivers) (Scotland) Act 1972. Similarly, holdings of floating charges granted by certain types of companies, such as public private partnerships, utility projects and registered social landlords, can still appoint administrative receivers – Insolvency Act 1986 ss. 72B–72GA.
108 Insolvency Act 1986 Sch. B1 para. 3.
109 Insolvency Act 1986 Sch. B1 para. 17.

to satisfy the debt then under Position one the creditor must submit a claim alongside unsecured creditors to rank in the insolvency of the debtor. Position two provides a middle ground – a secured creditor is entitled to a return ahead of (most) unsecured creditors.[110] Thus, not only does the floating charge provide a theoretical 'sweeper' for assets over which fixed security is not possible or desirable, it lets the creditor obtain a beneficial return over these assets in the insolvency of the debtor.

Thus Position two represents an improvement in efficiency for the secured creditor. It is able to receive security over more assets than it is under Position one. It provides a 'sweeper' or fall-back option in respect of future assets. It obtains insolvency appointment control, including an 'out of court' procedure not otherwise available to it. It receives a preferential return on the winding up of the debtor. It also is able to take security without interfering in the business of the debtor, especially important in the situations highlighted above where the debtor's profit is generated from, ultimately, trading assets. So far, accordingly, a move from Position one to Position two is Pareto superior for the debtor and the creditor.

(4) Effect on adjusting creditors

It is more difficult to establish how a move to Position two can be said in any manner to be efficient from the perspective of third parties. After all, the majority of benefits to secured creditors arise at the expense of unsecured creditors. It is, perhaps, an easier task to begin with adjusting creditors. As we have seen, adjusting creditors are able to, should they wish, adjust the price of their debt (or its non-financial terms) to reflect the risk of additional security being granted. There are reasons why they may not want to, but these result in an advantage for the debtor rather than the adjusting creditor themselves. There is, however, a reason why adjusting creditors are better off under Position two than they are under Position one. All security is open, subject to certain conditions, to being challenged if it is granted by a vehicle and if it unfairly prefers one creditor over another.[111] Thus creditors are protected generally from a debtor approaching insolvency and granting security in favour of its preferred creditor prior to its insolvency. Additional protections apply in respect of a floating charge: a floating charge is void within

110 See e.g. Insolvency Act 1986 Sch. B1 para. 116. However, as we shall see there are preferential creditors who rank ahead of floating charge holders and the 'prescribed part' that is to be paid to unsecured creditors out of floating charge realisations.
111 Insolvency Act 1986 s. 243.

one year of its grant (or two years if it is granted to a connected party) save to the extent that it secures new money advanced.[112] This section applies in England and Wales as well as Scotland.[113] When interpreting precursors to this section, it has been stated:

> 'what does the section mean? I think it means exactly what it says, that you have to measure the security by the amount of the cash received from the lender at or subsequently to the creation of the charge and in relation, therefore, to the amount which is to be applicable for the then future purposes of the company - not for discharging antecedent debts and certainly not for returning to the lender a large portion of the money either in payment of a former advance or past consideration or for any other consideration ... '.[114]

This has been held to mean that more than book entries are required: actual money has to be advanced to the debtor, which become part of the assets of the debtor.[115] The result is that a floating charge is only valid to the extent that new funds are actually advanced to the debtor. Thus, from the perspective of an adjusting creditor, the value of the assets of the debtor must be increased in order for the floating charge to be valid. Accordingly, from an adjusting creditor's perspective, the creation of a floating charge must be linked to additional money being injected into their debtor. This means that the floating charge can only be used in conjunction with the strengthening of the liquidity of the debtor. We have seen that the floating charge will make creditors more likely to lend in the marginal cases and is also likely to make creditors reduce the price of their debt. Putting these together, it is therefore possible that the move to Position two makes it more likely that additional liquidity will be advanced to the debtor. This additional liquidity will benefit the debtor – including making it less likely that they will not pay an amount due by an adjusting creditor.

As such, despite what it may seem, the operation of Position two is actually an improvement for adjusting creditors from Position one. They will either consider themselves benefitting from the increased liquidity or, if they are concerned by the additional leverage created, be able to adjust their pricing accordingly. Adjusting creditors are yet another category for whom the move from Position one to Position two represents a Pareto superior move.

---

112 Insolvency Act 1986 s. 245.
113 Insolvency Act 1986 s. 245(1).
114 *Re Matthew Ellis Ltd* [1933] Ch 458 at 465 per Eve J. This quotation was provided by the first instance judge – whilst this Court of Appeal judgment allowed the appeal from the first instance on the facts of the case, it agreed with the law as set out by Eve J.
115 *Re Fairway Magazines Ltd* [1992] BCC 924.

(5) Effect on non-adjusting creditors

The most difficult challenge arises in respect of non-adjusting creditors. After all, part of the advantage for adjusting creditors was that, if they were concerned by the additional leverage in the debtor created by the funds advanced to which the floating charge relates, then they could adjust and so avoid the harm. This is not the case for non-adjusting creditors.

Nevertheless, the advantage for adjusting creditors remains an advantage for non-adjusting creditors: under Position two, the debtor is not free to simply gratuitously grant floating charges, it must receive some worth for such grant and that worth must also be to the advantage of non-adjusting creditors.

More pertinently, however, there are two key advantages for non-adjusting creditors. First, courts and the legislature are increasingly keen to hold non-adjusting creditors as more senior to the claims of floating charge holders. Employees have long been considered preferential creditors, paid out in advance of floating charge holders (up to certain limits).[116] Part of amounts owed to HMRC now, following an announcement made in the 2018 budget, will be paid prior to floating charge holders on the insolvency of the debtor.[117] So will, generally, any statutory liability so long as it came into existence as a result of the commencement of the insolvency and that appears to be Parliament's intention.[118] This has been held to apply to certain pension liabilities,[119] rates owed to the local council[120] and environmental liabilities.[121] There are therefore many categories of non-adjusting creditors for whom the introduction of the floating charge carries no negative elements, only the positive increases in liquidity as once the money is advanced to the debtor, such non-adjusting creditors will have a preferential right to it.

In addition, non-adjusting creditors benefit from the 'prescribed part'.[122] This means that a part of floating charge realisations is set aside (as a

---

116 Insolvency Act 1986 s. 175.
117 Finance Act 2020 s. 98; R Caldwell, 'Enterprise Goes into Reverse for Floating Charge-Holders' 2019 Jur Rev 103.
118 *Re Nortel Companies* [2013] UKSC 52.
119 *Re Nortel Companies*.
120 In England – *Exeter City Council v Bairstow* [2007] EWHC 400 (Ch).
121 *Joint Liquidators of Doonin Plant Ltd, Noters* [2018] CSOH 89.
122 Insolvency Act 1986 s. 176A(2).

proportion of the debtor's estate and up to a maximum of £800,000[123]) to pay unsecured creditors. Thus non-adjusting creditors are further protected in respect of the prescribed part.

Accordingly, a large number of non-adjusting creditors have their positions actively improved by the move from Position one to Position two, and the other non-adjusting creditors benefit from the requirement to inject funds in the company, the increased access to finance provided and the prescribed part. Therefore for some non-adjusting creditors the position is improved and for others the position is neutral. Overall, for non-adjusting creditors, Position two is Pareto superior to Position one.

D. CRITIQUE AND CONCLUSION

(1) Critique

It therefore seems as if the author has achieved his goals. Every constituency appears to experience an improvement by the move from Position one to Position two. Consequently, it seems as if the high hurdle of Pareto superiority has been met, and the Challenge has been met.

However, on closer examination, this proves not to be the case. Working backwards, the author aggregated non-adjusting creditors (and the effect of the move from Position one to Position two) into one category, which causes all the issues that were flagged in respect of a Kaldor-Hicks analysis. Whilst governmental authorities are well protected by the floating charge, others are not. Delict sufferers, who are generally considered to be at risk of harm from the use of a corporate structure,[124] do not have any comfort gained. Even preferential creditors are subject to low caps.[125] The level of the prescribed part is, generally, too low to provide any meaningful protection to non-adjusting creditors.

---

123 The Insolvency Act 1986 (Prescribed Part) (Amendment) Order 2020 (SI 2020/211). See discussion in A D J MacPherson and D McKenzie Skene, 'Back to the Future? The Partial Reinstatement of the Crown Preference in Insolvency', available at *https://www.abdn.ac.uk/law/blog/back-to-the-future-the-partial-reinstatement-of-the-crown-preference-in-insolvency/* (last accessed 27 October 2021).

124 H Hansmann and R Kraakman, 'Towards Unlimited Shareholder Liability for Corporate Torts' (1991) 100 Yale LJ 1879.

125 For example, wages of employees are preferred only to the extent of work undertaken in the four months ending on the insolvency date and up to a maximum of £800 per employee – Insolvency Proceedings (Monetary Limits) Order 1986 (SI 1986/1996) art. 4.

The analysis that the floating charge is void save to the extent of new moneys appears to provide some protection for third parties. However, its operation is flawed. The rule in *Clayton's Case*[126] means that oldest debts are deemed to be repaid first. This, in turn, means that for a fluctuating account[127] each new drawing is deemed to be 'new money', which neuters the protection of this provision. Seen from this perspective, the move from Position one to Position two for both non-adjusting creditors and adjusting creditors is, in fact, a move that subordinates their claims on insolvency but means they have no benefits. Therefore some non-adjusting creditors lose from the move to Position two rather than gain. This means that Position two cannot be said to be Pareto superior to Position one.

The expansion of the prescribed part to other non-adjusting creditors and the expansion of the categories falling to be considered as preferential creditors may, in fact, harm the secured creditor themselves,[128] which may mean that there are no advantages in moving from Position one to Position two in adopting the floating charge. Similarly, there is a risk that a debtor could be bullied into granting a floating charge as a way to provide insolvency control to the creditor: which means a move to Position two harms them as well.

Ultimately, each argument advanced is a double-edged sword. Every advantage to one constituent is a disadvantage to another. This argument commenced with the author attempting to meet the Challenge set down. The fact that he was able to even purport to do so evidences the confirmation bias risked by undertaking any form of positive law and economics analysis.[129] As Gant puts it 'this is largely a retrospective exercise in which law and economics legal theorists transpose a theoretical construct onto the historic rule in question. It does not necessarily explain the true history of a legal rule's developmental process'.[130]

We have seen that the efficiency of any transaction is an inherently subjective matter. A move is efficient from the perspective of one person if they

---

126 *Devaynes v Noble* (1816) 35 ER 767 as accepted into Scots law by *Houston's Executor's v Speirs' Trustees* (1835) 13 S 945. For interactions between floating charges and *Clayton's Case* more generally see P Hood, 'Clayton's Case and Connected Matters' 2013 Jur Rev 501.

127 For example, an overdraft or revolving credit facility.

128 Indeed, this is the point of the article cited above – Caldwell (n 117).

129 For further, similar, critique see J Hardman, 'Law and Economics of Corporate Financial Difficulty' in P Omar and J L L Gant (eds), *Research Handbook on Corporate Restructuring* (Cheltenham: Edward Elgar Publishing, 2021).

130 J L L Gant, *Balancing the Protection of Business and Employment in Insolvency* (The Hague: Eleven International Publishing, 2017) 7.

value Position two more than they value Position one. Some efficiencies can be assumed, but when it comes to an internal balance between, for example, flexibility of receiving security over future assets versus more deductions from recoveries on insolvency, it is impossible to say which one creditors as a whole will value more. It is therefore impossible to undertake a deductive analysis of economic efficiency in the manner that we set out to do.

(2) Conclusion

To prove that the floating charge was Pareto superior in Scots law was always a challenge. Nonetheless, the author has provided arguments as to why the introduction of the floating charge can be said to be efficient from the perspective of one constituency or another. Sadly, this endeavour was always likely to fail. Ultimately, any policy decision that is truly Pareto superior, in that it provides only positive or neutral effects to everyone who it affects, is such a 'no-brainer' that such a move tends not to provide any controversy. The converse of this is that the presence of any controversy (as we have for the floating charge) tends to suggest that a proposal is not Pareto optimal.

This chapter has flagged up several advantages to several parties of a move from Position one to Position two. It is, however, possible that the very items that make the transition beneficial for one party may make it detrimental to another party. It is therefore probable that the introduction of the floating charge is Kaldor-Hicks efficient. Unfortunately, it is very difficult to measure. The Challenge lies unmet. However, hopefully the arguments advanced have sufficient merit in them for subsequent authors to develop them further in order to successfully meet the Challenge.

Perhaps, though, it is not for law and economics to conclusively answer this or any other question as to whether a law is advantageous. Calabresi and Melamed[131] adopted the example of Monet's paintings of Rouen Cathedral. Monet painted over thirty versions of the same angle of the cathedral. He painted it in sunshine and rain, first thing in the morning, at midday and at evening. The question is – which one shows what Rouen Cathedral looks like? Calabresi and Melamed use this analogy to argue that, without a coherent theory of law, such as law and economics, every argument or rule is simply a different view of the cathedral.[132] With respect to Calabresi and

131 Calabresi and Melamed (n 59).
132 Calabresi and Melamed (n 59) at 1128.

Melamed, however well developed a law and economics analysis may be, it can only ever show one view of the cathedral. Hopefully this chapter demonstrates that, even within the school of thought of law and economics, there are various different arguments – various views of the cathedral. It just depends how you look.

6 Floating Charges and Moral Hazard: Finding Fairness for Involuntary and Vulnerable Stakeholders

Jennifer L L Gant

A. INTRODUCTION
B. CONTEXT AND METHODLOGY
    (1) The impact of control and scope of the Scottish floating charge
    (2) Current provisions mitigating the impact of the floating charge
        (a) Super-priority/preferential creditors
        (b) The 'prescribed part'
        (c) The effect of insolvency on employees and other vulnerable stakeholders
    (3) Theoretical framework
    (4) Presentation of the chapter
C. PERSPECTIVES ON DEBT, INSOLVENCY AND MORAL HAZARD
    (1) The moral dimension of debt
    (2) Financial regulation and economic efficiency
    (3) Justifying priority for secured debt and floating charges
D. JUSTIFYING EMPLOYEE PREFERENCE OVER FLOATING CHARGES
    (1) Employment regulation and the free market
    (2) Employees in insolvency: contradiction of pre-insolvency priority entitlements
E. ARE FLOATING CHARGES FAIR TO VULNERABLE STAKEHOLDERS?

A. INTRODUCTION

Insolvency and bankruptcy are words that tend to conjure disappointment, fear and blame in most corners of the globe, with the notable exception of the US, which has the aura of rewarding risk-taking entrepreneurs by frequent do-overs. The same cannot be said for most of the rest of the world, particularly within the UK, which until quite recently has ever been hesitant to introduce insolvency or restructuring procedures that allow the debtor company's management to remain in control of the ailing firm. Along with these procedures, whether debtor in possession or otherwise, come adjustments to the rights and entitlements of creditors and other stakeholders associated with the company in financial distress. This includes, whether directly or indirectly, an impact on employees who are essentially involuntary creditors to an insolvency process entered by their corporate employer, along with other vulnerable and involuntary creditors such as franchisees and tort (or delict) claimants. Although there are a number of firebreaks that provide a buffer for employees under such circumstances in most countries, the underlying paradigm of the insolvency process resembles a recommoditisation of labour as one of a number of stakeholders who become categorised in terms of preference, priority and payment as creditors, reducing employees to the value of what they are owed for their labour.

While insolvency and restructuring have a significant impact on a debtor company's employees, there are also devices that may indirectly interfere with the full complement of employee rights, whether statutory or contractual. The UK also provides a device that gives a significant amount of power to a debtor company to continue to deal with its assets, despite those same assets being subject to the extensive charge of a lender: on the wind the floating charge arrives. Typically considered a common law device that is difficult to square with the law of security rights in civil law countries, the floating charge is a somewhat unusual device that is fairly unique in its form, scope and function to the UK, although other common law jurisdictions have versions of the same concept. However, differences do appear between the English and the Scottish versions of the device, which are discussed elsewhere in this book.[1]

The floating charge as a concept undoubtedly affords a considerable amount of preference and control to the creditor who holds it and to the

---

1 See M Raczynska, 'The Species and Structure(s) of the Floating Charge: The English Law Perspective on the Scottish Floating Charge', Chapter 8 within this volume.

debtor who can continue to deal with the charged assets and to potentially dissipate them in the normal course of business. Such power may overshadow any preferences and priorities available to vulnerable stakeholders, such as employees, and certainly over involuntary creditors such as tort victims, as there is no limitation on how such charged assets can be dealt with until and unless the collective format of insolvency and restructuring are put into place at a time of financial distress. The purpose of this chapter is to explore the socio-legal aspects of the floating charge as it affects employees as vulnerable and involuntary stakeholders specifically, and asks the question as to whether it is possible to achieve fairness by an employee preference and set priority position over the floating charge, or whether it could be open to abuse due to moral hazards created by the power inherent in the floating charge device however and wherever a line is drawn.

B. CONTEXT AND METHODOLOGY

(1) The impact of control and scope of the Scottish floating charge

It must be admitted at the beginning that this author is not a Scots lawyer nor a Scottish legal academic, therefore the content of this chapter will inevitably have a foundation in English law, but contrasts will be drawn wherever prudent and relevant. The concept of the floating charge is, however, fairly similar between the two jurisdictions and its creation in Scots law under the broadly worded statutory formulation[2] means it is substantially the same as the common law position in English law.[3] As employment law of both jurisdictions is the same as it relates to employees in insolvency given that most of these specific regulations are derived from EU law, the protections and entitlements available are essentially equivalent as employment law within *Great Britain* (England, Scotland and Wales) is not devolved from Westminster.[4] Further, English and Scots law often overlap and in the commercial law sphere they are frequently identical.[5]

---

2 See Companies Act 1985 s. 462.

3 J Hardman, 'Some Legal Determinants of External Finance in Scotland: A Response to Lord Hodge' (2017) 21(1) Edin L Rev 30 at 49 citing the example of *Re Panama, New Zealand and Australian Royal Mail Co* (1870) 5 Ch App 318.

4 L Furber, 'Employment Law in the United Kingdom – What Differences are there?', *Crunch.* (1 February 2020), available at *https://www.crunch.co.uk/knowledge/employment/employment-law-in-the-united-kingdom-what-differences-are-there/* (last accessed 27 October 2021).

5 Hardman (n 3) at 40.

There are, however, certain key differences in the enforcement of floating charges in England and Scotland that could have a different bearing on how employees are affected. In particular, the Scots floating charge attaches only to specific assets upon: the appointment of a receiver; the commencement of liquidation; an administrator providing notice that there are insufficient assets to satisfy all creditors in full; or the court giving an administrator permission to make a payment that is neither secured or preferential. This position differs from the English version, which can crystallise much earlier and with a greater potential for covering a broad range of assets of the company in existence from time to time. The Scots floating charge also cannot convert into a fixed charge automatically, rather there is a bond indicated in the documentation that refers to the chargor's undertaking to pay the underlying debt.[6] The Scottish floating charge is also statutory in nature as is the crystallisation process. As a result, certain characteristics of the English floating charge are lacking, such as the ability to draft the device in a document that allows for automatic crystallisation upon the occurrence of certain events or to include the ability for a creditor to provide notice of crystallisation under certain circumstances. Thus there are already limitations that may prevent the high level of freedom exercised by English floating charge holders as compared to those in Scotland, which will already reduce the risk of abuse. That said, there is still a great deal of scope for creditors offering floating charge security to get quite a large bite of the estate apple when it comes to the insolvency of a debtor owing a loan secured by a floating charge.

The floating charge has certainly raised controversy in Scotland, being described as 'utterly repugnant'[7] and, unlike the English floating charge, remains covered by the Companies Act 1985 s. 462(1).[8] It has been severely criticised as 'not fitting into the framework of Scottish security law'[9] and has been described as a blunt instrument, if an effective one.[10] The Scottish

---

6 R Edgar and S Cooley, 'Taking Security: Some Key Differences between Scotland and England & Wales', *Shoosmiths* (29 November 2019), available at *https://www.shoosmiths.co.uk/insights/articles/taking-security-some-key-differences-between-scotland-and-england-and-wales#:~:text=In%20Scotland%20there%20is%20no, 'bond%20and%20floating%20charge'* (last accessed 27 October 2021).

7 So described in *Carse v Coppen* 1951 SC 233 at 239, as cited in J Hardman, *A Practical Guide to Granting Corporate Security in Scotland* (Edinburgh: W. Green, 2018) para. 6–03. See also A D J MacPherson, 'The "Pre-History" of Floating Charges in Scotland', Chapter 1 within this volume.

8 Hardman, *Practical Guide* (n 7) para. 6–04.

9 Hardman, *Practical Guide* (n 7) para. 6–06.

10 Hardman, *Practical Guide* (n 7) para. 6–06; and see also on the academic debate around the Scottish floating charge: G L Gretton, 'What Went Wrong with the Floating Charge?' (1984) SLT

floating charge effectively puts the lender benefitting from the charge granted by a company in control of an insolvency process entered into by the company owing the debt under the charge. Because the holder of a floating charge can appoint an administrator without the need for application to a court[11] and can essentially overrule winding up petitions,[12] they retain a significant amount of control of the appointments and the process. As an administrator is appointed by the floating charge holder in such circumstances, there have been unsurprising allegations that such a practitioner may have conflicts upon appointment with some loyalty paid to the entity that appoints them.[13]

A floating charge can also cover all or substantially all of the assets of a company,[14] thus not only is the control of the floating charge holder significant, but so is the scope of its reach in terms of the assets available to it for realisation to satisfy the debt. The administrator is also able to deal with the floating charge property as if it were not charged at all, whereas fixed security charged property would require a court order in the absence of consent or discharge.[15] Thus, there is nothing apart from traditional corporate and securities law to protect against what would otherwise be perceived as an appropriate asset dissipation, but which could have a significant impact on returns to less powerful or vulnerable creditors in the event of an insolvency due to distributional priorities that favour security holders.

The floating charge holder also has an advantage when claiming from the insolvent estate as it will be entitled to returns before the body of unsecured creditors,[16] with some notable exceptions.[17] Fixed security, however, will rank prior in distribution to floating charges, unless there is an earlier floating charge with a negative pledge.[18] Although the 'prescribed part' was introduced under the Enterprise Act 2002, which ringfences up to (now)

(News) 172 and 'Should Floating Charges Be Abolished?' (1986) SLT (News) 325; D Cabrelli, 'The Case against the Floating Charge in Scotland' (2005) 9(3) Edin L Rev 407; R Jack, 'The Coming of the Floating Charge to Scotland: An Account and an Assessment' in D J Cuisine (ed), *A Scots Conveyancing Miscellany: Essays in Honour of Professor J M Halliday* (Edinburgh: W. Green, 1987) 45–46; Hardman (n 3).

11 Insolvency Act 1986 Sch. B1 para. 14. See also D McKenzie Skene, 'The Floating Charge and Insolvency Law', Chapter 10 within this volume.
12 Insolvency Act 1986 Sch. B1 para. 17.
13 Hardman, *Practical Guide* (n 7) para. 6–09.
14 Hardman, *Practical Guide* (n 7) para. 6–12.
15 Insolvency Act 1986, Sch. B1 paras 70 and 71.
16 Insolvency Act 1986 Sch. B1 para. 65(3).
17 Hardman, *Practical Guide* (n 7) para. 6–14.
18 Companies Act 1985 s. 464(1)–(4).

£800,000 of the assets covered by a floating charge,[19] this amount can look quite small if one considers the level of debts of some of the more recent large insolvencies, such as Nortel and Lehman Brothers and, even more recently, companies such as Carillion, British Home Stores and Thomas Cook. This prescribed part will be shared between not only standard unsecured creditors, but also employee wages that are not included in the employee preference or the state guarantee funds.[20] Given the level of debt that will be owed to employees as opposed to suppliers and banks, and the fact that such debts are paid by *pari passu* distributions to all those who participate in the prescribed part, employees are unlikely to benefit much from the prescribed part. The floating charge is therefore a powerful tool but, as queried by Hardman, why should society 'accept the concept of one creditor receiving a preferential return as a result of this private bargain'.[21] Although there are currently protections that aim to hedge against the impact of this preference on employees and other less powerful stakeholders, it is arguable that these do not go far enough given the invaluable contribution that employees make to a company that goes beyond the typical commoditisation of the value of their labour under the employment contract.

(2) Current provisions mitigating the impact of the floating charge

(a) Super-priority/preferential creditors

In the UK, the Insolvency Act 1986 provides a certain level of preference for employee claims, including up to eight weeks of unpaid wages and up to six weeks of accrued of holiday pay, along with a basic award for unfair dismissal.[22] Such payments are made by the Secretary of State out of the National Insurance Fund.[23] Insurance funds such as this can reduce the burden of the unemployed on the state during any interim period of unemployment that may require social protection following redundancy occurring

---

19 The Insolvency Act 1986 (Prescribed Part) Order 2003 (SI 2003/2097) paras 2 and 3, as amended by the Insolvency Act 1986 (Prescribed Part) (Amendment) Order 2020 (SI 2020/211) art. 2(2).
20 See V Finch and D Milman, *Corporate Insolvency Law: Perspectives and Principles*, 3rd edn (Cambridge: Cambridge University Press, 2017) 513–524.
21 J Hardman, 'Law and Economics of the Floating Charge', Chapter 5 within this volume. See also L LoPucki, 'The Unsecured Creditor's Bargain' (1994) 80 Virginia Law Review 1887 in which the author argues that any form of security is an agreement between A and B that C gets nothing, which runs counter to most contractual principles.
22 Insolvency Act 1986 s. 386 and Sch. 6.
23 Enacted under the Employment Rights Act 1996 ss. 166–170 and 182–190 as an implementation of Council Directive 80/987/EEC OJ 1980 L283.

as a result of a restructuring or insolvency.[24] The fund will cover unpaid wages and holiday pay as well as unfair dismissal settlements, redundancy payments and pay-outs for failure to consult in the event of collective redundancies or transfers of undertakings. The National Insurance Fund is then subrogated to the rights of employees against the debtor company including their right as preferential creditors.[25] It should also be noted, however, that the payments made as a result of this preference is capped in terms of both the period covered and the amounts that can be claimed. The limits are adjusted from time to time by statutory instrument.[26] Employee claims beyond the preferred portion rank equally to those of other unsecured creditors.

In addition, certain pension contributions are also preferential. Unpaid employee contributions are preferential insofar as sums have been deducted but not yet paid into the pension scheme four months prior to the time of insolvency, with no ceiling on the amount of pension contributions that can be considered preferential under this category. Unpaid employer contributions to an occupational pension scheme are preferred but limited to twelve months prior to insolvency and connected to the amount of the national insurance rebate that is applicable. The pension preference is therefore limited to a percentage of the relevant earnings.[27] Preferential payments are payable out of the available assets of a company prior to ordinary *unsecured* claims, but also prior to the claims owed to floating charge holders once regular secured claims and administrative expenses have been paid.[28] Thus on the face of it, it would appear that the preference already takes into account the issues of floating charge holders grabbing assets prior to other creditors. However, given the discussion in section C about the reality of value ascribed to floating charge holders, much of the asset value may have already been absorbed by paying out the secured creditors in priority.

---

24 G W Johnson, 'Insolvency and the Social Protection: Employee Entitlements in the Event of Employer Insolvency' (2006) Report written after the Fifth Forum for Asian Insolvency Reform 27–28 April 2006 in Beijing, China 7.

25 Finch and Milman, *Corporate Insolvency Law* (n 20) 648.

26 The Employment Rights (Increase of Limits) Order 2021 (SI 2021/208). See also Finch and Milman, *Corporate Insolvency Law* (n 20) 522–523.

27 D Pollard and I Carruthers, 'Pensions as a Preferential Debt' (2004) 17 Insolvency Intelligence 65.

28 Finch and Milman, *Corporate Insolvency Law* (n 20) 647.

(b) The 'prescribed part'

The Enterprise Act 2002 provided what could arguably be described as a buffer against the commodification of debt that the last several decades has seen evolve. The 2002 Act was the first of the UK's statutory shifts towards a corporate rescue ideology, reducing the power of the floating charge holder's power to commence a self-interested receivership to a clear favouring of the more communal, entity-based administration. It also introduced a mechanism aimed to mitigate the extent of losses that are generally borne by unsecured creditors.

The 'prescribed part' inserted into the Insolvency Act 1986 s. 176A 'applies where a floating charge relates to the property of a company which has gone into liquidation, administration, provisional liquidation, or receivership' and requires that the insolvency practitioner ringfences a portion of the company's assets available in order to satisfy a certain proportion of unsecured debt.[29] The quantum is established by the order of a statutory instrument and in 2020 was raised to £800,000 from £600,000.[30] Although a government paper noted in 2018 that 'the prescribed part payments very rarely reach the current cap', it is notable that the Government also observed that in those cases where the cap is reached, the raise will be to the benefit of unsecured creditors,[31] which will include most vulnerable creditors such as employees whose full claims were not covered in an alternative way, along with tort and environmental claimants.

Empirical evidence has also demonstrated some interesting facts about the realisation of floating charges during an insolvency and the impact this has had on the creation of a prescribed part, as well as how relevant it is in terms of mitigating the adverse impact on unsecured creditors. In research conducted between 2006 and 2011 on 2,129 companies entering insolvency, 1,160 of these companies had given floating charge security with 704 of those companies granting floating charges following the enactment of the Enterprise Act 2002. Only 95 out of the 704 post-Enterprise Act insolvency procedures surveyed saw the creation of a prescribed part by insolvency

---

29 V Finch, 'Corporate Rescue in a World of Debt' (2008) 8 JBL 756 at 764–766.
30 The Insolvency Act 1986 (Prescribed Part) (Amendment) Order 2020 art. 2(2) amending the Insolvency Act 1986 (Prescribed Part) Order 2003.
31 Department for Business Energy and Industrial Strategy, 'Insolvency and Corporate Governance: Government Response' (26 August 2018) available at *https://assets.publishing.service.gov. uk/government/uploads/system/uploads/attachment_data/file/736163/ICG_-_Government_ response_doc_-_24_Aug_clean_version__with_Minister_s_photo_and_signature__AC.pdf* (last accessed 27 October 2021).

office holders.[32] This was mainly because of the fragmented capital structure of the companies surveyed rather than any failure on the part of the office holder. The floating charge was used as a sweep-up security where other instruments were relied upon for most of the realisations instead. Where secured creditors' debts were fully repaid through exercising their rights under fixed charges, the floating charge was superfluous and no longer carried any value in terms of debt owed,[33] thus the prescribed part would have no value in such a case. As noted by Akintola, 'where the fragmentation of a company's capital structure prevents the operation of the prescribed part provision, it would seem that the redistributive policy under the Insolvency Act is self-defeating'.[34] The question of the floating charge's impact on vulnerable creditors in such a case is moot; rather, the whole modern debt financing apparatus needs to be considered insofar as it unfairly impacts vulnerable stakeholders. Although the Scottish floating charge may not be used in the same way, England's experience with the relative (in)effectiveness of the prescribed part in mitigating the losses of unsecured creditors may be instructive.

(c) The effect of insolvency on employees and other vulnerable stakeholders

There is no denying that an employer's insolvency can have a dramatic impact on its employees, whether this is due to a liquidation in which the company is wound up and all jobs are lost, or a restructuring or reorganisation, which may lead to uncertainties and redundancies as well as various insidious means of taking advantage of an employee's bargaining position as leverage to seek better terms that favour the position of the employing company. Although there are certain protections that may offer some solace to employees and allow them to mitigate their risk somewhat, employers will often account for the costs of failing to comply with employment obligations, such as consultation in the event of a collective redundancy,[35] which effectively monetises the rights of employees and leaves with them with the responsibility to press their rights in an employment tribunal. For example, Thomas Cook failed in their consultation duties during a collective redundancy process, which

---

32 K Akintola, 'What is Left of the Floating Charge? An Empirical Outlook' (2015) JIBFL 404 at 404.

33 K Akintola, 'What is Left of the Floating Charge? An Empirical Outlook' (n 32) at 406.

34 K Akintola, 'What is Left of the Floating Charge? An Empirical Outlook' (n 32) at 406.

35 Trade Union and Labour Relations (Consolidation) Act 1992 Ch. 2 "Procedure for Handling Redundancies".

led to 1,500 employees filing a claim that would amount to eight weeks pay, though this could only be claimed from the National Insurance Fund and capped given the lack of assets left in the company.[36] Such payments also do not attract a super-priority as wages and holiday pay do.

The recent demise of Debenhams brought a unique problem to the company's administrators. The insolvency occurred during the COVID-19 pandemic during which many of the Debenhams workers were furloughed.[37] Administrators have fourteen days within which to confirm they are adopting employment contracts, after which adoption is automatic. The employment contracts for the employees on furlough were incidentally adopted by administrators who continued to pay them beyond the fourteen days within which the decision to adopt their contracts had to be made. As a result, their salaries would be accorded the super-priority along with the employees that were intentionally retained. Salaries of adopted contracts would be counted as expenses of administration, which would accord those payments a super-priority over all other debts. With that said, by mid-August 2020, 6,500 employees had been made redundant, including those already furloughed and many who had continued to work during the pandemic. The administrators admitted openly that a full statutory consultation was not feasible in an insolvency situation 'where the options available are limited and the administrators must consider their own duty to creditors'.[38] Protective awards for failure to consult are paid preferentially in an administration, so will affect the distributions available to other creditors as well, which raises a whole other issue in terms of the fairness of employee entitlements and tribunal awards in such situations. As summarised by Chris Laughton, 'employees feel injustice, employment tribunals impose penalties which fall on innocent creditors, and administrators seek to treat all creditors fairly'.[39]

There is ample evidence of the effect that powerful creditors and their security can have on the more vulnerable stakeholders of a company. The liquidation of British Home Stores (BHS) included questions around a

---

36 A McCulloch, 'Up to 1500 Former Thomas Cook Employees Win Payout', *Personnel Today* (16 March 2021) *https://www.personneltoday.com/hr/up-to-1500-former-thomas-cook-employees-win-payouts/* (last accessed 28 October 2021).

37 Coronavirus Act 2020 ss. 71 and 76 provided the competence to create the Coronavirus Job Retention Scheme, the details of which can be found here: *https://assets.publishing.service. gov.uk/government/uploads/system/uploads/attachment_data/file/879484/200414_CJRS_ DIRECTION_-_33_FINAL_Signed.pdf* (last accessed 28 October 2021).

38 Chris Laughton, 'Debenhams: What the Insolvency Process Means for Employees', *Personnel Today* (20 August 2020) *https://www.personneltoday.com/hr/debenhams-what-the-insolvency-process-means-for-employees/* (last accessed 28 October 2021).

39 Chris Laughton, 'Debenhams: What the Insolvency Process Means for Employees'.

floating charge held in the name of Phillip Green, which would have entitled him to get essentially all of his money back from the proceeds of the insolvency process. The Pension Protection Fund (PPF) was the biggest creditor of BHS, which demonstrates just how extensive the social impact can be for a company with a large number of employees. Were the floating charge held to be valid, it would have meant £35 million would not be available to satisfy the claims of the PPF. As it stood, unsecured creditors were only going to get a maximum of 8 pence on the pound of what they were owed.[40] This group would include involuntary creditors such as tort claimants and any additional claims of employees that were not covered by the preference.[41]

Another well-known insolvency in the recent past also relied on its pension schemes to mitigate some effects of its financial distress. The Carillion collapse highlighted the bad behaviour of directors and shareholders insofar as choices were made to pay out more in dividends than the company generated in cash, despite an increase in borrowing and a growing pension deficit.[42] The company financed its debt by borrowing against the value of the pension scheme itself.[43] The pension scheme was left without £2.6 billion that it was owed by Carillion. It also owed £2 billion to 30,000 suppliers, sub-contractors and other short-term and unsecured creditors, who would not be likely to get very much at all in a liquidation.[44] To add insult to injury, Carillion often paid late or otherwise stretched payment terms while encouraging supply chain finance.

Carillion owed more than £1.3 billion to banks when it entered compulsory liquidation and only had £29 million in cash at the time.[45] Banks with security would, of course, be able to exercise their enforcement rights against the assets charged.[46] In addition, The GLAS Trust Corporation, which had facilitated the advancement of a series of loans to Carillion, held fixed and

40 Zoe Wood, 'BHS Placed into Liquidation after Pressure from Biggest Creditor', *Guardian* (2 December 2016) *https://www.theguardian.com/business/2016/dec/02/bhs-liquidation-pressure-biggest-creditor-ppf-philip-green-frank-field* (last accessed 28 October 2021).

41 For more on the BHS insolvency, see for example I Clark, 'The British Home Stores Pension Scheme: Privatised Looting?' (2019) 50(4) *Industrial Relations Journal* 331 and N Safari and M Gelter, 'British Home Stores Collapse: The Case for an Employee Derivative Claim' (2018) 19(1) *Journal of Corporate Law Studies* 43.

42 House of Commons Business Energy and Industrial Strategy and Work and Pensions Committees, *Carillion* (16 May 2018) 7.

43 Clark, (n 41) at 335.

44 House of Commons Business Energy and Industrial Strategy and Work and Pensions Committees, *Carillion* (n 42) 7.

45 F Mor et al., 'The Collapse of Carillion' (Briefing Paper No 8206, House of Commons Library 2018) 9.

46 F Mor et al., 'The Collapse of Carillion' 13.

floating charges over the company's assets and would be paid first in priority to unsecured creditors.[47] The overleveraging of Carillion and the way that its financing was structured resulted in the directors and shareholders both being the overall 'winners' in the failure, while unpaid traders and suppliers as well as employees would lose out. As noted in the House of Commons:

> 'The consequences of the collapse of Carillion are a familiar story. The Company's employees, its suppliers, and their employees face at best an uncertain future. Pension scheme members will see their entitlements cut, their reduced pensions subsidised by levies on other pension schemes …
>
> But this sorry tale is not without winners. Carillion's directors took huge salaries and bonuses which, for all their professed contrition in evidence before us, they show no sign of relinquishing …
>
> Carillion was not just a failure of a company, it was a failure of a system of corporate accountability which too often leaves those responsible at the top – and ever-present firms that surround them – as winners, while everyone else loses out.'[48]

There are clearly many issues that can cause unfairness in an insolvency, as indicated by the above examples. However, for the purpose of this chapter, the floating charge and security in general and the priority afforded to them during an insolvency will be the focus. While employees in particular are granted a certain level of priority and preference over that of the floating charge holder, creditors with fixed charges will still be able to fully exercise their rights in most circumstances. Given the nature of employment as part of the human condition, this chapter will query whether it is fair to place them within the realm of a factor of production once an insolvency has been commenced. Employees and involuntary creditors such as tort and environmental claimants, carry a certain vulnerability as they do not have the power or capacity to mitigate the risk that is taken when entering into a relationship with a company. To a lesser extent, many unsecured creditors are beset by information asymmetries and an imbalance in bargaining power as compared to banks and venture capitalists that makes their position also difficult to mitigate in terms of the risk they undertake. In short, vulnerable stakeholders such as employees are less resilient than unsecured creditors who, in turn, are less resilient than secured creditors. This chapter will argue that these vulnerabilities should be taken into account when considering the fairness of security instruments and, in particular, the floating charge. In

---

47 'Carillion Company Liquidation Case', *Business Rescue Expert*, available at *https://www.busi nessrescueexpert.co.uk/carillion-compulsory-liquidation-contracts-employees/* (last accessed 28 October 2021).
48 House of Commons Business Energy and Industrial Strategy and Work and Pensions Committees, *Carillion* (n 42) 93 (para. 39).

order to derive a justification for this position, a theoretical framework will be introduced in the next sub-section relying on the application of vulnerability theory as developed by Martha Fineman.

(3) Theoretical framework

One aim of this chapter is to examine the issue of the floating charge and its fairness relative to vulnerable and involuntary stakeholders from a socio-legal perspective, rather than the typical efficiency perspective so often embraced by company and commercial law scholars. This means treading a line that attempts to balance two often conflicting areas of law and society: the need for a regulatory framework that allows businesses to thrive by attracting investment and another often-competing regulatory framework that provides a buffer for more vulnerable corporate stakeholders against the impact of unbridled self-interested capitalism, such as was so acute during the early Industrial Revolution in the UK and the US in particular. The special nature of labour has often been a focus of democratic-socialists, labour politicians, religious leaders and social activists. The key tenet of the International Labour Organisation that 'labour is not a commodity'[49] echoes through the writings of Karl Marx[50] and Robert Owen.[51] The Encyclical *Rerum Novarum* 'The Workers Charter' written by Pope Leo XIII also places the value of labour in connection with natural justice rather than that of the 'invisible hand' of the market, as described by Adam Smith[52]:

> 'Let the working man and the employer make free agreements, and in particular let them agree freely as to the wages; nevertheless, there underlies a dictate of natural justice more imperious and ancient than any bargain between man and man, namely, that wages ought not to be insufficient to support a frugal and well-behaved wage-earner.'[53]

Fundamentally, a person's labour cannot be fairly valued without consideration of the wider implications of what that value must go on to support. The

---

49 Declaration of Philadelphia, Constitution of the International Labour Organisation (1992) 22.
50 See for example, K Marx, *Das Kapital* (1867) *https://www.marxists.org/archive/marx/works/1867-c1/* (last accessed 28 October 2021).
51 See R Owen, *A New View of Society Or, Essays on the Principle of the Formation of the Human Character and the Application of the Principle to Practice* (first published 1816, Political Economy Reference Archive) *https://www.marxists.org/reference/subject/economics/owen/index.htm* (last accessed 28 October 2021).
52 See A Smith, *An Inquiry into the Nature and Causes of the Wealth of Nations* (first published 1776, 1993).
53 Leo XIII, *The Workers' Charter: The Encyclical Rerum Novarum* (1950).

employee is not simply selling their labour, they are earning a livelihood that must be applied to daily needs and also put by for the unforeseen and for old age.[54] In addition, regardless of the choice that it has been said that workers have in accepting employment, particularly clear in the 'employment-at-will' doctrine still prevalent in the US, employees really have little choice when accepting and maintaining employment. This lack of choice makes them vulnerable to the uncertainties caused by an employer's financial distress, and less resilient to the impact that it can have compared to other less vulnerable stakeholders. Even when given a voice, insolvency processes tend to give the most power and the loudest voice to the creditor possessing the largest proportions of the debt owed. This would place individual employees on the bottom rung of the ladder. Even as a group, their voices are unlikely to be heard over the finance creditors holding floating charges over substantial assets of the employing company.

Given the clear vulnerability of employees in the context of an employer's financial distress and the clear uniqueness of employees as a group of creditors and stakeholders that are more dependent on the benefits of employment and therefore less resilient, a different approach to assessing fairness in their treatment during insolvency may add a new perspective on how their position should perhaps be reconsidered and how processes and devices such as the floating charge should be reconsidered as they impact these essential components of business. Such a perspective requires the consideration of values that cannot so easily be monetised and while modern law has gone some way to incorporating some non-economic values, it tends to be piecemeal dependent upon the particular fields of law in question. Thus, 'values may provide some of law's content but are typically subordinated to the formal rational qualities that dominate it'.[55]

A theoretical framework is therefore needed that considers the choices of all stakeholders affected by the decisions of a corporate entity and their relative resilience to the impact of those decisions. Law and economics considerations, and by extension the Jacksonian adherence to creditor wealth maximisation as the underpinning rational for insolvency procedures, is exclusionary.[56] It depends on legal ties connected to the law of contract. It

54 See for example P O'Higgins, "Labour is not a Commodity' – an Irish Contribution to International Labour Law' (1997) 26 ILJ 227.
55 R Cotterrell, 'Theory and Values in Socio-legal Studies' (2017) 44(S1) *Journal of Law and Society* 19 at 26.
56 See T H Jackson, *The Logic and Limits of Bankruptcy Law* (Harvard: Harvard University Press, 1986).

does not allow for a balancing of the vulnerabilities caused by involuntary parties and information asymmetries inherent in processes instigated at the behest of a large creditor who may hold a floating charge. In fact, the efficiency metrics (Kaldor-Hicks) used in law and economics calculations tend to benefit one party while harming the other over and over again. A socio-legal perspective, however, allows for an analysis of current legal structures in such a way that is directly linked with the social situation to which the law applies,[57] thereby allowing for a focus on the impact on stakeholders who may be involuntary parties to an insolvency and unable to adjust their level of risk accordingly.

One of the key underlying precepts of collective insolvency procedures globally is that of equal treatment,[58] although there are so many priority carveouts that it is arguable whether this remains the case.[59] Martha Fineman notes, in respect to equality of treatment between individuals, that where equality is 'reduced to sameness of treatment or a prohibition on discrimination, this has proved an inadequate tool to resist or upset persistent forms of subordination or domination'.[60] Further:

> 'This version of equality is similarly weak in its ability to address and correct the disparities in economic and social wellbeing among various groups in our society. Formal equality leaves undisturbed – and may even serve to validate – existing institutional arrangements that privilege some and disadvantage others.'[61]

Although the treatment of creditors already carries with it the obligations that were in place under contract for the repayment of debts due, the nature of debts for goods and services or for loans is different in nature from the obligations owed to employees under an employment contract and their social and economic dependence upon it. While there are certainly debts in terms of wages for work undertaken, the relationship is far more complex and far-reaching in terms of social implications. Equal treatment in such circumstances is not necessarily fair treatment given the varying degrees of power and resilience that different categories of stakeholders will have in an

---

57 D N Schiff, 'Socio-Legal Theory: Social Structure and Law' (1976) 39(3) MLR 287 at 287.

58 The *pari passu* principle is said to be the 'foremost principle in the law of insolvency around the world'. See A Keay and P Walton, 'The Preferential Debts Regime in Liquidation Law: in the Public Interest' (1999) CfiLR 84 at 85 as cited in R J Mokal, 'Priority as Pathology: the *Pari Passu* Principle' (2001) 60(3) CLJ 581.

59 For a full discussion on the realities of *pari passu* in the context of regulatory priorities, see Mokal 1 (n 58).

60 M Fineman, 'The Vulnerable Subject: Anchoring Equality in the Human Condition' (2008) 20(1) *Yale Journal of Law and Feminism* 1 at 3.

61 M Fineman, 'The Vulnerable Subject: Anchoring Equality in the Human Condition' at 3.

insolvency process. This is also why so many carveouts already exist to this so-called fundamental principle, such as the categorisation of preferential debts that is often applied to employee claims.[62] It should be noted that in the UK context this preference is extremely limited in terms of what is likely to be owed to employees, any excess of which would either have to rank as an unsecured debt or to be paid through the National Insurance Fund.

Although Martha Fineman's vulnerability theory was constructed with the very human dependencies associated with social and cultural discrimination that have not been mitigated fully by the models of equal protection that currently underpin civil rights law and discourse, with some adjustment it can also provide a new lens through which to view legitimately vulnerable stakeholders to a corporate insolvency. Equality may even be an unjust measure when it is applied to 'situations of inescapable or inevitable inequality where differing levels of authority and power are appropriate' such as in an employer/employee relationship.[63] Extending this to insolvency situations, it can serve to recalibrate fairness between the clearly differential power structure among the various stakeholders due to the rights attached to security and regulatory priorities where applicable.

Fineman observes that the term 'vulnerable' can be used to describe:

> 'a universal, inevitable, enduring aspect of the human condition that must be at the heart of our concept of social and state responsibility. Vulnerability thus freed from its limited and negative associations is a powerful conceptual tool with the potential to define an obligation for the state to ensure a richer and more robust guarantee of equality than is currently afforded under the equal protection model'.[64]

Fineman goes on to explain that 'the concept of vulnerability can act as a heuristic device, pulling us back to examine hidden assumptions and biases that shaped its original social and cultural meanings'.[65] Vulnerability can then provide a valuable context within which critical perspectives on political, societal and legal institutions can be constructed.[66] A focus on vulnerability goes beyond the normative claims for equality generally, whether formal or substantive, and suggests the interrogation of what may be 'just and appropriate mechanisms to structure the terms and practices of inequality'.[67]

---

62 Mokal (n 58) at 584.
63 M Fineman, 'Vulnerability and Inevitable Inequality' (2017) 4(3) *Oslo Law Review* 133 at 135.
64 Fineman (n 60) at 8–9.
65 Fineman (n 60) at 9.
66 Fineman (n 60) at 9.
67 Fineman (n 63) at 134.

Currently, insolvency procedures continue to be guided by economic paradigms, principally due to its association with corporate law which continues to be shielded to some extent in the UK, and to a larger extent in the US, by the continued reliance on the free-market of Western capitalism.[68] However, given the social implications of corporate insolvency, an adjusted perspective that takes in these non-economic features is overdue.

By placing vulnerability at the centre of the social policies that have come to influence the preferences and entitlements for employees in insolvency law, it is possible to re-evaluate current approaches and to also consider the resilience of the institutions themselves. As has been evident in the age of COVID-19, some institutions will fail in the face of market fluctuations caused by sudden economic shocks such as lockdowns. By focusing on stakeholder vulnerability, it is also possible to uncover the weaknesses of the institutions in place that were intended to respond to that vulnerability, such as, in the case of UK insolvency law, the prescribed part or certain preferences for employees.[69]

Vulnerability theory provides a different perspective from which the treatment of employees (and other vulnerable and involuntary creditors) can be viewed that considers the broader social implications of their role in society and the impact upon this that an insolvency of their employer may have, along with how they may be affected by the exercise of rights held by more powerful creditors, such as floating charge holders. Achieving a balance between the contractual obligations implicated and affected by security and the economic needs of the availability of security and the social impact that the control and priority of security provides, particularly in a situation of insolvency, is inherently value-laden. Although commentators and scholars of corporate and insolvency law often prefer to avoid the determination of social value in a corporate or commercial context as will be discussed in section C, there can be no denying that the social impact remains and should therefore at least be considered in the context of achieving fairness in the balance of power and resilience between social and business interests. As noted by Fineman, as 'law should recognise, respond to, and, perhaps, redirect unjustified inequality, the critical issue must be whether the balance of power struck by the law was warranted'.[70] Although she generally refers to equality between individuals, given the differences between powerful creditors and those who are invol-

---

68 Fineman (n 60) at 5.
69 Fineman (n 60) at 12–13.
70 Fineman (n 63) at 142.

untary creditors to an insolvency as well as the value-laden characteristics of some of the more vulnerable involuntary creditors, a rethinking of the equalities ascribed to insolvency procedures is also worth undertaking.

(4) Presentation of the chapter

This chapter will be examining the potential moral hazard associated with the power of floating charge holders and other security interests when considered in the context of vulnerable and involuntary stakeholders, primarily employees. Section C will present a number of theoretical perspectives that will help to contextualise the associated issues of debt, insolvency and financial regulation and the values ascribed thereto. The chapter will then discuss the theoretical justification for the interference with pre-insolvency entitlements that the priorities and preferences ascribed to employees present. The fairness of floating charges and other security devices to involuntary and non-adjusting creditors and stakeholders during an insolvency will then be considered within the context of the oft-conflicting priorities of capital versus labour. Finally, the chapter will return to vulnerability theory with a view to suggesting certain adjustments in perspective and approach that will account for the inherent vulnerability of employees in an employers' insolvency and whether the current framework of protection is adequate under the circumstances, which will be followed by a conclusion considering the current changes to law and society over the last few years and the potential impact this has had or will have on the need to protect vulnerable insolvency stakeholders going forward.

C. PERSPECTIVES ON DEBT, INSOLVENCY, AND MORAL HAZARD

(1) The moral dimension of debt

Debt used to have an intrinsic moral dimension tied to the human condition. While early banks could only advance loans against the deposits held within the bank, this is no longer the banking norm. Today dispensing with debt has become a financial decision as institutions tend to treat individual debt obligations as profit-making and capital freeing instruments. Granted, in order for banks to lend to individuals, they must first have capital to provide to borrowers and capital can only be freed if banks can also free themselves from the debt of their borrowers, often by selling it on through the complex securitisation transactions, such as those that were at least partially indicted by assessments of the financial crisis of 2007/2008. However, the extent to which debts can now be separated from the individual who owes them is reflective of fundamental changes in how debt is perceived in the modern financial context, particularly when compared to the anthropological origins of debt as a concept. Modern securities such as the floating charge are examples of how far debt has evolved from its early conception.

Debt and credit have an extraordinarily long history lying well outside their current financial aspects. It has been said that the origin of modern debt and credit lies in a sense of human community, mutual obligations, and morality.[71] It has been viewed as a product of humanity's existential condition owed by virtue of the natural mutual protections afforded by living in a society or, from a metaphysical perspective, the existential debt owed to a supreme being.[72] Those living proper and moral lives are obliged to constantly repay the existential debts owed to one another. This evolved into a social obligation over time related to a reputation for honesty and charity,[73] something that can be traced to the early developments of social contract theory as well.

Over time, this connection between debt and morality has changed fundamentally. The impersonal market and state regulation replaced moralistic social networks. The legalisation of lending with interest has allowed for the growth of the finance industry as it is known today.[74] While today debts and credits have taken on an impersonal and purely financial character within a specific legal framework, their derivation is in good faith, socially acceptable behaviour and reputation that create the 'credit' of an individual in society.[75]

It is rare today to find an individual or a company that does not live in a perpetual state of financial debt: it is the accepted status quo of the human condition and the conditions of the free market and capitalism, which has essentially commoditised the value of debt into something that has been separated from its moral roots and which also leads to the fragmentation of credit and invention of clever debt instruments such as the floating charge, which allows large creditors to further mitigate the risk of their lending.[76] It

---

71 D Graeber, *Debt: The First 5000 Years* (New York: Melville House, 2011) 1–19.
72 This is a primordial debt 'owed by the living to the continuity and durability of the society that secures their individual existence' from G Ingham, *The Nature of Money* (Cambridge: Polity Press, 2004) 90.
73 Graeber, *Debt* (n 71), and J H Munro, 'The Medieval Origins of the Financial Revolution: Usury, Rentes and Negotiability' (2003) 25(3) *The International History Review* 505, 506.
74 Graeber, *Debt* (n 71) 332–333.
75 Graeber, *Debt* (n 71) 56–57; according to Munro (n 73) at 506, usury is defined as the exaction of interest or of any specified return beyond the principal value of a loan.
76 Finch (n 29) at 765.

has become abstracted from any proprietary interest that a debtor may have had over it; banks do not ask a mortgagor if they can sell their 'IOU' on to hedge funds, insurance companies or other financial institutions, despite that by all appearances, debt has a proprietary nature. It also does not matter that security can be granted over non-specific assets and in relation to unspecified or generalised financial needs as is done by the granting of a floating charge.

(2) Financial regulation and economic efficiency

The financial sector has long benefitted from a neo-liberal economic approach to its regulation. This has allowed innovation in investment and profit-making, creating new and different debt instruments and ways of selling and packaging them in order to increase bank liquidity, permitting more and greater lending to individuals and businesses. However, much lending now lacks the moral underpinning that has traditionally characterised debt and credit, which raises the question of how abuse can be avoided without engaging in morally hazardous activities that may place more vulnerable and involuntary creditors of a company at greater risk of higher losses in an insolvency due to the power that debt instruments such as floating charges afford to both the secured creditor and the lender. It must be queried, then, if a purely economic approach to regulation of the financial market is adequate, particularly given the distance that has evolved between debt and the human element of it and the ease by which it is now disposed.

The principles of law and economics provide an analytical framework within which a balance between social and commercial interests is sought. The basis of an economic approach to legal rules assumes that the people involved in a legal system will act rationally to maximise their own satisfaction.[77] In an economic analysis of the law, if two opposing sides of an issue behave rationally, they will find a balance that maximises the benefits/happiness of each side when an outcome is uncertain at the outset.[78] Rational maximisation within a legal system suggests that by putting a conceptual price on legal rights and remedies, it will be possible to create legal rules that maximise effectiveness by finding the perfect balance of economic efficiency between competing aims.[79]

Law and economics define a good legal system as one that keeps the profit-

---

77 R A Posner, 'Utilitarianism, Economics and Legal Theory' (1979) 8(1) JLS 104.
78 R A Posner, 'Observation: The Economic Approach to Law' (1974) 53 Tex L Rev 761.
79 R A Posner, 'Observation: The Economic Approach to Law' at 764.

ability of businesses and the welfare of people aligned, so that the pursuit of profit also benefits the public. This is somewhat reflective of the ideals of utilitarianism, a fairly hedonistic and secular political theory that places the overall pleasure or perhaps satisfaction of humanity as the defining characteristic of what is 'right' for humanity in terms of political and legal structure.[80] However, while classical utilitarianism seeks to maximise the sum of all individuals' functions in terms of utility, law and economics aims to try to maximise social wealth rather than social utility. Goods should be awarded to those individuals who are willing to pay the most, not to those for whom those goods will have the highest utility. Fines and sanctions then become a deterrent if they are set at a level that people are unwilling to 'pay the price' for doing the unwanted behaviour. The trick is to set the price at a level that deters the behaviour but does not deter one from engaging in some risk, particularly if applied to economic activity.[81] While true that sanctions may prevent unwanted and costly behaviour, it would be economically inefficient in terms of regulating the financial market to set those sanctions at such a level that no one would want to lend, invest or follow entrepreneurial ideas. Thus, a balance needs to be struck to find the point that deters enough behaviour to retain some order in the market, while not discouraging some risk in the market.

One problem with the law and economics theoretical framework is that it has been perceived as being of a specifically free-market, capitalistic ideology and even an apology for conservatism. While it is not intended to paint capitalism as 'evil', it must also be acknowledged that it does not often consider those elements of society that fall outside of the markets and profit, or that are impacted by imbalances in the power of choice, such as employees and other involuntary creditors in an insolvency situation. If economic efficiency depends on what people are willing to pay, then by association, a person's willingness to pay is directly connected to what they are able to afford. Thus, the more wealth one has, the more likely it is that it can be increased in a system built on models of pure economic efficiency. Its precept tends to support unequal income distribution and can also be exemplified in the power differential between those holding little of the debt proportion in an insolvency and those that hold substantially all of the assets hostage as could be the case for a floating charge holder, which may have a detrimental effect upon the insolvency outcomes for other stakeholders.

---

80 M Freeman, *Lloyd's Introduction to Jurisprudence*, 9th edn (London: Sweet & Maxwell, 2014) Chs 2 and 3; B Bix, *Jurisprudence: Theory and Context*, 6th edn (London: Sweet & Maxwell, 2012) Ch. 3.

81 U Gneezy and A Rustichini, 'A Fine is a Price' (2000) 29(1) JLS 1.

Ronald Coase's theory, developed in the 1960s, on social costs posits that in circumstances where two activities conflict, the costs should be assessed as the combination of both activities. For example, where a train passing by a farmers' field causes crop damage, there should be a compensation that balances the requirements of supply and demand for the services of both the farmer and the railway. Both the train and the farmer provide a social benefit that can be quantified economically, which can make it difficult to assess where the compensatory obligation should lie in perfectly economic terms. A balanced approach would allocate the costs to both farmers and railways and allow for both to continue to co-exist and provide their benefits to society as a whole.[82] This analysis, however, tends to ignore transaction costs. Without such costs parties would tend to negotiate on an equal footing to achieve a mutually beneficial transaction while internalising the social costs. This does not reflect reality, however.

Applying Coase's theory to the need to achieve a balance between social costs and the highly complex and depersonalised characteristic of modern financial regulation does not necessarily amount to a true balance of fairness between society and economy. It does not consider external obstacles and influences or the inherent imbalance in bargaining power between the various parties. Regulation has been created to control industrial pollution, noise and other noxious or anti-social effects of industry, but the commoditisation of debt presents an entirely different social cost. If debt is fundamentally an obligation or promise, what happens when that promise is mixed with other promises, amalgamated, divided, sold and dispersed to the point that it can no longer be identified in connection with the goods or services to which it was originally connected? Granted, debt is itself only a concept having no true physical existence, at least not since the unpegging of major currencies from the gold standard, and even then money only represented a promise to pay something else of equivalent value, accepted only because it is assumed that others will also accept it as valuable in exchange.[83] That said, if debt is to remain a promise, surely the person who made that promise should remain connected to it in some way.

---

82 R H Coase, 'The Problem of Social Cost' (1960) 3 *Journal of Law and Economics* 1. See further discussion in Hardman, 'Law and Economics of the Floating Charge', Chapter 5.
83 Graeber, *Debt* (n 71) 47.

(3) Justifying priority for secured debt and floating charges

There are many rationales for the protection of the rights of creditors who bargain for security over their lending. There has long been a fairly widespread consensus among both legal scholars and economists that 'according full priority to secured creditors is desirable because it promotes economic efficiency'.[84] The accordance of a priority in repayment in respect of a secured loan, which is common in many legal systems, may not result in secured creditors obtaining the full value of their claims, but they still tend to be substantially advantaged over unsecured creditors or other more vulnerable involuntary (non-adjusting) stakeholders. Unsecured creditors will only have a claim to those assets that are left after the secured creditors have taken their share,[85] effectively subordinating the claims of unsecured and non-adjusting creditors to the creditor with security without their consent, which is theoretically contrary to the mandatory rules of insolvency that do not allow for the circumvention of distribution rules by way of subordination.[86]

In the case of England and Scotland, unsecured and non-adjusting creditors may only be left with what has been circumscribed by the prescribed part out of a floating charge, which, as has been described above, may not even exist if the same creditor retains a fixed charge that has already satisfied the fullness of their debt, leaving the floating charge valueless. In circumstances where vulnerable or involuntary creditors do not have the same kind of support or power that even the median group of unsecured creditors do, this could have an even more significant impact. See, for example, the discussion of British Home Stores in section B.

The consensus supported by these many rationales fall back on the premise supported by well-known insolvency law theorists such as Thomas Jackson and Douglas Baird that '[b]ankruptcy law should change a substantive non bankruptcy rule only when doing so preserves the value of assets for the group of investors holding rights in them'.[87] Further, Baird and Jackson have asserted that:

---

84 L A Bebchuk and J M Fried, 'The Uneasy Case for Priority of Secured Claims in Bankruptcy' (1996) 105 Yale LJ 857 at 859.

85 L A Bebchuk and J M Fried, 'The Uneasy Case for Priority of Secured Claims in Bankruptcy' at 861.

86 L A Bebchuk and J M Fried, 'The Uneasy Case for Priority of Secured Claims in Bankruptcy' at 857–858.

87 D G Baird and T H Jackson, 'Corporate Reorganisations and the Treatment of Diverse Ownership Interests: A Comment on Adequate Protection of Secured Creditors in Bankruptcy' (1984) 51(1) U Chi L Rev 97 at 99.

'Protecting the value of a secured creditor's non-bankruptcy rights – whatever they might be – actually reinforces the bankruptcy policy of putting the firm's assets to their best use by placing the costs of trying to keep the assets of a firm together on those who stand to benefit from such an effort.'[88]

Although the 'bankruptcy policy' referred to in the quote above is specifically US' policy, many jurisdictions reflect a similar approach to secured credit, offering protection to the point that they are excluded from the collective procedure in some cases. This leaves secured creditors in some jurisdictions free from the restrictions of a stay or moratorium and able to enforce their security despite the company being subject to a collective insolvency procedure. In addition, the Scottish floating charge has been described as an insolvency tool, rather than a traditional real right in security, which grants an additional level of security and risk mitigation for creditors holding such charges.[89] These priorities are based on the bargains made between debtor and creditor; however, only larger and powerful creditors tend to be able to afford the high level of risk mitigation provided by a floating charge. It therefore creates a higher level of priority that is justified as having been paid for by the secured creditor. This approach embraces the application of a law and economics approach to insolvency and restructuring law, which tends to follow the creditors' bargain theory in many respects still today.

The creditors' bargain theory supported the view that the objective of insolvency law was to provide a collective debt mechanism for the creditors of an insolvent entity and, therefore, the legitimacy of an insolvency procedure depended on its ability to maximise the value of the debtor's estate for distributions.[90] This theory also claimed that pre-insolvency entitlements should only be impaired in insolvency when necessary to maximise the net asset distribution to the collective of creditors and never to accomplish strictly distributional goals.[91] Thus insolvency laws influenced by this theory tended to be hostile toward the redistribution of wealth post-insolvency.[92]

---

88 D G Baird and T H Jackson, 'Corporate Reorganisations and the Treatment of Diverse Ownership Interests' at 101. 'Insolvency' and 'bankruptcy' will be used interchangeably in this section due to the discussion of American theorists. 'Bankruptcy' refers to both corporate and personal insolvency in the US, whereas 'bankruptcy' traditionally refers to personal insolvency in the UK.

89 See Hardman, 'Hohfeld and the Scottish Floating Charge', Chapter 7 within this volume and A D J MacPherson, *The Floating Charge* (Edinburgh: Edinburgh Legal Education Trust, 2020), especially Ch. 6.

90 Jackson, *Logic and Limits* (n 56) 2–3.

91 R E Scott, 'Through Insolvency with the Creditors' Bargain Heuristic' (1986) 53 U Chi L Rev 690 at 692.

92 D G Carlson, 'Bankruptcy Theory and the Creditors' Bargain' (1992) 61 U Cin L Rev 453 at 457.

There have only been limited successful explorations of alternative theories of insolvency law that take in the many social, involuntary and non-financial stakeholder interests that are inextricably associated with business and corporate failure. This is particularly true given that the creditors' bargain model is fraught with problems, not the least of which being that it was created to explain a process that has existed in some form for two millennia and longer in some ancient civilisations (for example, the Hammurabi dynasty in Babylon, 2,250 BC)[93] and was developed as a reaction to pre-existing conditions relating to debt. Rather, bankruptcy is not 'the logical outcome of ethical principles consciously adopted and consistently applied by perfectly rational legislators; it is instead the product of social exigency, moral conflict, and political compromise'.[94] In short, the result of over-indebtedness and financial failure is messy and it is the messiness that collective procedural frameworks have been created to control and improve for the benefit of all creditors and, more recently, stakeholders in the future of the company.[95] Add to that the pull of social policy issues that include vulnerable stakeholders who are unable to adjust their financial risk, and the issues becomes tortuous.

Some theorists have tried to depart from the creditors' bargain. For example, Donald Korobkin presents an 'insolvency choice' theory,[96] a value-based account that attempts to explain insolvency law,[97] which was necessary in his view because previous theories were 'limited by the economic account's vision of insolvency law as a mechanism for achieving superior economic returns',[98] which, in turn, limited choices to economic outcomes only.[99] Essentially, Korobkin viewed the economic accounts as being 'incapable of recognising noneconomic values essential to a vindicating explanation

---

93 See L Levinthal, 'The Early History of Bankruptcy Law' (1918) U Pa L Rev 223; for a detailed history of bankruptcy law over the last two millennia, see P Omar, *European Insolvency Law* (Surrey: Ashgate Publishing, 2004).

94 D G Carlson, 'Philosophy in Bankruptcy' (1987) 85(5/6) Mich L Rev 1341 at 1389 as summarised by D R Korobkin, 'Contractarianism and the Normative Foundations of Insolvency Law' (1993) 71 Tex L Rev 541 at 543.

95 See for example G-J Boon, 'Harmonising European Insolvency Law: The Emerging Role of Stakeholders' (2018) 27 *International Insolvency Review* 150.

96 A similar communitarian approach to the creditors' bargain theory based on a hypothetical situation in which the principles of an insolvency system are selected by participants. An explanation of the creditors' bargain theory will follow in this section.

97 D R Korobkin, 'Rehabilitating Values: A Jurisprudence of Insolvency' (1991) 91(4) Colum L Rev 717 at 721.

98 D R Korobkin, 'Rehabilitating Values: A Jurisprudence of Insolvency' at 737.

99 D R Korobkin, 'Rehabilitating Values: A Jurisprudence of Insolvency' at 738.

of corporate reorganisation'.[100] Indeed, insolvency law has emerged as a system with varied contours and dimensions that satisfy interests that go well beyond simple wealth maximisation.[101]

Korobkin's view recognises that the outcomes of financial distress, such as a foreclosure by a secured creditor or sale of assets to satisfy a floating charge holder, have more than just an economic impact on the company, rather they involve a range of issues such as loss of employment and economic activity. Furthermore, given the higher level of procedural complexity that reorganisation and restructuring present, which tend to be the current aims of most insolvency procedures, a purely economic account does not fully explain or justify their use. Rather than liquidate a company, reorganisations and restructurings aim to rehabilitate it with the success of such a procedure predicated on the corporation surviving as a going concern or at least existing long enough to maximise distributions to creditors.[102]

It is not only creditors that participate in Korobkin's model but rather all that are impacted by an insolvency within a society.[103] The aim is to define a 'procedure of choice that satisfies basic notions of fairness' while ensuring that the principles do not 'offend our most strongly considered judgments about how society ought to respond to the problem of financial distress'.[104] Where a solution that exclusively focuses on creditor wealth maximisation would often lead to the liquidation of the business to distribute proceeds to creditors, such an outcome would not necessarily satisfy the needs of employees or their dependents. For example, the application of creditor wealth maximisation would require that the business of a financially distressed company be sold whenever it would result in the largest distribution in money to creditors, despite the fact that the business might still be viable and also support numerous employees relying on it as their exclusive source of income.[105] Plainly, the preferential treatment of some parties in insolvency frameworks is a departure from normal priorities but meets a social need to protect more vulnerable parties. While this concept does not fit neatly within the definition of collective principles of insolvency law, it

---

100 D R Korobkin, 'Rehabilitating Values: A Jurisprudence of Insolvency' at 740.
101 D R Korobkin, 'Rehabilitating Values: A Jurisprudence of Insolvency' at 739.
102 M J Roe, 'Insolvency and Debt: A New Approach to Corporate Reorganisation' (1983) Colum L Rev 527 at 534–536.
103 Korobkin (n 94) at 554.
104 Korobkin (n 94) at 553–553.
105 Korobkin (n 94) at 579.

does allow such a framework to satisfy a broader set of needs than the strict adherence to contractual entitlements and priorities.

Elizabeth Warren has also challenged the creditors' bargain theory as a premise for insolvency law. She recognised that the distributional issues arising in insolvency have an inherent give-and-take character; for example, when a secured creditor enforces against an insolvent estate, this often defeats, at least partially, the collective rights of unsecured creditors who will not get their full contractual due.[106] Warren challenged the creditors' bargain theory, redefining it as an argument about economic rationality in which the aim of the policies underpinning insolvency law were to make sure that assets were managed to achieve the highest value in their use.[107] She also argued that the central job of insolvency law should be to apportion the losses of the debtor's default and that 'a variety of factors impinge on the difficult policy decision of where to let those losses fall'.[108] Warren also claimed that neither the simple nor enhanced creditors' bargain could justify or account for corporate rehabilitation, restructuring and rescue.

What has been apparent to Warren, Korobkin and others is that a more nuanced and thoughtful approach is more appropriate than a purely economic framework provided by the creditors' bargain theory, given the many competing interests in a rescue or restructuring procedure. Warren's approach promoted a design of an insolvency framework that would keep viable businesses running while allowing for the consideration of 'non normal' creditors such as employees.[109] With the focus on restructuring in today's global insolvency policy an insolvency framework should also provide for rescue, rehabilitation and restructuring where the business is viable, in order to protect the greater interests of the company and its stakeholders. Maximising value for the collective also means reducing strategic behaviour associated with individual creditors and debtors pressing whatever advantage they may have in the process, creating 'prisoners' dilemmas' by the exploitation of

---

106 E Warren, 'Insolvency Policy' (1987) 54(3) U Chi L Rev 755 at 789–790.
107 E Warren, 'Insolvency Policy' (1987) at 802.
108 E Warren, 'Insolvency Policy' (1987) at 810.
109 Douglas Baird, for example, agrees that such stakeholders are not always adequately protected, but argues that their protection is something that should sit outside of an insolvency framework. See D G Baird, 'Loss Distribution, Forum Shopping, and Insolvency: A Reply to Warren' (1987) 54 U Chi L Rev 815 at 815. The view of workers as 'non normal' stakeholders is a particularly American view in contrast to the European view of workers as being central stakeholders in corporate life. See generally I Lynch-Fannon, *Working Within Two Kinds of Capitalism* (Oxford: Hart Publishing, 2003).

superior information or greater bargaining power.[110] Although insolvency systems tend to be designed to reduce the risk of such dilemmas, the power afforded to secured creditors including floating charge holders undoubtedly continues to influence insolvency outcomes.

The argument for interfering with pre-insolvency rights and entitlements in order to respond to the social problems caused by insolvency has frequently been met with outright rejection to varying degrees of acceptance with caveats. It has been said that it should not be within insolvency or bankruptcy law that issues of social policy should be resolved.[111] Given the theoretical framework underpinning this discussion, the position of theorists such as Baird and Jackson within the paradigm of law and economics supporting wealth maximisation for contractual creditors cannot survive. It leaves aside the vulnerabilities inherent in the employment relationship and the involuntariness of other stakeholders who have suffered detriment and are owed recompense of some description by the company in financial distress, whereas the position of theorists such as Warren and Korobkin tend to support this paradigm shift. These are obligations owed by the company itself, the assets of which tend to be preserved first for creditors holding security and then unsecured creditors, covering a variety of vulnerable and involuntary stakeholders, who may (if they are fortunate) achieve a few pence on the pound of what they are owed. The obligations go beyond the debt itself in many cases, although they have been quantified in the only way that the typical capitalist system is able to do, which ranks them as an equivalent unsecured claim to be answered in the relevant order of priority.

Secured creditors are generally very well placed to influence the insolvency outcomes of a company in financial distress. Generally, secured creditors tend to be banks, which are key players who can also contribute to the rescue of a company by deferring payment demands, renegotiating terms, choosing not to exercise their enforcement rights and supplying rescue funds. They are more resilient because they usually have far more information about the financial situation of a company, so are better placed to make well-informed decisions about the risks of continuing to do business with

---

110 A prisoner's dilemma is a theory that says that rationally acting individuals will not act in a manner that is in their collective interest if they are not able to communicate with each other and co-ordinate their actions. See A Rapoport and A M Chammah, *Prisoner's Dilemma* (Ann Arbor: University of Michigan Press, 1965) and J Hardman, 'Law and Economics of Corporate Financial Difficulty' in P Omar and J L L Gant, *Research Handbook on Corporate Restructuring* (Cheltenham: Edward Elgar Publishing, 2021) 500–512.

111 D G Baird and T H Jackson (n 87) at 102.

the company. They also are well resourced with funds, skills and expertise to exercise their power over the insolvency process, which will also be mostly to their ongoing benefit.[112] Employees and other vulnerable stakeholders, in contrast, are plagued by information asymmetries and as their funds are also tied up in the ongoing success of the company in question, will not have anywhere near the same level of resourcing to ensure they get an equal hearing.

The last several decades have also seen a shift in how corporate financing is arranged while the perspective on debt as a concept has changed dramatically from its moralistic roots. This has involved a considerable fragmentation of debt,[113] which has created greater and greater distances between the original debtor and lenders in a credit relationship. Although the floating charge has been around arguably in one form or another for more than a thousand years, it has also been affected by the more modern views on debt, which have created that moral distance between debtor and creditor on the financial markets. The buying and selling of debt have also led to the commodification of debt,[114] which adds further distance from that fundamental moral dimension of repaying what is owed.

Although the Enterprise Act 2002 introduced some mitigation upon the power of the floating charge holder, the existence of the floating charge has been viewed as having an overall positive effect on corporate finance and rescue. It has 'played a cardinal role in the provision of debt finance to companies'.[115] While it has undergone a number of changes both under legislation such as the Enterprise Act 2002 and through case law, such as *Spectrum Plus*,[116] the instrument remains an important form of security today. As noted by Kayode Akintola, '[i]n spite of insolvency legislation, the floating charge is still capable of performing one of the cardinal functions of security – debt realisation'.[117] The facility of the floating charge is particularly useful as a modern debt realisation device due to the nature of smaller companies in particular, which tend to have more current assets than fixed assets, making fixed security less effective in protecting a secured lender.

The floating charge itself also offers a certain level of power to floating charge holders in terms of commencing insolvency and exercising some control over appointments, despite the changes introduced by the Enterprise

---

112 V Finch, 'Corporate Rescue: Who is Interested?' (2012) 3 JBL 190 at 195.

113 Finch (n 29) at 759.

114 Finch (n 29) at 765.

115 Akintola (n 32) 404.

116 *Spectrum Plus Ltd v National Westminster Bank Plc* [2005] UKHL 41; [2005] 3 WLR 58.

117 Akintola (n 32) at 404.

Act 2002.[118] Though an administration can be commenced by directors or the floating charge holder in many cases, in a high number of those commenced by the company or its directors in the aforementioned study there was also evidence that secured creditors, including floating charge holders, were also actively involved in appointments under the process, often by applying leverage associated with the continuation or granting of new lending.[119] Thus, while the banks that often hold the floating changes may not take full control by commencing a process and appointing a professional to see it through, they will still exercise significant influence over the process, not the least reason being that they could also be a source of rescue finance should a restructuring be possible.

D. JUSTIFYING EMPLOYEE PREFERENCE OVER FLOATING CHARGES

(1) Employment regulation and the free market

In classic neo-liberal economic tradition, labour was considered a mere factor of production: a commodity to be bought and sold freely on the market.[120] The Industrial Revolution in the UK revealed how much labour could be dehumanised by this *laissez faire* approach. However, once the untenable position of workers during the Industrial Revolution was recognised, it was declared that labour should not be treated as a commodity. Even Adam Smith observed that there was an inequality of bargaining power between employers and employees. He noted that:

> 'Many workmen could not subsist a week, few could subsist a month, and scarce any a year without employment. In the long run, the workman may be as necessary to his master as his master is to him; but the necessity is not so immediate.'[121]

The following century, Karl Marx described the commoditisation of labour as leading to exploitation of workers and constituting a barrier to free human development.[122] Contrary to this commoditisation premise, labour is unlike any other commodity insofar as it has a distinctly human aspect as

---

118 V Finch, 'Re-Invigorating Corporate Rescue' (2003) JBL 527 at 541.

119 Akintola (n 32) at 406.

120 Smith, *Wealth of Nations* (n 52) 36–44.

121 Smith, *Wealth of Nations* (n 52) 65.

122 See K Marx, 'Economic and Philosophic Manuscripts' in T B Bottomore (ed), *Early Writings* (first published 1844, 1963) 76, discussed at length in E Tucker, 'Renorming Labour Law: Can we Escape Labour Law's Recurring Regulatory Dilemmas?' (2010) 39(2) ILJ 99 at 105–106.

individuals can decide how hard they work and with what level of care. The environment in which someone works also affects their behaviour, which affects their decision-making and the work that they provide. It is not as simple as providing work under a contract as employees have other concerns that may limit their choices with regards to the jobs they can take, such as the costs of changing location and other human factors such as the stigma that can be associated with changing jobs regularly.[123] Were labour a mere commodity, as Marx notes, there would be little or no possibility for growth or advancement of individuals once they have taken their first job, which is clearly not how the labour market works in reality.

Eventually workers' vulnerability was confirmed by the International Labour Organisation in the Declaration of Philadelphia.[124] The welfare state gave the plight of workers a central concern, recognising that due to asymmetry of information between employees and employers, perfect competition could not exist in the labour market.[125] Social justice, fair income distribution and even job security can be linked to the need for the welfare state to preserve and protect human dignity.[126] Labour regulation has also been justified by reference to the stability it can provide to the labour market.[127] The preferential legislative treatment that employees often receive during insolvency procedures and EU Directives that provide protection can be seen as a product of these justifications.

The development of the employment relationship has a long history. In most jurisdictions, it can be characterised by the subordination of an employee to the needs of the employer, who will generally have control over hours, workplace, tools and work performance. There is an inherent imbalance in employment relationships that historically allowed for the exploitation of employees.[128] Employment law today is concerned with equalising

---

123 J Stiglitz, 'Employment, Social Justice, and Societal Well-Being' (2002) 141(1–2) *International Labour Review* 9 at 10.
124 Declaration Concerning the Aims and Purposes of the International Labour Organisation, adopted at the 26th Session of the ILO, Philadelphia, 10 May 1944.
125 B E Kaufman, 'Labor Law and Employment Regulation: Neoclassical and Institutional Perspectives' in K G Dau-Schmidt et al. (eds), *Labor and Employment Law and Economics: Volume 2, Encyclopaedia of Law and Economics*, 2nd edn (Cheltenham: Edward Elgar Publishing, 2009) 4 at 14–16.
126 See art. 1 of the Charter of Fundamental Rights of the European Union 2012/C 326/02: 'Human dignity is inviolable. It must be respected and protected'.
127 Kaufman (n 125) at 49.
128 J L L Gant, 'Proletarianisation and the Emergence of Labour Regulation in France and Britain' in *Balancing the Protection of Business and Employment in Insolvency: An Anglo-French Perspective* (The Hague: Eleven International Publishing, 2017) 33–78.

the bargaining power of the employment relationship and accounting for the weaker resilience of employees in that relationship. This is generally through legislation preventing employers from unfairly exercising their power over employees and protecting employees' right to continued employment. While countries such as the US, with only a few individual state exceptions, continue to embrace the 'employment-at-will' doctrine,[129] most countries, including the UK, have evolved systems that acknowledge the social risks of employment, including the cost of unemployment, and provide some protection to try to prevent the vagaries of a regulation-free labour market.

Workers provide more than a simple quantifiable service that can be equated to a cost or value. They also provide firm specific skills and expertise that become integrated into the business of a company, which goes far deeper than a nut or bolt, or machinery. Where such human capital is invested, it is reasonable that it should be protected from arbitrary treatment by management along with other guarantees to protect employment.[130] Firm specific human capital can be as important if not more so than the value of equity capital and will often contribute at a higher level to the firm's wealth than its physical assets.[131] Employees contribute to productivity, innovation and firm synergies, along with labour and loyalty over an extended period, all of which will often significantly enhance firm value. These employee investments confer value on the company in return for an implicit or explicit promise of job security,[132] which is of course compromised in the event of an insolvency or restructuring in terms of the certainty of that security and often at the expense of continued employment. In addition, most employees are essentially undiversified, working full time at a single firm, thus they are less resilient if a firm then fails. A job loss and/or loss of compensation can therefore have a devastating effect on both the individual employees and

---

129 The employment-at-will doctrine is best articulated by Horace Gray Wood in 1877: 'With us the rule is inflexible, that a general or indefinite hiring is *prima facie* a hiring-at-will, and if the servant seeks to make out a yearly hiring, the burden is upon him to establish it by proof … '; S F Befort, 'Labor and Employment Law at the Millennium: a Historical Review and Critical Assessment' (2001–2002) 43 Boston College L Rev 351 at 355–356.

130 S Deakin and F Wilkinson, 'Labour Law and Economic Theory: A Reappraisal' (1998) ESRC Centre for Business Research, University of Cambridge Working Paper No 92, 1.

131 M M Blair, 'Firm-Specific Human Capital and Theories of the Firm' in M M Blair and M J Roe (eds), *Employees and Corporate Governance* (Washington DC: Brookings Institution Press, 1999) 58 at 71.

132 J Sarra, 'Widening the Insolvency Lens: The Treatment of Employee Claims' in Paul J Omar (ed), *International Insolvency Law: Themes and Perspectives* (Surrey: Ashgate Publishing, 2008) 295 at 297.

their families, as well as communities and local economies that their wages support.[133]

The time and effort expended by employees on the firm for which they work will often be overlooked when valuing their contribution, for example, when it comes to a redundancy situation resulting from a restructuring. A conservative estimate by Blair suggests that employees who have worked for a long time for a single firm and who are laid off during a corporate restructuring typically will earn 15–20% less in their next position.[134] A substantial part of the investment that the employee has made is therefore lost when they are laid off with no prospect for recovery.[135] As noted by Easterbrook and Fischel, employees 'may make formidable investments in the firm (in the sense of irrevocable, specialised commitments of physical or human capital)' but account for this on the basis that employees are equally empowered to bargain for adequate compensation in their employment contract.[136] Although true that a firm will equally invest in an employee, it is impossible to define or quantify the value gained by the company as a result of an employee gaining skills and expertise on the job, an investment by an employee that is lost when they are terminated during a restructuring or otherwise.[137]

The argument for protecting employees with some priority in insolvency stems from various justifications. A reorganisation is generally commenced with the hope that the business will continue and that by retaining employees, corporate knowledge will also be retained. Also, an employee's wages represent a large part of that person's wealth; they do not enter the relationship consciously factoring in the risk of their employer's default in the way that a trade creditor signing a negotiated contract might. From a business protection point of view, prioritising employee claims may prevent valuable employees from seeking work elsewhere while a reorganisation is taking place.[138]

In relation to the passing of social legislation and a focus on social policy in political agendas, it has historically been argued by proponents of efficiency in the law and economics movement that these are an illegitimate

133 J Sarra, 'Widening the Insolvency Lens: The Treatment of Employee Claims' (n 132) at 297.
134 Blair (n 131) at 61.
135 W Njoya, 'Employee Ownership and Efficiency: An Evolutionary Perspective' (2004) 33(3) ILJ 211 at 230.
136 F H Easterbrook and D R Fischel, *The Economic Structure of Corporate Law* (Harvard: Harvard University Press, 1991) 38 as cited in Njoya (n 135) at 230.
137 Njoya (n 135) at 230.
138 D R Korobkin, 'Employee Interests in Bankruptcy' (1996) 4 Am Bankr Inst L Rev 5, 6.

interference with market relations.[139] While freedom, autonomy, liberty and individualism are central to the benefits perceived in following a neo-classical economic model, giving individuals choices free from constraint and coercion,[140] these positive effects are not always accessible. It is not reflective of the real position of employees in the labour market. In terms of welfare economics, if markets are competitive, information must be perfect in order to reach a true competitive equilibrium. This presumes that government intervention should not be necessary to maintain market efficiency in an optimal competitive situation.[141]

The premise that perfect competition can exist within the labour market is spurious. The labour market is imperfectly competitive due to inequality of bargaining power, unequal access to information and resources and unequal balance of rights that exist within it as demonstrated in the foregoing sections. While employment regulation often impedes the perceived efficiency of the free market, it is justified as restoring balance to an otherwise exploitative and imbalanced relationship that, without control, would be socially inefficient and unjust due to the unilateral reduction in wages and conditions of labour.[142] Market failures owing to informational problems that cause an inefficient allocation of resources provide a premise for the argument in favour of social policy as a factor for improving that market efficiency.[143] The early days of the Industrial Revolution throughout Europe exemplify this imbalance in competition. While it could be argued that the same moral conditions do not exist today, it is only necessary to observe the exploitation of workers that occurs in developing countries to realise that such conditions persist.[144]

Fundamentally, the protection of employment rights and labour are justified due to the human element from a moral perspective as well as a human investment perspective. Labour protection and regulation 'addresses the idiosyncratic problems that arise in relation to contracts of employment through a mixture of special contract law and market regulation'. It also

---

139 S Deakin and F Wilkinson, 'Rights vs Efficiency? The Economic Case for Transnational Labour Standards' (1994) 23(4) ILJ 289 at 292.

140 Kaufman (n 125) at 6–9.

141 D Fourage, 'Costs of Non-Social Policy: Towards and Economic Framework of Quality Social Policies – and the Costs of not Having them' (Report for the Employment and Social Affairs DG, European Commission, 3 January 2003).

142 Kaufman (n 125) at 30–41.

143 D Fourage (n 141).

144 J L L Gant, 'Conflict and Resolution: Path Dependent Influences on the Evolution of Acquired Rights in Corporate Rescue in the UK and France', in *Balancing the Protection of Business and Employment in Insolvency: An Anglo-French Perspective* (2017) 195–208.

'appeals to considerations of a fair distribution of wealth, power, and other goods in society'.[145] The prevalence of labour and employment protection even in places such as the US where such protection is generally quite limited, indicates the broad recognition that employees and workers should be a special case when considered as a 'factor of production'. However, when insolvency arises, labour appears to be recommoditised with employees becoming creditors valued by reference to the debt owed under their employment contracts. Although there are some additional protections and preferences, it is arguable that these do not go far enough to account for the investments made by employees in terms of their time and skill. This is even more relevant in the context of the power wielded by secured creditors including floating charge holders whose priorities effectively subordinate unsecured claims.

(2) Employees in insolvency: contradiction of pre-insolvency priority entitlements

The majority of insolvency scholars and policymakers tend to ignore or eschew non-contractual interests, such as the social policy matters associated with employees, community interests and other non-adjusting involuntary stakeholders. Rather, most insolvency scholars still tend to view insolvency from a law and economics perspective and focus on creditor wealth maximisation as the main or sole goal for an insolvency or restructuring process.[146] These goals tend to favour the creditors with the most power (holding the highest value of debt with the highest level of priority). Although the argument goes that creditors can choose how to mitigate their risk when entering into contracts and that the information is there for them to do so, the reality is not so black and white as discussed in section C. Some creditors do not have the information, the money, time or power to adjust to the changing situation, which puts them at a disadvantage to those who can. As observed by Elizabeth Warren, there is clearly nothing simple about insolvency policy or the social issues affected by it. Rather, insolvency is 'a dirty, complex, elastic, interconnected view ... from which [she] can neither predict outcomes nor even necessarily fully articulate all the factors relevant to a policy

---

145 H Collins, 'Theories of Rights as Justifications for Labour Law' in G Davidov and B Langille (eds), *The Idea of Labour Law* (Oxford: Oxford University Press, 2011) 137 at 137.

146 N D Martin, 'Noneconomic Interests in Bankruptcy: Standing on the Outside Looking in' (1998) 59 Ohio State L J 428 at 438.

decision'.[147] Non-contractual interests are, of course, far more difficult to quantify, which explains to some extent why those interests tend to be left out of economic evaluation of insolvency law. However, their existence and importance have a significant value to society, particularly when those non-quantifiable up-front costs then have to be borne by governments and, by extension, tax-payers.[148]

Corporate failure affects more than banks, trade creditors and share-holders who all have a contractual claim against the assets or value of the company. Clearly, the employees of a company may find themselves jobless and perhaps even pension-less if the company is dissolved. As an employee's purely contractual claim is unsecured, it will have little hope of claiming back lost wages, entitlements and other benefits unless additional protections are provided under the law.

Most jurisdictions have recognised the social problem associated with this situation and provided some level of priority or preference to ensure that employees will get a commensurately larger bite of the apple, at the expense of both secured and unsecured creditors depending on the jurisdiction. These privileges are supported by international organisations such as the World Bank,[149] UNCITRAL,[150] the International Labour Organisation[151]

---

147 E Warren, 'Bankruptcy Policy' (1987) 54 U Chi L Rev 775 at 811.

148 See for example, K Gross, 'Taking Community Interests into Account in Bankruptcy: An Essay' (1994) 72 Wash U L Q 1031.

149 The World Bank, 'Principles for Effective Insolvency and Creditor/Debtor Regimes', *World Bank Group* (2016), available at *https://openknowledge.worldbank.org/bitstream/ handle/10986/35506/Principles-for-Effective-Insolvency-and-Creditor-and-Debtor-Regimes. pdf?sequence=1&IsAllowed=y* (last accessed 30 October 2021). Principle C.12.4 calls for special recognition and treatment of labour claims on the basis that 'workers are a vital part of an enterprise and careful consideration should be given to balancing the rights of employees with those of other creditors'.

150 UNCITRAL Legislative Guide on Insolvency Law (United Nations 2005) *https://uncitral.un. org/sites/uncitral.un.org/files/media-documents/uncitral/en/05-80722_ebook.pdf* (last accessed 30 October 2021). See paras 72 and 73 on pp. 287–288 in which the priority for workers claims provided by a majority of states is discussed as well as the guarantee funds that some states provide to cover claims not met by the insolvent estate.

151 See the International Labour Organisation, C095 Protection of Wages Convention (1949) *https://www.ilo.org/dyn/normlex/en/f?p=NORMLEXPUB:12100:0::NO::P12100_ILO_ CODE:C095* (last accessed 30 October 2021). See art. 11(1): 'In the event of the bankruptcy or judicial liquidation of an undertaking, the workers employed therein shall be treated as privileged creditors either as regards wages due to them for service rendered during such a period prior to the bankruptcy or judicial liquidation as may be prescribed by national laws or regulations, or as regards wages up to a prescribed amount as may be determined by national laws or regulations'. See also International Labour Organisation, C158 Termination of Employment Convention (1982) art. 11 and C173 Protection of Workers Claims (Employer's Insolvency) Convention 1992 arts 6 and 12.

and European Union institutions[152] and extend well beyond the protection of direct financial costs in respect of wages. In particular, the EU institutions have laid down Directives that require the approximation of minimum standards for protecting job security and continuity of employment,[153] as well as ensuring fairness for collective economic dismissals.[154]

Employees are afforded greater consideration for a number of reasons. They are often considered 'involuntary creditors' as they have little choice but to provide their labour in exchange for their livelihood. However, it could also be argued that an employee can choose whether or not to take a job, but the reality is far more complicated. The capitalist societies of the Western World require as a matter of fundamental importance to society and even the individual identity that people work to support themselves financially. Their labour investment is undiversified so if the firm fails, an employee will likely lose their job with the unavoidable effect on local economies supported by their wages. This can also impact future support through the adverse impact an insolvency may have on employee pensions.[155] It is therefore difficult to accept that there really is a choice in whether a person undertakes work to earn their livelihood, or even a particular job depending on the circumstances of the individual and market conditions at the time.

Employees contribute more than just their labour for livelihood, particularly in today's service economies requiring a high level of skill and intellect. They contribute to 'productivity, innovation and firm synergies' that frequently enhance firm value and may have done so over an extended period, exhibiting difficult to quantify values such as loyalty. These confer 'value on the corporation on the basis of implicit or explicit promises of job security'.[156] Sarra observes further that:

> 'The promise gives rise to contributions to the firm in the form of time, energy and creativity over and above the current wage/labour exchange. On insolvency, the employees' investments in this respect are not adequately protected by employment contracts or statutory minimum protections as these provisions are aimed solely at fixed capital claims.'[157]

---

152 Directive 2008/94/EC OJ 2008 L283/36.
153 Directive 2001/23/EC OJ 2001 L82/16.
154 Directive 98/59/EC OJ 1998 L225/6.
155 Sarra (n 132) at 297.
156 Sarra (n 132) at 297.
157 J Sarra, *Creditor Rights and the Public Interest, Restructuring Insolvent Corporations* (Toronto: University of Toronto Press, 2003) 70 as cited in Sarra (n 132) at 297.

Whereas wealth maximisation can be justified if humanity is removed from the equation entirely, along with the costs of involuntariness and information asymmetry, when looking at the circumstances of insolvency as a reality and all of its associated impacts on society and global economies, people (and other non-financial stakeholders) must be considered in order to perform a full execution of the social contract to which we are all a party. This includes the corporation, which benefits from legal systems 'perpetuated by the government and the public' and should therefore bear some responsibility and accountability to the human beings upon which the corporation is built.[158] The need to consider employees as integral parts of the business has been supported by discussions around firm-specific human capital and the integral part that humans play as a defining feature of a firm itself.[159] A key takeaway of labour theory in this area is that 'employee investments in firm-specific human capital cannot be well protected by explicit and complete contracts. Other institutional arrangements are needed, and those arrangement often have the effect of tying the fortunes of the employee together with those of the firm'.[160]

The relationship between employee and employer (debtor/company) is therefore far more interrelated and connected than a supplier/debtor relationship as suppliers can choose the terms of the contract and adjust interest rates, for example, to account for insolvency risk. A secured creditor will have an even greater separation as their risk is protected by the ability to exercise their security. Employees have no such choice or flexibility in the role that they play in a firm.

158 E M Dodd Jr, 'For Whom Are Corporate Managers Trustees?' (1932) 45 Harv L Rev 1145 at 1148 as cited in N D Martin, 'Noneconomic Interests in Bankruptcy: Standing on the Outside Looking In' (1998) 59 Ohio State L J 429 at 439.
159 On this discussion, see for example G S Becker, *Human Capital: A Theoretical and Empirical Analysis with Special Reference to Education* (New York: National Bureau of Economic Research, 1964); Peter B Doeringer and Michael J Piore, *Internal Labour Markets and Manpower Analysis* (Cambridge, MA: MIT, 1971); S M Jacoby, 'The New Institutionalism: What can it Learn from the Old?' 29(Spring) *Industrial Relations* 316; M Hashimoto, 'Firm-Specific Human Capital as a Shared Investment' (1981) 71(June) *American Economic Review* 475; and R C Topel, 'Specific Capital and Unemployment: Measuring the Costs and Consequences of Job Loss' in A H Meltzer and C I Ploser (eds), *Studies in Labour Economics in Honor of Walter Y Oi* (Amsterdam: North-Holland, 1990) 181.
160 M M Blair, 'Firm-Specific Human Capital and Theories of the Firm' (2003) Georgetown University Law Centre, Business, Economic and Regulatory Policy Working Paper No. 167848, 58, 61.

E. ARE FLOATING CHARGES FAIR TO VULNERABLE STAKEHOLDERS?

Security with priority has been described as fair because: (1) it has been freely bargained for; (2) it does not deprive the company of value; and (3) parties are given notice of security arrangements and so cannot justifiably complain about it.[161] These arguments are based on the premise that other creditors will be aware of such activities and will be able to adjust their loan rates accordingly. However, this applies rationally only to voluntary contractual parties and even then, the information asymmetries persist, whether voluntary or not. There are vastly differing negotiating positions between banks holding floating charges and trade suppliers extending a line of credit.[162] The bargain argument also does not stand up for those creditors who are truly involuntary nor where the bargain itself effectively lays costs on other creditors without their consent insofar as a floating charge allows for a debtor to increase the insolvency share for a secured creditor, which will inevitably come at the expense of unsecured and involuntary creditors.[163]

The contention that granting security does not deprive the company of value also has difficulties. As new assets are acquired following the granting of a security, more security builds up without the injection of additional value. Finch notes '[t]hat creditor enjoys the windfall benefit of diminishing risks of default and the existing interest proves increasingly advantageous to it. New assets do not enter the pool for the potential benefit of unsecured creditors but create such windfalls'.[164] The floating charge effectively allows for a charge to be placed on future property without bargaining for that specific security, which seems fundamentally inequitable when it comes to the fairness with regards to unsecured and involuntary creditors. This can have a particularly acute impact on employees given that their future claims are not accounted for in the insolvency waterfall.

---

161 J Hudson, 'The Case Against Secured Lending' (1995) 15 Int Rev of Law and Econ 47 at 55 and R Goode, 'Is the Law too Favourable to Secured Creditors?' (1983–1984) 8 Can Bus Rev 53 as cited in V Finch, 'Security, Insolvency and Risk: Who Pays the Price?' (1999) 62(5) MLR 633 at 660.
162 B Carruthers and T Halliday, *Rescuing Businesses: The Making of Corporate Bankruptcy Law in England and the United States* (Oxford: Oxford University Press, 1998) 171 and L LoPucki, 'The Unsecured Creditors' Bargain' (1994) 80 Va L Rev 1887 at 1896–1898 as cited in Finch (n 161) at 660–661.
163 Finch (n 161) at 661.
164 Finch (n 161) at 662.

Finally, the third argument rests on adequate information for creditors to make adjustments to their loan rates. Although floating charges and other rights in security must be registered, and this is considered as a form of notice, the reality is much different. The register itself is static and will not account for the fluctuations of value within the property of the company over which a charge floats. Furthermore, if a floating charge includes bank overdrafts, these can fluctuate on a daily basis, so no information available on a register will give a full picture of a company's finances at any given point in time. In addition, this information is valueless to involuntary or non-adjusting creditors in any event as they do not have the freedom to mitigate their risks by adjusting their loan rates.[165]

The creation of security in general will divert value from creditors that cannot adjust the size of their claims to take into account the effect of the security held by floating charge and fixed security holders. Any security given will effectively subordinate their unsecured claims without any need to inform them or allow them to mitigate the risks that such actions by a debtor may entail.[166] Essentially, the private contract of the floating charge instrument will have an effect on third parties to their detriment, which under contract law would not normally be acceptable.[167] Such third parties will suffer from information asymmetries, particularly if they are involuntary creditors, and will generally be unable to adjust their terms to account for the increased risk presented by the granting of additional security.[168] There are also creditors whose claims may simply be too small to justify the cost of making additional searches to determine the leveraging of the debtor prior to contracting and will be 'rationally uninformed' about the borrower's financial structure.[169] They will thus be disadvantaged by the information asymmetries between themselves and those creditors who are more closely involved with the debtor's financial decision-making, such as fixed security and floating charge holders.

Security interests giving full priority essentially make the lender better off by effectively transferring insolvency value from creditors that cannot adjust the size of their claims.[170] As noted by Vanessa Finch, the floating charge in particular is a 'mechanism that is particularly conducive to the transfer

---

165 Finch (n 161) at 662.
166 Bebchuk and Fried (n 84) at 964.
167 Hardman, 'Law and Economics of the Floating Charge', Chapter 5.
168 Hardman, 'Law and Economics of the Floating Charge', Chapter 5.
169 Bebchuk and Fried (n 84) at 864.
170 Bebchuk and Fried (n 84) at 882.

of insolvency value from unsecured to secured creditors'.[171] It allows large lenders to exploit their dominant bargaining position and effectively to arrange for a transfer of value to what would have been distributed to unsecured creditors out of the working capital of a debtor, which is instead tied up by the floating charge.[172] This will clearly harm employees who are owed for their labour and for pension contributions that are contractually guaranteed and fundamentally should also not be adjustable on the basis that employees should not be treated as a commodity that can be valued simply as a factor of production.

If one considers the information asymmetries naturally present between the banks, which generally hold the majority of security, including the floating charges, and the relatively weak position of employees and other involuntary and non-adjusting creditors, there is clearly a power bias toward the entity wielding the security and/or the highest level of debt. Such secured creditors will wield considerably more control over the governance of an insolvency process.[173] Banks are significantly better informed about the financial state of a company to which it is lending due to the due diligence and auditing requirements that are often applied prior to lending a sum of money. They also have access to expertise on corporate funding, which further assists in assessing the risks of lending.[174] In addition, floating charge holders continue to exercise a great deal of power over procedure and appointment, despite the general abolition of administrative receiverships under the Enterprise Act 2002,[175] creating a moral hazard risk of making opportunistic appointments suiting their self-interests while potentially further unbalancing the playing field for less powerful stakeholders in an insolvency. They are aware of the risks to a high level of detail, whereas regular employees will be dependent upon the company fully for livelihood and pension contributions along with the support this provides for families and communities. They will not be privy to the same level of information and even if they were, they are caught in the ubiquitous need for a job without any true instrument or tool to mitigate the risks of continuing to work for their current financially distressed employer. The choice is simply not there.

171 Finch (n 161) at 658.
172 Finch (n 161) at 658.
173 E J Janger, 'The Logic and Limits of Liens' (2017) Brooklyn Law School Legal Studies Research Papers Accepted Paper Series (No. 539) 589, 592.
174 Finch (n 118) at 541.
175 Finch (n 118) at 540.

Floating charges and other forms of security can have a clear and some-times extreme effect on third parties who are unable to mitigate their risk. A shift in approach to regulation in this area could reorient corporate decision-making, whether that is preserving assets, asset value, and entering into financing transactions, including the creation of floating charges, that may subordinate the rights of other stakeholders. Reorienting corporate decision-making towards vulnerabilities would mean reconsidering the cor-porate governance relationship from the top down. Whereas directors are generally tasked with maximising and growing the value of the corporation's assets, if that role shifts to that of a 'trustee', the responsibility shifts from dollar (or pound) signs to sustaining the corporate assets for the benefit of all those who depend upon it. A trustee in this context replaces the tradi-tional director concept, whose duty is narrower and focused on maximising shareholder value; whereas a director with a trustee type of role would be in charge of a corporation as a social institution rather than an entity created solely through private contracts.[176] Directors then shift from being agents of the shareholders to being trustees of the corporate entity that would include the duty to protect all of the corporation's tangible and intangible assets for the benefit of all stakeholders who depend on the corporation in one way or another.[177]

A shift towards trusteeship rather than an agent/principal type of model that typifies most corporations in England and Scotland would also mean a shift in the way corporate assets are valued as such valuations would have to include characteristics that are far more difficult to monetise. Assets sepa-rated from straightforward value maximisation will also include firm specific human capital, the expectations of customers and suppliers and the com-pany's influence on and importance to the community within which it exists. Thus, a trustee's duties are not just to the financial interests of its sharehold-ers, but also to the broader purposes of the corporation as a social construct built upon a number of social institutions beyond the financing of banks.[178] This shift requires a consideration of 'social capital', described as 'the set of resources, tangible or virtual, that accrue to an organisation through social

176 T Clarke, 'Accounting for Enron: Shareholder Value and Stakeholder Interests' (2005) 13(5) *Corporate Governance: An International Review* 598 at 606.
177 J Kay, 'The Stakeholder Corporation' in G Kelly et al. (eds), *Stakeholder Capitalism* (London: Palgrave Macmillan, 1997) 125 at 135 as cited in Clarke (n 176) at 606–607.
178 Kay (n 177) at 135 as cited in Clarke (n 176) at 607.

stricture, facilitating the attainment of goals',[179] all of which are difficult to value in money, but without which no corporation could survive. These are deeper and more complex social relationships based in the reality of how business works within the world, rather than a strict adherence to law and economics limitations that see only contractual relationships and monetary value.[180]

These expanded interests can be justified in insolvency considerations if one looks to the needs of the community as a social construct upon which corporations rest.[181] Without the community within which a corporation exists, a corporation will not exist. It is not merely an entity built on legal contracts and relationships – there are far more considerations, which were first clearly recognised in modern times by leaders of the early labour and social movements of the industrial revolution such as Marx, Owen, and even the Pope. Although 'vulnerability theory' may not have been the defining factor of their philosophy, Fineman's theory provides a new paradigm that highlights the fundamental unfairness of security rights that neglect social concerns, some of which are absolutely fundamental to the survival of a corporation beyond the value of their contractual contribution. The human factor must be taken into account if a more equitable global community is to be created in the future. This includes a more nuanced approach to enforcing securities such as floating charges and the relative priorities ascribed to them during an insolvency.

---

179 R Leenders and S Gabbay, *Corporate Social Capital and Liability* (Boston, Springer, 1999) 3 as cited in Clarke (n 176) at 607.
180 Clarke (n 176) 607.
181 See K Gross, 'Taking Community Interests into Account in Bankruptcy: An Essay' (1994) 72 Wash U L Q 1031.

7 Hohfeld and the Scots Law Floating Charge

Jonathan Hardman[*]

A. INTRODUCTION
B. HOHFELDIAN ERRORS
    (1) Transposition errors
    (2) Case law
        (a) Pre-history
        (b) Cases following the statutory introduction
    (3) Legislation
    (4) Relevance
C. HOHFELDIAN PROGNOSIS
    (1) Dyads: jural correlatives and jural opposites
    (2) Application
        (a) Security interests
        (b) Floating charges
    (3) Critique
D. CONCLUSION

A. INTRODUCTION

What is a Scots law floating charge? In different chapters we can see various places where the floating charge does not act like a security interest in its traditional sense. From insolvency law,[1] cross-border

---

[*] In addition to my co-editor, I would like to thank Prof Ben McFarlane of the University of Oxford, Prof Lionel Smith of McGill University, Prof Antonios Karampatzos of National and Kapodistrian University of Athens, and all other participants at the Third Edinburgh/Oxford Private Law Workshop held at Worcester College, Oxford on 28 February 2020 for their helpful and insightful comments on navigating the complexities of Hohfeld. All errors, mistakes and misunderstandings remain the sole responsibility of the author.

1 D W McKenzie Skene, 'The Floating Charge and Insolvency Law', Chapter 10 within this volume.

analysis,[2] potential for reform,[3] and historical analysis[4] we can see what Professor Gretton has been holding true for a number of years[5]: that the Scottish floating charge does not neatly fit within Scots law of security interests. This is important in and of itself, but it also begs a further question: what, exactly, is a modern Scottish floating charge?

To answer that question, the author will borrow the analysis of a thinker from the early twentieth century, Wesley Newcomb Hohfeld. Hohfeld unfortunately died at the age of thirty-nine, having published only seven articles over the course of eight years, yet became a professor at both Stanford and Yale in that time.[6] Of those seven articles, two in particular have had a lasting impact.[7] Hohfeld's main contribution was to bring a (much needed) clarity to legal analysis. The problem, as he saw it, was repeated judicial and scholarly laxness of language that led to a confusion and conflation of legal concepts. This could be solved by way of atomisation[8] – separating out legal relationships, distilling any legal relationship into its core elements and then reconstructing from those core elements to provide a clarity that the analyses of most courts were lacking.

This chapter will use Hohfeld's techniques to attempt to find clarity for analysis of the floating charge.[9] First, it shall review problems that Hohfeld identified in early twentieth century American jurisprudence, and establish whether such errors can be seen in the case law of the Scots law floating charge and the relevant legislation. Secondly, it shall review Hohfeld's atomisation approach and apply this analysis to the Scottish floating charge. The aim is to see whether such a Hohfeldian analysis can provide us with any particular insight into the operation of the floating charge in Scotland.

---

2 From the perspective of English law, see M Raczynska, 'The Species and Structure(s) of the Floating Charge: The English Law Perspective on the Scottish Floating Charge', Chapter 8 within this volume.

3 A Steven, 'Reform of the Scottish Floating Charge', Chapter 12 within this volume.

4 A D J MacPherson, 'The "Pre-History" of Floating Charges in Scotland', Chapter 1 within this volume.

5 For example, G L Gretton, 'What went wrong with the floating charge?' 1984 SLT (News) 172 and G L Gretton, 'Should floating charges and receivership be abolished?' 1986 SLT (News) 325. This line of analysis has received a modern development in A D J MacPherson, *The Floating Charge* (Edinburgh: Edinburgh Legal Education Trust, 2020) Ch. 6.

6 See the obituary 'Wesley Newcomb Hohfeld' (1918) 28 Yale LJ 166 for a biographical overview.

7 For example, D Kennedy, *Sexy Dressing etc. Essays in the Power and Politics of Cultural Identity* (Harvard: Harvard University Press, 1993) 89.

8 P Schlag, 'How to do things with Hohfeld' (2015) 78 *Law and Contemporary Problems* 185.

9 There has been very little theoretical analysis of the Scots law floating charge. In addition, there has been no application of Hohfeldian concepts to the Scots law floating charge, except a brief reference in MacPherson, *Floating Charge* (n 5) at para. 2–21.

It seems that the outcome of this deconstruction and reconstruction is clear: the floating charge is not a security interest. It shares none of the characteristics of a security interest but instead has a parallel set of characteristics, which mostly become relevant on the insolvency of the granter. We therefore need to stop considering the floating charge as being a security interest in Scotland and, instead, find a new area of analysis in which to fit the floating charge. However, on closer reflection, this may be an over-simplification: just because the floating charge is different from other security interests does not entirely detach the concept of a security interest from the floating charge.

B. HOHFELDIAN ERRORS

(1) Transposition errors

Hohfeld's analysis has been characterised as dry. Schlag states of it: 'A thrilling read it is not – more like chewing on sawdust. The arguments are dense, the examples unwieldy and the prose turgid'.[10] Nevertheless, at the time his analysis was quite incendiary.[11] At the start of his ground-breaking article, 'Some fundamental legal conceptions as applied in judicial reasoning',[12] he lists nine commentators in the field of trusts, ranging from Lord Coke to then-modern writers, and states 'it is believed that all of the discussions and analyses referred to are inadequate'.[13] The reasons for such inadequacy is the same reason for inadequacy across all areas of law: 'the tendency – and the fallacy – has been to treat the specific problem as if it were far less complex than it really is'.[14]

Quite precocious stuff. He explains further that the word 'property' is inevitably used to refer to several different concepts. It is used to refer both to the physical land that is the object of rights and obligations (my property is located in Leith) and the legal rights and obligations relating to such property (that flat in Leith is my property).[15] Hohfeld states that in judgments

---

10 Schlag (n 8) at 186.
11 A L Corbin, 'Jural Relations and Their Classification' (1920) 30 Yale LJ 226.
12 W N Hohfeld, 'Some Fundamental Legal Conceptions as Applied in Judicial Reasoning' (1913) 23 Yale LJ 16.
13 Hohfeld (n 12) at 18.
14 Hohfeld (n 12) at 19.
15 See discussion in K G C Reid, *The Law of Property in Scotland* (London: Butterworths Law, 1996) paras 3 and 11.

'frequently there is a rapid and fallacious shift from the one meaning to the other'.[16] The same issue arises in the field of contracts:

> 'Passing to the field of contracts, we soon discover a similar inveterate tendency to confuse and blur legal discussions by failing to discriminate between the mental and physical facts involved in the so-called "agreement" of the parties, and the legal "contractual obligation" to which those facts give rise. Such ambiguity and confusion are peculiarly incident to the use of the word "contract." One moment the word may mean the agreement of the parties; and then, with a rapid and unexpected shift, the writer or speaker may use the term to indicate the contractual obligation created by law as a result of the agrement.' [Sic][17]

The word 'contract' therefore can mean several things. It can mean the physical document giving rise to contractual relationship (they signed the contract), it can mean the act of entering into a contractual relationship (you and I contracted for this) or it can mean the contractual relationship that arises as a result (you are bound by contract to do X).[18] Schlag states:

> 'the fact that we use the term "contract" to refer to all of these things (and then some) would not be a problem if we could be sure which was which when. But, as Hohfeld notes, there is an inveterate tendency among jurists and scholars to confuse the legal relations with the mental and physical facts that bring them into being.'[19]

For Schlag, this conflation produces three linked problems. First, discussion of the term (e.g. 'contract') becomes ambiguous – in any given situation it becomes difficult to establish whether we are discussing the physical evidence, the act of creating the legal relations arising from the physical evidence or the rights arising thereunder. This leads into the second problem of slippage – where discussion slips between the three elements over the course of analysis:

> 'Thus, in one sentence, the court is discussing the agreement between the parties ("the contract"), and in the next, unbeknownst to itself and perhaps to the reader, the court has switched to a discussion of the legal relations established (also "the contract").'[20]

When slippage occurs over time, the result is blending – legal analysis of the various elements becomes blended into one. These problems create confusion (does (and should) a particular judgment have an impact on all

---

16 Hohfeld (n 12) at 21–22.
17 Hohfeld (n 12) at 24–25.
18 A L Corbin, 'The Law of Contracts. By Samuel Williston' (1919) 29 Yale LJ 942 at 943.
19 Schlag (n 8) at 192.
20 Schlag (n 8) at 193.

of the three elements or only one), and makes legal analysis seem complete and coherent when it is, in fact, not. It is one thing for a court to consider that the same rules should apply to each element, but another for this to happen without reflection.[21] Whilst the former is the result of reasoned legal analysis, the second happens accidentally and confuses the legal position.

We shall therefore review whether clarity arises under Scots law in respect of the floating charge. This shall be split into the case law in respect of the floating charge (both prior to the introduction of the floating charge and after it) and the current legalisation that governs the floating charge under Scots law.

(2) Case law

(a) Pre-history

Prior to the statutory introduction of the floating charge, Scots law struggled to comprehend what one was. The words 'floating charge' were not mentioned in the judgment that is often seen[22] as being the first rejection of a floating charge by the Scottish courts.[23] *Ballachulish Slate Quarries*[24] was the first case to discuss the 'floating charge' per se, in which the Lord President stated:

'We have nothing to do with the law of England, but at the same time it is common knowledge that it is possible to create a floating charge over moveable estate in England; and if there is a proper authorisation to that effect under the articles and memorandum of association, you can make a floating charge include uncalled capital. But the whole method of creating a floating charge, which I do not propose to detail, is absolutely foreign to our law, and consequently the form which was here used was perfectly inappropriate to create a valid security over uncalled capital according to the forms of the law of Scotland.'[25]

Similarly Lord M'Laren stated:

'I think it is evident on the face of the documents that what was desired was to constitute what is known in the law of England as a 'floating charge' over the whole property of the Company, for the clauses purport to give a general security

21 Schlag (n 8) at 196 and Corbin (n 18) at 944.
22 See discussion in A J P Menzies, 'Is the Creation of a Floating Charge Competent to a Limited Company Registered in Scotland?' (1909) 21 Jur Rev 87 at 87–88.
23 *Clark v West Calder Oil Co* (1882) 9 R 1017.
24 *Ballachulish Slate Quarries v Bruce* (1908) 16 SLT 48.
25 *Ballachulish Slate Quarries v Bruce* 48 at 52.

over the undertaking. It is well known that such a floating security has no effect in the law of Scotland.'[26]

Thus neither the Lord President nor Lord M'Laren actually reviewed the fundamental features of the putative floating charge, the methods of creating it or its effects. Both their arguments proceeded along the basis of: we know English law has this concept. We will not discuss what this concept is, but it is 'absolutely foreign to our law' and 'well known that such a floating security has no effect in the law of Scotland'. It is certainly the case that a floating charge would not constitute a security interest under Scots law. But as neither of their Lordships explained why the English law concept of a floating charge was unacceptable to Scots law it is difficult to garner a concept of what the floating charge is under Scots law. It is therefore easy to establish how a commentator was querying whether an argument could be constructed for the competence of some form of floating charge in Scotland, even after *Ballachulish Slate Quarries*.[27] The same issue arose in *Carse v Coppen*[28] with the oft-quoted phrase 'it is clear in principle and amply supported by authority that a floating charge is utterly repugnant to the principles of Scots law and is not recognised by us as creating a security at all'.[29] The authority the Lord President cited to 'amply support' this? *Ballachulish Slate Quarries*. There are therefore three increasingly strident opinions, which use increasingly firm language, which neither analyse the precise reasons why no element of the floating charge may be upheld, nor provide (despite claiming to) extensive authority from other cases. Lord Keith does provide some authority by reference to analogy with diligence cases,[30] but the Lord President relies primarily on *Ballachulish Slate Quarries*, which merely asserted that the floating charge just did not work under Scots law. The Lord President does provide some analysis of the subject matter by stating:

'Putting aside the rare and exceptional cases of hypothec, we require for the constitution of a security which will confer upon the holder rights over and above those which he enjoys in common with the general body of unsecured creditors of a debtor, (a) the transfer to the creditor of a real right in specific subjects by the method appropriate for the constitution of such rights in the particular classes of property in question, or (b) the creation of a nexus over specific property by

---

26 *Ballachulish Slate Quarries* (n 24) at 52.
27 Menzies (n 22).
28 *Carse v Coppen* 1951 SC 233.
29 *Carse v Coppen* at 239.
30 *Carse v Coppen* at 247.

the due use of the appropriate form of diligence. A floating charge, even after appointment of a receiver, satisfies none of these requirements.'[31]

This conclusion arises, however, without an active discussion of what a floating charge (at the time) was considered to be. Accordingly, prior to the statutory introduction of the floating charge under Scots law, it did not have a clear conception of what a floating charge was. The lack of such a conception means that there were no blending or transposition errors – rather a more fundamental lack of clarity.

(b) Cases following the statutory introduction

Having seen that prior to the statutory introduction of the floating charge Scottish courts were unclear as to its application, it is necessary to review how Scottish courts have treated the floating charge since its statutory introduction. Our first stage, then, is to analyse whether we see any transposition errors appearing in respect of the modern floating charge: is any of the discussion confused? Here, the main potential areas for such ambiguity/slippage/ blending arise between the document constituting the floating charge and the floating charge itself. This is because the act of granting the floating charge contains sufficiently different language to avoid such risk: whilst referring to 'the floating charge' can mean the document constituting it or the legal relations arising as the result of it, it cannot, in ordinary English, mean the creation of the floating charge itself.[32] Accordingly, we only need to examine for slippage between the document creating it and the legal relationships arising from entering into such document. Incidentally, most terms that can be used to mean 'the physical evidence' contain an embedded ambiguity. 'Document' can be used to refer to the noun (this document is signed) and the verb (we should document that),[33] and the word deed implies even more of an action. We shall, to be clear, in the rest of this chapter contradistinct 'floating charge' with the 'floating charge instrument' or merely the

---

31 *Carse v Coppen* at 239.
32 There is no concept of 'floating' a real right in security, never mind a 'charge', under Scots law.
33 Although in such cases (as with contract), the emphasis is placed on different syllables when referring to the noun and the verb – contrast DOCument (the piece of paper) with docuMENT (the act of writing it), and CONtract (the piece of paper) with conTRACT (the act of forming contractual relations). However, this applies only to the spoken word and not the written word. It has been judicially recognised that there is occasional conflation under Scots law between a written document creating rights and the rights thereby created – see *The Advice Centre for Mortgages v McNicoll* 2006 SLT 591 at [19].

'instrument' as applicable. Is there any evidence of such slippage or blending occurring in judicial discussion of the floating charge?

Unfortunately, the answer is yes. We can split the judicial errors of the floating charge into two categories: first, where courts deployed different terms to refer to the instrument and the security interest, and there was slippage between the two; and secondly where the same term was used to refer to the instrument and the floating charge. The first category represents slippage between the two concepts and the second category is evidence of the two concepts blending into one.

The first category consists of cases that identified a separation between the 'floating charge' and the 'floating charge instrument', but failed to maintain an adequate separation between the two concepts. Thus in *Tay Valley*[34] the court drew a distinction between the 'floating charge' and the 'floating charge debenture'.[35] The use of the word 'debenture' is flawed,[36] but nonetheless provided the framework for a clear differentiation – the former applied to the legal relationship and the latter to the instrument creating the legal relationship. Even so, their Lordships frequently slipped between the two. Lord Robertson started with ambiguity – he referred to the floating charge debenture (i.e. the instrument) being 'granted' by the company.[37] The author would have preferred a formulation that clarified that the floating charge debenture was executed that constituted the grant of a floating charge, but this is perhaps semantic – it is arguable that the instrument itself could be construed to be 'granted' and so Lord Robertson was correct. However, Lord Dunpark referred to the bank as the 'holders of a floating charge debenture'[38] and also as the 'holder of the floating charge'.[39] The latter formulation must be correct – the important factor was that the 'secured creditor' side of the legal relationship sat with the bank, not that they physically held the instrument. Lord Macdonald made the same initial

---

34 *Tay Valley Joinery Ltd v C F Financial Services Ltd* 1987 SLT 207 – the case known for establishing the interaction between trusts and the floating charge in Scotland – see A D J MacPherson, 'Floating Charges and Trust Property in Scots Law: A Tale of Two Patrimonies?' (2018) 22 Edin L Rev 1.

35 *Tay Valley* (n 34) at 210.

36 As it is a term of art under English law without Scots law equivalents – see the discussion in *Fons Hf v Corporal Ltd* [2014] EWCA Civ 304 at [37]–[40]. Whilst a definition of 'debenture' is provided in the Companies Act 2006 s. 738 ('"debenture" includes debenture stock, bonds and any other securities of a company, whether or not constituting a charge on the assets of the company'), this is a non-exhaustive definition that does not identify exactly what a debenture is.

37 *Tay Valley* (n 34) at 210.

38 *Tay Valley* (n 34) at 213.

39 *Tay Valley* (n 34) at 217.

mistake as Lord Dunpark.[40] Similar slippage is seen in other cases. In *AIB Finance Ltd v Bank of Scotland*,[41] the concept of the 'instrument creating the floating charge' is used in several places.[42] Even so, this does not stop the following passages in the judgment that evidence slippage:

1. 'the provisions which the floating charge contains'[43];
2. 'the execution of the floating charge'[44];
3. 'the construction to be placed on the restrictive clause in the floating charge'[45]; and
4. 'provisions contained in the floating charge'[46],

all of which should have referred to the instrument rather than the security interest.

In *Forth & Clyde*[47] Lord Johnson differentiated between a 'floating charge' and a 'bond and floating charge'.[48] The latter phrase is still commonly used to describe an instrument creating a floating charge, and arose because prescription periods for personal bonds used to be forty years compared to six for other personal obligations.[49] Since 1973, this distinction has been redundant.[50] Lord Cowie's opinion states that 'the said bond and floating charge was granted over the whole of the property of the petitioners'.[51] Whilst, as noted above, it may be possible to construe the word 'grant' to apply to the execution of an instrument rather than the creating of the legal relationship arising therefrom, it is slippage to refer to the instrument being

---

40 *Tay Valley* (n 34) at 217.
41 *AIB Finance Ltd v Bank of Scotland* 1993 SC 588. This is the case known for establishing the implications on timing of creation of a floating charge *vis-à-vis* a standard security – see J Hardman, *A Practical Guide to Granting Corporate Security in Scotland* (Edinburgh: W. Green, 2018) para. 9–11.
42 For example, *AIB* (n 41) at 597, 601, 602.
43 *AIB* (n 41) at 601.
44 *AIB* (n 41) at 590.
45 *AIB* (n 41) at 592.
46 *AIB* (n 41) at 594.
47 *Forth & Clyde Construction Co Ltd v Trinity Timber & Plywood Co Ltd* 1984 SC 1, known as the case which held that the rules of catholic and secondary creditors do not apply to receivers: see Hardman (n 41) para. 6–31.
48 *Forth & Clyde* (n 47) at 4.
49 W D Esslemont, *A Popular Handbook of Commercial Law in Scotland*, 2nd edn (Edinburgh: Hodge & Co, 1921) 162–165.
50 Prescription and Limitation (Scotland) Act 1973 s. 6 – and yet it continues to pervade modern instruments constituting floating charges. The statutory regime for floating charges does refer to an 'instrument', which is then defined as the relevant bond or other written instrument – Companies Act 1985 s. 462(4). The reference to bond in this formulation is interesting, but the breadth of the 'or other written instrument' means that the reference to a bond is not necessary.
51 *Forth & Clyde* (n 47) at 4.

granted over certain assets. Lord Cowie evidences this by also using in the same paragraph of his judgment the (correct) phrase 'the sum secured by the floating charge was'[52] and the (incorrect) phrase 'the amount of money secured by the bond and floating charge is'.[53] Whilst the security interest can be said to secure a certain sum, and the instrument can be said to create (or purport to create) a floating charge that secures a certain sum, the only way in which the instrument itself can be used to secure it is if it is used as a paperweight.[54] By the time that Lord Cowie refers to the 'property attached by the bond and floating charge',[55] the unreflective slippage is complete and so it becomes difficult to establish which elements of Lord Cowie's *dicta* is intended to apply to the instrument and which is intended to apply to the legal concept arising therefrom.

The judgment in *Libertas-Kommerz GmbH v Johnson*[56] also applied the term 'bond and floating charge' to the instrument and 'floating charge' to the legal relationship arising therefrom.[57] There is evidence in that case of these concepts being used correctly – for example: 'in my judgment the bond and floating charge is the document governing the contractual relations of the parties, i.e. between the company and the persons advancing money to it in security of the floating charge'.[58]

This is a particularly clear use as it shows the difference between the instrument and the security interest. However, slippage appears in the judgment with the phrase 'ground for rejecting the bond and floating charge as a security'.[59] Whilst the floating charge itself can be classified 'as a security',[60] the instrument constituting it cannot be. Therefore, even within judgments that otherwise differentiate the concepts, we see evidence of slippage.

The second category provides evidence of 'blending'. In the House of Lords decision of *Sharp v Thomson*,[61] only the term 'floating charge'

---

52 *Forth & Clyde* (n 47) at 5.
53 *Forth & Clyde* (n 47) at 4.
54 This, of course, does not itself stand up to Hohfeldian scrutiny as it conflates the physical embodiment of the money (either coin or promissory bank notes) with the legal conception of money.
55 *Forth & Clyde* (n 47) at 5.
56 *Libertas-Kommerz GmbH v Johnson* 1977 SC 191, known as the case that provides clarity on the transferability of the floating charge – see W Lucas, 'Assignation of Floating Charges', 1996 SLT (News) 203 for criticism of the law as it stands.
57 *Libertas-Kommerz* (n 56) at 200.
58 *Libertas-Kommerz* (n 56) at 210.
59 *Libertas-Kommerz* (n 56) at 209.
60 The phrase 'security' is problematic in and of itself as it can refer to multitude of items, including a right in security or a security or a share in a company depending on the precise context.
61 *Sharp v Thomson* 1997 SC (HL) 66. This is a seminal case on the interaction of the floating charge and conveyancing principles under Scots law – for evidence of its remaining import see

was used. Whilst Lord Clyde's judgment made a few references to 'the instrument',[62] these were related to general statements of law rather than being linked to the specific legal relations that were at issue in the judgment of the case. It is, of course, possible to only refer to the security interest and not the instrument constituting the security interest, but only if no mention of the instrument is included. In the majority of the judgment this line is adhered to – Lord Jauncey of Tullichettle discussed whether the floating charge had attached[63] and discussed rights available to holders of floating charges,[64] as did Lord Clyde.[65] However, the difficulty of relying on one concept became apparent when Lord Clyde stated: 'that is a question of the construction of the terms of the floating charge',[66] and '[i]n my view there are sound reasons for preferring a construction of the floating charge which looks to the ordinary use of language'.[67] It is possible to construct an argument in which it is correct to refer to 'construction' of the security interest rather than the words in the instrument creating it, but it would seem to the author that such language would ordinarily refer to construing the instrument instead. By the time that Lord Clyde states 'the particular construction of the phrase 'property and undertaking' in the floating charge',[68] it is clear that there is blending of the two concepts. Rather than the security interest, Lord Clyde clearly is referring to the instrument creating the security interest. The blending is understandable given that the key terms of the security interest are contained in the instrument (including the property the security interest purports to be over, and circumstances in which the holder of the security interest can appoint an insolvency practitioner to the secured assets). Nonetheless, different legal concepts apply to the security interest and to the instrument. In the First Division judgment of *Gordon Anderson*,[69] the Lord President and Lords Avonside and Thomson each also attempted to only refer to the security interest rather than the instrument. Whilst Lord

---

K G C Reid 'Smoothing the Rugged Parts of the Passage: Scots Law and its Edinburgh Chair' (2014) 18 Edin L Rev 315 at 338. See also Scottish Law Commission, *Report on Sharp v Thomson* (Scot. Law Com. No. 208, 2007) Appendix B of a list of literature generated by this case, and MacPherson, *Floating Charge* (n 5) Ch. 7 for details of ongoing issues in respect of the case.

62 *Sharp* (n 61) at 78–79.
63 *Sharp* (n 61) at 68 and 75.
64 *Sharp* (n 61) at 70.
65 *Sharp* (n 61) at 78.
66 *Sharp* (n 61) at 79.
67 *Sharp* (n 61) at 82.
68 *Sharp* (n 61) at 83.
69 *Gordon Anderson (Plant) Ltd v Campsie Construction Ltd and Anglo Scottish Plant Ltd* 1977 SLT 7.

Thomson's judgment shows no evidence of blending or slippage, the other two judgments do. The Lord President stated, '[i]n terms of cl. 9 thereof any receiver appointed as provided for in the floating charge was empowered to "collect and get in all or any of the assets" of the second-named defenders'.[70]

This clearly refers to the instrument rather than the legal relationship created thereunder. Similarly, Lord Avonside's judgment includes the words '[i]t is stated on record that by virtue of cl. 9 of the floating charge any receiver appointed had power …'.[71] This only makes sense if referring to the instrument, not the legal relationship arising therefrom. In *Scottish & Newcastle plc v Ascot Inns Ltd*,[72] Lord Milligan also attempted to only refer to the relevant legal relationship created by the instrument rather than the instrument itself. And yet he referred to the floating charge being 'dated 29 March 1990'.[73] Whilst it is normal to refer to a security interest being created on a certain date, it cannot be the case that such security interest is in any way 'dated' such date. His next sentence begins '[t]he floating charge bears to be granted over the whole property'.[74] Once more this is truncation – the instrument constituting the floating charge provides that such charge is over all assets of the granter. By undertaking such truncation, Lord Milligan fell into the traps that Hohfeld warned about.

As Hohfeld identified over 100 years ago: if courts cannot be clear about whether their legal analysis applies to the document or the legal relationship arising therefrom, how can anyone else?

(3) Legislation

It is, perhaps, inevitable that the courts are unclear in their analysis of the floating charge, as the underlying legislation that currently governs the floating charge is inherently confused.[75] The current section reads:

'It is competent under the law of Scotland for an incorporated company (whether a company within the meaning of this Act or not), for the purpose of securing any debt or other obligation (including a cautionary obligation) incurred or to be incurred by, or binding upon, the company or any other person, to create in favour of the creditor in the debt or obligation a charge, in this Part referred to as

---

70 *Gordon Anderson (Plant) Ltd* (n 69) at 11.
71 *Gordon Anderson (Plant) Ltd* (n 69) at 14.
72 1994 SLT 1140.
73 *Scottish & Newcastle plc v Ascot Inns Ltd* (n 72) at 1142.
74 *Scottish & Newcastle plc v Ascot Inns Ltd* (n 72) at 1142.
75 Obviously, a large number of cases cited pre-date the current formulation of the floating charge in Scotland.

a floating charge, over all or any part of the property (including uncalled capital) which may from time to time be comprised in its property and undertaking.'[76]

The author has previously tried to identify several defining features of the floating charge:

(1) The granter only has to be an incorporated company to grant a floating charge that is recognised under Scots law. Accordingly, non-Scots companies can also grant floating charges that Scots law will consider valid.

(2) The obligation secured can be monetary or non-monetary. Therefore, a floating charge can secure ad factum praestandum obligations.

(3) The obligation secured can be either incurred by the granter, or by a third party. If the latter, it can either secure a guarantee or be a third party charge.

(4) There are no timing constraints on the obligation secured: it can be a future, past or present obligation.

(5) The charge can be over all or any of the assets of the granter.

(6) The charge can cover future assets.[77]

These are all clearly features that a floating charge can have. However, they are not defining, that is to say exclusive, features of the floating charge. Points 1–4 could also be said to apply to standard securities.[78] Point 5 is question of fact from time to time: if a granter only owns a property in Scotland then, as a matter of fact, a standard security over such property could be said to also cover all the assets of the granter. This only leaves point 6, which has been proposed to be the case for registered assignations and statutory pledges under the Scottish Law Commission's proposals.[79] Whilst these characteristics therefore do apply to the floating charge, they are

---

76 Companies Act 1985, s. 462(1).

77 Hardman (n 41) para. 6–05.

78 There are no limits on the identity of who can enter into a standard security in the Conveyancing and Feudal Reform (Scotland) Act 1970 s. 9(2), *ad factum praestandum* obligations can be secured by standard securities under Conveyancing and Feudal Reform (Scotland) Act 1970 s. 2(8)(c), a standard security can be created over debts due by third parties (see discussion in *3D Garages Ltd v Prolatis Co Ltd* 2017 SLT (Sh Ct) 9), and standard securities can secure any debt including any which will or may become due according to s. 2(8)(c). This is the subject of proposed reform – see Scottish Law Commission, *Discussion Paper on Heritable Securities* (Scot. Law Com. DP No. 168, 2019).

79 See discussion in J Hardman, 'Three Steps Forward, Two Steps Back: A View from Corporate Security Practice of the Moveable Transactions (Scotland) Bill' (2018) 22 Edin L Rev 266. Then, however, a creditor would receive an interest in particular property upon the acquisition by the debtor of the property and so the debtor would not be able to generally deal with the property, differentiating these proposals from the commonly considered implications of a floating charge.

hardly an exclusive definition of a floating charge as they can also apply to other security interests. Most of these features are merely permissive, stating that a floating charge 'can' be this or that. Indeed, once we remove all such enabling features from the current definition of the floating charge, the definition reverts to a floating charge being a 'charge ... over all or any part of the property'. This leads to two interesting observations.

First, the word 'charge'. This is now defined (for the purposes of registration of securities only) in the Companies Act 2006, which provides that a charge includes a mortgage, a standard security, assignation in security and 'any other right in security constituted under the law of Scotland, including any heritable security, but not including a pledge'.[80] This means that we do not have an exhaustive list of the types of legal relationships that constitute 'charges', they simply include fixed securities under Scots law and anything else Scots law recognises. The definition of 'charge' therefore provides no further clarity on the fundamental nature of the floating charge itself, this term would apply equally to a standard security as a pledge or an assignation in security. The placement of the use of the defined term 'floating charge' in the statutory definition is not helpful as it is the defined term rather than any inherent part of the definition. This means that the use of 'floating charge' acts as a defined term to describe what falls before it, and all that we have prior to it is the rather bare 'charge'. If the word 'charge' were replaced with 'standard security', then any standard security granted by a corporate vehicle would fall to be defined as a 'floating charge' under Scots law given the rest of the paragraph. Under the current formulation, if a standard security fell within the other non-permissive elements of the definition then it could be argued that it qualified as a 'floating charge' for s. 462 purposes.

Secondly, such charge can be over 'all or any part of the property'. This provides no defining features either. If this element provided that a floating charge only qualifies as such if it is over all the assets of the granter then this would at least provide some definitional perimeter – a standard security would NOT fall within the definition of 'floating charge' unless it was over the entire property of the granter. Similarly, we would have clarity if such a charge was to be expressed in the relevant instrument as being over all of the property (or any formulation of words that included part). However, this is not the case, meaning that this element of the definition also provides no meaning.

80 Companies Act 2006 s. 859A(7).

In other words, the only core part of the definition of a 'floating charge' under modern Scots law is that it is a 'charge' – a word that provides no clarity under the existing framework. There are two possible extensions to this argument. First, it could be argued any security interest that is granted by a company qualifies as a floating charge for the purposes of s. 462 so long as it is over some or all of the property of the granter. Secondly, it could be argued that we have borrowed more from English law than expected: English law has always held that a purported fixed charge in respect of which the necessary perfections steps have not been completed is a floating charge.[81] Nineteenth century Scots case law held that this was not the case in Scotland.[82] However, given the lack of adequate definition of 'floating charge' in the statutory definition, an argument can be constructed that a purported standard security over an asset that does not meet the relevant criteria for a standard security (for example because the amount secured is rent for the property[83]) falls to be a floating charge. In other words, the operation of this provision could be that any failed fixed security falls to be a floating charge.

There is, of course, no support for either of these arguments. Indeed, commentary (including by the author) is strongly against the latter.[84] However, suffice it to note that in the text of the current enabling statute, there is as much support for either of these as there is for the current conventional wisdom in respect of a floating charge: that it is a statutory implant into Scots law based on the English equitable floating charge and adapted in a few areas, that it must be separately constituted and must use the word 'floating' in the relevant instrument.[85]

It is important to note that this ambiguity is a relatively modern creation. When the Companies Act 1985 formulation was enacted, an additional subsection provided:

> 'A floating charge may be created, in the case of a company which the Court of Session has jurisdiction to wind up, only by the execution, under the seal of the company, of an instrument or bond or other written acknowledgment of debt or obligation which purports to create such a charge.'[86]

---

81 See R Goode and L Gullifer, *Goode and Gullifer on Legal Problems of Credit and Security*, 6th edn (London: Sweet & Maxwell, 2017) Ch. 4.

82 *Clark* (n 23).

83 Conveyancing and Feudal Reform (Scotland) Act 1970 s. 9(8)(c).

84 See Hardman (n 41) para. 6–05.

85 See Hardman (n 41) para. 6–05.

86 Companies Act 1985 s. 462(2). The form of the charge itself was also included in the Companies (Floating Charges) (Scotland) Act 1961 Sch. 1.

In the framework, this section therefore performed an important function. Whilst s. 462(1) (which remains in force) provided details of the assets that the floating charge *could* cover and the obligations that it *could* secure, s. 462(2) told companies how to create a floating charge – an instrument was entered into that purported to create a floating charge. The logic was, therefore, less than ideal but workable: we know that something is a floating charge because it stated on its face it was and was signed in a certain way. The more permissive language of s. 462(1) then contained several enabling features as to what this security interest could (but did not have to) include, and insolvency legislation told us the effect of the presence of this security interest. However, s. 462(2) was repealed in 1990[87] and replaced with a broader concept of how companies sign Scots law documents.[88] This would have been all well and good if s. 462(2) only provided how a company executed a floating charge instrument. However, it did so much more than that – it provided the only statutory statement of how to identify a floating charge under Scots law. Whilst the wording 'which purports to create such a charge' may hint towards circularity (it is a floating charge because it states that it is), it was the only element of the framework that told a reader how to identify what a floating charge *is*. Accordingly, repealing this subsection, and not replacing it with any provision that deals with the same subject matter, created a lacuna at the heart of the concept of the 'floating charge'.

(4) Relevance

So, to recap, judicial decisions often conflate analysis of the instrument creating a floating charge with the security interest constituted by that instrument. In addition, the modern statutory framework has a fundamental hole that undermines the entire framework. It is possible that there is an overlap between these two issues.[89] As the conceptual framework of the floating charge security interest eroded in coherence, it is possible that it became easier for all to conflate the security interest with the form of instrument that, by now, practitioners (and judges) were familiar with.

Schlag highlights that such conflation creates an inherent conservative outlook and ties the legal relationships to the current physical manifestations: if we conflate the 'object' and the 'rights attaching to the object', then

---

87 Law Reform (Miscellaneous Provisions) (Scotland) Act 1990 s. 74(1), (2).
88 This was, itself, replaced by the Requirements of Writing (Scotland) Act 1995.
89 This, of course, only applies to cases decided under the framework since 1990, not older cases.

it becomes difficult to apply the latter to new objects. Take the example of cryptocurrency – so long as we conflate the legal relationships applicable to currencies with physical currencies, cryptocurrencies become almost impossible to comprehend.[90] Schlag uses the example of the company, 'the corporation as a legal concept should be fashioned not simply with regard to visible present socioeconomical uses of the corporate form but with regard to the uses (desirable and not) that might be made of that form'.[91]

In other words, conflating the legal relationship and the form inherently ties the legal relationship to the current form. This phenomenon, when combined with the weakness of the floating charge framework, explains some elements of practice. Whilst there is no evidence that the current statutory framework will (or should) be interpreted such that a 'failed fixed security' will be considered to be a floating charge, there is nothing inherently in the statutory framework that prevents each fixed security document from containing a clause granting a floating charge over the relevant assets, at all times or limited to when the fixed security was not valid for any reason. Yet this does not happen.[92] Similarly, there is nothing in the framework that provides anymore that the words 'floating charge' must be used in a document creating a floating charge (or even that such floating charge needs to be documented).[93] In English law, it has been held that it is not necessary for a floating charge to state that it is a floating charge so long as several conditions are met.[94] It is possible for English law to arrive at such a position because it enjoys a better understanding of what a floating charge is. Based on its long understanding, and application, of these principles, the English courts are able to identify when a particular legal relationship constitutes a floating charge. Under Scots law, our only definitive method of doing so – the simplistic but effective tool of saying it is a floating charge if created under an instrument that says it is – has been removed. It is therefore difficult to say how a Scots court would be able to identify a floating charge without the use of the word 'floating' in the instrument constituting it. In other words, not only is our judicial reasoning suspect, our underlying framework is also. In the absence of being able to understand the Scottish floating charge in the

---

90 For a high-quality work resolving this issue see D Fox and S Green (eds), *Cryptocurrencies in Public and Private Law* (Oxford: Oxford University Press, 2019).
91 Schlag (n 8) at 198.
92 See Hardman (n 41) at para. 6–12.
93 See discussion in Hardman (n 41) at para. 6–26.
94 *Brumark Investments Ltd, Re* [2001] UKPC 28, [2001] 2 AC 710. See also *National Westminster Bank plc v Spectrum Plus Ltd* [2005] UKHL 41, [2005] 2 AC 680.

abstract, we look to (possibly semi-deliberately) conflate the unclear legal relationship with the clear formulation we have of what a floating charge instrument looks like. This is a perfect example of Schlag's argument that Hohfeldian mistakes lead to a fundamental conservatism of action.

C. HOHFELDIAN PROGNOSIS

(1) Dyads: jural correlatives and jural opposites

Hohfeld noticed that judicial decision-making was flawed because it conflated concepts together (primarily the physical object, the legal relationships attaching to such physical object and the method of creating such legal relationships) by lack of linguistic clarity. We have seen the same arise in Scotland in respect of the floating charge. It is therefore possible that Hohfeld's solutions can provide us with some guidance for better analysis of the Scots law floating charge.

For Hohfeld, any form of legal relationships could be atomised into eight fundamental building blocks. The atomisation is a very important part of this process – it not only involves breaking down the legal relations into these blocks,[95] but acknowledging that in any given relationship there are likely to be a number of different legal relationships ongoing at the same time. He used the example of the fee simple and deconstructed that into a series of rights, privileges, powers and immunities.[96] The process is therefore to isolate each legal relationship from all others within the same subject matter and analyse the relationship as to which of these building blocks applies to each element of the relationship. The eight building blocks are:

Rights

This has a strict meaning (one that has not been used throughout this chapter). It is also called a 'claim-right'. In order to have a claim-right, other people must be obliged to provide you with it. Hohfeld uses the example of a right that someone else stays off your land.[97] It is important to note that such a right can never be to do something, or to not do something, in the abstract.

---

95 Schlag (n 8) at 218.
96 See W N Hohfeld, 'Fundamental Legal Conceptions as Applied in Judicial Reasoning' (1917) 26 Yale LJ 710 at 746–747.
97 Hohfeld (n 12) at 32. It has also been described as a right to have things done to or for you – see H M Hurd and M S Moore, 'The Hohfeldian Analysis of Rights' (2018) 63 *The American Journal of Jurisprudence* 295.

Instead, it is a claim that is held against someone else[98] – I don't have a right to £5, I have a right that *you* pay me £5.

Privilege

This is narrower than a right – a privilege is an ability to do something without a corresponding requirement on others to provide you with it. To continue the land analogy, a privilege is your ability to enter your own land.[99] No one else is under an obligation to help you enter the land (or, indeed, to not hinder you) but you can do it. In modern language, privileges tend to be called liberties,[100] or even 'liberty nots' as they enable the putative privilege holder to not do something.[101] Wenar adds that liberties are often 'paired' – at the same time one is often at a liberty to do X and not to do X.[102] It has also been argued that Hohfeld's privilege analysis is too simplistic and needs to be further subdivided.[103] This has been criticised as being overly complicated.[104] It should be noted, however, that privileges or liberties sometimes do not exist in isolation. Often privileges can be supported by claim-rights. Finnis uses the example of a privilege to walk on your own land. In most jurisdictions, this is re-enforced by a series of claim-rights that support this privilege.[105] Finnis uses this example to demonstrate how a number of then-leading commentators on Hohfeld had confused their analysis by conflating together this relation with other, parallel relations.

Power

A power is an ability to make something happen – Hohfeld refers to it as a '(legal) power to effect the particular change of legal relations that is involved in the problem'.[106] Thus an ability to create a right or a privilege (or to transform, say, a privilege into a right) is a 'power'. For example, in

98 J Finnis, 'Some Professorial Fallacies about Rights' (1972) 4 Adel L Rev 377 at 380.

99 Hohfeld (n 12) at 32. This is distinguished from a right on the grounds that a privilege gives you a right to do something (rather than a right to have things done to or for you) – Hurd and Moore (n 97).

100 See the discussion in L D D'Almeida, 'Fundamental Legal Concepts: The Hohfeldian Framework' (2016) 11 *Philosophy Compass* 554.

101 See G Williams, 'The Concept of Legal Liberty' (1956) 56(8) Colum L Rev 1129 at 1135.

102 L Wenar, 'The Nature of Rights' (2005) 33(3) *Philosophy and Public Affairs* 223 at 226.

103 For example, V Brown, 'Rights, Liberties and Duties: Reformulating Hohfeld's Scheme of Legal Relations?' (2005) 58 *Current Legal Problems* 343.

104 See D'Almeida (n 100).

105 Finnis (n 98) at 378.

106 Hohfeld (n 12) at 44.

the ownership of land, I have a selection of legal relations *vis-à-vis* you – I have the privilege to enjoy my land, I have the right to exclude you from my land and the power to change these relations by, for example, selling my land to a third party. Hohfeld states that in order to have a power, one side must have 'volitional control'.[107] This means that the putative power holder has 'decisional control' – 'the power holder *alone* must decide whether or not the power is exercised'.[108] We can discern narrow and wide conceptions of powers.[109] A narrow conception of a power relates purely to the legal framework: in order to have a power, law needs to not just recognise that power but also to approve it as a legitimate choice. Conversely, the broad conception of a power includes the power to break the law: I have a power not to pay a debt that I acknowledge is due.[110] The broad conception is thought-provoking and has a cohesion with Hohfeldian thought. However, it misses that there are legal consequences for me exercising such putative power. It is therefore analytically cleaner to define a power as a change of relations that the law will recognise as legitimate, and therefore adopt a narrow conception of power. This is because whilst I could be said to be able to refuse payment, the law can force me to pay (and, in the case of other breaches, demand some form of redress). Accordingly, this cannot be said to be a legal power. Instead, I have a duty to pay and a disability to adjust this duty.

Immunity

Hohfeld considered that:

> 'a power enjoys the same general contrast to an immunity that a right does to a privilege … a power is one's affirmative "control" over a given legal relation as against another; whereas an immunity is one's freedom from the legal power or "control" of another as regards some legal relation'.[111]

Thus whilst a power is an active ability to change legal relations, an immunity is a veto to any change in your legal relations.

---

107 Hohfeld (n 12) at 44.
108 A Reilly, 'Is the "Mere Equity" to Rescind a Legal Power? Unpacking Hohfeld's Concept of "Volitional Control"' (2019) 39(4) OJLS 779 at 781.
109 A Reilly, 'Is the "Mere Equity" to Rescind a Legal Power? Unpacking Hohfeld's Concept of "Volitional Control"' (n 108) at 785.
110 See M Kramer, 'Rights Without Trimmings' in M Kramer et al. (eds), *A Debate Over Rights: Philosophical Enquiries* (Oxford: Oxford University Press, 2000) 104.
111 Hohfeld (n 12) at 55.

Disability

A disability is something that you are not allowed to do. If, in respect of an isolated legal relation, you have an immunity from something being done, I therefore have a disability from doing that thing.

Liability

A liability is something that may happen to you. More precisely, it refers to the fact that your legal relation with someone else may change without your control – by the counterparty exercising a power that they have. If (once more in respect of an isolated legal relation) you have a power to do something, I have a liability in respect of what the subject of that power may be.

Duty

A duty is the correlative of a right. If you have a claim-right then I must be under a duty to uphold it. Thus in the example of my right that you stay off my land, you have a duty to not enter my land. Conceptually, there is a difference between duties owed to specific individuals (so called directed duties) and those owed more generally: if I owe duties not to you, but generally, how can the analysis be dissolved into dyads?[112] This can be resolved by reviewing such duties as being owed to everyone in the world.[113] Once we adopt this analysis, we can see each such duty being reduced to dyads (it is just that the duty holder has such dyads with each person in the world).

No right

A 'no right' is simply the absence of a legal position. It means that a party has 'no right' to a particular action (or to stop a particular action, as the case may be).

Hohfeld describes these as 'the lowest common denominators of the law',[114] going further to state:

> 'Ten fractions (1-3, 2-5, etc) may superficially seem so different from one another as to defy comparison. If, however, they are expressed in terms of their lowest

---

112 D'Almeida (n 100).

113 See K Barker, 'Private Law, Analytical Philosophy and the Modern Value of Wesley Newcomb Hohfeld: A Centennial Appraisal' (2018) 38 OJLS 585.

114 Hohfeld (n 12) at 58.

common denominations (5-15, 6-15, etc) comparison becomes easy, and fundamental similarity may be discovered. The same thing is of course true as regards
the lowest generic conceptions to which any and all "legal quantities" may be
reduced.'[115]

On their own, there is nothing intrinsic in these eight categories that makes
them a definitive taxonomy – nothing immediately stands out as proving
that this should be used instead of other taxonomies of legal rules.[116] The
real value of this taxonomy, however, becomes apparent when we consider
two different types of pairing of these blocks. Indeed, we can see from the
definitions of several of the blocks that they are defined by reference to how
they relate to others of the blocks. This means that they cease to be standalone concepts and become dyads – the importance ceases to be what each
building block is and instead arises from the interaction between that block
and the other block in the dyad. There are two fundamental categories of
dyad that Hohfeld identifies as applying to his building blocks.[117] Indeed, so
vital are the dyadic relations to Hohfeld that he *commences* his discussion of
these building blocks by reference to the two types of dyads. The two types
are jural correlatives and jural opposites.

Jural correlatives are those that apply to any given isolated legal relationship. As we can isolate each relationship to the interaction between two
people, a jural correlative is therefore 'in order for the block applicable to
me in this relationship to be X, the block applicable to you in this relationship has to by Y'. Indeed, Llewellyn states that jural correlatives are merely
looking at the same legal relationship from the perspectives of the two
different parties to that relationship.[118]

Thus our four jural correlatives are[119]:

Right and duty

For me to have a claim-right to X, you have to have a duty to me to provide X. Thus in the example of land use, in order for me to have a right to

---

115 Hohfeld (n 12) at 58–59.
116 For example, rules can be divided into property rules, liability rules and inaliena-
    ble entitlements – G Calabresi and A D Melamed, 'Property Rules, Liability Rules, and
    Inalienability: One View of the Cathedral' (1972) 85 Harv L Rev 1089, 1092, or default,
    mandatory and permissive rules. See B R Cheffins, *Company Law Theory, Structure and
    Operations* (Oxford: Clarendon Press, 2008, reprint) 227–263.
117 Hohfeld (n 96) at 710.
118 K Llewellyn, *The Bramble Bush* (Oxford: Oxford University Press, 2008 (reprint)) at 90.
119 Hohfeld (n 96) at 710.

exclude you from my land, you must be under a duty to not enter my land. This therefore can be applied the other way: if I have a duty to provide you with something, then you have a claim-right in respect of that thing from me. However, and this was a fundamental point of Hohfeld's analysis, in the absence of you having a duty to provide me with something, I cannot be said to have a claim-right in respect of that thing from you. Rights and duties are therefore correlative – if one exists then the counterparty experiences the other, and conversely if you look at a legal relationship and one of these does not apply (there is no right on one side or no duty on the other), then the other does not. Hohfeld uses this distinction to provide some clarity to discourse on the rather emotive subject of 'rights'.[120]

Privilege and no right

A privilege corresponds to a 'no right'. If I am able to enter my own land but you are neither able to stop me nor under a duty to help me, then you have a 'no right' in the legal relation – it is, quite simply, unlinked to you.

Power and liability

If I have a power to do something – to change our legal relation, say, from a privilege to a right – then you are under a liability for the exercise of such power. My ability to exert this power happens to you and you must suffer that exercise of this power as a liability. Once more the converse of this is, of course, that if we can see that one person has such a liability, then the other must have such a power.

Immunity and disability

If I am immune to you changing the legal relationship, then you are disabled from making such a change – the corollary to my immunity is your disability. Once again the same is true in the inverse – my disability to change the legal relation provides you with an immunity from me doing so.

Every legal relationship therefore fits in to one of these jural correlatives. The first two describe the current legal relationship and the second two describe potential changes that can (or cannot) be made to that legal relationship.

---

120 Hohfeld (n 96) at 710.

In addition to the correlatives, we can also identify dyads of jural opposites. Whilst jural correlatives are different sides of the same legal relationship, jural opposites are seen from one party's perspective and show that such party cannot have both of any dyad in respect of the same legal relationship. These opposites are therefore:

1. **Right and no right:** It is not possible for me to have a claim-right to something and no right to it in respect of the same legal relationship.
2. **Privilege and duty:** It is not possible for me to have a privilege to be able to do something and a duty not to do it in respect of the same legal relationship.
3. **Power and disability:** It is not possible for me to have a power to change a legal relationship and be disabled from changing the same legal relationship. If I have a power to change relations by selling my land, I cannot be disabled from selling my land; and
4. **Immunity and liability:** It is not possible for me to be immune from a change of legal relationship and have a liability that such change may occur. Thus if I am immune from a change of landowner changing my legal relations (e.g. I have a consent 'right' to such transfer) then I do not have a liability that such owner will change without my consent.[121]

Once again, points 1 and 2 relate to the current state of matters: on a static basis, a party can enjoy a right or a no-right; a privilege or a duty in respect of their relationship with another. Points 3 and 4 relate to the ability to change this static position – a party either has the power to change it or is disabled from changing it or has immunity from their counterparty changing it or is liable to suffer any changes that are made. It is worth pausing on the nature of the change relations: they relate to the party's abilities to effect a change relation. Thus the 'power' to do something is a power that a party must be able to exercise. This exercise involves two steps: a normative intention to exercise the power and an objectively verifiable decision by the power holder.[122] The analysis becomes less clear when it comes to changes over time. Say I am due to pay £5 to you following the passage of ten years. If we follow a strict Hohfeldian approach, we have to adopt one of two approaches. We can either concentrate on the position as at the date of analysis, or assume that the contingency has occurred. The former would mean that we would characterise our relations as a

---

121 There would, of course, still be AN owner, and my rights against the NEW owner would be the same as my rights against the old owner. However, for measuring interactions between people, my rights *vis-à-vis* the old owner are altered.
122 Reilly (n 108) at 791.

no-right and privilege relationship, as I do not currently have a duty to pay you £5. The latter would mean that we assume that I owe you £5 now – and characterise it as a duty to pay you £5. The situation is starker if we factor in a contingency – if I have to pay you £5 upon the occurrence of a certain extrinsic event, should we assume that event will not happen or pretend that it has already happened? Neither seems to provide conceptual clarity. The same issues arise if the contingent event is actually in my control but has automatic effect.

We can resolve this by adding a concept of 'contingency' into the analysis. Something arising in the future that the party cannot influence is merely a contingent static relation – if I am due to be paid something today by you then I have a claim-right to payment and you are under a corresponding duty to pay me. If we change the date from today to next week this does not change the nature of the relationship – it is still a right/duty dyad, merely one that will occur in the future. Similarly if you are due to pay me something contingent upon a particular occurrence, then we have a contingent right/duty dyad, not a power/liability dyad. In order to classify as a power/liability dyad, the party with the putative power must be the party with the power to effect the change – and so must enjoy Reilly's 'decisional control'.[123] In other words – an obligation to pay me money if I ask for it is a power/liability dyad. It seems as if this is the same as a contingent right/duty dyad as if X happens in the future then Y occurs. However, this is not the case as the contingent right/duty provides no power to the putative power holder. In order to qualify as a power, it must be the actions of the power holder that effect it. Thus we can also discern contingent powers in addition to contingent rights – if I have the ability *to ask you for money* (which you must pay) contingent upon a particular occurrence but that occurrence does not automatically trigger a payment obligation, then I have a contingent power, whereas if you have to pay me money contingent upon a particular occurrence then we have a contingent right/duty dyad.[124] In addition, a right/duty dyad requires some form of reciprocal arrangement between the parties, which is lacking from a privilege/no right dyad.[125] We can use this analysis to help differentiate between contingent rights and contingent privileges.

It has been stated that static and change relations exist in different universes.[126] However, this obscures the reality. For any given set of obligations,

---

123 Reilly (n 108).

124 This reflects Lord Drummond Young's discussion of contingency in *Liquidation of Ben Line Steamers Ltd, Noter* [2010] CSOH 174, 2011 SLT 535 at 553.

125 See A Arvantis and A Karampatzos, 'Negotiation as an intersubjective process: Creating and validating claim-rights' (2013) 26 *Philosophical Psychology* 89 at 95.

126 M Radin, 'A Restatement of Hohfeld' (1938) 51(7) Harv L Rev 1141 at 1157.

I must have a static relation *and* a change relationship. We must be able to describe what the relationship currently is and also whether I have an ability to change it or not. The issue is not that they are different universes, but that they portray different tenses; the current and the future. This helps enrich the discussion of contingencies: for a future payment, we simply have a right/duty analysis contingent upon the passing of time, with both sides at the same time immune and disabled from changing it. For a contingent payment based on extrinsic factors, we have a right/duty analysis contingent upon that extrinsic event, once more with both sides at the same time immune and disabled from changing that. For a contingent payment based on my actions, we have a privilege/no right analysis, coupled with a contingent power/liability analysis to change that to a right/duty relationship.

For Hohfeld, obtaining clarity in legal analysis was a case of breaking down the legal relations into those that could fit into these building blocks and dyads. Finnis clarifies that this means realising that:

> 'each Hohfeldian relation … concerns only one activity of one person … To sharpen the point, let it be particularly noted that, while somebody's activity is one topic for Hohfeldian relationships between that person and other persons, interference with that person's activity always another topic for other Hohfeldian relationships. Thus the correlative of X's privilege is Y's no-right that X shall not exercise this privilege; and that is all that can be said about this relationship. The matter of Y's possible privilege (or even duty) to interfere with X's exercise of his (X's) privilege is always a further problem requiring a distinct solution by positive law; nothing can be asserted about it by inference from the first-mentioned relationship'.[127]

Thus, other than identifying a legal relationship and the ability for either side to change it, we cannot identify any further implications from a particular relation: I may have a privilege that is supported by a claim-right, or I may have a privilege that is not supported by a claim-right. In either case, each relation needs to be analysed on its own: what is the static relation and what is the dynamic relation on an atomised, relation-by-relation basis. By reconstituting the legal analysis accordingly we can gain clarity as to the precise nature of the legal relationship between two parties that we are analysing.

(2) Application

Having seen that the floating charge has a Hohfeldian problem (lack of clarity in judicial decision-making), we can therefore try to apply Hohfeldian solutions to the analysis. The function of this enquiry is to establish what

127 Finnis (n 98) at 378.

the nature of a Scottish floating charge really is. In order to do so, we shall examine the features of other security interests in a Hohfeldian manner and then analyse features of the floating charge, to establish whether the floating charge can truly be said to be a security interest at all.

(a) Security interests

It has been stated that 'the core of proper security is not a right at all, but rather a set of Hohfeldian powers and privileges'.[128] If we can state that the purpose of a security interest is to realise money,[129] then according to Smith, a Hohfeldian power is required to sell the secured asset, backed with a Hohfeldian privilege to keep the money.[130] This perception is important, but simplistic: we can provide further Hohfeldian atomisation than this. First, the security holder obtains certain rights in respect of the specific asset in question. In terms of traditional non-Hohfeldian dialogue, the security holder obtains either a subordinated real right or (for an improper security) the real right of ownership itself, subject to some restrictions.[131] Their security interest is inherent to the asset and the security granter is unable to sell the asset free of the security without the consent of the creditor.[132] A static analysis of this is complicated and varies depending on type of asset. However, a unifying feature is the dynamic immunity that the holder of each security right enjoys: they are immune from their security interest being removed from the property without their consent (or receiving full repayment). The security granter is subject to a corresponding disability – they are disabled from changing the static relations.[133] Attached to these immunities are contingent powers for the security holder, and a contingent liability for the security granter.

128 L Smith, 'Powership and its Objects' in A J M Steven et al. (eds), *Nothing So Practical as a Good Theory* (Edinburgh: Avizandum, 2017) 229.
129 See G L Gretton, 'The Concept of Security' in D J Cusine (ed), *A Scots Conveyancing Miscellany* (Edinburgh: W. Green, 1987) at 128.
130 Smith (n 128) at 230.
131 See A J M Steven and H Patrick, 'Reforming Secured Transactions law in Scotland' in L Gullifer and O Akseli (eds), *Secured Transactions Law Reform* (London: Bloomsbury, 2016) 260.
132 In an assignation in security the granter has alienated the incorporeal moveable property and so cannot transfer it, in a pledge the granter has delivered the property to the creditor and so cannot transfer it (the ownership right could be transferred but it would remain subject to the pledge right) and whilst the debtor can still transfer the land if a standard security is granted, the standard security will continue to encumber the land (Conveyancing and Feudal Reform (Scotland) Act 1970 s. 11).
133 The author is indebted to Professor Lionel Smith for providing this insightful analysis.

Secondly, the security holder is under a corresponding duty to any potential other holder of security under the rules pertaining to catholic and secondary creditors. Consider the example whereby we have two security holders. The first security holder has security over asset X AND asset Y (the catholic creditor), whereas the second security holder has security only over asset Y. The first security holder is under a duty to enforce against asset X first, and the second security holder has a claim-right to ensure that the common security pool is not used up prior to enforcement over asset X.[134] Accordingly, the secondary creditor has a contingent Hohfeldian claim-right to require the catholic creditor to enforce against asset X first. The catholic creditor has a corresponding duty. In terms of change relations, these can be changed by both the catholic and the secondary creditor: either releasing their charge over X will alter the static relationship. Accordingly, in the same way as paired liberties were noted above, we can also have paired powers and liabilities.

There are two further change relations related to the grant of fixed security. First, fixed security provides recipients of security with a power to, on the occurrence of a breach of the term of the document, enforce against a specific asset.[135] The act of enforcement changes the relationship to a realisation process – no longer does a latent subordinate (non-Hohfeldian) right exist in respect of the specific asset but instead the asset is subject to the enforcement and realisation. This provides an equivalent liability for the security granter – they must suffer the enforcement of the security should enforcement occur. Prior to enforcement, the security holder has no right in respect of the sale of the asset and the security granter is at liberty in respect of the use of the asset. Post-enforcement, the exercise of the power changes the legal relationship to one of right and duty. The security recipient has a claim-right to sell the secured assets, whereas the security granter has a corresponding duty to not hinder such sale. However, it is the exercise of the power that makes it so.

The security recipient themselves is also under a liability to release the security on repayment by the debtor.[136] This means that the security granters have a power to compel the release upon repayment of the relevant debt. Prior to repayment, the security holder has a privilege as to whether

---

134 *Littlejohn v Black* (1855) 18 D 207.
135 Being the asset that they have the real right in.
136 In the context of an assignation in security, see *Crerar v Bank of Scotland* 1921 SC 736 at 760, in the context of a standard security, see Conveyancing and Feudal Reform (Scotland) Act 1970 s. 18 and in the context of a pledge, see e.g. *Hunter and Co v Slack* (1860) 22 D 1166.

to release the security or not, and the security granter has no claim-right to demand it. The security granter has the power to change the legal relationship by repaying the debt and requesting the release of security, and if they do so then the legal relationship changes to the security granter having a claim-right to the release of the security and the security holder being under a corresponding duty to release the security. This is a power as the change between statuses is under the control of the security granter.

(b) Floating charges

Discussion so far has all been rather general. The reason for this is that these features are all common to all types of fixed security: be it a standard security over heritable property, a pledge over corporeal moveable property or an assignation in security over incorporeal moveable property. Does a floating charge share the same characteristics? The answer to each is no. A granter of a floating charge may sell floating charge property without the consent of the floating charge holder, meaning that the floating charge holder has a liability that the granter will exercise their Hohfeldian power to change this dynamic in respect of each individual asset. If the holder of a fixed charge over a certain piece of machinery is immune from the granter changing this, and the granter is so disabled from amending it (without a full repayment of the secured obligation); the holder of a floating charge over such machinery has a liability that the floating charge holder will exercise their power to change this. Such a power can be exercised by selling the machine, thus removing it from the ambit of the floating charge. The holder of a floating charge does not gain a claim-right from the granter to enforce against any specific asset.[137] The law of catholic and secondary creditors has been held to not apply to receivers appointed under floating charges.[138] Indeed, this was couched in wider terms – that default rules applicable to security interests do not apply to the floating charge. This may mean that there is no liability on a security holder to release a floating charge upon repayment of the secured debt.[139] We can therefore say that the floating charge does not share any of the core Hohfeldian characteristics of 'security' as known under

---

137 Technically their remedy is to attempt to appoint an insolvency practitioner to the assets that are, at the time of enforcement, subject to the floating charge (or, in the case of administration, to the person of the security granter themselves), but it gives no right to any specified assets.

138 *Forth & Clyde* (n 47).

139 See Hardman (n 41) para. 10–34.

Scots law.[140] What features, then, can we discern of a floating charge in Scotland?

The floating charge under Scots law provides for three key Hohfeldian rights and a power. Each of the rights is contingent upon the insolvency of the security granter. First, the security holder will obtain a ranking on insolvency ahead of unsecured creditors.[141] Secondly, contingent upon the floating charge containing a negative pledge, the security holder is able to ensure that their security ranks ahead of any subsequently granted real rights in security.[142] Thirdly, contingent upon someone else trying to appoint an insolvency practitioner to the security granter, the security holder has the claim-right to make their own appointment of an insolvency practitioner to the granter.[143]

A floating charge also provides a contingent power to the security holder: if there is a breach of the terms of the floating charge instrument, the holder of a qualifying floating charge is able to appoint an administrator (or, in limited circumstances, an administrative receiver) to the assets of the granter.[144] The granter of the floating charge therefore suffers a liability that, upon breach, an insolvency practitioner will be appointed to the assets of the company. The floating charge holder is not able to do so until there is a breach and such breach is out of their control. However, once the breach occurs, this power arises.

We can therefore see that the floating charge does not, in fact, share any characteristics with traditional, fixed security. Indeed, we can identify some further differences in the characteristics: a floating charge holder is more passive as their primary remedy falls in the place of contingent rights and the contingent power to appoint a third party to the security granter on breach of the floating charge. By contrast, the fixed charge holder obtains an immunity from their specific relation changing, a contingent duty in the form of the rules of catholic and secondary creditors, a power to enforce against the specific assets in question and a liability to release their security interest on repayment.[145] These characteristics are all shared by all security

---

140 This is a purely descriptive argument based on textual analysis of judgements – the author passes no comment on whether any of the case law examined is correct.

141 Insolvency Act 1986 Sch. B1 para. 65(3). This is a right that the floating charge has in common with other security rights.

142 Companies Act 1985 s. 463(1).

143 Insolvency Act 1986 Sch. B1 para. 14 and Insolvency Act 1986 Sch. B1 para. 17.

144 Enterprise Act 2002 s. 250 and related amendments.

145 In addition, an enforcing security holder has an obligation to distribute any excess proceeds to other, e.g. for standard securities Conveyancing and Feudal Reform (Scotland) Act 1970 s. 27.

interests other than the floating charge, which has its own unique characteristics. Accordingly, the floating charge cannot be said to be a security interest.

What, then, is it? All rights that the security holder has are contingent upon, ultimately, insolvency or a process involving an insolvency practitioner.[146] Security interests, however, exist and have relevance outside of insolvency. Seen in the light of Hohfeldian analysis, the floating charge ceases to be a security interest at all: it is an insolvency concept – a legal relation that only exists to create a power to put a security granter into an insolvency process (or quasi-insolvency process) and provide contingent rights that only become relevant when the security granter is otherwise in insolvency. Thus the floating charge provides one simple ability for the floating charge holder – to press the 'nuclear launch button' should the worst happen and to be slightly preferred should it happen (either as a result of their button-pushing or otherwise). When we stop considering the floating charge as a security concept and start thinking of it as an insolvency concept, clarity can prevail.[147] Until then, due to problems with legislation and judicial reasoning, we will be left in the dark.

(3) Critique

Whilst the foregoing analysis creates a neat and simple narrative to argue that the floating charge is so inherently different from other security interests that it should be considered an insolvency concept rather than a security concept, there are some severe critiques of the analysis that require to be clarified.

First, the analysis as to contingency in the right/power differentiation are the author's own. They cannot be said to be 'Hohfeldian' other than to the extent that the author used Hohfeldian concepts and twisted them towards his own analysis. Indeed, the need to refer to a new concept of contingency, which is not in Hohfeld's work, could risk implying that the author has blended some concepts together: his atomisation of the floating charge may not be accurate and could be the subject of further atomisation. In undertaking such blending, the author could be said to be guilty of the

---

146 See J Hardman, 'Some Legal Determinants of External Finance in Scotland: A Response to Lord Hodge' (2017) 21 Edin L Rev 30 at 49–50.
147 The idea that the floating charge may not be purely a security right is not novel – see MacPherson (n 5) Ch. 6, which characterises the floating charge as a patrimonial preference right with some security incidences.

same crimes that he identified courts had committed over the years: and the same crime that Finnis identified is commonly committed when people use Hohfeldian analysis.[148]

Similarly, when reconstructing, the author deliberately ignored any overlapping features between security interests and the floating charge: such as obligations to register security and floating charges to ensure their effectiveness[149] and that the possessory nature and/or subordinated real right status of fixed security could be argued to be a functional equivalent of a negative pledge: they act to ensure priority over subsequent security. To put the same subject in a neater way: the negative pledge was only necessary in the floating charge as it is the only form of security in which the problem of being trumped by a later security could arise.[150]

The chapter is also very simplistic when it comes to elements of the floating charge – whilst the author's analysis is generally correct for the holder of a qualifying floating charge,[151] it is not applicable to a floating charge that is not a qualifying floating charge. Both are conceptually the same security interest, just applicable to different assets, and yet different characteristics apply to them. By over-simplifying matters, the author has ignored a potential area for analysis. In a similar vein, it is overly simplistic to state that the holder of a qualifying floating charge has enhanced rights to appoint an insolvency practitioner to the security granter. This is only the case if the insolvency process is administration and the insolvency practitioner is satisfied that the appointment satisfies the purposes of administration.[152] In all other circumstances, the holder of a qualifying floating charge has an almost identical ability as other creditors to attempt to persuade the court to make their own appointment.[153]

There are two overriding criticisms of the foregoing analysis. First, none of the judicial reasoning errors identified by the author were determinative of a case – no cases were decided incorrectly (or differently) as a result of blending or slippage. Accordingly, even if the analysis is correct, its relevance is open to questioning. Secondly, the floating charge is *meant* to be different from existing security interests. That was the point in introducing

---

148 Finnis (n 98).
149 Companies Act 2006 s. 859A onwards.
150 See discussion in J Hardman and A D J MacPherson, 'The Ranking of Floating Charges', Chapter 9 within this volume.
151 Insolvency Act 1986 Sch. B1 para. 14(3).
152 Insolvency Act 1986 Sch. B1 para. 3.
153 A qualifying floating charge holder does not need to show that the company is unable to pay its debts – Insolvency Act 1985 Sch. B1 para. 35.

it – to provide much needed flexibility. If the floating charge fitted neatly with Scots law then it is likely that its introduction would not have required to be so blunt. That it now has different characteristics is, in fact, evidence that the floating charge plays an important role in the sphere of voluntary security in Scotland. Indeed, it can be argued that the presence of a floating charge under Scots law has expanded the notion of what a right in security is under Scots law.[154]

Despite these criticisms, however, by applying such an established theory of private law into the detailed nuance of some of the floating charge, we gain further insights. The analysis advanced in this chapter may be ripe for further refinement but this does not negate its insights: which are a methodological development and insight into a previously neglected area.

D. CONCLUSION

The floating charge suffers from a distinctly Hohfeldian illness. Its analysis is frequently flawed, as the language used to describe it is not precise enough. Without certainty as to whether one is analysing the instrument creating the floating charge or the floating charge itself, confusion is bound to arise. This confusion, however, is rooted in a statutory problem – under the current formulation, it is very unclear what is necessary to constitute a 'floating charge'.

This much is undoubtable. However, market participants, lawyers, insolvency practitioners and judges are aware of the majority of what constitutes a floating charge. Like obscenity, this is currently undertaken on an 'I know it when I see it' basis.[155] This does cause problems at the margin and does feed in to Schlag's concept that obfuscating the relationship and the document creating the relationship leads to a fundamental conservatism. It would be preferable for Scots law to remedy this.

It is not, ultimately, necessary to provide any clarifications in respect of the floating charge under Scots law, nor is it possible to conclude that the floating charge is so different that it ceases to be in the same category as other security.

---

154 See MacPherson, *Floating Charge* (n 5) Ch. 6.
155 See the US case of *Jacobellis v Ohio* 378 US 184 (1964).

8 The Species and Structure(s) of the Floating Charge: The English Law Perspective on the Scottish Floating Charge

*Magda Raczynska**

A. INTRODUCTION
B. PARTIES' FREEDOM TO CREATE AND SHAPE THE CHARGE
    (1) A common forerunner: charge over an undertaking under 1845 Acts
    (2) Different attitudes towards parties' agreement
    (3) Person of the chargor
    (4) Charged assets
    (5) Debentures
    (6) Registration
    (7) Crystallisation
    (8) Enforcement
C. THE NATURE OF THE FLOATING CHARGE PRIOR TO CRYSTALLISATION ('ATTACHMENT' IN SCOTS LAW)
    (1) Property right v personal right
    (2) The extent to which the floating charge binds third parties
    (3) Not a personal right
    (4) Not a preference right
    (5) Property right with a broad authority to dispose free of the charge
D. CONCLUSION

* I am very grateful to both editors for their invaluable comments on an earlier version of this chapter and their time taken to answer my queries about Scots law. All errors remain mine.

A. INTRODUCTION

The floating charge is one of the most useful developments facilitated by the English Chancery courts.[1] It has played an important role since the mid-nineteenth century in enabling corporate businesses[2] to raise finance.[3] One of its practical selling points is that the charged assets are at free disposal of the chargor, so the chargor may sell or otherwise dispose of them without the chargee's consent, as if they are not charged, for as long as the disposition is within the terms of the charge, until the charge is crystallised.[4]

The adoption of an identically-named device into Scots law was motivated by the desire to improve borrowing opportunities for Scottish companies.[5] It was introduced by the Companies (Floating Charges) (Scotland) Act 1961,[6] and it currently finds its basis in the Companies Act

1 Note that references to 'England' and 'English' are meant to encompass the jurisdiction of England and Wales unless stated otherwise.

2 The discussion in this chapter focuses on floating charges granted by companies, as companies are the main type of grantor of this type of security interest in English and Scots law, but see section B(3) below.

3 See e.g. J Armour, 'The Law and Economics Debate about Secured Lending: Lessons for European Lawmaking? Part 1: The Conceptual and Legal Framework' (2008) *European Company and Financial Law Review* 3 at 22 (suggesting that, in a debtor's insolvency, the enforcement mechanism associated with a general floating charge – running the process for the benefit of secured creditors – is more efficient than reorganisation procedures where the process is run for the benefit of all creditors collectively). Note J Getzler, 'The Role of Security over Future and Circulating Capital: Evidence from the British Economy Circa 1850 to 1920' in J Getzler and J Payne (eds), *Company Charges: Spectrum and Beyond* (Oxford: Oxford University Press, 2006) 227.

4 This is also seen as the hallmark of the floating charge, distinguishing it from a fixed charge: *Agnew v Commissioner of Inland Revenue (Brumark)* [2001] UKPC 28, [2001] 2 AC 710 at paras 23, 32 per Lord Millett (delivering the judgement of the Board); *In re Spectrum Plus (in liquidation)* [2005] 2 AC 680 (HL) at paras 107–111 per Lord Scott (with whom Lord Brown and Baroness Hale were in full agreement; and at 53 per Lord Hope agreeing with what Lord Scott said about the relevant authorities).

5 Law Reform Committee for Scotland, *Eighth Report of the Law Reform Committee for Scotland: The Constitution of Security over Moveable Property; and Floating Charges* (Cmnd 1017: 1960). See also *Sharp v Thomson* 1997 SC (HL) 66 at 78 per Lord Clyde (with whom Lords Keith, Browne-Wilkinson and Steyn agreed): 'since it was believed that [floating charges in English law] were convenient and advantageous for commercial business, provision was made by statute to enable this form of security to be available in Scotland'; *Spectrum* (n 4) at para. 50 per Lord Hope: 'This situation [i.e. the inability to create the floating charge in Scotland prior to the statutory reforms] was thought to be to the disadvantage of Scottish companies'. See also A D J MacPherson, 'The Genesis of the Scottish Floating Charge', Chapter 3 within this volume.

6 The Companies (Floating Charges) (Scotland) Act 1961 was superseded by the Companies (Floating Charges and Receivers) (Scotland) Act 1972.

1985.[7] There is little doubt that the Scottish floating charge was inspired by the English floating charge[8] but it does not follow that they are the same institution.

It is surprising how little analysis there has been of the similarities and differences between the English and the Scottish floating charges. Many accounts focus on a different question, namely the poor fit of the Scottish floating charge into Scots property law,[9] which is Civilian and 'based on the more rigorous conceptual structure of Roman law'.[10] The point of comparison with English law is generally reduced to an assertion that the English floating charge is equitable while the Scottish one is not[11] and so the two charges are very different 'by nature'.[12] Such a line of thinking has a long tradition. It is epitomised in the stark words of Lord President Cooper in a case preceding the introduction of the floating charge in Scotland, *Carse v Coppen*,[13] in which he said that the equitable nature of the English floating charge is the reason why this form of security is 'utterly repugnant to the principles of Scots law … In Scotland the term "equitable security" is meaningless'.[14] The consequence of this reasoning is that English authorities, practice and even analyses are thought to be of no (or little) assistance

---

7 Note that Part 2 of the Bankruptcy and Diligence etc. (Scotland) Act 2007 repeals and replaces the provisions in the Companies Act 1985 but the relevant provisions of the 2007 Act are not yet in force, for which see G L Gretton, 'The Story of the Scots Law Floating Charge: 1961 to Date', Chapter 4 within this volume, section D(5)(c).

8 See e.g. *National Commercial Bank of Scotland Ltd v Liquidators of Telford Grier Mackay & Co Ltd* 1969 SC 181 at 184 per Lord Fraser.

9 See e.g. G L Gretton, 'Floating Charges: The Scottish Experience' (1984) *Journal of Business Law* 255 at 256–257; G L Gretton, 'Floating Charges in Scots Law: the Saga Continues' (1995) *Journal of Business Law* 212; G L Gretton, 'Reception without Integration – Floating Charges and Mixed Systems' (2003) 78 Tul L Rev 307; G L Gretton and A J M Steven, *Property, Trusts and Succession*, 4th edn (London: Bloomsbury Professional, 2021) para. 21.38; D Cabrelli, 'The Case against the Floating Charge in Scotland' (2005) 9(3) Edin L Rev 407; R Goode, 'Commercial Law and the Scottish Parliament' (1999) 4 SLPQ 81 at 89: 'the method of incorporation of this concept [of the floating charge] into Scots law was not the happiest'.

10 *MacMillan v T Leith Developments Ltd (in receivership and liquidation)* [2017] CSIH 23, 2017 SC 642 para. 121 per Lord Drummond Young.

11 The most extensive discussion to date appears in S C Styles, 'The Two Types of Floating Charge: The English and the Scots' (1999) SLPQ 235, who argues that the 'legal logic' underlying the operation of the English and Scots floating charges is very different.

12 *Telford* (n 8) at 184 per Lord Fraser: '[t]he theoretical basis of the floating charge is unfamiliar, and even alien, to the general law of Scotland'.

13 1951 SC 233.

14 1951 SC 233 at 239 per Lord President Cooper, referred to in various subsequent authorities, e.g. *Gordon Anderson (Plant) Ltd v Campsie Construction Ltd and Anglo Scottish Plant Ltd* 1977 SLT 7 at 14 per Lord Avonside; *Sharp* (n 5) at 69 per Lord Jauncey (with whom Lord Keith, Lord Browne-Wilkinson and Lord Steyn agreed).

in Scotland.[15] Such a negative stance is misleading and unfortunate. It seems to be underpinned by an incorrect premise that every aspect of the English floating charge is explained by the equitable nature of the security, omitting entirely, e.g. the statutory regulation. Secondly, it precludes a comparative line of analysis that might illuminate the understanding of the concept of the floating charge in England and in Scotland and, more generally, it debars any insights into how a concept derived from one legal system could operate in another, whose property law is built upon different principles.

The primary purpose of this chapter is to compare the Scottish and the English floating charge. The central claim, drawn from insights in modern property theory, is that the basic structure of the floating charge in the two jurisdictions is the same but that there is a difference in the legal basis of its components, and the parties' freedom in shaping them. The differences are important but, it is argued, they do not warrant a conclusion that the two floating charges are entirely 'alien' to one another. This chapter offers a more nuanced understanding of the two interests. In so doing, it provides a new frame of analysis of some of the key concepts in property law across common law and civil law jurisdictions. At a theoretical level, the significance of this analysis is in demonstrating how a common conceptual framework operates across the different jurisdictions and so it addresses one of the key challenges in comparative law, namely the difficulty in finding the

---

15 *Telford* (n 8) at 184 per Lord Fraser: 'the machinery for working out the rights of creditors under floating charges differs materially in Scotland from that in England, and I do not consider that any assistance … can be derived from the law or practice in England' and at 203 per Lord Cameron: 'while admittedly the concept of a floating charge is derived from England, it is essential to limit consideration of the character, effect and operation of a floating charge in Scotland to interpretation of the language of the statute by which it has been introduced'; Styles (n 11) at 237: 'any analysis of the *nature* of the floating charge in English law is completely inapplicable in Scotland because [the Scots] lack the very category of equitable rights which is the fundamental presumption upon which the English floating charge is based' [emphasis in the original] and at 239: 'consideration of English authorities must be eschewed… [as] completely and utterly irrelevant in Scots law'; see, too, A D J MacPherson, *The Floating Charge* (Edinburgh: Edinburgh Legal Education Trust, 2020) para. 2–02: 'interpretations of English law [of the floating charge prior to crystallisation] are of limited value in the Scottish context as they are dependent upon the background system of English law and equity' and cf para. 1–09. Cf R Rennie, 'The Tragedy of the Floating Charge in Scots Law' (1998) 3 SLPQ 169 at 170 (arguing that the '[examination of the English law concept in English cases before interpreting of the statute] would have … spared [the Scots courts] some of the agonising … every time the courts have had to adjudicate in a dispute between the holder of a crystallised floating charge and another creditor or party which an interest in the company's property').

common language, the 'grammar of property',[16] especially around equitable interests. At a practical level, this chapter shows that some parallels between English and Scottish floating charges can be drawn and suggests where they can be drawn.

The argument develops as follows. First, it is shown that the Scottish floating charge is relatively rigidly regulated, allowing parties to the charge agreement generally less freedom in shaping the content of the charge than under English law. However, it will be seen that the statutory regulation of the Scottish floating charge should not be viewed as always more limiting than the framework of English law. The second part of the analysis focuses on the conceptual nature of the floating charge. It will be argued that, contrary to some theories in both Scottish[17] and English[18] scholarship, floating charges in England and Scotland are best explained as a form of property right in charged assets, whose basic structure is the same across both jurisdictions, although some elements of this structure are modified more easily under English law. This applies the insights of the first part of the argument to the second and explains how the greater freedom that parties enjoy in shaping the charge under English law corresponds to the structure of the floating charge. An explanation is also provided as to why this new perspective matters.

16 M Graziadei, 'The Structure of Property Ownership and the Common Law/Civil Law Divide' in M Graziadei and L Smith (eds), *Comparative Property Law: Global Perspectives* (Cheltenham: Edward Elgar Publishing, 2017) 71, 76 and the literature cited there.

17 Styles (n 11) (conditional property right); MacPherson, *The Floating Charge* (n 15) para. 2–13 (potential (real) interest) and paras 6–88–6–91 (preference right); J Hardman, 'Hohfeld and the Scots Law Floating Charge', Chapter 7 within this volume (insolvency concept). See, too, sections C(3) and C(4) below.

18 W Gough, *Company Charges*, 2nd edn (London: Butterworths, 1996) Ch. 13 (floating charge as an unattached and non-immediate interest); R Pennington, 'The Genesis of the Floating Charge' (1960) 23 MLR 630 at 644–646 (mortgage of future assets theory); B McFarlane, *Structure of Property Law* (Oxford: Hart Publishing, 2007) at 599–601 (power to acquire a persistent right theory); R Stevens, 'Contractual Aspects of Debt Financing' in D Prentice and A Reisberg (eds), *Corporate Finance Law in the UK and EU* (Oxford: Oxford University Press, 2010) 213 at 221–222 (power *in rem* theory); R Goode, originally in *Legal Problems of Credit and Security* (London: Centre for Commercial Law Studies, 1982), now L Gullifer (ed), *Goode and Gullifer on Legal Problems of Credit and Security*, 6th edn (London: Sweet & Maxwell, 2017) para. 4–04 (fund theory).

B. PARTIES' FREEDOM TO CREATE AND SHAPE THE CHARGE

This section considers the extent to which parties are free to create the floating charge and to shape its contents under Scots and English law. The legal framework underpinning the floating charge in Scotland is entirely statutory whilst in England the charge is based primarily on judge-made law with some statutory regulation. The theme that this section explores is whether the greater statutory regulation necessarily means more restriction on parties' freedom.

It will first be seen, in section (1), that the early statutory attempts to facilitate lending against a charge over an undertaking (a precursor of the floating charge) were similarly restrictive in Scotland and England. The development of the English floating charge in the Chancery has been marked by the general willingness of the judges to enforce the terms of parties' agreement, even at the price of imposing obligations on third parties (section (2)). The Scottish Companies (Floating Charges) (Scotland) Act 1961 and now the Companies Act 1985 replicated the bare bones of the English floating charge but did not instil in Scots law the relaxed approach associated with the Chancery. The statutory regulation in England in some ways restricted parties' freedom in designing the charge but in others it played a facilitative role, promoting the exercise of parties' freedom. Sections (3)–(8) below illustrate these points.

(1) A common forerunner: charge over an undertaking under 1845 Acts

Before the boom of private companies in the UK, spurred on by the freedom to incorporate by registration,[19] the limitation of shareholders' liability on company's insolvency[20] and the recognition of private companies,[21] a

---

19 Joint Stock Companies Act 1844, which did not apply to Scotland with the exception of Scottish companies with premises in England, but it seems that it 'did not much needed to be applied': H A Shannon, 'The Coming of General Limited Liability' (1931) 2 *Economic History* 267 at 279.

20 Limited Liability Act 1855, which did not apply to Scotland. However, this Act and the Joint Stock Companies Act 1844 were later consolidated into Joint Stock Companies Act 1856, which applied across the UK. Subsequently, various consolidating statutes were passed, the most important of which was the Companies Act 1862.

21 Companies Act 1907. See also R Harris, 'The Private Origins of the Private Company: Britain 1862–1907' (2013) 33 OJLS 339.

number of entities,[22] especially of public utility, were incorporated by an Act of Parliament.[23] In relation to such statutory companies, a model set of rules was compiled in the Companies Clauses Consolidation Act 1845 (in England), and in the Companies Clauses Consolidation (Scotland) Act 1845. These rules apply[24] if the statute constituting the company incorporates the relevant 1845 Act.

One rule, contained in both of the 1845 Acts, is that statutory companies have a power to borrow by mortgaging 'the undertaking, and the future calls on the shareholders' of the company.[25] English courts interpreted this phrase under the 1845 Act to mean not the assets of the company but that the secured loan is to be paid from the earnings and returns on the completed work.[26] Under the 1845 (Scotland) Act, unlike the 1845 Act in England, a mortgage over an undertaking is said to take the 'full effect of an assignation in security duly completed'.[27] Prima facie the Scottish wording differs from the English rule, and suggests that assets within the undertaking become the property of the mortgagee. However, it appears to have been interpreted that the security operates similarly to the mortgage under the 1845 Act in England.[28] This means that under neither Act can the mortgagee

22 Other entities were incorporated by a royal charter.

23 Note, however, that at least some of the advantages of incorporation were available under Scots law earlier than in England: see R H Campbell, 'The Law and the Joint-Stock Company in Scotland' in P L Payne (ed), *Studies in Scottish Business History* (Oxford: Routledge, 1967) at 136; M Freeman et al., "Different and Better?' Scottish Joint-Stock Companies and the Law, c. 1720–1845' (2007) 122 *The English Historical Review* 61 at 62.

24 Both Acts continue to be in force.

25 Companies Clauses Consolidation Act 1845 s. 38 and Companies Clauses Consolidation (Scotland) Act 1845 s. 40: '[i]f the company be authorized by the special Act [i.e. act of incorporation] to borrow money on mortgage or bond, it shall be lawful for them … for securing [sic!] the repayment of the money so borrowed, with interest, to mortgage the undertaking and all future calls on shareholders'. Note, too, s. 2 in both Acts, defining 'undertaking' of a company as 'the undertaking or works, of whatever nature, which shall by the special Act be authorized to be executed'. The provisions to borrow against a mortgage on company's undertaking can be found also in special Acts of Parliament, see e.g. the Newburgh and North Fife Railway Act 1897. See also R G Anderson, 'Borrowing on the Undertaking: Scottish Statutory Companies', Chapter 2 within this volume.

26 *Gardner v London, Chatham and Dover Railway* (1866) 2 Ch App 201 at 217 per Cairns LJ: '[t]he term "undertaking" is the proper style, not for the ingredients, but for the completed work, and it is from the completed work that any return of moneys or earnings can arise', and 211 (Turner LJ agreeing); *Re Parker, sub nom Wignall v Park* [1891] 1 Ch 682 at 689–690 per Stirling J.

27 Companies Clauses Consolidation (Scotland) Act 1845 s. 43.

28 See W Gloag and J Irvine, *Law of Rights in Security, Heritable and Moveable: Including Cautionary Obligations* (Edinburgh: W. Green, 1897) 632–633, citing English cases: *Gardner* (n 26); *Potts v The Warwick and Birmingham Canal Navigation Co* (1853) Kay 142.

interfere with the going concern,[29] for example, by selling the company on a break-up basis.[30] However, the mortgagee does have a power to apply to the court to appoint a receiver[31] (judicial factor[32] in Scotland) to collect the income (tolls) and profits, and has priority over a judgment creditor of a company[33] as well as over other creditors in respect of proceeds of sale of an undertaking of an insolvent company.[34]

The 1845 legislation is sometimes said to have played a role in the emergence of the floating charge in England,[35] but it is not entirely clear what this role has been.[36] The comparison with Scots law suggests that it could not have been critical given that the Scots statute did not spur an analogous development, nor even influence the attitudes towards a security interest of this kind. That said, the charge over an undertaking under the 1845 Acts does functionally resemble the modern floating charge in broad terms[37]: it enables the company to carry on as a going concern whilst placing the creditor taking the charge over an undertaking in a relatively strong position against at least some other creditors of the company on enforcement, or against creditors seeking enforcement. Nevertheless, by comparison to the modern floating charge in England and Scotland, the statutory charge is a

29 *Furness v The Caterham Railway Co* (1859) 27 Beav 358 at 361 per Sir John Romilly MR; *Gardner* (n 26) at 217 per Cairns LJ.
30 *Walker v Milne* (1849) 11 Beav 507 at 518 per Lord Langdale MR.
31 Such a power was typically set out under the special Acts of Parliament that incorporated statutory companies: see *Fripp v The Chard Railway Company* 68 ER 1264; *Gardner* (n 26). And see Companies Clauses Consolidation Act 1845 s. 54. The receivership was of tolls and not profits only: *Griffin v Bishop's Castle Railway* (1867) 15 WR 1058, cited in P Walton and T Robinson (eds), *Kerr & Hunter on Receivers and Administrators*, 20th edn (London: Sweet & Maxwell, 2017) para. 2–48 fn 287. See, too, *Potts* (n 28) at 147 per Sir Page Wood VC and *Ames v The Trustees of Birkenhead Docks* (1855) 20 Beav 332 at 342–343 and 348 per Sir John Romilly MR.
32 See Companies Clauses Consolidation (Scotland) Act 1845 ss. 56–57; and *Harrington Evans Broad v Samuel Henry Day* (1888) 15 R 641 (note that the court would appoint the person nominated by the mortgagees unless there were objections).
33 *Furness* (n 29) at 362 per Sir John Romilly MR; *Legg v Mathieson* (1860) 2 Giff 71 (the mortgagee could restrain judgment creditors from taking possession of the company's land and chattels where taking chattels would interfere with the mortgagee's right to the undertaking and tolls). See too, *William Russell v The East Anglian Railway Co* (1850) 3 Mac & G 104.
34 *Re Liskeard and Caradon Railway Co* [1903] 2 Ch 681 at 688 per Swinfen Eady J. This has not been uncontroversial: *William Russell* (n 33) at 144 per Lord Truro LC.
35 Pennington (n 18) 638.
36 Lord Millett in *Brumark* (n 4) para. 5 suggests that the 1845 Act made it 'natural' to later use the formula that the company assigns 'its undertaking' but this is probably an overstatement given the earlier use of the phrase, e.g. in earlier Acts of Parliament incorporating companies, see e.g. *Hill v The Manchester and Salford Water Works Co* (1833) 5 B & Ad 866; *Doe d Myatt v St Helen's & Runcorn Gap Railway Co* (1841) 2 QB 364; *R v The Hull and Selby Railway Co* (1854) 5 De G M & G 872; *Steele v Harmer* (1845) 14 M & W 831.
37 J McGhee (ed), *Snell's Equity* (London: Sweet & Maxwell, 2020) para. 40–004.

rigid institution that does not allow the company and the chargee to modify the content of the charge through an agreement.

(2) Different attitudes towards parties' agreement

In England, the real catalyst for the emergence of the floating charge was the willingness of Chancery judges[38] to give effect to what parties agreed, even if it meant that third parties became bound.[39] This can be seen in two aspects in particular. One is the recognition of the grantor's power to grant a security interest over assets that the grantor does not own at the time when parties agree to create security in such assets, and to do so in a way that makes the security interest effective from the date of the agreement, not merely from, e.g. the date of acquisition of them by the grantor. The interest created binds execution creditors seeking to levy enforcement against encumbered assets, trustees in bankruptcy (insolvency officers) and certain other third parties. It is the agreement itself that creates a security interest and confers on the secured creditors rights in future assets, once these assets are acquired, as if they belonged to the grantor at the time of the contract. The principle was stated authoritatively by the House of Lords in *Holroyd v Marshall*[40] in the 1860s and again in the 1880s in *Tailby v Official Receiver*[41] but it had been well established before.[42]

Another aspect was the judicial recognition of parties' agreement to charge all present and future assets of the business.[43] In *Re Panama*, it was held that the charge over the company's 'undertaking, and the sums of money arising therefrom' meant 'a charge upon all the property of the company, past and future'.[44] Sir Giffard LJ expressed no doubts as to its validity and said that it entitled the chargee to be paid out of the property of the

---

38 More precisely, judges in the Court of Chancery, and since the Supreme Court of Judicature Acts 1873–75, the Chancery Division.

39 See generally *Brumark* (n 4) para. 5 per Lord Millett.

40 (1862) 10 HL Cas 191.

41 (1888) 13 App Cas 523.

42 (1888) 13 App Cas 523 at 546 per Lord Macnaghten: '*Holroyd v Marshall* laid down no new law, nor did it extend the principles of equity in the slightest degree'. See, e.g. *Hobson v Trevor* (1723) 2 P Wms 191; *Wright v Wright* (1750) 1 Ves Sen 409; *Lyde v Mynn* (1831) 4 Sim 505; *Douglas v Russell* (1831) 4 Sim 524; *Metcalfe v The Archbishop of York* (1836) 1 My & C 547; *Langton v Horton* (1842) 1 Hare 549.

43 Note that the floating charge in English law is thought to have originated from the cases referred to in this paragraph: see Pennington (n 18) at 630 and *Brumark* (n 4) para. 5 per Lord Millett.

44 *In re Panama, New Zealand, and Australian Royal Mail* (1869–1870) LR 5 Ch App 318 at 322 per Sir GM Giffard LJ (rejecting the argument that the charge covered only contracts and income arising from business, but not capital assets).

company on its winding up in priority to the general creditors.[45] The argument that a generic description of the assets covered by the security interest could make it invalid was firmly rejected by the highest authority in *Tailby*.[46]

A related development was that a charge over an undertaking/all assets was held not to preclude the chargor from conducting its business until default.[47] The argument that a charge over all assets would paralyse the business was rejected.[48]

There is no equivalent of the *Holroyd/Tailby* rule in Scotland; an obligation to assign a security over an asset or to transfer ownership of an asset does not create any proprietary interest in the asset (e.g. no trust).[49] Scots law requires an external act such as delivery of an asset to the creditor. For the same reason, only assets that are held by the grantor at the time the security interest is created can be subject matter of the security. In relation to goods and documentary intangibles, only assets that the grantor owns, or in relation to which it is authorised to create a pledge by its owner, can be pledged.[50]

As for intangible assets, assignment (assignation) of rights or claims not yet in existence is not generally possible. For example, if A is a trader of goods, and sells goods on credit to its customers, A cannot assign to B contractual rights against the future customers because an assignation under Scots law requires notice (intimation) to the debtor.[51] It is not possible to notify those who are not identifiable. There exists, however, the doctrine of accretion. It operates where A purports to assign to B its future claim that it might have against an identifiable person, say X. If before the claim against X arises, X is notified of the assignment to B, and A later does acquire a

---

45 *In re Panama, New Zealand, and Australian Royal Mail* at 322 per Sir GM Giffard LJ.

46 *Tailby* (n 41) at 534–535.

47 *Re Marine Mansions Company* (1867) LR 4 Eq 601; *Re Panama* (n 44) at 322–323 per Sir GM Giffard LJ; *In re Florence Land and Public Works Co, ex p Moor* (1878) 10 Ch D 530; *Moor v Anglo-Italian Bank* (1879) 10 Ch D 681; *In re Hamilton's Windsor Ironworks; ex p Pitman & Edwards* (1879) 12 Ch D 707 and *In re Colonial Trusts Corpn; ex p Bradshaw* (1879) 15 Ch D 465.

48 See *re Florence* (n 47) at 541 per Sir George Jessel MR; *Biggerstaff v Rowatt's Wharf Ltd* [1896] 2 Ch 93 at 101, 103 per Lindley and Lopes LJJ.

49 *Inglis v Mansfield* (1835) 3 Cl & F 362 (HL) at 382 per Lord Brougham; *Bank of Scotland v Liquidators of Hutchison, Main & Co Ltd* 1914 SC (HL) 1; *Gibson v Hunter Home Designs Ltd* 1976 SC 23.

50 Bell, *Principles* §1364; W M Gloag, 'Pledge' in *Encyclopaedia of the Laws of Scotland*, 3rd edn, Vol. 11 (1931) para. 773; A J M Steven, *Pledge and Lien* (Edinburgh: Edinburgh Legal Education Trust, 2008) para. 6–35.

51 Scottish Law Commission, *Report on Moveable Transactions* (Scot. Law Com. No. 249, 2017) at para. 3.11.

claim against X, the claim passes immediately and automatically from A to B, without the need for any further act.[52] The doctrine of accretion in Scots law operates as a very limited *Holroyd/Tailby* rule in the sense that it results in an effective assignment from the moment of agreement to assign (i.e. from the moment of the purported assignation), once a set of conditions is satisfied.

This shows that, by contrast to England, courts in Scotland have shown little willingness to depart from the relatively rigid property law principles, so much so that creation of a security interest in a future asset is only possible under Scots law in certain limited circumstances set out in statutes (under the floating charge; the charge under the Agricultural Credits (Scotland) Act 1929).[53]

(3) Person of the chargor

The type of person who can create a floating charge in Scotland and England is broadly similar, although in Scotland the person of the grantor is generally simpler to ascertain because no one can create a floating charge without a statute conferring on them the power to do so. The key example is the Companies Act 1985 s. 462(1),[54] which provides that:

> 'It is competent under the law of Scotland for an incorporated company (whether a company within the meaning of this Act or not), for the purpose of securing any debt or other obligation (including a cautionary obligation) incurred or to be incurred by, or binding upon, the company or any other person, to create in favour of the creditor in the debt or obligation a charge, in this Part referred to as a floating charge, over all or any part of the property (including uncalled capital) which may from time to time be comprised in its property and undertaking.'

---

52 *Buchanan v Alba Diagnostics Ltd* 2004 SC (HL) 9. See, too, R G Anderson, '*Buchanan v Alba Diagnostics*: Accretion of Title and Assignation of Future Patents' (2005) 9(3) Edin L Rev 457.

53 Note that landlord's hypothec is sometimes also listed as a form of security interest in after-acquired property in Scots law: see Scottish Law Commission, *Report on Moveable Transactions* (n 51) xi (definition of 'after-acquired property/assets'). Landlord's hypothec is a common law security for rent over the tenant's moveable property on the rented premises, and is now regulated under the Bankruptcy and Diligence etc. (Scotland) Act 2007 s. 208. It is a tacit security interest (arising by operation of law), and as such is not 'created': G Morse (ed), *Palmer's Company Law* release 171 (2020) para. 13.402.

54 See also Companies Act 1985 ss. 410–424, 463–466. See also Insolvency Act 1986 Parts II and III, especially s. 51 (a power of the chargee to appoint a receiver), and see paras 14–21 of Sch. B1 of the Insolvency Act 1986 (a power of a qualifying floating charge holder to appoint an administrator).

There is no equivalent provision in English law mandating registered companies to create a floating charge.[55] Their power to do so is based on common law.[56] There are, however, statutes in England as well as in Scotland that vest the power to create floating charges in various other corporate bodies. This is so in relation to limited liability partnerships,[57] registered co-operative and community societies,[58] building societies[59] and European economic groupings.[60]

It would seem that in neither jurisdiction an unincorporated person (an individual, sole trader, a Scots law regular partnership or partner in either an English or Scots law regular partnership) can create a floating charge. However, while in Scots law this appears to be a clear rule without exceptions, in English law the position is not uncontroversial, and there is at least one exception: floating charges can be created by farmers,[61] that is persons who are not incorporated companies or societies and who cultivate the holding for profit.[62] In Scotland, there are provisions for a floating charge in an agricultural context but the person of the grantor is a corporate body, a registered agricultural society.[63]

---

55 Note that in both jurisdictions, companies incorporated by a special Act of Parliament can create charges over their undertaking, as discussed at section B(1) above.

56 See discussion in section B(2) above.

57 Limited Liability Partnerships (Application of Companies Act 2006) Regulations 2009 (SI 2009/1804) reg. 32 and, in relation to Scotland, see too Limited Liability Partnerships Regulations 2001 (SI 2001/1090) Sch. 2, as amended by Limited Liability Partnerships (Application of Companies Act 2006) Regulations 2009 (SI 2009/1804) Sch. 3 para. 13.

58 Co-operative and Community Benefit Societies Act 2014 s. 59 (for registered societies whose registered office in England or Wales) and Co-operative and Community Benefit Societies Act 2014 s. 62 (for registered societies with a registered office in Scotland).

59 In England: Financial Services (Banking Reform) Act 2013 Sch. 9, para. 4 (repealing the restriction on building societies' power to create floating charges, contained in Building Societies Act 1986 s. 9B); in Scotland. Financial Services (Banking Reform) Act 2013 (Commencement (No. 8) and Consequential Provisions) Order 2015 (SI 2015/428) art. 4 (application of Part 18 of the Companies Act 1985).

60 In both England and Scotland: European Economic Interest Groupings Regulations 1989 (SI 1989/638) reg. 18 (applying the provisions of the Companies Acts 1985 and 2006 to these groupings).

61 Agricultural Credits Act 1928 s. 5. An agricultural charge (under s. 5(2)) can be fixed and/or floating. Note that the agricultural charge (under s. 5(1)) is a charge created by instrument in writing in favour of a 'bank' over 'the farming stock and other agricultural assets', which are defined in s. 5(7) and (7A). The charge must be registered at the Land Registry within seven clear days after the execution of agricultural charges: Agricultural Credits Act 1928 s. 9, otherwise it is void against everyone except the farmer.

62 Agricultural Credits Act 1928 s. 5(7).

63 Agricultural Credits (Scotland) Act 1929. Registration of these charges was abolished (under the Financial Services and Markets Act 2000 (Consequential Amendments and Repeals) Order 2001 (SI 2001/3649)) although it is not entirely clear why: Scottish Law Commission, *Discussion Paper on Moveable Transactions* (Scot. Law Com. DP No. 151) para. 6.21. In addition, considering that

In relation to other unincorporated persons under English law, it is in theory possible[64] to create a floating charge over some assets at least in the sense that the power to do so is not dependent on legislation mandating it (as in Scotland).[65] However, in practice, there are at least three key reasons why unincorporated persons do not grant floating charges (and why in relation to some assets they effectively cannot do that). First, English law imposes[66] various formal requirements in relation to security interests granted by individuals in a document (a bill)[67] over 'personal chattels' (goods).[68] This includes a requirement that goods must be 'specifically described' in the bill and that the grantor must own them at the time of the bill of sale.[69] Otherwise, the document, and the security interest, is void against everyone except the grantor in relation to the goods not specifically described,[70] or those that are not owned by the grantor.[71] This means that in practice a floating charge cannot be created over the goods within the Acts without falling foul of the formal requirements given that it is often created over generically described present and future assets. Floating charges by unincorporated grantors over assets that fall outside the Bills of Sale Acts, e.g. shares, book debts and other contractual rights[72] are theoretically possible but highly unlikely in practice

---

sequestration for rent for the landlord's hypothec has been abolished in Scotland, their enforceability outside insolvency is unclear: MacPherson, *The Floating Charge* (n 15) para. 4–32 fn 80, and the Scottish Law Commission recommended that agricultural charges be abolished: Scottish Law Commission, *Report on Moveable Transactions* (n 51) para. 38.13, and Draft Bill cl. 115.

64 Note, however, that as a matter of authority this has been doubted: *Aquachem Ltd v Delphis Bank Ltd* [2008] UKPC 7, [2008] BCC 648 at para. 6 per Lord Hoffmann; cf *National Westminster Bank Plc v Jones* [2001] 1 BCLC 98 para. 116 per Neuberger J.

65 See *Re Anchor Line Ltd* [1937] Ch 483 at 488 per Luxmoore J.

66 The main acts are Bills of Sale Act 1878 and the Bills of Sale Act 1878 (Amendment) Act 1882 (referred to as the 1878 Act and the 1882 Act respectively; and jointly as the Bills of Sale Acts). The Bills of Sale Acts have no application to Scotland: see *Scottish Transit Trust v Scottish Land Cultivators* 1955 SC 254 at 263 per Lord Russell.

67 The Bills of Sale Acts do not apply to security interests granted orally but security interests are nearly always, if not always, taken in documents.

68 The expression 'personal chattels' means 'goods, furniture, and other articles capable of complete transfer by delivery': the Bills of Sale Act 1878 s. 4. The term used here is 'goods' instead of 'personal chattels'.

69 The only exceptions are growing crops and replacement plant, trade machinery, fixtures in substitution for those specifically described: the Bills of Sale Act 1878 (Amendment) Act 1882 s. 6.

70 See the Bills of Sale Act 1878 (Amendment) Act 1882 s. 4 (a bill is void against everyone except the grantor in relation to specifically described chattels, which the grantor does not own at the time of the execution of the bill of sale).

71 See Bills of Sale Act 1878 (Amendment) Act 1882 s. 5. See, e.g. *Chapman v Wilson* [2010] EWHC 1746.

72 See, too, P Giddins, 'Floating Mortgages by Individuals: Are They Conceptually Possible?' (2011) 3 JIBFL 125 at 128 (an argument that not-yet-manufactured goods are not capable of delivery and so fall outside the definition of 'chattels').

for the remaining reasons, now discussed. Secondly, assets over which a floating charge might theoretically be created might not be available to some individuals: for example, some consumers might not have shares or contractual rights they could offer as security. Even if individuals do have such assets available (which might be the case in relation to, e.g. traders), they might prefer to use other forms of raising finance against such assets, e.g. outright assignment.[73] Thirdly, the lack of provision for the publicity (registration) of such charges makes any potential lending against such security unattractive from the lender's perspective.[74] This is because floating charges, as equitable interests, are defeasible by, e.g. disponees of legal title to the asset without notice of the charge, such as lenders, taking a legal security right. Without a register of security, facilitating provision of actual or constructive notice of the security, it would be easy to defeat the chargee's interest. This is an example of an area where a statutory framework that provides for registration of the charge promotes secured lending. In practice, lenders do not usually lend against such an unregistrable and unregistered charge where the risk of fraud is high, especially where there exist readily available alternatives (such as assignment) of achieving the same goal.[75]

In result, the question of who can grant the floating charge is answered similarly in England and in Scotland, despite the different routes of arriving at the answer.

(4) Charged assets

Any asset can be subject to a floating charge in English law. If the chargor has only a limited interest in charged asset while another party also has an interest in that asset, the position of the creditor holding the floating charge *vis-à-vis* that other will depend on general priority rules, but this does not preclude the chargor from creating a floating charge. At first glance, Scots law appears to be the same as the statute provides that the floating charge is

---

73 If it is a general assignment of book debts (i.e. other than specified debts or debts owed under specified contracts), it is registrable under the Bills of Sale Acts by virtue of the Insolvency Act 1986 s. 344.

74 This is not to suggest that the registration system under the Bills of Sale Acts is conducive to lending; quite the opposite. See e.g. M Bridge, 'Form, Substance and Innovation in Personal Property Security Law' (1992) JBL 1 at 4.

75 If it is a general assignment of book debts (i.e. other than specified debts or debts owed under specified contracts), it is registrable under the Bills of Sale Acts by virtue of the Insolvency Act 1986 s. 344.

granted over 'property and undertaking'.[76] However, these words appear to be interpreted restrictively by the House of Lords in *Sharp v Thomson* as not including property that the chargor agreed to sell and in relation to which the disposition was delivered but not yet registered in the land register.[77]

A related issue is whether a trustee company can create a floating charge over trust property. In English law, it is not unusual for a trustee to have a power to borrow,[78] which generally includes the power to borrow against trust assets and so, to create a floating charge.[79] It is a separate issue whether such borrowing is within the proper exercise of the power, is defective or outside the power altogether. If it is outside the power, creation of a charge over trust assets will constitute a breach of trust,[80] but does not necessarily invalidate the charge.

For some time, it was not entirely clear whether such a charge over trust assets was registrable at Companies House as it was not clear against whose name (trustee's or beneficiary's) such a charge could be registered: neither the trustee company's name nor the beneficiaries' names seem appropriate: the trustee does not own the trust assets beneficially while the beneficiaries' names (even assuming they are companies) are not the ones 'creating' the charge over the trust assets.[81] The Companies Act 2006, following the 2013 reform,[82] clarifies that registration of a charge over trust assets is against the name of the corporate trustee. It is possible to deliver to the registrar a statement to the effect that the company, acting as a trustee, granted a charge over the trust property or undertaking.[83]

By contrast, in Scotland, there is a view that trust assets cannot be the subject matter of the floating charge, not even if the debenture provides that

---

76 Companies Act 1985 s. 462(1).

77 *Sharp* (n 5).

78 An unrestricted power to borrow under general law is limited (see *Suenson-Taylor's Settlement Trusts* [1974] 1 WLR 1280) but broad powers are often expressly or impliedly conferred: see STEP's *The Standard Provisions of the Society of Trust and Estate Practitioners*, 2nd edn (2011) para. 14 (power to borrow for any purpose). See generally L Tucker et al., *Lewin on Trusts*, 20th edn (London: Sweet & Maxwell, 2020) paras 36–120–36–123.

79 In practice, this relates to corporate trustees only; see below.

80 *Royal Brunei Airlines v Tan* [1995] 2 AC 378 at 390 per Lord Nicholls.

81 The arguments are laid out in more detail in *Goode and Gullifer on Legal Problems* (n 18) para. 2–22. Note the Companies Act 2006 in s. 859A (and its predecessor, s. 860) provides for registration 'where a company creates a charge'. There is no mention of the charge being over, e.g. the company's assets but see text below in this section.

82 Companies Act 2006 (Amendment of Part 25) Regulations 2013 (SI 2013/600) reg. 2 and Sch. 1.

83 Companies Act 2006 s. 859J.

the floating charge covers trust property.[84] MacPherson, for example, argues that in Scots law a floating charge can cover (at most) the whole of the company's property and undertaking, 'and this does not include trust property'.[85] The reason is that the company trustee holds in fact two patrimonies: a general patrimony (comprising company's property and undertaking) and a special trust patrimony, which are separate.[86] This view is consistent with the decision in *Tay Valley v CF Financial Services*.[87] A company (Tay Valley) granted a floating charge in favour of a bank over all of its assets. It later entered into an invoice discounting agreement with CF, meaning it agreed to sell to CF its present and future book debts. The arrangement did not constitute a formal assignment (assignation) under Scots law. The question was whether these book debts continued to be part of the company's property and undertaking. If they did, the floating charge would have attached to them when the bank appointed a receiver. The Second Division held that the invoice discounting agreement amounted to a declaration of trust over the book debts. It also held that the creation of a trust was 'sufficient to divest the company of the beneficial right to the debts'[88] on the facts. Thus, the debts, as trust assets, did not become encumbered with the floating charge. The reasons why trust assets are no longer trustee company's assets are relatively brief, as all three Lords focus on the logically prior question, namely why the arrangement was a trust.[89] The court noted that the counsel for the bank had raised a point whether the trust over debts could be a 'latent trust which could not defeat the rights of the bank as holder of the floating charge' but that this was not argued because the 'parties had been unable to agree whether the holder of the floating charge knew ... of the existence of the invoice discounting agreement before the charge crystallised'.[90]

Thus, at one level, Scots and English are very different, with English law

84 G Morse (ed), *Palmer's Company Law* (n 53) para. 13.402; H L MacQueen and Lord Eassie (eds), *Gloag and Henderson: The Law of Scotland*, 14th edn (Edinburgh: W. Green, 2017) para. 36.03; I M Fletcher and R Roxburgh, *Greene and Fletcher on the Law and Practice of Receivership in Scotland*, 3rd edn (London: Bloomsbury Professional, 2005) para. 2.42.

85 A D J MacPherson, 'Floating Charges and Trust Property in Scots Law: A Tale of Two Patrimonies?' (2018) 22(1) Edin L Rev 1 at 9.

86 G L Gretton, 'Trusts Without Equity' (2000) 49(3) ICLQ 599.

87 1987 SLT 207.

88 1987 SLT 207, the header.

89 See 1987 SLT 207 at 212 per Lord Robertson, and at 218–219 per Lord McDonald (at 218–219); see, too, *Allan's Trustees v Lord Advocate* 1971 SC (HL) 45, 1971 SLT 62 at 63–64 per Lord Reid.

90 *Tay Valley* (n 87) at 217 per Lord Dunpark and see 213 per Lord Robertson and 219 per Lord McDonald.

appearing more flexible in allowing for a floating charge to be created over all assets while Scots law does not. However, in some circumstances there is less to this difference than first meets the eye. A charge over trust assets is a good example. It is not entirely clear what consequences follow the lack of registration of such a charge under English law. Section 859H of the Companies Act 2006 provides that a charge that is not registered within the prescribed period is invalid 'so far as any security on the company's property or undertaking is conferred by it' against the insolvency officers and creditors of the company.[91] It is not entirely clear what 'company's property' means but on literal reading it seems unlikely to include trust assets. If this is true, failure to file the charge over trust assets would not invalidate it. Even if the charge over trust assets does become invalid, it does not necessarily mean that the insolvency officer or creditor could access the trust assets as if no trust had been created. Under English law, the trust assets do not become part of the trustee's estate. On the commencement of administration or winding-up, assets held on trust by the insolvent company-trustee fall outside the regime,[92] so the liquidator or administrator of the insolvent trustee cannot use trust assets to distribute to the trustee's creditors.[93]

(5) Debentures

In English law, unlike in Scots law, floating charges are often granted by companies in debentures that also include fixed security interests. Debenture means an 'instrument [that] imports an obligation or covenant to pay ... [which is] in most cases ... accompanied by some charge or security'.[94]

---

91 See section B(8) below.
92 See *Barclays Bank Ltd v Quistclose Investments Ltd* [1970] AC 567 (HL); *Carreras Rothmans Ltd v Freeman Matthews Treasure Ltd* [1985] Ch 207; *Re Kayford Ltd* [1975] 1 WLR 279; *In re Carluccio's Ltd (in administration)* [2020] EWHC 886 (Ch) para. 33 per Snowden J.
93 The same applies to other insolvency officers (such as an administrative receiver or provisional liquidator). Note that the insolvency officer might inadvertently seize or dispose of property not belonging beneficially to the company. When this happens, the statute provides the liquidator with a broad protection under the Insolvency Act 1986 s. 234(3) and (4).
94 *Edmonds v Blaina Furnaces Co* (1887) 36 Ch D 215 at 219 per Chitty J (noting also that '[t]he term itself imports a debt – an acknowledgment of a debt' and that debentures can either be secured or unsecured). See, too, *British India Steam Navigation Co v The Commissioners of Inland Revenue* (1881) 7 QBD 165 at 172 (Lindley J); *Lemon v Austin Friars Investment Trust Ltd* [1926] Ch 1 at 12–13, 15 per Sir Frederick Pollock MR, at 17 per Warrington LJ; *Knightsbridge Estates Trust Ltd v Byrne* [1940] AC 613 at 621–622 per Viscount Maugham. Note, however, that what a debenture means is a matter of contractual interpretation: *Fons HF v Corporal Ltd, Pillar Securitisation S.à.r.l.* [2014] EWCA Civ 304 at paras 38–39 per Patten LJ, and see para. 47 per Gloster LJ.

Fixed charges, which put the creditor in a better position on the chargor's insolvency than floating charges (as discussed in section B(8) below), are taken over assets such as land, equipment, certain bank accounts and insurance policies, while the floating charge is taken over any other assets of the chargor. By structuring the security in this way, the chargee obtains the benefit of the best possible security interest over as many assets as it can, while the floating charge, which offers worse protection than the fixed charge, 'sweeps' any assets not covered by the fixed charge. Related to this in practice is a situation where the parties expressed the charge to be fixed in the debenture but the charge fails as a fixed charge and is recharacterised as floating.[95] The risk of recharacterisation is problematic but it exists whether or not a fixed charge is created in the same document as the floating charge. In any case, 'demotion' of a fixed charge to a floating charge upon recharacterisation is better, from the lender's perspective' than its avoidance, which could in theory be another way of levying consequences against a chargee who fails to ensure the charge is fixed but it is not a way that has ever been considered in this context by English courts.

In Scotland, secured and unsecured debentures are taken, too, but where the debenture is secured it cannot effectively provide for both fixed and floating charges. The obvious reason is that Scots law does not recognise a non-possessory fixed security over moveable property. Scots law does, however, recognise pledge of tangibles (corporeal moveable) and assignment (assignation) of intangible (incorporeal moveable) assets, so theoretically, it would be possible for debentures to include floating charges and, say, assignations. However, assignation requires more than an intention to assign immediately and unconditionally (expressed typically in a document, which in theory could be a debenture). They require a notification (intimation) to the debtor.[96] It might, therefore, be thought that there is little advantage of including the agreement for a pledge or assignment in the debenture except perhaps any cost-saving associated with negotiating two or more documents rather than one.

It may well be that the practice of granting various types of security in standalone documents in Scotland, and in one document in England, is driven by the conservatism of practitioners, more than the law.[97]

---

95 See *Brumark* (n 4); *Spectrum* (n 4).
96 See *Stamfield's Creditors v Scot's Children* (1696) IV Bro Supp 344.
97 Thanks to Jonathan Hardman for this point regarding Scotland. I borrowed the 'conservatism' tag from him, which helps explain English practice, too.

(6) Registration

Registration of the floating charge created by companies is governed in both jurisdictions by the Companies Act 2006 and, since the reforms of this Act in 2013,[98] one registration scheme applies in both jurisdictions[99] with some small differences noted below. The floating charge, once created by a company, is registered at Companies House when a statement of particulars is delivered to the registrar together with a certified copy of the instrument creating the floating charge. Considering the similarity of the regime in England and Scotland, it would not be productive to discuss its details in this chapter, but it is illuminating to make two observations.

The first point is that while the registration regime could be seen as limiting parties' freedom in English law (as explained below), in Scotland, it is just part of the wider statutory regulation that institutes how the floating charge takes effect. Under the Companies Act 2006, any charge[100] granted by a UK-registered[101] company is registrable at Companies House.[102] Failure to register the charge within twenty-one days[103] from the moment of its creation means that it is void against certain persons: the liquidator, administrator and creditors.[104] 'Creditors' has been interpreted by the courts to mean creditors who have a property right or interest in the charged

---

98 Companies Act 2006 (Amendment to Part 25) Regulations 2013 (SI 2013/600).

99 It also applies to companies registered in Wales and Northern Ireland. For charges created prior to 6 April 2013, the regime was governed by Companies Act 2006 Part 25 Ch. 2 for companies registered in Scotland, and by Companies Act 2006 Pt 25 Ch. 1 for companies registered in England, Wales or Northern Ireland.

100 There are some exceptions: Companies Act 2006 s. 859A(6).

101 Charges granted by overseas companies are no longer registrable at Companies House since the so-called 'Slavenburg register' (*NV Slavenburg's Bank v Intercontinental Natural Resources Ltd* [1980] 1 All ER 955) has been abolished under Overseas Companies (Execution of Documents and Registration of Charges) (Amendment) Regulations 2011 (SI 2011/2194). Recognition of a floating charge created overseas is a different issue: unlike in English law, in Scots law, the key problem is whether it was created by an entity incorporated in the relevant jurisdiction, see Scottish Law Commission and the Law Commission, *Partnership Law: A Joint Consultation Paper* (Law Com. CP No. 159 and Scot. Law Com. DP No. 111, 2000) para. 23.13.

102 Companies Act 2006 s. 859A(1).

103 Companies Act 2006 s. 859A(4), but the period can be extended by court order: s. 859F. Note that the period was extended by legislation to thirty-one days due to the pandemic for charges created between 6 June 2020 and 4 April 2021: Companies etc. (Filing Requirements) (Temporary Modifications) Regulations 2020 (SI 2020/645).

104 Companies Act 2006 s. 859H.

assets,[105] for example, secured creditors,[106] execution creditors[107] and lienees.[108] An unregistered charge is not void against third parties that are not mentioned in the statute: it does not become void for want of registration against, e.g. unsecured creditors (up until the company goes into administration or liquidation), or outright purchasers of charged assets.[109]

Thus, a charge agreement itself creates an 'imperfect' charge, which is only perfected when registered at Companies House. In English law, this is a good illustration of the limits on the parties' freedom to create a security interest enforceable against third parties in a way other rights (e.g. trusts) are. Chancery judges have not been willing to go against the statute to impose obligations on third parties.[110] This limitation exists for a good reason: to protect third parties dealing with the company. By contrast, from the perspective of Scots law, a security right that takes effect upon its creation but before an additional act, such as registration or delivery of an asset to the creditor, is very unusual.[111] It is unsurprising that the floating charge in Scotland is so controversial.

The second point is about how the statutory regime facilitates (in Scotland) and enhances (in England) parties' freedom to shape the content of the floating charge, specifically its priority in relation to other security interests through registration of ranking agreements and negative pledges.

---

105 *Re Ehrmann Brothers Ltd* [1906] 2 Ch 697 at 704 per Vaughan Williams LJ; *Re Cardiff Workmen's Cottage Co Ltd* [1906] 2 Ch 627 at 628–629 per Buckley J.

106 *Re Monolithic Building Co* [1915] 1 Ch 643 (CA); *Re Ashpurton Estates Ltd* [1983] Ch 110 at 119 and 123 per Lord Brightman.

107 *Ashpurton Estates* (n 106) at 123 per Lord Brightman.

108 *Goode and Gullifer on Legal Problems of Credit and Security* (n 18) para. 2–23.

109 See *Re Overseas Aviation Engineering (GB) Ltd* [1963] Ch 24 (CA) at 38 (Lord Denning MR); *Stroud Architectural Services Ltd v John Laing Construction Ltd* [1994] 2 BCLC 276. There was an attempt to make an unregistered charge void against purchasers of charged asset under Companies Act 1989 but the relevant provisions never entered into force. And see a similar attempt prior to the 2013 reform of Companies Act 2006 (n 98) under proposal F of the Department for Business, Innovation and Skills, *Government Response, Consultation on Registration of Charges Created by Companies and Limited Liability Partnerships* (December 2010) prior to the 2013 reform (see n 99), which was later abandoned: see Department for Business, Innovation and Skills, *Revised Scheme for Registration of Charges Created by Companies and Limited Liability Partnerships: Proposed Revision of Part 25, Companies Act 2006* (August 2011, URN 11/1108) para. 37.

110 See the discussion in *Re Monolithic Building Co* [1915] 1 Ch 643 (CA).

111 This is one of the key reasons why the 'fit' of the floating charges with the general principles of Scots property law has been lambasted. See, e.g. Styles (n 11) 84: 'It would be much more satisfactory if floating charges only came into effect, like standard securities, on the day of their registration. This would … fit better … with … Scots property law'. Note that this assumes it is correct to treat the floating charge as a form of a property right, on which see the discussion below part C.

One example is an inter-creditor agreement whereby two (or more) lenders each hold or seek to take a floating charge from the same company (or one holds a floating charge while the other a fixed security). Another is a provision in the floating charge for a negative pledge, i.e. a clause that prohibits or restricts the creation of a fixed or floating security that would rank prior to, or *pari passu* with, the floating charge. Unlike English law, Scots law requires such 'instruments of alteration' to be registered against each floating charge within twenty-one days of the date of the execution of the instrument.[112] If not filed, the alteration is void against the liquidator, administrator or a creditor of the company. [113] Under English law, their registration is voluntary.[114]

The restrictive treatment in Scotland of ranking agreements and negative pledges illustrates the more cautious approach, compared to English law, regarding the recognition of the third-party effect of contractual provisions and unilateral grants. In Scotland, such provisions are not effective unless publicised on the public register. Under English law, their enforceability depends on notice that the relevant third party has of them.[115] While it is not entirely clear what registration is a notice of and to whom, it seems that a party actually searching the register has actual notice of what they search,[116] which at the very least will be the particulars.[117] This is one reason why the introduction in 2013 of the facility to indicate the existence of the negative pledge in the particulars of the charge[118] has been useful.

---

112 Companies Act 1985 s. 466.
113 Companies Act 1985 s. 466(4)(a).
114 See Companies Act 2006 ss. 859D and 859O. These also apply to companies registered in Scotland, but they do not preclude the operation of the Companies Act 1985.
115 There are complex issues surrounding the extent to which registration at Companies House constitutes as notice under English law: see H Beale, M Bridge, L Gullifer and E Lomnicka, *The Law of Security and Title-based Financing*, 3rd edn (Oxford: Oxford University Press, 2018) paras 12.04–12.17.
116 The issue of who has constructive notice, and of what, is more complex: see L Gullifer and M Raczynska, 'The English Law of Personal Property Security: Under-reformed?' in L Gullifer and O Akseli (eds), *Secured Transactions Law Reform: Principles, Policies and Practice* (London: Bloomsbury, 2016) 271 at 284–286.
117 See *English & Scottish Mercantile Investment Co v Brunton* [1892] 2 QB 700; *Wilson v Kelland* [1910] 2 Ch 306; *Siebe Gorman & Co Ltd v Barclays Bank* [1979] 2 Lloyd's Rep 142 at 160; *Welch v Bowmaker (Ireland) Ltd* [1980] IR 251; *Re Salthill Properties Ltd* (2004) IEHC 145.
118 Companies Act 2006 s. 859D.

(7) Crystallisation

There is a difference between the two jurisdictions in relation to crystallisation ('attachment' in Scots law, although the two terms seem to be interchangeable[119]). Crystallisation of the charge terminates the authority of the chargor to dispose of the assets in the ordinary course of business. In that sense it is correct to say (as is often the case) that the floating charge becomes a fixed charge. In English law, crystallisation takes place on the occurrence of certain events such as cessation of business[120] or appointment of a receiver[121] but it is also possible (and, indeed, common) to specify in the debenture when the charge is to crystallise, which could be events that denote cessation of trading but need not.[122] Parties are also free to agree whether the charge is to crystallise upon the chargee giving the chargor a notice or whether it is to crystallise automatically on the occurrence of a particular event.[123] These provisions are included in debentures as a way of controlling the behaviour of the chargor (if nothing else, by providing the chargee with a negotiating leverage) and protecting the chargee's interests. However, automatic crystallisation clauses may well be counterproductive as they could lead to the entire clause being ignored on the basis of a waiver, if normal trading continues once a crystallising event takes place, so care when drafting them is advised.[124]

Such crystallisation clauses are not effective in Scots law.[125] Floating charges in Scots law crystallise in circumstances prescribed by the statute,

---

119 Scottish Law Commission, *Report on Moveable Transactions* (n 51) para. 17.31.
120 *Re Brightlife Ltd* [1987] Ch 200 at 212 per Hoffmann J; *Re The Real Meat Co Ltd* [1996] BCC 254 at 261 per Chadwick J.
121 *Evans v Rival Granite Quarries Ltd* [1910] 2 KB 979 at 986–987 per Vaughan Williams LJ and at 1000 per Buckley LJ.
122 See e.g. *Goode and Gullifer on Legal Problems of Credit and Security* (n 18) paras 4–31–4.61.
123 *Re Brightlife* (n 120) at 212–215 per Hoffmann J. For some statutory restrictions, see Insolvency Act 1986 s. A22(3) introduced by the Corporate Insolvency and Governance Act 2020.
124 *Goode and Gullifer on Legal Problems of Credit and Security* (n 18) paras 4–57 and 4–62–4–63. Note, too, that crystallisation under English law, especially in the context of automatic crystallisation clauses, has led to a question whether de-crystallisation ('re-floating') of the charge is possible. The balance of opinion is that it is (see e.g. Lightman, Moss, Anderson, Fletcher and Snowden, *Lightman & Moss on The Law of Administrators and Receivers of Companies*, 6th edn (London: Sweet & Maxwell, 2017) paras 3–095–3–099; Beale et al., *The Law of Security and Title-based Financing* (n 115) para. 6.86; T N Parsons, *Lingard's Bank Security Documents*, 7th edn (London: LexisNexis, 2019) para. 9.31). A comparison with Scotland provides an additional reason in support of this view because decrystallisation is recognised in Scots law under statute: Insolvency Act 1986 s. 62(6).
125 *Norfolk House Plc (in receivership) v Repsol Petroleum Ltd* 1992 SLT 235; D Cabrelli, 'The Curious Case of the 'Unreal' Floating Charge' 2005 SLT (News) 127 at 130–131. See also J Hardman, *A Practical Guide to Granting Corporate Security in Scotland* (Edinburgh: W. Green, 2018) para. 6–23; MacPherson, *The Floating Charge* (n 15) para. 3–10.

namely: (i) appointment of the liquidator[126]; (ii) appointment of a receiver in respect of the charged assets[127]; (iii) filing of notice by the administrator at Companies House that the company's assets are insufficient to satisfy all creditors' claims in full[128]; and (iv) when the court gives the administrator the permission to pay a creditor who is neither secured nor preferential.[129] The reason why the statute does not permit for the parties to provide in the agreement that the charge would crystallise automatically is that an attached floating charge is equivalent to a fixed charge, which Scots law does not recognise. If the reform proposals[130] to introduce a new fixed non-possessory security (a statutory pledge) in Scotland are adopted, and it would in principle be possible to grant statutory pledge and floating charge over the same type of assets, this policy argument would fall away because parties could agree that the floating charge would crystallise into a statutory pledge. Whether this would be desirable or compatible with the rest of the proposed new regime is another matter and not addressed here.

Until Scotland adopts the Moveable Transactions (Scotland) Bill, it is clear that parties enjoy greater freedom under English law to shape the content of the floating charge when it comes to determining when the charge crystallises.

(8) Enforcement

Under both Scots and English law, where the charge is a 'qualifying floating charge', parties can set out in the security agreement the circumstances in which the chargee has a power to enforce the floating charge by appointing an administrator.[131] The events that the parties list as triggers for the appointment of an administrator are similar.[132] In relevant circumstances, parties can also state the circumstances for the appointment of an administrative receiver (in Scotland – a receiver).[133] If the floating charge is not a qualifying floating charge, in both jurisdictions the chargee may appoint a receiver (in this context, in Scotland, the word 'receiver' does not mean administrative receiver). In England the power to appoint a receiver and

---

126 Companies Act 1985 s. 463(1).
127 Insolvency Act 1986 ss. 53(7) and 54(6).
128 Insolvency Act 1986 Sch. B1 para. 115(3).
129 Insolvency Act 1986 Sch. B1 para. 115(1B) *juncto* para. 65(3)(b).
130 See Scottish Law Commission, *Report on Moveable Transactions* (n 51).
131 Insolvency Act 1986 Sch. B1 para. 14.
132 See Insolvency Act 1986 Sch. B1 para. 14(2)(c) and 14(2)(d).
133 Insolvency Act 1986 ss. 52 and 72A–72GA.

the receiver's powers are almost invariably a matter of charge agreement whereas in Scotland the power is based on statute[134] and its exercise and scope appears more limited than in England. For example, there is a belief in Scots law that a receiver cannot be appointed over part of the assets subject to the charge.[135]

Distribution of proceeds of assets by a distributing administrator or liquidator in both jurisdictions follows the same ranking[136]: the holder of a floating charge is subordinated to claims secured by a fixed security (in England),[137] or a standard security, an assignation or a pledge (in Scotland), insolvency expenses,[138] preferential claims[139] and prescribed part set aside for unsecured creditors.[140]

While enforcement of floating charges through an administrator and on liquidation is in both jurisdictions very similar, it does seem that parties under English law generally make greater use of the freedom to provide in the charge agreement for enforcement outside administration and insolvency.

C. THE NATURE OF THE FLOATING CHARGE PRIOR TO CRYSTALLISATION ('ATTACHMENT' IN SCOTS LAW)

One of the most difficult issues in both English and Scots law is determining the nature of the right that the creditor has when it holds a floating charge prior to crystallisation. The question typically asked is whether it is a property (real) right or a personal right that only becomes a property

---

134 Insolvency Act 1986 s. 51.
135 See discussion and literature cited in Hardman, *A Practical Guide to Granting Corporate Security in Scotland* (n 125) para. 6–28.
136 The distribution waterfall is not spelled out in insolvency legislation, but see *Re Nortel GmbH (in liquidation)*, also known as *Bloom v Pensions Regulator* [2013] UKSC 52 para. 39 per Lord Neuberger (with whom Lord Mance, Lord Clarke and Lord Toulson agreed), *Re Lehman Brothers International (Europe) (in administration) (No. 4)* [2017] UKSC 38 para. 17 per Lord Neuberger, *Re LB Holdings Intermediate 2 Ltd (In Administration)* [2020] EWHC 1681 (Ch) para. 87 per Marcus Smith J. An inter-creditor agreement may well change the order of priority between consensual creditors.
137 Technically, assets secured by a fixed charge are outside the insolvency waterfall: see *LB Holdings Intermediate* (n 136) para. 87 per Marcus Smith J.
138 See e.g. Insolvency Act 1986 s. 176ZA and Sch. B1 paras 99(3) and 116.
139 See Insolvency Act 1986 s. 175 and Sch. B1 paras 65(2) and 116; and Companies Act 1985 s. 463(3). Note that the Crown has gained the status of a secondary preferential creditor in respect of some taxes as of 1 December 2020: Insolvency Act 1986 Sch. 6 para. 15D (and consequential amendment to s. 386 of the 1986 Act).
140 See Insolvency Act 1986 s. 176A.

right on crystallisation.[141] This conceptual issue matters in practice as in various contexts different rules apply to rights depending on whether they are personal or proprietary, e.g. in conflict-of-laws rules. In short, the difficulty is as follows. If the floating charge is a personal right, it is hard to see why in certain circumstances it is capable of binding third parties and how it can transform into a property right without a fresh act, enabling the creditor at a critical moment to gain a significant advantage over unsecured creditors on insolvency, where the general preferred approach is that creditors share *pari passu*. If it is a property right, the challenge is to explain the susceptibility of this right to disposals of the charged assets by the chargor without chargee's consent, and why the susceptibility ceases on, for example, crystallisation.

Taking a view in this debate requires first to consider what right constitutes a property right[142] (section (1) below).[143] It will then be seen that the best view is that the floating charge prior to crystallisation can be seen as a weak form of property right in both English and Scots law (section (2) below), and that it is unsatisfactory to view it as a conditional real right (section (3) or a preference right (4). However, it will be argued that property law principles are insufficient to explain the nature of the right, and it is necessary to also resort to principles underpinning agency law (section (5) below).

(1) Property right v personal right

The issue how a property right differs from a personal right has been much debated in both Civilian[144] and common law scholarship. In each, it is

---

141 That the floating charge becomes a property right on crystallisation in Scotland was said in, e.g. *Telford* (n 8) 194 per Lord President Clyde and 198 per Lord Guthrie (this is in the context of the Companies (Floating Charges) (Scotland) Act 1961 s. 1(2), but the wording of the current Companies Act 1985 is very similar except that the charge is said to crystallise in a wider range of circumstances). However, note discussion below regarding preference right: section C(4).

142 For the purpose of the discussion, it is assumed the terms 'proprietary right' or 'proprietary interest', which are sometimes encountered in the context of English law, are synonyms of 'property right'.

143 It might be thought that an alternative method of checking whether a particular right is a property right is to see whether it is included on the list of property rights (*numerus clausus*): K Reid, 'Obligations and Property: Exploring the Border' (1997) *Acta Juridica* 225 at 227–228. However, this would not be a particularly helpful method when faced with the need to determine *which* rights are on the list, and whether a right not generally on the list should be on it. In any case, this still requires an understanding of what a property right is.

144 The discussion of Civilian scholarship is based mainly on French scholarship, which has rarely influenced Scottish authors but since Scots law is also a product of *ius commune*, similar

possible to identify two major sets of views. One Civilian theory (referred to as 'traditional' or 'classical') is that a property right confers various 'powers' (liberties)[145] over an asset,[146] which are enforceable against the world, whilst a personal right confers powers against a person.[147] A broadly similar view of property that developed in common law scholarship is the 'bundle of rights' view.[148] Taking ownership as its focal point, it states that an owner enjoys various incidents (rights/liberties) such as a right to use, possess or manage.[149] One key problem with those views is that the emphasis on incidents or liberties fails as a criterion of distinction between property and personal rights.[150]

reasoning has developed: S Demeyere, *Real Obligations at the Edge of Contract and Property* (Cambridge: Intersentia, 2020) para. 46. See also Gretton and Steven, *Property, Trusts and Succession* (n 9) at para. 1.18.

145 It is unclear in what sense the proponents of the 'traditional' theory use the word 'power'. It probably is used to denote acts within volitional control of the actor that rely on substantial factual element (e.g. being in a position to make use of something, or to destroy it), so they could be seen as a Hohfeldian privileges (liberties): see W N Hohfeld, 'Some Fundamental Conceptions as Applied in Judicial Reasoning' (1913) 23 Yale LJ 16 at 32. Where these acts have legal consequences (e.g. a physical destruction of a thing destroys anyone's legal entitlements relating to that thing), this might fit within what Hohfeld refers to as 'power' (Hohfeld at 44) but that is because Hohfeld's understanding is very broad. For a useful critique of the breadth of Hohfeldian powers, see J Raz, *Practical Reason and Norms* (Oxford: Oxford University Press, 1990) at 102–104; J E Penner, *Property Rights: A Re-Examination* (Oxford: Oxford University Press, 2020) at 71–72.

146 In property theory, and various legal systems, it is controversial whether property rights can exist in intangible (incorporeal) assets. For the purpose of the discussion here, it is assumed that they can.

147 Its proponents include C Aubry and C Rau, *Droit Civil Français II* (1897) at 72, para. 172; L Rigaud, *Le Droit Reél. Histoire et Théories; Son Origine Institutionelle* (Toulouse: A Nauze, 1912) at 11–13; C Atias, *Droit Civil: Les Biens* (London: LexisNexis, 2014) at 49–55. Some Scottish authors also seem to emphasise property right holder's 'powers' over a thing above third party effectiveness of the right: see Stair, *Institutions* II, 2; Gretton and Steven, *Property, Trusts and Succession* (n 9) at paras 1.16–1.18.

148 See e.g. A M Honoré, 'Ownership' in A G Guest (ed), *Oxford Essays in Jurisprudence* (Oxford: Oxford University Press, 1961) 107; S Munzer, 'A Bundle Theorist Holds on to His Collection of Sticks' (2011) 8 Econ Journal Watch 265.

149 Honoré (n 148). The 'bundle of rights' view is said to be underpinned not only by Honoré but also Hohfeld: see S Munzer, *A Theory of Property* (Cambridge: Cambridge University Press, 1990) at 17–27. Hohfeld sought to provide an exhaustive list of relations comprising the legal position of any person as against others: Hohfeld (n 145); W N Hohfeld, 'Fundamental Legal Conceptions as Applied in Judicial Reasoning' (1917) 26 Yale LJ 710. As Penner notes, however, it is a mistake to cluster the analytical work of Hohfeld with the functional description offered by Honoré: J Penner, 'Property' in A Gold, J Goldberg, D Kelly, E Sherwin and H Smith (eds), *The Oxford Handbook of The New Private Law* (Oxford: Oxford University Press, 2021) 277 at 279.

150 The reason the incidents fail is because they are not juridical norms: Penner (n 149) at 281. This is one of the reasons why the 'bundle of rights' theory of property rights fails, but there are others: see generally Penner at 279–285, and J Penner, 'The 'Bundle of Rights' Picture of Property' (1996) 43 UCLA L Rev 711. The idea of 'powers' on the 'traditional view' probably fails for the same reason.

For example, someone to whom the owner gives a one-off permission to cross their land one afternoon (which is a personal right) has the same power to use the land as the owner's neighbour who has a right of way, i.e. an easement in common law, or a servitude in Civilian systems (a property right).[151] Another problem with those views is that the absence of liberties in relation to an asset would suggest that the right holder has no property right over an asset but this does not correspond to law. For instance, a pledge under Scots or English law is widely known to be a property right,[152] but it would probably not be one under this set of views of property because its holder does not necessarily have any liberties in relation to the asset,[153] at least not until the debtor's default on the debt secured by the pledge. In particular, the pledgee is not generally free to use the pledged asset,[154] or to take fruits from it,[155] and might not even have physical control of the asset.[156] Therefore, the 'traditional'/'bundle of rights' theories are not useful in determining the nature of the floating charge.

Another view in Civilian scholarship (the 'personalist' view) centres on the idea that a property right corresponds to duties owed by everyone to the right holder not to interfere with (not to violate) the right holder's right while a personal right is a right enforceable against a specific person.[157] This is loosely similar to the 'exclusion' theory developed by scholars in common

---

151 For further critique of the 'traditional' view, see Reid (n 143) at 225–226; Demeyere, *Real Obligations* (n 144) para. 41, and the literature cited there.

152 In English law, cases refer to the pledgee having special property by contrast to a merely personal right to possess, see *Coggs v Bernard* (1703) 2 Ld Raym 909 at 917 per Holt CJ; *Franklin v Neate* (1844) 13 M & W 481 at 486 per Rolfe B; *Donald v Suckling* (1866) LR 1 585 at 610 per Mellor J, at 613 per Blackburn J, at 619 per Cockburn J; *Sewell v Burdick* (1884) LR 10 (App Cas) 74 at 78 per Earl of Selborne LC. In Scots law, see *Robertson & Baxter v Inglis* (1897) 24 R 758 at 777 per Lord M'Laren; Gloag and Irvine, *Rights in Security* (n 28) at 199–200; Steven, *Pledge and Lien* (n 50) para. 2–01.

153 Such powers can, however, be conferred by an agreement, see *R A Barrett v Livesey* (6 November 1980, unreported) cited in Beale et al., *The Law of Security and Title-based Financing* (n 115) para. 5.08 (English law), and Steven, *Pledge and Lien* (n 50) at para. 7–08 citing *Moore v Gledden* (1869) 7 M 1016 (Scots law).

154 In English law, see *The Odessa* [1916] 1 AC 145 (PC) at 159 per Lord Mersey, cf *Coggs* (n 152) at 917 per Holt CJ, and see Beale et al., *The Law of Security and Title-based Financing* (n 115) para. 5.08. In Scots law, see Steven, *Pledge and Lien* (n 50) paras 7–05–7–07.

155 Steven, *Pledge and Lien* (n 50) para. 7–10.

156 In English law, see *Inglis v Robertson* [1898] AC 616 (HL), *Dublin City Distillery v Doherty* [1914] AC 823 (HL (Irl)) at 852 per Lord Parker, *Official Assignee of Madras v Mercantile Bank of India Ltd* [1935] AC 53 (PC) at 58–59 per Lord Wright. In Scots law, see *Robertson & Baxter* (n 152); Steven, *Pledge and Lien* (n 50) para. 6–26.

157 M Planiol, *Traité Élémentaire de Droit Civil I* (Paris: Librairie générale de droit et de jurisprudence, 1922) at 656–657.

law jurisdictions over the last two decades.[158] The 'exclusion' view of property sees the distinctiveness of property rights in the duty owed to the right holder by the rest of the world not to interfere with the asset. One key objection sometimes raised is that the distinction between property and personal rights collapses because it looks like the difference between them is in the number of people who owe a duty to the right holder.[159] This is not persuasive because the 'game' is about more than numbers: there is a qualitative difference between the source of duties. What distinguishes a property right from a personal right is that a property right binds others (third parties) because the law imposes a legal norm that places a general duty on them not to interfere with the asset in order to protect the corresponding right in an asset.[160] The general duty applies to third parties by virtue of them being alive (or, in the case of corporate entities, being in existence).[161]

A right can be classed as a property even if it is not enforceable against absolutely everyone in the world, despite what the oft-cited Latin tag describing the enforceability of such rights – 'erga omnes' – might suggest. This is because a duty does not cease to be general just because it applies with exceptions[162] in the sense that the law might give some third parties a defence.[163] It might seem odd to a Civilian property lawyer to speak of a property right that binds third parties whilst furnishing some of those third parties with a defence. Yet, examples of such property rights are not hard to find. In Scots law, for example, where A enters into a contract of sale with B and places B in possession of goods before property (ownership) is transferred to B, C who buys from B (a non-owner) in good faith is protected should A argue that ownership never left them.[164]

---

158 J Penner, *The Idea of Property in Law* (Oxford: Oxford University Press, 1997) 71; T Merrill, 'Property and the Right to Exclude' (1998) 77 *Nebraska Law Review* 730; H Smith, 'Exclusion versus Governance: Two Strategies for Delineating Property Rights' (2002) 31 *The Journal of Legal Studies* 453; H Smith, 'Property as the Law of Things' (2012) 125 *Harvard Law Review* 1691; S Douglas and B McFarlane, 'Defining Property Rights' in J Penner and H Smith (eds), *Philosophical Foundations of Property Law* (Oxford: Oxford University Press, 2013) at 219; Penner (n 149) at 287–288.

159 Reid (n 143) 226.

160 A similar point is made by Penner, *Property Rights. A Re-Examination* (n 145) 91.

161 Penner, *Property Rights. A Re-Examination* (n 145) 91.

162 Penner, *Property Rights. A Re-Examination* (n 145) 91.

163 See e.g. *Akers v Samba* [2017] UKSC 6, [2017] AC 424 at para. 82 (Lord Sumption).

164 Sale of Goods Act 1979 s. 25; Factors Act 1889 s. 9. The 1889 Act applies in Scotland by virtue of the Factors (Scotland) Act 1890. Other defences, regarding goods, can be raised under the Sale of Goods Act 1979 ss. 23, 24; Factors Act 1889 ss. 2, 8; Hire Purchase Act 1964 s. 27. In relation to land, see Land Registration etc. (Scotland) Act 2012 s. 86. For defences in other Civilian property law systems, see e.g. French Civil Code art. 2276 (formerly art. 2279);

It follows that a useful test determining the nature of a right with respect to an asset is to ask whether the right binds third parties, i.e. whether there exist legal norms that impose a general duty on third parties not to interfere with the asset. In the context of secured finance, a third party (C) can be said to interfere with an asset subject to a security right in favour of A where C acts (or fails to act) in a way that deprives A of the possibility to treat the asset as a source of payment of the secured debt. This means that a security right can be said to 'bind' third parties if the secured creditor can treat the charged asset as a source of repayment of the secured debt in priority to third parties and the rights they might wish to assert with respect to the asset. For the purposes of this chapter, it is convenient to split third parties into groups: outright purchasers of asset; disponees taking a security interest in the asset; judgment and execution creditors; and insolvency officers of the asset-holder. It does not defeat the proprietary character of a right if some third parties are bound but not others.

(2) The extent to which the floating charge binds third parties

In both English and Scots law, there is much to be said against the idea that the floating charge pre-crystallisation is a property right because in many circumstances it does not bind third parties in the sense just defined. First, under the statutory priority rules[165] in both jurisdictions, the floating charge ranks behind any fixed security rights,[166] even if the fixed security was created later than the floating charge.[167] Only once crystallised, it ranks above any later-created (i.e. post-crystallisation) fixed security interests.

Secondly, the holder of the floating charge cannot enforce the charge prior to crystallisation against a third party buyer of assets that fell within the scope of the charge. In Scotland, this seems to follow from the statutory wording of

---

German Civil Code (BGB) §§ 932 and 935; Italian Civil Code art. 1153; Polish Civil Code art. 169.

165 This is subject to any ranking agreement and negative pledge clauses: see section B(6) above, and also immediately below.

166 'Fixed security right' is a convenient shorthand used here to mean a standard security, an assignation in security or a pledge and any other security right other than a floating charge.

167 In English law: *Re Hamilton's* (n 47) (subsequent assignment of a debt by way of security had a priority over a floating charge); *Re Castell and Brown Ltd* [1898] 1 Ch 315; *Re Benjamin Cope & Sons Ltd* [1914] 1 Ch 800. In Scots law: Companies Act 1985 ss. 464(4)(a) (ranking) and 463(1)(b) (effect of the floating charge on winding up), Insolvency Act 1986 ss. 55(3)(b) (on the subordination of the powers of a receiver) and 60(1)(a) (on distribution of money paid to creditors by the receiver). As discussed below, under the Scots law statutory regime a negative pledge in a floating charge adjusts this such that the floating charge can rank first.

the subject matter of the charge as 'all or any part of the property ... which may from time to time be comprised in its property and undertaking'.[168] This suggests changes to the composition of the 'property and undertaking' on any account are possible, including dispositions of assets within it, and there is no suggestion that the buyer would take assets subject to the charge. By contrast, in England, the question whether a third party takes free of the floating charge is generally answered by checking whether the disposition of the charged asset is within the terms of the charge, i.e. whether it is in the ordinary course of business. On the face of it, the English approach seems much narrower. However, what constitutes ordinary course of business has been understood widely by the courts,[169] so in practice the position is close to that in Scotland. To illustrate, in English law many transactions involving charged assets fall within ordinary course of business,[170] e.g. disposals of the assets in the course of the trade,[171] even if it is a quick sale to raise finance[172] or a substantial portion of charged assets are disposed[173]; use of proceeds of sale of charged assets to meet expenses of the business[174]; sale and lease-back of charged assets.[175] It should be added for completeness that even if the disposition is outside the ordinary course of business, in English law a third party disponee may still take the assets free of the charge if they have a defence, for example if they are a bona fide purchaser of legal title for value without notice, although the circumstances when this might happen in practice are very rare.[176]

Thirdly, in neither jurisdiction does a floating charge bind creditors who complete execution (enforcement) before the charge crystallised.[177] It is worth adding that in Scots law, after crystallisation, floating charge holders

168 Companies Act 1985 s. 462(1).
169 See in particular *Willmot v London Celluloid Co* (1886) 34 Ch D 147 (CA) at 151 per Cotton LJ.
170 See L Gullifer and M Raczynska, 'Secured Transactions' in S Paterson and R Zakrzewski (eds), *McKnight, Paterson, and Zakrzewski on The Law of International Finance*, 2nd edn (Oxford: Oxford University Press, 2017) at paras 14.6.5.1–14.6.5.2.
171 *In re Florence* (n 47).
172 *Hamer v London, City & Midland Bank Ltd* (1918) 87 LJKB 973.
173 *Re HH Vivian & Co* [1900] 2 Ch 654; *Ashborder BV v Green Gas Power Ltd* [2004] EWHC 1517 (Ch) at para. 227 per Etherton J; *Bulbinder Singh Sandhu (t/a Isher Fashions UK) v Jet Star Retail Ltd (in administration)* [2011] EWCA Civ 459 at para. 10 per Moore-Bick LJ.
174 *Re Panama* (n 44).
175 *Reynolds Bros (Motors) Pty Ltd v Esanda Ltd* [1977] 1 WLR 578.
176 See R Calnan, *Taking Security*, 4th edn (London: Jordan Publishing, 2018) paras 5.48–5.49.
177 In England, see *Re Standard Manufacturing Co* [1891] 1 Ch 627 (CA) at 640; *Evans* (n 121) at 995 per Fletcher Moulton LJ. In Scotland, see MacPherson, *The Floating Charge* (n 15) para. 2–12.

rank below creditors with 'effectually executed diligence'[178] by contrast to those who have not effectually executed,[179] but prior to crystallisation there is no need to draw this distinction with effectual execution.

That said, in both jurisdictions the floating charge prior to crystallisation binds some third parties, so there are arguments in favour of it being a property right, although in Scotland they are weaker than in England.

In English law, the holder of a floating charge can, prior to the charge crystallising, protect itself from disposals of charged assets that are otherwise than in the ordinary course of business by appointing a receiver[180] or apply for an injunction against a third party to prevent them from interfering with the rights of the floating chargee over the charged assets.[181] In addition, a disposition of charged assets outside the ordinary course of business (which might not crystallise the charge) means that a third party disponee (e.g. a purchaser) does not take ownership of the asset free of the floating charge unless the disponee has a defence, e.g. bona fide purchaser defence.[182]

In Scotland, the holder of the floating charge does not benefit from third-party effectiveness just described, but it does not mean it never binds third parties, in the sense that the word 'bind' was explained above in section C(1). First, ranking of two or more floating charges over the same assets is in the order of their registration at Companies House.[183] This means that the holder of the first floating charge binds a subsequent holder of a floating charge so long as the former was registered first. In English law, the floating charge also binds a subsequent floating charge, although the binding effect is more limited than under Scots law. In English law, the earlier floating charge binds a later floating charge where the latter covers the assets subject

---

178 Companies Act 1985 s. 463(1)(a), Insolvency Act 1986 ss. 55(3)(a) (on the subordination of the powers of a receiver) and 60(1)(b) (on distribution of money paid to creditors by the receiver).

179 *Lord Advocate v Royal Bank of Scotland* 1977 SC 155; *MacMillan* (n 10).

180 *Hubbuck v Helms* (1887) 56 LJ Ch 536; *McMahon v North Kent Ironworks Co* [1891] 2 Ch 148 at 150 per Kekewich J; *Edwards v Standard Rolling Stock Syndicate* [1893] 1 Ch 574 at 577 per North J.

181 *In re London Pressed Hinge Co Ltd* [1905] 1 Ch 576 at 583 per Buckley J (granting a relief by appointment of a receiver to prevent a judgment creditor from issuing execution against charged assets, even though the chargor was not in default; he did so through gritted teeth); *Wily v St George Partnership Banking Ltd* (1999) 30 ACSR 204 (Fed Crt of Aus) at 213 per Finkelstein J.

182 *Re Bartlett Estates Pty Ltd (in liquidation)* (1988) 14 ACLR 512 (Sup Crt of Queensland) at 516 per Dowsett J; *Wily v St George Partnership Banking Ltd* (1999) 30 ACSR 204 (Fed Crt of Aus) at para. 9 (Sackville J).

183 Companies Act 1985 s. 464(4)(b).

to the first floating charge[184] but it does not bind a creditor who takes a floating charge of a more limited scope than the first one.[185]

Secondly, in Scotland, a floating charge with a registered negative pledge clause[186] takes priority over any consensual[187] security (whether a subsequent fixed security or another floating charge) created after the date of the instrument under the default statutory priority rules.[188] In English law, the position of a floating chargee with a registered negative pledge clause is very similar, although, as mentioned earlier,[189] the priority the chargee is governed not by statutory but by general judge-made priority rules and the doctrine of notice.

On balance, in both jurisdictions, the floating charge, even without a negative pledge clause, prior to crystallisation binds at least some third parties, which suggests that it could class as a property right, albeit a weak one, and with the Scots floating charge being an even weaker property right than the English floating charge. The case in favour of it being a property right is much strengthened when the charge contains a registered negative pledge clause.

If this is right, as this chapter argues, it is necessary to provide an explanation why the right appears to be so weak, i.e. why various third parties are not bound, which is what section C(5) attempts to offer. Before turning to that discussion, the sections immediately below will address the possibility that the Scots floating charge pre-crystallisation is a form of personal right only.

(3) Not a personal right

Some authors suggest that the Scots floating charge prior to crystallisation is a personal right, and only becomes a property right upon crystallisation (attachment). One key argument against the charge creating a property right, made by MacPherson, is that 'the chargeholder has [no] rights exercisable against the property [prior to crystallisation]' and that there is no 'direct

---

184 *Benjamin Cope* (n 167).
185 *Re Automatic Bottlemakers* [1926] Ch 412.
186 See above section B(6).
187 In Scots law, a fixed security arising by operation of law takes priority over the floating charge: Companies Act 1985 s. 464(2).
188 Companies Act 1985 s. 464(1)–(1A). The insertion of subsection (1A) effectively confirmed that a negative pledge clause is also a priority clause, which was a point decided in *AIB Finance v Bank of Scotland* 1995 SLT 2, [1994] BCC 184. See SC Styles, 'Floating Charges and Subsequent Securities' (2001) 6 SLPQ 73 at 79.
189 See earlier, section B(6).

effect on property before attachment'.[190] One problem with this view is that in focusing on the charge holder's rights in charged assets, it appears to rest on the 'traditional'/'bundle of rights' views of property rights discussed and rejected earlier.[191] If the argument presented here is correct, pledge should also not be a property right[192]; powers over an asset are not a good test of whether the right is personal or proprietary.

Another argument advanced by the proponents of the personal right view is that the fact that the chargor can trade charged assets free of the charge undermines the proprietary character of the charge.[193] This is true, but it does not mean it prevents it from being proprietary. It was seen earlier that a right can be a property right even if it is not enforceable against all third parties.[194] The same can be said in response to the arguments that the charge does not bind other secured creditors and execution creditors.[195] The rebuttal is even stronger when one notices the point made earlier that the floating charge does bind some third parties: a (registered) floating charge binds subsequent floating chargees and, if it contains a negative pledge clause, the holders of subsequent fixed security interests.[196] It does not matter that the holder of the floating charge cannot enforce their rights against the assets, and realise the third party effect, until enforcement.[197] A pledge (which is a property right) does not cease to be a property right from the moment of its creation just because the pledgee cannot enforce the pledge until the debtor defaults on the secured obligation, which risk might, of course, never even materialise.

Another problem with the view that the floating charge is a personal right is: (i) the need to explain how it becomes a property right upon crystallisation; whilst (ii) accounting for the effect of the dealings prior to the charge crystallising. Styles suggested that the Scots floating charge is a 'conditional real right'.[198] This view addresses (i) in the sense that it is a personal right to

---

190 See earlier, section B(6). MacPherson, *The Floating Charge* (n 15) para. 2–08, and see para. 2–13.
191 See section C(1).
192 See section C(1).
193 MacPherson, *The Floating Charge* (n 15) para. 2–09.
194 See section C(1).
195 MacPherson, *The Floating Charge* (n 15) paras 2–10–2–11.
196 See section C(1).
197 This is a concern raised by MacPherson, *The Floating Charge* (n 15) at para. 2–10.
198 Styles (n 11) 240 (a view developed prior to the Enterprise Act 2002). Other attempts to explain the Scots floating charge prior to crystallisation include the 'potential-interest theory' (MacPherson, *The Floating Charge* (n 15) para. 2–13) and a parallel with the German concept of *Gestaltungsrecht* ('right to shape'), which confers on its holder a power to establish, define,

appoint a receiver, and becomes a real right when the condition precedent (one of the conditions for crystallisation) is fulfilled.[199] However, it fails to address (ii) because up until crystallisation, on this view, the floating charge cannot take any third party effect. This is problematic for two reasons. First, if the proprietary nature of the floating charge were only to emerge on crystallisation, the ranking as between two floating charges should be determined by the date of crystallisation, but it is not; instead, it is determined by the date of registration.[200] Secondly, this view does not explain how a floating charge that contains a registered negative pledge could rank ahead of a fixed security interest that is created in the period between creation of a floating charge and its crystallisation. It could perhaps be counter-argued that a floating charge with a negative pledge clause is a property right, while one without such a clause is a conditional property right, but this would create an odd situation where two very similar rights have different natures merely because one is binding on one additional category of third parties. It is preferable not to treat a floating charge as a different type of right depending on whether it contains a registered negative pledge clause.

(4) Not a preference right

A novel view has emerged recently that could be described as a stronger version of the personal right view just addressed.[201] On this new view, the floating charge is not a real right, whether before or *after* crystallisation, or at least not an ordinary property right. The fact that it prevails over the general body of unsecured creditors[202] is considered a matter of redistribution in insolvency, when some creditors holding personal rights are given priority over property rights for policy reasons. Hence, it is referred to as a 'preference right'.

---

amend a particular legal relation (MacPherson, *The Floating Charge* (n 15) para. 2–22). The 'potential-interest theory' seems to resemble Styles' 'conditional right' idea and so fails for the same reasons, which are set out here. The parallel with the German concept does not work very well because, unlike *Gestaltungsrechten* (e.g. an option to repurchase: Bürgerliches Gesetzbuch §456, or the right of pre-emption: Bürgerliches Gesetzbuch §463), crystallisation in Scots law is not (not exclusively or directly at least) an act within the right holder's volitional control.

199 Styles (n 11) 240.
200 See section C(2).
201 MacPherson, *The Floating Charge* (n 15) paras 6–88–6–91; J Hardman, 'Hohfeld and the Scots Law Floating Charge', Chapter 7 (insolvency concept).
202 See section B(8) above.

The existence of preferential status (privilege) of some claims on insolvency is, in some ways, not uncommon. In various jurisdictions certain policy-protected claims take priority over all secured creditors, or at least some of them[203] – as is the case in both Scotland and England in relation to preferential creditors *vis-à-vis* the floating charge.[204] On this reasoning, claims secured by the floating charge enjoy privileged status over unsecured creditors after expenses of insolvency, preferential creditors and the prescribed part have been paid. In addition, an appeal of the preference right view is that it would not be necessary to explain why the floating charge pre-crystallisation, and to some extent also post-crystallisation, does not bind many third parties.

There are some important problems with this view, however. First, it is necessary to consider what goal insolvency law serves as far as distribution of assets on liquidation (or administration) is concerned. This is widely debated[205] but the prevailing view continues to be that its focus should be on collection efforts of creditors with property rights in assets of the insolvent whilst balancing them with creditors who deserve protection as a matter of fairness, e.g. some claims under environmental law, labour law or pensions law.[206] If this is true, the proponents of the preference view should explain why a holder of a floating charge (on their view – not a real right) would be deserving of a preferential status (ranking above unsecured creditors). If the answer is that they facilitate the raising of finance, then the question is why other creditors who also do so should not similarly be protected, e.g. when they lend without any security, or lend taking only personal security in the form of guarantees or indemnities.[207] Even if one views insolvency as 'an attempt to reckon with a debtor's multiple defaults and to distribute the consequences among a number of different actors [in accordance with

---

203 See Dutch Civil Code, art. 3:279 (referred to by MacPherson, *The Floating Charge* (n 15) para. 6–89); Polish Insolvency and Restructuring Law of 28 February 2003 (Dz U 60, 535, 2003), arts 336, 345–346.

204 See section B(8) above.

205 For a useful overview, see V Finch, *Corporate Insolvency Law: Perspectives and Principles*, 2nd edn (Cambridge: Cambridge University Press, 2009) Ch. 2.

206 For this so-called 'creditors' bargain' and emphasis on property rights, see e.g. T H Jackson, *The Logic and Limits of Bankruptcy Law* (Harvard: Harvard University Press, 1986) 2; D G Baird and T H Jackson, 'Corporate Reorganizations and the Treatment of Diverse Ownership Interests: A Comment on Adequate Protection of Secured Creditors in Bankruptcy' (1984) 51 U Chi L Rev 97 at 103; T H Jackson and R Scott, 'On the Nature of Bankruptcy: An Essay on Bankruptcy Sharing and the Creditors' Bargain' (1989) 75 Va L Rev 155. See, too, *Report of the Review Committee on Insolvency Law and Practice* (Cmnd 8558, 1982) para. 232.

207 In practice, personal security interests are often, but not always, taken alongside real security. In any case, the point raised in the text is one of principle.

different values]',[208] without necessarily prioritising property right holders, it is still necessary to justify the value of the floating charge as against other creditors before the priority status can be conferred.

Secondly, the preference-right view of the floating charge does not account, and cannot account (given its focus is insolvency), for the third party effects of the floating charge prior to insolvency, discussed above,[209] especially where the floating charge contains a negative pledge clause.

Additionally, the preference-right view is inconsistent with Scottish judicial authority, which states that the floating charge becomes a property (real) right on crystallisation.[210]

As this section and section C(3) have shown, the explanations of the floating charge as a personal (non-real) right, whether just before crystallisation, or both before and after crystallisation (the preference-right view), have not been convincing. The preferable view is that the floating charge constitutes a (weak) property right in the sense that it binds some third parties.[211] If this is true, a question arises why other third parties are not bound by it, which the section immediately below goes on to address.

(5) Property right with a broad authority to dispose free of the charge

When taking a floating charge, the chargee recognises the chargor's power to dispose of the encumbered assets.[212] 'Disposition' is understood here as any transaction that grants a third party a property right (a proprietary interest) in the charged assets, which could be e.g., by way of sale, lease, creation of other security interests, or even an execution levied against these assets. The chargor's power to dispose of charged assets is based on the chargor's ownership of the assets or some other interest that comprises a power to dispose of the assets. If the power were unrestricted the chargor would be able to defeat (or subordinate)[213] the chargee's interest through any disposition, perhaps even on insolvency and this would undermine the usefulness

---

208 E Warren, 'Bankruptcy Policy' (1987) 54 U Chi L Rev 775 at 777.
209 See section C(2).
210 *Telford* (n 8) at 194 (Lord President Clyde) and 198 (Lord Guthrie).
211 As set out in section C(1).
212 The discussion in this section is based on M Raczynska, *The Law of Tracing in Commercial Transactions* (Oxford: Oxford University Press, 2018) paras 1.54–1.63.
213 For convenience, in the analysis below reference is made to dispositions that defeat the charge, but this should be read to include transactions that would not *prima facie* lead to extinction of the charge in the asset disposed of but would instead result in its subordination (e.g. creation of a security interest in the charged assets will not, as a matter of principle, extinguish the floating charge but might cause it rank behind another interest).

of the charge. It is, therefore, sensible to control the exercise of the chargor's power by determining when the chargor may (is 'authorised'[214] to) defeat the charge as between the chargor and the chargee.

In English law, the chargor's authority to dispose of the encumbered assets free of the charge is shaped primarily by the terms of the charge. While the authority is generally very wide, especially given the broadly-interpreted term used in debentures that the chargor is free to dispose of charged assets 'in the ordinary course of business',[215] parties to the charge agreement are free to restrict it, e.g. by introducing various negative pledge clauses or crystallisation clauses.[216] Any exercise of power outside this authority results in the charge continuing against a third party disponee, or might give the chargee a right to the proceeds of the disposition.[217]

By contrast, in Scots law, the scope of the chargor's authority to defeat the charge pre-crystallisation is based primarily on statute, with only a limited role given to the parties' agreement (through inclusion of negative pledge clauses[218]). Where the charge contains no negative pledge, the chargor's authority to defeat the charge prior to crystallisation is wider than in English law: the only limits appear to be the grant of another floating charge (when the first floating charge takes priority, if registered first), and crystallisation (when the authority to defeat the charge is terminated). Where the charge contains a registered negative pledge, the additional limit is that the chargor lacks authority to create fixed security interests that would rank above the floating charge.

The idea of a person taking a property right whilst allowing for it to be defeated might at first seem surprising, but it should be remembered that consensually granted property rights can also be consensually extinguished (discharged) or disclaimed.[219] From this perspective, the floating charge is a weak 'disclaimable' property right in charged assets.

This power-authority explanation shows that drawing on concepts familiar from agency law accounts for both the external as well as internal aspects of the floating charge, providing a more complete picture than one that emerges based solely on the concepts of property law, on which a number

---

214 The concept of authority here is similar to that found in agency law: Raczynska, *The Law of Tracing* (n 212) paras 1.55–1.59.
215 See section C(2).
216 See section B(6).
217 Raczynska, *The Law of Tracing* (n 212) Ch. 6.
218 See section B(6).
219 Gretton and Steven, *Property, Trusts and Succession* (n 9) paras 1.29 and 31.4.

of existing theories of the floating charge are based.[220] It also shows that it is possible to view both English and Scots floating charges as property rights that are based on the same (power-authority) structure, thus illustrating how formalism can help develop common language in difficult comparative law discussions, where previously such common language was lacking. The identification of the common structural framework also allows us to see more clearly where the differences between legal systems lie (here: the differences between the English and Scottish floating charges).

D. CONCLUSION

It has been seen that under Scots and English law, the question of who can create the floating charge, and how, is answered similarly; the treatment of the floating charge on insolvency is also similar. This is not a result of the fact that the Scottish charge is based on statute while the English charge is mainly based on judge-made law. Some aspects of market confidence benefit from statutory and public framework (e.g. registration of security and various priority clauses). The lack of provision of registration framework of floating charges in England for most individuals and unincorporated entities[221] is in practice as limiting as the Scots delimitation of the person of the grantor of the floating charge as a corporate person only. In a number of other instances, however, English law offers parties more freedom to determine the terms on which the charge is granted. This is so in particular in relation to: (i) clauses restricting the chargor in creating security interests that would rank ahead of the creditor taking the floating charge (negative pledge clauses); and (ii) crystallisation clauses. Under English law the parties can

---

220 The existing theories that developed in English law tend to focus on explaining the changeability of the subject matter and why the disponee takes free of the charge: the fund theory: R Goode, originally in *Legal Problems* (n 18), now *Goode and Gullifer on Legal Problems* (n 18) para. 4–04; license theory: S Worthington, 'Floating Charges: Use and Abuse of Doctrinal Analysis' in *Company Charges: Spectrum and Beyond* (n 3) 25 at 39–44; S Worthington, *Proprietary Interests in Commercial Transactions* (Oxford: Clarendon Press, 1996) at 79–86; S Worthington, 'Floating Charges: An Alternative Theory' (1994) 53 CLJ 81; a similar theory of a defeasible equitable interest was advanced by J Farrar, 'The Crystallisation of a Floating Charge' (1976) 40 Conv 397 at 397–398, and 'World Economic Stagnation Puts the Floating Charge on Trial' (1980) 1 *The Company Lawyer* 83 at 83–87; overreaching theory: R Nolan, 'Property in a Fund' (2004) 120 LQR 108 at 129–130.
221 The desirability of a system that makes it easier for individuals and other non-corporates to grant floating charges is a separate issue, and not addressed here, but see Secured Transactions Law Reform Project's discussion paper on *To Whom Should Registration of Security Apply?* (2013) available at *https://stlrp.files.wordpress.com/2013/12/paper-2-the-person-of-the-gran tor-of-security.pdf* (last accessed 1 November 2021).

also restrict what constitutes transactions in 'ordinary course of business'. Taking advantage of this freedom to shape the floating charge leads to issues that are not known in Scots law, and which can lead to complex results, as is the case, for example, with automatic crystallisation clauses or transactions that are outside the ordinary course of business whilst the charge remains uncrystallised. The differences between the English and Scottish law in this area is unsurprising given their different legal traditions and cultures: the greater willingness of judges to impose obligations on third parties in England,[222] and the more rigorous and less flexible tradition of property law in Scotland.

For all their differences, it is notable that in both jurisdictions the nature of the floating charge has proved problematic to conceptualise. In the analyses to date, in each jurisdiction, there has been little interest in the debates that developed on the other side of the border. Such a state of affairs is unfortunate but to be expected considering the difficulties in comparative property law to develop common conceptual framework, or 'common grammar',[223] especially across the civil and common law divide. This chapter has shown how to conceptualise one practically important property law institution across the civil and common law, and that it can be based on the same structural framework whilst preserving unique features of the different traditions. In so doing, it is hoped it has broken the ground in using formal and conceptual analysis to manage discourse across divergent systems.

---

222 For discussion that such willingness is one of equity's distinctive features, see L Smith, 'Fusion and Tradition' in S Degeling and J Edelman (eds), *Equity in Commercial Law* (Sydney: Lawbook Co, 2005) 19 at 33–35.

223 M Clark, 'Foucault, Gadamer and the Law: Hermeneutics in Post-Modern Legal Thought' (1995) 26 U Tol Law Rev 111 at 114: '[D]iscourses become incommensurable with one another, when something beyond a simple disagreement reigns. Such a disagreement is not limited to the minutiae of a particular rule or statute, but concerns the general rules of the game. At this point, the hegemonic "discourse" becomes multiple "discourses" and debates are conducted by listeners who no longer share a common grammar'.

PART 3
PRACTICE, DOCTRINE
AND THE FUTURE

9 The Ranking of Floating Charges

Jonathan Hardman and Alisdair D J MacPherson

A. INTRODUCTION
B. GENERAL RANKING RULES
C. DEFAULT RANKING RULES FOR FLOATING CHARGES
    (1) Against voluntary fixed securities
    (2) Against fixed securities arising by operation of law
    (3) Against other floating charges
    (4) Against diligences
    (5) Against other security rights
D. NEGATIVE PLEDGES
E. RANKING AGREEMENTS
F. ATTACHMENT, RANKING AND ENFORCEMENT
    (1) Attachment and ranking
    (2) Appointing and enforcing
G. RANKING AND DISTRIBUTION
    (1) Liquidation
    (2) Receivership
    (3) Administration
    (4) Enforcement by fixed security holder
H. FURTHER RANKING ISSUES
    (1) Circles of priority
    (2) Catholic and secondary security
    (3) Offside goals rule
I. CONCLUSION

A. INTRODUCTION

A floating charge and the debt it secures do not exist in isolation. They need to interact with other obligations due by the granter and other claims on the granter's property. In common parlance it is said to be necessary to establish how security 'ranks'.[1] Ranking denotes a comparison between two things: whether X is preferred to Y. In a legal context, ranking often focuses on respective priorities as far as an asset is concerned: how X ranks against Y in respect of asset Z.[2] However, the term ranking in its wider sense actually aggregates two key concepts together. First, the freedom enjoyed by the granter in respect of the assets over which security is granted prior to its enforcement: is the granter free to dispose of the asset (and, if so, what happens to any proceeds), and are there any other restrictions on what can be done with the relevant asset? This can be seen as a form of ranking between a secured creditor and the granter as to control over the use of the asset in question. Secondly, the respective priorities of creditors' claims in competitions involving assets, which is particularly relevant in the context of insolvency. The most thorough and systematic categorisation of commercial law principles in Scotland comes from George Joseph Bell, who himself had a considerable underlying interest in insolvency law.[3] Indeed, Bell discussed ranking issues at length in the context of the division of a bankrupt's estate and codified certain court decisions dealing with competitions between secured creditors (including diligence creditors) in his 'canons of ranking'.[4] Although those canons of ranking have limited relevance under the current law, it is still no surprise that Scots law generally has prioritised the second question over the first when considering the 'ranking' of securities. For the

---

1 See J Hardman, *A Practical Guide to Granting Corporate Security in Scotland* (Edinburgh: W. Green, 2018) Ch. 9; L Macgregor et al., *Commercial Law in Scotland*, 6th edn (Edinburgh: W. Green, 2020) para. 7.3.6.2; J MacLeod 'Non-Judicial Real Security' in I G MacNeil (ed), *Scots Commercial Law* (Edinburgh: Avizandum, 2014) paras 11.13–11.15.

2 There may, however, be claims that are ranked in relation to an entire estate, rather than in relation to one or more particular assets.

3 Indeed, his *Commentaries on the Law of Scotland and on the Principles of Mercantile Jurisprudence*, an institutional work, started out as *A Treatise on the Law of Bankruptcy in Scotland* (1800), with the title of the work changing to *Commentaries on the Municipal and Mercantile Law of Scotland Considered in Relation to the Subject of Bankruptcy* by the time the second volume of the first edition was published in 1804. See K G C Reid, 'From Text-book to Book of Authority: The Principles of George Joseph Bell' (2011) 15 Edin L Rev 6; L Macgregor, 'Partnerships and Legal Personality: Cautionary Tales from Scotland' (2020) 20 *Journal of Corporate Law Studies* 237 at 250 onwards.

4 See G J Bell, *Commentaries on the Law of Scotland*, 7th edn, J McLaren (ed) (Edinburgh: T&T Clark, 1870) at 401 onwards for discussion of ranking and see 413, in particular, for the canons of ranking. For further discussion and practical examples, see G L Gretton, *The Law of Inhibition and Adjudication*, 2nd edn (London: LexisNexis, 1996) Ch. 7. Given that the necessity of using the canons of ranking has usually depended on the ranking effects of inhibitions, their role has been greatly diminished by the Bankruptcy and Diligence etc. (Scotland) Act 2007 s. 154, which provides that an inhibition does not confer any preference in any sequestration, insolvency proceedings or other ranking process. And see Scottish Law Commission, *Report on Diligence* (Scot. Law Com. No. 183, 2001) paras 6.39 onwards.

purposes of the floating charge it is also helpful: the granter retains freedom to utilise its assets prior to enforcement,[5] rendering the first question irrelevant.

Accordingly, our enquiry can be limited to the second question: which rights[6] held by creditors of the granter, against certain assets of the granter, prevail in a competition with other such rights, particularly upon an insolvency of the granter. Although the ranking of security rights can provide some enforcement advantages outside the context of insolvency, it is in insolvency that this issue becomes crucial – on a solvent winding up, all debts can be repaid, rendering rights in security essentially redundant. This chapter will review general rules of ranking, the default rules for ranking floating charges and voluntary variations of that regime. The latter will be split into amendments made *ex ante* to the grant of the floating charge (the negative pledge) and amendments made *ex post* (ranking agreements).[7] It will then cover the ranking of the floating charge upon its enforcement, with respect to attachment and distribution of proceeds recovered. Finally, some further problems with the current Scots law ranking regime for floating charges will be outlined and discussed. Given the significance of the Companies Act 1985 for the ranking of floating charges in Scots law, all section references are to that legislation unless specified or the context indicates otherwise.

B. GENERAL RANKING RULES

Our first enquiry is to identify the general rules of ranking. Having established that by 'ranking' we principally mean ranking creditors' rights in specific assets in the insolvency of the granter, we can move to the question of what needs to be ranked. The core question is ranking securities against each other. There are two aspects to this, both established on an asset-by-asset basis: ranking between categories of security; and ranking within a

---

5 See Hardman, *Granting Corporate Security* (n 1) paras 6–06 and 6–08; A D J MacPherson, *The Floating Charge* (Edinburgh: Edinburgh Legal Education Trust, 2020) Ch. 2.
6 All creditors enjoy a claim (personal right) for the amount of their debt due and can prove in the insolvency of their debtor. The order in which such debts (secured or unsecured) are paid in the absence of insolvency is principally a contractual matter. Our concern is, instead, to establish which creditors have rights against which assets of the granter (or the proceeds of the sale thereof) and to determine the order of priority of those rights.
7 Ranking agreements can also be entered into at the same time as, or in advance of, the creation of the relevant security. For simplicity, our principal focus in this chapter is on ranking agreements that are entered into after the security is created.

category of security. In respect of the former, this is not normally an issue for most voluntary real rights in security. This is because voluntary security under Scots law matches the property type of the collateral[8]: heritable property must be subject to a proper security right of a standard security, and cannot be transferred in security[9]; corporeal moveable property can only be pledged and cannot be assigned[10]; incorporeal moveable property can be transferred in security but cannot be pledged.[11] Accordingly, by way of example, a standard security cannot be in competition with a pledge. Only the floating charge transcends various property classes to allow for one voluntary right to be granted over all types of property. This therefore means that ranking across different categories of voluntary security is, in general terms, an enquiry that is limited to the floating charge in its interaction with other securities.[12] However, it must be acknowledged that voluntary securities can, of course, interact with involuntary securities, such as tacit or judicial securities, in which case the other general rules outlined in this part will largely apply.

Within a particular category of voluntary security, the question of ranking also arises less frequently than would be expected. Securities over incorporeal property are achieved by way of improper security, an actual transfer of ownership of the asset from the granter to the creditor.[13] As they involve

---

8 See W M Gloag and J M Irvine, *Law of Rights in Security Heritable and Moveable including Cautionary Obligations* (Edinburgh: W. Green, 1897) 4; Macleod (n 1) para. 11.09; Hardman, *Granting Corporate Security* (n 1) para. 5–06; and A D J MacPherson, 'The "Pre-History" of Floating Charges in Scots Law', Chapter 1 within this volume.

9 Conveyancing and Feudal Reform (Scotland) Act 1970 s. 9(3). This was a change from the earlier law, see e.g. Scottish Law Commission, *Discussion Paper on Heritable Securities: Pre-default* (Scot. Law Com. DP No. 168, 2019) Ch. 2. And see MacPherson, *Floating Charge* (n 5) paras 7–82 onwards, for the interaction of those earlier security rights with the floating charge following its introduction.

10 See R Anderson, *Assignation* (Edinburgh: Edinburgh Legal Education Trust, 2008) para. 1–09. There are, however, a number of examples where the language of 'assignation' of corporeal moveables has, confusingly, been used in Scots law, see the sources cited at MacPherson, *Floating Charge* (n 5) para. 8–36.

11 To be pledged, the property in question needs to be capable of physical delivery, which incorporeal moveable property is not – see *Darling v Wilson's Trustee* (1887) 15 R 180. Despite this, the terminology of 'pledging' of incorporeal property is sometimes used in Scots law – see J Hardman, 'Scottish Share Pledges and Recent Legislative Developments: Lessons for the Great Repeal Bill' 2018 Jur Rev 64; MacPherson, *Floating Charge* (n 5) para. 9–43.

12 See Hardman, *Granting Corporate Security* (n 1) para. 9–11. As with all these general statements, there are exceptions to this general principle – a statutory non-possessory aircraft mortgage granted under the Mortgaging of Aircraft Order 1972 (SI 1972/1268) could, in theory, be in competition with a pledge of the same aircraft.

13 MacLeod (n 1) paras 11.84–11.86; Macgregor et al., *Commercial Law in Scotland* (n 1) para. 7.3.5: MacPherson, *Floating Charge* (n 5) paras 9–16 onwards; and see A J M Steven and

an actual transfer, the granter retains no interest in the property to grant a second security over.[14] Accordingly, there cannot be competition between real rights in security over incorporeal moveable property. Yet the floating charge represents something of an exception to this, with multiple floating charges over the same incorporeal property being possible.[15] Whilst a pledge is a proper security, it involves delivering the asset to the creditor.[16] The result is that the granter no longer has possession of the pledged asset to deliver to a new creditor to create a pledge.[17] This will, of course, change with the introduction of the statutory pledge,[18] but until then, there is no ability for the same asset to be subject to two pledges. Accordingly, most moveable property cannot be subject to competing voluntary security rights within the same category,[19] again with the exception of the floating charge. The position is different for heritable property, as standard securities, introduced in 1970, are proper securities and therefore create a subordinate real right in the property. As they are non-possessory (unlike pledge), there can be more than one of such subordinate real right created.[20] Similarly, multiple floating charges can be granted but this regime was only introduced in 1961.[21] Accordingly, ranking issues across different voluntary security types is limited to interactions between the floating charge and other securities,

H Patrick, 'Reforming Secured Transactions Law in Scotland' in L Gullifer and O Akseli (eds), *Secured Transactions Law Reform* (London: Bloomsbury, 2016) 261.

14 Other than a reversionary interest – *Bank of Scotland v Crerar* 1922 SC (HL) 137. Such a reversionary interest is, however, a different type of asset (a personal right to a retrocession of the transferred right, rather than the transferred right itself). Whilst this separate asset can be subject to its own separate assignation in security, it is a discrete right in security over a different asset rather than a second ranking assignation in security. See also MacPherson, *Floating Charge* (n 5) para. 9–53.

15 And is generally viewed as conferring a real right upon its attachment. See further below.

16 *Hamilton v Western Bank of Scotland* (1856) 19 D 152.

17 See discussion in A J M Steven, *Pledge and Lien* (Edinburgh: Edinburgh Legal Education Trust, 2008) Ch. 6.

18 See Moveable Transactions (Scotland) Bill s. 43(2); See discussion in J Hardman 'Three Steps Forward, Two Steps Back: A View from Corporate Security Practice of the Moveable Transactions (Scotland) Bill' (2018) 22 Edin L Rev 266; A D J MacPherson, 'The Future of Moveable Security in Scots Law? Comments on the Scottish Law Commission's Report on Moveable Transactions' 2018 Jur Rev 98.

19 There is, however, the possibility of competitions for certain types of assets, e.g. ship mortgages (see Merchant Shipping Act 1995 Sch. 1 para. 7) and aircraft mortgages (see Mortgaging of Aircraft Order 1972 (SI 1972/1268)). And note the (essentially obsolete) non-possessory securities known as bonds of bottomry and respondentia at common law for ships and their cargo.

20 Conveyancing and Feudal Reform (Scotland) Act 1970 s. 9.

21 Companies (Floating Charges) (Scotland) Act 1961 s. 5(3).

and ranking issues within a given type of voluntarily granted security are limited to the standard security and the floating charge.[22]

The existence of floating charges in Scots law has made the ranking of security rights more complicated in various respects, including in relation to both voluntary and involuntary securities. Before proceeding to specific rules regarding floating charges, we will first set out five general rules of ranking. These general rules are subject to a number of exceptions,[23] which will be unpacked in this chapter as we explore whether the floating charge is subject to such rules. Prior to establishing exceptions to the rules, however, we need to identify the general rules. The first three apply broadly to security rights, the fourth to the ranking relationship between the categories of fixed securities and floating charges and the fifth applies to ranking within a category and across categories. The first rule is that secured creditors rank ahead of unsecured creditors.[24] Indeed, this is the point of a system allowing the grant of security[25] and is one of the primary objections to a system allowing the grant of rights in security.[26] Accordingly, the recipient of a right in security will rank ahead of those who have not received a right in security, including unsecured creditors and the shareholders of the granter.[27] While floating charges generally adhere to this, they are subject to the prescribed part (a ringfenced amount of a chargor's assets for the benefit of unsecured creditors), which will be discussed further below.

Secondly, the rule(s) relating to catholic and secondary creditors regulate ranking. The intention is to stop a creditor with a wide security package trying to enforce against an asset that has one or more other securities granted over it prior to enforcing against assets that only they have security

22 For discussion of ranking of the bond and disposition in security, which was replaced by the standard security, see e.g. Gloag and Irvine, *Rights in Security* (n 8) 73 onwards. The *ex facie* absolute disposition with back-bond did not allow for multiple ranking voluntary securities in the same way as it involved a transfer of the property (see Gloag and Irvine Ch. 4). For an overview of the natures of these securities and the disputes regarding such matters, see MacPherson, *Floating Charge* (n 5) paras 7–90 onwards; and G L Gretton, 'Radical Rights and Radical Wrongs: A Study in the Law of Trusts, Securities and Insolvency' 1986 Jur Rev 51 and 192.

23 It is a phenomenon noted across many disciplines that more general rules, or models, tend to be inaccurate, but that does not always reduce their utility – see G E P Box, 'Science and Statistics' (1976) 71 *Journal of the American Statistical Association* 791.

24 See Lord Kinnear in *Colquhoun's Trustees v Campbell's Trustees* (1902) 4 F 739 at 743–744; Insolvency (Scotland) (Receivership and Winding up) Rules 2018 (SSI 2018/347) r. 7.27.

25 MacLeod (n 1) para. 11.04.

26 L LoPucki, 'The Unsecured Creditor's Bargain' (1994) 80 Va L Rev 1887.

27 See L Gullifer and J Payne, *Corporate Finance Law: Principles and Policy*, 3rd edn (Oxford: Hart Publishing, 2020) 104–105. Shareholders of the granter will ordinarily rank behind all creditors of the granter, whether secured or unsecured.

over. Consider the situation whereby creditor A has a standard security over property X and also a standard security over property Y, and creditor B, a lower-ranking creditor, has only a standard security over property X. In this situation, creditor A is the catholic creditor and creditor B is the secondary creditor. The rule on catholic and secondary creditors prevents creditor A enforcing against property X before they have enforced against property Y.[28] If A does enforce first against X, they will be required to assign their (remaining) security over Y to B. This is the Scots law equivalent to the English concept of 'marshalling'.[29] The doctrine can be rationalised as follows: if it is accepted that secured creditors should rank ahead of unsecured creditors, one secured creditor should not be able to exhaust the security of another if there is a way to avoid this taking place. An English court has stated 'a person having resort to two funds shall not by his choice disappoint another, having one only'.[30] In the leading Scottish case on the doctrine, the Lord President (Colonsay) summed up the Scots law position in 1855:

> 'In the ordinary case of a catholic creditor—i.e., a creditor holding security over two subjects, which for the sake of simplicity I shall suppose to be heritable subjects—and another creditor holding a postponed security over one of them, there can be no doubt that the catholic creditor is entitled to operate payment out of the two subjects as he best can for his own interest, but he is not entitled arbitrarily or nimiously to proceed in such a manner as to injure the secondary creditor without benefiting himself—as, for instance, capriciously to take his payment entirely out of the subjects over which there is a second security, and thereby to exhaust that subject, to the detriment of the second creditor, leaving the other subject of his own security unaffected or unexhausted. The second creditor will be protected against a proceeding so contrary to equity, and the primary creditor will be compelled either to take his payment in the first instance out of that one of the subjects in which no other creditor holds a special interest, or to assign his right to the second creditor, from whom he has wrested the only subject of his security.'[31]

As will be discussed below in section H, it has been held that the doctrine of catholic and secondary creditors does not apply to floating charges, at least in some contexts; however, the appropriateness of such an approach may be disputed.

---

28 See the passage from *Littlejohn v Black* (1855) 18 D 207 quoted below.
29 *Szepietowski v National Crime Agency* [2013] UKSC 65, [2014] AC 338; P A U Ali, *Marshalling of Securities: Equity and the Prior-Ranking of Secured Debt* (Oxford: Oxford University Press, 1999).
30 *Trimmer v Bayne (No. 2)* (1803) 9 Ves 209 at 211.
31 *Littlejohn v Black* (1855) 18 D 207 at 212; Hardman, *Granting Corporate Security* (n 1) para. 9.04. See also Bell, *Commentaries*, II, 417.

The third general rule is the property law rule of 'offside goals', otherwise known as the rule penalising private knowledge of a prior right. This rule prevents a bad faith second purchaser (or donee) from perfecting their title prior to the first purchaser doing so.[32] The football analogy is of dubious accuracy, especially as the effect is to make the second transaction voidable rather than void (unlike an offside goal).[33] The rule does not just apply to double sales but also to circumstances involving the granting of real rights other than ownership (as well as to rights capable of being made real).[34] It therefore can apply where a security right is created in breach of a prior obligation to transfer or create a real right in favour of someone else.[35] However, the precise ambit of this doctrine for rights in security is unclear. As Dr Patrick has stated: 'while the offside goals rule also applies to undermine security interests completed in the knowledge of breach of conflicting personal obligations of the granter of the security, the scope of application of the rule in this context is quite obscure'.[36]

The doctrine has been expressly applied in the context of rights in security, with the Lord Ordinary (Emslie) stating that a creditor receiving a security over an asset who is aware that someone else may have an uncompleted real right over the asset has to inquire into the nature of that uncompleted real right or may find their security struck down.[37] This could clearly apply to an uncompleted transfer (either outright or in security) or potentially the grant of a security right.[38] It has been suggested, however, that the case stated the obligations on the creditor too strongly.[39]

There is a weaker case for the application of the offside goals rule where both grantees have obtained, or are seeking to obtain, real security rights. As is pointed out in *Professor McDonald's Conveyancing Manual* and *Scottish*

---

32 The leading modern case is *Rodger (Builders) Ltd v Fawdry* 1950 SC 483 at 501. For discussion of the doctrine, see e.g. K G C Reid, *The Law of Property in Scotland* (London: Butterworths Law, 1996) paras 695 onwards; J MacLeod, *Fraud and Voidable Transfer* (Edinburgh: Edinburgh Legal Education Trust, 2020) Ch. 7.

33 See G L Gretton and A J M Steven, *Property, Trusts and Succession*, 4th edn (London: Bloomsbury Professional, 2021) para. 4.48.

34 *Wallace v Simmers* 1960 SC 255.

35 See Hardman, *Granting Corporate Security* (n 1) para. 9–03.

36 H Patrick, 'Charge Registration Reform—Further BIS Consultation', 2011 SLT 81 at 84; see discussion in Hardman, *Granting Corporate Security* (n 1) para. 9–03.

37 *Gibson v Royal Bank of Scotland* [2009] CSOH 14; Hardman, *Granting Corporate Security* (n 1) para. 9–03. The security granted in the *Gibson* case was a standard security.

38 The comments of the Lord Ordinary in *Gibson* were agreed with by the Lord Ordinary (McEwan) in *Wheeldon's Executor Nominate v Spence's Executrix Nominate* [2014] CSOH 69 at [16]; however, the earlier case was distinguished on the facts.

39 R G Anderson and J MacLeod, 'Offside Goals and Interfering with Play' 2009 SLT 93 at 96.

Land Law, certain multiple security rights are compatible or co-existent real rights with the issue being one merely of ranking rather than whether a party can validly obtain a real right.[40] This is in contrast to other situations, such as where there is a transfer of land by X to Z, where X is already bound to grant a standard security to Y, but Z's acquisition of ownership of the property means Y is not able to obtain the security (without invoking the offside goals rule).[41] It may be that the doctrine does not apply to cases involving multiple security rights and that the 'normal' rules of ranking are used.[42] The limited case law on the topic can be considered to support this view.[43] Security rights are obtained in order to acquire a ranking priority over other creditors, so penalising a party for doing exactly that would appear illogical.[44] Due to the nature of floating charges, the application of the doctrine to that form of security is even more unlikely and will be discussed further in section H.

The fourth general rule is that, as between categories of security, fixed security ranks ahead of floating security.[45] This is understandable, and appropriate, given the different characteristics of the two types of security and the different points in time at which creditors obtain rights.[46] However, as we shall see, it is very frequently departed from in practice due to the specific effect of negative pledges. The final general rule applies within specific categories and also between securities in different categories: first in time, stronger by right, or *prior tempore potior jure*.[47] In other words, the sooner a security is established as a real right, the higher its priority. Scots law cases

---

40 D A Brand et al., *Professor McDonald's Conveyancing Manual*, 7th edn (Haywards Heath, Tottel Publishing, 2004) para. 32.61; W M Gordon and S Wortley, *Scottish Land Law*, 3rd edn (Edinburgh: W. Green, 2020) Vol. II paras 19–94 onwards.

41 Despite some mixed case law on the subject, it is suggested in Gordon and Wortley, *Scottish Land Law* (n 40) para. 19–93 that the prospective security holder should be able to assert their personal right against the new owner.

42 Brand et al., *Conveyancing Manual* (n 40) para. 32.61.

43 See *Blackwood v Creditors of Sir George Hamilton* (1749) Mor 4898; *Henderson v Campbell* (1821) 1 S 103; *Leslie v McIndoe's Trustees* (1824) 3 S 48. It is suggested in D A Brand et al., *Conveyancing Manual* (n 40) para. 32.61, that one of the reasons why these cases have never been overturned is that applying the offside goals rule where there are three or more securities may create circles of priority. For instance, securities A, B and C are created in turn but C uses the offside goals rule to obtain priority over A. This would mean that A ranks ahead of B, who ranks ahead of C, who ranks ahead of A. See Gordon and Wortley, *Scottish Land Law* (n 40) para. 19–99 for additional consideration of this. And see below for further discussion of circles of priority.

44 See Gordon and Wortley, *Scottish Land Law* (n 40) para. 19–97.

45 See MacLeod (n 1) para. 11–63; Companies Act 1985 s. 464(4).

46 See J Hardman, 'Hohfeld and the Scots Law Floating Charge', Chapter 7 within this volume; MacPherson, *Floating Charge* (n 5) Ch. 6.

47 MacLeod (n 1) paras 11.13–11.15.

on real rights in security confirmed this principle at common law.[48] The rule is also reflected in legislation for the principal category of fixed security for which it is relevant: standard securities rank in order of their creation (with registration in the Land Register being required).[49] The Scottish Law Commission proposes equivalent rules for the statutory pledge, i.e. priority based on when a real right is acquired by registration (in the Register of Statutory Pledges).[50] The policy is simple: it is only fair that those who have received security cannot have their ranking altered by the granter subsequently creating security. The position for floating charges is less straightforward and depends on whether or not there is a negative pledge and also which type(s) of security the floating charge is in competition with.

Having identified the general rules, we will now turn our attention to discussing the specific rules for floating charges in more detail.

C. DEFAULT RANKING RULES FOR FLOATING CHARGES

In addition to the foregoing general rules of ranking, there are a number of default rules specifically for the ranking of floating charges against other types of security right: voluntary fixed securities, fixed securities arising by operation of law, other floating charges, diligences and other security rights. The ranking relationship between a floating charge and each of these forms of security will be considered in turn in this section. Rules involving preferential creditors and the prescribed part are not dealt with here but are discussed later in relation to ranking and distributions.

(1) Against voluntary fixed securities

Voluntary fixed securities encompass standard securities, pledges and assignations in security. As well as these general forms of security in Scots law, the term also includes special types of voluntary security, such as aircraft and ship mortgages.[51] The default ranking rules for competitions between floating

---

48 See e.g. *Blackwood v Creditors of George Hamilton* (1740) Mor 4898; *Henderson v Campbell* (1821) 1 S 103; *Leslie v McIndoe's Trustees* (1824) 3 S 48.

49 See Conveyancing and Feudal Reform (Scotland) Act 1970 ss. 11(1) and 13(1); and Titles to Land Consolidation (Scotland) Act 1868 s. 120.

50 See Scottish Law Commission, *Report on Moveable Transactions* (Scot. Law Com. No. 249, 2017) paras 26.3 onwards and Draft Bill ss. 48 and 64(1)–(3).

51 For these forms of security, see Merchant Shipping Act 1995 s. 16(1) and Sch. 1 paras 7–13 (and formerly Merchant Shipping Act 1894 ss. 31–46); Civil Aviation Act 1982 s. 86; Mortgaging of Aircraft Order 1972 (SI 1972/1268).

charges and voluntary fixed securities are contained in the Companies Act 1985 s. 464(3)–(5). It is provided in s. 464(3) that the order of ranking between a floating charge and a fixed security, whether subsisting or future, is determined by s. 464(4) and (5). This is, however, subject to the order being determined by s. 464(1)(a) (negative pledges) or (b) (ranking agreements), both of which involve a departure from the default rules and will be discussed in the following sections. While the provisions in s. 464(3)–(5) refer to 'fixed security' and 'fixed securities' broadly, they, in fact, exclude fixed securities arising by operation of law. This is because there is a separate rule for fixed securities arising by operation of law, which will be examined in the next sub-section.

According to s. 464(4)(a), 'a fixed security, the right to which has been constituted as a real right before a floating charge has attached to all or any part of the property of the company, has priority of ranking over the floating charge'. Thus, in order to ascertain whether a floating charge ranks ahead of a voluntary fixed security (under the default rule) one must take into account the date when the fixed security was constituted as a real right and the date when the floating charge attaches to the relevant property. If the fixed security becomes a real right before the floating charge attaches, the fixed security ranks first, if the floating charge attaches before the fixed security is constituted as a real right, the floating charge ranks first. In the event that the floating charge attaches on the same day that the fixed security is created, they may rank equally with one another, unless perhaps it can be shown that one was created before the other on that date.[52]

As noted above, it is reasonable for floating charges to rank behind fixed securities while the charge remains floating. However, once the charge attaches, it does so as if it were a fixed security.[53] It is therefore logical for the competition to be viewed, from this point, as if it involved two (or more) voluntary fixed securities and, therefore, for it to be determined by the general rule that the earlier in time has priority. And the relevant time point for each is when the security has real effect, which, for the floating charge, is attachment.[54]

---

52 There is no equivalent rule for such a competition as there is for floating charges that are received for registration in the same postal delivery, which are to rank equally (s. 464(4)(c)).

53 Companies Act 1985 s. 463(2); Insolvency Act ss. 53(7) and 54(6) and Sch. B1 para. 115(4).

54 Floating charges do have some real effect upon attachment and have been described as a real right at this point: see e.g. *National Commercial Bank of Scotland v Liquidators of Telford Grier Mackay & Co* 1969 SC 181; Reid, *Property* (n 32) para. 5 and fn 5; S Styles, 'The Two Types of Floating Charge' (1999) 4 SLPQ 235 at 240. However, whether a floating charge can

It is somewhat problematic, from a doctrinal Scots law point of view, that the ranking rule does not depend on publicity with respect to the floating charge. As regards fixed securities, publicity is ordinarily provided by registration (such as for standard securities) or by the giving of possession (such as for pledges), and this is necessary in order to create the relevant securities.[55] But for floating charges, a publicity event is not a pre-requisite for the creation of the charge nor its attachment. It is true that the creation of a charge requires to be followed by registration in the charges register within twenty-one days from the day after the creation date for the charge to be fully effective and that the events surrounding attachment in relation to receivership, administration and liquidation involve elements of publicity.[56] However, the floating charge is unusual in Scots law by its non-adherence to the publicity principle in terms of its creation and the point at which it has real effect.[57] Separating creation of a security right from its having real effect is also unusual in Scots law. While the absence of publicity is not too much of a problem for the creation of the charge in the context of the default ranking rule, as it will rank behind fixed securities, the problem is more pronounced if the charge has a negative pledge and is therefore to rank from its creation date. It is also an issue for unsecured creditors, including potential unsecured creditors, who may wish to ascertain whether a security exists that will lower their ranking priority. Yet it is perhaps unlikely that many unsecured creditors would check for such security and, in any event, they would be faced with the possibility that a later-granted security would also have priority over them.

(2) Against fixed securities arising by operation of law

A clear statement is provided in s. 464(2) regarding the ranking relationship of floating charges and fixed securities arising by operation of law. It states: '[w]here all or any part of the property of a company is subject both

accurately be described as a real right in the normal sense of the term is a vexed question – see MacPherson, *Floating Charge* (n 5) paras 5–32 onwards and 6–83 onwards.

55 See Conveyancing and Feudal Reform (Scotland) Act 1970 s. 11 for standard securities, and for the required forms of delivery for pledge, see Steven, *Pledge and Lien* (n 17) paras 6–07 onwards and Scottish Law Commission, *Report on Moveable Transactions* (n 50) paras 17.17 onwards and 25.2 onwards. The Scottish Law Commission propose that legislation should render ineffective the rule in *Hamilton v Western Bank* (1856) 19 D 152, that actual delivery is required to create a pledge.

56 See MacPherson, *Floating Charge* (n 5) paras 3–16 onwards.

57 Albeit that the extent to which the publicity principle more broadly is a description of reality or a normative policy goal may be debated.

to a floating charge and to a fixed security arising by operation of law, the fixed security has priority over the floating charge'. The provision raises the question: what is a fixed security arising by operation of law? This form of security is also known in Scots law as tacit security and arises automatically in certain circumstances, rather than being voluntarily created. The principal security rights within the category are the landlord's hypothec and lien.

Yet the position for the landlord's hypothec has not been without controversy. In a sheriff court case from 1983, *Cumbernauld Development Corporation v Mustone*,[58] it was held that a landlord's hypothec was not a fixed security but rather 'a charge having the nature of a floating charge'.[59] This decision was heavily criticised and was contrary to what was intended when the floating charge was introduced.[60] In a subsequent sheriff court case, around a decade later, *Grampian Regional Council v Drill Stem (Inspection Services) Ltd*,[61] the sheriff correctly held that a landlord's hypothec is a fixed security arising by operation of law and thereby has ranking priority over an attached floating charge. This has not changed with the abolition of sequestration for rent,[62] but a landlord will now need to rely on a distribution from a liquidator, administrator or receiver ahead of a floating charge holder.[63]

As far as liens are concerned, the definition of fixed security arising by operation of law encompasses general liens and special liens.[64] The term almost certainly includes statutory liens, such as the lien of a seller in possession under s. 39(1)(a) of the Sale of Goods Act 1979.[65] Thus, if a creditor of the granter of a floating charge holds a lien over that party's property, it will give that creditor priority over a floating charge holder. This will allow

---

58 1983 SLT (Sh Ct) 55.

59 This is a term used in the definition of 'fixed security' and is utilised to help define fixed security by being excluded from its meaning (see Companies Act 1985 s. 486(1) and Insolvency Act 1986 s. 70(1)).

60 See MacPherson, *Floating Charge* (n 5) paras 8–61–8–62 and the sources cited there.

61 1994 SCLR 36.

62 Bankruptcy and Diligence etc. (Scotland) Act 2007 s. 208(1).

63 For discussion of the enforcement of the landlord's hypothec in the context of the tenant's insolvency, see A Sweeney, *The Landlord's Hypothec* (Edinburgh: Edinburgh Legal Education Trust, 2021) Ch. 11. Outside insolvency processes, it may be possible for the landlord's hypothec to be enforced using diligence, namely attachment or arrestment – see A Sweeney, *The Landlord's Hypothec* Ch. 10.

64 See MacPherson, *Floating Charge* (n 5) paras 8–62–8–63. For details of these lien types, see Steven, *Pledge and Lien* (n 17) Chs 16–17. See also Macgregor et al., *Commercial Law in Scotland* (n 1) para. 7.4.

65 See MacPherson, *Floating Charge* (n 5) para. 8–63.

the lienholder to seek the court's authority to sell the relevant property and obtain payment prior to the chargeholder or to receive distribution from a liquidator, administrator or receiver before the holder of the floating charge.

It is clear that if a floating charge is in a competition with a fixed security arising by operation of law created prior to the floating charge attaching then the fixed security prevails, even if created after the floating charge. But is the position different if the tacit security only comes into existence after the floating charge has *attached*? This could occur where, for example, payment is due to the repairer of the chargor's property some time after attachment has taken place but the repairer is not paid and retains possession of the property, giving rise to the repairer's lien. Alternatively, the chargor may, prior to their insolvency, have failed to pay rent and then goods are brought onto leased premises, causing the landlord's hypothec to extend to such property, after a floating charge has attached. It could be contended that the ranking relationship outlined in s. 464(2) is limited to where the fixed security has been created while the floating charge is floating and that once the floating charge attaches it should be treated as a fixed security (as per its attachment mechanism), allowing it to rank ahead of a later fixed security. However, Dr Sweeney persuasively argues that this view is incorrect.[66] In his study of the landlord's hypothec, he points out that the statement in s. 464(2) is clear and without exception and if it had been intended that a floating charge could rank ahead of such security this could have been specified in the legislation, as is done for other forms of fixed security.[67] He also notes that floating charges are still treated as floating charges under relevant legislation if they are created as such, even if they have subsequently attached.[68] This approach is the preferable one and is also supported by the fact that upon attachment a floating charge does not become a fixed security, it is merely treated as one for certain purposes. Consequently, the references to floating charges in the legislation still apply to an attached floating charge, meaning that it will rank behind a post-attachment tacit security.

---

66 Sweeney, *The Landlord's Hypothec* (n 63) paras 11–30 onwards.
67 Under Companies Act 1985 s. 464(4)(a), whereby a floating charge can rank ahead of a fixed security if the charge attaches before the fixed security has been constituted as a real right.
68 Sweeney, *The Landlord's Hypothec* (n 63) para. 11–31. Insolvency Act 1986 s. 251 defines 'floating charge' as 'a charge which, as created, was a floating charge and includes a floating charge within section 462 of the Companies Act [1985] (Scottish floating charges)'.

(3) Against other floating charges

It is, of course, possible for multiple floating charges to be granted by the same company. This necessitates ranking rules to regulate the priority between floating charges. Section 464(4)(b) provides that floating charges rank against one another 'according to the time of registration' in the charges register. Meanwhile, s. 464(4)(c) clarifies that 'floating charges ... received by the registrar [of companies] for registration by the same postal delivery rank with one another equally'.[69] This latter rule is, however, of reduced relevance nowadays due to the reliance on online filing.[70]

The key point then is that the timing of registration determines the default ranking between floating charges, irrespective of their creation dates. Thus, if floating charge A is granted on day one, and floating charge B is granted on day two, but B is registered on day three and A is only registered on day four, B has priority. This is, however, subject to the major caveat that the existence of a negative pledge clause for floating charge A could have prohibited or otherwise restricted the creation of a later-granted floating charge, such as B, and thus allowed A to rank ahead despite the registration situation. These clauses are used in the vast majority of floating charges and are discussed further below. Nevertheless, it is interesting to note that the default ranking rule between floating charges involves a publicity event (i.e. registration), which contrasts with the ranking of floating charges in other respects.

Where a floating charge holder, whose charge has been registered in the charges register, receives written intimation that another floating charge has subsequently been registered, the ranking of the first floating charge is limited in certain respects.[71] Section 464(5) provides that the preference is restricted to security for: (a) the holder's present advances; (b) future advances they may be required to make under the charge instrument or any ancillary document; (c) interest due or to become due on all such advances; (d) any expenses or outlays which may be reasonably incurred by the holder; and (e) if the floating charge is to secure a contingent liability other than a

---

69 The provision refers to the receipt of floating charges by the registrar, but this should be read to mean the floating charge instruments. It should be noted that when charges (floating or otherwise) are being registered with Companies House, there may be a delay between the documentation being received and it being processed, but the registration date will be backdated to the date of receipt.

70 As well as reasons such as cost, simplicity and certainty of receipt by the registrar of companies favouring online filing, there is also a risk that between documentation being sent by post and being received, another party may have filed a security online, which would have priority.

71 Companies Act 1985 s. 464(3)-(5).

liability arising under any further advances made from time to time, then the maximum sum to which the contingent liability is capable of amounting, whether or not it is contractually limited. The provision is similar to s. 13 of the Conveyancing and Feudal Reform (Scotland) Act 1970, which outlines the priority restrictions for a standard security holder who receives notice of the creation of a subsequent standard security. Depending on the nature of the sum secured by the first floating charge (all sums provided by way of overdraft or a set figure), this could interact with the rule in *Clayton's Case*.[72]

Rather strangely, s. 464(5) may not apply to floating charges where the ranking is determined by a negative pledge clause or ranking agreement. This is because s. 464(3) provides that s. 464(4)–(5) determines the order of ranking *except* where s. 464(1)(a) or (b) apply.[73] As such, it is possible that if there is a floating charge with negative pledge then, subject to contrary agreements, it has priority for all sums, even if sums are voluntarily extended to the debtor after a subsequent floating charge comes to the attention of the first charge holder. This statutory construction may be at odds with what practitioners consider the law to be regarding the effect of notice of a second floating charge but the statutory construction is relatively clear. To combat this issue, any ranking agreement should specify the exact extent of the priority conferred. There is also no equivalent to s. 464(5) for the relationship between floating charges and fixed securities and s. 13 of the Conveyancing and Feudal Reform (Scotland) Act 1970 does not appear to apply to floating charges ranking against standard securities, as floating charges are not registered in the land register. This means that a prior-ranking fixed security is likely to have priority for all sums, whether or not yet provided, at least prior to the charge's attachment. The extent to which the floating charge approximates the relevant form of fixed security upon its attachment may then determine whether the priority effect of the fixed security is to be restricted (e.g. if the floating charge attaches to heritable property as if it were a registered standard security,[74] this could cause restrictions due to the existence of s. 13 of the Conveyancing and Feudal Reform (Scotland) Act 1970). However, it is unlikely that a floating charge transforms into a fixed

72 See part E below.
73 With s. 464(1)(a) allowing negative pledges and s. 464(1)(b) giving effect to ranking agreements.
74 As per the view of the attachment mechanism taken in cases such as *Forth & Clyde Construction Co Ltd v Trinity Timber & Plywood Co Ltd* 1984 SC 1; and *Sharp v Thomson* 1995 SC 455, especially per Lord Coulsfield at 488. Despite the House of Lords (1997 SC (HL) 66) reversing the decision of the Inner House, they did not disagree with the Inner House on this point, see at 70 per Lord Jauncey and at 79 per Lord Clyde. But see MacPherson, *Floating Charge* (n 5) Ch. 5 for some of the problems with this type of attachment effect.

security to such an extent that it would enable these restrictions to apply.[75] If, instead, the floating charge ranks ahead, whether due to a negative pledge or by attaching before the real right is created, the construction of s. 464 of the 1985 Act may mean that it will have priority for all sums, whether already provided or to be provided in future. This highlights the importance of carefully drafted ranking agreements to reflect the intentions of the parties, especially if the intention departs from the default rules.

(4) Against diligences

Diligences are judicial securities, a form of involuntary security. The principal types of diligence are arrestment and attachment (which replaced poinding) for moveable property[76] and inhibition and adjudication for heritable property.[77] Given the potential scope of the floating charge, it can be in competition with any of the diligences. The relationship between floating charges and diligence has been one of the most controversial and vexed aspects of floating charges in Scotland.[78] The ranking position is not, however, outlined in s. 464 of the Companies Act 1985. Instead, s. 463(1) provides that where a floating charge attaches to property as a result of the granter company's liquidation, it does so:

'subject to the rights of any person who:
(a) has effectually executed diligence on the property or any part of it; or
(b) holds a fixed security over the property or any part of it ranking in priority to the floating charge; or
(c) holds over the property or any part of it another floating charge so ranking'.

Consequently, those who have 'effectually executed diligence' have priority over a floating charge holder in the chargor's liquidation, as do those with prior-ranking fixed securities and floating charges. In the context of receivership, the powers of a receiver are 'subject to the rights of any person who

---

75 See MacPherson, *Floating Charge* (n 5) paras 5–21 onwards and 6–07 onwards.
76 With attachment applicable to corporeal moveables and arrestment mainly used for incorporeal property but available if corporeal moveables are in the hands of a third party.
77 There are, however, variants of these (e.g. money attachment and earnings arrestment) and adjudication can be used for certain types of moveable property, but only if no other form of security is available for such property (e.g. intellectual property). The Bankruptcy and Diligence etc. (Scotland) Act 2007 Part 4 provides that adjudication is to be replaced by land attachment and residual attachment but the relevant provisions have not been brought into force and it is not clear if they will be. For more details regarding diligence, see Macgregor et al., *Commercial Law in Scotland* (n 1) Ch. 9.
78 See G L Gretton, 'The Story of the Scots Law Floating Charge: 1961 to Date', Chapter 4 within this volume.

has effectually executed diligence on all or any part of the property of the company prior to the appointment of the receiver'.[79] And a party who has effectually executed diligence is one of the parties to receive distribution payments from a receiver prior to a floating charge holder.[80]

The key issue then is to determine what constitutes effectually executed diligence. In 1977, the Inner House in *Lord Advocate v Royal Bank of Scotland Ltd*[81] held that an arrestment without furthcoming[82] was not effectually executed diligence on property for the purposes of the (then-applicable) floating charges legislation. The case received significant academic criticism due to it creating illogical results and ranking problems and because it did not conform to the intention of parliament, which was to give priority to diligence creditors over floating charge holders.[83] However, the courts accepted the decision as correct and its ratio was considered to apply to inhibitions, so that an inhibition without adjudication was deemed not to be effectually executed diligence.[84] *Lord Advocate v RBS* also cast some doubt on the ranking relationships between floating charges and other diligences. While the courts did not show any sign of overturning the decision, the Scottish Law Commission suggested doing so by legislation.[85]

Legislative intervention has not proved necessary, however, as in 2017 a five-judge First Division bench in *MacMillan v T Leith Developments Ltd*[86]

---

79 Insolvency Act 1986 s. 55(3)(a). The powers of a receiver are also subject to the rights of any person who has a floating charge or fixed security that has priority over or ranks equally with the floating charge by virtue of which the receiver was appointed: s. 55(3)(b).

80 Insolvency Act 1986 s. 60(1)(b).

81 1977 SC 155.

82 An action of furthcoming is used to enable the arrester to receive arrested funds from the arrestee and thereby complete the diligence. Its importance has been reduced as arrested funds are now released automatically from the arrestee to the arrester after fourteen weeks from the date of service of the schedule of arrestment unless there is an objection: Debtors (Scotland) Act 1987 ss. 73J and 73L–73M.

83 See, e.g. W A Wilson, 'Prior Arrestment of Funds and Floating Charges (Scotland)' [1978] JBL 367; W A Wilson, 'Effectively Executed Diligence', 1978 Jur Rev 253; G L Gretton, 'Diligence, Trusts and Floating Charges—I: "Effectually Executed Diligence"' (1981) 26 JLSS 57; G L Gretton, 'Inhibitions and Company Insolvencies', 1983 SLT (News) 145; A J Sim, 'The Receiver and Effectually Executed Diligence' 1984 SLT (News) 25; S Wortley, 'Squaring the Circle: Revisiting the Receiver and "Effectually Executed Diligence"', 2000 Jur Rev 325. See also Gretton, 'The Story of the Scots Law Floating Charge: 1961 to Date', Chapter 4.

84 See *Armour and Mycroft, Petitioners*, 1983 SLT 453; *Taymech Ltd v Rush and Tompkins Ltd*, 1990 SLT 681; *Iona Hotels Ltd (In Receivership) v Craig*, 1990 SC 330, per Lord President Hope at 334–335, who agreed with the decision in *Lord Advocate v RBS*, but distinguished it.

85 See Scottish Law Commission, *Discussion Paper on Moveable Transactions* (Scot. Law Com. DP No. 151, 2011) paras 22.33–22.34.

86 [2017] CSIH 23, 2017 SC 642.

correctly overturned *Lord Advocate v RBS*.[87] *MacMillan* involved an inhibition in competition with a floating charge but the decision has wider effect for the meaning of effectually executed diligence.[88] Diligence will be effectually executed if is validly executed and is not rendered ineffectual by being executed within close proximity to liquidation.[89] The term also extends to arrestment and inhibition on the dependence and interim attachment, but the underlying action will need to be successful for the diligence creditor to be entitled to payment before the floating charge holder.

Yet diligence being effectually executed is not enough by itself for it to rank ahead of a floating charge. Attention needs to be paid to the effects of the diligence in question. Despite *MacMillan* involving inhibition and the court concluding that it could be effectually executed diligence, the case dealt with the law prior to provisions in the Bankruptcy and Diligence etc. (Scotland) Act 2007 coming into effect. Under s. 154(1) of that Act, it is stated that an inhibition 'does not confer any preference' in any sequestration, insolvency proceedings (including liquidation, receivership, administration and company voluntary arrangements) or other process in which there is ranking.[90] How far the section extends is unclear, but given that inhibition can be effectually executed diligence and one of its effects is to prohibit voluntary dealings relating to land, the grant of a subsequent floating charge would seem to be subject to the inhibition, but how this could be given effect to without conferring a preference in a ranking process is unknown.

Thus, although *MacMillan* has resolved certain difficulties involving floating charges and diligence, other problems remain.[91] These include the status of diligence in administration. Diligence cannot be carried out in

---

87 For consideration of the case, see A D J MacPherson, 'The Circle Squared? Floating Charges and Diligence after *MacMillan v T Leith Developments Ltd*' 2018 Jur Rev 230.

88 See the discussion in A D J MacPherson, 'The Circle Squared?'.

89 If an arrestment, attachment or inhibition is executed within sixty days of liquidation, it will be ineffectual: Bankruptcy (Scotland) Act 2016 s. 24, as applied to liquidation by the Insolvency Act 1986 s. 185(1)(a). There may be other situations that cause diligence not to be 'effectually executed' – see MacPherson (n 87) at 239 and 247. It is also arguable that the effect of the Diligence Act 1661, as applied to adjudications by the Adjudications Act 1672, in combination with the effect of liquidation under Insolvency Act 1986 s. 185(1)(a) applying Bankruptcy (Scotland) Act 2016 s. 24(2)(a), renders an adjudication ineffectual if it became effective within a year and a day prior to the liquidation.

90 Consequently, if the circumstances in *MacMillan* came before a court now, the charge holder would prevail, holding as it did a charge that was granted prior to the execution of the inhibition (albeit that the debts due to the charge holder post-dated the inhibition).

91 See MacPherson (n 87) at 240 onwards.

administration[92] but it is not obvious what effect administration has on diligence executed prior to commencement of the administration. The distribution provisions relating to Scottish floating charges in administration in fact do not even mention diligences. It is desirable for them to be given priority over floating charges in that context but it is questionable whether the legislative wording supports this approach.[93] Although the law of floating charges deserves criticism for ranking confusion and incoherence, part of the blame must lie with uncertainty regarding the nature and effects of diligences.

A further ranking matter involving diligences and floating charges is whether a floating charge would have ranking priority if it attached prior to the diligence being effectually executed. If the floating charge attached in liquidation or administration it would not generally be possible for diligence to be effectually executed afterwards. This is due to liquidation rendering diligences a short time prior to its commencement and thereafter ineffectual and because of the moratorium on executing diligence in administration.[94] The position is different in receivership. There are no express provisions to preclude the execution or completion of diligence; however, given that the floating charge attaches as if it were a fixed security, the ordinary ranking rule of *prior tempore potior jure* should apply to confer priority on the charge ahead of any diligence.[95]

(5) Against other security rights

If the rules in the Companies Act 1985 are comprehensive as to the ranking of floating charges against other security rights, then it must be possible for every type of security right to be included in one of the categories covered by those rules. With this in mind, two further types of security right will be

---

92 Insolvency Act 1986 Sch. B1 para. 43(6), which imposes a moratorium on legal processes. The provision states: '[n]o legal process (including legal proceedings, execution, distress and diligence) may be instituted or continued against the company or property of the company except– (a) with the consent of the administrator, or (b) with the permission of the court'.

93 For further details, see MacPherson (n 87) at 242 onwards.

94 For liquidation, see Bankruptcy (Scotland) Act 2016 s. 24, as applied to liquidation by the Insolvency Act 1986 s. 185(1)(a); and for administration, see Insolvency Act 1986 Sch. B1 para. 43(6) – for the diligence to be instituted or continued in administration it would require the consent of the administrator or permission of the court.

95 For discussion, see MacPherson, *Floating Charge* (n 5) paras 6–68 onwards. In *Forth & Clyde* (n 74), the floating charge was considered to attach to book debts as if it were an assignation in security, which meant that the property was deemed to be assigned to the chargeholder. This rendered a post-attachment arrestment by a creditor of the chargor ineffective.

discussed here: agricultural charges; and charging orders.[96] It will be seen that although such securities can fit into the rules within the floating charges legislation, sometimes ranking rules are expressly provided in other legislation instead.

As discussed in an earlier chapter, the agricultural charge can be considered something of a precursor of the floating charge in Scots law, having been introduced by the Agricultural Credits (Scotland) Act 1929.[97] It is more limited in its scope than the floating charge and can only be granted by agricultural cooperatives in favour of banks.[98] It covers 'stocks of merchandise from time to time belonging to and in the possession of' the granter.[99] The fact that the agricultural charge covers property within a class, as that class changes over time, and property can be sold and thereby released from the charge without the permission of the creditor[100] makes it comparable to the floating charge. Yet it seems as if the agricultural charge creates a security interest in the security property items immediately rather than awaiting an 'attachment' event.[101] In this respect, it could be considered a fixed security.

Consequently, the agricultural charge is perhaps on the borderline between a fixed security and a floating security. The definition of 'fixed security' in both s. 486(1) of the Companies Act 1985 and s. 70(1) of the Insolvency Act 1986 contrasts such security with 'a floating charge or a charge having the nature of a floating charge'. While the agricultural charge is not a 'floating charge' in the strict sense in the legislation, not being the form of security that can be granted by companies under the Companies Act 1985 s. 462, it could be considered a security 'having the nature of a floating charge'.[102] However, any dubiety about its nature and ranking position as against a floating charge is removed by statutory provision. The Cooperative and Community Benefit Societies Act 2014 s. 62(5)–(6), provides that if assets

---

96 Gretton and Steven, *Property, Trusts and Succession* (n 33) paras 21.32 and 21.57, divide security rights into voluntary securities and involuntary securities, with the latter consisting of tacit securities, judicial securities and charging orders.

97 MacPherson, 'The "Pre-History" of Floating Charges in Scots Law', Chapter 1.

98 Agricultural Credits (Scotland) Act 1929 s. 5(1). The organisations that can grant such a charge were known as industrial and provident societies but are now co-operative societies or community benefit societies (Cooperative and Community Benefit Society Act 2014).

99 Agricultural Credits (Scotland) Act 1929 s. 5(2).

100 Agricultural Credits (Scotland) Act 1929 s. 6(5).

101 For enforcement, see Agricultural Credits (Scotland) Act 1929 s. 6(1).

102 There are other forms of security that could be considered to be a security 'having the nature of a floating charge' such as a mortgage of the undertaking of a company created by private Act – for details of this type of security, see R G Anderson, 'Borrowing on the Undertaking: Scottish Statutory Companies', Chapter 2 within this volume; MacPherson, *Floating Charge* (n 5) paras 4–28 onwards; and MacPherson, 'The "Pre-History" of Floating Charges', Chapter 1.

of a registered society are subject to a floating charge (which can be granted by such societies by virtue of s. 62(1)–(4)) and an agricultural charge, the relevant ranking provisions apply as if the agricultural charge were a floating charge registered at the same time as it was registered under Part 2 of the 1929 Act.[103] The removal of the registration requirement for agricultural charges by the Financial Services and Markets Act 2000 (Consequential Amendments and Repeals) Order 2001[104] therefore creates a problem in this regard. In any event, the likelihood of any such ranking competition is nevertheless low, given how few agricultural charges exist, in part because of the ability of entities involved in agriculture to create floating charges instead. The Scottish Law Commission has recommended that the law should be amended so that no new agricultural charges can be created.[105]

Charging orders are a more common form of security than agricultural charges. Professors Gretton and Steven classify them as one of the three sub-categories comprising involuntary securities, along with tacit securities and judicial securities (i.e. diligences).[106] A charging order is a security over heritable property established by a public body owed money by the owner of the property. They exist by way of legislation and there are, in fact, a number of different types of charging order. The term charging orders as used here includes 'repayment charges' under the Housing (Scotland) Act 2006 s. 172. Other examples of legislation that provide for charging orders are the Housing (Scotland) Act 1987, the Town and Country Planning (Scotland) Act 1997 and the Building (Scotland) Act 2003.[107]

In terms of the ranking of charging orders against other security rights, this depends on whether the legislation concerning the charging order makes provision for its ranking. Public policy considerations mean that charging orders are often expressly given a high ranking due to them being created in favour of public bodies. For instance, s. 173(2) of the Housing (Scotland) Act 2006 provides that a registered repayment charge constitutes a charge on the property and has priority over all existing and future 'burdens and incumbrances on the same property' with some exceptions relating to public

---

103 Previously, the Industrial and Provident Societies Act 1967 s. 3 was to the same effect.
104 SI 2001/3649 art. 216. This is noted by the Scottish Law Commission, *Report on Moveable Transactions* (n 50) paras 17.34 and 38.13.
105 Scottish Law Commission, *Report on Moveable Transactions* (n 50) para. 38.15 and Draft Bill s. 115.
106 Gretton and Steven (n 33) para. 21.57.
107 For more details about charging orders, see Gordon and Wortley, *Scottish Land Law* (n 40) paras 22–11 onwards. The charging order provisions in ss. 158B-158F of the 1997 Act have not yet been brought into force.

bodies. The ranking rules for charging orders under the Housing (Scotland) Act 1987 are expressed in substantially the same terms.[108] As such, this type of security would have priority over a floating charge, whether or not the floating charge was created or attached earlier or later than the creation of the repayment charge.

If, instead, the legislation for a particular charging order makes no express provision for ranking, then it will ordinarily rank against other security rights according to *prior tempore potior jure*.[109] In relation to floating charges, a charging order can be considered a 'fixed security'. However, it is neither a 'fixed security arising by operation of law' (as its creation depends on the public body's action) nor a fixed security that can be prohibited by a negative pledge (as it is not voluntarily granted by the chargor). Consequently, s. 464(4)(a) will apply so that the charging order will rank ahead of the floating charge if it is constituted as a real right through registration in the land register prior to the floating charge's attachment, whereas the floating charge will rank ahead if it attaches before the charging order becomes a real right.

Depending on how broadly or narrowly the meaning of security rights is drawn, there are other forms of asset security available in Scots law.[110] However, functional securities such as retention of title, transfer of ownership as a security device and trust mechanisms do not involve ranking in the strict sense, as the relevant creditor has ownership of the property or it is held in a trust patrimony on their behalf. This means that the floating charge does not attach to the property and so there is no direct ranking competition between the charge holder and the creditor with the functional security. As such, these securities have not been discussed here but are mentioned later in this chapter and are also discussed in detail elsewhere.[111]

Furthermore, this section has not considered preferential creditors, the prescribed part, or expenses in insolvency processes, which provide priority over a floating charge holder. This is because these do not constitute security rights. They are, however, referred to in the distribution section below and in the chapter of this book by Professor McKenzie Skene.

---

108 See Housing (Scotland) Act 1987 Sch. 9 para. 4.
109 See *Sowman v City of Glasgow District Council* 1984 SC 91; Gordon and Wortley, *Scottish Land Law* (n 40) para. 22–11.
110 For discussion, see G L Gretton, 'The Concept of Security' in D J Cusine (ed), *A Scots Conveyancing Miscellany: Essays in Honour of Professor J M Halliday* (Edinburgh: W. Green, 1987) 130.
111 See e.g. A D J MacPherson, 'Floating Charges and Trust Property in Scots Law: A Tale of Two Patrimonies?' (2018) 22 Edin L Rev 1; and MacPherson, *Floating Charge* (n 5) especially Chs 8 and 9.

D. NEGATIVE PLEDGES

This combination of default rights leaves a floating charge holder in an invidious position. Whilst they can be sure that they will rank ahead of subsequently registered floating charges, there is a risk that another floating charge is granted afterwards but obtains ranking priority by being registered first. There is also a much greater and more significant risk of a charge holder being 'trumped' by a grant of a fixed security. The fixed security would have priority if constituted as a real right before the charge's attachment, due to the default rule outlined above. The floating charge is the only type of voluntary security for which this is relevant. The recipient of a standard security can be sure that they will rank ahead of any subsequent floating charges and standard securities, as can the holder of a pledge or an assignation in security. Each of these provide an inherent protective measure: they each rank ahead of floating charges, the requirements of delivery[112] and transfer[113] in respect of moveable property prevent a subsequent fixed security being granted and standard securities fall under the *prior tempore* rule.[114] The risk of being trumped is, therefore, unique to the floating charge amongst voluntary securities.

This risk has been consistently ameliorated by statute. The original formulation stated that a floating charge could rank ahead of a subsequently granted fixed security if the floating charge contained a prohibition on the granter granting any subsequent security having priority over, or ranking *pari passu* with the relevant floating charge.[115] This remains the case under the current regime – if a floating charge instrument contains in it a provision that states that the granter cannot grant a security (fixed or floating) having priority over, or ranking *pari passu* with, the floating charge, then the floating charge has priority over any subsequently granted security (whether fixed or floating).[116] Such a provision provides the functional equivalent to the protections enjoyed by the holders of other securities, and is referred to as a negative pledge.[117] The phrase negative pledge appears to have been borrowed from English law, although under English law, the effect of a

---

112 *Hamilton v Western Bank of Scotland* (1856) 19 D 152.

113 Anderson, *Assignation* (n 10) Ch. 6.

114 This is provided for by Conveyancing and Feudal Reform (Scotland) Act 1970 ss. 11(1) and 13(1); Titles to Land Consolidation (Scotland) Act 1868 s. 120.

115 Companies (Floating Charges) (Scotland) Act 1961 s. 5(2)(c).

116 Companies Act 1985 s. 464(1)(a) and (1A).

117 See Hardman, *Granting Corporate Security* (n 1) para. 6–24.

negative pledge is less absolute and automatic than in Scots law.[118] For a floating charge holder to rank ahead of a fixed chargee in English law, the latter needs to have (actual or constructive) notice of the negative pledge. Due to the requirement to include details of a negative pledge in the particulars of a floating charge sent for registration in the register of charges, third party chargees will ordinarily be deemed to have notice of a negative pledge once registration has taken place.[119] The surprising result is that in terms of negative pledges affecting third parties, English law may be considered more compliant with the publicity principle than Scots law. Yet when the Scottish floating charge was first introduced, a floating charge with negative pledge required to be registered prior to the constitution of a fixed security as a real right in order for the floating charge to rank ahead.[120] This was, however, unfortunately omitted from subsequent legislation, allowing a floating charge to rank ahead of a later fixed security even if the holder of the latter has no means to know of the existence of the floating charge (i.e. it has not yet been registered).[121]

There are two key elements of any negative pledge, the external and the internal. First, the external. It is important that any negative pledge prevents securities granted in favour of third parties from having priority over the floating charge held by the creditor. To cover this, there are two options: the wording of the negative pledge can prevent the grant of subsequent ranking security that would rank prior absolutely, or it can prevent such grant without the prior consent of the floating charge holder. The second is common[122] but its operation needs to be used carefully: a holder of a floating charge needs to be very clear and explicit as to what they are agreeing to. Thus in *Bank of Ireland v Bass Brewers (No. 2)*, a consent under such a provision was deemed to have the effect of consenting not just to the grant of security, but to such security ranking ahead of the initial floating charge, which does not seem to have been the intention of the parties.[123]

---

118 R Hardwick, 'The Negative Pledge and Disposal Restrictions: Carve-outs and Remedies for Breach' 2017 JIBFL 510; Gullifer and Payne, *Corporate Finance Law* (n 27) 335.

119 Companies Act 2006 s. 859D(2)(c); and see E McKendrick, *Goode and McKendrick on Commercial Law*, 6th edn (London: LexisNexis, 2020) paras 24.42 onwards.

120 Companies (Floating Charges) (Scotland) Act 1961 s. 5(2); and see MacPherson, *Floating Charge* (n 5) paras 2–29 onwards, for discussion.

121 See Gretton, 'The Story of the Scots Law Floating Charge: 1961 to Date', Chapter 4 for more details of this invisibility period.

122 See Hardman, *Granting Corporate Security* (n 1) para. 6–24.

123 *Bank of Ireland v Bass Brewers Ltd (No. 2)* 2000 GWD 28–1077. See D Cabrelli, 'Negative Pledges and Ranking Reconsidered' (2002) 7 SLPQ 18.

Secondly, the internal aspect needs to be considered by a creditor. It is common for the holder of a floating charge to have the benefit of other securities, from the granter and others, known in the collective as the security package.[124] It is important that the floating charge ranks where it should do within the creditor's own security package, normally behind their fixed securities.[125] However, as floating charges are (seemingly) created on the date that the relevant underlying document is delivered to the creditor (formerly when execution of the instrument took place),[126] but fixed securities are created the date that a further completion step after this has been taken,[127] a structural issue arises in that floating charges are created prior to fixed securities, even if all documents constituting them are signed and delivered on the same date.[128] As well as applying externally in interactions with other parties, this means that a creditor's floating charge ranks ahead of the standard security taken in the same security package, which is not an ideal result for a creditor, as recoveries under a floating charge are subject to leakages that recoveries under fixed securities are not. As a result, a negative pledge affects not only external interactions, but also internal interactions within the security package. Accordingly, within a negative pledge, it is normal to carve out any fixed security granted in favour of the same creditor.[129]

E. RANKING AGREEMENTS

If a negative pledge is an *ex ante* way to ensure that the floating charge ranks where it is intended to, an *ex post* method is to subsequently enter into a ranking agreement. A ranking agreement can also be entered into *ex ante*, at the same time as (or even in advance of) the grant of the relevant

---

124 See Steven and Patrick (n 13) 261; Gullifer and Payne, *Corporate Finance Law* (n 27) 834.

125 This will avoid any danger of the fixed security ranking behind other claims that have priority over the floating charge, such as expenses of an insolvency process, preferential creditors and the prescribed part. See also J Hardman and A D J MacPherson, 'The Empirical Importance of the Floating Charge in Scotland', Chapter 11 within this volume.

126 Companies Act 2006 ss. 859A and 859E. This is the date of creation for registration of charges purposes. There is some uncertainty as to whether it or the date of execution is the relevant date for ranking purposes, see A D J MacPherson, 'Registration of Company Charges Revisited' (2019) 23 Edin L Rev 153 at 165 onwards.

127 Be it delivery of the pledged item, intimation of assignation or registration of the standard security.

128 *AIB Finance Ltd v Bank of Scotland*, 1993 SC 588.

129 With security trusts, or more complicated arrangements, additional care needs to be taken to ensure that the provision reflects the intention of the parties.

floating charge[130] but it is the only *ex post* way to overcome the foregoing default rules. The legal basis of an *ex post* ranking agreement is that the Companies Act 1985 enables a floating charge to be altered after its grant by the granter, the holder of the floating charge and any other holder of security that would be adversely affected executing an 'instrument of alteration' of the floating charge.[131] This alteration then brings the security within the confines of s. 464(1)(b) of the 1985 Act, which states that an instrument creating a floating charge over all or part of the company's property may contain:

> 'with the consent of the holder of any subsisting floating charge or fixed security which would be adversely affected, provisions regulating the order in which the floating charge shall rank with any other subsisting or future floating charges or fixed securities over that property or any part of it'.

This serves to oust the default rules of ranking against other floating charges and fixed securities. As such, ranking agreements relating to floating charges do not merely have personal effect, they have real effect in determining ranking outcomes, assuming that registration requirements have been complied with.

It is easy to envisage scenarios whereby a creditor receives a floating charge with a full negative pledge, with no intention of ranking anything other than first, but this intention changes with the passage of time. For example, if a floating charge is granted to a financial institution who is, and is intended to continue to be, the company's sole secured creditor, then there may seem to be no downside of including a full negative pledge. Should this change, such that a second secured creditor (with the first secured creditor's consent) agrees to fund a particular project of the company's in exchange for security, the original floating charge would not match the current needs of parties. In such circumstances, the initial creditor will not want to release and retake their floating charge, as they will not want to restart 'hardening' periods[132] in respect of their floating charge.[133] In order to avoid this, a ranking agreement can be entered into in respect of the existing floating charge.

---

130 Companies Act 1985 s. 464(1)(b). If the ranking agreement is entered into prior to the creation of the floating charge, it will need to be incorporated into the floating charge instrument to have full effect.

131 Companies Act 1985 s. 466(1). And see s. 466(3).

132 These are the periods of time prior to the granter's insolvency in which a challengeable transaction can be so challenged – see D McKenzie Skene, 'The Floating Charge and Insolvency Law', Chapter 10 within this volume.

133 See Hardman, *Granting Corporate Security* (n 1) paras 2–21–2.23.

In addition, given that the priority of a floating charge may be limited if a creditor becomes aware of the creation of a subsequent floating charge to the amount that the creditor was then owed (or under a commitment to advance) as at the date of receipt,[134] then upon receipt of any such notice a creditor is likely to request that a ranking agreement is entered into. Even if the charge is not so limited by notice of a later floating charge (as discussed above), a ranking agreement is desirable for the clarity it provides to the parties regarding their respective priorities. The uncertainty of the law in this area reinforces the point.

When considering voluntary ranking in a ranking agreement, there are a number of options. First, an absolute ranking can be included, stating that one security (or one creditor's security) ranks ahead of the others. If security packages are present, it will be important to ensure that the ranking agreement does not just place one package above the other, but that the securities within the packages are adequately ranked to avoid the issues highlighted in the negative pledges section above. Secondly, it is possible to provide that security ranks differently depending on different levels of recovery: for example, that the first £1m realised from the relevant assets go to Creditor X, but thereafter everything from such assets goes to Creditor Y, and only after they have been repaid does any balance get paid to Creditor X.[135] Thirdly, it is possible to provide for different rankings across different assets. If Creditor X has a standard security over Property A, and Creditor Y has a standard security over Property B, and both have floating charges over all assets of the company that owns both properties, it is possible to agree that Creditor X will rank first in respect of Property A (and all moveable assets related to Property A), whereas Creditor Y will rank first in respect of Property B (and all moveable assets related to Property B). This is particularly helpful if two creditors are funding two entirely different projects, operations or businesses managed or owned by the same legal entity. Any such options will need to include a 'turnover' clause – one which states that if a creditor recovers sums they were not meant to from the realisation of an asset, they will turn it over to the relevant creditor and hold it on trust in the interim.[136]

When drafting a ranking agreement, it is common to narrate all the default rules that the ranking is to overcome. In the case of a floating charge,

---

134 Companies Act 1985 s. 464(5).
135 Once Creditor X is repaid in full, any balance would of course become part of the granter's estate to be dealt with in accordance with insolvency law.
136 Gullifer and Payne, *Corporate Finance Law* (n 27) 266–270.

it is commonly worded that the ranking set out will apply notwithstanding the nature of security,[137] the time of grant,[138] the timing of advances[139] and any other securities that the granter has granted in favour of either or both creditors.[140] It is also common to state that the granter obtains no rights under the agreement – the purpose is only to regulate rights as between security holders on enforcement. As a result, it is common to regulate not just the ranking of securities but also any restrictions on the enforcement of security.[141] This is especially important if two secured creditors are funding their own separate projects in relation to the same company and part of the common costs between the two projects. In such a circumstance, one creditor enforcing in respect of their project is likely to bring down the project funded by the second creditor, even if the second project would otherwise be successful. Accordingly, creditors are likely to impose a 'standstill' obligation – which states that a creditor cannot enforce without the expiry of prescribed events (such as the passage of time, agreement of the other secured creditor or some other event). The precise scope of that obligation will depend on the agreement between the creditors. If Creditor A is to rank first for all purposes, it is likely to impose such an obligation on Creditor B, but not likely to agree to provide such an obligation. On the other hand, if both creditors have agreed to rank *pari passu*, it is likely that each will want prior notice from the other before enforcement. Sometimes such standstill arrangements can be absolute, or they can be subject to terms: for example, Creditor A may only be able to enforce after a default under their documentation has been outstanding for six months, and they have provided at least six months' notice to Creditor B of such default. Technically, a ranking agreement will only rank security rights and not liabilities. Accordingly, a usual ranking agreement will only cover enforcement proceeds and standstills. If an agreement between the creditors goes further and regulates not just the security granted by the parties but also the liabilities owed to them (for example, if it prevents one creditor being repaid other than in certain circumstances), then it tends to be called an intercreditor agreement rather

---

137 To overcome the rule that fixed security ranks ahead of floating.
138 To overcome the *priore tempore* rule.
139 To overcome the rule in *Clayton's Case – Devaynes v Noble* (1816) 35 ER 781, adopted into Scots law by *Buchanan v Main* (1900) 3 F 215; see P Hood 'Clayton's Case and Connected Matters' 2013 Jur Rev 501. This may also potentially be used to overcome statutory limitations in priority noted above.
140 To overcome any rules in respect of catholic and secondary creditors.
141 Hardman, *Granting Corporate Security* (n 1) para. 9–24.

than a ranking agreement.[142] Intercreditor agreements can also regulate floating charges in the same way as ranking agreements can.

As noted above, any ranking agreement or intercreditor agreement affecting a floating charge has to be signed by the granter of the security and any other creditor adversely affected. There are no requirements for any such agreement to be governed by Scots law and English law intercreditor agreements are common.[143] The effect of a ranking agreement is to amend the floating charge under s. 466 and so the provisions contained in s. 464 apply to the amended floating charge. Any instrument of alteration in respect of a floating charge has to be registered at Companies House within twenty-one days of its execution.[144] This ostensibly applies to all companies who have granted Scots law floating charges, but is usually only taken to apply to Scottish companies (and then to all floating charges granted by the granter – English law governed floating charges will also be subject to the same requirements).[145] For English law governed intercreditor agreements, this merely risks commercial embarrassment, as features that may have been intended to be private (e.g. levels of debt, key beneficiaries of security trusts, other commercial terms, etc.) will become publicly available. For Scots law intercreditor agreements or ranking agreements, the retention of the word 'executed' to start the twenty-one-day registration period creates further practical issues. For unilateral documents, or documents executed in counterpart, the effective date of a document will be linked to the date of delivery of the document rather than the date of execution.[146] If a Scots law intercreditor agreement is executed in counterpart at the same time as security documents, but all are only delivered twenty-five days later, the twenty-one day period will start for the security on the date of delivery, but will already have expired for the intercreditor agreement.[147] Failure to register an intercreditor agreement within twenty-one days of its execution renders it invalid.[148] This mismatch therefore causes real issues in practice and a real concern for practitioners. In

---

142 See L Gullifer, *Goode & Gullifer on Legal Problems of Credit and Security*, 6th edn (London: Sweet & Maxwell, 2017) para. 5–63.

143 Hardman, *Granting Corporate Security* (n 1) para. 9–19.

144 Companies Act 1985 s. 466(4C).

145 Hardman, *Granting Corporate Security* (n 1) para. 10–17.

146 See J Hardman, 'Necessary and Balanced? Critical Analysis of the Legal Writings (Counterparts and Delivery) (Scotland) Act 2015' 2016 Jur Rev 177.

147 J Hardman, 'Necessary and balanced? Critical analysis of the Legal Writings (Counterparts and Delivery) (Scotland) Act 2015'; Hardman, *Granting Corporate Security* (n 1) para. 10–19.

148 Companies Act 1985 s. 466(4A).

addition, the relevant form used for registering instruments of alteration is based on historical Companies House forms, which required large amounts of text to be copied and pasted from the underlying document. This is no longer the approach used for charge registration documents, which now adopt a mere 'tick box' approach.[149] Accordingly, ranking agreements create issues not only in terms of filing deadlines but also issues with familiarity of the filing requirements. There are no proposals to amend either of these major practical issues.

The foregoing has proceeded on the basis that the instrument of alteration affects the ranking of the floating charge. However, there are four circumstances in which an instrument of alteration requires to be filed with Companies House, two of which relate to ranking.[150] The third is if a floating charge is altered to release property from the floating charge.[151] This has been interpreted narrowly – it only applies if the floating charge is amended, not if property just happens to be released from the ambit of the floating charge.[152] The fourth is if the floating charge is amended to increase the amount secured by it.[153] This requires the floating charge to be amended in some way. It has been asserted elsewhere that:

'if:
(1) the floating charge secures all amounts due under the facility agreement;
(2) the floating charge expressly states that it will do so regardless of any amendments to the facility agreement; and
(3) the facility agreement is amended so as to add a new tranche to increase the amounts due under the same facility agreement,
then there will be no filing requirement under s.466 of the Companies Act 1985'.[154]

It is possible for multiple floating charges granted by Scottish vehicles to be amended by the same ranking agreement, in which case filings will need to be made against each floating charge. In addition, should such ranking agreement also rank a standard security, then additional requirements under

---

149 Compare Hardman, *Granting Corporate Security* (n 1) para. 10–20 (which deals with how to complete the forms in respect of instruments of alteration) to para. 10–10 (which deals with how to complete forms in respect of registration of security).

150 The introduction of a negative pledge and any variation of ranking – Companies Act 1985 s. 466(4)(a) and (b).

151 Companies Act 1985 s. 466(4)(c).

152 *Scottish and Newcastle Breweries plc v Ascot Inns Ltd (in receivership)* 1994 SLT 1140; [1994] BCC 634; Hardman, *Granting Corporate Security* (n 1) para. 10–17.

153 Companies Act 1985 s. 466(4)(d).

154 Hardman, *Granting Corporate Security* (n 1) para. 10–17.

the standard security regime should be considered, particularly if there are multiple standard securities.[155]

The Scottish Law Commission has proposed that a pledgee, including the holder of a new statutory pledge, should be able to enter into a ranking agreement with other pledgees and creditors holding other types of security, including floating charges.[156] However, any such agreement would only have effect as between the parties to it and their successors and it would not be registrable in the Register of Statutory Pledges.[157] The interaction between this type of ranking agreement and those discussed above could raise difficult and interesting questions.

F. ATTACHMENT, RANKING AND ENFORCEMENT

(1) Attachment and ranking

A floating charge holder can of course receive payment of debt from a chargor in accordance with agreed repayment terms, even if their floating charge has not attached. However, in relation to enforcement, the attachment of a floating charge is necessary for its holder to receive a right to the proceeds of charged property. In other words, to obtain payment on the granter's insolvency the creditor's charge must have already attached. This is true whether enforcement is taking place in liquidation,[158] receivership,[159] administration[160] or if another secured creditor is enforcing against property

---

155 See Conveyancing and Feudal Reform (Scotland) Act 1970 s. 13(4).
156 Scottish Law Commission, *Report on Moveable Transactions* (n 50) paras 26.35 onwards and Draft Bill s. 64(6).
157 Scottish Law Commission, *Report on Moveable Transactions* (n 50) paras 26.37 onwards and Draft Bill s. 64(7).
158 Liquidation itself causes the floating charge to attach – Companies Act 1985 s. 463(1).
159 If a charge holder appoints a receiver under the floating charge or the court appoints a receiver under the floating charge upon the charge holder's application, the floating charge will attach – Insolvency Act 1986 ss. 53–54. A receiver's powers are subject to, *inter alia*, the rights of a floating charge with priority over, or ranking equally with, the floating charge by virtue of which the receiver was appointed. However, if there are other floating charges over the same property, whatever their ranking, their holders will not receive a distribution unless their charges have also attached. This incentivises the attachment of other floating charges if a receiver is appointed. For the distribution list in receivership, see Insolvency Act 1986 s. 60, and see further below.
160 Insolvency Act 1986 Sch. B1 para. 115(1). Administration itself does not cause attachment, but attachment can occur in administration in two circumstances – Insolvency Act 1986 Sch. B1 para. 115(1B) and (3).

covered by the floating charge.[161] Thus, a charge holder should ensure that their charge has attached or should seek to bring this about if they wish to receive payment of proceeds.

The ranking of a floating charge in relation to charged property and its proceeds therefore depends upon attachment. It is attachment that allows the above-noted rules of ranking, including those for negative pledges, to be given effect to as regards items of property.[162] This means that if a floating charge does not attach to particular property then there is no ranking (in the strict sense of the term) between a charge holder and other creditors in relation to that property. If property is beyond the ambit of a charge's attachment, the charge holder has no legal interest in the property. Of course, there is some uncertainty as to when property becomes unattachable, in large part due to the House of Lords decision in *Sharp v Thomson*.[163] Nevertheless, whether a floating charge can attach to property will ordinarily depend on whether the chargor is owner of the property in question at the relevant time (as well as whether the property is of a type encompassed by the particular floating charge).[164] A floating charge cannot attach to property that is not owned by the chargor.

A consequence of this is that if property is subject to a functional security, a floating charge granted by the debtor will not be able to rank against that security. In the event that a creditor retains ownership of property for security purposes, the chargor does not acquire ownership and therefore the floating charge cannot attach, but will attach to the chargor's right to obtain ownership if certain conditions are fulfilled. If the security consists of a sale and leaseback of corporeal moveable property (with or without an option to repurchase), the creditor will own the property and the floating charge will only be able to attach the chargor's personal rights, including any right of repurchase.[165] Likewise, if the chargor validly holds property in trust for a creditor, a floating charge is not able to rank against that creditor as floating charges do not attach to property held in a chargor's trust

---

161 Such as a standard security holder enforcing, see Conveyancing and Feudal Reform (Scotland) Act 1970 s. 27(1) for the order of priority for payment of proceeds. For discussion, see MacPherson, *Floating Charge* (n 5) paras 6–09 onwards.

162 For negative pledges and attachment, see MacPherson, *Floating Charge* (n 5) paras 2–29 onwards.

163 *Sharp* (n 74). For discussion, see MacPherson, *Floating Charge* (n 5), Ch. 7 in particular.

164 A more accurate description of the floating charge's attachment may be to say that it attaches to rights (personal and real) held by the chargor at a given time, rather than to property owned by the chargor, see MacPherson, *Floating Charge* (n 5) paras 4–36–4–38.

165 For further details of attachment of floating charges and retention of title and sale and leaseback, see MacPherson, *Floating Charge* (n 5) paras 8–26 onwards.

patrimony.[166] The result of each of these scenarios is that the creditor with a functional security prevails over the floating charge holder and this seems to apply whether or not the floating charge is accompanied by a negative pledge. Negative pledges cannot stop the transfer of ownership to another party (or a creditor holding on to ownership) and their effect for ranking in relation to property depends upon attachment, which is not possible if the property has been transferred (or the chargor does not obtain ownership). All of this raises considerable questions about assignation in security, which is a transfer of incorporeal property to a creditor for security purposes. This is discussed in detail elsewhere and, consequently, will not be dealt with further here.[167] In any event, it will often be desirable for a charge holder to be wary of functional securities and they may seek to use personal covenants or otherwise monitor the chargor's activities to avoid being disadvantaged.[168]

(2) Appointing and enforcing

So far, the focus has been almost exclusively on ranking as far as it involves priority in relation to property upon attachment of a charge. Ranking does, however, also have significance with respect to the enforcement of floating charges as far as appointing insolvency practitioners and their powers are concerned. Administration is now the principal means of enforcing a floating charge. The holder of a 'qualifying floating charge'[169] may appoint an administrator of the company (out of court).[170] Unlike other creditors, who have to apply to court for an administration order, the holder of a qualifying floating charge does not need to show that the company is or is likely to become unable to pay its debts or that an administration order is reasonably likely to achieve the purpose of administration.[171] If the holder of a qualifying floating charge seeks to appoint

---

166 *Tay Valley Joinery Ltd v C F Financial Services Ltd* 1987 SLT 207. See MacPherson (n 111).
167 MacPherson, *Floating Charge* (n 5) Ch. 9. In brief, if there is an assignation in security it may be contended that a floating charge created by the cedent only attaches to their retrocession right and not to the transferred property itself.
168 See Gullifer and Payne, *Corporate Finance Law* (n 27) Ch. 6 for details regarding contractual creditor protection.
169 See Insolvency Act 1986 Sch. B1 para. 14(2)–(3). This requires *inter alia* that the floating charge must (on its own or with other security) cover all or substantially all the assets of the company – see Hardman, *Granting Corporate Security* (n 1) paras 6–11–6–12.
170 Insolvency Act 1986 Sch. B1 para. 14(1). The holder of a qualifying floating charge holder also has certain rights in relation to applications for administration made to the court – paras 35–37.
171 Insolvency Act 1986 Sch. B1 paras 10–13. For the purpose of administration, see Sch. B1 para. 3.

an administrator, it does, however, have to give at least two business days' written notice to the holder of any prior qualifying floating charge, or obtain that party's written consent to the making of the appointment.[172] The notice provision enables the prior-ranking charge holder to appoint their own administrator, if they are so inclined. In this context, a floating charge has priority if 'it has priority of ranking in accordance with section 464(4)(b)' (i.e. is registered before the other floating charge) or 'it is to be treated as having priority in accordance with an agreement to which the holder of each floating charge was a party'.[173] The possibility of a floating charge ranking ahead of another due to the first-created one containing a negative pledge (even if registered later than a subsequently created floating charge) seems to have been overlooked, probably inadvertently.[174] The same priority rule as for the prior notice provision is also included in the provision that allows the holder of a qualifying floating charge to apply to the court for an administrator to be replaced by an administrator nominated by the holder of that prior floating charge.[175] This is unfortunate and likewise appears to be an error.

It is still possible in some circumstances for a receiver to be appointed, whether by a charge holder or the court.[176] If receivers are appointed by or on the application of holders of two or more floating charges, the law determines which of those receivers will be prioritised. The receiver (or receivers) for the highest-ranking floating charge holder has the powers of a receiver to the exclusion of any other receiver.[177] This enables that prioritised receiver to, amongst other things, sell the attached property and distribute proceeds to 'their' charge holder with any other receiver only receiving sums after that charge holder and various other parties have been paid.[178] If a receiver has already been appointed and another receiver is subsequently appointed by or for a higher-ranking floating charge holder, the powers of the first-appointed receiver are suspended to the extent necessary to enable the receiver for the higher-ranking floating charge to exercise their powers.[179] Any suspended powers take effect once again when the floating

---

172 Insolvency Act 1986 Sch. B1 para. 15(1).
173 Insolvency Act 1986 Sch. B1 para. 15(2)–(3).
174 For further discussion, see S Wortley, 'When is a Prior Ranking Floating Charge not a Prior Ranking Floating Charge?' 2020 SLT (News) 191.
175 Insolvency Act 1986 Sch. B1 para. 96.
176 See Insolvency Act 1986 ss. 51–54, and 72B onwards. And see McKenzie Skene, 'The Floating Charge and Insolvency Law', Chapter 10 for details.
177 Insolvency Act 1986 s. 56(1).
178 Insolvency Act 1986 s. 60(1)–(2).
179 Insolvency Act 1986 s. 56(4).

charge with priority ceases to attach to the property subject to the charge.[180] If floating charges rank equally, the appointed receivers are deemed to have been appointed as joint receivers.[181] The enforcement of floating charges is discussed further in the next section and in 'The Floating Charge and Insolvency Law' by Professor McKenzie Skene in this volume.

G. RANKING AND DISTRIBUTION

The payment of proceeds from attached property to a charge holder, in accordance with their ranking priority, depends upon distribution by a liquidator, administrator or receiver, as a charge holder cannot 'self-enforce'.[182] Distribution rules generally seek to give effect to the ranking rules. However, there are complicating factors due to additional types of claim that entitle payment and require distribution. There are also ranking complications that are not taken account of by the distribution rules, which can create unfairness and uncertainty.

(1) Liquidation

In liquidation, security holders generally have priority over other types of creditor, including preferential creditors, ordinary unsecured (non-preferential) creditors and postponed creditors, as well as priority in relation to general liquidation expenses.[183] The position for floating charges differs notably compared to other security rights. A floating charge ranks behind the claims of preferential creditors.[184] These preferential debts comprise ordinary preferential debts and secondary preferential debts and are outlined in the Insolvency Act 1986.[185] Ordinary preferential debts include contributions to occupational pension schemes,[186] employee wage claims

---

180 Insolvency Act 1986 s. 56(4).
181 Insolvency Act 1986 s. 56(2).
182 On self-enforcement, see MacPherson, *Floating Charge* (n 5) paras 6–04–6–08.
183 See Insolvency (Scotland) (Receivership and Winding up) Rules 2018 (SSI 2018/347) r. 7.27(1) and (6). But if the liquidator realises security property and distributes proceeds to a secured creditor, the expenses of that realisation will be paid before the secured creditor receives anything. See e.g. *Buchler v Talbot* [2004] UKHL 9, [2004] 2 AC 298 per Lord Nicholls of Birkenhead at para. 19 and Lord Millett at para. 63; and see Sweeney, *The Landlord's Hypothec* (n 63) para. 11–06 for this issue in the context of the landlord's hypothec.
184 See Companies Act 1985 ss. 463(3) and 464(6); and Insolvency Act 1986 s. 175(2)(b).
185 See Insolvency Act 1986 s. 386 and Sch. 6 paras 8 onwards.
186 Insolvency Act 1986 Sch. 6 para. 8.

to a limited extent[187] and accrued holiday remuneration for parties whose employment has been terminated.[188] Following the recent partial reinstatement of the Crown's preference in insolvency, secondary preferential debts (for insolvency processes since 1 December 2020) now include HMRC's claims with respect to certain types of tax payments that are held by the debtor for onward transfer to HMRC, including VAT, PAYE income tax and employee national insurance contributions.[189] It has been pointed out that this change is particularly disadvantageous to secured creditors in Scotland, as the difficulties in creating fixed securities under Scots law mean that there is more reliance on floating charges, which rank behind HMRC's preferential claims, while fixed securities do not.[190]

Since the changes enacted by the Enterprise Act 2002 came into force, the 'prescribed part' is also prioritised over floating charges.[191] This enables unsecured creditors to receive a proportion of proceeds ahead of a floating charge holder. If the company's 'net property'[192] does not exceed £10,000 in value, the prescribed part is 50 per cent of that property, while if its value exceeds £10,000, the prescribed part is 50 per cent of the first £10,000 in value and 20 per cent of the net property that exceeds £10,000 in value, with the maximum value of the prescribed part being £800,000.[193]

Thus, a possible order of priority in an insolvent liquidation would be as follows: fixed security (including a diligence creditor), preferential creditors, the prescribed part, floating charge, ordinary unsecured creditors, postponed creditors. Of course, each party in the priority list will only

---

187 For a period of four months prior to the relevant date but limited to £800 – see Insolvency Act 1986 Sch. 6 para. 9; and Insolvency Proceedings (Monetary Limits) Order 1986 (SI 1086/1996).

188 Insolvency Act 1986 Sch. 6 para. 10.

189 Insolvency Act 1986 Sch. 6 para. 15D, as inserted by Finance Act 2020 s. 98; and see s. 99 of the 2020 Act and the Insolvency Act 1986 (HMRC Debts: Priority on Insolvency) Regulations 2020 (SI 2020/983).

190 See R Caldwell, 'Enterprise goes into Reverse for Floating Charge-holders' 2019 Jur Rev 103. This is discussed further in McKenzie Skene, 'The Floating Charge and Insolvency Law', Chapter 10.

191 For the prescribed part, see Insolvency Act 1986 s. 176A (added by the Enterprise Act 2002 s. 252). It has been held that a floating charge creditor cannot claim in the prescribed part with respect to any unsecured balance: *Thorniley v HMRC* [2008] EWHC 124 (Ch); *Re Permacell Finesse Ltd* [2007] EWHC 3233 (Ch).

192 The company's net property is 'the amount of its property which would, but for [section 176A of the Insolvency Act 1986], be available for satisfaction of claims of holders of debentures secured by, or holders of, any floating charge created by the company' – Insolvency Act 1986 s. 176A(6).

193 Insolvency Act 1986 (Prescribed Part) Order 2003 (SI 2003/2097). The figure of £800,000 was increased from £600,000 by the Insolvency Act 1986 (Prescribed Part) (Amendment) Order 2020 (SI 2020/211).

receive something if the prior-ranking parties have been paid in full. The position of liquidation expenses has been intentionally omitted as its status is problematic. In English law, the controversial case of *Buchler v Talbot*,[194] where a floating charge was held to rank ahead of liquidation expenses, led to the introduction of s. 176ZA of the Insolvency Act 1986,[195] which now provides that the expenses of winding up in England and Wales have priority over a floating charge. There is no such statutory provision for liquidation in Scotland. A floating charge granted by a Scottish company, as a form of security right, could, from one perspective, be expected to have priority over liquidation expenses but the necessity of realisation by the liquidator for the charge holder may mean that some or all of the expenses of liquidation must be paid before the charge holder receives payment.[196] In practice, the same approach as in English law appears to be followed in Scotland, with all liquidation expenses paid before there is a distribution to the charge holder.[197]

(2) Receivership

The distribution list in receivership is at least more clearly outlined than the position in liquidation. Section 60(1) of the Insolvency Act 1986 states that a receiver is to pay moneys received by them to the holder of a floating charge by virtue of which they were appointed, subject to the rights of various categories of persons. Except to the extent otherwise provided in any instrument, those rights are stated to have the following order of priority:

(a) The holder of a fixed security over property subject to the floating charge that ranks prior to (or *pari passu* with) the floating charge.
(b) All persons who have effectually executed diligence on any part of the property subject to the floating charge.
(c) Creditors in respect of all liabilities, charges and expenses incurred by or on behalf of the receiver.

---

194 [2004] UKHL 9, [2004] 2 AC 298.
195 The provision was inserted by the Companies Act 2006 s. 1282(1). See e.g. A Keay and P Walton, *Insolvency Law: Corporate and Personal*, 4th edn (London: Jordan Publishing, 2017) 515.
196 See J St Clair and Lord Drummond Young, *The Law of Corporate Insolvency in Scotland*, 4th edn (Edinburgh: W. Green, 2011) para. 6–44 for discussion.
197 See the insolvency dataset used in Hardman and MacPherson, 'The Empirical Importance of the Floating Charge in Scotland', Chapter 11 for more details.

(d) The receiver in respect of their liabilities, expenses and remuneration, and any indemnity to which they are entitled out of property of the company.

(e) The preferential creditors entitled to payment (under s. 59 of the 1986 Act).

On the surface, this list appears unproblematic. However, one notable issue is that because of its seemingly inflexible application, it subordinates all diligences to fixed securities, no matter what their ranking relationship actually is. Thus, if property is subject to a diligence, which is effectually executed, and this is followed by a voluntary security that ranks behind the diligence due to *prior tempore potior jure*, distribution by a receiver appointed by the holder of a floating charge also affecting the property would unfathomably and unfairly involve payment to the fixed security holder ahead of the diligence creditor. This creates an incentive for enforcement by a diligence creditor rather than letting a receiver do so, in order to give effect to the proper priority status of the diligence.

In addition to the parties mentioned above, a receiver is also required to make a prescribed part of the company's net property available for the satisfaction of unsecured debts.[198] The prescribed part will therefore also usually need to be paid before payment is made to the floating charge holder. Once the parties above and the floating charge holder are paid in full, any balance of moneys is to be paid to, and in accordance with the rights and interests of, the following persons, as the case may require[199]:

(a) Any other receiver.

(b) The holder of a fixed security that is over property subject to the floating charge.

(c) The company or its liquidator, as the case may be.

The phrase 'as the case may require' used in the provision indicates that the party to whom payment is to be made will depend on the particular circumstances. If a lower-ranking floating charge holder has appointed a receiver, payment can be made to that receiver to allow for onward transmission to the charge holder.[200] This will also be the case if there is a fixed security holder who ranks below the second floating charge holder. If, instead, there

---

198 Insolvency Act 1986 s. 176A(1)–(2). Under certain circumstances, the prescribed part does not require to be paid – s. 176A(3)–(5).

199 Insolvency Act 1986 s. 60(2).

200 It may also be necessary for this second receiver to pay a prescribed part of the net property to unsecured creditors under s. 176A of the Insolvency Act 1986.

is a fixed security holder who ranks between the floating charge holders or there is no second charge holder, then the receiver can pay the fixed security holder. If there are no lower-ranking security holders, payment can be made to the company or, if the company is in liquidation, to the liquidator, which would also be the course of action if another floating charge had attached by virtue of the chargor entering liquidation.

(3) Administration

Any payment that an administrator seeks to make to the holder of an attached floating charge, is subject to the rights of various categories of persons. And these rights, except to the extent provided in any instrument, have the following order of priority[201]:

(a) The holder of any fixed security that is over property subject to the floating charge and that ranks prior to, or *pari passu* with, the floating charge.

(b) Creditors in respect of all liabilities and expenses incurred by or on behalf of the administrator.

(c) The administrator in respect of their liabilities, expenses and remuneration and any indemnity to which they are entitled out of the property of the company.

(d) The preferential creditors entitled to payment in accordance with para. 65 (of Sch. B1 of the Insolvency Act 1986).

(e) The holder of the floating charge in accordance with the priority of that charge in relation to any other floating charge that has attached.

(f) The holder of a fixed security, other than one referred to in para. (a), which is over property subject to the floating charge.

The preliminary wording of the provision and the list itself are reminiscent of the position for receivership, and as with receivership the prescribed part payment also needs to be made,[202] but there are also key differences. Strangely, there is no express mention of diligence in the administration list. The implications of this are unknown. It may be that it is included in the meaning of fixed security, despite these forming two different categories in

---

201 Insolvency Act 1986 Sch. B1 para. 116.
202 Insolvency Act 1986 s. 176A.

the context of the ranking list for receivership. However, this is by no means certain.[203]

There is also a potential problem with the administration distribution order if there are multiple security rights over particular property. Let us assume that three security rights rank in the following order: floating charge one; fixed security; floating charge two. Despite these rankings, the list above, and in particular the order of entries (e) and (f), would suggest that floating charge two would have priority over the fixed security. This was probably an oversight when the provisions were drafted but it is difficult to see how the order of the distribution list could be departed from. If, instead, (e) does not require payment to a lower-ranking floating charge holder, there is no other provision for such payment in the distribution priority list for administration (in Sch. B1 para. 116 of the Insolvency Act 1986), and so a fixed security holder ranking behind the second floating charge holder would nevertheless (unfairly) receive payment in priority to that charge holder, due to provision (f). Whatever the position is, the uncertainty caused and the disjointedness of the rules across the different ranking contexts is undesirable.

(4) Enforcement by fixed security holder

It is also possible for the holder of a fixed security to seek to enforce their right by realising property despite the existence of an attached floating charge. There are certain complexities regarding this that cannot be considered here but are discussed in detail elsewhere.[204] The preferable course of action if the fixed security ranks higher than the floating charge is for the holder of the fixed security to satisfy the debt due to itself first, and then to transfer the whole remainder of the realised sum to the liquidator, receiver or administrator. This will enable payment to be made to parties ranking ahead of the charge holder, such as preferential creditors and the prescribed part, and then to the charge holder itself.[205] If the fixed security ranks lower than the floating charge but its holder is nevertheless able to itself enforce, it will probably not be advisable for it to do so and instead it should let the

---

203 For further discussion and alternative approaches regarding diligence in administration, see MacPherson (n 87) at 242 onwards.
204 MacPherson, *Floating Charge* (n 5) paras 6–09 onwards.
205 This is true whether the enforcing secured creditor holds a standard security (see Conveyancing and Feudal Reform (Scotland) Act 1970 s. 27(1)) or another form of fixed security, see MacPherson, *Floating Charge* (n 5) paras 6–15 onwards for discussion.

liquidator, receiver or administrator realise the property.[206] Otherwise, the fixed security holder will have little certainty as to how much ought to be paid over (to satisfy the charge holder and others) prior to it being able to use the realised sums to pay off the debt due to itself.

H. FURTHER RANKING ISSUES

In the discussion above, a number of ranking problems have been identified. This section pays attention to some further issues that arise as a result of the nature of the floating charge and the ranking rules that apply to it.

(1) Circles of priority

Ranking two securities against each other tends to provide simple and clear outcomes. Matters get more complicated when three or more securities or other claims are ranked. One unfortunate outcome of the current rules is the risk of circles of priority. A 'circle of priority' or 'circularity problem' is a scenario in which the ranking rules do not produce a hierarchy from highest to lowest but instead the overall ranking outcome is incoherent.[207] For example, security A ranks ahead of B, which ranks ahead of C, which has priority over A.

Circles of priority exist in other legal systems[208] and are also a long-standing phenomenon in Scots law.[209] However, the multiplicity of different ranking

---

206 Again, this is true irrespective of the form of fixed security that the enforcing creditor holds. See MacPherson, *Floating Charge* (n 5) paras 6–29 onwards for discussion.

207 See also A D J MacPherson, 'A Vicious Circle: The Ranking of Floating Charges and Fixed Securities' (2014) *Edinburgh Student Law Review* 67 at 67. In most priority circles, each interest ranks higher and lower than at least one other interest but there is also the possibility that, e.g. A and B rank equally, B ranks ahead of C but C ranks ahead of A. If not a priority circle in a narrow sense of the term, it certainly approximates one.

208 See e.g. G Gilmore, *Security Interests in Personal Property* (Boston: Little, Brown & Co, 1965) Ch. 39; R J Wood, 'Circular Priorities in Secured Transactions Law' (2010) 47 Alberta L Rev 823; McKendrick, *Goode and McKendrick* (n 119) paras 24.62 onwards; K R Haug, *Transfer of Movables: A Comparison of the Unitary Approach and the Scandinavian Functional Approach* (2021) 251 onwards. For a recent contribution dealing with other complicated priority conflicts, see A Waldman, 'Resolving Priority Competitions between PPSA Security Interests and Non-PPS Interests' (2021) 44 UNSW LJ 811.

209 See e.g. J Steuart, *Dirleton's Doubts and Questions in the Law of Scotland, Resolved and Answered* (1715) 322 onwards; H Home, *Essays upon Several Subjects in Law* (1732) 61 onwards; H Home, Lord Kames, *Principles of Equity*, 3rd edn (1778) [2013] 3.190; H Home, Lord Kames, *Elucidations Respecting the Common and Statute Law of Scotland* (1777; 1800 (new edition)) 201 onwards; J G Stewart, *A Treatise on the Law of Diligence* (Edinburgh: W. Green, 1898) 145 onwards. And see G Mackenzie, 'Observations on the First Parliament of

rules accompanying floating charges, in combination with external rules for other security types, has led to a proliferation of priority circles. Some commentators have pointed to a circle of priority arising from the decision in *Lord Advocate v RBS* if there were a competition between a floating charge, an arrestment and an intimated assignation.[210] It can be questioned whether this would have given rise to a true priority circle.[211] But, in any event, the case of *MacMillan v T Leith Developments Ltd*[212] has removed any such possibility. The ranking position as decided in *MacMillan* does, however, create a different circularity problem involving diligence.[213] This exists where there is a floating charge with negative pledge, followed by a fixed security (e.g. a standard security or a pledge), which in turn is followed by diligence (e.g. adjudication or attachment or arrestment) and the floating charge attaches at a later date. Taking each competition in turn, the outcome is as follows:

- The floating charge has priority over the fixed security due to the negative pledge.
- The fixed security ranks ahead of the diligence due to *prior tempore potior jure*.
- The diligence has priority over the floating charge due to it being effectually executed diligence (see Figure 9.1 below).

There are, in fact, many priority circles involving floating charges. It is something of a parlour game, for a certain type of person (such as the authors), to seek to identify as many as possible. Due to reasons of space, we are not able to discuss all such circles here, but a number of further priority circles will now be mentioned.

King Charles II' in *The Works of Sir George Mackenzie of Rosehaugh* (1716–1722) Vol. I 408 onwards; and J Erskine, *Institute of the Law of Scotland*, 6th edn, by J Ivory (Edinburgh: Bell & Bradfute, 1824–1828) III.6.11, n 302, where the future Lord Ivory reviews relevant authorities and ponders a competition between an executor-creditor, an assignee and an arrester.

210 See Sim (n 83); Wortley (n 83). It was suggested that this circle would arise because a floating charge would rank ahead of an arrestment, which would have priority over a later assignation, which would rank ahead of a floating charge due to the charge attaching after the assignation was constituted as a real right.

211 As the assignation with intimation would cause the property to leave the patrimony of the chargor, meaning that the floating charge could no longer attach to the property and so the competition would be merely between the arrestment and the assignation. Even if a floating charge could attach to property assigned *in security*, the circle would be dependent upon the floating charge not having a negative pledge (as otherwise it would rank ahead of the later assignation in security). See MacPherson (n 87) at 246; MacPherson, *Floating Charge* (n 5) paras 9–08 and 9–16 onwards.

212 *Macmillan* (n 86).

213 See also MacPherson (n 87) at 246 onwards.

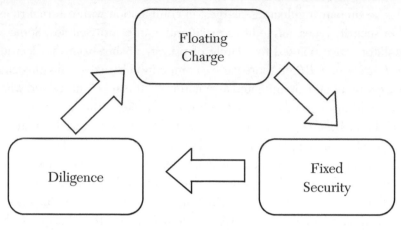

Figure 9.1

First, a circle of priority arises where[214]:

- A company grants a floating charge with no negative pledge (security A).
- The same company grants a second floating charge that does have a negative pledge prohibiting at least the creation of prior-ranking (or equal-ranking) fixed securities (security B).
- That company then grants a standard security (or other fixed security) (security C).
- The floating charges attach.

In that situation, security A ranks ahead of B, assuming that A is registered in the charges register first. B ranks ahead of C due to the existence of the negative pledge. And security C ranks ahead of A as it was constituted as a real right prior to the attachment of A. The order in which recoveries should be paid out is uncertain. Each of the documents creating the security rights can be unilateral and signed only by the granter. As a result, there is a possibility for the granter to cause this ranking scenario without the other creditors being aware of it.

Another circle of priority is created in the following circumstances[215]:

- A company grants a floating charge (security one) in favour of X, with a negative pledge that prevents the grant of any prior-ranking fixed security to a third party (however, it allows prior ranking fixed security to be granted in favour of X).

214 This circle is outlined and discussed in more detail in MacPherson (n 207).
215 Hardman, *Granting Corporate Security* (n 1) para. 9–13.

- That company acquires a property funded by Y, and grants a standard security in favour of Y (security two).
- The company grants X a standard security over the new property (security three) that is expressly subordinated to Y's standard security.

This produces a similar circle of priority: security one ranks ahead of security two, security two ranks ahead of security three and security three ranks ahead of security one. Yet it is interesting to note that this circle is created because of the second standard security granted in favour of X. If this were not granted, then X's floating charge would simply have ranked ahead of Y's standard security. However, the grant of an ostensibly additional right to X has the effect of moving a clear priority position into an unclear priority position. As standard securities are granted unilaterally, the company can unilaterally amend X's ranking, and X may not even be aware in advance that the company has done so. The risk of this has become even greater following the introduction of the 'advance notice' mechanic in respect of standard securities[216]:

- An advance notice is lodged for standard security X.
- Standard security Y is granted and created.
- Floating charge Z is granted, containing a full negative pledge.
- Standard security X is granted and created.[217]

This problem occurs because advance notices only apply to documents registered with the Keeper, and not to floating charges.[218] The result of the scenario is that standard security X ranks ahead of standard security Y. The nature of the security and timing mean that standard security Y ranks ahead of floating charge Z. And the negative pledge means that floating charge Z ranks ahead of standard security X.[219]

A further circle of priority seems to arise where there is a floating charge with negative pledge that ranks ahead of a fixed security and there are also preferential creditors.[220] The fixed security ranks ahead of the preferential

---

216 Land Registration etc. (Scotland) Act 2012 ss. 56–64.
217 Hardman, *Granting Corporate Security* (n 1) para. 9–14.
218 See Hardman, *Granting Corporate Security* (n 1) para. 8–11.
219 See also Hardman, *Granting Corporate Security* (n 1) para. 9–14.
220 This is a priority circle previously identified by others, see e.g. Gullifer, *Goode & Gullifer* (n 142) para. 8–58; and Scott Wortley's comments at the University of Edinburgh, https://media.ed.ac.uk/media/Scott+Wortley-Commercial+Law-Research+In+A+Nutshell-School+of+Law-26+11+2012/1_t19aa8kc (last accessed 3 November 2021).

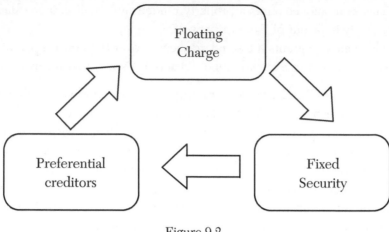

Figure 9.2

creditors and the claims of those creditors have priority over a floating charge.[221]

In at least some circumstances, it appears possible to resolve this priority circle using the distribution provisions discussed above. If a floating charge ranks ahead of a fixed security, the rules for distribution in receivership and administration seem to require that the preferential creditors will be paid first, followed by the floating charge holder and then the fixed security holder. In other words, by being subordinated to the floating charge, the fixed security holder also falls behind the claims that rank ahead of the floating charge. The priority circle does not appear so easy to resolve in liquidation, but it is possible that the same approach could be adopted in that context too. In any event, all of this provides a key incentive for a creditor to make sure that a relevant charge specifies that a floating charge they hold ranks behind any fixed security they receive from the same party.

Another possible circle of priority involving floating charges and preferential creditors arises where there are liquidation expenses. On one view, a floating charge can rank ahead of liquidation expenses in Scots law,[222]

---

221 For floating charges and preferential creditors, see Companies Act 1985 s. 464(6); Insolvency Act 1986 s. 176(1)–(2); and the distribution provisions discussed above. For fixed securities and preferential creditors, see Insolvency (Scotland) (Receivership and Winding up) Rules 2018 (SSI 2018/347) r. 7.27(1) and (6); and Insolvency (Scotland) (Company Voluntary Arrangements and Administration) Rules 2018 (SI 2018/1082) r. 3.115(1) and (6). Also, the mere fact that fixed security holders have real rights in the property gives them priority over preferential creditors (a type of unsecured creditor) in the absence of any statutory provision to the contrary.

222 See J St Clair and Lord Drummond Young, *The Law of Corporate Insolvency in Scotland* (n 196) para. 6–44. But it will not do so to the extent that the liquidator is realising property for the charge holder's benefit.

those expenses have priority over the claims of preferential creditors,[223] and those creditors rank ahead of the floating charge (as noted above).[224] Yet, if Scots law uses the same approach as English law instead,[225] which appears to be done in practice,[226] and ranks liquidation expenses ahead of floating charges, a different priority circle could be created where a floating charge with negative pledge is followed by a fixed security and the floating charge attaches due to the chargor's liquidation. The negative pledge means the floating charge would rank ahead of the fixed security, which would have priority over liquidation expenses, but those expenses would rank ahead of the floating charge.[227]

The existence of the prescribed part may also be viewed as creating a priority circle in some circumstances, as it ranks ahead of the floating charge, and the claims of unsecured creditors (whether in the context of the prescribed part or not) rank behind fixed security holders.[228] But this is perhaps a circle that can be resolved by viewing the prescribed part as accompanying or connected to the floating charge, so that a fixed security that is subject to the floating charge is also always subject to the prescribed part. Thus a party acquiring a voluntary fixed security over property already subject to a floating charge with negative pledge should be aware that the prescribed part is payable ahead of them too.

Another circle of priority can occur in the following scenario:

- A company grants a floating charge with negative pledge.
- The company then grants a standard security.
- A charging order is created over the company's property.
- The floating charge attaches.

The floating charge ranks ahead of the standard security; the standard security has priority over the charging order but only if the charging order is of a type that ranks according to *prior tempore potior jure*; and the charging order has priority over the floating charge, as it cannot be prohibited by the

223 Insolvency (Scotland) (Receivership and Winding up) Rules 2018 (SSI 2018/347) r. 7.27(1).
224 The potential for difficulties arising from such an approach have been recognised in relation to English law, see e.g. *Re Portbase Clothing Ltd* [1993] Ch 388 per Chadwick J at 408 onwards.
225 As per s. 176ZA of the Insolvency Act 1986.
226 See the insolvency dataset used in Hardman and MacPherson, 'The Empirical Importance of the Floating Charge in Scotland', Chapter 11.
227 Such a circle of priority can be avoided in relation to administration and receivership due to the distribution rules that provide an express hierarchy.
228 See Insolvency (Scotland) (Receivership and Winding up) Rules 2018 (SSI 2018/347) r. 7.27(1) and (6); and Insolvency (Scotland) (Company Voluntary Arrangements and Administration) Rules 2018 (SI 2018/1082) r. 3.115(1) and (6).

charge's negative pledge and is constituted as a real right before the floating charge attaches.[229]

Additionally, it can be debated whether a priority circle will appear in some situations where there is floating charge with negative pledge, a voluntary fixed security and a fixed security arising by operation of law. The floating charge will rank ahead of the later voluntary fixed security due to the negative pledge and the fixed security arising by operation of law will rank ahead of the floating charge.[230] In rare circumstances it may be possible for there to be both types of fixed security in existence over the same property, and (on one view) the voluntary fixed security could have priority either on the basis of *prior tempore potior jure* or because possession was obtained in the normal course of business by (for example) a pledgee where the property was already subject to a landlord's hypothec.[231] The Scottish Law Commission have, however, recommended an express statutory rule that a pledge (whether possessory or statutory) would rank behind a fixed security arising by operation of law.[232]

The priority circles above can be made more complicated, even fiendish, if additional parties are involved. For example, one can become utterly bamboozled by contemplating the ranking outcome in the following circumstances:

- X Ltd grants a floating charge without negative pledge to A.
- X Ltd then grants a floating charge with a negative pledge to B.
- X Ltd grants a standard security over property Y to C.
- Y is the subject of an adjudication (for debt) by D.
- Y is the subject of a charging order (that ranks *prior tempore potior jure*) in favour of E.
- X Ltd enters liquidation and the floating charges attach.
- There are liquidation expenses.
- There is a prescribed part.
- There are preferential creditors.

Thankfully, in reality, circularity problems are unlikely to be quite as complicated as this. But they can still be very complex in some more plausible situations.

---

229 See Companies Act 1985 s. 464(4)(a). For charging orders, see the discussion above.
230 Companies Act 1985 s. 464(1A) and (2).
231 See Sweeney, *The Landlord's Hypothec* (n 63) paras 9–61 onwards and the sources cited there.
232 Scottish Law Commission, *Report on Moveable Transactions* (n 50) paras 26.27 onwards and Draft Bill s. 64(4).

Priority circles can, particularly for voluntary security, be resolved by entering into ranking agreements, which will often provide a welcome pragmatic solution. This may partly explain the lack of circularity problems to have appeared before the courts. However, given that the floating charge needs to rank against non-voluntary security and other types of right that are unlikely to be known at the time the floating charge is granted, circles of priority remain a concern for a creditor. It would be interesting to see how a court in Scotland would approach resolving a priority circle.[233] Such scenarios have come before the courts in England resulting in varying outcomes.[234] With respect to judges encountering circles of priority, the renowned American scholar Grant Gilmore has colourfully written:

'A judge who finds himself face to face with a circular priority system typically reacts in the manner of a bull who has been goaded by the picadors: He paws the ground and roars with rage. The spectator can only sympathize with judge and bull.'[235]

One would expect Scottish judges to be a little more restrained. Nevertheless, identifying solutions to circularity problems is no easy task.[236] Breaking the circle by selecting a particular order of preference contrary to the applicable rules can appear arbitrary, even if, for example, a chronological order is chosen. It may also not be possible for a judge to depart from clear statutory authority. In some cases, a more complicated approach using, for instance, Bell's canons of ranking could provide a desirable outcome.[237] Alternatively,

---

233 The possibility of a circle of priority arising can dissuade courts from reaching a solution that would cause this – see e.g. *MacMillan* (n 86) at paras [92]–[93] per Lord Drummond Young.

234 Compare e.g. *Re Woodroffes (Musical Instruments) Ltd* [1986] Ch 366 and *Re Portbase* (n 224). The cases involved ranking competitions between floating charges, fixed security and preferential creditors, with issues arising from agreed subordination among the securities and consideration of the extent to which subrogation should apply to alter the general priority positions. For discussion, see McKendrick, *Goode and McKendrick* (n 119) paras 24.62 onwards; and Gullifer, *Goode & Gullifer* (n 142) para. 5–62, where the decision in *Re Portbase* is criticised. If a fixed security holder subordinated their claim to that of a floating charge holder in a ranking agreement under Scots law, there could be similar difficulties resolving the matter, albeit that the automatic application of the Scottish ranking provisions might lead to different outcomes.

235 G Gilmore, 'Circular Priority Systems' (1961) 71 Yale LJ 53 at 53; and see Gilmore, *Security Interests* (n 208) §39.1 at 1020–21.

236 See Gilmore (n 208) Ch. 39; Wood (n 208), for a range of different approaches that may be adopted to try and resolve circularity problems. Some of these involve complicated mathematics, which may make them less attractive than alternative solutions. However, in other contexts, mathematical approaches have been used to resolve seemingly intractable ranking problems – see e.g. R J Aumann and M Maschler, 'Game Theoretic Analysis of a Bankruptcy Problem from the Talmud' (1985) 36 *Journal of Economic Theory* 195.

237 In the context of the Scottish Law Commission's project on moveable transactions, John MacLeod suggested using Bell's canons of ranking to solve a potential priority circle – Scottish

the outcome could be determined on the basis of preferring certain parties for policy reasons, e.g. to protect more vulnerable parties who perhaps have less control over their ranking relationships with others. A straightforward approach, in the event that no other solution were available or suitable, would be to divide the proceeds between all of the parties in proportion to the debts due to each of them (i.e. *pari passu* ranking).[238]

(2) Catholic and secondary security

In *Forth & Clyde*,[239] the court rejected the argument that the common law doctrine of catholic and secondary security applied to constrain a receiver's freedom to realise property, whose actions were only governed by the 'code, complete in itself' formed by the legislation.[240] The case can also be interpreted more widely so that the doctrine is disapplied entirely for floating charges.[241] The following discussion, however, challenges the correctness of such interpretations.[242] It is true that the floating charges legislation (past and present) does not expressly state that the doctrine, or other general rules concerning security rights, apply to floating charges. Yet the attachment of a floating charge as if it were a fixed security and its operation within the field of security rights, including in competition with other security interests, perhaps should be viewed as causing the application of rules relating to security rights more broadly. This could include an administrator or liquidator (or even a receiver) treating the attached charge like a fixed security subject to the doctrine of catholic and secondary security. Given that the doctrine is intended to provide fairness to creditors and the charge holder would suffer

Law Commission, *Report on Moveable Transactions* (n 50) paras 32.36 onwards. However, although acknowledging it as a solution to the issue, the Scottish Law Commission considered that the complexity of the approach 'reduces its attractiveness' and noted their earlier recommendation to abolish the canons of ranking in relation to inhibition 'specifically because of their complexity' (para 32.41).

238 See also MacPherson (n 207) at 73 onwards.

239 *Forth & Clyde* (n 74) per LP Emslie at 11.

240 *Forth & Clyde* (n 74) per LP Emslie at 11 onwards. The 'code' was provided by the Companies (Floating Charges and Receivers) (Scotland) Act 1972, which would now be the Insolvency Act 1986.

241 As well as the Inner House's description of the legislation as a complete code, at the Outer House stage in *Forth & Clyde* (1983 SLT 372), the Lord Ordinary (Cowie) stated (at 374): 'I am of the opinion that the legislature has made it very clear that the provisions relating to floating charges in the 1972 Act overrule that doctrine in spite of the fact that it is not specifically stated'. This was not departed from by the Inner House.

242 *Forth & Clyde* has also been criticised by others for the decision not to apply the doctrine of catholic and secondary creditors to floating charges and receivers, see e.g. G L Gretton, 'Receivers and Arresters' 1984 SLT (News) 177 at 179.

no loss as a result of its application, it seems strange to disapply it, at least in policy terms.

In the leading catholic and secondary security case it was held that in a sequestration the rules on catholic and secondary creditors continued to apply, even where the court considered it expedient for the trustee in sequestration to preside over the property involved.[243] By extending this to other insolvency processes, a liquidator or administrator could be obliged to give effect to the doctrine in cases involving attached floating charges. If it did apply, and property X was subject to: (i) A's attached floating charge; and (ii) B's lower-ranking fixed security (e.g. a standard security); and property Y was only subject to A's charge, then it would be necessary for A to first be allocated payment from the realisation of Y before the allocation of proceeds arising from realising X.[244] This does not involve a reordering of ranking or distribution, which would be unacceptable given their express statutory form. Rather, the liquidator or administrator is merely obliged to deal with property in a way that gives effect to the doctrine. This is most obviously applicable to liquidation, due to it being the closest equivalent to sequestration, but there is also a strong case for it affecting an administrator. In the relatively recent English case of *McLean v Berry*,[245] Norris J held that marshalling (the English equivalent of the catholic and secondary creditors doctrine) applied to agricultural charges created under the Agricultural Credits Act 1928, on the basis that nothing within the Act excluded the principle's application.[246] A similar approach could be taken for a Scottish company in administration as there are no legislative provisions that negate the application of the doctrine, including with respect to floating charges.[247] Admittedly, that would be at odds with the approach in *Forth & Clyde*, but it would be a preferable approach and one that allows floating charges to fit more coherently with wider Scots law.

As a receiver acts in the interests of the charge holder alone, and only as regards attached property, it is more difficult to argue that limitations on

---

243 *Littlejohn v Black* (1855) 18 D 207.
244 This should not matter for the liquidator as they will be selling off all the property in due course.
245 [2016] EWHC 2650, [2017] Ch 422.
246 The secondary creditor was entitled to stand in place of the primary creditor and thereby claim proceeds from administrators; the proceeds were derived from property charged by the primary creditor.
247 Insolvency Act 1986 Sch. B1 paras 115–116. The administrator has control over whether, and when, to make a distribution to the charge holder – para. 115(1). The proposed approach would also be reconcilable with the order of priority in para. 116.

their enforcement powers incorporate the common law doctrine of catholic and secondary security. However, it seems that there may have been an intention for a receiver to be so bound. The Scottish Law Commission's *Memorandum No. 10*, which was followed by a report[248] and the Companies (Floating Charges and Receivers) Act 1972, states clearly that where a creditor with heritable security is postponed to the charge holder, the 'ordinary rules of law relating to catholic and secondary securities would apply'.[249] There seems no good reason to limit the application of the doctrine in the floating charges context to heritable securities, or even voluntary securities, despite what was decided in *Forth & Clyde*. Given that: (i) the floating charge is a deemed fixed security upon attachment; (ii) the doctrine applies to fixed securities; (iii) the doctrine confers rights upon the secondary creditor exercisable against the catholic creditor and, apparently, against those dealing with insolvent estates; and (iv) the charge holder enforces through a party dealing with (normally) insolvent estates, it appears appropriate to oblige a receiver, administrator and liquidator to give effect to the doctrine. Due to a floating charge's wide-ranging scope, the doctrine's application would usually confer no benefit on a charge holder, whereas it could provide considerable advantage to lower-ranking fixed security holders, in line with the equitable basis of the doctrine.[250] Of course, as well as the authority provided by *Forth & Clyde*, which is now decades old, there would be some practical issues in requiring insolvency practitioners to apply the doctrine of catholic and secondary creditors when dealing with assets attached by a floating charge. However, these would certainly not be insurmountable.

(3) Offside goals rule

The doctrine of offside goals and the uncertainty of its application in relation to security rights has been mentioned above. The doctrine has less relevance for floating charges than for other security rights. The very nature of the floating charge allows for a chargor company to transfer property to others and to create security rights before the floating charge has real effect,

---

248 Scottish Law Commission, *Report on the Companies (Floating Charges) (Scotland) Act 1961* (Scot. Law Com. No. 14, 1970).

249 Within the Report of the Working Party chaired by Professor Halliday, in Scottish Law Commission, *Memorandum No. 10: Examination of the Companies (Floating Charges) (Scotland) Act 1961* (1969) para. 41.

250 It could theoretically benefit a floating charge holder if there was a limited assets floating charge and another party held higher-ranking security over multiple items of property, including at least one item beyond the coverage of the floating charge.

without this constituting a breach entitling the floating charge holder to reduce the other transaction. This is also the case if the company has merely contractually obliged itself to grant a floating charge but has not yet done so and then proceeds to transfer specific property or create another security in favour of a different party. A floating charge is connected to the patrimony of the chargor: it only covers that party's property as it changes from time to time. As such, a charge holder does not have the right to render transactions involving particular property void on the basis of the offside goals rule. To do so, express statutory provision would be required.

This need for express provision differs from the position for catholic and secondary creditors above, as the non-application of offside goals is a reflection of the nature of the floating charge, which separates it from the background law where the doctrine applies. By contrast, there is no inherent incompatibility between the doctrine of catholic and secondary creditors and the floating charge's nature. An alternative approach that relies on applying *Forth & Clyde* analogously to the offside goals rule also supports the inapplicability of offside goals to floating charges due to the absence of express legislative provision.[251]

If a floating charge instrument contains a restriction on the chargor transferring property to another (as they commonly do),[252] this is merely a personal obligation, creating only personal liability for the chargor if it is breached. It will not affect the transfer itself, whether or not the transferee is aware of the prohibition. The charge holder's personal right to enforce this obligation is not capable of being made real as it is not directly connected to the floating charge itself. Even if we consider a floating charge to become real upon attachment,[253] the obligation's content is contrary to the nature of a floating charge and if it was considered part of the security itself it would likely mean that it was not a floating charge and was in fact an invalid form of security (as a non-possessory security that does not conform to any of the other existing types in Scots law). If there is a prohibition on the creation of

---

251 That is, if it is true that broader rules of law relating to security rights do not apply to floating charges without statutory provision, in line with the decision in *Forth & Clyde*, then this is a further argument in favour of the offside goals doctrine not applying to floating charges.

252 This could be an absolute prohibition on transferring a specific item or a certain type of property (e.g. heritable property) or, more likely, a prohibition on such a transfer without the consent of the charge holder. For discussion of restrictions on asset disposal and other forms of restriction on the activities of a borrower, see Gullifer and Payne, *Corporate Finance Law* (n 27) 206 onwards. And see Hardman and MacPherson, 'The Empirical Importance of the Floating Charge in Scotland', Chapter 11.

253 This, in itself, is arguably too removed from the relevant personal right for the offside goals rule to operate.

security rights, rather than on transfer of ownership, this is a negative pledge and just affects priority rather than invalidating the subsequent security.[254]

The previous discussion has involved consideration of whether a charge holder is able to rely upon the offside goals rule. We must also consider whether the grant of a floating charge could be a breach of an obligation in favour of another party, which would allow for the use of the offside goals doctrine. If a transferee has not yet completed title and then a floating charge is created by the chargor/transferor and the charge holder is aware of the impending transfer, the transferee can still complete title, which will cause the property to leave the ambit of the floating charge. This may still be the case even after a floating charge attaches or, alternatively, depending on the circumstances, it may no longer be possible for the transferee to complete the transfer as the chargor will be in the midst of an insolvency process.[255] As such, there is either no need or no possibility of relying on the offside goals rule. If, instead, a floating charge with negative pledge has been granted despite the chargor already being bound to create another security right, and the charge holder is aware of this, it is not wholly clear whether the floating charge would be voidable (or perhaps simply rank behind the other security). Two security rights can mutually exist in relation to property and the only effect arising from the grant of the floating charge in the scenario would be that it would have priority over the other security (rather than the other way around).[256] But given that parties seek to obtain security rights in order to gain priority over others it would perhaps be odd to penalise a charge holder for doing exactly that, as mentioned in the general rules of ranking section above. It therefore seems as if the floating charge would rank ahead of the other security and would not be voidable.

CONCLUSION

As will be evident from reading this chapter, ranking issues concerning floating charges are many and varied. This is further emphasised by the fact that keeping the chapter to this length was challenging: there were some issues that were omitted or had to be dealt with only briefly. Although the ranking and distribution provisions relating to floating charges may seek to cover all forms of competing security right or insolvency preference, they can be

254 See Companies Act 1985 s. 464(1A).
255 See MacPherson, *Floating Charge* (n 5) paras 6–37 onwards.
256 Due to the existence of the negative pledge – Companies Act 1985 s. 464(1)(a) and (1A).

inconsistent and unclear. Thus, if the ranking rules for floating charges are a 'complete code', it is a fragmentary code that is scattered throughout legislation, requires references to background law and is unfathomable in places.

Due to the nature of floating charges, a number of general rules applicable to security rights either do not apply to floating charges or apply in unusual ways. Yet it may be that some rules ought to apply to floating charges to a greater extent than has been considered to be the case in Scots law to this point, for example, with respect to the doctrine of catholic and secondary security. The chapter has also demonstrated the many ranking problems that exist due to the various rules that determine the outcomes between competing rights. This is typified by the large number of circles of priority that the law of floating charges creates.

Perhaps it is unsurprising that the ranking rules for floating charges give rise to difficulties. After all, it is a security right that covers all types of property and has to interact with a wide range of different types of interest. The ranking rules often represent policy choices to prefer particular parties in the face of the power of the floating charge holder. Thus, the floating charge may be considered inescapably dysfunctional as far as ranking is concerned. We should not, however, let this undermine the search for clarity and certainty that this chapter has sought to embark upon.

10 The Floating Charge and Insolvency Law

Donna McKenzie Skene

A. INTRODUCTION
B. THE NATURE OF THE FLOATING CHARGE
C. SCOPE OF FLOATING CHARGE
D. ENFORCEMENT OF THE FLOATING CHARGE GENERALLY
E. ENFORCEMENT THROUGH RECEIVERSHIP
 (1) Appointment of receiver
 (2) Status and powers of receiver
 (3) Duties of receiver
 (4) Distribution in receivership
 (5) Re-floating of charge
F. THE FLOATING CHARGE AND OTHER INSOLVENCY PROCESSES
 (1) Liquidation
 (2) Administration
 (3) Other receivers
 (4) Company voluntary arrangements
 (5) Moratorium and arrangements and reconstructions introduced by the 2020 Act
  (a) Moratorium
  (b) Arrangements and reconstructions
 (6) Challenge of floating charges within insolvency processes
G. RETRENCHMENT
H. CONCLUSION

A. INTRODUCTION

The floating charge is intimately bound up with insolvency law and this chapter explores that relationship with particular reference to Scots law. The chapter commences with a discussion of the nature of the floating charge as a security in the context of insolvency law. It then turns to issues relating to the scope of the floating charge and their implications in the context of insolvency law. Thereafter, it considers enforcement of the floating charge, particularly through the process of receivership, and the charge's interaction with other insolvency processes. Finally, it examines the retrenchment brought about by the Enterprise Act 2002. It concludes with an assessment of how well, or otherwise, the law has been able to accommodate the floating charge into the insolvency framework and what this tells us about the nature and operation of the floating charge.

B. THE NATURE OF THE FLOATING CHARGE

Like other securities, the floating charge is intended to give its holder an advantage over other creditors on the insolvency of the granter,[1] insolvency generally being considered the 'acid test' of a security.[2] Insolvency law generally, although not invariably or completely, respects pre-existing rights including security rights.[3] In many ways, however, the floating charge is

---

1 A floating charge may be granted only by a company or a limited liability partnership (LLP) or by certain other less common forms of corporate entities, for which see G L Gretton, 'The Story of the Scots Law Floating Charge: 1961 to Date', Chapter 4 within this volume. In this chapter, where possible, neutral terminology is used to reflect the fact that the granter of the floating charge may be either a company, an LLP or another entity, and that LLPs are subject to a modified version of the insolvency processes (or processes treated for the purpose of this chapter as insolvency processes) that apply to companies that are discussed in this chapter. Where this is not practicable, this will be noted at the time.

2 For the classic definition of security, see W M Gloag and J M Irvine, *Law of Rights in Security Heritable and Moveable Including Cautionary Obligations* (Edinburgh: W. Green, 1897) 1–2, which defines security as 'any right which a creditor may hold for ensuring the payment or satisfaction of his debt, distinct from, and in addition to, his right of action and execution against the debtor under the latter's personal obligation'.

3 There are a variety of different theories as to the proper functions and purposes of insolvency law with correspondingly different views on the proper extent of the protection to be afforded to pre-insolvency entitlements, including security rights: for a useful summary, see V Finch and D Milman, *Corporate Insolvency Law: Perspectives and Principles*, 3rd edn (Cambridge: Cambridge University Press, 2017) Ch. 2; K van Zwieten (ed), *Goode on Principles of Corporate Insolvency Law*, 5th edn (London: Sweet & Maxwell, 2018) Ch. 2. The Scottish Law Commission in their *Memorandum No. 16, Insolvency, Bankruptcy and Liquidation in Scotland* (1971), in setting out four objectives which they thought the law should and did seek to obtain, specifically included 'the protection of security and other rights and preferences lawfully obtained ... ' (para. 5). Their subsequent *Report on Bankruptcy and Related Aspects of Insolvency and Liquidation* (Scot. Law Com. No. 68, 1982) did not include a specific statement to the same effect in the extended list of twelve objectives underpinning its recommendations for reform but, as will be seen further below, it is clear that the law continues to protect pre-existing security rights on insolvency to a large extent.

different from other types of security, and this means that it is not always possible to treat it in the same way as other securities on insolvency.

First, at the risk of stating the obvious, the floating charge is floating. Unlike other securities, at least those created consensually,[4] the floating charge does not in itself confer a real right in the property subject to the security: it floats over that property until something causes it to attach. Attachment, sometimes referred to as 'crystallisation',[5] occurs automatically on the appointment of a receiver under the floating charge and on liquidation and may occur in specified circumstances on administration.[6] In contrast to the position in England and Wales, it is not possible in Scots law to provide for the charge to attach in any other circumstances. Attachment causes the floating charge to attach to property 'as if' it is a fixed security,[7] although it is not clear that a real right is created in that property even then.[8] As a consequence, it has been questioned whether the floating charge can be characterised as a real security at all.[9] It is, however, generally regarded as such and will be so regarded for the purposes of this discussion.

Secondly, unlike most other securities, which generally create real rights in a specific piece of the granter's property,[10] the floating charge has the potential, generally utilised in practice, to affect multiple pieces of the granter's property of different types. This raises particular issues of fairness to other, especially unsecured, creditors where the granter is absolutely insolvent.[11]

---

4 The landlord's hypothec, which arises by operation of law, has been viewed by some as a form of floating security, but despite some of its characteristics appearing to justify that view at first blush, the better view would appear to be that it is not: see A Sweeney, *The Landlord's Hypothec* (Edinburgh: Edinburgh Legal Education Trust, 2021).

5 Although that term appears nowhere in the legislation, with the very recent exception of the Corporate Insolvency and Governance Act 2020.

6 See further below. The fact that administration, unlike the appointment of a receiver or liquidation, does not cause the charge to crystallise automatically has been described as 'odd': see D Cabrelli, 'The Curious Case of the 'Unreal' Floating Charge' 2005 SLT (News) 127.

7 See Insolvency Act 1986 ss. 53(7) (attachment on appointment of receiver by holder of floating charge) and 54(6) (attachment on appointment of receiver by the court); Companies Act 1985 s. 463(2) (attachment on liquidation); Insolvency Act 1986 Sch. B1 para. 115(4) (attachment in specified circumstances in administration).

8 See A D J MacPherson, *The Floating Charge* (Edinburgh: Edinburgh Legal Education Trust, 2020), especially at paras 5–32 onwards and 6–83 onwards.

9 See Cabrelli (n 6).

10 Cf the landlord's hypothec, which extends to a category of property (generally referred to as *invecta et illata*) that will generally include multiple pieces of individual property.

11 See, for example, the discussion of secured creditors generally and floating charge holders in particular, in the *Report of the Review Committee on Insolvency Law and Practice* (Cmnd 8558: 1982) Ch. 34.

This is discussed further below.[12] The scope of the floating charge is discussed in greater detail in the following section.

C. SCOPE OF FLOATING CHARGE

As noted in the previous section, the floating charge has the potential to affect multiple pieces of property of different types. While it is perfectly possible for a floating charge to be drawn in such a way as to affect only some, or certain types, of the granter's property, historically it has typically been drawn in such a way as to affect all of the granter's property, including future property. What exactly is encompassed by a floating charge drawn in this way has been the subject of some controversy. One example is the case of *Sharp v Thomson*,[13] which raised issues about whether heritable property owned by a company in respect of which a disposition had been delivered to its purchasers but not registered at the time of the appointment of a receiver was caught by the floating charge, a question ultimately answered in the negative by the House of Lords.[14] Another is the controversy over whether (the fruits of) officeholder claims such as misfeasance claims, claims for fraudulent and wrongful trading and claims relating to challengeable transactions were caught by a floating charge. This was ultimately resolved only by the introduction of s. 176ZB of the Insolvency Act 1986,[15] which provides that claims for fraudulent and wrongful trading as well as claims under the statutory provisions relating to gratuitous alienations, unfair preferences and extortionate credit transactions are not caught by a floating charge.[16]

The extent of the property affected by the floating charge has important consequences, including whether or not the floating charge is a 'qualifying floating charge' for the purpose, *inter alia*, of making an out-of-court appointment of an administrator and whether or not the holder of the

---

12 And see also J Hardman and A D J MacPherson, 'The Ranking of Floating Charges', Chapter 9 within this volume and J L L Gant, 'Floating Charges and Moral Hazard: Finding Fairness for Involuntary and Vulnerable Stakeholders', Chapter 6 within this volume.

13 1994 SC 503 affd 1995 SC 45 rev 1997 SC (HL) 66.

14 And see Gretton, 'The Story of the Scots Law Floating Charge: 1961 to Date', Chapter 4.

15 Inserted by the Small Business, Enterprise and Employment Act 2015 s. 119 as from 1 October 2015.

16 Insolvency Act 1986 s. 176ZB(1)–(3). Note that the provisions do not apply to claims under s. 212 of the Insolvency Act 1986, (the fruits of) which are caught by a floating charge. The provisions may be disapplied by a voluntary arrangement under Part 1 of the Insolvency Act 1986 or a scheme of arrangement under Part 26 or 26A of the Companies Act 2006: Insolvency Act 1986 s. 176ZB(4) as amended by the Corporate Insolvency and Governance Act 2020 Sch. 9(2) para. 6(2).

floating charge is able to exercise the so-called 'floating charge holder's veto' on the appointment of an administrator by the court.[17] Furthermore, a receiver in a case where the whole, or substantially the whole, of the debtor's property is attached by the floating charge is an administrative receiver,[18] while a receiver appointed under any other floating charge is not.[19] This has a number of implications.[20] For example, only an administrative receiver is required to be a qualified insolvency practitioner[21]; only an administrative receiver is required to carry out certain functions, such as reporting on the conduct of the directors for the purposes of the director disqualification regime[22]; and only an administrative receiver is required to vacate office automatically on the appointment of an administrator[23] (although the administrator may at their discretion require a non-administrative receiver to do so).[24] This can perhaps be explained by the fact that, as discussed further below, while all receiverships are effectively a form of insolvency process in themselves, an administrative receivership that is dealing with the whole or substantially the whole of the debtor's assets can be regarded as more closely akin to the truly collective insolvency processes of administration and liquidation, while a non-administrative receivership that is not dealing with the whole or substantially the whole of the debtor's assets can be regarded as less closely akin to these collective insolvency processes and more akin to the normal enforcement process for a security relating to a specific piece of property (notwithstanding that the receiver may nonetheless be dealing with multiple pieces of property).

D. ENFORCEMENT OF THE FLOATING CHARGE GENERALLY

Enforcement of a security is normally carried out by the secured creditor and it is a long-standing principle of Scots law that, subject to certain provisos, a secured creditor may proceed to enforce their security notwithstanding the granter's entry into an insolvency process. The secured creditor can

---

17 See further below.
18 Insolvency Act 1986 s. 251.
19 Such a receiver is hereafter referred to as a non-administrative receiver.
20 For a fuller discussion, see G Morse (ed), *Palmer's Company Law* (London: Sweet & Maxwell, looseleaf) para. 14.202.
21 See Insolvency Act 1986 s. 388.
22 See Company Directors Disqualification Act 1986 s. 7A(9).
23 Insolvency Act 1986 Sch. B1 para. 41(1), discussed further below.
24 Insolvency Act 1986 Sch. B1 para. 41(2), discussed further below.

therefore effectively stay outside the insolvency process if so inclined.[25] The floating charge, however, is different in this respect as in so many others. As discussed in the chapter of this volume by Professor Gretton, when floating charges were first introduced in Scotland the only mechanism for enforcement was through liquidation.[26] Liquidation caused the floating charge to attach, and the realisation of the property attached was carried out by the liquidator. The liquidator then ranked the floating charge holder as appropriate when distributing the company's property in accordance with the statutory scheme.

The Companies (Floating Charges and Receivers) (Scotland) Act 1972 subsequently allowed the floating charge holder to appoint, or to apply to the court for the appointment of, a receiver to enforce the charge without waiting for or initiating liquidation.[27] The appointment of a receiver caused the floating charge to attach and the realisation of the property attached was carried out by the receiver. However, in contrast to the position in England and Wales, there was, and remains, no mechanism in Scots law for the floating charge holder to enforce the security directly through what has been described as 'self-enforcement'.[28] Enforcement of the charge can take place only through liquidation, receivership or now, in certain circumstances, administration, and as will be seen below, this has had implications for the way in which insolvency law has developed. The interaction between receivership and liquidation and between receivership and administration, as well as the position with regard to company voluntary arrangements under Part 1 of the Insolvency Act 1986 and the new statutory moratorium and arrangement and reconstruction procedure introduced by the Corporate Insolvency and Governance Act 2020 is discussed further in section F. The next section, however, concentrates on receivership itself.

E. ENFORCEMENT THROUGH RECEIVERSHIP

As mentioned above, as well as being a mechanism for enforcement of a floating charge, receivership is in effect a form of insolvency process. It therefore has what might be described as a dual personality. As an insolvency process,

---

25 See, for example, Scottish Law Commission, *Report on Bankruptcy* (n 3) para. 18.2. The discussion relates to sequestration but is equally applicable to corporate insolvency.
26 See Gretton, 'The Story of the Scots Law Floating Charge: 1961 to Date', Chapter 4.
27 The position where there is both a receivership and a liquidation is discussed further below.
28 See *Palmer's Company Law* (n 20) para. 13.204; MacPherson, *Floating Charge* (n 8) paras 6–04 onwards.

however, it is different in important respects from the other main insolvency processes of liquidation and administration. In particular, it is not a truly collective process dealing with the claims of all creditors: rather, it deals with the claims of certain categories of creditors only.[29] One consequence of this is that it is not always recognised as an insolvency process for all purposes: for example, it is not an insolvency process for the purpose of the EU regulation on insolvency proceedings[30] or the UNCITRAL Model Law as enacted in the Cross Border Insolvency Regulations 2006.[31] This feature of receivership was also one of the main factors leading to the introduction of restrictions on the use of administrative receivership and the change of focus to administration as the primary means of enforcing a floating charge brought about by the Enterprise Act 2002. This is discussed further below. The remainder of this section, however, considers both the enforcement and insolvency process aspects of receivership itself in more detail.

(1) Appointment of receiver

A receiver may be appointed on the grounds provided for in the floating charge itself or on the statutory grounds set out in s. 52 of the Insolvency Act 1986. It is possible for joint receivers to be appointed but, for the sake of simplicity, this chapter will refer only to the appointment of a receiver. The appointment need not be made as a result of any financial difficulties or insolvency of the granter, although in practice it usually will be.[32] Irrespective of the grounds for the appointment, the receivership will proceed in the same way and in this respect receivership is no different to other corporate insolvency processes: inability to pay debts[33] is only one ground for liquidation, and even if a liquidation proceeds on this ground, the debtor may ultimately turn out to be solvent, while a debtor entering administration

---

29 This is discussed further below.
30 Regulation of the European Parliament and of the Council of 20 May 2015 on insolvency proceedings (recast), 2015/848 OJ L141/58 Annex A. The same was true of its predecessor, Council Regulation of 29 May 2000 on insolvency proceedings, 1346/2000 OJ L160/1 Annex A.
31 The Cross-Border Insolvency Regulations 2006 (SI 2006/1048) enact a modified version of the UNCITRAL Model Law on Cross-Border Insolvency in Great Britain.
32 The statutory grounds for the appointment of a receiver are largely reflective of financial difficulties/insolvency, but the floating charge itself may, and generally will, permit the appointment of a receiver where there is a failure to comply with any of the granter's obligations, not just financial ones. In this respect the floating charge is no different from, for example, a standard security, where the creditor may be entitled to enforce the security as a result of failure to implement obligations other than financial ones.
33 See Insolvency Act 1986 s. 122(1)(f).

may similarly not (yet) be insolvent or may ultimately turn out to be solvent. As noted above, the receiver is required to be a qualified insolvency practitioner only where they are an administrative receiver. As also noted above, the appointment of a receiver causes the floating charge to attach to the property then subject to the charge. It will be seen further below that the receiver has the right to deal with the property so attached, and only the property so attached. Like other corporate insolvency processes, however, the property does not vest in the receiver and, in contrast to the position in liquidation where the liquidator may apply to the court for a vesting order,[34] there is no statutory mechanism for vesting property in a receiver.

A debtor may have granted more than one floating charge. In such a case, it is possible for a receiver (or joint receivers) to be appointed under any or all such floating charges. The relationship between receiverships is discussed further below.

(2) Status and powers of receiver

As in other corporate insolvency processes, a receiver is deemed to be the agent of the company.[35] Subject to the restrictions discussed below, a receiver has the powers given to them by the instrument creating the floating charge, if any,[36] and, in addition, the statutory powers contained in Sch. 2 of the Insolvency Act 1986 so far as not inconsistent with any provisions in the instrument creating the floating charge.[37] These powers are virtually identical to the powers given to an administrator and to an administrative receiver in England and Wales by Sch. 1 of the Insolvency Act 1986.[38] They also mirror to a large extent the powers given to a liquidator by Sch. 4 and other provisions of the Insolvency Act 1986.

Of particular note is the power in para. 1 of Sch. 2, which gives the receiver power to take possession of, collect and get in the property attached by the charge 'from the company *or a liquidator thereof* or any other person' [emphasis supplied]. This makes clear that a receiver may be appointed or remain in position following liquidation and is entitled

---

34 Insolvency Act 1986 s. 145.
35 Insolvency Act 1986 s. 57. The agency extends only to the property attached by the charge under which the receiver was appointed and to contracts of employment adopted by them in carrying out their functions: s. 57(1), (1A).
36 Insolvency Act 1986 s. 55(1).
37 Insolvency Act 1986 s. 55(2).
38 It may be noted that a Scottish receiver has these powers whether or not they are an administrative receiver.

to take the necessary steps to enforce the floating charge notwithstanding the liquidation. This reflects the normal principle, referred to above, that a creditor may enforce their security notwithstanding the granter's entry into an insolvency process.[39] Also of note is the power in para. 2 of Sch. 2, which gives the receiver power to sell, hire out or otherwise dispose of property. Following the decision in *Sharp v Thomson*,[40] a practical question that may arise is whether the receiver does in fact have the power to sell any particular piece of heritable property since, as discussed above, the effect of the decision is that heritable property owned by a company in respect of which a disposition has been delivered to its purchasers but not registered at the time of the receiver's appointment is not caught by the floating charge and so cannot be dealt with by the receiver. As it is impossible to establish conclusively that no delivered but unregistered disposition exists, there may be a question over the receiver's ability to deliver a good title. However, while the Scottish Law Commission in their consideration of the implications of the decision recognised the problem, they did not recommend any legislative solution to it on the basis that it did not seem to have caused serious difficulties and receivership was in decline.[41] Where the receiver wishes to sell or dispose of property but is unable to obtain the consent of a creditor with a security over the property or effectually executed diligence, they can apply to the court for authority to sell or dispose of the property free of the security or diligence.[42] This is a corollary of the fact that the powers of a receiver, whether conferred by the charge or Sch. 2, are subject to the rights of any person who has effectually executed diligence on all or any part of the property prior to the appointment of the receiver and to the rights of any person who holds over all or any part of the property a fixed security or floating charge having priority over, or ranking *pari passu* with, the floating charge under which the receiver was appointed.[43] The meaning of effectually executed diligence was also previously the subject of some controversy

---

39 The interaction of receivership and liquidation is discussed in more detail in the next section.
40 *Sharp* (n 13).
41 See Scottish Law Commission, *Discussion Paper on Sharp v Thomson* (Scot. Law Com. DP No. 114, 2001) para. 2.15; Scottish Law Commission, *Report on Sharp v Thomson* (Scot. Law Com. No. 208, 2007) para. 2.8.
42 Insolvency Act 1986 s. 61. The section sets out a number of conditions that apply before and after any such authorisation. For the corresponding (but not identical) provisions in administration, see paras 70 and 71 of Sch. B1.
43 Insolvency Act 1986 s. 55(3).

that has now, however, been resolved by the decision of the Inner House in *MacMillan v T Leith Developments Ltd.*[44]

In addition to the powers referred to, certain other powers also enjoyed by other insolvency officeholders are enjoyed by either all receivers or administrative receivers. For example, all receivers have the power (and duty) to obtain a statement of affairs from specified persons[45] and to apply to the court for directions,[46] while administrative receivers also have the power to obtain the continued supply of specified services,[47] the power to seek the court's assistance in getting in property to which they are entitled,[48] the power to require specified persons to give them specified information[49] and the power to apply to the court for examination of specified persons and related orders.[50] One power that no receiver has, however, is the power to challenge prior transactions of the granter of the floating charge under either the statutory provisions relating to gratuitous alienations, unfair preferences and extortionate credit transactions or the corresponding common law rules. This reflects the fact, referred to above, that receivership, even administrative receivership, although a form of insolvency process, is not a truly collective process that deals with the claims of all creditors, and the fruits of any such challenge are intended to be for the benefit of the general body of unsecured creditors and, at least in the case of recoveries under the statutory provisions, are not caught by the floating charge. It may be noted, however, that the floating charge holder *qua* creditor may have the right to challenge gratuitous alienations or unfair preferences where the relevant

---

44 *MacMillan v T Leith Developments Ltd* [2017] CSIH 23, 2017 SC 642. See also Insolvency Act 1986 s. 61(1A) inserted by the Bankruptcy and Diligence etc. (Scotland) Act 2007 s. 155(2). Insolvency Act 1986 s. 61(1B), which was prospectively inserted by the Bankruptcy and Diligence etc. (Scotland) Act 2007 s. 155(3), has never come into force. For a detailed discussion, see A D J MacPherson, 'The Circle Squared? Floating Charges and Diligence after *MacMillan v T Leith Developments Ltd*' 2018 Jur Rev 230. See also J Hardman and A D J MacPherson, 'The Ranking of Floating Charges', Chapter 9.
45 Insolvency Act 1986 s. 66. This section is specific to receivership, but there are similar provisions in administration and liquidation.
46 Insolvency Act 1986 s. 63. This section is specific to receivership, but there are similar provisions in administration and liquidation.
47 Insolvency Act 1986 s. 233. This section also applies to an administrator, the supervisor of a company voluntary arrangement, a provisional liquidator and a liquidator.
48 Insolvency Act 1986 s. 234. This section also applies to an administrator, a provisional liquidator and a liquidator.
49 Insolvency Act 1986 s. 235. This section also applies to an administrator, a provisional liquidator and a liquidator.
50 Insolvency Act 1986 s. 236. This section also applies to an administrator, a provisional liquidator and a liquidator.

conditions are satisfied.[51] The provisions of s. 245 of the Insolvency Act 1986 (avoidance of certain floating charges) apply only where the debtor is (also) in administration or liquidation. In addition, although it is now possible for an administrator as well as a liquidator to bring proceedings for fraudulent or wrongful trading,[52] no receiver may do so. Again, this reflects the fact that receivership, even administrative receivership, although a form of insolvency process, is not a truly collective process that deals with the claims of all creditors and the fruits of fraudulent or wrongful trading claims are intended to be for the benefit of the general body of unsecured creditors and are not caught by the floating charge.

(3) Duties of receiver

A receiver has a number of statutory duties that also mirror in many respects those of the officeholders in other insolvency processes. For example, a receiver must take steps to publicise their appointment[53] and to report on the receivership to specified parties,[54] although commensurate with the more limited nature of receivership, the requirements to report are more limited than in other processes. A committee of unsecured creditors may be formed,[55] but again commensurate with the nature of receivership, such a committee has less functions and powers than the committees that may be established in other insolvency processes. As noted above, an administrative receiver also has a duty to report on the conduct of the directors for the purposes of the director disqualification regime.[56]

All receivers also owe certain duties at common law to, *inter alia*, the floating charge holder and the granter. Thus, while a receiver has discretion as to which parts of the property attached by the charge to ingather and realise and is not subject to the common law rules in relation to catholic and secondary creditors,[57] they have a duty to take reasonable steps to obtain

---

51 For a detailed discussion of the provisions on challengeable transactions, see D W McKenzie Skene, 'Corporate Insolvency', in *The Laws of Scotland: Stair Memorial Encyclopaedia*, Reissue (2008) paras 323 onwards.

52 See Insolvency Act 1986 ss. 213 and 214 (liquidation) and 246ZA and 246ZB (administration). In the case of an LLP, the provisions on fraudulent and wrongful trading apply on the liquidation of an LLP but not its administration.

53 Insolvency Act 1986 ss. 64 and 65.

54 Insolvency Act 1986 s. 67.

55 Insolvency Act 1986 s. 68.

56 Company Directors Disqualification Act 1986 s. 7A(9).

57 *Forth and Clyde Construction Co Ltd v Trinity Timber and Plywood Co Ltd* 1984 SC 1. But see Hardman and MacPherson, 'The Ranking of Floating Charges', Chapter 9.

a proper price for the property, although the precise nature and extent of that duty remains less than entirely clear,[58] in particular whether the receiver's duty in this respect is to be equiparated with that of a creditor with fixed security.[59] The receiver must also act in good faith,[60] and may also have a general duty of care to those affected by their actions other than in relation to the realisation of the property, for example in managing the property or business.[61] Furthermore, like other insolvency officeholders, a receiver may be held liable for misfeasance[62] and fraudulent trading.[63] The receiver's primary duty is, however, to the floating charge holder[64] and can be summed up as being to realise the assets attached by the charge and pay the floating charge holder after first paying certain other specified debts.[65] It is this feature of receivership that was the other main factor leading to the introduction of restrictions on the use of administrative receivership and the change of focus to administration as the primary means of enforcing a floating charge brought about by the Enterprise Act 2002.[66]

(4) Distribution in receivership

Commensurate with the nature of receivership as an enforcement process, a receiver is required to pay the monies received by them to the holder of the floating charge under which they are appointed but, commensurate with the nature of receivership as an insolvency process, only after payment

---

58 See *Forth and Clyde* (n 57); *Jackson v Clydesdale Bank plc* 2003 SLT 273; cf *Imperial Hotel (Aberdeen) Ltd v Vaux Breweries Ltd* 1978 SC 86. In *Clydesdale Bank plc v Spencer* 2001 GWD 17-667, Lord Macfadyen specifically declined to consider whether the duty was owed to a guarantor, although it is thought that it should be so owed. The floating charge holder will not normally be liable for the receiver's failure to fulfil the duty unless they give the receiver directions or otherwise interferes in the realisation of the property. For a fuller discussion, see McKenzie Skene 'Corporate Insolvency' (n 51) para. 167; *Palmer's Company Law* (n 20) para. 14.219.

59 Differing views on this point have been expressed: see *Palmer's Company Law* (n 20) para. 14.219 and I M Fletcher and R Roxburgh, *Greene and Fletcher, The Law and Practice of Receivership in Scotland*, 3rd edn (London: Bloomsbury, 2005) paras 3.44 and 3.50.

60 See *Downsview Nominees Ltd v First City Corporation* [1993] AC 295. Although this is an English case, it is thought that the same principle applies in Scotland.

61 See, for example, *Larsen's Executrix v Henderson* 1990 SLT 498; *Palmer's Company Law* (n 20) para. 14.219.

62 Insolvency Act 1986 s. 212, which also applies to liquidators; for administrators, see Sch. B1, para. 75.

63 Insolvency Act 1986 s. 213.

64 *Imperial Hotel* (n 58).

65 Distribution is discussed further below; see also Hardman and MacPherson, 'The Ranking of Floating Charges', Chapter 9.

66 This is discussed further below.

of certain other persons.[67] These include the receivership expenses and, where the granter is not already in the course of being wound up at the time of the receiver's appointment, the preferential creditors.[68] The requirement to pay preferential creditors out of the proceeds of the security property is unique to floating charges and reflects the fact that because a floating charge can potentially affect all of the granter's assets, there might be nothing left to pay such creditors absent such provision. Any payments to the preferential creditors are, however, to be recouped so far as possible out of the assets available for the payment of ordinary creditors.[69] This seeks so far as possible to put the floating charge back on the same footing as other secured creditors, who are not required to pay preferential creditors out of the proceeds of their security irrespective of whether or not there are other assets available to pay such creditors. In reality, however, where the floating charge does affect all of the granter's assets, there are likely to be no assets available for the payment of ordinary creditors, even though, as discussed above, there are certain assets that are not caught by a floating charge and that, if extant, would be available in principle for the payment of ordinary creditors and thus the preferential debts.[70] Where the floating charge affects only part of the granter's assets, however, it may be more likely that the floating charge holder will not have to bear the cost of payment of the preferential debts and will thus be in the same position as other secured creditors in this respect.

In addition, the Enterprise Act 2002 introduced provisions requiring a prescribed part of a debtor's net property to be set aside for the satisfaction of unsecured debts,[71] the debtor's 'net property' being defined as the amount of its property that would, but for the provisions, be available for the satisfaction of the claims of floating charge holders.[72] The provisions

---

67 Insolvency Act 1986 s. 60 and see further Hardman and MacPherson, 'The Ranking of Floating Charges', Chapter 9.

68 Insolvency Act 1986 s. 59.

69 Insolvency Act 1986 s. 59(3).

70 As noted above, property not caught by a floating charge includes (the fruits of) certain office-holder claims, but these would only exist where the granter was subject to the relevant insolvency process and the claims had either been successfully pursued by the relevant officeholder or assigned by them in return for a payment. Such property also includes property in a *Sharp v Thomson* situation and it is arguable that such property, although not caught by the floating charge, is still the granter's property because title remains with the granter, with the result that the property is available for the payment of ordinary creditors, but even if this is correct, such a situation is likely to be vanishingly rare.

71 See Insolvency Act 1986 s. 176A.

72 Insolvency Act 1986 s. 176A(6).

apply to floating charges created after 15 September 2003[73] and, unless the requirement to set aside the prescribed part either does not apply or is disapplied in the circumstances provided for,[74] it will reduce the amount available for payment of the floating charge holder. The provisions and the policy reasons for their introduction are discussed further below, but for the moment, it may be noted that the quid pro quo of these provisions was a reduction in the categories of preferential debt, meaning that the effect on the floating charge holder would in fact be neutral.[75] The partial reintroduction of Crown preference,[76] also discussed further below, however, alters this position. The receiver must deliver the sums representing the prescribed part to any liquidator or administrator or, in the absence of a liquidator or administrator, apply to the court for directions.[77] Irrespective of who is responsible for distribution of the prescribed part, the expenses relating to it are borne by the prescribed part itself, so there is no further encroachment on the monies due to the charge holder.[78]

In the unlikely event of any surplus remaining once the floating charge holder has been paid, this is to be paid to any other receiver, the holder of a fixed security that is over property subject to the floating charge, the company or its liquidator as the case may be.[79] The relationship between a receivership and any other receivership and between receivership and liquidation, as well as other insolvency processes, is discussed in the next section.

(5) Re-floating of charge

The legislation envisages that a floating charge which has attached may cease to do so. Section 62(2) of the Insolvency Act 1986 provides that if by the expiry of a period of one month following the removal of a receiver or

---

73 Insolvency Act 1986 s. 176A(9) and Insolvency Act 1986 (Prescribed Part) Order 2003 (SI 2003/2097).
74 See Insolvency Act 1986 s. 176A(3)–(5).
75 See Insolvency Service, *Insolvency – A Second Chance* (Cm 5234: 2001) para. 2.19.
76 See Finance Act 2020 s. 98.
77 Insolvency (Scotland) (Receivership and Winding Up) Rules 2018 (SSI 2018/347) r. 2.20. The interaction of receivership with liquidation and with administration is discussed further below.
78 Insolvency (Scotland) (Receivership and Winding Up) Rules 2018 r. 7.28(2) for liquidation and Insolvency (Scotland) (Company Voluntary Arrangements and Administration) Rules 2018 (SI 2018/1082) r. 3.50(2) for administration. There is no corresponding rule for receivership itself, presumably on the basis that it is anticipated that distribution will normally be carried out by the liquidator or administrator, but where there is no liquidation or administration and the receiver applies to the court for directions, it is anticipated that the court would make an appropriate order to the same effect.
79 Insolvency Act 1986 s. 60(2).

their ceasing to act as such no other receiver has been appointed, the floating charge will cease to attach to the property then subject to the charge and again subsist as a floating charge. Unlike other securities, therefore, the floating charge may continue post-enforcement and, in theory, may be enforced again in future, although in practice it is more likely that the company will go into liquidation, or perhaps administration.

F. THE FLOATING CHARGE AND OTHER INSOLVENCY PROCESSES

This section explores how the law has developed to accommodate the principle that secured creditors may generally enforce their securities notwithstanding the granter's entry into an insolvency process where the security in question is a floating charge. It will therefore consider the enforcement of the floating charge in the context of: (i) liquidation; (ii) administration; (iii) a receivership under another floating charge; (iv) a company voluntary arrangement under Part 1 of the Insolvency Act 1986; and (v) the new moratorium and arrangement and reconstruction procedure introduced by the Corporate Insolvency and Governance Act 2020, although the last two may not strictly be considered to be insolvency processes as such.

(1) Liquidation

As noted above, liquidation causes a floating charge to attach.[80] Where no receiver has been appointed, as in the days before receivership was available, enforcement of the charge is effectively carried out by the liquidator, who will realise the property attached by the charge and pay the floating charge holder as appropriate when distributing the granter's property in accordance with the statutory scheme.[81]

A receiver may, however, be appointed either before or after liquidation, and as mentioned above, a receiver is entitled to take possession of the property attached by the charge from, *inter alia*, a liquidator.[82] The receiver therefore takes precedence over the liquidator so far as the property attached by the charge is concerned, and this reflects the normal principle that a creditor may generally enforce their security notwithstanding

---

80 Companies Act 1985 s. 463(2).
81 See further below and Hardman and MacPherson, 'The Ranking of Floating Charges', Chapter 9.
82 Insolvency Act 1986 Sch. 2 para. 1.

the granter's entry into an insolvency process. There may, however, be a question as to exactly what property is attached by the charge. As noted above, both receivership and liquidation cause a floating charge to attach. The question is therefore whether, where there is both a receivership and a liquidation, the charge attaches more than once, sometimes referred to as 'double crystallisation'. In the case of *Ross v Taylor*,[83] where liquidation followed receivership, that question was answered in the affirmative. However, the decision, and the concept of double crystallisation, has been criticised, and since the statutory wording is now different, it is not clear whether the decision would now be followed.[84] The better approach would seem to be to regard the floating charge as attaching only once unless it has re-floated in the interim.[85]

Another question that may arise is liability for the liquidation expenses. In Scotland, there is no provision for the payment of liquidation expenses out of the property attached by the floating charge. Where a receiver is appointed, the statutory scheme for the distribution of monies in receivership[86] makes no mention of liquidation expenses. Where there is no receiver and the property attached by the charge is realised by the liquidator,[87] the costs of realisation will fall to be met from that property in the same way as for any other security. There will, however, inevitably be liquidation expenses that are not attributable to the realisation of the charged property, even where that property comprises all the granter's assets. But there is nothing in the statutory scheme for distribution in liquidation providing or allowing for payment of the liquidation expenses from the property attached by the floating charge, even where a receiver is appointed after the commencement of the liquidation and liquidation expenses have therefore been incurred prior to the receiver's appointment. It is understood that, at least hitherto, it was the practice in Scotland for the whole of the liquidation expenses to be paid out of the property attached by the floating charge where realisation of the charged property was carried out by the liquidator,[88] but while this may have been a matter of agreement or acceptance by floating charge holders, it does not represent the legal position. The position in Scotland

---

83 1985 SC 156.

84 See *Palmer's Company Law* (n 20) paras 13.208–13.210; J St Clair and Lord Drummond Young, *The Law of Corporate Insolvency in Scotland*, 4th edn (Edinburgh: W. Green, 2011) para. 6–09.

85 Re-floating of the charge is discussed above.

86 Insolvency Act 1986 s. 60.

87 Or where a receiver is appointed, but it is agreed that the liquidator will carry out the realisation.

88 See St Clair and Drummond Young, *Corporate Insolvency* (n 84) para. 6–44.

may be contrasted with the position in England and Wales. There, prior to the decision of the House of Lords in *Buchler v Talbot*,[89] it had been held that the expenses of liquidation could be paid out of floating charge assets if necessary.[90] The House of Lords in *Buchler v Talbot*, however, overruled that earlier authority, holding that it was incorrect and that liquidation expenses (other than the expenses of realising the property subject to the charge where that realisation was carried out by the liquidator) could not be paid from floating charge assets. The decision, which reflected the true position in Scotland as discussed above, was reversed by statute in England and Wales,[91] but the position in Scotland remains as stated. This means that in this respect, if not in others, the floating charge is treated in the same way as other securities, which are not obliged to bear the general expenses of liquidation. On the other hand, the position in England and Wales can be seen as recognising more effectively the different nature of the floating charge as a security, at least where it affects all of the granter's assets.

A floating charge holder who wishes to claim in the liquidation for any unsecured balance due to them must deduct the value of their security from their claim,[92] thus ranking as an ordinary creditor in the liquidation for the unsecured element of their claim. Alternatively, the floating charge holder may surrender their security and rank as an unsecured creditor for their whole claim.[93] The liquidator has the power to require a floating charge holder, at the expense of the company's assets, to discharge their security or convey or assign it to the liquidator on payment of the security value as specified by the floating charge holder, whereupon the floating charge creditor will rank as an ordinary creditor for any remaining balance of the sums due to them.[94] Where the security has been realised, the floating charge creditor must deduct the amount received or entitled to be received by them, less the expenses of realisation, from their claim.[95] In these respects, the floating charge holder is treated in the same way as other creditors, although the position with a floating charge will tend to be more complicated, particularly where the floating charge relates to the whole or substantially the whole of the company's assets.

---

89 [2004] UKHL 9. The case is also known as *Re Leyland Daf International Ltd*.
90 *Re Barleycorn Enterprises Ltd* [1970] Ch 465.
91 Insolvency Act 1986 s. 176ZA.
92 Insolvency (Scotland) (Receivership and Winding Up) Rules 2018 (SSI 2018/347) r. 7.24(1).
93 Insolvency (Scotland) (Receivership and Winding Up) Rules 2018 (n 92) r. 7.24(2).
94 Insolvency (Scotland) (Receivership and Winding Up) Rules 2018 (n 92) r. 7.24(3), (4).
95 Insolvency (Scotland) (Receivership and Winding Up) Rules 2018 (n 92) r. 7.24(5).

Where the prescribed part applies to any floating charge,[96] the liquidator will be responsible for its distribution, having either received the prescribed part from the receiver[97] or having set it aside as required by the statutory provisions where there is no receiver.[98] As noted above, the expenses relating to the prescribed part are borne by the prescribed part itself. The prescribed part is discussed further below.

(2) Administration

The position for administration is somewhat more complex than the position with regard to liquidation. This perhaps reflects the different purpose of administration that, at least in theory, is concerned primarily with the rescue of the debtor[99] and can therefore be seen as justifying a different approach.

As noted above, administration does not automatically cause a floating charge to attach. Where a receiver has been appointed or the company has gone into liquidation prior to the administration, however, the floating charge will have attached by virtue of that event. If the floating charge has not attached, the administrator may cause it to do so in certain circumstances in order to enable a distribution to be made to the floating charge holder. This is discussed further below.

When administration was first introduced, an administrator could only be appointed by the court on the application of specified persons. The reforms introduced by the Enterprise Act 2002 made provision for the out-of-court appointment of an administrator in certain cases,[100] but it remains possible for an administrator to be appointed by the court. As a general rule, the court may make an administration order only where it is satisfied that a debtor is, or is likely to become, unable to pay its debts and the administration order is reasonably likely to achieve the purpose of administration.[101] The applicant is required to give notice of the application to, *inter alia*, any person who has appointed an administrative receiver of the company, any person who is or may be entitled to appoint an administrative receiver of the company and any person who is or may be entitled to appoint an administrator of the

---

96 See above and further below.
97 See above.
98 Insolvency Act 1986 s. 176A(2).
99 See Insolvency Act 1986 Sch. B1 para. 3.
100 See further below.
101 Insolvency Act 1986 Sch. B1 para. 11. The position is different, however, where the application is made by a qualifying floating charge holder: see further below.

company via the out-of-court route available to a qualifying floating charge holder.[102] On hearing the application, the court has a wide discretion as to the order it may make, if any.[103] Where, however, an administrative receiver has been appointed to the company, whether before or after the making of the application,[104] the court must dismiss the application unless: (i) the holder of the floating charge under which the administrative receiver was appointed consents to the making of the administration order[105]; (ii) the court thinks that the floating charge would be avoided under s. 245 of the Insolvency Act 1986 if an administration order were to be made[106]; or (iii) the court thinks that the floating charge would be challengeable as a gratuitous alienation or unfair preference under the relevant statutory provisions or at common law.[107] This is the so-called floating charge holder's veto, which effectively gives a floating charge holder who is in a position to appoint an administrative receiver the power to insist on an administrative receivership rather than an administration. This can be seen as comparable to the position in liquidation where any receiver (administrative or otherwise) takes precedence over the liquidator, only more so, since a floating charge holder in a position to appoint an administrative receiver is able to prevent the initiation of administration in the first place. In the light of the restrictions on the use of administrative receivership introduced by the Enterprise Act 2002, however, the ability of a floating charge holder to appoint an administrative receiver and so veto an administration will now, of course, apply in very few cases.[108]

Where an administration application is made by someone who is not the holder of a qualifying floating charge, the holder of a qualifying floating

---

102 Insolvency Act 1986 Sch. B1 para. 12(2). The definition of qualifying floating charge holder is discussed further below.

103 Insolvency Act 1986 Sch. B1 para. 13(1).

104 Insolvency Act 1986 Sch. B1 para. 39(2). The interim moratorium that comes into force under para. 44 of Sch. B1 of the Insolvency Act 1986 pending a decision on the application does not prevent the appointment of an administrative receiver after the making of an application. It does, however, prevent the appointment of a non-administrative receiver without the permission of the court. In this respect, a floating charge under which a receiver is a non-administrative receiver is treated like any other security.

105 Insolvency Act 1986 Sch. B1 para. 39(1)(a).

106 Insolvency Act 1986 Sch. B1 para. 39(1)(c). Insolvency Act 1986 s. 245, which relates to the avoidance of certain floating charges, and which applies only where a debtor is in administration or liquidation, is discussed further below.

107 Insolvency Act 1986 Sch. B1 para. 39(1)(d). Paragraph 39 also applies where the court thinks that the floating charge would be challengeable under the corresponding statutory provisions in England and Wales: see para. 39(1)(b).

108 See further below.

charge may apply to the court to have a person other than the person nominated in the application appointed as administrator, and the court must grant that application unless it thinks it right to refuse it in the circumstances of the case.[109] In effect, this maintains the floating charge holder's right to choose the person who may end up enforcing the floating charge, although as will be seen further below, the administrator is not a direct replacement for an administrative receiver and, in theory at least, the identity of the appointee should make no difference.

Whether or not they have a right to appoint an administrative receiver, the holder of a qualifying floating charge in respect of the granter's property may be able to appoint an administrator using the out-of-court procedure introduced by the Enterprise Act 2002. For this purpose, a qualifying floating charge is one that states that para. 14 of Sch. B1 of the Insolvency Act 1986 applies to it, purports to empower the holder to appoint an administrator or purports to empower the holder (in Scotland) to appoint a receiver who would be an administrative receiver.[110] A person is the holder of a qualifying charge if they hold a qualifying floating charge that relates to the whole or substantially the whole of the debtor's property, a number of qualifying floating charges that together relate to the whole or substantially the whole of the debtor's property, or charges (of which at least one is a qualifying floating charge) and other forms of security that together relate to the whole or substantially the whole of the debtor's property.[111] An appointment may only be made under these provisions if the holder of the floating charge has given notice of intention to appoint to, or obtained the consent of, any prior-ranking floating charge holder[112] and the floating charge is enforceable,[113] and it may not be made where a provisional liquidator of the company has been appointed or an administrative receiver is in office.[114] The holder of

---

109 Insolvency Act 1986 Sch. B1 para. 36. The definition of a qualifying floating charge is discussed further below.

110 Insolvency Act 1986 Sch. B1 para. 14(2).

111 Insolvency Act 1986 Sch. B1 para. 14(3).

112 Insolvency Act 1986 Sch. B1 para. 15(1). For a useful discussion of an oddity in the meaning of prior-ranking floating charge holder under these provisions, see S Wortley, 'When is a Prior Ranking Floating Charge not a Prior Ranking Floating Charge?' 2020 SLT (News) 191.

113 Insolvency Act 1986 Sch. B1 para. 16.

114 Insolvency Act 1986 Sch. B1 para. 17. Although it does not specifically say so, the appointment of the administrative receiver may have been made before or after the giving of notice of intention to appoint since the interim moratorium that comes into force under para. 44 of Sch. B1 pending the appointment of the administrator taking effect does not prevent the appointment of an administrative receiver and the notice to the prior-ranking floating charge holder gives them an opportunity to appoint an administrative receiver where that remains possible. As noted above, the interim moratorium does, however, prevent the appointment of a

a prior-ranking floating charge may apply to the court for an administrator appointed under these provisions to be replaced by an administrator nominated by the holder of the prior-ranking floating charge.[115] Once again, this gives the holder of the prior-ranking floating charge the right to choose the person who may be responsible for enforcing the floating charge, although as noted above, in theory at least the identity of the appointee should make no difference.

As an alternative to using the out-of-court procedure, the holder of a qualifying floating charge may apply to the court for the appointment of an administrator without establishing that the debtor is or is likely to become unable to pay its debts, provided that the floating charge is enforceable and the holder could appoint an administrator using the out-of-court procedure.[116] Finally, where the holder of a qualifying floating charge would be in a position to appoint an administrator using the out-of-court procedure but for the fact that the debtor is being wound up by the court (administration and liquidation being unable to co-exist), they may apply to the court for the appointment of an administrator and, if the application is granted, the winding up order will be discharged.[117]

As well as introducing a procedure for the holder of a qualifying floating charge to appoint an administrator out-of-court, the Enterprise Act 2002 introduced a procedure for the debtor or its directors to appoint an administrator out-of-court. The procedure cannot be used, however, where there is, *inter alia*, an administrative receiver in place.[118] The debtor/its directors must give notice of their intention to appoint an administrator to, *inter alia*, any person who is or may be entitled to appoint an administrative receiver of the company and any person who is or may be entitled to appoint an administrator of the company via the out-of-court route available to the holder of a qualifying floating charge.[119] Once again, therefore,

---

non-administrative receiver without the permission of the court, and in this respect, a floating charge under which a receiver is a non-administrative receiver is treated like any other security.

115 Insolvency Act 1986 Sch. B1 para. 96.

116 Insolvency Act 1986 Sch. B1 para. 35. It has been suggested that one reason for seeking a court appointment rather than appointing out-of-court is to clarify that the statutory conditions have been met: see D Milman and P Bailey (eds), *Sealy & Milman: Annotated Guide to the Insolvency Legislation*, 24th edn (London: Sweet & Maxwell, 2021) commentary to Sch. B1 para. 35.

117 Insolvency Act 1986 Sch. B1 para. 37.

118 Insolvency Act 1986 Sch. B1 para. 25(c). See n 114 for how an administrative receiver may have been appointed.

119 Insolvency Act 1986 Sch. B1 para. 26(1). The notice gives the floating charge holder the opportunity to appoint an administrative receiver (where that remains possible) or an administrator where the conditions for doing so are satisfied.

administrative receivership, where available, is given precedence over administration, although as noted above, the ability of a floating charge holder to appoint an administrative receiver will now, of course, apply in very few cases.[120]

Where an administration order takes effect, any administrative receiver must vacate office.[121] As was seen above, however, an administration order could only have been made where an administrative receiver was in place if the floating charge holder who had appointed the administrative receiver had consented or the court thought that the floating charge would be avoided if an administration order was made or would be challengeable as a gratuitous alienation or unfair preference. A non-administrative receiver need not vacate office unless the administrator (however appointed) requires them to do so.[122] Again, this reflects the difference between a receivership that relates to the whole or substantially the whole of the debtor's assets and a receivership that does not (and which may not therefore impede the administration). Where a non-administrative receiver is not required to vacate office, this is consistent with the principle that a secured creditor can continue to enforce their security notwithstanding the debtor's entry into insolvency proceedings, but with the difference that in this case, they are doing so not as of right, but at the discretion of the administrator.

Where an administrative receiver vacates office on the taking effect of an administration order or a non-administrative receiver is required to vacate office by the administrator, their remuneration (which includes expenses properly incurred and any indemnity to which they are entitled out of the assets of the company)[123] is to be charged on and paid out of the property that was in their custody or under their control immediately before they vacated office.[124] The charge imposed is given priority over the sums due to the floating charge holder,[125] which reflects the position that would have obtained had the receivership been completed in the normal way, but the receiver will not be able to enforce payment without the consent of the administrator or the court.[126] On vacating office, the receiver is released from the requirement to take any further steps to pay the preferential creditors.[127]

---

120 See further below.
121 Insolvency Act 1986 Sch. B1 para. 41(1).
122 Insolvency Act 1986 Sch. B1 para. 41(2).
123 Insolvency Act 1986 Sch. B1 para. 41(4)(a).
124 Insolvency Act 1986 Sch. B1 para. 41(3)(a).
125 Insolvency Act 1986 Sch. B1 para. 41(4)(b).
126 Insolvency Act 1986 Sch. B1 para. 41(4)(c).
127 Insolvency Act 1986Sch. B1 para. 41(3)(b).

Once a debtor is in administration, an administrative receiver may not be appointed[128] and no step may be taken to enforce any security over the debtor's property except with the consent of the administrator or the court.[129] This includes the appointment of a non-administrative receiver.[130] The principle that a secured creditor may enforce their security notwithstanding the debtor's entry into insolvency proceedings is therefore tempered in so far as any such enforcement is at the discretion of the administrator (or the court). This reflects the different nature of administration, referred to above, which is seen as justifying a different approach to the rights of secured creditors. In this respect, the position of the holder of a floating charge who is not in a position to, or who has chosen not to, appoint an administrative receiver is the same as that of any other secured creditor.

As noted above, the powers of the administrator are almost identical to the statutory powers of a receiver in Scotland (and are identical to the statutory powers of an administrative receiver in England and Wales). Of particular note is the power in the Insolvency Act 1986 Sch. 1 para. 1, which gives the administrator power to take possession of, collect and get in the property of the company, and the power in Sch. 1 para. 2, which gives the administrator the power to sell, hire out or otherwise dispose of the property of the company. So far as property subject to a floating charge is concerned, Sch. B1 para. 70 gives the administrator power to dispose of or take action relating to any property that is subject to a floating charge as if it were not subject to the charge,[131] although this is subject to the proviso that the floating charge holder retains the same priority as they had in relation to the property disposed of in relation to any property directly or indirectly representing it.[132] The position of a floating charge can be contrasted with the position of other securities, since the administrator requires the consent of the court to dispose of property subject to a security other than a floating charge as if it were not subject to the security.[133]

---

128 Insolvency Act 1986 Sch. B1 para. 43(6A). This is an absolute prohibition.
129 Insolvency Act 1986 Sch. B1 para. 43(1).
130 The principles to be applied in determining whether any such consent will be given were set out in *Re Atlantic Computer Systems plc* [1992] Ch 505 and have been applied in a number of subsequent cases including in Scotland: see *Scottish Exhibition Centre Ltd v Mirestop Ltd* 1993 SLT 1304. Space precludes a detailed discussion here, but see *Palmer's Company Law* (n 20) para. 14A.028; St Clair and Drummond Young, *Corporate Insolvency* (n 84) paras 5–66–5–67.
131 Insolvency Act 1986 Sch. B1 para. 70(1).
132 Insolvency Act 1986 Sch. B1 para. 70(2). These provisions apply whether or not the floating charge has attached.
133 Insolvency Act 1986 Sch. B1 para. 71.

The administrator is required to prepare a statement of their proposals for achieving the purpose of administration[134] that, except in certain cases, will be voted on by the creditors.[135] The proposals may not, however, include any action which, *inter alia*, affects the right of a secured creditor to enforce their security,[136] except with the consent of the secured creditor or where the proposal is part of, *inter alia*, a proposal for a company voluntary arrangement under Part 1 of the Insolvency Act 1986 or a proposal for a compromise or arrangement under Part 26 or, now, Part 26A, of the Companies Act 2006.[137] This applies to a floating charge holder in the same way as to other secured creditors and reflects the recognition of the security holder's pre-existing rights discussed above. In addition, a floating charge holder, in common with any other creditor of the company, may apply to the court for an appropriate remedy where they claim that the administrator is acting or has acted in such a way as to unfairly harm their interests or proposes to act in a way that would unfairly harm their interests.[138]

As originally introduced, administration was not intended to be a distributive process: any distributions to creditors were intended to take place through a company voluntary arrangement under Part 1 of the Insolvency Act 1986, a compromise or arrangement under what is now Part 26 of the Companies Act 2006 or a subsequent liquidation. Following the changes brought about by the Enterprise Act 2002, however, administration may now in some circumstances be a distributive process, thus avoiding a double process in appropriate cases.

Even absent the prospect of receiving any distribution, creditors have always submitted claims in an administration for voting purposes. A floating charge holder who submits a claim in the administration must deduct the value of their security from their claim.[139] Alternatively, the floating charge

---

134 Insolvency Act 1986 Sch. B1 para. 49(1).
135 Insolvency Act 1986 Sch. B1 paras 51–52.
136 Insolvency Act 1986 Sch. B1 para. 73(1)(a).
137 Insolvency Act 1986 Sch. B1 para. 73(2). In the case of a company voluntary arrangement under Part 1 of the Insolvency Act 1986, this is without prejudice to s. 4(3) of the Insolvency Act 1986, which provides that any proposal or modification that affects the right of a secured creditor to enforce their security may not be approved except with the consent of the secured creditor. In the case of a compromise or arrangement under Part 26 or Part 26A of the Companies Act 2006, any alteration of the secured creditor's rights would fall to be voted on as part of the process for approving the relevant compromise or arrangement.
138 Insolvency Act 1986 Sch. B1 para. 74.
139 Insolvency (Scotland) (Company Voluntary Arrangements and Administration) Rules 2018 (SI 2018/1082) r. 3.113(1).

holder may surrender their security and become an unsecured creditor.[140] An administrator has the same power as a liquidator to require a floating charge holder, at the expense of the company's assets, to discharge their security or convey or assign it to the administrator on payment of the security value as specified by the floating charge holder, whereupon the floating charge creditor will be an ordinary creditor for any remaining balance of the sums due to them.[141] Where the security has been realised, the floating charge creditor must deduct the amount received or entitled to be received by them, less the expenses of realisation, from their claim.[142] In these respects, the floating charge holder is treated in the same way as other creditors, although the position with a floating charge will tend to be more complicated, particularly where the floating charge relates to the whole or substantially the whole of the company's assets.

An administrator is given the power to make a payment to the holder of a floating charge that has attached to the property subject to the charge in or towards the satisfaction of the debt secured by the floating charge.[143] As noted above, the floating charge may have attached as a result of a receivership or liquidation. Where it has not so attached, it must be made to attach in order to allow the administrator to make a payment to the floating charge holder. This may happen in one of two ways. The first is where the court gives permission to the administrator to make a distribution under para. 65 of Sch. B1[144]; the second is where the administrator thinks that the company has insufficient property to enable a distribution to be made to unsecured creditors other than via the prescribed part and files a notice to that effect with the registrar of companies.[145] In either case, the floating charge attaches to the property that is subject to the charge[146] as if it was a fixed security.[147] In making a payment to the floating charge holder under these provisions, the administrator is required to do so subject to the rights of certain

---

140 Insolvency (Scotland) (Company Voluntary Arrangements and Administration) Rules 2018 (n 139) r. 3.113(2).
141 Insolvency (Scotland) (Company Voluntary Arrangements and Administration) Rules 2018 (n 139) r. 3.113(3), (4).
142 Insolvency (Scotland) (Company Voluntary Arrangements and Administration) Rules 2018 (n 139) r. 3.113(5).
143 Insolvency Act 1986 Sch. B1 para. 115(1).
144 Insolvency Act 1986 Sch. B1 para. 115(1A).
145 Insolvency Act 1986 Sch. B1 para. 115(2).
146 Insolvency Act 1986 Sch. B1 para. 115(1B) (permission by the court), (3) (notice by the administrator).
147 Insolvency Act 1986 Sch. B1 para. 115(4).

specified persons.[148] The list of persons is similar to, but not exactly the same as, the persons who must be paid by a receiver prior to paying the floating charge holder.[149] In particular, they include the expenses of the administration (which take the place of the expenses of receivership since the floating charge is being enforced by the administrator)[150] and the preferential creditors (in so far as the assets available for the payment of general creditors are insufficient to pay them).[151] It may be noted, however, that the expenses of the administration may be considerably greater than the expenses of a receivership would have been.[152]

Where the prescribed part applies to a floating charge,[153] the administrator will be responsible for its distribution, having either received it from a receiver appointed under the floating charge[154] or having set it aside as required by the statutory provisions where there is no receiver.[155] As noted above, the expenses relating to the prescribed part are borne by the prescribed part itself. The prescribed part is discussed further below.

The picture with respect to administration is therefore complicated. Where it is still possible for a floating charge holder to appoint an administrative receiver and the floating charge holder chooses to do so, the administrative receivership will take precedence over the initiation of an administration. In this respect, a floating charge holder in a position to appoint an administrative receiver is in a better position than other secured creditors, including a floating charge holder in a position to appoint only a non-administrative receiver. This is because, as noted above, even where the procedure for appointing an administrator is underway, the interim moratorium does not prevent the appointment of an administrative receiver, while steps to enforce other securities, including the appointment of a non-administrative receiver, require the permission of the court. On the other hand, as already stated, the ability of a floating charge holder to appoint an administrative receiver will now apply in very few cases. In addition, once the debtor is in administration, in contrast to the position in liquidation, there can be no

---

148 Insolvency Act 1986 Sch. B1 para. 116.
149 The list in para. 115 does not mention persons who have effectually executed diligence, who are specifically mentioned in Insolvency Act 1986 s. 60. This is discussed further in Hardman and MacPherson, 'The Ranking of Floating Charges', Chapter 9.
150 Insolvency Act 1986 Sch. B1 para. 116(c).
151 Insolvency Act 1986 Sch. B1 para. 116(d).
152 The same point was made above in relation to liquidation.
153 See above and further below.
154 See above.
155 Insolvency Act 1986 s. 176A(2).

administrative receivership. A pre-existing non-administrative receivership may, however, be allowed to continue at the discretion of the administrator and the appointment of a non-administrative receiver, like steps to enforce other securities, may be allowed with the consent of the administrator or the court. Once again, this reflects the different purpose of administration referred to above and the difference between an administrative and a non-administrative receivership. If a non-administrative receiver is allowed to remain in place, the enforcement of the floating charge will be carried out by that receiver in the normal way and the proceeds of the property attached by the charge will be distributed in accordance with the statutory scheme for receivership.

It may be noted that the statutory scheme for the distribution of monies in receivership makes no mention of administration expenses, so there is no provision for any part of the administration expenses to be paid out of the property attached by the floating charge.[156] Where administration results in a distribution in the administration itself, however, a floating charge where there is no (non-administrative) receiver in place will effectively be enforced by the administrator through the administration in much the same way as in a liquidation where there is no receiver. As indicated, where the administrator makes a distribution to a floating charge holder, this is done in a similar, but not identical, way to receivership. In particular, and in contrast to the position in liquidation, the whole of the administration expenses and not just the expenses relating to realisation of the property attached by the floating charge fall to be paid out of the floating charge assets.

(3) Other receivers

It has been mentioned already that since a debtor may have granted more than one floating charge, it is possible for there to be receivers appointed under more than one floating charge at any given time.[157] In this case, the receiver appointed under the most senior-ranking floating charge is entitled to exercise their powers to the exclusion of any other receiver[158] and where the floating charges under which receivers have been appointed rank equally, the receivers are deemed to have been appointed as joint

---

156 This reflects the position in relation to liquidation expenses, discussed above.
157 Insolvency Act 1986 s. 56(1).
158 Insolvency Act 1986 s. 56(1).

receivers.[159] The powers of any other receivers are suspended *pro tem*[160] but the floating charges under which they were appointed remain attached.[161]

As noted above, in the unlikely event of any surplus remaining once the floating charge holder has been paid, this is to be paid to any other receiver if there is one.[162] This preserves the preference given to receivership.

(4) Company voluntary arrangements[163]

Although it might be said that a company voluntary arrangement under Part 1 of the Insolvency Act 1986 is not an insolvency process like other insolvency processes such as liquidation and administration, the provisions for such an arrangement are included in the Insolvency Act 1986 and so are considered here. The process is designed to provide a simple mechanism for a debtor to bring about 'a composition in satisfaction of its debts or a scheme of arrangement for its affairs' with its members and creditors.[164]

A proposal for a company voluntary arrangement may be made by the directors of the company where it is not in administration or liquidation,[165] or by the administrator or liquidator where it is in one of these processes.[166] The proposal must be approved by the prescribed majorities of the company and its creditors.[167] However, it is not possible for a proposal to be

---

159 Insolvency Act 1986 s. 56(2).
160 Insolvency Act 1986 s. 56(4).
161 Insolvency Act 1986 s. 56(6).
162 Insolvency Act 1986 s. 60(2)(a). In the unlikely event of there being more than one such other receiver, it is suggested that the surplus would fall to be paid to the receiver under the most senior ranking of the charges under which those receivers were appointed.
163 As noted at the beginning of this chapter, a modified version of the insolvency processes (or processes treated for the purpose of this chapter as insolvency processes) that apply to companies, including company voluntary arrangements, apply to LLPs, but it is more difficult with company voluntary arrangements to employ neutral terminology encompassing both companies and LLPs and any other entities that may grant a floating charge, so the term 'company' and related terminology is used in this section purely for ease of reference.
164 Insolvency Act 1986 s. 1(1).
165 Insolvency Act 1986 s. 1(1).
166 Insolvency Act 1986 s. 1(3).
167 The requisite majority of members is a majority in value of those voting, subject to any express provision to the contrary in the articles: Insolvency (Scotland) (Company Voluntary Arrangements and Administration) Rules 2018 (SI 2018/1082) r. 2.35(1), (2). The requisite majority of creditors is at least 75 per cent in value of those voting (r. 5.31(3)(a)). This is subject to the proviso that more than half the total value of unconnected creditors do not vote against (r. 5.31(4), (5)). Every creditor, secured or unsecured, is entitled to vote on the proposed company voluntary arrangement (r. 5.26(4)). However, where a debt is wholly secured, its value for voting purposes is nil, and where it is partly secured, its value for voting purposes is the value of the unsecured part (r. 5.28(4) and (5)). In this respect, a floating charge holder is treated in the same way as any other secured creditor.

approved where the proposal affects, *inter alia*, the right of a secured creditor to enforce their security except with the concurrence of the creditor concerned.[168] This reflects the principle of respect for pre-existing rights in insolvency proceedings. Unless, therefore, the company voluntary arrangement alters the rights of a floating charge holder to enforce their security with their consent, the floating charge holder will remain in a position to enforce their security in the normal way even after approval of the company voluntary arrangement.

When company voluntary arrangements were first introduced, there was no provision for a moratorium on creditor action while the proposal for a company voluntary arrangement was being considered.[169] However, the Insolvency Act 2000 introduced provision for an optional moratorium for certain eligible companies that could be obtained by the directors prior to making a proposal for a company voluntary arrangement.[170] As introduced, the moratorium provided, *inter alia*, that no administrative receiver might be appointed during the moratorium[171] and that no other steps might be taken to enforce any security over the company's property except with the leave of the court and subject to such conditions as the court might impose.[172] This included the appointment of a non-administrative receiver. Following the reforms introduced by the Enterprise Act 2002, the moratorium was extended to provide that no administrator of the company might be appointed under the provisions for an out-of-court appointment of an administrator by a qualifying floating charge holder.[173] Unusually, therefore, a floating charge holder was prevented from enforcing their security either absolutely (in the case of a floating charge holder seeking to appoint an administrative receiver or, later, an administrator) or without the permission of the court (in the case of a floating charge holder seeking to appoint a non-administrative receiver). However, some protection was intended to be provided for creditors generally during the moratorium by the monitoring to be carried out by the nominee[174] and, if appointed on the extension

---

168 Insolvency Act 1986 s. 4(3).

169 This was considered one of the main drawbacks of the process and one of the reasons for its lack of use.

170 Insolvency Act 1986 s. 1A and Sch. A1.

171 Insolvency Act 1986 Sch. A1 para. 12(1)(e).

172 Insolvency Act 1986 Sch. A1 para. 12(1)(g).

173 Insolvency Act 1986 Sch. A1 para. 12(1)(da). The moratorium already provided that no administration application might be made, preventing any such application by the floating charge holder: Insolvency Act 1986 Sch. A1 para. 12(1)(d).

174 The nominee being the person named in the proposal to act as trustee or otherwise for the purpose of supervising the implementation of the voluntary arrangement and required to be

of the moratorium beyond the initial period, the moratorium committee.[175] In addition, specific protection was intended to be provided for secured creditors by the provision that during the moratorium, the company could dispose of property subject to a security as if it were not subject to that security only if the security holder consented or the court gave leave,[176] and where the property disposed of was subject to a security that, as created, was a floating charge, the holder had the same priority as they would have had in that property in any property directly or indirectly representing it.[177] The moratorium provisions, including the restrictions on enforcement of security, were regarded as justified on the basis that they were temporary restrictions only, to allow the possibility of an arrangement that might result in the rescue of the company to be explored. Once again, they reflected the difference between an administrative receivership and a non-administrative receivership and, in the latter case, equiparated the floating charge holder with other secured creditors. The moratorium provisions have now been repealed by the Corporate Insolvency and Governance Act 2020, which instead makes provision for a free-standing moratorium that is discussed in the following section.

(5) Moratorium and arrangements and reconstructions introduced by the 2020 Act[178]

The Corporate Insolvency and Governance Act 2020 introduced, *inter alia*, a new, free-standing moratorium designed to give eligible companies a breathing space to seek the rescue of the company as a going concern and a new arrangement and reconstruction procedure designed to provide an additional rescue process. The introduction of these provisions had been the subject of previous consultation resulting in a commitment by the Government in 2018 to legislate,[179] but legislation was not brought forward

a qualified insolvency practitioner: Insolvency Act 1986 s. 1(2). The nominee's obligation to monitor the company's affairs during the moratorium was set out in Sch. A1 para. 24.

175 Insolvency Act 1986 Sch. A1 para. 35.

176 Insolvency Act 1986 Sch. A1 para. 20(1), (2).

177 Insolvency Act 1986 Sch. A1 para. 20(4).

178 As in the preceding section dealing with company voluntary arrangements, it is more difficult to employ neutral terminology encompassing both companies and LLPs in this section, so the term 'company' and related terminology is used in this section purely for ease of reference.

179 The reforms were first consulted on by the Insolvency Service in *A Review of the Corporate Insolvency Framework: A consultation on options for reform* in May 2016. Although not specifically referred to in the consultation, the proposals were developed against the background of proposals for what is now Directive (EU) 2019/1023 of the European Parliament and of

until the COVID-19 pandemic made their introduction a perceived matter of urgency.[180] The legislation was passed using the fast-track procedure[181] and came into force on 26 June 2020.[182] The provisions were subject to certain temporary modifications as a result of the COVID-19 pandemic, but on the basis that these were temporary, they are not be considered here.

(a) Moratorium

The moratorium can be obtained by the directors of certain eligible companies[183] by lodging the relevant documents with the court (where the company is not subject to an outstanding winding up petition[184]) or by application to the court (where the company is subject to an outstanding winding up petition[185] or is an overseas company[186]).

The moratorium is similar but not identical to the optional moratorium for company voluntary arrangements that, as noted above, has now been repealed and replaced by the moratorium discussed in this section. It provides, *inter alia*, that during the moratorium, no administration application may be made in respect of the company except by the directors[187]; no notice of intention to appoint an administrator of the company may be lodged with the court under the provisions for an out-of-court appointment of an administrator by a qualifying floating charge holder[188]; no appointment of

the Council of 20 June 2019 on preventative restructuring frameworks, on discharge of debt and disqualifications, and on measures to increase the efficiency of procedures concerning restructuring, insolvency and discharge of debt, and amending Directive (EU) 2017/1132 (Directive on restructuring and insolvency), OJL 172, 26/06/2019. The Insolvency Service duly published its *Summary of Responses: A Review of the Corporate Insolvency Framework* in September 2016, but it was not until the publication of the Department for Business, Energy and Industrial Strategy's *Insolvency and Corporate Governance: Government Response* in August 2018, following a separate Department for Business, Energy and Industrial Strategy consultation *Insolvency and Corporate Governance* in March 2018, that firm proposals to legislate were set out.

180 See Corporate Insolvency and Governance Bill Explanatory Notes, paras 3 and 81.
181 The justifications for using this procedure are set out in the Corporate Insolvency and Governance Bill Explanatory Notes, paras 78–96. The Bill was introduced into the House of Commons on 20 May 2020 and completed all its stages in the House of Commons on 3 June 2020. Following its passage through the House of Lords, it received Royal Assent on 25 June 2020.
182 Corporate Insolvency and Governance Act 2020 s. 49(1).
183 Eligible companies are defined in Insolvency Act 1986 s. A2 and Sch. ZA1.
184 Insolvency Act 1986 s. A3.
185 Insolvency Act 1986 s. A4.
186 Insolvency Act 1986 s. A5.
187 Insolvency Act 1986 s. A20(1)(e).
188 Insolvency Act 1986 s. A20(1)(f).

an administrator of the company may be made under those provisions[189]; and no administrative receiver may be appointed.[190] In addition, with certain limited exceptions, no other steps may be taken to enforce any security over the company's property except with the permission of the court,[191] which may impose conditions.[192] However, an application may not be made for permission to enforce a security for the purposes of enforcing a pre-moratorium debt for which the company has a payment holiday during the moratorium.[193] Furthermore, an application for such permission may not be made with a view to obtaining, *inter alia*, the crystallisation of a floating charge.[194] This would preclude an application for permission to appoint a non-administrative receiver since that would result in the crystallisation of the floating charge and so a floating charge holder is prevented from enforcing their security to an even greater extent than under the previous company voluntary arrangement moratorium. Again, however, some protection is intended to be provided for creditors generally during the moratorium by the monitoring to be carried out by the monitor.[195] In addition, specific protection is given for secured creditors by the provision that during the moratorium, the company can dispose of property subject to a security as if it were not subject to that security only with the permission of the court.[196] Furthermore, where the property disposed of is subject to a floating charge, the holder has the same priority as they would have had in that property in any property directly or indirectly representing it.[197] The moratorium provisions, including the restrictions on enforcement of security, are again regarded as justified on the basis that they are temporary restrictions only, allowing options for the rescue of the company to be explored. In some respects, however, a floating charge holder is subject to greater restrictions than other secured creditors, as the circumstances in which the permission

---

189 Insolvency Act 1986 s. A20(1)(g).
190 Insolvency Act 1986 s. A20(1)(h).
191 Insolvency Act 1986 s. A21(1)(c).
192 Insolvency Act 1986 s. A21(4).
193 Insolvency Act 1986 s. A21(2).
194 Insolvency Act 1986 s. A21(3).
195 The monitor must be a qualified person, is an officer of the court and has an obligation to monitor the company's affairs during the moratorium: see Insolvency Act 1986 ss. A6(1)(a), A34 and A35 respectively. The Insolvency Service has published guidance for monitors: Insolvency Service, *Insolvency Act 1986 part A1: moratorium – guidance for monitors* (2020) available at *https://www.gov.uk/government/publications/insolvency-act-1986-part-a1-moratorium-guidance-for-monitors* (last accessed 4 November 2021).
196 Insolvency Act 1986 s. A31(1).
197 Insolvency Act 1986 s. A31(5), (6).

of the court to enforce their security may be applied for are, in fact, more restricted.

(b) Arrangements and reconstructions

The Corporate Insolvency and Governance Act 2020 adds a new Part 26A to the Companies Act 2006 entitled 'Arrangements and Reconstructions: Companies in Financial Difficulties'. The provisions of Part 26A apply where a company 'has encountered, or is likely to encounter, financial difficulties that are affecting, or will or may affect, its ability to carry on business as a going concern'.[198] It is therefore specifically designed for companies that are in financial difficulty or may become so. For that reason, although it appears in the Companies Act 2006 and not the Insolvency Act 1986 and could not be described as an insolvency process as such, it is considered briefly here, while Part 26 of the Companies Act 2006, which can be, and often is, used by companies that are or are in danger of becoming insolvent, but that are not confined to such cases, is not.[199] It may be noted, however, that the new Part 26A procedure does share a number of key features with the Part 26 procedure.

So far as floating charge holders are concerned, the key points are that the proposed compromise or arrangement may be with the company's creditors or any class of them or its members or any class of them[200]; the purpose of the compromise or arrangement must be to eliminate, reduce or prevent, or mitigate the effect of, any of the aforementioned financial difficulties[201]; the necessary application to the court to call the relevant meetings to consider the compromise or arrangement can be made by, *inter alia*, a creditor,[202] which would include a floating charge holder; every creditor whose rights are affected by the proposed compromise or arrangement must be permitted to participate in the meetings, except for creditors who do not have 'a genuine economic interest' in the company[203]; creditors are divided into classes[204]; a number representing 75 per cent in value of the creditors or

---

198 Companies Act 2006 s. 901A(1), (2).
199 The provisions that were the precursor of what is now Part 26 of the Companies Act 2006 when first introduced applied only to companies in liquidation, but were gradually extended in subsequent Companies Acts and are now available to all companies whether solvent or insolvent.
200 Companies Act 2006 s. 901A(1), (3)(a).
201 Companies Act 2006 s. 901A(1), (3)(b).
202 Companies Act 2006 s. 901C(1), (2)(b).
203 Companies Act 2006 s. 901C(3), (4).
204 Companies Act 2006 s. 901C(1).

class of creditors is required to approve the compromise or arrangement[205]; and the compromise or arrangement must be sanctioned by the court[206] that may, in specified circumstances, impose a cross-class cramdown.[207] Where a compromise or arrangement is sanctioned by the court, it is binding on all creditors or the relevant classes of creditors (as the case may be) and on the company.[208] Thus, as in a Part 26 arrangement, but in contrast to a company voluntary arrangement, a floating charge holder may be bound to a compromise or arrangement that affects their rights without their consent where the relevant compromise or arrangement is sanctioned by the court in accordance with the statutory provisions.

(6) Challenge of floating charges within insolvency processes

It was noted above that the floating charge holder's veto on administration does not operate where the court thinks, *inter alia*, that the floating charge would be avoided under s. 245 of the Insolvency Act 1986 if an administration order were to be made or that the floating charge would be challengeable as a gratuitous alienation or unfair preference under the relevant statutory provisions[209] or at common law.

Section 245 of the Insolvency Act 1986 contains specific provisions relating to the avoidance of certain floating charges where the debtor is in administration or liquidation. In this respect, floating charges are unique since there are no corresponding provisions specifically providing for the avoidance of other types of security.

Floating charges may also be subject to challenge under the statutory provisions relating to gratuitous alienations,[210] unfair preferences[211] and extortionate credit transactions[212] where the company is in administration or liquidation or under the corresponding common law provisions. In this respect, floating charges are not unique, since other types of security may also be subject to challenge under these provisions.

---

205 Companies Act 2006 s. 901F(1).
206 Companies Act 2006 s. 901F.
207 Companies Act 2006 s. 901G. A cross-class cramdown was imposed in *Re Deep Ocean 1 UK Ltd* [2021] EWHC 138 (Ch). See also, although not involving cross-class cramdown, *Re Virgin Atlantic Airways Ltd* [2020] EWHC 2191 (Ch) and [2020] EWHC 2376 (Ch).
208 Companies Act 2006 s. 901F(5).
209 See Insolvency Act 1986 ss. 242 and 243 respectively.
210 Insolvency Act 1986 s. 242.
211 Insolvency Act 1986 s. 243.
212 Insolvency Act 1986 s. 244.

G. RETRENCHMENT

This section returns to discuss in more detail the reforms introduced by the Enterprise Act 2002 that led to the restriction on the use of administrative receivership and the change of focus to administration as the primary means of enforcing a floating charge. These reforms represented a significant sea change in attitude to floating charge security in the context of insolvency that brought about major changes to insolvency law and so deserve further consideration.

The background to the changes can be found in the White Paper *Insolvency – A Second Chance* which was published in July 2001.[213] The White Paper contained proposals for changes to both bankruptcy law and corporate insolvency law. The proposals relating to bankruptcy law were almost entirely confined to England and Wales and are not relevant here. The proposals relating to corporate insolvency law were, however, intended to extend to Scotland, subject to the consent of the Scottish Parliament for those (few) elements that were devolved.[214]

The underlying rationale of the reforms was set out in the foreword to the White Paper: companies in financial difficulty must not be allowed to go to the wall unnecessarily. The focus of the reforms was therefore firmly on enhancing the rescue culture. The White Paper referred to 'widespread concern as to the extent to which administrative receivership as a procedure provides adequate incentives to maximise economic value' and 'concern about whether it provides an acceptable level of transparency and account-ability to the range of stakeholders with an interest in a company's affairs, particularly creditors'.[215] It recognised the importance of administrative receivership to secured lenders, not least because of their complete control over its inception, but highlighted the fact that the administrative receiver's principal obligation is to the floating charge holder, with the result that there was substantially no accountability to other creditors for the way in which the company's assets were dealt with and no equivalent of the duty owed by an administrator to act in the best interests of the creditors as a whole.[216] The maximisation of recoveries and the minimisation of costs were seen as areas where the lack of a wider and more general accountability could impact very substantially on the interests of unsecured creditors in an

---

213 Insolvency Service, *A Second Chance* (n 75).
214 Insolvency Service, *A Second Chance* (n 75) para. 2.21.
215 Insolvency Service, *A Second Chance* (n 75) para. 2.2.
216 Insolvency Service, *A Second Chance* (n 75) para. 2.2.

administrative receivership.[217] Reference was also made to the increasing importance of the international dimension in insolvency highlighting the 'poor fit' between international law, based on collective procedures, and administrative receivership.[218] Taking all of these factors into account, it concluded that the existing framework for administrative receivership did not provide an adequate basis for accountability or properly aligned incentives in relation to the bulk of cases giving rise to administrative receivership.[219] It therefore intended that administrative receivership should cease to be a major insolvency process.[220]

Building to some extent on earlier work,[221] the reforms intended to address these concerns were essentially three-fold: restricting the right to appoint an administrative receiver (with limited exceptions)[222]; streamlining administration, which would effectively replace administrative receivership, to make it more effective and accessible[223]; and abolishing Crown preference and ensuring that the benefit of that abolition enured to the unsecured creditors.[224] The White Paper stated confidently that secured creditors [sic] should not feel at any risk from the proposals: there was no reason why their interests should not be protected equally well by an administrator as by an administrative receiver and it was anticipated that, over time, secured creditors would come to see administration as their remedy of choice for maximising value.[225]

Perhaps unsurprisingly, the proposed reforms proved far from uncontroversial, but the Enterprise Act 2002 went on to give effect to all the main elements discussed above with the consent of the Scottish Parliament in so far as they related to devolved matters.

The right to appoint an administrative receiver was abolished with limited exceptions.[226] The reforms were not retrospective, however, so it remains possible to appoint an administrative receiver under a floating charge created prior to 15 September 2003. Nonetheless, as noted above, the number of cases in which it is still now possible to appoint an administrative receiver will be relatively few.

---

217 Insolvency Service, *A Second Chance* (n 75) para. 2.3.
218 Insolvency Service, *A Second Chance* (n 75) para. 2.3.
219 Insolvency Service, *A Second Chance* (n 75) para. 2.3.
220 Insolvency Service, *A Second Chance* (n 75) para. 2.5.
221 Insolvency Service, *A Second Chance* (n 75) Annex B.
222 Insolvency Service, *A Second Chance* (n 75) paras 2.5 and 2.18.
223 Insolvency Service, *A Second Chance* (n 75) paras 2.6–2.17.
224 Insolvency Service, *A Second Chance* (n 75) para. 2.19.
225 Insolvency Service, *A Second Chance* (n 75) para. 2.6.
226 See Insolvency Act 1986 ss. 72A–72GA.

The streamlining and reform of administration included provisions already discussed, such as the introduction of out-of-court routes into administration allowing, *inter alia*, a floating charge holder to appoint an administrator out-of-court, and the introduction of other rights for floating charge holders such as the right to choose the administrator even where the appointment is made or sought by someone else. These rights were intended to compensate the floating charge holder for the loss of the ability to appoint an administrative receiver.

Crown preference was abolished[227] and the prescribed part was introduced with a view to giving the benefit of that abolition to the unsecured creditors, who now included the Crown.[228] The prescribed part was the mechanism chosen to address the issue, referred to above, of the unfairness to unsecured, non-preferential creditors arising from a floating charge holder with a charge over all of the debtor's assets being able to 'scoop the pool' and leave nothing for those creditors. The idea of such a mechanism was not new. The Cork Committee had previously recommended the introduction of a 'ten per cent fund', a fund equal to 10 per cent of the net realisations of assets subject to a floating charge to be made available for distribution to the ordinary unsecured creditors.[229] Like the prescribed part, the 'ten percent fund' was seen as a *quid pro quo* for the reduction in the number and amount of preferential debts that the committee had also recommended.[230] The calculation of the prescribed part is more complex than the simple 10 per cent recommended by the Cork Committee,[231] but while the stated intention was that the prescribed part would allow the benefit of the abolition of Crown preference to enure to the unsecured creditors, meaning that the effect on the floating charge holder would effectively be neutral, there is an absence of empirical evidence as to whether or to what

---

227 Enterprise Act 2002 s. 251.
228 See Insolvency Act 1986 s. 176A, discussed above, and the Insolvency Act 1986 (Prescribed Part) Order 2003 (SI 2003/2097). The prescribed part applies only to floating charges created on or after 15 September 2003: Insolvency Act 1986 s. 176A(9). This means that in insolvency proceedings commenced after that date, a floating charge created before that date enjoys the benefit of the abolition of Crown preference without being subject to the prescribed part, creating a windfall for the floating charge holder. There may, of course, be more than one floating charge to which the prescribed part provisions apply, in which case there will be a prescribed part in each case.
229 See the *Report of the Review Committee on Insolvency Law and Practice* (n 11) Ch. 36.
230 *Report of the Review Committee on Insolvency Law and Practice* (n 11) para. 1531.
231 See the Insolvency Act 1986 (Prescribed Part) Order 2003 (SI 2003/2097) as amended by the Insolvency Act 1986 (Prescribed Part) (Amendment) Order 2020 (SI 2020/211), which increased the cap on the prescribed part from £600,000 to £800,000.

extent the prescribed part in fact equates to the sums that would otherwise have been payable to the Crown.[232] The prescribed part is available for the satisfaction of unsecured debts and it is specifically provided that it may not be distributed to the proprietor of a floating charge except in so far as it exceeds the amount required for the satisfaction of the unsecured debts.[233] It has been held in England that this means that a floating charge holder is not entitled to claim on the prescribed part for any unsecured balance of their debt,[234] although it has also been held that a floating charge holder may do so where they have surrendered their security and thus become an unsecured creditor for all purposes.[235] The reasoning in these decisions has, however, been criticised.[236]

While the extent to which these reforms may have enhanced the rescue culture may be debateable, their impact on the floating charge is undeniable. In terms of both control of the inception of the process leading to enforcement of the floating charge and the nature of that process, the position in relation to floating charges where the receiver appointed under the charge is a non-administrative receiver has remained more or less unchanged, in so far as the floating charge holder may still appoint (only) a non-administrative receiver whose primary purpose is the enforcement of the floating charge and whose duties are owed primarily to the floating charge holder. However, in the case of a floating charge where the holder would, absent these reforms, have been able to appoint an administrative receiver, the position is different. The holder of such a charge does still have an element of control over the inception of the process, although it may be noted that the process of appointment of an administrator is less quick and straightforward than the appointment of a receiver. The holder of the floating charge also still has an element of control over the choice of officeholder, for what that may be worth. The process is, however, administration rather than receivership and it is a very different process.

Administration is not primarily about enforcement of the floating charge: indeed, administration may not even result in the enforcement of the

232 For more detailed discussion, which includes consideration of some empirical data relating to the prescribed part, see K Akintola, 'The Prescribed Part for Unsecured Creditors: A Further Review' (2019) 32 *Insolvency Intelligence* 67; K Akintola, 'The Prescribed Part for Unsecured Creditors: A Pithy Review' (2017) 30 *Insolvency Intelligence* 55.
233 Insolvency Act 1986 s. 176A(2).
234 See *Re Permacell Finesse Ltd* [2007] EWHC 3233 (Ch); *Re Airbase Services Ltd* [2008] EWHC 124 (Ch).
235 See *Re PAL SC Realisations 2007 Ltd* [2010] EWHC 2850 (Ch).
236 See St Clair and Drummond Young, *Corporate Insolvency* (n 84) para. 5–93.

floating charge as such, although where it does, the outcome in practice may be much the same as in a receivership, subject to the point made above in relation to the expenses of the administration. Furthermore, the administrator does not owe their duties primarily to the floating charge holder but to the creditors as a whole, and decisions made in the interests of the creditors as a whole may be quite different to those made primarily in the interests of the floating charge holder. In addition, there is the effect of the introduction of the prescribed part. Even if the effect of the prescribed part when it was first introduced was effectively neutral for a floating charge holder as a result of the abolition of Crown preference, this is unlikely to be the case following the partial reintroduction of Crown preference brought about by the Finance Act 2020.[237] This is because the floating charge holder has to bear an increase in the preferential creditors but there is no corresponding reduction in the prescribed part.[238] Combined with the recent increase in the maximum value of the prescribed part referred to above,[239] the detrimental effect on the floating charge holder could be considerable.[240] This does not, however, seem to have been considered when the partial reintroduction of Crown preference was proposed, or perhaps continuing to maintain a neutral effect on floating charges when making such changes is no longer considered to be important. There has, however, been concern that the detrimental effects for floating charge holders could impact on lending to the detriment of business and the rescue culture that the Government is still seeking to promote, most recently through the reforms in the Corporate Insolvency and Governance Act 2020 referred to above.[241]

---

237 Finance Act 2020 s. 98.
238 This may, of course, be to the benefit of the (remaining) unsecured creditors depending on the amount available to them through the prescribed part. For a more detailed discussion of the possible effects, see A D J MacPherson and D McKenzie Skene 'Back to the Future? The Partial Re-instatement of the Crown Preference in Insolvency', available at *https://www. abdn.ac.uk/law/blog/back-to-the-future-the-partial-reinstatement-of-the-crown-preference-in-insolvency/* (last accessed 4 November 2021).
239 Insolvency Act 1986 (Prescribed Part) (Amendment) Order 2020 (SI 2020/211).
240 See MacPherson and McKenzie Skene (n 238). During the passage of the Corporate Insolvency and Governance Act 2020, amendments were tabled at committee stage in the House of Commons seeking to make the prescribed part at least 30 per cent of the sums due to the floating charge holder: see HC Deb 3 June 2020, col 957. The amendments were, however, unsuccessful.
241 See R Caldwell, 'Enterprise goes into Reverse for Floating Charge-holders' 2019 Jur Rev 103. R3, the Association of Business Recovery Professionals, has spearheaded a campaign against the partial re-introduction of Crown preference: for full details, see 'Royal Assent for the Finance Bill – but R3's opposition to Crown Preference continues', at *https://www.r3.org.uk/press-policy-and-research/r3-blog/more/29492/page/1/royal-assent-for-the-finance-bill-but-r3-s-opposition-to-crown-preference-continues/?utm_source=Association%20of%20Business%20*

CONCLUSION

It has been seen that the floating charge, like other securities, is designed to give its holder an advantage on the granter's insolvency. It is, however, a security like no other in Scots law. That being the case, how well, or otherwise, can the floating charge be said to have been assimilated into insolvency law in Scotland?

In seeking to answer that question, it is necessary to take account of the following points. First, the floating charge is a floating, not fixed security, and attachment is necessary before it can be enforced as if it were a fixed security. This has given rise to questions about, *inter alia*, the property caught by a floating charge on attachment and the relationship between the floating charge and diligence that have in turn raised difficult issues regarding the relationship between Scots property law and the law relating to floating charges, receivership and other insolvency processes.

Secondly, the floating charge is capable of affecting all of the granter's property, including future property, heritable and moveable, corporeal and incorporeal, and while it can be used to affect only some, or only certain types, of the granter's property, historically at least it has generally been used to affect the whole or substantially the whole of that property. The potentially wide scope of the floating charge gives rise to issues of fairness on the granter's insolvency and has led to a degree of differential treatment of floating charges depending on the extent of the security, as well as specific provisions designed to alleviate its unfairness to unsecured creditors such as provisions for the payment of preferential creditors and the prescribed part.

Thirdly, the floating charge stands in direct contrast to most other securities[242] where enforcement can generally be carried out by the creditor directly.[243] It is this ability to enforce the security directly that means that a secured creditor can effectively stay outside any insolvency process affecting the granter and the insolvency processes generally reflect this in the way that they deal with secured creditors. But this is not the case with a floating charge. A floating charge can only be enforced by the appointment

---

Recovery%20Professionals&utm_medium=email&utm_campaign=11734878_Newsletter%20 06%2F08%2F2020&dm_i=133C,6ZIOU,5JHV6R,S502X,1 (last accessed 4 November 2021).

242 The exception would be the landlord's hypothec, where the process of sequestration for rent formerly used to enforce the security was abolished by the Bankruptcy and Diligence etc. (Scotland) Act 2007 s. 208(1), with the result that the security can be given effect to only in the relevant insolvency or other ranking process.

243 As noted above, this is also in contrast to the position in England and Wales.

of a receiver (where that is still possible) or through liquidation or administration. It is therefore not possible to apply fully the same approach that applies in the case of other securities in an insolvency process, especially where the floating charge affects the whole or substantially the whole of the granter's property. This can be seen most clearly where enforcement is by the appointment of a receiver. The resulting receivership has a dual personality: it is both an enforcement process and, most obviously in the case of administrative receivership, a form of insolvency process. Yet while it has features of both, it cannot be wholly equiparated with either. Thus, as has been seen, receivership as an enforcement process is not, and in some respects cannot be, treated in the same way as the enforcement of other securities in the context of other insolvency processes. In addition, while receivership, particularly administrative receivership, as an insolvency process shares a number of features with the collective insolvency processes of liquidation and administration, it also differs from them in other ways precisely because it is not collective. In colloquial terms, therefore, one might say that it is neither fish nor fowl.

Fourthly, the interplay between the enforcement of a floating charge and insolvency processes is, at best, complex. It is perhaps less complex in the case of liquidation than administration, which might be explained at least partly because of the different nature of the processes: liquidation is intended to wind up the debtor while administration is intended to be primarily a rescue process, at least in theory if not often in practice. In the case of multiple receiverships, the position is relatively more straightforward, with priority in enforcement according to the ranking of the floating charges under which receivers are appointed. So far as the other processes discussed here are concerned, floating charges are treated largely in the same way as other securities. The notable exception to this is the new moratorium introduced by the Corporate Insolvency and Governance Act 2020, which again might be explained by the nature of the process as a mechanism to promote rescue.

The answer to the question posed above is therefore that the floating charge (and its enforcement) have been assimilated into insolvency law in Scotland less than seamlessly. At a technical level, there is scope for improvement in the drafting of the legislation and the clarification of difficult points. At a more fundamental level, however, the real problem remains the nature of the floating charge and how it is enforced, which simply cannot be made to fit neatly into insolvency law in the same way as other securities, particularly where the floating charge affects the whole or substantially the whole of the granter's property. The fact that the floating charge relies on insolvency processes for its enforcement has meant that insolvency law has had to change and develop to accommodate it, and in this respect the floating charge has clearly had a major impact on the development of insolvency law. The general trend of reform from the Enterprise Act 2002 onwards can, however, be regarded as anti-floating charge, or perhaps more accurately anti-receivership, at least where the floating charge affects the whole or substantially the whole of the granter's property. This is interesting because it is floating charges that affect the whole or substantially the whole of the granter's property that are perhaps seen as the most valuable to creditors but at the same time are the most difficult to accommodate in the context of insolvency law.

Yet it seems that the floating charge is destined to remain part of the insolvency landscape. The Cork Committee, while seeking to remedy at least some its acknowledged defects, thought that the floating charge was 'too convenient a form of security to be lightly abolished',[244] and the White Paper that preceded the Enterprise Act 2002 reforms, while also seeking to address what it perceived as problems with administrative receivership, made no mention of the possibility of the abolition of the floating charge itself. More recently, the Scottish Law Commission's proposals for reform of the law relating to security over moveable property,[245] which include the introduction of a new type of security that is easier to assimilate into insolvency law and potentially reduces if not eliminates the need for the floating charge, similarly included no proposals for its abolition, noting rather that there had been strong resistance by consultees to any such possibility. It therefore seems that for the foreseeable future, insolvency law will have to continue to accommodate the floating charge as best it can, however imperfectly that may be.

---

244 See the *Report of the Review Committee on Insolvency Law and Practice* (n 11) paras 1486–1487.
245 Scottish Law Commission, *Report on Moveable Transactions* (Scot. Law Com. No. 249, 2017) para. 20.8.

11 The Empirical Importance of the Floating Charge in Scotland

Jonathan Hardman and Alisdair D J MacPherson

A. INTRODUCTION
B. THE MACRO PICTURE
    (1) Methodology
    (2) Results
    (3) Implications
C. THE MICRO PICTURE: RECENTLY LIQUIDATED COMPANIES
    (1) Methodology
    (2) Results
    (3) Implications
D. THE MICRO PICTURE IN CONTEXT: TERMS OF FLOATING CHARGES
E. CONCLUSION
APPENDIX

A. INTRODUCTION

The rest of this book outlines the historical, theoretical and practical elements of the floating charge in Scotland. In this chapter, we explore empirically how important the floating charge is for Scottish companies. Empirical research provides an original[1] method of reviewing the world as we find it. Companies are usually brought into existence by registration at Companies House.[2] Fixed securities and floating charges created by a company must

---

1 M M Siems, 'Legal Originality' (2008) 28(1) OJLS 147.

2 Companies Act 2006 ss. 1 and 16. There are some exceptions to this, such as companies incorporated by Act of Parliament or by letters patent/charter – see R G Anderson, 'Borrowing on the Undertaking: Scottish Statutory Companies', Chapter 2 within this volume; J J du Plessis,

be registered against that company at Companies House within twenty-one days of their creation to be valid.[3] The records of Companies House are freely available and ripe for empirical study.[4] This chapter examines Companies House data and uses three different empirical techniques to review the floating charge in practice.

First, Companies House is subject to freedom of information requirements[5] and therefore we submitted freedom of information requests to ascertain the macro picture regarding the creation of floating charges.[6] Secondly, we utilised data obtained on Scottish companies who filed certain insolvency (liquidation) forms between 1 October 2019 and 30 September 2020[7] to review this set of companies and identify their use of floating charges. Thirdly, we reviewed a sample of the floating charges granted by such companies to identify and examine certain key terms included in these instruments.

Legal empirical research has been compared to attempts to verify a pre-existing hunch[8] and, as such, legal empirical research does not need to be held up to the same level of statistical scrutiny that other social sciences require.[9] Our first method of analysis overcomes any risk, as it presents a holistic overview of the floating charges granted by Scottish companies. Our second and third methods rely on a smaller sample, and therefore

---

'Corporate Law and Corporate Governance Lessons From the Past: Ebbs and Flows, But Far From "the End of History": Part 1' (2009) 30(2) Co Law 43.

3   Companies Act 2006 s. 859A. This is subject to some exceptions. See A D J MacPherson, 'Registration of Company Charges Revisited: New and Familiar Problems' (2019) 23(2) Edin L Rev 153. Due to the COVID-19 crisis the period was extended to thirty-one days for charges created between 6 June 2020 and 4 April 2021: Companies etc. (Filing Requirements) (Temporary Modifications) Regulations 2020 (SI 2020/645). Given the timing of our freedom of information requests detailed below, this temporary change did not affect the data gathered.

4   See J Hardman, 'The Moral Hazard of Limited Liability? An Empirical Scottish Study' (2018) 6 *Nottingham Insolvency and Business Law eJournal* 3; J Hardman, 'Articles of Association in UK Private Companies: An Empirical Leximetric Study' (2021) 22 EBOR 517; J Hardman, 'The Slow Death of the Scottish plc Listed in London: An Empirical Study' [2022] JBL 118.

5   Freedom of Information Act 2000.

6   Freedom of Information request dated 5 February 2021 from J Hardman to informationrights@companieshouse.gov.uk, responded to on 1 March 2021 with reference number 'FOI 32-02-21'; and Freedom of Information request dated 5 March 2021 from A MacPherson to information-rights@companieshouse.gov.uk, responded to on 19 March 2021 with reference number 'FOI 63-03-21'. For a copy of these requests and responses, please contact either of the authors.

7   J Hardman and A MacPherson, 'Scottish Companies Who Have Filed Certain Insolvency Forms between 1 October 2019 and 30 September 2020' (2021) [dataset], available at *https://doi.org/10.7488/ds/3040* (last accessed 4 November 2021).

8   A Dignam and P B Oh, 'Disregarding the *Salomon* Principle: An Empirical Analysis, 1885–2014' (2019) 39(1) OJLS 16.

9   L M LoPucki, 'A Rule-Based Method for Comparing Corporate Laws' (2018) 94(1) Notre Dame LRev 263.

there may be limits as to their extrapolability. Nonetheless, our results are stark – the floating charge is an integral part of Scottish corporate finance. In addition, our examination of the terms of a sample of floating charges shows some commonplace terms and variations thereof and highlights the potential for future research.

There have been few empirical studies of the Scottish floating charge. The most notable examples are a survey conducted for the Scottish Law Commission outlined briefly in their *Report on Registration of Rights in Security by Companies*,[10] and a qualitative study for the Scottish Executive.[11] The present contribution, however, provides the most detailed and extensive exploration of the use of the floating charge, and is the first to combine the aforementioned different empirical techniques to present an overview of the use of the floating charge as a whole. This chapter proceeds as follows. Part B outlines our empirical analysis as to the macro position, part C outlines our analysis as to the presence of floating charges in relation to a selection of companies and part D outlines our analysis as to the terms of certain of those floating charges. Part E concludes.

B. THE MACRO PICTURE

(1) Methodology

Our first empirical study relied on freedom of information requests asked of Companies House.[12] The Companies House registration regime changed as of 6 April 2013 to replace the previous system, which relied on qualitative copying of data from the instrument into the form, to a simple box ticking system.[13] From then on, to register the grant of a charge,[14] including a

---

10 Scottish Law Commission, *Report on Registration of Rights in Security by Companies* (Scot. Law Com. No. 197, 2004) para. 2.1. They identified floating charges as the second most common form of security registered by Scottish companies with Companies House, after standard securities. Together, standard securities and floating charges accounted for around 95 per cent of applications for registration in the survey.

11 J Hamilton, S Wortley, A Coulson and D Ingram, *Business Finance and Security over Moveable Property* (Scottish Executive Central Research Unit, 2002).

12 See n 6 above.

13 See discussion in H Patrick, 'Charges Changing' (2013) 58(2) JLSS 20; J Hardman, *A Practical Guide to Granting Corporate Security in Scotland* (Edinburgh: W. Green, 2018) Ch. 10.

14 Charge is, of course, the English term – see R G Anderson, 'Security over Bank Accounts under Scots Law' (2010) 4(6) LFMR 593. Nonetheless, it is the statutory term (Companies Act 2006 Part 25) and the term used by Companies House to refer to registrable rights in security. As such, throughout this chapter, we will refer to 'charge' to refer to the wider category of registrable rights in security. It is likely that standard securities and assignations in security are the other

floating charge, a form MR01 needed to be filled in.[15] It should be noted that individual charges are not registered – instruments constituting charges are. There can therefore be multiple charges covered by the same instrument. Box six of the form MR01 asks two questions: first, whether the instrument being registered contains a floating charge; and secondly if there is such a floating charge, whether it is expressed to cover all the property and undertaking of the company. This phrase has been subject to extensive discussion,[16] but nevertheless is the settled term used in the legislation.[17] Box seven of the form MR01 asks whether 'any of the terms of the charge prohibit or restrict the company from creating further security that will rank equally with or ahead of the charge?'.[18] This refers to a 'negative pledge'.[19] A negative pledge has special importance for the Scottish floating charge as it overrides the default rule that floating security ranks behind fixed security and, as such, the negative pledge affects the ranking of the floating charge.[20] We used this information to identify the data we required. We requested the number of charges granted generally. Of these, we explored the number of floating charges granted, and within that category two sub-questions, is any floating charge an 'all assets' floating charge,[21] and is there a negative pledge.

We asked for details of our variables across various different samples and periods. First, we asked for the number of Scottish companies and

most common forms of registrable charge created by Scottish companies; however, we do not have data to confirm this.

15 Companies Act 2006 s. 1117; available at *https://assets.publishing.service.gov.uk/govern ment/uploads/system/uploads/attachment_data/file/933654/MR01_v2.1__2_.pdf* (last accessed 4 November 2021).

16 It was interpreted in the important case of *Sharp v Thomson* 1997 SC (HL) 66. See Scottish Law Commission, *Report on Sharp v Thomson* (Scot. Law Com. No. 208, 2007); A D J MacPherson, *The Floating Charge* (Edinburgh: Edinburgh Legal Education Trust, 2020) Chs 4 and 7.

17 Companies Act 1985 s. 462(1).

18 See Companies Act 1985 s. 464.

19 Hardman, *Granting Corporate Security* (n 13) para. 6–24; MacPherson, *Floating Charge* (n 16) paras 2–29–2–34.

20 See J Hardman and A D J MacPherson, 'The Ranking of Floating Charges', Chapter 9 within this volume. The effect of the Scottish negative pledge on ranking can be contrasted with the English effect, which is more contractual in nature – see R Hardwick, 'The Negative Pledge and Disposal Restrictions: Carve-outs and Remedies for Breach' (2017) 32(8) JIBFL 510.

21 The primary enforcement mechanism for a floating charge is now administration, which is open to the 'holder of a qualifying floating charge', being someone who holds floating charges over all or substantially all the assets of the company, at least one of which must be qualifying – Insolvency Act 1986 Sch. B1 para. 14. Whether a charge is an 'all assets' charge therefore affects the availability of this enforcement mechanic – see D McKenzie Skene, 'The Floating Charge and Insolvency Law', Chapter 10 within this volume; MacPherson, *Floating Charge* (n 16) Ch. 6.

(separately) English companies who filed MR01s for charges created[22]: (i) between 6 April 2013 and 31 December 2020 inclusive; (ii) between 1 January 2019 and 31 December 2019 inclusive; and (iii) between 1 January 2020 and 31 December 2020 inclusive. Secondly, we asked for the number of Scottish companies and (separately) English companies who filed MR01s in respect of instruments that included floating charges created: (i) between 6 April 2013 and 31 December 2020 inclusive; (ii) between 1 January 2019 and 31 December 2019 inclusive; and (iii) between 1 January 2020 and 31 December 2020 inclusive. Thirdly, we asked for the number of floating charges, in each of the foregoing categories, that covered all of the property and undertaking of the company. Fourthly, we asked for the number of floating charges in each of the categories (including the all assets floating charges) that contained negative pledges. Due to the COVID-19 pandemic[23] (which remains ongoing at the time of writing), we worried that 2020 may be an outlier and therefore requested details for Scottish and English companies from 2019 too. The number of companies who have granted securities tells parts of the picture, however, it would show the same results whether a company had granted one charge or 1,000 charges. Thus we asked not only for the number of companies that had granted charges and floating charges, but also the number of times that companies had successfully applied to register charges and floating charges – which will be referred to as 'applications'. We also requested details of the aggregate number of charges granted by those sample groups across that period, to be able to see how prevalent it was for an instrument to contain a floating charge.

Identifying the sheer numbers are helpful but can be misleading, due to the difference in number of English and Scottish companies. As at 31 March 2021,[24] there were 4,129,873 English companies, and 220,083 Scottish companies on the corporate register. Companies are continually created by the 'mysterious rite' of incorporation[25] and removed from the register for a

---

22 It should be noted that charges are created and then registered. Failure to register the charge within twenty-one days (or such subsequent period as a court may permit) results in the charge being invalid against creditors and insolvency practitioners – Companies Act 2006 s. 859H.

23 For an overview of insolvency changes made to accommodate the COVID-19 crisis, see J Hardman, 'The Law and Economics of Lockdown Mitigation: Bankruptcy Errors in the UK' (2021) *International Insolvency Review* 344.

24 Companies House, *Incorporated companies in the UK January to March 2021 (revised)*, available at *https://www.gov.uk/government/statistics/incorporated-companies-in-the-uk-january-to-march-2021* (last accessed 5 November 2021).

25 E M Dodd, 'For Whom Are Corporate Managers Trustees' (1932) 45(7) HarvLRev 1145 at 1160.

number of purposes, including dissolution and liquidation.[26] The overall numbers, though, are increasing – as of 31 March 2013 the figures were 2,588,340 and 151,248 respectively.[27] As such, as at 31 March 2021, Scottish companies made up 5.06 per cent of the aggregate Scottish and English companies, whereas English companies made up 94.94 per cent. Whilst the absolute numbers have changed slightly, as at 31 March 2013 the relevant percentages were 5.52 per cent and 94.48 per cent respectively.[28] Thus whilst the total number of companies has increased by 58.7 per cent in the eight years between the relevant data, the percentages of companies that are English and Scottish have remained roughly similar. The UK Office of National Statistics figures for mid-2019 provided that England had a population of 56,287,000 compared to Scotland's population of 5,463,300. This meant England had 91.15 per cent of the combined population, with Scotland having 8.85 per cent.[29] As such, the Scottish percentage of companies by number is slightly lower than Scotland's population percentage compared to England.[30] Given the dramatic growth of the corporate register, we cannot state with precision what percentage of Scottish and English companies have granted registrable charges or floating charges at any given moment. However, we can establish proportions between the two jurisdictions and the percentages of floating charges granted by companies incorporated within the two jurisdictions that have each of the two features we are exploring.

(2) Results

The results are shown in tables one to five in the appendix to this chapter. Table one shows the aggregate number of charge instruments registered over the three periods. Over the entire period, an aggregate of 401,946 English and Scottish companies granted instruments containing charges, with a total number of 1,025,295 applications to register instruments

---

26 See Companies Act 2006 Part 31 Ch. 1 in respect of voluntary striking off. This can be contrasted with limited partnerships, where there is no ability to remove defunct vehicles – see J Hardman, 'Reconceptualising Scottish Limited Partnership Law' (2021) 21(1) JCLS 179.

27 Companies House, *Incorporated companies in the UK January to March 2021 (revised)* (n 24).

28 It should be noted that percentages given in this chapter will not always add up to 100 per cent due to rounding.

29 Office for National Statistics, *Population Estimates*, available at *https://www.ons.gov.uk/peoplepopulationandcommunity/populationandmigration/populationestimates#timeseries* (last accessed 5 November 2021).

30 See also Hardman, 'Slow Death' (n 4).

containing charges across those companies. This means that, overall, each company who granted a charge granted 2.55 charge instruments. When we divide this between England and Scotland, we can see that 22,407 Scottish companies granted charges (5.57 per cent of the aggregate) compared to 379,539 English companies (94.43 per cent of the aggregate). This means that more Scottish companies have granted charges than would proportionately be expected, but not significantly. Scottish companies accounted for 60,379 applications (5.89 per cent of the aggregate), with English companies accounting for 964,916 applications (94.11 per cent of the aggregate). Scottish companies averaged 2.69 applications per company granting security, whereas English companies averaged 2.54 applications per company granting security. This is perhaps not surprising given the noted English tendency to create 'composite' security documents, as opposed to the Scots law tradition of separate security documents being used in respect of each right in security.[31]

These patterns are slightly different in respect of the individual years examined. Thus in 2019, 88,663 Scottish and English companies granted instruments containing registrable[32] security rights, of which 4,321 (4.87 per cent) were Scottish and 84,342 (95.13 per cent) were English. This shows Scottish companies were granting slightly below their proportion of security for the number of companies existing on the register. This was more pronounced in 2020, which saw a 7.4 per cent decrease in grant of security to 82,585, consisting of 3,637 (4.4 per cent) Scottish companies and 78,948 (95.6 per cent) English companies. Applications followed suit, with 152,876 total applications in 2019, of which 8,364 (5.47 per cent) were Scottish and 144,512 (94.53 per cent) were English, Applications dropped 17.19 per cent in 2020, to 130,452, of which 6,537 (5.01 per cent) were Scottish, and 123,915 (94.99 per cent) were English. In 2019, Scottish companies averaged 1.94 applications per company granting charges compared to English companies' 1.71, with each of these figures dropping in 2020 to 1.80 and 1.57 respectively.

Table two shows the granting of instruments containing floating charges by Scottish companies, and table three shows the corresponding granting of such instruments by English companies. Over the entire period, an aggregate of 318,160 Scottish and English companies granted floating charges, being

---

31 See Hardman, *Granting Corporate Security* (n 13) para. 6–12.
32 Possessory pledges are a particular example of a security that is not registrable – see Companies Act 2006 s. 859A(7).

79.15 per cent of all English and Scottish companies who granted charges. In other words, nearly 80 per cent of companies who granted instruments containing charges since the 2013 reforms of charge registration granted an instrument containing a floating charge. 17,606 of these (5.53 per cent) were Scottish, which is roughly in line with the overall proportion of companies. This means that 78.57 per cent of Scottish companies who granted instruments containing charges granted floating charges.

Between Scotland and England there were 559,193 applications to register instruments containing floating charges, which corresponds to 54.54 per cent of all applications. This is lower than the percentage of the number of companies granting floating charges, which implies that whilst a lot of overall applications contain floating charges, companies that have created floating charges are also likely to grant other instruments that do not include floating charges. Of these applications, 24,551, or 4.39 per cent, were Scottish. This is below the overall proportion of companies that are Scottish and runs counter to the traditional narrative that the floating charge plays a more significant role in Scottish rights in security (in comparison to English law) due to the difficulty in taking fixed security.[33] Over the entire period, there were 1.394 applications for floating charges per Scottish company granting a floating charge, meaning that each Scottish company that has granted a floating charge within that period had granted on average 1.394 floating charges.

This disparity between the overall proportions of English and Scottish companies and those granting floating charges was greater in the two individual years examined. Thus in 2019, there were 56,843 companies granting instruments containing floating charges (64.11 per cent of the total charges granted), of which 2,641 (4.65 per cent) were Scottish companies, meaning that 61.12 per cent of Scottish companies who granted instruments containing charges in this period granted floating charges. In 2020, this dropped to 53,225 companies granting floating charges, being 64.45 per cent of the total charges granted, of which 2,103 (or 3.95 per cent) were Scottish companies. It is, of course, impossible to tell from the data received whether this means lenders to Scottish companies did not have floating charges or already had floating charges from those companies – in other words whether such companies were granting brand new security packages or adding to existing security packages. The latter would explain the comparative lack of floating

33 For example, see R B Jack, 'The Coming of the Floating Charge to Scotland: an Account and an Assessment', in D J Cusine (ed), *A Scots Conveyancing Miscellany: Essays in Honour of Professor J M Halliday* (Edinburgh: W. Green, 1987) 33.

charges granted within an individual year, as it would also explain the comparatively lower number of new applications for floating charges granted by a company who has already granted a floating charge. Applications within the two individual years reflect the same trend – 2019 saw 74,044 applications for floating charges, being 48.43 per cent of the total applications for charges, of which 3,150 (4.25 per cent) were Scottish. In 2020, this dropped 13.3 per cent to 65,355 applications, of which 2,482 (3.8 per cent) were Scottish. Certainly, the disparity between the proportions of companies in the two jurisdictions and the number of applications that contained floating charges is greatest in 2020.

Tables four and five tell us of the features of floating charges granted by Scottish and English companies respectively. For the overall period, 87.53 per cent of Scottish companies who granted floating charges had granted a floating charge with a negative pledge, 95.52 per cent of Scottish companies who had granted a floating charge did so over all of their assets, and 83.7 per cent of Scottish companies who had granted a floating charge granted one that contained a negative pledge and over all of their assets. These figures are roughly the same in England, at 88.9 per cent, 93.11 per cent and 83.01 per cent respectively. Applications followed the same trend, with 85.17 per cent of applications for floating charges granted by Scottish companies containing a negative pledge, 92.47 per cent covering all assets, and 79.12 per cent of applications for floating charges granted by Scottish companies covering all assets and containing a negative pledge. The English percentages are, once again, similar, at 84.22 per cent, 82.98 per cent and 70.24 per cent respectively.

When looking at our individual years, though, the position changes markedly. Thus in 2019, 97.96 per cent of Scottish companies who granted floating charges granted them containing a negative pledge, rising to 98.05 per cent in 2020. Similarly, in 2019 95.19 per cent of Scottish companies who had granted floating charges had granted a floating charge over all of their assets, which rose to 96.05 per cent in 2020. This means that in 2019, 93.64 per cent of Scottish companies who granted a floating charge granted one with a negative pledge and over all their assets, rising to 94.72 per cent in 2020. These figures are reflected in the number of applications as well, with 97.4 per cent of applications by Scottish companies for floating charges containing a negative pledge in 2019, rising to 98.03 per cent in 2020; 92.73 per cent of applications in 2019 for floating charges granted by Scottish companies covering all assets increasing to 93.997 per cent in 2020; and 90.67 per cent of applications for floating charges granted by Scottish companies in 2019 containing a negative pledge and being over all assets of the company, rising to 92.75 per cent in 2020.

These figures are reflected for English companies, with Table 11.1 below being an extract of the relevant figures from table five for the two relevant years.

In both jurisdictions the grant of a negative pledge is more common in the two relevant years than the grant of an all assets floating charge, which reverses the aggregate trend across all years.

(3) Implications

There are six major implications of the foregoing results. First, the floating charge is a commonly used security interest in both England and Scotland, empirically demonstrating the importance of the study of its features in both jurisdictions. 79.15 per cent of English and Scottish companies who granted charges granted a floating charge, with 54.4 per cent of all applications containing a floating charge. Secondly, this percentage difference shows that whilst a large number of companies grant floating charges, many applications do not contain them – indicating that stand-alone fixed securities are also prevalent. This provides two possible implications. First, if there is only one secured creditor, they are comfortable to rely on an initial floating charge to provide floating security over new assets, but have required additional fixed security. Secondly, if there are multiple secured creditors, floating charge

Table 11.1

	1 January 2019 – 31 December 2019	1 January 2020 – 31 December 2020
% of English companies granting floating charges with negative pledge	97.52%	97.41%
% of English companies granting floating charges covering all assets	88.93%	91.71%
% of English companies granting floating charges with negative pledge and covering all assets	86.96%	89.65%
% of English floating charge applications with negative pledge	95.80%	96.53%
% of English floating charge applications covering all assets	83.36%	86.66%
% of English applications for floating charges with negative pledge and covering all assets	79.09%	84.05%

holders are more keen to agree to a subsequent creation of a fixed security than they are a competing floating charge. Either of these implications, once again, emphasises the empirical importance of the floating charge and suggests that the floating charge is the cornerstone of a secured creditor's security package, buttressed as necessary with fixed securities, with the secured creditor more readily agreeing to the subsequent creation of fixed security rather than a floating charge.

Thirdly, in both jurisdictions there were a high number of 'all assets' floating charges with negative pledges, being 79.12 per cent of applications by Scottish companies and 70.24 per cent of applications by English companies. The prevalence of this type of security is unsurprising, given that there are marked advantages to enforcement for an 'all assets' floating charge[34] and the ranking effect of the negative pledge prevents the floating charge being subsequently 'trumped' by the grant of a fixed security.[35] Nevertheless, whilst these are clearly the majority of floating charges, they are not all floating charges. 14.83 per cent of applications by Scottish companies apparently contained no negative pledge, and 7.53 per cent of applications by Scottish companies were not over all assets. The percentage figures are similar in England, with 15.78 per cent of applications by English companies containing no negative pledge and 17 per cent of applications by English companies not being over all assets of the company. Thus whilst the existence of the negative pledge and enforcement through an out-of-court appointment of an administrator remain the norm, we cannot ignore that other enforcement routes may be required, and floating charges holders do not always demand that they receive the protection to their ranking that law allows for them.

The next two implications relate to differences between English and Scottish companies. Fourthly, English numbers of applications per company granting a charge were generally lower than their Scottish equivalents (but the opposite seems to be true for the number of floating charge applications per company granting such security). There are a number of potential causes of this, which range from those that are dramatic for the corporate landscape (e.g. that Scottish companies needed to grant more security than English companies to obtain the same levels of debt), to those than are more mundane (e.g. that Scottish legal practice tends towards individual documents for security interests, whereas English legal practice tends towards composite security interests being granted within one document). More

---

34 See McKenzie Skene, 'The Floating Charge and Insolvency Law', Chapter 10.
35 See Hardman and MacPherson, 'The Ranking of Floating Charges', Chapter 9.

research is needed to explain why this is the case and why the position appears to be reversed for the number of floating charge applications per company granting floating charges, with the figure for each time period lower for English companies than for Scottish companies. However, fifthly, it is important to note that the percentage of the combined totals being granted by Scottish companies is declining over time. This implies that factors (legal or non-legal) are driving changes to the balance between England and Scotland. Once more, it is impossible to tell from these figures whether the English aspects are growing or the Scottish aspects are shrinking, but it is worth noting that this balance is changing over time.

Sixthly, there is an evident COVID-19 drop from 2019 to 2020 across the figures. This is clearly rationalised by a retrenchment driven by global contraction: fewer securities are granted (perhaps because lawyers' fees for the grant of security are an avoidable transaction cost), there are fewer applications for each company that does grant security (perhaps demonstrating a more simplified capital structure), more floating charges proportionately were granted (perhaps as creditors aim to ensure their position on the insolvency of the granter), and proportionately more floating charges contained negative pledges and covered all assets. It will be interesting to trace this trajectory after the COVID-19 crisis has abated to establish whether these trends ultimately represent a long-term major realignment of the terms of security documents, or were a short term response to a discrete global challenge.

However, these implications, and the analysis that flows from them, need to be qualified by the limitations of the study, of which there are a number. The figures are entirely derived from those received from Companies House. As such, any errors in the freedom of information requests will correspond to errors in our analysis. Even if Companies House have their figures correct, they are based on those filed at the public registry – so if participants have not filed charges, then they will not show in our figures.[36] Perhaps more importantly, any mistakes in the forms filed will correspond to errors in our figures. As such, if there is no negative pledge but the box is ticked, then our figures would be skewed, as they would also be if there is a negative pledge but the box is not ticked. Companies House undertakes cursory detail verification but seeks to minimise its role in verifying any information filed on the public register.[37] As such, any errors in filing will also be compounded

---

36 However, should this be the case then it would be correct to exclude them as they will also not be
   enforceable against creditors or an insolvency practitioner – see Companies Act 2006 s. 859H.
37 See *Sebry v Companies House* [2015] EWHC 115 (QB).

into our statistics. This is especially the case if widespread market-based errors subsist, especially if it is thought that the form can influence the legal regime, rather than merely being reflective of the document that influences the regime (e.g. if it was commonly thought that ticking the 'yes' box in respect of the negative pledge was sufficient to create one, even if the document itself is silent). Also, given the dramatic growth in companies over the time of study, it could be that the COVID-19 figures provide a bigger skew to the aggregate statistics than initially thought. Finally, even if none of these come to pass, the foregoing only identifies the 'what', not the 'why'. Further research is needed to explore why any of these phenomena have occurred. We can advance supposition, and have done where we consider it appropriate. However, this does not verify that any such supposition is the root cause of the issues identified. We leave that to subsequent commentators who use these statistics.

C. THE MICRO PICTURE: RECENTLY LIQUIDATED COMPANIES

(1) Methodology

Our second empirical study used an existing dataset compiled by the authors for empirical research into insolvency recoveries in Scotland.[38] This dataset contains data derived from a freedom of information request to Companies House. This request sought to ascertain the number of particular forms[39] submitted within a twelve month period in respect of Scottish companies (i.e. between 1 October 2019 and 30 September 2020), with the said forms representing the end stages of liquidations of the companies, specifically compulsory liquidations and creditors' voluntary liquidations.[40] We then obtained company information and details of insolvency recoveries from the Companies House database. One of the variables that we identified in this dataset was whether the company in question had granted security that was outstanding at the time when the liquidation ended or not. It should be

---

38 Hardman and MacPherson (n 7). This dataset identifies the relevant companies, with additional work undertaken by the authors for this chapter. Such work is on file with the authors and available upon request.

39 These forms are: (i) Notice of final account prior to dissolution in CVL (LIQ14 (Scot)); and (ii) Notice of final account prior to dissolution in a winding up by the court (WU15 (Scot)).

40 Freedom of Information Request dated 14 October 2020 from A MacPherson to information-rights@companieshouse.gov.uk, responded to on 22 October 2020 with reference number 'FOI 303-10-20'. For a copy of the request and response, please contact either of the authors.

noted, therefore, that this study will exclude a company that had granted a raft of security that was redeemed[41] prior to the end of the company's insolvency process.

For the purposes of this chapter, we then reviewed the type of security granted. We first explored the number of charge documents registered over the life of the company in total – regardless of whether these were outstanding, partially satisfied or wholly satisfied.[42] Charge documents can contain multiple charges.[43] We also explored the number of these that contained floating charges and, in each case, the number of these that pre-dated the 2013 registration reforms. We then noted whether the company in question had granted charge documents in favour of multiple creditors over their life and whether multiple creditors had received multiple floating charges over the life of the company.

We then narrowed our search by excluding those charges that were wholly satisfied.[44] In theory, this should remove historic charges. The charges registration regime provides an ability to register a charge as satisfied. However, unlike the regime for registering charges[45] there is no mandatory time period for such a release to be registered. Given that removing the wrong charge will require a court order to rectify,[46] anecdotal evidence reveals that solicitors are reticent to register charges as satisfied at Companies House unless required to do so by an incoming lender. As such, there is a distinct

41 As any companies whose security has been listed as being satisfied at Companies House prior to the conclusion of insolvency is excluded from this dataset.

42 These are the operational options that Companies House provide – see the blog post by Companies House, *Mortgage Charges: save time, file online*, available at *https://companieshouse. blog.gov.uk/2018/10/10/mortgage-charges-save-time-file-online/* (last accessed 5 November 2021).

43 It is commonly the case that an English charge document will contain multiple charges within the same document, with the floating charge covering all assets not caught by fixed charges elsewhere – see L Gullifer, *Goode and Gullifer on Legal Problems of Credit and Security*, 6th edn (London: Sweet & Maxwell, 2017) Ch. 4. This is no doubt because charges that are expressed to be fixed may instead be characterised under English law as floating and it can be difficult to determine whether a charge is one or the other – see *Re Spectrum Plus* [2005] UKHL 41.

44 A charge is satisfied in full if it is registered as satisfied using an MR04, available at *https://assets. publishing.service.gov.uk/government/uploads/system/uploads/attachment_data/file/878473/ MR05_statement_that_part_or_the_whole_of_the_property_charged.pdf* (last accessed 11 November 2021), and can be partially released if some property (even if all property) is noted as being released from the scope of the charge – see *https://assets.publishing.service.gov.uk/ government/uploads/system/uploads/attachment_data/file/878473/MR05_statement_that_part_ or_the_whole_of_the_property_charged.pdf* (last accessed 5 November 2021).

45 Compare Companies Act 2006 s. 859H, setting out consequences of failing to register the charge within the timescale provided, with Companies Act 2006 s. 859L, which states that charges can be released but contains no timescale requirements as to when they are to be released.

46 Companies Act 2006 s. 859M.

possibility that the number of outstanding charges registered against a company is overinclusive. There is also a chance that a charge was removed inadvertently. Nonetheless, the number of outstanding charges should provide good indicative figures. We counted the same variables for only outstanding charges: being the number of outstanding charge documents; the number of outstanding charge documents that contained a floating charge; how many for each of these represent charge documents pre-dating the 2013 reform; whether multiple creditors had been granted live charge documents; and whether multiple creditors had been granted live charge documents containing a floating charge.

(2) Results

Table six outlines the headline results in respect of the grant of security by those within our sample group. The initial dataset revealed that a total of 505 Scottish companies had filed the relevant insolvency forms at Companies House within the relevant timescales.[47] Of these, 136 (26.93 per cent) had outstanding charges registered at Companies House at the time of the conclusion of their insolvency process. These 136 companies had granted a total of 655 charges, at an average of 4.82 charges per company. It should be noted that this is heavily skewed by one company[48] that had granted 283 charges – if this is excluded, then the average number of charges granted over the life of companies within our sample is reduced to 2.76 per company with an outstanding charge at the conclusion of its insolvency process. Of these 655 charges, 531 (81.07 per cent of the total charges granted by those companies within the sample group) pre-dated the 2013 reforms. Of the 655 charges granted in total, 206 (or 31.45 per cent) were floating charges, of which 143 (or 69.42 per cent of floating charges granted) pre-dated the 2013 reforms. There was an average of 1.51 floating charges granted by every company within the sample over its life.

A number of these charges were not relevant at the time of the insolvency of the company – only 315 charges (or 48.09 per cent of all charges) were outstanding at the conclusion of the company's insolvency.[49] Of these, 161 (51.11 per cent of those outstanding as at completion of the relevant

47 Of which, 184 of the forms relate to companies in creditors' voluntary liquidations and 321 relate to companies in compulsory liquidations (i.e. winding up of companies by the court).
48 Kelvin River Properties Ltd, registered number SC210158.
49 It is worth re-emphasising that this can only state whether the charge is stated to be outstanding, rather than whether it actually is or not.

insolvency process) related to floating charges. Accordingly, a company had an average of 2.32 charges, and an average of 1.18 floating charges, outstanding at the time that its insolvency process was concluded.

Over the life of the company, forty-five (or 33.09 per cent) had granted charges in favour of more than one creditor.[50] Forty-one (91.11 per cent of those who had granted charges in favour of multiple creditors) had also granted floating charges in favour of different creditors over their life. When we exclude those charges listed as satisfied in advance of the conclusion of insolvency proceedings, these figures drop to thirty and twenty-six respectively – meaning that 66.67 per cent of companies who had granted charges in favour of multiple creditors continued to be subject to charges in favour of multiple creditors until the end of their insolvency, and 86.67 per cent of those companies were also subject to different floating charges in favour of different creditors.

Table seven outlines the overall picture for the number of charge documents granted by each company. Sixty-two companies (45.59 per cent of the sample) only ever created one charge over their life – and for sixty of those companies (96.77 per cent) this was a floating charge. Thirty-two companies granted two charges over their life, and all thirty-two granted a floating charge as part of that (seventeen granted one document that contained a floating charge, and both charge documents for the remaining fifteen contained a floating charge). Twenty companies granted three charges over their life, with nineteen of those companies granting a floating charge (seven such companies granting one floating charge, three granting two and nine companies for whom all three charge documents registered contained floating charges). Five companies granted four charges each and six granted five charges each and all but one granted at least one floating charge. Eleven companies granted more than five charges and all companies within this category granted at least one floating charge.

When we narrow down the selection to those live at the conclusion of the insolvency, the picture shown is very similar. Seventy-two (52.94 per cent) companies had only one charge outstanding at the conclusion of their insolvency,

---

50 By this, we mean that different charges have been granted in favour of different creditors. Thus it would not include one charge granted in favour of joint recipients, nor two charges granted in favour of the same joint recipients. It also does not include charges granted in favour of multiple creditors under a security trust mechanic. We also carved out known change of name/restructurings, such as The Governor and Company of the Bank of Scotland transferring its entire business and assets to Bank of Scotland plc – these were not counted as different creditors for this purpose.

and for sixty-nine of those companies (95.83 per cent) this contained a floating charge. Thirty-six companies had two charges outstanding at the conclusion of their insolvency process, of which thirty-three (91.67 per cent) had at least one charge outstanding (for seventeen companies there was one floating charge outstanding, for sixteen companies there were two). Fifteen companies had three charges outstanding, of which fourteen had outstanding floating charges (five had one floating charge outstanding, five had two, and four had three). Three companies had four charges outstanding, and all had a floating charge outstanding (two had two outstanding floating charges, and one had three outstanding floating charges). One company had five charges outstanding and none of them contained floating charges. Nine companies had more than five charges outstanding at the completion of their insolvency process, and six of these had granted floating charges.

A final point to note here is that the sample included eighteen companies who had granted pre-Enterprise Act 2002 floating charges that remained outstanding at the end of the company's liquidation.

(3) Implications

There are four key implications of the foregoing. First, whilst a lot of companies in our base data did not have outstanding charges registered at the conclusion of their liquidation, it is evident that for those that made it into the sample that the floating charge was a key part of the security package. More than half of the charges granted by those within the sample were floating charges, and more than half of those outstanding at the conclusion of liquidation were floating charges. This shows that the floating charge was a major component of the security received by secured creditors within this sample. Secondly, this importance increased when few security documents were granted, and decreased when more security documents were granted. This would seem to reinforce the implication noted in section B that the floating charge acts as a cornerstone and key security document, that is often relied upon, with multiple fixed securities being subsequently granted on top of that cornerstone.

Thirdly, the companies within our sample frequently granted securities in favour of more than one creditor, but the existence of multiple secured creditors in relation to one company was less common at the time of their insolvency. This implies that lenders prefer to be the only secured creditor at any given time, but that moving between different secured creditors is common within the sample group.

Fourthly, it seems that older security documents were highly valued by creditors, with a number of outstanding charges being created prior to the change in registration process in 2013. We consider that there are three potential explanations for this. First, creditors value older securities because they are less challengeable – the three key grounds to challenge a security under legislation expire after the passage of time.[51] As such, there is a quantifiable benefit for the creditor in maintaining a charge for which these periods have expired. If holding security is a zero-sum game, a creditor may prefer to maintain an older charge rather than release it and retake a new charge. Secondly, granting new security incurs transaction costs.[52] Not only are there costs incurred in registering the new security with relevant registers, but also there are costs involved in engaging lawyers – likely for the creditor and for the granter. As such, it may be cheaper for both creditor and granter to ensure that security is drafted in as future-proof and robust a manner as possible, and to ensure that subsequent alterations to amounts secured are captured by that framework. As the granter traditionally pays the secured creditor's legal fees in Scotland, pressure is likely to come from the granter. Thirdly, pre-Enterprise Act 2002 floating charges still enable the appointment of an administrative receiver, rather than requiring an administrator.[53] These earlier charges bring a myriad of advantages to the creditor: in addition to the administrative receiver primarily owing duties to the creditor, a prescribed part does not require to be paid to unsecured creditors.[54] We focused on whether charges preceded the 2013 reforms rather than the 2002 reforms and yet it provides another rationale for creditors preferring to maintain older charges.

As with section B above, the foregoing analysis is subject to a number of limitations. The first here relates to sample selection: our sample consists of only insolvent companies who undertook a particular insolvency process, liquidation. It may be that the picture is different for companies who did not enter insolvency processes within a set timescale, or those who entered

---

51 For unfair preferences, the challengeability expires if the granter has not entered liquidation or administration after six months (Insolvency Act 1986 s. 243(1)), for gratuitous alienations, the relevant time period is two years if the recipient is not an associate of the granter, and five years if they are (Insolvency Act 1986 s. 242(3)), and for the avoidance of floating charges regime, the relevant time period is a year if the granter is not an associate of the recipient, and two years if they are (Insolvency Act 1986 s. 245(3)).

52 See discussion in J Hardman, 'Some Legal Determinants of External Finance in Scotland: A Reply to Lord Hodge' (2017) 21(1) Edin L Rev 30.

53 Insolvency Act 1986 s. 72A.

54 See McKenzie Skene, 'The Floating Charge and Insolvency Law', Chapter 10.

different insolvency processes. Indeed, it is possible for other insolvency processes to occur first and then for the company to move into liquidation and, as such, we miss anything that would be captured by that first process. Once we pass sample selection, the above figures only reflect what was filed at Companies House, as such any errors in filing by Companies House or in submissions will be ignored. In particular, as noted above, we consider that there is a likelihood of defunct charges being retained on the registers unless another creditor is particularly pushing for the register to be tidied up. This is especially likely to be the case for a floating charge, as assets can be freely sold from under its ambit. As such, purchasers are likely to be less concerned about a defunct charge remaining on the public register than, say, a purchaser of an asset subject to a standard security would be. Ultimately, again, our outcomes can only represent a qualified 'what' rather than a 'why' – further research will be required to identify why any of the results of this part has occurred.

D. THE MICRO PICTURE IN CONTEXT: TERMS OF FLOATING CHARGES

Much could be said about the terms of floating charge instruments, including with respect to why particular terms are used, how common they are, the variations that exist, and the legal effects of the terms. Indeed, as noted above, there are a number of situations in which the terms of the instrument creating the floating charge impact upon the security interest created, be it the amount secured, whether ranking is future proof (the negative pledge) and enforcement (the assets covered/qualifying floating charge status). However, in the confines of this present contribution, only a few select terms can be mentioned below. From the floating charges discussed in part C above, we have examined the terms of thirty floating charge instruments identified on Companies House as outstanding upon the conclusion of each relevant company's liquidation. To choose these floating charge instruments, we used the list of companies that we compiled for the study in part C and selected the first thirty companies from the list that had granted a floating charge that was still recorded as outstanding. In order to avoid complications in the study, and to maximise comparability, we did not select companies for which there was more than one floating charge recorded as outstanding. The company numbers of the chosen companies are given in table eight below. Given the variations across the different instruments, the complexity involved in the language and the limited space available here, we have not utilised numerical analysis of these instruments. Nevertheless, the work undertaken enables us to make noteworthy points regarding some of the terms of floating charges created by Scottish companies.

Of the floating charge instruments examined, a significant majority expressly state that the charges are qualifying floating charges for the purposes of the Insolvency Act 1986 Sch. B1 para. 14, thus enabling the charge holder to appoint an administrator where the floating charge covers the whole (or substantially the whole) of the company's property. Although the remaining floating charge instruments do not directly state that the created charges are qualifying floating charges, they nevertheless meet the test by purporting to allow for the appointment of an administrator and/or administrative receiver.[55] This does not, of course, automatically allow an out of court appointment of an administrator, as this depends on the assets covered by the charge.

Perhaps unsurprisingly given the findings above and the legal implications involved, the instruments examined all contain negative pledges providing that the floating charge being granted ranks ahead of subsequent fixed securities and floating charges granted by the chargor.[56] In most instruments, however, it is stated that the floating charge ranks behind any fixed security created by the company in favour of the chargee. This is a sensible provision from the creditor's perspective, as if the floating charge was to rank ahead there would be various other claims, such as preferential creditors, the prescribed part and insolvency expenses that would arguably be entitled to payment before the secured creditor.[57] Yet the precise effectiveness of this type of term is unclear if there is another secured creditor with a security right that ranks behind the first creditor's floating charge but ahead of its fixed security.

In addition to prohibitions on the creation of later security rights, many of the instruments contain prohibitions on the sale or other disposal of charged property by the chargor. These prohibitions come in different forms. Some contain outright prohibitions on dealing with heritable property and stipulate that other property can only be disposed of in the ordinary course of business (or equivalent), while others provide that all charged property can only be disposed of in the ordinary course of business, with certain instruments providing more detail as to what would constitute dealing in such a way (e.g. for market value, on an arms' length basis and for consideration

---

55 See Insolvency Act 1986 Sch. B1 para. 14(2).
56 For the ranking of negative pledges, see Companies Act 1985 s. 464(1)(a) and (1A); and Hardman and MacPherson, 'The Ranking of Floating Charges', Chapter 9.
57 See Hardman and MacPherson, 'The Ranking of Floating Charges', Chapter 9, for more details.

payable in cash on normal commercial terms).[58] Various instruments also deal specifically with book debts and other types of debt and stipulate that factoring and invoice discounting do not constitute dealing with the assets in the ordinary course of business and the chargor's consent would be required to do so. This is an attempt to address the possibility of the assets being transferred to another party or placed in trust for their benefit, both of which would mean that the floating charge would not attach to the property.[59]

As the Scottish floating charges legislation does not specify that dealing with charged property outside the ordinary course of business is proscribed, it is worthwhile for floating charge instruments to address this expressly.[60] However, given that the nature of a floating charge necessitates allowing for the chargor to deal with the property, it seems that all of the restrictions on transfer in the instruments, for all types of property, are only personal obligations. Consequently, any transfer (or other dealing) contrary to these terms would be effective but a breach of a contractual obligation that would enable enforcement of the floating charge. It seems likely that this is the intention behind the inclusion of such terms.

As well as the conditions already mentioned, the floating charge instruments disclose various other restrictions and requirements in relation to the charged property. These include terms stating that the charged property is to be kept in good condition and repair and that the chargor is not to cause or permit anything that may depreciate, jeopardise or otherwise prejudice the value or marketability of the assets. Professor Kenneth Reid has written that conditions accompanying a floating charge are 'an obvious ... candidate' for being 'non-neighbourhood [real] conditions', at least once the floating charge has attached.[61] If they are real conditions, they would seem to have this status for all types of property and, as Reid suggests, would be a (rare) example of a real condition for moveable property.[62] The assertion that floating charge conditions could be real conditions presumably emerges

---

58 Some of the instruments also seek to restrict actions by subsidiary and/or other associated companies in the context of these terms.
59 See *Tay Valley Joinery Ltd v CF Financial Services Ltd* 1987 SLT 207; A D J MacPherson, 'Floating Charges and Trust Property in Scots Law: A Tale of Two Patrimonies?' (2018) 22(1) Edin L Rev 1.
60 For the English position, which only allows for dealing in the ordinary course of business (albeit interpreted widely), see E McKendrick, *Goode and McKendrick on Commercial Law*, 6th edn (London: LexisNexis, 2020) para. 25.26 and the authorities cited there.
61 K G C Reid, 'Defining Real Conditions' 1989 Jur Rev 69 at 81. In K G C Reid, 'Real Conditions in Standard Securities' 1983 SLT (News) 169 at 171, he also suggests that 'conditions contained in floating charges' may bind successor proprietors of the burdened property.
62 Reid, 'Defining Real Conditions' (n 61) at 85.

from deemed equivalence to the standard conditions relating to heritable property that complement standard securities, and which can affect successor owners.[63] These conditions include obligations to maintain the subjects, not to let them out without the prior written consent of the security holder and to insure them. It is true that conditions like these are often included within floating charge instruments (such as those examined for the purposes of the present study). However, a standard security is a real right upon its creation (by way of registration) and the standard conditions have real effect from their creation too. By contrast, floating charges do not have real effect when created and accompanying conditions must therefore be mere personal obligations at this stage. These obligations are only enforceable against the chargor, and if the property to which the obligations relate is transferred to another it becomes unattachable by the floating charge and thus the conditions are no longer enforceable by the chargee. As with the terms restricting transfers discussed above, it appears that these provisions act to let the creditor threaten the chargor with a 'nuclear option' enabling enforcement should these terms be breached: as such, the creditor may consider that these provisions simply give them leverage against the chargor, rather than being conditions with real effect.

In line with the suggestion by Reid noted above, for the charge conditions to be real conditions, they would need to become real as accessories to the floating charge when the latter obtains real effect upon attachment. However, by this point the chargor's property will be dealt with by an administrator, liquidator or receiver. The content of floating charge conditions are also not statutorily identifiable. Under the current registration regime, it is possible to access details of conditions in relation to particular charges via Companies House, as with the instruments examined here, but there is no standard set of conditions. In any event, if property is transferred to a third party, the floating charge is no longer enforceable against that property, and this seems to be the case even if the transfer is completed after the charge's attachment.[64] This suggests that conditions accompanying floating charges do not merit the status of real conditions and instead merely add leverage to the creditor.

It is clear that the provisions within the floating charge instruments examined can raise interesting doctrinal questions, including in relation to issues

---

63 Conveyancing and Feudal Reform (Scotland) Act 1970 s. 11(2) provides that the standard conditions (specified in Sch. 3), as varied by the parties, 'shall regulate every standard security'.

64 See MacPherson, *Floating Charge* (n 16), especially Ch. 6.

that have not been addressed by the courts. Considering the terms of various different floating charges may be of value to practitioners with a view to amending their own floating charge styles. Obtaining access to floating charge instruments drafted by others via Companies House is an option nowadays in a way that it was not in the past. Many other terms beyond the ones discussed here could also usefully be considered, such as the range of different undertakings specified in instruments, the events allowing for enforcement of floating charges, and the specified powers available to an appointed administrator or receiver. In methodological terms, further work could be done using leximetric techniques[65] – by reducing certain terms to variables and coding them on a binary[66] basis to establish whether certain terms are used or not.

E. CONCLUSION

Space limitations have precluded this chapter from providing concrete definitive answers as to the operation of the floating charge in the marketplace and the reasons for such deployment. However, there are three substantive advances that this chapter has made. First, it has provided modern empirical analysis as to the importance of the floating charge. There can be no doubt that the empirical data unveils the frequency of use of the floating charge. Companies in England and Wales and Scotland who grant registrable charges grant floating charges. This demonstrates the importance of the clear conceptual, historical and practical understanding of this key security device outlined throughout the rest of this book. On that basis alone, the chapter has demonstrated its value.

The second and third advances made by this chapter are methodological. Secondly, we have demonstrated this by reference to new sources of material – the Companies House records are ripe for empirical study, and large amounts of corporate finance law and practice can be better informed by insights gleaned from this source. Thirdly, we have provided different methods to interrogate the data: first, an analysis of headline statistical

---

65 See M M Siems, 'Convergence in Corporate Governance: A Leximetric Approach' (2010) 35(4) JCorpL 729; P P Lele and M M Siems, 'Shareholder Protection: A Leximetric Approach' (2007) 7(1) JCLS 17.

66 Leximetrics has traditionally used binary variables – e.g. R La Porta et al., 'Law and Finance' (1998) 106(6) *Journal of Political Economy* 1113, but modern leximetric techniques sometimes use non-binary variables – e.g. I-M Esser, I MacNeil and K Chalaczkiewicz-Ladna, 'Engaging Stakeholders in the UK in Corporate Decision Making through Strategic Reporting: An Empirical Study of FTSE 100 Companies' (2018) 29(5) *European Business Law Review* 729.

data, obtained through freedom of information requests from the registrar, provides an overview of what has happened within a set period of time. Secondly, we conducted a detailed examination of the overview of a sample of companies, in this case chosen by reference to liquidation concluding within a certain time period. Whilst these results may not be universalisable, they nevertheless demonstrate the utilisation of the floating charge within a discrete sample of companies. Thirdly, by exploring some of the terms of the instruments creating floating charges, we gain further insights into how floating charges operate in practice, and how they are intended to operate. None of these three methods tell us all of the answers about the deployment of the floating charge in the marketplace. In particular, none tell us 'why' certain decisions were taken. However, the data outlined here provides the start of a research agenda to complete the picture of both what happens in practice and why. This, in turn, will be invaluable for the future development of all corporate finance law: including the floating charge.

APPENDIX

Table 1 Total number of charges granted

	6 April 2013 – 31 December 2020	1 January 2020 – 31 December 2020	1 January 2019 – 31 December 2019
Total number of companies granting charges	401,946	82,585	88,663
Scottish companies granting charges	22,407	3,637	4,321
Scottish % of total companies granting charges	5.57%	4.40%	4.87%
English companies granting charges	379,539	78,948	84,342
English % of total companies granting charges	94.43%	95.60%	95.13%
Total number of applications	1,025,295	130,452	152,876
Applications by Scottish companies	60,379	6,537	8,364

Table 1 (Continued)

	6 April 2013 – 31 December 2020	1 January 2020 – 31 December 2020	1 January 2019 – 31 December 2019
Scottish % of total applications	5.89%	5.01%	5.47%
Scottish applications per company granting charge	2.69	1.80	1.94
Applications by English companies	964,916	123,915	144,512
English % of total applications	94.11%	94.99%	94.53%
English applications per company granting charge	2.54	1.57	1.71

Table 2 Total number of floating charges granted by Scottish companies

	6 April 2013 – 31 December 2020	1 January 2020 – 31 December 2020	1 January 2019 – 31 December 2019
Total number of companies granting floating charges	318,160 (79.15% of total)	53,225 (64.45% of total)	56,843 (64.11% of total)
Scottish companies granting floating charges	17,606	2,103	2,641
% of Scottish companies who granted charges who granted floating charges	78.57%	57.82%	61.12%
Scottish % of companies granting floating charges out of total companies granting floating charges	5.53%	3.95%	4.65%
Total number of applications for floating charges	559,193 (54.54% of total)	65,355 (50.10% of total)	74,044 (48.43% of total)
Applications for floating charges by Scottish companies	24,551	2,482	3,150
Scottish % of total applications for floating charges	4.39%	3.80%	4.25%
Scottish applications for floating charges per company granting floating charges	1.39	1.18	1.19

Table 3 Total number of floating charges granted by English companies

	6 April 2013 – 31 December 2020	1 January 2020 – 31 December 2020	1 January 2019 – 31 December 2019
Total number of companies granting floating charges	318,160 (79.15% of total)	53,225 (64.45% of total)	56,843 (64.11% of total)
English companies granting floating charges	300,554	51,122	54,202
% of English companies who granted charges who granted floating charges	79.19%	64.75%	64.26%
English % of companies granting floating charges out of total companies granting charges	94.47%	96.05%	95.35%
Total number of applications for floating charges	559,193 (54.54% of total)	65,355 (50.1% of total)	74,044 (48.43% of total)
Applications for floating charges by English companies	534,642	62,873	70,894
English % of total applications for floating charges	95.61%	96.20%	95.75%
English applications for floating charges per company granting floating charges	1.78	1.23	1.31

Table 4 Features of Scottish floating charges

	6 April 2013 – 31 December 2020	1 January 2020 – 31 December 2020	1 January 2019 – 31 December 2019
Scottish companies granting floating charges with negative pledge	15,410	2,062	2,587
% of Scottish companies granting floating charges with negative pledge	87.53%	98.05%	97.96%
Scottish companies granting floating charges covering all assets	16,818	2,020	2,514
% of Scottish companies granting floating charges covering all assets	95.52%	96.05%	95.19%

Table 4　(Continued)

	6 April 2013 – 31 December 2020	1 January 2020 – 31 December 2020	1 January 2019 – 31 December 2019
Scottish companies granting floating charges with negative pledge and covering all assets	14,736	1,992	2,473
% of Scottish companies granting floating charges with negative pledge and covering all assets	83.70%	94.72%	93.64%
Scottish applications for floating charges with negative pledge	20,911	2,433	3,068
% of Scottish floating charge applications with negative pledge	85.17%	98.03%	97.40%
Scottish applications for floating charges covering all assets	22,703	2,333	2,921
% of Scottish floating charge applications covering all assets	92.47%	94.00%	92.73%
Scottish applications for floating charges with negative pledge and covering all assets	19,425	2,302	2,856
% of Scottish applications for floating charges with negative pledge and covering all assets	79.12%	92.75%	90.67%

Table 5　Features of English floating charges

	6 April 2013 – 31 December 2020	1 January 2020 – 31 December 2020	1 January 2019 – 31 December 2019
English companies granting floating charges with negative pledge	267,182	49,800	52,860
% of English companies granting floating charges with negative pledge	88.90%	97.41%	97.52%
English companies granting floating charges covering all assets	279,833	46,884	48,204

Table 5 (Continued)

	6 April 2013 – 31 December 2020	1 January 2020 – 31 December 2020	1 January 2019 – 31 December 2019
% of English companies granting floating charges covering all assets	93.11%	91.71%	88.93%
English companies granting floating charges with negative pledge and covering all assets	249,482	45,833	47,135
% of English companies granting floating charges with negative pledge and covering all assets	83.01%	89.65%	86.96%
English applications for floating charges with negative pledge	450,253	60,689	67,915
% of English floating charge applications with negative pledge	84.22%	96.53%	95.80%
English applications for floating charges covering all assets	443,644	54,488	58,389
% of English floating charge applications covering all assets	82.98%	86.66%	83.36%
English applications for floating charges with negative pledge and covering all assets	375,523	52,843	56,070
% of English applications for floating charges with negative pledge and covering all assets	70.24%	84.05%	79.09%

Table 6 Issues arising under the second empirical study

Issue	Number
Total number of charges granted by sample	655
Total number of charges granted by sample which pre-date 2013 reforms	531 (81.07% of total charges granted)
Total number of floating charges granted by sample	206 (31.45% of total charges granted)
Total number of floating charges granted by sample which pre-date 2013 reforms	143 (69.42% of total floating charges granted)

Table 6 (Continued)

Issue	Number
Total number of charges granted by sample outstanding at conclusion of insolvency	315 (48.09% of total charges granted)
Total number of pre-2013 charges granted by sample outstanding at conclusion of insolvency	242 (76.83% of total charges outstanding at conclusion of insolvency)
Total number of floating charges granted by sample outstanding at conclusion of insolvency	161 (51.11% of total charges outstanding at conclusion of insolvency)
Total number of pre-2013 floating charges granted by sample outstanding at conclusion of insolvency	105 (65.22% of total floating charges outstanding at conclusion of insolvency)
Companies granting charges over their life to more than one creditor	45 (33.09% of companies within sample)
Companies granting floating charges over their life to more than one creditor	41 (91.11% of companies who granted charges in favour of multiple different creditors over their life)
Companies granting charges to more than one creditor which were outstanding at the conclusion of insolvency	30 (66.67% of companies who granted charges in favour of multiple different creditors over their life)
Companies granting floating charges to more than one creditor which were outstanding at the conclusion of insolvency	26 (86.67% of companies who had granted charges in favour of multiple different creditors which were outstanding at conclusion of insolvency)

Table 7 How many charge documents each company had granted

Number	Number of companies who granted this number of charge documents over company life	How many of those companies from previous column granted a floating charge over their life	Number of companies with this number of charge documents live at conclusion of insolvency	How many of those companies from previous column granted a floating charge which was live at the conclusion of insolvency
1	62	60	72	69
2	32	32 (17 had 1 document with a floating charge, 15 had 2 documents with a floating charge)	36	33 (17 with one, 16 with two)

Table 7 (Continued)

Number	Number of companies who granted this number of charge documents over company life	How many of those companies from previous column granted a floating charge over their life	Number of companies with this number of charge documents live at conclusion of insolvency	How many of those companies from previous column granted a floating charge which was live at the conclusion of insolvency
3	20	19 (7 with one, 3 with 2, 9 with 3)	15	14 (5 with 1, 5 with 2, 4 with 3)
4	5	5 (1 with 1, 2 with 2, 1 with 3, 1 with 4)	3	3 (2 with 2, 1 with 3)
5	6	5 (2 with 2, 2 with 3 and 1 with 4)	1	0
More than 5	11	11	9	6 (3 with 1, 3 with 2)
Total	136	132	136	125

Table 8 Companies examined for terms of floating charges study

Number	Company number
1	SC345645
2	SC367598
3	SC413001
4	SC289281
5	SC523283
6	SC602858
7	SC315304
8	SC508473
9	SC397024
10	SC599225
11	SC482266
12	SC516687
13	SC443921
14	SC469417
15	SC501952
16	SC518424
17	SC489686
18	SC496030
19	SC402376
20	SC417482
21	SC406741

Table 8 (Continued)

Number	Company number
22	SC404332
23	SC313081
24	SC459321
25	SC388133
26	SC481564
27	SC447081
28	SC403380
29	SC452588
30	SC494056

12 Reform of the Scottish Floating Charge

Andrew J M Steven

A. INTRODUCTION
B. PREVIOUS REFORM ATTEMPTS
   (1) General
   (2) Failed expansionism: the Murray Report
   (3) Failed revisionism: the Bankruptcy and Diligence etc.
      (Scotland) Act 2007 Part 2
C. THE SLC MOVEABLE TRANSACTIONS PROJECT
   (1) Beginnings
   (2) Discussion paper
   (3) Consultation
   (4) Report
D. REFORM OF ENGLISH LAW
   (1) Impetuses
   (2) City of London Law Society
   (3) Secured Transactions Law Reform Project
E. FUTURE REFORM IN SCOTLAND
   (1) Introduction
   (2) UK PPSA
   (3) UK Secured Transactions Code
   (4) Insolvency law (plus?) reform
   (5) Reform leading to single security rights in England and
      Scotland
F. CONCLUSION

A. INTRODUCTION

In *MacMillan v T Leith Developments Ltd (in receivership and liquidation)*,[1] towards the end of his judgment, Lord Drummond Young states:

> 'The introduction of the floating charge into Scots law, and subsequently the concept of receivership, have created significant practical problems. A large part of the difficulty has, I think, been an attempt to reproduce concepts of English equity in a legal system that has no similar institution … It is difficult to translate the institutions of English equity into another legal system, especially one based on the more rigorous conceptual structure of Roman law, as is the case with Scots law and most other European legal systems other than English law.'[2]

He goes on to say that the solution to the difficulty is reform, citing in particular the Scottish Law Commission's work on moveable transactions. I declare an interest here as the lead commissioner responsible for the report on that subject, which was published in 2017.[3] That role reinforced to me the persistent difficulties of achieving reform in this area and in the law of security over moveable property more generally. As shall be seen,[4] a similar pattern has been observable south of the Scottish border. To a certain extent this is unsurprising given the commonality of the law in relation to floating charges, their source, of course, being English law.

This chapter focuses with some tentativeness on future prospects. It begins by trying to learn lessons from the past. Part B looks relatively briefly at previous attempts to reform floating charge law in Scotland that proved unsuccessful. There is particular emphasis on the Murray Report and Part 2 of the Bankruptcy and Diligence etc. (Scotland) Act 2007 (the 2007 Act). Part C then considers the moveable transactions project. At the time of writing there is reasonable confidence that its recommendations will lead to legislation, although progress has been hindered by the COVID-19 pandemic. Part D examines the reform debate in England and Wales. A significant aspect of that is the move by other common law legal systems to a functional approach to security rights over moveable property as exemplified by art. 9 of the Uniform Commercial Code (UCC) of the USA and

---

1 [2017] CSIH 23.
2 [2017] CSIH 23 at para. 121. His view contrasts with the position in England where it has been commented that the judiciary have 'nurtured' the floating charge in the face of hostility from the legislature. See R Calnan, *Proprietary Rights and Insolvency*, 2nd edn (Oxford: Oxford University Press, 2016) para. 1.153.
3 Scottish Law Commission, *Report on Moveable Transactions* (Scot. Law Com. No. 249, 2017).
4 See D below.

the Personal Properties Securities Act (PPSA) approach of Canada, New Zealand, Australia and elsewhere. Part E attempts to map out possibilities for Scotland. It looks at the likelihood of: (i) a UK PPSA; (ii) a UK Secured Transactions Code; (iii) the more limited option of the reform of UK corporate insolvency law but with significant implications for the scope of the floating charge in Scotland; and (iv) the introduction of single security rights in Scotland and England to replace the multiple types currently available. Part F is the conclusion.

B. PREVIOUS REFORM ATTEMPTS

(1) General

The floating charge's Scottish story begins with law reform. Our common law of rights in security in relation to moveable property had long been considered unduly restrictive.[5] In both the nineteenth and twentieth centuries there was remarkably more legislation on reform of security over land (heritable security) than in relation to security over moveables. The former now almost entirely rests on statute.[6] In contrast, pledge, the principal security for corporeal moveables, is a creature of our heavily Roman-influenced common law apart from the legislation on pawnbroking (now consumer credit).[7] The shortcomings of pledge are well known. It is a *possessory* security and it is impractical for businesses to be able to go about their activities when they have to give up possession of their assets to their bank.[8]

The wider inadequacies of the common law are considered in detail in Dr MacPherson's chapter on 'the "Pre-History" of Floating Charges in Scots Law'.[9] These led of course to the Law Reform Committee for Scotland's recommendation in 1960 that the floating charge should be transplanted

---

5 See e.g. W M Gloag and J M Irvine, *Law of Rights in Security Heritable and Moveable Including Cautionary Obligations* (Edinburgh: W. Green, 1897) 187–188.

6 Notably the Conveyancing (Scotland) Act 1874, the Conveyancing (Scotland) Act 1924 and now the Conveyancing and Feudal Reform (Scotland) Act 1970. The legislation on heritable securities is currently the subject of a major review by the Scottish Law Commission on which generally see A J M Steven, 'Mortgage Law Reform in Scotland: Fifty Years Apart' in S Farran et al. (eds), *Modern Studies in Property Law*, Vol. 11 (Oxford: Hart Publishing, 2021) 215.

7 See A J M Steven, *Pledge and Lien* (Edinburgh: Edinburgh Legal Education Trust, 2008) Ch. 3. Pawnbroking is currently regulated by the Consumer Credit Act 1974 ss. 114–122.

8 See e.g. D J Y Hamwijk, *Publicity in Secured Transactions Law: Towards a European public notice filing system for non-possessory security rights in movable assets?* (doctoral thesis, University of Amsterdam, 2014) 7–10.

9 See Chapter 1 within this volume.

from English law.[10] That recommendation was swiftly implemented by the Companies (Floating Charges) (Scotland) Act 1961.

The policy choices made by the committee in its brief report[11] have had an enduring impact that has profoundly affected law reform attempts ever since. Chief amongst these was the decision to adopt what might be termed a 'company law approach' rather than a 'property law approach' to reform of security rights. The 1961 legislation and its successors enable UK companies to create a floating charge over their assets throughout the UK. Before that the law of rights in security in England and Scotland reflected the fact that property law in the two jurisdictions was markedly different.[12] The result of this policy choice is undoubtedly very convenient for companies but has led to significant issues in trying to make floating charges fit within wider Scottish law.[13] A second important policy choice, which naturally followed, was that as under English law the floating charge introduced by the 1961 Act covers land (heritable property) as well as moveable property. Thus, the reform went further than addressing the inadequacies of the common law of security over moveables.

Over the last sixty years there have been numerous attempts to reform floating charges law in Scotland and, it might be also said, to reform the area in England or in the UK as a whole. These are traced by Professor Gretton in his chapter in this book[14] and it would not be a sensible use of space to repeat the exercise here. This history was, however, something that weighed heavily on him and on me as his successor as lead commissioners on the moveable transactions project, which is discussed in the next part of this chapter. Moreover, history is important when trying to assess what should best be done in the future.[15] This is particularly true considering the lack

---

10 Law Reform Committee for Scotland, *Eighth Report of the Law Reform Committee for Scotland: The Constitution of Security over Moveable Property; and Floating Charges* (Cmnd 1017:1960). And see A D J MacPherson, 'The Genesis of the Scottish Floating Charge', Chapter 3 within this volume.

11 The contrast in depth with law reform papers of the 1960s and today is marked, a comment that I have made elsewhere. See Steven (n 6) at 230–231. The same applies with slightly less force in relation to the 1980s. See section E(2) below in relation to the Halliday Report.

12 That is *not* to say they were entirely different. For example, the English law of possessory lien as mediated by Bell in the early 1800s clearly had an influence on its Scottish counterpart. See Steven, *Pledge and Lien* (n 7) Ch. 10.

13 A subject on which much has been written, including in this book. See also generally A D J MacPherson, *The Floating Charge* (Edinburgh: Edinburgh Legal Education Trust, 2020).

14 See G L Gretton, 'The Story of the Scots Law Floating Charge: 1961 to Date', Chapter 4 within this volume and see also section D(1) below.

15 Cf Lord Rodger of Earlsferry, 'Developing the Law Today: National and International Influences' 2002 TSAR 1 at 11.

of success in achieving reform in the past. The discussion here will confine itself to two of the most significant and specific earlier attempts to reform floating charges within Scottish law alone.

(2) Failed expansionism: the Murray Report

What is now referred to as the Murray Report was a consultation paper with draft Bill issued in 1994 by the Department of Trade and Industry.[16] It was prepared by a committee chaired by Professor John Murray QC. This appeared in the year I commenced my doctorate on rights in security and it led to my first ever published article.[17] The Murray Report favoured incremental change to the law of security over moveables. The radical functional approach of art. 9 UCC was eschewed.[18] Instead, a binary structure of: (i) a reformed floating charge; and (ii) a new 'moveable security' was proposed. On (i), the floating charge would be rolled out to non-corporate businesses, notably sole traders and partnerships. This was to be achieved by removing the statutory limitation on the persons permitted to grant floating charges. But consumer goods were to be excluded and for non-company granters the floating charge would not be able to extend to land.[19] As to (ii), this too would not be restricted as to granter, with consumer goods once again being excluded. It would be a fixed security for corporate insolvency law purposes. Only in respect of receivables would it be allowed to cover after-acquired assets.[20] Both the reformed floating charge and the moveable security would be registered in a new Register of Security Interests, to be held at Companies House, but there was to be a procedure for company granters whereby the entry created in the new register would be transmitted to the Companies Register.[21] The securities would only be effective against third parties on registration. There would no longer be an invisibility period

---

16 Department of Trade and Industry, *Security over Moveable Property in Scotland: a Consultation Paper* (1994) (hereafter, 'Murray Report').

17 A J M Steven, 'Reform of Security over Moveable Property' 1995 SLT (News) 120.

18 This marked a departure from a report published eight years earlier by a working party set up by the Scottish Law Commission under the chairmanship of Professor Jack Halliday: *Report by the Working Party on Security over Moveable Property* (1986). This is discussed at section E(2) below.

19 Murray Report (n 16) para. 3.3.

20 Murray Report (n 16) para. 3.4.

21 Murray Report (n 16) paras 3.11 and 3.17. The transmission recommendation is the precursor of the Companies Act 2006 s. 893.

following the creation of a floating charge prior to its registration within twenty-one days.[22]

No legislation followed the Murray Report. It is not exactly clear why.[23] The reason may simply be one that dogs technical law reform projects to this day: competition with more political priorities of government, coupled with a shortage of civil service resources and Bill slots. Here there was the additional challenge of securing pre-devolution Scotland-only commercial law reform. This point may be pressed further in the light of later developments: it may well have been felt unattractive by key stakeholders such as banks to 'Scottify' (or as practitioners would say 'put a kilt on') what was effectively a UK law of floating charges, certainly as regards registration requirements. Another issue was that the proposals were not without difficulty at a technical level,[24] something probably not helped by the speed at which Professor Murray's committee reported.[25] Finally, any likelihood that there would be implementation in the early years following devolution disappeared following the publication of a report[26] commissioned by the Justice Minister on the 'perception that businesses in Scotland are being inhibited in raising capital because under Scots law, they cannot create a security over moveable property without giving up possession'.[27] The report concluded that there was a lack of empirical evidence to justify this perception.

(3) Failed revisionism: the Bankruptcy and Diligence etc. (Scotland) Act 2007 Part 2

Despite not being taken forward, the Murray Report's proposals on floating charges influenced what became Part 2 of the 2007 Act. The genesis of this legislation lay in the decision of the Department of Trade and Industry in 1998 to review company law.[28] An offshoot of this review was work by

---

22 The current provision on this is the Companies Act 2006 s. 859A(4).
23 For earlier theorisation on the reasons see Scottish Law Commission, *Report on Moveable Transactions* (n 3) paras 18.38–18.39.
24 For example, as regards the fixed nature of the new moveable security in relation to incorporeal moveables. See comments by Scottish Law Commission on the consultation paper by Department of Trade and Industry on *Security over Moveable Property in Scotland* (November 1994) 16 March 1995, discussed in Scottish Law Commission, *Report on Moveable Transactions* (n 3) paras 22.12–22.15.
25 See Gretton, 'The Story of the Scots Law Floating Charge: 1961 to Date', Chapter 4.
26 Scottish Executive Central Research Unit, *Report on Business Finance and Security over Moveable Property* (2002).
27 Parliamentary Written Answer S1W–1719 (29 September 1999).
28 See Gretton, 'The Story of the Scots Law Floating Charge: 1961 to Date', Chapter 4.

both the Law Commission for England and Wales and the Scottish Law Commission (SLC) on security rights granted by companies. More about the work south of the border will be said later,[29] but the efforts at 140 Causewayside, Edinburgh[30] led to the *Report on Registration of Rights in Security by Companies* published in 2004.[31] This recommended that floating charges granted by companies over assets in Scotland would need to be registered in a new Register of Floating Charges, to be maintained by the Keeper of the Registers of Scotland.[32] Registration would be necessary for third party effect.[33] There would be no twenty-one-day invisibility period. Floating charges and other securities granted by companies would no longer have to be registered at Companies House.[34] The ranking rules on floating charges would be reformed.[35] The report was almost entirely implemented by Part 2 of the 2007 Act, apart from the recommendation ending the need for securities to be registered at Companies House, which is probably outwith the legislative competence of the Scottish Parliament.[36]

As is well known, however, Part 2 has never been brought into force. The Committee of Scottish Clearing Bankers, who had previously been supportive of the SLC's proposed reforms,[37] wrote to the Cabinet Secretary for Justice opposing the legislation on the basis that it would increase costs for business. The objection centred principally on the fact that under the existing law a single registration of a floating charge in the Companies Register would suffice to make it effective against creditors in respect of assets UK-wide. Under Part 2, it was argued that a second registration would be needed in the Register of Floating Charges by any company who

---

29 See section D(1) below.
30 The address of the Scottish Law Commission.
31 Scottish Law Commission, *Report on Registration of Rights in Security by Companies* (Scot. Law Com. No. 197, 2004).
32 Scottish Law Commission, *Report on Registration of Rights in Security by Companies* (n 31) para. 2.7.
33 Scottish Law Commission, *Report on Registration of Rights in Security by Companies* (n 31) para. 2.5.
34 Scottish Law Commission, *Report on Registration of Rights in Security by Companies* (n 31) para. 3.25.
35 Scottish Law Commission, *Report on Registration of Rights in Security by Companies* (n 31) para. 2.19.
36 The law of business associations is reserved to the UK Parliament by the Scotland Act 1998 Sch. 5 Part C1 but there is an exception for floating charges in Part C2. For discussion, see Scottish Law Commission, *Report on Registration of Rights in Security by Companies* (n 31) part 6.
37 When serving as a Scottish Law Commissioner, I inspected the project files. There was a supportive response from the committee to the discussion paper that preceded the 2004 report.

could potentially have assets in Scotland.[38] In a story told in more detail in Professor Gretton's chapter,[39] a technical working group was set up under the auspices of Registers of Scotland to attempt to resolve the problem through information-sharing arrangements with Companies House. But the committee was split on the way forward leading to stalemate in relation to implementation. It can safely be stated that Part 2 will never be brought into force.[40]

The reason for the failure of this reform was considered by the SLC in its *Report on Moveable Transactions*.[41] In a nutshell the powerful opposition of the banks carried the day. Their demand was for a continued UK regime of floating charges, at least as regards registration. Such an approach places floating charges firmly within commercial law and corporate insolvency where there is considerable UK harmonisation and sometimes uniformity. The differences in property law north and south of the Scottish border become something of an afterthought. The fate of Part 2 of the 2007 Act weighed heavily on the SLC in its work on moveable transactions.

C. THE SLC MOVEABLE TRANSACTIONS PROJECT

(1) Beginnings

Moveable transactions was one of the largest and most ambitious projects carried out in the history of the SLC. It started out more narrowly. In the SLC's *Seventh Programme of Law Reform* published in 2005 a project was announced on the assignation of, and security over, incorporeal moveable property.[42] It was perhaps unsurprising that corporeal moveable property was excluded given the conclusion in the 2002 report commissioned by

---

38 See G Yeowart, 'A Register of Floating Charges over Scottish Assets: A New "Slavenburg" Problem?' (2012) 27 JIBFL 470.

39 See Gretton, 'The Story of the Scots Law Floating Charge: 1961 to Date', Chapter 4. The one footnote that I will add is a memory when at the Scottish Law Commission of one my fellow commissioners, a Queen's Counsel, expressing surprise at the number of members of the working group being based in London and there being no representatives from the Faculty of Advocates or the Law Society of Scotland.

40 See also H Patrick and A J M Steven, 'Reforming the Law of Secured Transactions in Scotland' in L Gullifer and O Akseli (eds), *Secured Transactions Law Reform: Principles, Policies and Practice* (London: Bloomsbury, 2016) 253.

41 Scottish Law Commission, *Report on Moveable Transactions* (n 3) paras 18.41–18.43.

42 Scottish Law Commission, *Seventh Programme of Law Reform* (Scot. Law Com. No. 198, 2005) paras 2.31–2.39.

the Justice Minister referenced above.[43] The driver for the project was the restrictive nature of the law of security over incorporeals that was said to have been 'largely unchanged since the Institutional writers'.[44] The necessity for formal imitation to account debtors in the case of assignation in security of claims was clearly cumbersome. Floating charges were described as a 'partial solution'[45] being available only to companies and more recently limited liability partnerships (LLPs). The restriction on the appointment of a receiver by the Enterprise Act 2002[46] and the ranking below the 'prescribed part'[47] for unsecured creditors were also stated to be shortcomings of the floating charge. But the plan clearly was not to reform the law of floating charges, but rather the law of assignation.

The Seventh Programme noted that the project would be a long-term one that would be unlikely to begin until work on land registration concluded.[48] By the time, however, that the *Eighth Programme of Law Reform* was announced in 2010 that work had only just finished.[49] Following support from consultees in the run-up to this,[50] the project was widened to include security over corporeal moveable property. It was commented that the law here 'is regarded by many as being outmoded'.[51] There is no mention of the floating charge. But reference is made to developments internationally, including the functional approaches of art. 9 UCC and the PPSAs.[52]

(2) Discussion paper

When the SLC issued its discussion paper in 2011 the subject had acquired the snappier title of 'moveable transactions'.[53] An outline scheme

---

43 At section B(2).
44 Scottish Law Commission, *Seventh Programme of Law Reform* (n 42) para. 2.34.
45 Scottish Law Commission, *Seventh Programme of Law Reform* (n 42) para. 2.36.
46 See Insolvency Act 1986 s. 72A as inserted by the Enterprise Act 2002 s. 150(1).
47 Insolvency Act 1986 s. 176A.
48 Scottish Law Commission, *Seventh Programme of Law Reform* (n 42) para. 2.31.
49 See Scottish Law Commission, *Report on Land Registration* (Scot. Law Com. No. 222, 2010), implemented by the Land Registration etc. (Scotland) Act 2012.
50 For example, the Lord President of the Court Session at the time, Lord Hamilton said that the subject 'appears to be in urgent need of consideration'. See Scottish Law Commission, *Report on Moveable Transactions* (n 3) para. 1.15.
51 Scottish Law Commission, *Eighth Programme of Law Reform* (Scot. Law Com. No. 220, 2010) para. 2.5.
52 Scottish Law Commission, *Eighth Programme of Law Reform* (n 51) para. 2.6.
53 Scottish Law Commission, *Discussion Paper on Moveable Transactions* (Scot. Law Com. DP No. 151, 2011).

was produced,[54] grounded in a new Register of Moveable Transactions. Registration there would offer an alternative to intimation in the case of assignation of claims. It would also be where a new security right over moveable property would be registered. This security right would give the creditor a subordinate real right in the property. For corporeals, registration would replace the delivery requirement of pledge and for incorporeals it would mean that title to the asset would not have to be transferred to the creditor. The new security would be generally available, but with certain consumer protections. There was some flirting with a functional approach to security over moveables but with limited enthusiasm.[55]

What though of the floating charge? The discussion paper devotes two chapters to the subject. Chapter 9 sets out the current law and Chapter 22 considers reform. The aim of the first of these is to show that the existence of the floating charge does not obviate need for reform more generally. The inability of a natural person or partnership (other than an LLP) to grant this form of security is noted.[56] The chapter subsequently highlights a number of practical weaknesses of the floating charge, many of which relate to its lower ranking when compared with a fixed security.[57] It goes on to discuss conceptual weaknesses, asking 'whether, given the technical shortcomings of the floating charge, something better might be devised, something that would deliver, in practical terms, more or less what the floating charge can deliver, but deliver it better'.[58] In this regard what is suggested is drawing on art. 9 UCC and the PPSAs to introduce a 'floating lien'. At first sight, this is rather surprising because these jurisdictions have a common law system of property law, but what would matter would be the level of appropriate adaptation.

Chapter 22 considers the future of floating charges and the introduction of floating liens. The case for the latter is concluded to be threefold. First, the new security being proposed would automatically be a floating security unless it was confined to present assets. It would be a case of 'buy one, get one free'.[59] Secondly, unlike the floating charge, the floating lien would be

---

54 Scottish Law Commission, *Discussion Paper on Moveable Transactions* (n 53) Ch. 3.
55 Scottish Law Commission, *Discussion Paper on Moveable Transactions* (n 53) Ch. 21.
56 Scottish Law Commission, *Discussion Paper on Moveable Transactions* (n 53) para. 9.2.
57 Scottish Law Commission, *Discussion Paper on Moveable Transactions* (n 53) para. 9.13. The relevant statutory provisions are listed in n 92 below.
58 Scottish Law Commission, *Discussion Paper on Moveable Transactions* (n 53) para. 9.15.
59 Scottish Law Commission, *Discussion Paper on Moveable Transactions* (n 53) para. 22.22. As discussed below at section C(3), however, the attitude of many of the consultees to the proposal unfortunately might be summed up by the acronym for this marketing expression.

available to unincorporated businesses. Thirdly, compared with the floating charge the new security right would have a 'superior inner logic'.[60] Consultees are then asked whether they agree that the new right should not be limited to present assets except in consumer cases. In hindsight, however, this discussion inadequately captures the fixed and floating security distinction recognised in English law and now throughout the UK in relation to corporate insolvencies. The key to a floating security is not that it can cover future assets. A fixed security can do that.[61] Rather, the hallmark of a floating security is that prior to enforcement the debtor is free to deal with the assets without the permission of the security holder and to give a purchaser an unencumbered title.[62]

The chapter then goes on to consider the fate of the floating charge, given the proposed introduction of the floating lien. It suggests that there is a strong case for prospective abolition but notes that financial institutions are generally 'conservative'[63] in relation to law reform. Therefore, the idea would be that both security rights would co-exist but that the floating charge might be less and less used, because of the availability of the floating lien.[64] The question then asked of consultees is whether they agree that 'the floating charge should not be abolished, at least for the time being'.[65] The chapter also asks for their view as to whether in the future floating charges should be restricted to moveable property.[66] Further, it proposes that floating charges should continue to be unavailable to non-corporate businesses.[67] Finally, there are some miscellaneous questions, including whether the decision of *Lord Advocate v Royal Bank of Scotland*[68] on the interaction of floating charges with 'effectually executed diligence' should be overturned[69] and whether the ranking rules in relation to negative pledge clauses should be altered.[70]

60 Scottish Law Commission, *Discussion Paper on Moveable Transactions* (n 53) para. 22.22.
61 *Re Yorkshire Woolcombers Association Ltd* [1903] 2 Ch D 284 at 294 per Vaughan Williams LJ.
62 *Re Spectrum Plus Ltd* [2005] UKHL 41, [2005] 2 AC 680 at para. 107 per Lord Scott. See generally H Beale et al., *The Law of Security and Title-Based Financing*, 3rd edn (Oxford: Oxford University Press, 2018) para. 6.101.
63 Scottish Law Commission, *Discussion Paper on Moveable Transactions* (n 53) para. 22.28.
64 Earlier in the discussion paper (n 53) at para. 22.13 the rather colourful (in more senses than one) analogy of red and grey squirrels is used to make the point.
65 Scottish Law Commission, *Discussion Paper on Moveable Transactions* (n 53) para. 22.28.
66 Scottish Law Commission, *Discussion Paper on Moveable Transactions* (n 53) para. 22.29.
67 Scottish Law Commission, *Discussion Paper on Moveable Transactions* (n 53) para. 22.35.
68 1977 SC 155.
69 Scottish Law Commission, *Discussion Paper on Moveable Transactions* (n 53) paras 22.33–22.34.
70 Scottish Law Commission, *Discussion Paper on Moveable Transactions* (n 53) paras 22.30–22.31.

(3) Consultation

During the consultation period for the discussion paper, there was a change of the guard at the SLC. George Gretton, who had been the lead commissioner on the project completed his term and was succeeded by me. Prior to my appointment I had arranged for there to be a symposium on the discussion paper at the University of Edinburgh.[71] Invitations were issued to both academics and practitioners, with a flier setting out the context. The first inkling of the likely response to the floating charge proposals came when the Committee of Scottish Clearing Bankers contacted me. The flier contained the statement: 'The introduction of floating charges fifty years ago led to many problems'. I was asked to provide examples.[72] On reflection this had perhaps not been the wisest thing to put in the flier, given the experience of Part 2 of the 2007 Act. Nevertheless, the statement is true in terms of the hard cases that the courts have been called upon since 1961 to decide upon floating charges. But from a banking perspective the benefits of having the floating charge, compared with the situation pre-1961 far outshine the difficulties in making it fit within Scottish law.

The reforms proposed in the discussion paper in relation to the reform of the law of assignation and the introduction of a new fixed security over moveable property were to be strongly supported by consultees. Not so those on floating charges. In response to the proposal that there should be no abolition 'for the time being', the Law Society of Scotland said that it was 'strongly against any move to abolish floating charges'.[73] A major law firm, Dundas and Wilson,[74] stated: 'We strongly believe that steps to replace the floating charge with a system that differs from that currently existing will be *retrograde*. The system as currently operated is *entrenched* and works

---

71 The papers are published at (2012) 16 Edin L Rev 261.
72 My response was to refer to *Sharp v Thomson* 1997 SC (HL) 66 and *Lord Advocate v Royal Bank of Scotland* 1977 SC 155.
73 See Scottish Law Commission, *Report on Moveable Transactions* (n 3) para. 20.8. The discussion paper in fact only suggested possible future abolition if the floating lien proved successful. As I have commented elsewhere, it is reasonable to speculate that the depth of the opposition was heightened by the knowledge that the principal author of the discussion paper was George Gretton, who is widely regarded as the floating charge's top critic in Scotland. See A J M Steven, 'George Gretton and the Scots Law of Rights in Security' in A J M Steven et al. (eds), *Nothing so Practical as a Good Theory: Festschrift for George L Gretton* (Edinburgh: Avizandum, 2017) 235 at 250.
74 Now subsumed into CMS Cameron McKenna Nabarro Olswang LLP.

extremely well in practice' [my emphasis].[75] The floating lien, despite its 'superior inner logic', held little attraction to those in practice. In this regard, two particular points can be drawn out. The first is the fact that it would be possible for the proposed new security to be a fixed security, even though it could extend to future assets, as discussed above.[76] The second is that the proposed new security could not encumber land.[77] Consultees, particularly those in practice carrying out banking work, perhaps unsurprisingly saw the ability of the floating charge to cover all assets as a clear advantage. The question in the discussion paper asking whether floating charges should be restricted to moveable property inevitably drew submissions supporting the status quo.

(4) Report

As a result of these responses, the *Report on Moveable Transactions* recommended a narrower scheme for reform of security over moveable property than that proposed in the discussion paper.[78] The new security, to be termed the 'statutory pledge', would in a corporate insolvency context be a fixed security. It would be available in respect of corporeal moveable property, intellectual property and financial instruments.[79] In property law terms, it would be a real right, like a standard security over land. It would be incompetent to grant a mandate to the debtor enabling it to deal freely with the property without the creditor's consent because that would make the security like a floating charge and undeserving of the higher ranking in insolvency of a fixed security.[80] There would be no floating lien. Clearly, the suggestion in the discussion paper that its introduction would lead to the floating charge fading away was misplaced. In addition to the opposition

---

75 See Scottish Law Commission, *Report on Moveable Transactions* (n 3) para. 20.8. See also J Hardman, *A Practical Guide to Granting Corporate Security in Scotland* (Edinburgh: W. Green, 2018) para. 6–06: 'The floating charge under Scots law is definitely a blunt instrument, but as with all blunt instruments it can be particularly effective'.

76 See section C(2) above.

77 See Scottish Law Commission, *Report on Moveable Transactions* (n 3) para. 20.22.

78 In a direct parallel to what had happened in relation to proposals by the Law Commission for England and Wales in the early 2000s in this area. It should be stressed, however, that the SLC's initial proposals were far less ambitious than those originally made south of the border where wholesale reform based on art. 9 UCC and the PPSAs was proposed.

79 The reason for the limitation, at least initially, for incorporeal moveable property to only intellectual property and financial instruments was driven primarily by the technical difficulties of the fixed/floating distinction in relation to security over receivables and their proceeds. See section D(1) below.

80 See Scottish Law Commission, *Report on Moveable Transactions* (n 3) paras 20.27–20.36.

from consultees, a policy issue that now motivated the SLC was that in relation to non-corporate granters, personal insolvency law did not have the
rules that corporate insolvency law has to keep in check a security capable of
attaching to all a debtor's assets.[81]

Chapter 38 of the report deals with reform of floating charges and agricultural charges. The latter are a specialist form of security limited both as
to granter and types of asset. While they have similar features to floating
charges they are beyond scope here.[82] There are only three formal recommendations on floating charges, none of which necessitate draft Bill provisions. One, in line with consultee views mentioned above, is that the security
should remain competent over land. Another is that it should continue to be
unavailable to sole traders and partnerships. On this issue, consultees had
been split. A reason given by the SLC for the status quo was the likelihood of
opposition to reform of floating charges on a Scotland-only basis given what
happened with Part 2 of the 2007 Act.[83] The aforesaid consequences for personal insolvency law are also relevant. The third recommendation, that there
should be no change to ranking rules in relation to negative pledge clauses,
was influenced by a reform to English law since the publication of the discussion paper.[84] Finally, although there was no formal recommendation, the
report considered the issue of 'effectually executed diligence'. Here once
again there had been a major development since the discussion paper. *Lord
Advocate v Royal Bank of Scotland*[85] had been overruled by the five-judge
Inner House in *MacMillan v T Leith Developments Ltd (in receivership
and liquidation)*.[86] While noting that there remained difficulties, the SLC
took the view that the issues were best left to a future reform of corporate
insolvency law.[87]

The overall approach here, with its absence of reform recommendations given the strong opinions of consultees, might be termed, following

---

81 See Scottish Law Commission, *Report on Moveable Transactions* (n 3) para. 20.18–20.19. In
  particular the rules on preferential creditors and the prescribed part mentioned at section C(1)
  above.
82 See Scottish Law Commission, *Report on Moveable Transactions* (n 3) paras 38.13–38.15. And
  see MacPherson, 'The "Pre-History" of Floating Charges in Scots Law', Chapter 1.
83 See Scottish Law Commission, *Report on Moveable Transactions* (n 3) para. 38.4, noting also
  that the law of business associations is reserved to the UK Parliament, although floating charges
  are devolved.
84 See Scottish Law Commission, *Report on Moveable Transactions* (n 3) paras 38.7–38.9. The
  change in England is that such clauses can now be registered in the Companies Register.
85 See above n 68.
86 See above n 1.
87 Scottish Law Commission, *Report on Moveable Transactions* (n 3) paras 38.10–38.12.

the debacle of Part 2 of the 2007 Act, as once bitten twice shy. To which the reader might expect this chapter to draw to a close. But that would be premature. There is no doubt that there will be future reform of the floating charge. The principal reason for this is significant dissatisfaction as to the current state of the law of security rights in England.

D. REFORM OF ENGLISH LAW

(1) Impetuses

The problematic nature of the floating charge results primarily from its lack of conceptual fit with the underlying law, as noted by Lord Drummond Young in the statement that opened this chapter. It is a creature of equity and Scottish property law does not recognise equity in this sense.[88] The same cannot obviously be said of England. The impetuses for reform therefore differ from those that drove Part 2 of the 2007 Act.[89] Moreover, floating charge reform is almost universally considered in the context of reform of rights in security law more generally. A number of general themes have emerged.

First, current English law is over-complex and uncertain.[90] There is no accessible modern statute. Rather, for the most part there is a body of judge-made law. Commercial parties want certainty.[91] In some places, this is not possible. The epitome of this is the distinction between fixed and floating charges.[92] This issue is crucial in a corporate insolvency where, by statute, a fixed charge has a higher ranking.[93] But statute does not define the two types of charge. That is left to the courts, the leading modern case being *National*

---

88 Compare D Carr, *Ideas of Equity* (Edinburgh: Edinburgh Legal Education Trust, 2017).

89 That said, there has been a longstanding debate on the nature of a floating charge in English law prior to crystallisation.

90 See e.g. L Gullifer and M Raczynska, 'The English Law of Personal Property Security: Under-reformed?' in Gullifer and Akseli (eds), *Secured Transactions Law Reform: Principles, Policies and Practice* (n 40) 271.

91 In the famous words of Lord Mansfield in *Vallejo v Wheeler* (1774) 1 Cowp 143 at 153: 'In all mercantile transactions the great object should be certainty'. See more generally I MacNeil, 'Uncertainty in Commercial Law' (2009) 13 Edin L Rev 68.

92 See e.g. Beale et al., *The Law of Security and Title-Based Financing* (n 62) paras 6.109–6.22; M Raczynska, *The Law of Tracing in Commercial Transactions* (Oxford: Oxford University Press, 2018) paras 1.39 and 5.46–5.66.

93 Insolvency Act 1986 ss. 40, 175, 176A, 386 and Sch. B1 paras 65 and 99(3). The partial reintroduction of the Crown preference for taxation on 1 December 2020 by the Finance Act 2020 s. 98 has accentuated this position. See R Caldwell, 'Enterprise Goes into Reverse for Floating Charge-holders' 2019 Jur Rev 103.

Westminster Bank plc v Spectrum Plus Ltd,[94] which reversed previous case law. The Financial Law Committee of the City of London Law Society has said that the issue of whether a charge is fixed or floating is 'a running sore in our legal system'.[95] This is one problem that the generally inadequate Scottish law does not have because there is no direct equivalent of a fixed charge. Our existing fixed securities such as pledge and standard security are readily distinguished from it. The problem of differentiation is, however, one that the SLC encountered in its moveable transactions project. It had no English statute to draw on to set out the fixed nature of the new statutory pledge. The definitional difficulties were central to the decision to exclude receivables from the types of asset over which a statutory pledge may be granted, because determining the nature of charges over these has been particularly problematic south of the border.[96]

Secondly, the law is fragmented.[97] It recognises a number of different securities that can be available in respect of the same types of asset. Thus, there is: (1) mortgage; (2) charge; (3) pledge; and (4) contractual lien. It is possible to have either a legal or equitable mortgage. Charges, which are always equitable, can be fixed or floating. The different securities have different methods of creation and enforcement, as well as their own priority rules. In fact what has been said here is confined to formal security types. It excludes functional securities such as retention of title.

Thirdly, therefore, there is the view that the law is unsatisfactory because it takes a formalistic rather than functional approach to security rights.[98] This issue is most germane to the question of publicity. Where a company grants a mortgage or charge, that security will be ineffective against other creditors without registration at Companies House. Pledge and lien require possession by the creditor. Functional securities do not require to be registered. Yet they

---

94 See above n 62. See J Getzler and J Payne (eds), *Company Charges: Spectrum and Beyond* (Oxford: Oxford University Press, 2006).

95 City of London Law Society Financial Law Committee, *Discussion Paper: Secured Transactions Reform* (2012) para. 4.24.

96 See Scottish Law Commission, *Report on Moveable Transactions* (n 3) Ch. 22.

97 I draw here on Louise Gullifer's terminology in 'Conclusions and Recommendations' in Gullifer and Akseli (eds), *Secured Transactions Law Reform: Principles, Policies and Practice* (n 40) 505. Accounts of English law can be found in standard texts such as Beale et al., *The Law of Security and Title-Based Financing* (n 62) and R Calnan, *Taking Security*, 4th edn (Bristol: Jordan Publishing, 2018).

98 For discussion, see e.g. I Davies, 'The Reform of English Personal Property Security Law: Functionalism and Article 9 of the Uniform Commercial Code' (2004) 24 *Legal Studies* 295 and L Gullifer, 'Quasi-security Interests: Functionalism and the Incidents of Security' in I Davies (ed), *Issues in International Commercial Law* (Oxford: Routledge, 2005) 11.

have the same economic purpose as formal securities, namely to protect the creditor in the event of the debtor's insolvency. It is this fact that has led to the functional approach to security over moveable property, as exemplified by art. 9 UCC and the PPSAs. This has attracted some law reformers in the UK now for over fifty years.[99] In the early 2000s, the most serious attempt to date to implement it at the behest of the Law Commission for England and Wales in relation to security rights granted by companies foundered after substantial opposition from the legal profession.[100] Recent years have seen the functional approach become increasingly dominant internationally as evidenced in the UNCITRAL's *Legislative Guide on Secured Transactions* (2007) and *Model Law on Secured Transactions* (2016), as well as being supported by the World Bank.[101]

Despite the fact that the Law Commission's proposals were not taken forward there is unanimity that reform of English law is required, but inevitably dissensus on how this should be achieved. In the last few years the Law Commission has worked on reform of bills of sale, a particular type of security over chattels (corporeal moveables) available to non-corporate granters.[102] That too has not (yet) been taken forward. In relation to wider reform two groups are in the forefront. The first is the City of London Law Society and the second is the Secured Transactions Law Reform Project.[103]

---

99 Since at least the Crowther Report, *Consumer Credit: Report of the Committee* (Cmnd 4956, 1971), on which see section E(2) below. See J de Lacy, 'The evolution and regulation of security interests over personal property in English law' in J de Lacy (ed), *The Reform of UK Personal Property Security Law: Comparative Perspectives* (Oxford: Routledge, 2010) 3 at 43 onwards.

100 See e.g. L Gullifer, 'Will the Law Commission Sink the Floating Charge' [2003] LMCLQ 125; H Beale, 'The Exportability of North American Chattel Security Regimes: The Fate of the English Law Commission's Proposals' (2006) 43 Canadian Business LJ 177 and G McCormack, 'Pressured by the Paradigm: The Law Commission and Company Security Interests' in J de Lacy (ed), *The Reform of UK Personal Property Security Law: Comparative Perspectives* (n 99) 83. See also section E(2) below on attempts in the 1970s and 1980s to achieve this type of reform.

101 See S V Bazinas, 'The UNCITRAL Legislative Guide on Secured Transactions and the Draft UNCITRAL Model Law on Secured Transactions Compared' in Gullifer and Akseli (eds), *Secured Transactions Law Reform: Principles, Policies and Practice* (n 40) 481; D Sheehan, *The Principles of Personal Property Law*, 2nd edn (Oxford: Hart Publishing, 2017) 386; M Dubovec and L Gullifer, *Secured Transactions Law Reform in Africa* (Oxford: Hart Publishing, 2019) 8–13 and Ch. 2; and L Gullifer and D Neo, 'Introduction' in L Gullifer and D Neo (eds), *Secured Transactions Law in Asia: Principles, Perspectives and Reform* (Oxford: Hart Publishing, 2021) 1 at 9–10.

102 Law Commission, *Goods Mortgages* (Law Com. No. 369, 2016). Implementation of this report was announced in the 2017 Queen's Speech but the UK Government subsequently changed its mind, apparently over concerns that the Bill might be amended to include wider consumer issues.

103 See too Beale et al., *The Law of Security and Title-Based Financing* (n 62) paras 23.178–23.179.

(2) City of London Law Society

The City of London Law Society (CLLS) was one of the principal opponents of the reform on the basis of a functional approach as proposed by the Law Commission.[104] For the CLLS, current English law is nevertheless in an imperfect state. To that end its Financial Law Committee has published a series of discussion papers on reform[105] and more recently begun work on a draft Secured Transactions Code.

For present purposes it is discussion paper two, issued in February 2014, which is most germane. It considers fixed and floating charges on insolvency. The paper notes that the need to differentiate the two types of charge 'creates material practical problems'[106] that result in transactions being more complicated and costly. A number of examples of where it may be unclear as to whether a charge is fixed or floating are given. These include: (i) a property finance transaction where the debtor may collect the rents until default; (ii) a share charge where the debtor can receive the dividends or vote until default; and (iii) where security is taken over assets held by a custodier but the debtor has management powers prior to default.[107] In relation to fixing the problem, the paper highlights two key policy issues.[108] First, there is the requirement for certainty in financial transactions. Secondly, there is the funding of administrations. As these aim to keep a company trading, usually by its sale as a going concern, there is a need to fund the administrator. There is a powerful argument that this funding should come from realisation of at least some of the assets that are encumbered by security rights.

The paper proceeds to offer three options for reform. CLLS option one is to clarify the distinction between fixed and floating charges. This is recognised as the most conservative approach, which has attractions in relation to ease of implementation. But given that the question of whether a charge is fixed or floating is ultimately fact-specific depending on the drafting of individual documents, the paper is sceptical about this being a reform with

---

104 See McCormack, 'Pressurised by the Paradigm' (n 100) at 84–85.
105 Discussion paper one on secured transactions reform was issued in November 2012. For an account from a Scottish perspective, see A J M Steven, 'Secured Transactions Reform' (2013) 17 Edin L Rev 251.
106 City of London Law Society's Financial Law Committee, *Secured Transactions Reform: Discussion Paper 2 Fixed and Floating Charges on Insolvency* (2014) para. 4.
107 CLLS, *Secured Transactions Reform: Discussion Paper 2 Fixed and Floating Charges on Insolvency* (n 106) para. 19.
108 CLLS, *Secured Transactions Reform: Discussion Paper 2 Fixed and Floating Charges on Insolvency* (n 106) paras 24–30.

much value.[109] CLLS option two is to abolish the distinction for insolvency purposes and instead to have new rules under which certain debts would have a prioritised right to be paid out of the proceeds of certain assets.[110] For example, an administrator's expenses might be funded by the sale of stock-in-trade or receivables.[111] As the paper notes,[112] the choice of relevant assets for these purposes may be controversial. Alternatively, the expenses could be paid out of, say, current assets (to use accountancy terminology) generally as opposed to fixed assets. But here once again there may be definitional challenges. CLLS option three, like CLLS option two, would abolish the fixed/floating distinction but this time the debts with prioritised status would be paid from a levy: a small percentage of all the encumbered assets up to a cap.[113] The 'prescribed part'[114] is noted as a model. This approach would be relatively simple, but its implementation would require policy decisions as to exactly which debts would be covered by the levy. There would inevitably be differences of opinion between secured lenders and insolvency practitioners. Achieving consensus would be difficult. The paper seeks to commence a debate about the best way forward.

The CLLS has continued its contribution to law reform by preparing a Secured Transactions Code and Commentary. The principal author is Richard Calnan[115] and the most recent version was published in 2020.[116] It runs to fifty-five sections. The introductory session of the commentary notes:

'The purpose of the Code is to create a new law of secured transactions, based on the existing law but simplifying and modernising it … The reason we start with

---

109 CLLS, *Secured Transactions Reform: Discussion Paper 2 Fixed and Floating Charges on Insolvency* (n 106) paras 31–34.

110 CLLS, *Secured Transactions Reform: Discussion Paper 2 Fixed and Floating Charges on Insolvency* (n 106) paras 35–40.

111 The paper references here Companies Act 1993 Sch. 7, para. 2(b) (New Zealand).

112 CLLS, *Secured Transactions Reform: Discussion Paper 2 Fixed and Floating Charges on Insolvency* (n 106) para. 39.

113 CLLS, *Secured Transactions Reform: Discussion Paper 2 Fixed and Floating Charges on Insolvency* (n 106) para. 19.

114 Insolvency Act 1986 s. 176A. See also section C(1) above.

115 See also R Calnan, 'What is Wrong with the Law of Security?' in J de Lacy (ed), *The Reform of UK Personal Property Security Law: Comparative Perspectives* (n 99) 162, R Calnan, 'What Makes a Good Law of Security?' in F Dahan (ed), *Research Handbook on Secured Financing in Commercial Transactions* (Cheltenham: Edward Elgar Publishing, 2015) 451 and R Calnan, 'A Secured Transactions Code' (2015) 30 JIBFL 215.

116 See CLLS, *https://www.citysolicitors.org.uk/clls/committees/financial-law/* (last accessed 6 November 2021). See also P Moffat, 'Why Reforming Secured Transactions Law is a Good Thing for Everyone – Including Law Students', *Legal Cheek* (30 November 2020), available at *https://www.legalcheek.com/lc-journal-posts/why-reforming-secured-transactions-law-is-a-good-thing-for-everyone-including-law-students/* (last accessed 6 November 2021).

the existing law is that, as a general rule, it works well in practice ... But, because the law has developed over 400 years, the underlying principles have become encrusted with detailed rules which are much more complicated than they need to be and which often do not reflect current practices. What we have attempted to do here is to remove the barnacles and to create a system which is simpler and clearer than the current law and which reflects more closely what parties actually need in practice.'[117]

The code is not drafted in the style of a normal UK statute. Its brevity and directness is much more like the French *Code civil*. This may pose challenges for implementation.

Some key features of the code are as follows. First, it would replace the existing forms of security with a single type known as a 'charge'.[118] Secondly, a charge could be granted over any type of property, both land ('real property') and moveables ('personal property') including present and future assets.[119] Thirdly, both individuals and legal persons could grant a charge, but there would be restrictions in relation to the former.[120] Fourthly, the code takes a formal rather than functional approach to the definition of a charge. Arrangements such as leases and retention of title are excluded.[121] Fifthly, the usual way for a charge to be effective against third parties would be registration at Companies House. This would be transaction filing rather than the notice filing approach of a PPSA.[122] Special types of assets may have further registration requirements.[123] For example, for land priority would also be dependent on registration with HM Land Registry. It would continue to be possible to achieve priority by taking possession in the case of goods. The possessory pledge in effect would become a sub-species of the new 'charge'. Sixthly, the code as far as possible avoids the distinction between law and equity in English law.

Seventhly, and most importantly for present purposes, the code also generally eschews the fixed/floating distinction. It does, however, make it clear towards the start that a charge can be created even where the chargor has authority to deal with the encumbered assets so that an acquirer takes these

117 CLLS, Financial Law Committee, *Secured Transactions Code and Commentary* (2020) paras 1 and 3–4.
118 CLLS, *Secured Transactions Code* (n 117) Part 1.
119 CLLS, *Secured Transactions Code* (n 117) Part 3.
120 CLLS, *Secured Transactions Code* (n 117) s. 22.
121 CLLS, *Secured Transactions Code* (n 117) s. 6.
122 See e.g. H Beale, 'An Outline of a Typical PPSA Scheme' in Gullifer and Akseli (eds), *Secured Transactions Law Reform: Principles, Policies and Practice* (n 40) 7 at 11–12.
123 CLLS, *Secured Transactions Code* (n 117) s. 3 and Part 7.

free of the charge.[124] The cardinal feature of the floating charge thus survives if this is what the parties wish. In this regard, there are subsequent provisions governing 'dispositions' of assets. Here a distinction is made between 'current assets' and 'fixed assets'. The former are defined as being financial collateral or 'goods other than ships or aircraft which, in the transaction concerned, a reasonable acquirer would expect the chargor to be able to sell free from a charge without the acquirer having to check'.[125] Assets that are not current assets are fixed assets.[126] As a general rule a third party acquirer of current assets will take these free of the charge whereas for fixed assets they will not.[127] In relation to insolvency, however, the code is silent on the fixed/floating distinction. The commentary says that it is expected as a result of the difficulties in the current law here 'that the legislation which will bring the code into force will repeal the statutory provisions which give priority to preferential creditors, unsecured creditors and insolvency practitioners over floating charges'.[128] As to what will replace these there is reference to further discussions based on CLLS discussion paper two.[129] Further iterations of the code are to follow.

(3) Secured Transactions Law Reform Project

The second group working on reform are the members of the Secured Transactions Law Reform Project (STR).[130] These include practitioners, academics and industry representatives from the financial sector. The STR's original executive director was Professor Sir Roy Goode and the current executive co-directors are Professor Louise Gullifer and Dr Magda Raczynska. Its website contains a statement setting out 'the case for reform'.[131] There is an immediate similarity with the CLLS position in relation to the first impetus for reform that is mentioned: complexity. This is unsurprising. Neither is the following further impetus:

124 CLLS, *Secured Transactions Code* (n 117) s. 4.3.
125 CLLS, *Secured Transactions Code* (n 117) s. 41.2.
126 CLLS, *Secured Transactions Code* (n 117) s. 41.3.
127 CLLS, *Secured Transactions Code* (n 117) ss. 42 and 43.
128 CLLS, *Secured Transactions Code* (n 117) s. 55.2 commentary para. 3.
129 CLLS, *Secured Transactions Code* (n 117) s. 55.2 commentary para. 4.
130 See *https://securedtransactionslawreformproject.org/* (last accessed 6 November 2021). The website uses 'STR' as the abbreviation for the project.
131 Secured Transactions Law Reform Project, *The Case for Reform*, available at *https://securedtransactionslawreformproject.org/the-case-for-reform/* (last accessed 6 November 2021).

'The law relating to the distinction between fixed and floating charges is in an unsatisfactory state. This makes it difficult to give clear advice when structuring transactions, and the cost of credit may be raised because steps have to be taken to avoid potential problems.'[132]

The statement goes on to suggest that this difficulty could be solved by the law using 'a simpler criterion with much the same practical effects'.[133] No further elaboration is given at this stage but later it is stated once again that the law here is 'unacceptably unclear'.[134]

Elsewhere, however, the statement takes a markedly different approach to that of the CLLS. It advocates 'major change',[135] the embracing of functionalism and the introduction of a PPSA. Fixed and floating charges would disappear and instead there would be a single security interest over all personal property. Given that the statement was authored by Sir Roy, one would not have expected otherwise.[136] Following his retirement as executive director, however, the stance on functionalism has become diluted. In a draft policy paper of April 2016 primacy is given to six core aspects of a reform agenda. These are:

(1) A simplified and codified law of secured transactions.
(2) Adoption of a single concept of a (consensual) security interest.
(3) A regime of secured transactions that enables security to be taken over any asset, present and future.
(4) A regime of secured transactions, including registration, that covers security interests granted by all debtors (whether corporate or non-corporate), although there could be different rules for consumers.
(5) A fully electronic system of registration, where registration takes effect without human intervention.
(6) A set of clear priority rules based on rational distinctions and, at its core, a rule that priority between registered interests is by date of registration.[137]

---

132 STR, *The Case for Reform* (n 131).
133 STR, *The Case for Reform* (n 131).
134 STR, *The Case for Reform* (n 131).
135 STR, *The Case for Reform* (n 131).
136 See e.g. R Goode, 'The Exodus of the Floating Charge' in D Feldman and F Meisel (eds), *Corporate and Commercial Law: Modern Developments* (London: Lloyds of London Press, 1996) 193 and R Goode, 'The Case for the Abolition of the Floating Charge' in Getzler and Payne (eds), *Company Charges: Spectrum and Beyond* (n 94) 11.
137 Secured Transactions Law Reform Project, *April 2016 Draft Policy Paper*, available at *https://securedtransactionslawreformproject.org/draft-policy-paper/* (last accessed 6 November 2021) para. 1.3.

There follows a list of subsidiary areas requiring further consideration and policy choices. These include 'whether other interests, not presently treated as security interests, should be included within the regime'.[138] A subsequent discussion paper issued in January 2017 and authored by Dr Raczynska discusses the arguments for and against here in relation to asset finance.[139] But there is no definitive advocation of a PPSA. Like the CLLS Secured Transactions Code, the STR bears to include both land and personal property within its remit. Land is mentioned in a section on financing of particular assets along with financial collateral, aircraft, ships and some types of intellectual property.[140] But it is noted that in some cases the current regimes are satisfactory and can be left as they are. In contrast, others merit reform. Where land lies in this regard is not made clear.

As to floating charges, the draft policy paper describes the distinction from fixed charges as being 'troublesome'.[141] The introduction of a single security interest would bring an end to the difficulty, but work would be needed on reform of insolvency law and, in particular, on the funding of insolvencies as a result of the new security law.[142] That work was progressed by a discussion paper on the insolvency consequences of the fixed/floating charge distinction issued in January 2017 under the authorship of Sarah Paterson.[143] This paper takes account of CLLS discussion paper two discussed above and considers a number of options.

STR option one is to reform corporate insolvency law to abolish partly or wholly the categories of claims such as those of preferential creditors and the

---

138 STR, *April 2016 Draft Policy Paper* (n 137) para. 1.4.
139 See Secured Transactions Law Reform Project, *Discussion Paper on Asset Finance as Part of Secured Transactions Reform: Registration without Recharacterisation?* (January 2017) available at *https://stlrp.files.wordpress.com/2017/01/raczynska-asset-finance-2.pdf* (last accessed 6 November 2021). And see also the discussion paper by Professor Hugh Beale issued at the same time dealing with sales of receivables available at *https://stlrp.files.wordpress.com/2017/01/beale-sale-of-receivables.pdf* (last accessed 6 November 2021). See too W Chan, 'Secured Transactions Law Reform: The Long and Winding Road' (2017) 32 JIBFL 215.
140 STR, *April 2016 Draft Policy Paper* (n 137) para. 3.29.
141 STR, *April 2016 Draft Policy Paper* (n 137) para. 3.17.
142 See also here Dubovec and Gullifer, *Secured Transactions Law Reform in Africa* (n 101) 23–26 and 440–441.
143 See Secured Transactions Law Reform Project, *Discussion Paper on the Insolvency Consequences of the Abolition of the Fixed/Floating Charge Distinction* (January 2017) available at *https://stlrp.files.wordpress.com/2017/01/paterson-fixed-and-floating-charges.pdf* (last accessed 6 November 2021). See also S Paterson, 'Finding Our Way: Secured Transactions and Corporate Bankruptcy Law and Policy in America and England' (2018) 18 *Journal of Corporate Law Studies* 247.

'prescribed part', which trump floating but not fixed charges.[144] This superficially is the position in the US, but as the paper points out in a detailed comparison there are other judicial mechanisms in that jurisdiction that can be used to protect creditors who are not secured.[145] The paper therefore recommends against this approach.

STR option two is essentially the opposite: for current prioritised claims to trump both fixed and floating charges.[146] This is given fairly short shrift, on the basis that fixed charge holders do not have the levers open to them in an insolvency as floating charge holders, such as ordinarily the right without judicial approval to appoint an administrator.[147]

STR option three, after being outlined, is dismissed even more cursorily.[148] This is CLLS option three of prioritised claims being drawn from a levy over all charged assets up to a cap.[149] Two reasons are given for ruling it out: (i) doubt about how a cap would be calculated; and (ii) the difficulties in maintaining the balance between the rights of secured and unsecured creditors. Neither of these, however, seem completely insoluble.

STR option four is close to CLLS option one,[150] namely keeping the distinction but clarifying it.[151] The specific suggestion, however, is drawing on the 'circulating assets' definition in the Australian personal property security legislation[152] as a replacement for what is currently regarded as floating security. But having reviewed the position in Australia, it is concluded that there would still be problems of definition[153] and this approach too is quickly discarded.

---

144 STR, *Discussion Paper on the Insolvency Consequences of the Abolition of the Fixed/Floating Charge Distinction* (n 143) paras 2.1–2.15.
145 STR, *Discussion Paper on the Insolvency Consequences of the Abolition of the Fixed/Floating Charge Distinction* (n 143) paras 2.4–2.9.
146 STR, *Discussion Paper on the Insolvency Consequences of the Abolition of the Fixed/Floating Charge Distinction* (n 143) paras 3.1–3.3.
147 If they are a 'qualifying' floating charge holder. See Insolvency Act 1986 Sch. B1 para. 14.
148 STR, *Discussion Paper on the Insolvency Consequences of the Abolition of the Fixed/Floating Charge Distinction* (n 143) paras 4.1–4.2.
149 See section D(2) above.
150 See section D(2) above.
151 STR, *Discussion Paper on the Insolvency Consequences of the Abolition of the Fixed/Floating Charge Distinction* (n 143) paras 5.1–5.3.
152 Personal Property Securities Act 2009 s. 340 (Australia).
153 A point borne out by litigation. See e.g. *In re RCR Tomlinson Ltd* [2020] NSWSC 735 discussed extra-judicially by one of the judges in A Black, 'Some recent case law and statutory developments in insolvency', ARITA conference 12 November 2020, available at *https:// www.supremecourt.justice.nsw.gov.au/Documents/Publications/Speeches/2020%20Speeches/ Black_20201112.pdf* (last accessed 6 November 2021). See also B Whittaker, *Review of the Personal Property Securities Act 2009: Final Report* (2015) para. 9.2.1 which recommended some amendment.

Finally, STR option five mirrors CLLS option two.[154] It is to reclassify what is currently a floating charge with a charge over particular types of assets.[155] Charges over such assets would be subordinated to the prioritised claims recognised by corporate insolvency law. The assets suggested for this categorisation are: inventory (stock in trade); book debts; and money, with perhaps also some other types of assets that may be regarded as circulating, such as raw materials and crops. This seems similar to STR option four but with a tighter definition. It is the approach that the paper ultimately favours. The paper then examines a number of problematic issues that would need to be addressed even under this favoured approach[156] and by considering wider insolvency reform.[157] It concludes by emphasising the need for clarity as to how the law is to apply.[158] The STR will no doubt continue to refine its thinking as its work progresses.

E. FUTURE REFORM IN SCOTLAND

(1) Introduction

Having considered recent developments south of the Scottish border, the time has now come to crystal ball gaze and to attempt to sketch out possible future developments in our own jurisdiction.[159] In its 2021–2022 legislative programme the Scottish Government included a Moveable Transactions (Scotland) Bill which would implement the SLC's 2017 Report.[160] Work here had previously been suspended as a result of the COVID-19 pandemic. Therefore what follows generally tries to proceed on the assumption that the

---

154 See section D(2) above.
155 STR, *Discussion Paper on the Insolvency Consequences of the Abolition of the Fixed/Floating Charge Distinction* (n 143) paras 6.1–6.2.
156 STR, *Discussion Paper on the Insolvency Consequences of the Abolition of the Fixed/Floating Charge Distinction* (n 143) para. 7.1. These include capital adequacy rules and the continued or otherwise relevance of the concept of 'control' of certain assets.
157 STR, *Discussion Paper on the Insolvency Consequences of the Abolition of the Fixed/Floating Charge Distinction* (n 143) para. 8.1.
158 STR, *Discussion Paper on the Insolvency Consequences of the Abolition of the Fixed/Floating Charge Distinction* (n 143) para. 7.1.
159 It is to be hoped that developments in Scotland will be watched with interest in England. In this regard it is gratifying to note that the final paragraph of Professors Beale, Bridge, Gullifer and Lomnicka's standard English text, *The Law of Security and Title-Based Financing* (n 62), para. 23.181 is on reform in Scotland.
160 Scottish Government, *A Fairer, Greener Scotland: Programme for Government* 2021-22 (2021) 77, available at *https://www.gov.scot/publications/fairer-greener-scotland-programme-government-2021-22/documents/* (last accessed 6 November 2021)..

new statutory pledge will be introduced in the coming years. But clearly that is only one step, albeit a major one. We consider now further possibilities beyond that.

(2) UK PPSA

We begin with the prospect of radical reform. Given the difficulties that the floating charge has caused in Scottish law, an argument can be made for discarding it in favour of a brand new system. Such an approach would avoid the pitfalls of piecemeal reform. Professor Louise Gullifer has cogently pointed these out and they include the risk of further complicating what is there already.[161] Given the desire for a single UK-wide approach as evidenced by the failure of Part 2 of the 2007 Act,[162] let us be even bolder. Is the answer to replace floating charges and the rest of English and Scottish secured transactions law with a UK PPSA? Certainly, this is the usual method of radical reform and it would bring our law in line with the preferred approach of the World Bank and the UNCITRAL Legislative Guide and Model Law.[163]

For several reasons, however, this does not seem the way forward, certainly in the short term and even in the longer term. First, it will be apparent from the previous part of this chapter and the discussion of the work of the CLLS and the STR that there is no consensus in favour of such an approach in England.[164] The CLLS is clearly against this, as initially evidenced by its views when the Law Commission proposed reform on this basis in the early 2000s. Its Secured Transactions Code eschews notice filing and functionalism, the hallmarks of a PPSA. The STR, while initially in favour, seems to have taken a step back. It may be highlighted here too that a PPSA, as its name indicates, does not extend to land. As discussed above,[165] the floating charge does. The new 'charge' that would be created under the CLLS code would cover all assets. This approach, while attractive in some ways,[166] is not

---

161 L Gullifer, 'Piecemeal Reform: Is it the Answer?' in F Dahan (ed), *Research Handbook on Secured Financing in Commercial Transactions* (n 115) 421. For the SLC response to this, see Scottish Law Commission, *Report on Moveable Transactions* (n 3) paras 18.52–18.54. See now also L Gullifer, 'Conclusion' in Gullifer and Neo (eds), *Secured Transactions Law in Asia: Principles, Perspectives and Reform* (n 101) 425 at 440–444.
162 See section B(3) above.
163 See section D(1) above.
164 See section D(2) and (3) above.
165 See sections B(1) and C above.
166 See Calnan 'What Makes a Good Law of Security'? (n 115) at 456–457.

without difficulty and would require to be the subject of detailed technical consideration.[167]

Secondly, there is presently little support for a PPSA in Scotland as the SLC found out when it consulted on the issue.[168] This, however, needs to be contextualised. A functional approach in Scotland under which a retention of title clause in a sale of goods transaction needs a registered notice to have third party effect is entirely unpalatable when no such registration is required in England and both jurisdictions are currently subject to common legislation in this area.[169] Were English law to embrace a PPSA-type approach, views north of the border might change.[170] But not necessarily.[171]

Thirdly, while the introduction of a pan-UK PPSA approach would displace the current secured transaction regimes, the different property laws in England and Scotland would remain. In the striking words of the SLC on art. 9 UCC, which has much in common with a PPSA: '[it] lies over the top of the underlying property law, like a tea towel laid over a pile of unwashed dishes'.[172] There are therefore considerable risks of incoherence. These risks would be accentuated under a pan-UK project. A leading English scholar, Professor Michael Bridge, has rightly commented that: 'A free-standing version of [UCC-9] cannot be transplanted into another legal system without considerable thought being given to all features of the legal terrain, especially the property law of the receiving jurisdiction, into which it is being transplanted'.[173] In this regard, a particular challenge is that

---

167 See Sheehan, *The Principles of Personal Property Law* (n 101) 372. For a negative view from a jurisdiction that already has a PPSA, see M Gedye, 'The New Zealand Perspective' Gullifer and Akseli (eds), *Secured Transactions Law Reform: Principles, Policies and Practice* (n 40) 115 at 129–130. See further L Gullifer, 'Conclusion' in Gullifer and Neo (eds), *Secured Transactions Law in Asia: Principles, Perspectives and Reform* (n 101) 425 at 461–462.

168 Scottish Law Commission, *Report on Moveable Transactions* (n 3) paras 18.44–18.49. See also section C(2) and (3) above.

169 Sale of Goods Act 1979, Consumer Rights Act 2015. See also A J M Steven, 'Reform of Moveable Transactions Law in Scotland' in O Akseli and J Linarelli (eds), *The Future of Commercial Law: Ways Forward for Change and Reform* (Oxford: Hart Publishing, 2020) 318 at 330.

170 In the same way as Louisiana, a mixed legal jurisdiction eventually decided to implement art. 9 UCC to facilitate secured transactions with neighbouring states. See 2001 La Acts No. 128 and J A Stuckey, 'Louisiana's Non-Uniform Variations in UCC Chapter 9' (2002) 62 Louisiana L R 793.

171 See J MacLeod, 'Thirty Years After: The Concept of Security Revisited' in Steven et al. (eds), *Nothing so Practical as a Good Theory: Festschrift for George L Gretton* (n 73) 177 at 190–192.

172 Scottish Law Commission, *Discussion Paper on Moveable Transactions* (n 53) para. 13.10.

173 M Bridge, 'Secured Credit Legislation: Functional or Transactional Co-Existence' in S V Bazinas and N O Akseli (eds), *International and Comparative Secured Transactions Law: Essays in honour of Roderick A Macdonald* (London: Bloomsbury, 2017) 1 at 16. But compare Gedye (n 167) at 143 who, while accepting the need for local policy choices, in general favours following 'tried and true precedent legislation'.

Scottish property law, like other Germanic property law systems, in principle rejects 'limping' rights.[174] Under Scottish law a right in security, like other property rights, is either good against the world or not good against any-one.[175] In contrast, in a PPSA approach there is the attachment/perfection distinction whereby the right can be good as between the parties ('attach-ment') but requires an external act, typically registration ('perfection'), to be effective against other parties, in particular other creditors.[176] To some extent, the system of company charges registration that was introduced to Scotland along with the floating charge mirrors this approach, with the gap period between creation and third party effectiveness by registration.[177] Nevertheless, this is a leading example of why the floating charge does not fit with our underlying property law and was at the core of the failed 2007 Act Part 2 attempted reform.[178] There are other ways in which a PPSA would give rise to significant challenges for Scottish property law, including in relation to the approach to both priority and publicity.[179] In this regard it is noteworthy that the PPSAs that have been enacted over recent times have typically been in common law jurisdictions.[180] It would take considerable efforts to create a system which would fit well into Scottish law. As Professor Sir Roy Goode has recently commented, harmonisation 'depends on respect for legal systems within other legal families, notably the civil law'.[181]

---

174 See G Gretton, 'Security over Moveables in Scots Law' in J de Lacy (ed), *The Reform of UK Personal Property Security Law: Comparative Perspectives* (n 99) 270 at 280. Professor Gretton argues at 284 that it is not clear that the attachment/perfection is 'really an essential part of a PPSA' having earlier cited the European Bank for Reconstruction and Development's Model Law on Secured Transactions, but it is certainly the standard approach.

175 For example, *Bank of Scotland v Liquidators of Hutchison, Main & Co Ltd* 1914 SC (HL) 1.

176 See Beale (n 122) at 8 and Sheehan, *The Principles of Personal Property Law* (n 101) 375–379.

177 See G L Gretton, 'Registration of Company Charges' (2002) 6 Edin L Rev 146 and A D J MacPherson, 'Registration of Company Charges Revisited: New and Familiar Problems' (2019) 23 Edin LR 153 at 168–172.

178 It was also a reason why the Scottish Law Commission did not favour registration of the new statutory pledge in the Companies Register. See Scottish Law Commission, *Report on Moveable Transactions* (n 3) para. 36.27 n 42. Compare J Hardman, 'Three Steps Forward, Two Steps Back: A View from Corporate Security Practice of the Moveable Transactions (Scotland) Bill' (2018) 22 Edin L Rev 266 at 272–273.

179 Gretton, 'Security over Moveables in Scots Law' (n 174) at 278–282.

180 For example, Australia, Malawi, New Zealand, Papua New Guinea and Zimbabwe. See also Dubovec and Gullifer, *Secured Transactions Law Reform in Africa* (n 101) 444–446 and T Rodríguez de las Heras Balell, 'Secured Transactions Law Reform in Civil Law Jurisdictions' in Gullifer and Neo (eds), *Secured Transactions Law in Asia: Principles, Perspectives and Reform* (n 101) 101.

181 R Goode, 'Creativity and Transnational Commercial Law: From Carchemish to Cape Town' (2021) 70 ICLQ 1 at 3.

Fourthly, there is the constitutional dimension. Legislative competence in relation to rights in security law in general and floating charges law in particular lies with the Scottish Parliament, as demonstrated by the passing of the 2007 Act.[182] This makes the enactment of a UK PPSA a more complex task. A joint project of the Scottish Law Commission and Law Commission for England and Wales would probably be necessary in the first place. The former is already fully committed with other work, not least a large project on reform of heritable securities.[183] Following the May 2021 Scottish Parliament election there is a more profound constitutional question. The Scottish National Party, which now forms the Scottish Government with the Scottish Greens, has committed to a second independence referendum within the lifetime of the current Scottish Parliament, in other words by 2026.[184] A pan-UK PPSA, if Scotland were to leave the UK, would seem unlikely.[185] And even if this does not happen, the current political climate appears against such a development.

Fifthly and lastly, we have been here before. Fifty years ago, the Crowther Report recommended reform of the law on security over moveable property in the UK based on art. 9 UCC.[186] But it concluded that because of the marked differences between Scottish law and English law, it would be desirable for there to be two separate statutes.[187] As a result of that the Scottish Law Commission established a working party to 'consider the legal and technical problems'[188] that this approach to secured transactions would cause for Scottish law. The working party was chaired by a former Scottish Law

---

182 On floating charges see the Scotland Act 1998 Sch. 5 Part II Head C2 and see generally Scottish Law Commission, *Report on Moveable Transactions* (n 3) paras 1.38–1.52.

183 See n 6 above.

184 See Scottish Parliament, Official Report, Meeting of the Parliament (Hybrid), 26 May 2021, col 16 (Nicola Sturgeon MSP, First Minister).

185 Of course, Scottish independence would also have major consequences for areas of law with a close connection to secured transactions law, including company law, intellectual property law and corporate insolvency law. See also section E(5) below.

186 Crowther Report (n 99) Part 5. The committee was chaired by Geoffrey Crowther and its members included Roy Goode.

187 Crowther Report (n 99) para. 5.2.21. For trenchant criticism of the impact of this reform in Scotland see the wonderfully titled D M Walker, 'Crowther's Consumer Credit Chaos Contemplated' 1972 SLT (News) 81 at 85.

188 Scottish Law Commission, *Report by Working Party on Security over Moveable Property* (March 1986), foreword, available at *https://www.scotlawcom.gov.uk/files/8812/8024/7156/Halliday_Report.pdf* (last accessed 6 November 2021) (hereafter, 'Halliday Report'). For background, see Lord Davidson, 'The Scottish Law Commission 1965–1995' (1995) 1 SLPQ 18 at 21 to 22. It was an earlier Halliday Report of 1966 which led to reform of the law of heritable security. See Steven 'Mortgage Law Reform' (n 6).

Commissioner, Professor Jack Halliday.[189] It submitted its report in 1983, but this was not published until 1986 and can be referred to by the name of its chairman. By today's standards the Halliday Report is brief. Many issues seem insufficiently covered, not least floating charges, where the intention was that they would continue to exist.[190] That, plus the planned exclusion of certain assets such as consumer goods and intellectual property,[191] would mean that the reform was not all-encompassing in relation to moveable property unlike under art. 9 UCC or a PPSA. The Halliday Report prompted no action. It would be foolish not to acknowledge that much has changed since the 1980s, in particular the increasing dominance of the PPSA-type approach as supported by UNCITRAL and the World Bank. Nevertheless, for the reasons set out here, a UK-wide PPSA or even a Scotland-only PPSA in the foreseeable future can be excluded.

(3) UK Secured Transactions Code

As we have seen the CLLS is working on a Secured Transactions Code to replace current English law.[192] This would be a more conservative reform than the introduction of a PPSA. In particular, there would be no function-alism and notice filing would be rejected. But in other ways English law would change, in particular with the replacement of the multiple forms of security with a single 'charge', a subject to which we return below.[193] It may be wondered, therefore, whether trying to widen the work of the CLLS and producing a UK Secured Transactions Code should be considered. This may be answered shortly in the negative. Several of the reasons given above against a UK PPSA apply here, in particular the marked differences between current secured transactions laws north and south of the border.

This can be demonstrated by considering a few examples in the current draft of the CLLS Secured Transactions Code. For example, s. 1.1 states that a charge is 'a proprietary interest in an asset'. In Scotland, we have

---

189 On whom, see D J Cusine (ed), *A Scots Conveyancing Miscellany: Essays in Honour of Professor J M Halliday* (Edinburgh: W. Green, 1987).

190 The Halliday Report (n 188) para. 31 states: 'The proposed scheme relates to the creation of fixed securities. Floating charges are outwith its scope and nothing in the new scheme would affect the operation of the Companies (Floating Charges and Receivers) (Scotland) Act 1972'. See also the Crowther Report (n 99) para. 5.7.7 and Scottish Law Commission, *Discussion Paper on Moveable Transactions* (n 53) para. 10.17.

191 Halliday Report (n 188) para. 31.

192 See section C(2) above.

193 See section E(5) below.

real rights rather than proprietary interests and this is not just a difference in language.[194] Section 3.1 provides that once a charge has been created it is 'effective between the chargor and chargee'. This is in effect the attachment/perfection distinction discussed in the previous section.[195] Section 9.2 goes on to provide that a charge is created 'when the chargor intends it to be created'. Such an approach is an anathema to Scottish law, which generally insists on an external act, typically delivery or registration. Finally, para. 28.3 provides for a possessory charge (in place of a pledge) to be created by attornment. But the law here in England and Scotland is different.[196]

It also worth drawing again on history and noting that trying to codify modern private or commercial law in the UK has proved problematic. The most germane example is the failed attempt by the Scottish Law Commission and the Law Commission for England and Wales to codify contract law in the 1970s.[197] Even codification of significant areas of law at a Scotland-only level has proved impossible.[198] This is disappointing given the obvious benefit of making the law more accessible. Scotland should keep a close eye on the CLLS Secured Transactions Code as it develops but seeking to widen it to cover the whole of the UK does not seem practicable.

(4) Insolvency law (plus?) reform

Having ruled out radical reform (at least in the short term) and codification, we consider now something that would be more limited. Such an approach immediately seems appealing given the fate of Part 2 of the 2007 Act and the response of consultees to the SLC *Discussion Paper on Moveable Transactions* discussed above.[199] There is clearly significant satisfaction with the current position within the Scottish legal and banking sector,

---

194 See e.g. G L Gretton and A J M Steven, *Property, Trusts and Succession*, 4th edn (London: Bloomsbury Professional, 2021) Ch. 2.

195 Previous drafts of the code took the Scottish approach of creation and third party effect being simultaneous, normally on registration at Companies House, but this was opposed by stakeholders at a conference to discuss the code in November 2019.

196 In Scotland the custodier must be told of the pledge but does not require to inform the creditor that the goods are now being held on their behalf. See Scottish Law Commission, *Report on Moveable Transactions* (n 3) para. 25.6.

197 See A E Anton, 'Obstacles to Law Reform' 1982 Jur Rev 15 and C K Davidson, 'Law Reform: The Case for Caution in an Age of Revolution' (1990) 35 JLSS 219.

198 See A J M Steven, 'Codification: A Perspective from a Scottish Law Commissioner' in A Parise and L van Vliet (eds), *Re-De-Co-dification? New Insights on the Codification of Private Law* (The Hague: Eleven International, 2018) 75.

199 See sections B(3) and C(3) above.

notwithstanding the grumbles of property law academics and occasionally judges. But as we have also seen there is dissatisfaction as regards the fixed/floating distinction in England. Having considered both the CLLS and STR proposals to date there is some commonality between them as to a possible way forward, although it is premature to suggest that there is any consensus on reform here.[200]

Nevertheless, drawing on this commonality the fixed/floating distinction in corporate insolvency law could be replaced with a new two-part classification of a charge. In respect of some types of asset ('category one'), it would be akin to the current fixed charge as it would trump other types of prioritised claim. In respect of other types of asset ('category two') it would be subordinated to these prioritised claims. This is CLLS option two; under it the category two assets provisionally suggested are stock-in-trade and receivables. Its equivalent is STR option five, which proposes the same category two assets (albeit using different names: inventory and book debts) but suggests a few others. It hardly needs to be stated that these assets are the classic subject matter of a floating charge.

In English law a floating charge rests primarily in equity rather than statute, although insolvency law is primarily statutory. Perhaps all that would be needed technically once consensus has been reached (assuming it could be reached) would be an amendment to the relevant provisions of the Insolvency Act 1986 dealing with claims that are prioritised over a floating charge.[201] This might be achieved simply by a new definition of 'floating charge' for these purposes as being a charge over category two assets. Separately and importantly, however, consideration would need to be given to the provision that currently allows qualifying floating charge holders to appoint an administrator without going to court.[202]

In Scotland, the floating charges provisions in the Companies Act 1985 would also require alteration, something that would, in principle, be a matter for the Scottish Parliament for the legislative competence reason given above.[203] Section 462(1), the provision on creation of floating charges, might be reformed along the following lines:

---

200 See e.g. J Lim En Lun, 'The Concept of a Charge and the Fragility that Lies Beneath its Fixed and Floating Dichotomy: Should its Distinction be Abolished?' (2021) 32 *International Company and Commercial Law Review* 398.

201 Insolvency Act 1986 ss. 175(2)(b), 176ZA, 176ZB and 176A.

202 Insolvency Act 1986 Sch. B1 para. 22.

203 See section E(2) above. Although a legislative consent motion (a 'Sewel motion') could be passed by the Scottish Parliament in respect of the UK Parliament passing legislation on the issue. See "Standing Orders of the Scottish Parliament" Ch. 9B, available at *https://www.*

'(1) An incorporated company may for the purpose of securing any debt grant in favour of another person a security over all or part of the property which it owns from time to time.

(2) This security is known as a 'floating charge'.

(3) The person in whose favour the floating charge is granted is known as the 'secured creditor'.

(4) A floating charge may only be granted over the following types of property:
(a) inventory;
(b) receivables;
... ['204]

Some of the terms, such as 'incorporated company' would need more definition and there are some other deliberate departures from the current drafting.[205] More significant, however, is the fact that such a reform would considerably reduce the classes of asset over which a Scottish floating charge could be granted, from everything to only some. In England, other (category one) assets could still be the subject of a charge that ranks above prioritised claims. In contrast, in Scotland security over these assets would have to be taken by other means: a standard security over land and the new statutory pledge for moveable assets. An obvious attraction of this approach is that because the new floating charge would be restricted to certain categories of asset there should not, in general, be ranking questions as between it and other securities.[206] There would still be priority issues with diligence.[207]

Nevertheless, there may be resistance to such an approach in Scotland on the basis that in England the registration requirements would be less onerous. But the difference is not as material as that which caused Part 2 of the 2007 Act to fail. While registration of a single charge document at Companies House would suffice for most personal property (moveables), elsewhere English law too demands a second registration. For land, priority in relation to a fixed (legal) charge can only be achieved by registration at

parliament.scot/about/how-parliament-works/parliament-rules-and-guidance/standing-orders/ chapter-9b-consent-in-relation-to-uk-parliament-bills (last accessed 6 November 2021).

204 The drafting has been considerably simplified from the previous version.

205 In particular, only allowing a floating charge to secure debts and not non-monetary obligations and not restricting the creditor to the creditor in the debt. On the former see Scottish Law Commission, *Discussion Paper on Heritable Securities: Pre-default* (Scot. Law Com. DP No. 168, 2019) Ch. 4 and on the latter see the same discussion paper at paras 3.28–3.41 and Scottish Law Commission, *Report on Moveable Transactions* (n 3) para. 19.24.

206 See e.g. S Wortley, 'When is a Prior Ranking Floating Charge not a Prior Ranking Floating Charge?' 2020 SLT (News) 191; J Hardman and A D J MacPherson, 'The Ranking of Floating Charges', Chapter 9 within this volume.

207 See section C(4) above.

HM Land Registry[208] and for registered intellectual property such as patents a charge needs to be registered at the appropriate specialist registry otherwise it will not have third party effect.[209] The same is true for aircraft[210] and ships.[211] Thus a second registration would commonly be required.[212]

Despite this some would still argue for the Companies Act 1985 to be amended to allow companies to grant security over the assets not included in category two in respect of which the new Scottish floating charge could be granted. The familiar arguments about the desirability of harmonisation of company law in the UK and the need to keep transaction costs low would be made.[213] The difficulty, however, with such an approach would be a very untidy overlap with the new statutory pledge. This must be avoided. It could be done by amending the statutory pledge provisions to make them unavailable to companies,[214] and therefore only available to private individuals, sole traders and partnerships. This, however, would be to sacrifice a scheme that was designed to be universal and coherent with the rest of Scottish law. Amending the Companies Act 1985 to allow a 'charge' that would trump prioritised claims would, in contrast, be a recipe for more of the incoherence that the introduction of the floating charge to Scotland sixty years ago has caused. It would be far better to address the issue at the level of transaction costs by having information sharing arrangements between the Register of Statutory Pledges (RSP) and the Companies Register. There is a legislative framework in place for this[215] and despite the previous failure here in relation to Part 2 of the 2007 Act,[216] with ongoing advances in technology

---

208 Land Registration Act 2002 s. 27(2)(f).

209 For example, Patents Act 1977 s. 33.

210 As well as domestic aircraft mortgages registered with the Register of Aircraft under the Civil Aviation Act 1982 s. 86 it is possible also to create an international interest in aircraft objects under the International Interests in Aircraft Equipment (Cape Town Convention) Regulations 2015 (SI 2015/912). The international registry is based in Dublin. See further R Goode, *Official Commentary on the Convention on International Interests in Mobile Equipment and Protocol thereto on Matters specific to Aircraft Equipment*, 4th edn (UNIDROIT, 2019), Beale et al., *The Law of Security and Title-Based Financing* (n 62) paras 14.50–14.65 and A Veneziano and W Brydie-Watson, 'A Modern International Approach to Equipment Financing in Africa: The Cape Town Convention and its Protocols' in Dubovec and Gullifer, *Secured Transactions Law Reform in Africa* (n 101) 377.

211 Merchant Shipping Act 1995 s. 16 and Sch. 1.

212 See in this regard generally CLLS, *Secured Transactions Code* (n 117) ss. 38.2 and 38.6.

213 See e.g. J Hardman, 'Some Legal Determinants of External Finance: A Response to Lord Hodge' (2017) 21 Edin L Rev 30 and J Hardman, 'Further Legal Determinants of External Finance in Scotland: An Intra-UK Market for Incorporation?' (2021) 25 Edin L Rev 192.

214 And the other entities such as LLPs that can grant floating charges.

215 Companies Act 2006 s. 893.

216 See section B(3) above.

this should surely be possible. It must be admitted, however, that having both the statutory pledge and the reformed floating charge is not the optimum position. There is much to be said for having a unified system.

(5) Reform leading to single security rights in England and Scotland

Revision of corporate insolvency law alone would still leave English law with a fragmented system of security rights and at odds with a growing international consensus on the benefits of reform that leads to a single security right at least over moveable property.[217] As discussed above,[218] both CLLS and STR also favour such an approach, with the former advocating a single 'charge' over all types of property including land. The result would be to spell the end of the floating charge as a distinct form of security, although its signal feature of allowing security over property present and future in respect of which the granter of the security can freely deal prior to enforcement would continue in the new single security right.[219]

In Scotland, the *Report on Moveable Transactions* takes the first step towards a single security right. The new statutory pledge will sit alongside the existing possessory pledge, but crucially both will have effectively the same enforcement rules.[220] As discussed above,[221] it will be a fixed security only and at least initially have limitations in respect of the incorporeal moveable property over which it could be granted. But it would not be difficult technically to amend the legislation to remove these restrictions. Similarly, the RSP could easily become the home for the new single security right. The SLC in designing its legislative framework deliberately took account of best practice in relation to modern registers of security rights over moveable property. The RSP is to be electronic and for the most part automated.[222] While in response to stakeholder views it is to work on the basis of transaction

217 But for a recent example of a unitary approach not being taken, see E Dirix, 'Belgian Reform on Security Interests in Movables' in Gullifer and Akseli (eds), *Secured Transactions Law Reform: Principles, Policies and Practice* (n 40) 391.

218 See section D(2) and (3) above.

219 See e.g. CLLS, *Secured Transactions Code* (n 117) ss. 12, 14, 41 and 43 and STR, *April 2016 Draft Policy Paper* (n 137) para. 2.3.

220 See Scottish Law Commission, *Report on Moveable Transactions* (n 3) paras 19.6 and 19.7 and Chs 27 and 28. Occasional refinements are necessary. In particular, with the statutory pledge there needs to be a procedure to allow the secured creditor to take possession of the property on enforcement. With possessory pledge, for obvious reasons, this is unnecessary.

221 See section C(4) above.

222 See Scottish Law Commission, *Report on Moveable Transactions* (n 3) paras 19.22–19.24.

rather notice filing,[223] even that aspect could be adjusted down the line if a PPSA-type approach eventually found favour. Other important features of the RSP are that it is not restricted to corporate security granters[224] and would be searchable in respect of certain types of property by serial number,[225] things not currently available at Companies House. While the SLC recognised that its *Report on Moveable Transactions* does not codify the law on security over moveable property, it said that 'the possibility of future codification would remain'.[226]

There remains a totemic issue if English law and Scottish law were to reform to recognise their own single security rights in respect of moveable property or indeed a single security right over all property. Currently, a floating charge works on a UK-wide basis with a single registration at Companies House. As we saw, it was the concern over more than one registration that resulted in the failure of Part 2 of the 2007 Act.[227] There would accordingly doubtless be opposition to a new system requiring separate registrations north and south of the border. The issue could conceivably be overtaken by Scottish independence. If this were to happen it may be assumed that there would be a new separate Scottish company register.[228] Recognition of the other country's security rights would be a question of international private law. In this regard it may be noted that modern secured transactions legislation or international instruments often make express provision on the matter.[229] If, on the other hand, Scotland remains part of the UK the solution would surely lie in mutual recognition by the two jurisdictions of the two security types and appropriate information sharing arrangements. Thus a Scottish security right registered in the RSP or its successor could be electronically transmitted from the Scottish register to the English register and thus be recognised south of the border. Vice versa for English charges.

---

223 See Scottish Law Commission, *Report on Moveable Transactions* (n 3) paras 6.13–6.30 and 29.13–29.14.

224 See Scottish Law Commission, *Report on Moveable Transactions* (n 3) paras 19.31–19.35.

225 See Scottish Law Commission, *Report on Moveable Transactions* (n 3) para. 34.5.

226 See Scottish Law Commission, *Report on Moveable Transactions* (n 3) para. 16.27.

227 See section B(3) above.

228 See J Bille, J Farley, S Hawes and M McIntosh, 'Scottish Independence: Contracts and Other Obligations', *Herbert Smith Freehills* (22 April 2021) available at *https://www.herbertsmithfree-hills.com/latest-thinking/scottish-independence-contracts-and-other-obligations* (last accessed 6 November 2021). The 670-page Scottish Government document published in the run-up to the 2014 referendum, *Scotland's Future* (2013) (available at *https://www.gov.scot/publications/scotlands-future/* (last accessed 6 November 2021)) is silent on the issue. In contrast, it is mentioned on p. 419 that there was an intention for Scotland to set up its own Shipping Register.

229 See e.g. Dubovec and Gullifer, *Secured Transactions Law Reform in Africa* (n 101) 60.

While, as we have seen, attempts at information sharing to salvage the implementation of Part 2 of the 2007 Act failed,[230] this does not seem good reason to give up on trying to achieve this in the future. The result of English and Scottish law being reformed to introduce single security rights would mean that the floating charge in its present form would disappear.

F. CONCLUSION

Since establishing itself by statute in Scotland in 1961, the floating charge has proved remarkably resistant to change. The Murray Report's recommendation in 1994 to roll it out further came to nothing as did the attempt by Part 2 of the 2007 Act to tame it into having greater coherence with the underlying law. The Scottish Law Commission in its *Report on Moveable Transactions* in 2017 decided following consultation simply to leave it alone and not to introduce a rival floating lien. Nevertheless, the signs now are that the days of the floating charge may slowly be coming to an end. In its mother country, England, there is consensus that it needs to go, although not on how this is to be done. There is a strong possibility that there will be reform of insolvency law to remove the priority difference between floating charges and fixed securities, replacing it with alternative rules. Beyond that the future is likely to see both England and Scotland moving to an approach where there is a single security right, although whether this would be restricted to moveables or include land is a subject of debate. It is not in doubt, however, that such a security right, like the floating charge, could cover assets present and future and allow the granter of the security to deal with these freely until enforcement. In that sense, if not in others, the floating charge will definitely live on.

---

230 See section B(3) above.

Index

adjusting and non-adjusting creditors,
203–4, 210, 217, 221–4, 225, 250,
262, 267, 268; *see also* insolvency
policy; involuntary creditors
administration
attachment events, 165, 185, 231, 326,
356, 402, 417, 424–5
consistency with liquidation and
receivership, 420, 440
distribution, 327, 384–5, 423, 424, 425,
426
generally, 164, 220, 327, 417, 437–8,
490, 491
purpose, 417, 423, 426, 435, 437–8,
440
secured creditors, 327, 423, 425
see also enforcement of floating
charges; *Sharp v Thomson*
administrative receivers, 64, 300, 326,
404, 407, 409, 410, 417, 418, 419,
420–1, 422, 425, 428, 434, 435, 436,
459, 461
administrative receivership
generally, 175, 404, 409, 410, 418,
420–1, 425–6, 429, 434–5, 440, 441
restriction on: exceptions, 435;
generally, 268, 406, 411, 418, 435
see also receivership
administrators
adoption of contracts, 237
appointment, 64, 184, 185, 231, 232,
257, 300, 302, 326, 378–9, 403–4,
417–21, 428, 430–1, 436, 437, 452,
461, 496, 504
duties, 423, 434, 438
powers, 101, 232, 407, 410, 421, 422,
424, 426, 427
agency law, 340, 407
agricultural charges
commentary, 50–2
generally, 48–50, 314, 315, 395, 486

relationship with floating charges, 52–3,
365–6
'all assets' floating charges
prevalence, 450–1, 452, 453, 467–9
appointment
administrative receivers, 64, 300, 417,
418, 422, 425, 428, 435, 436, 459,
461
administrators, 64, 184, 185, 231, 232,
257, 300, 302, 326, 378–9, 403–4,
417–21, 428, 430–1, 436, 437, 452,
461, 496, 504
liquidators, 64
receivers, 64, 231, 235, 326–7, 334,
379–80, 406–7, 422, 428, 431, 437,
440, 481
assignation in security
generally, 15–16, 74, 78, 215–16, 299,
310, 327
requirement of intimation, 15, 16, 97,
215–16, 313, 321, 481
statutory mortgage and assignation in
security, compared, 75, 81–2
attachment events
administration events, 165, 185, 231,
326, 356, 402, 417, 424–5
appointment of receivers, 185, 231,
326, 356, 402, 405, 407, 417
contractual events, 231, 325, 326–7, 402
English and Scots law compared, 231,
325–6, 402
generally, 325–6, 402
liquidation, 185, 231, 326, 356, 402,
405, 414, 417
publicity *see* publicity principle
attachment of floating charges
attachment and functional security,
377–8
automatic attachment clauses, 200, 231,
325, 326, 341–2, 402
definition, 402

English law, 325
generally, 135–8, 171–2, 325–6, 355

book debts, 29, 40, 54, 113, 121, 137, 147, 148, 180, 316, 319, 462, 497, 504

Carse v Coppen, 55–9, 63, 100, 103, 105, 276, 306
catholic and secondary creditors, 298, 299, 300, 350–1, 394–6, 397, 399, 410
challengeable transactions
generally, 221, 403, 409–10, 418, 421, 433, 459
see also fraudulent preferences; gratuitous alienation; unfair preferences
chargeholder, rights and powers of
enforcement powers, 162, 418, 462, 463
generally, 255, 423
legal history, 159, 162, 164
power to appoint insolvency practitioner, 64, 184, 185, 220, 232, 235, 257, 268, 300, 326–7, 334, 378–9, 403–4, 417–21, 436, 437, 452, 459, 461, 496, 504
'sweeper' function of floating charge, 219, 221, 236, 321
charge instruments
debentures, 25, 37, 38, 55–6, 82, 142, 143, 278, 320–1
real conditions, 462–3
registration, 445, 447–9
restrictions on dealing, 397, 461–2
terms, 407, 450–1, 460–4, 467–9
charge over an undertaking, 27, 310–12; *see also* statutory mortgage and assignation
circles of priority, 386–94
City of London Law Society
reform proposals, 490–3
Secured Transactions Law Reform Project proposals, compared, 494, 495–7
Clauses Acts
use as pro forma legislation, 27–8, 65, 67, 71, 72, 310
Committee of Scottish Clearing Bankers, 191, 479, 484

Companies House *see* registers
company arrangements and reconstructions, 432–3
company voluntary arrangements, 363, 423, 427–9
Cook, W. A., 111–12, 138–9, 144, 145, 147, 150, 151
Cork Committee
Report of the Review Committee on Insolvency Law and Practice, 436, 441
corporate governance
directors as trustees, 269–70
corporeal moveable property
pledges *see* pledges
COVID-19
impact on granting security, 446, 453, 454
insolvency legislation, 429–33
creation of floating charges
date, 149, 356, 370
generally, 165, 176–7, 188, 277, 314, 315, 341
in English law, 312–13, 315–17, 318, 341
lack of publicity *see* publicity principle
power to grant, 166, 314, 341, 481
Crowther Report, 168, 169, 501
cryptocurrency, 287
crystallisation
decrystallisation *see* re-flotation
generally, 231, 402
Scots and English law compared, 325–6, 402
see also attachment events; attachment of floating charges

debenture holders, 25, 29, 30, 88, 147
debenture stock, 77, 82–3
delivery
corporeal moveable property, 19, 96, 106, 107, 114, 130, 199
dispositions of heritable property, 318, 403, 408
generally, 10, 13, 14, 15, 37, 121, 124, 129, 313, 323, 368, 503
pledges *see* pledges
transfer of ownership, 136

Department of Trade and Industry
  Diamond Report, 167, 170, 174
  Murray Report, 167, 174–5, 179,
    477–8, 509
diligence
  'effectually executed diligence', 145,
    186, 333–4, 361–3, 408–9, 483, 486
  inapplicability to rolling stock, 76, 88
  ranking issues with floating charge,
    145–6, 158, 172, 361–4, 383, 387–8,
    505
  receivership, 408–9
double crystallisation, 415; *see also*
    attachment of floating charges;
    crystallisation

efficiency
  Coase theorem, 206–7, 209, 211, 249
  externalities, 205–6, 210, 211
  generally, 205–9, 225–6, 241–2,
    247–8
  Kaldor-Hicks efficiency, 212–13, 224,
    226, 241–2
  and law, 209–10, 250, 260–1
  measurement, 211–13
  Pareto efficiency, 211, 213–24, 226
employee rights
  National Insurance Fund, 233–4, 237,
    243
  preferential creditors, 223, 233–4,
    242–3, 461
employee vulnerability
  bargaining power, 236, 239, 249,
    257–9, 261
  Declaration of Philadelphia, 258
  employment – at – will, 241, 259
  firm specific human capital, 259–60,
    265, 269
  see also vulnerability theory
enforcement of floating charges
  challenge during insolvency, 433
  English and Scots law compared,
    326–7, 405
  fixed-security holders, relationship
    with, 408, 413
  generally, 376–7, 404–5, 440–1
  in administration: claims in, 423, 424;
    distribution, 327, 384–5, 423, 424,
    425, 426; expenses, 384, 425, 426,

  490, 491; generally, 164, 417–26,
    437–8; moratorium, 364, 425;
    purpose, 235, 417
  in liquidation: distribution, 327, 380–2,
    415, 417; expenses, 382, 391, 415–16;
    generally, 183, 414–17
  in receivership: expenses, 411–12;
    generally, 162, 183–4, 379–80,
    405–14; differences from
    administration, 235, 437–8;
    distribution, 382–4, 411–13, 415,
    427
  self-enforcement, 380, 405
English law
  crystallisation, 231, 325
  development of floating charge, 23–9,
    161, 287, 312–13
  interpretation, 25–6
  power to grant floating charge, 312–13,
    315–17, 318, 341
  and Roman law, 21–3
  scope of floating charge, 317, 318,
    319–20
equity
  generally, 21, 23, 24, 39, 115, 121, 187,
    219, 306–7, 487
ex facie absolute disposition, 14, 138–9,
    149–50
extortionate credit transactions, 403, 409,
    433

fixed charges
  English law, 25, 26, 114, 159, 321, 369,
    487, 495–6, 504
  Scots law, 326, 488
  see also fixed/floating distinction
fixed/floating distinction, 483, 487–8,
    490–1, 492–3, 494, 495–6, 504
fixed securities
  generally, 297–99, 385, 386, 422, 483,
    488
  priority, 232, 327, 353, 354–8, 360, 368,
    381, 382, 384, 461, 482, 485
  see also assignation in security; *ex facie*
    absolute dispositions; fixed-security
    holders; pledges; standard securities;
    tacit securities
floating charges, creation *see* creation of
    floating charges

floating charges, importance
  economic, 27, 193, 305, 444, 451–2, 464
  prior Scots law arguments, 198–200
  Scots and English law compared, 159
floating charges, introduction of *see* introduction of floating charges
floating charges, legal history of
  controversy, 29–34
  demand, 27, 45–8
  floating security: comparative law, 16–19; doctrinal obstacles, 19–20; early Scots law, 8–10; Institutional period, 10–20; terminology, 34–5
  opposition, 42–5
  rejection at Scots common law: *Carse v Coppen*, 63, 100, 276; commentary, 41–2; generally, 36–40, 275–6
floating charge literature, 179–82
floating charge, nature of
  pre-attachment, 327–41, 396–7, 402, 463
  upon attachment, 337, 360–1, 397, 402, 463
  see also chargeholder, rights and powers of; pre-attachment floating charge
floating charges, pre-introduction
  difficulties, 106–10, 112, 113–14
fraudulent trading, 403, 410
functional approach to security rights
  attachment/perfection distinction, 500, 503
  formalism, compared, 488–9
  Personal Property Securities Act, 474–5, 481, 482, 489, 492, 494, 495, 502
  potential UK Personal Property Securities Act, 168, 169, 174, 498–502
  single security right, 507–9
  Uniform Commercial Code, Article 9, 117, 167, 168, 169, 174, 193, 204, 474–5, 477, 482, 489, 499, 501–2
functional securities
  assignation in security *see* assignation in security
  generally, 367, 377–8
  hire purchase, 114

retention of title, 367, 488, 492, 499
sale and leaseback transactions, 377
see also transfer of ownership

Gibson, J. H., 112, 130
going concerns, 253, 490
goodwill, 148
Gower, L. C. B., 115, 116
gratuitous alienations, 165, 172, 403, 409, 418, 421, 433, 459

Halliday, J. M., 112, 167
Hendry, A. F.
  private member's Bill, 125, 128–32
heritable property
  attachment: generally, 136, 360, 403; *see also Sharp v Thomson*
  generally, 19, 46, 110, 112, 113, 114, 121, 122, 129, 150, 154–5, 159, 214, 408, 461, 476
  heritable securities *see* heritable securities
heritable securities
  attachment issues *see Sharp v Thomson*
  bond and disposition in security, 14, 35, 70
  commentary, 13–15, 19, 46, 159, 188, 192, 193, 214, 217–18, 475, 501
  ex facie absolute disposition in security, 14, 138–9, 149–50
  standard securities *see* standard securities
Hohfeldian dyads
  application to floating charges, 299–301
  atomisation, 272, 288
  contingency, 295–6
  correlatives, 292–3
  opposites, 293–5
Hohfeldian errors
  application to floating charges: blending, 280–2, 302; consequences, 286–8; slippage, 278–80, 302
  transposition errors, 273–5

immoveable property *see* heritable property

immoveable property, security over *see*
 heritable securities
incorporation of companies
 by private Act of Parliament, 64–6, 69
 by Royal Charter, 68–9
incorporeal property
 assignation in security *see* assignation in
  security
 intellectual property, 16, 148, 485, 495,
  502, 506
insolvency policy
 alternatives to creditor's bargain theory,
  252–5
 corporate rescue, 235, 434–5, 438
 creditor's bargain theory, 250–1, 254,
  338–9
 see also vulnerability theory
international private law
 problems concerning floating charges,
  54–9, 173–4
introduction of floating charges
 effect on adjusting creditors, 221–2
 effect on debtors, 217–18
 effect on non-adjusting creditors,
  223–4
 effect on the secured creditor, 218–21
 in English law, 23–9, 311, 312–13
 legislative progression, 63, 130–2,
  160–7, 305
 pressures relating to, 127–8
 responsibility for, 125–7
 specific provisions: assignation, 150–1;
  attachment, 135–8; definition, 133–5;
  diligence, 144–6; fixed security,
  138–9; ranking, 139–44; receivership,
  151–3; registration, 146–50, 160–1
 subsequent legislative development,
  160–7
involuntary creditors, 203, 229, 230, 238,
 239, 244, 247, 248, 264, 266, 267;
 see also adjusting and non-adjusting
 creditors

landlord's hypothec, 15, 20, 41, 49, 50,
 139–40, 357, 358
law and economics
 creditor wealth maximisation, 241, 253,
  255, 265
 economic approach to legal rules, 247

free market, 243–4, 246, 248, 257,
 261
 generally, 193
 information asymmetries, 239, 241,
  256, 258, 265, 266, 267, 268
 Modigliani-Miller theorem, 193, 201
 perfect competition, 258, 261
 rational maximisation, 247
 and security rights, 201–5
 see also efficiency
Law Commission for England and Wales,
 177, 478–9, 489, 501, 503
Law Reform Committee for Scotland
 attachment, 133
 comparative law, 115–21
 definition of floating charge, 133
 difficulties granting security, 107,
  113–14
 establishment, 111
 ranking, 139, 140–1, 142, 143
 reactions to recommendations, 123–5
 registration, 146–7
 scope of floating charge, 121–3
 'undertaking and assets', 135
liens, 21, 24, 80–1, 90–1, 140, 357–8,
 488
'limping' security rights, 500
liquidation
 analysis of insolvent companies,
  454–60
 attachment events, 231, 326, 356,
  402
 challengeable transactions, 403, 433
 consistency with administration and
  receivership, 420, 440
 diligence, 361–2, 363, 364
 distribution, 327, 380–2, 415, 417
 voluntary liquidation, 454
 see also enforcement of floating
  charges; *Sharp v Thomson*
liquidators
 appointment, 64
 powers, 407, 410, 416, 427

moratoria, 364, 425, 428–9, 430–2
mortgage, 21, 22, 23–4, 26, 28, 31, 35, 40,
 51, 70, 121, 284, 354, 488
moveable transactions *see* Scottish Law
 Commission

moveables *see* corporeal moveable
property, incorporeal property

negative pledges
before attachment, 335, 336, 337
in form MR01, 445
prevalence, 450–1, 452, 461, 467–9
publicity, 369
ranking, 141, 219, 232, 300, 302, 324,
335, 359, 360, 368–70, 445, 483,
486
Scots and English Law compared, 324,
341–2, 368–9, 445
notable insolvencies
British Home Stores, 233, 237–8
Carillion, 233, 238–9
Debenhams, 237
Thomas Cook, 233, 236–7
notice of title
registration, 317, 324

offside goals, 352–3, 396–8

partnerships
separate legal personality, 68
pledges
corporeal moveable property, 106, 214,
299, 321, 348, 475
generally, 6, 8–9, 13, 21, 23, 24, 106,
118, 214–15, 313, 321, 327, 330, 336,
488, 503
need for possession, 6, 13, 24, 106, 118,
215, 349, 475, 482
pre-attachment floating charge
nature of, 327–41, 396–7, 402, 463
nature upon attachment compared,
402, 463
negative pledge, 335, 336, 337
restrictions on dealing, 340, 461–2
see also chargeholder, rights and
powers of
preferences *see* fraudulent preferences;
unfair preferences
preferential creditors
crown preference: abolition, 158, 164,
185, 435, 436; reintroduction, 186,
223, 438, 381, 413
prejudice to, 413
priority, 223, 233–4, 242–3, 327, 338,

380–1, 383, 384, 403, 412, 425,
495–6
prescribed part, 30–1, 158, 164, 186,
223–4, 232–3, 235–6, 244, 250, 327,
338, 381, 383, 384, 412–13, 417, 424,
425, 436–7, 438, 459, 461, 481, 491,
495–6
priority circles *see* circles of priority
'property and undertaking'
interpretation, 318, 319, 333
legislative usage, 135, 183, 317–18,
332–3, 445
limits to property attached, 318, 319
see also Sharp v Thomson
property law
nature of real/property rights, 328–32,
502–3
publication of attachment events *see*
publicity principle
publicity principle
floating charges, lack of publicity at
creation, 356
floating charges, lack of publicity upon
attachment, 178, 187
generally, 32–3, 36, 58, 60, 141, 161,
178, 187, 188–9, 356, 369
negative pledge, 324, 369
publicity requirements, 12–13, 14,
15, 18, 19–20, 24, 31, 32–3, 40, 59,
60, 117, 118, 120–1, 122, 141–2,
143, 146–7, 154, 160–1, 188, 201,
317, 324, 356, 359, 369, 410, 488,
500

qualifying chargeholder, 220, 378–9,
418–20, 428, 430, 504
'qualifying floating charge', 185, 220, 300,
302, 326, 378–9, 403–4, 418–20,
461

ranking
assignation in security, 327, 359–61,
368
between floating charges, 142–4, 334–5,
408, 426–7, 440
Crown preference, 158, 164, 185, 186,
223, 381, 413
diligence, 144–6, 186, 333–4, 361–4,
383, 387–8, 408–9, 505

ranking (*cont.*)
  fixed securities, 140–2, 232, 321, 327,
    332, 353, 354–8, 360, 368, 381, 382,
    384, 408, 413, 461, 482, 485
  negative pledges, 149, 232, 300, 324,
    335, 337, 359, 360, 368–70, 445, 461,
    483, 486
  pledge, 327
  preferential creditors, 223, 234, 327,
    338, 380–1, 383, 384, 412, 425, 461,
    495–6
  prescribed part, 223–4, 235, 327, 338,
    381, 383, 384, 412–13, 425, 459, 461,
    481, 495–6
  prior tempore potior jure, 67, 353, 364,
    367, 368, 383, 387, 392
  standard securities, 327, 354, 360,
    368
  tacit securities, 140, 357–8
  unsecured creditors, 220–1, 232, 300,
    328, 337, 338, 381
  upon introduction of floating charge,
    139–44
  see also circles of priority; fixed-security
    holders; negative pledges; ranking
    agreements
ranking agreements
  generally, 143–4, 323–4, 355, 360,
    370–6
  registration, 323–4, 374–5
  Scots and English law compared, 324,
    374
receivers
  appointment, 64, 231, 235, 326–7, 334,
    379–80, 405, 406–7, 428, 431, 437,
    440, 481
  duties, 409, 410–11
  multiple, 379–80, 383, 406, 407, 426–7,
    440
  relationship to administrators and
    liquidators, 384, 407–8, 413, 414–15,
    417, 418, 421, 425
  status and powers, 101, 407–10
receivership
  attachment events, 326, 356, 402, 405,
    407
  consistency with liquidation and
    administration, 384, 406, 407, 409,
    410, 411

distribution, 382–4, 411–13, 415, 426,
    427
  enforcement of diligence, 361–2, 364,
    408–9
  generally, 162, 163, 164, 183–4, 404,
    405–14
  introduction to Scots law, 153, 157,
    161, 162, 405
  'limited asset' floating charges, 185,
    412
  nature of, 405–6, 440
  publication of attachment events, 410
  replacement by administration, 157,
    163–4, 175, 184, 235
  Scottish Law Commission, 153, 170–1,
    173, 408, 481
  see also administrative receivership;
    enforcement of floating charges;
    Sharp v Thomson
re-flotation, 413–14, 415
registers
  Companies Register, 159, 160–1, 176,
    177, 178, 188–9, 190–1, 322, 356,
    359, 374, 424, 442–3, 444, 446–7,
    453, 454, 455, 456, 460, 463, 464,
    477, 479, 506
  General Register of Sasines, 13, 150,
    161, 188
  Land Register, 159, 190, 354, 367
  Register of Floating Charges, 165,
    176–7, 178, 190–1, 479
  Register of Statutory Pledges, 354, 376,
    506, 507–8
registration
  age of charges, 149, 456, 458, 459,
    465–70
  assignation in security, 482
  automatic registration, 190, 477, 506
  central bank exemption, 187–8
  charges, 146–50, 320
  company charges, 160–1, 168, 176, 284,
    442–3, 444–5, 447–8, 457–8, 465–7,
    500
  double registration, 160–1, 190–1
  floating charges, 160, 165, 176–7, 178,
    187–92, 320, 322–4, 356, 359, 369,
    442–3, 448–54, 457–8, 465–7, 479
  introduction, 32, 146
  issues at Scots common law, 12

ranking agreements, 323–4, 374–5
Scots and English law compared, 320, 322–4
Scottish and English companies compared, 446–53, 465–7
volume of floating charges, 448–50, 465–7, 469–71
21-day invisibility period, 143, 165, 172–3, 188, 356, 477–8, 479
Roman law
and English law, 21–3
and security rights, 6–8
Scots law compared, 8, 10, 11, 12–13

Schemes of Arrangement
railway companies, 76, 89, 94
Scottish Council for Development and Industry, 106, 114
Scottish Law Commission
assignation in security, 481, 484
floating lien, 482–3, 485, 509
Halliday Report, 167, 169, 179, 501–2
receivership, 408
registered assignation, 283, 482
Register of Floating Charges, 176–7, 178, 190–1, 479
Register of Statutory Pledges, 354, 376, 506, 507–8
statutory pledge, 16, 179, 283, 326, 354, 376, 441, 485, 488, 498, 505, 506–7
21-day invisibility period, 172–3
see also Sharp v Thomson
Secured Transactions Law Reform Project
City of London Law Society proposals, compared, 494, 495–7
reform proposals, 493–7
security function of floating charges, 256, 401
security rights
in absence of floating charge, 213–17
law and economics, 201–5
volume of registration, 447–8, 456–8, 465–7, 469–71
see also assignation in security; pledges; standard securities
self-enforcement
chargeholder's powers, 405

Sharp v Thomson
beneficial interest, 187
blending, 280–1
controversy, 159
generally, 135–6, 318, 408
impact of Burnett's Trs v Grainger, 178, 187
'property and undertaking', 135–6, 317–18, 377
ratio, 318, 403
Report on Sharp v Thomson, 177–8
standard securities, 14, 139, 190–1, 214, 218, 283–5, 299, 327, 348, 349, 350, 351, 353, 354, 356, 360, 368, 372, 375–6, 389, 460, 463, 485, 488, 505; see also heritable property; heritable securities
statutory companies
market capitalisation of, 65–6
monopolies, 67, 69, 74
see also incorporation of companies
statutory mortgage and assignation in security
'Bond and Assignation', 79–80
common law assignation in security, compared, 75, 81
delivery, 82
enforcement by judicial factor, 67, 75, 77, 88–92, 98–100, 311
intimation, 74, 78, 80, 97
requirements of form, 74, 78, 80
'undertaking', meaning of, 83–6, 310–311
statutory pledge, 16, 179, 283, 326, 354, 376, 485, 488, 498, 505, 506–7

tacit securities, 12, 15, 20, 140, 357–8
third parties
protection of, 323, 331
publicity for benefit of, 142, 146, 154, 188, 323
real rights, 330–2
transferred property see transferred property
transfer of floating charges, 150–1
transferred property, 332–3, 334, 336, 339–41, 378, 396–7, 462, 463, 493
trust property

Scots and English law compared,
318–20
Tweedsmuir, Lady (P. Buchan), 108, 110,
127

unfair preferences, 165, 221, 403, 409,
418, 421, 433, 459

voluntary security rights
generally, 348
see also assignation in security; pledges;
standard securities
vulnerability theory, 242–4, 270

White Fish Authority, 106–8
winding up *see* liquidation